Also by America's Test Kitchen

Praise for America's Test Kitchen Titles

"Foolproof and high proof, this thoroughly researched and easy to follow volume will steady the hand of any home mixologist."

PUBLISHERS WEEKLY ON *HOW TO COCKTAIL*

"True to its name, this smart and endlessly enlightening cookbook is about as definitive as it's possible to get in the modern vegetarian realm."

MEN'S JOURNAL ON *THE COMPLETE VEGETARIAN COOKBOOK*

Selected as the Cookbook Award Winner of 2019 in the Health and Special Diet Category

INTERNATIONAL ASSOCIATION OF CULINARY PROFESSIONALS (IACP) ON *THE COMPLETE DIABETES COOKBOOK*

"Diabetics and all health-conscious home cooks will find great information on almost every page."

BOOKLIST (STARRED REVIEW) ON *THE COMPLETE DIABETES COOKBOOK*

"This is a wonderful, useful guide to healthy eating."

PUBLISHERS WEEKLY ON *NUTRITIOUS DELICIOUS*

"*The Perfect Cookie*. . . is, in a word, perfect. This is an important and substantial cookbook. . . . If you love cookies, but have been a tad shy to bake on your own, all your fears will be dissipated. This is one book you can use for years with magnificently happy results."

THE HUFFINGTON POST ON *THE PERFECT COOKIE*

Selected as one of the 10 Best New Cookbooks of 2017

THE LA TIMES ON *THE PERFECT COOKIE*

"The sum total of exhaustive experimentation . . . anyone interested in gluten-free cookery simply shouldn't be without it."

NIGELLA LAWSON ON *THE HOW CAN IT BE GLUTEN-FREE COOKBOOK*

"Use this charming, focused title to set a showstopping table for special occasions."

LIBRARY JOURNAL ON *ALL-TIME BEST HOLIDAY ENTERTAINING*

"If you're a home cook who loves long introductions that tell you why a dish works followed by lots of step-by-step hand holding, then you'll love *Vegetables Illustrated*."

THE WALL STREET JOURNAL ON *VEGETABLES ILLUSTRATED*

"A one-volume kitchen seminar, addressing in one smart chapter after another the sometimes surprising whys behind a cook's best practices. . . . You get the myth, the theory, the science, and the proof, all rigorously interrogated as only America's Test Kitchen can do."

NPR ON *THE SCIENCE OF GOOD COOKING*

"The 21st-century *Fannie Farmer Cookbook* or *The Joy of Cooking*. If you had to have one cookbook and that's all you could have, this one would do it."

CBS SAN FRANCISCO ON *THE NEW FAMILY COOKBOOK*

"Some 2,500 photos walk readers through 600 painstakingly tested recipes, leaving little room for error."

ASSOCIATED PRESS ON *THE AMERICA'S TEST KITCHEN COOKING SCHOOL COOKBOOK*

"This encyclopedia of meat cookery would feel completely overwhelming if it weren't so meticulously organized and artfully designed. This is Cook's Illustrated at its finest."

THE KITCHN ON *THE COOK'S ILLUSTRATED MEAT BOOK*

"The go-to gift book for newlyweds, small families, or empty nesters."

ORLANDO SENTINEL ON *THE COMPLETE COOKING FOR TWO COOKBOOK*

"Some books impress by the sheer audacity of their ambition. Backed by the magazine's famed mission to test every recipe relentlessly until it is the best it can be, this nearly 900-page volume lands with an authoritative wallop."

CHICAGO TRIBUNE ON *THE COOK'S ILLUSTRATED COOKBOOK*

"This impressive installment from America's Test Kitchen equips readers with dozens of repertoire-worthy recipes. . . . This is a must-have for beginner cooks and more experienced ones who wish to sharpen their skills."

PUBLISHERS WEEKLY (STARRED REVIEW) ON *THE NEW ESSENTIALS COOKBOOK*

THE COMPLETE
SUMMER
COOKBOOK

Beat the Heat with 500 Recipes That
Make the Most of Summer's Bounty

AMERICA'S TEST KITCHEN

Library of Congress Cataloging-in-Publication Data

Names: America's Test Kitchen (Firm), author.
Title: The complete summer cookbook : beat the heat with 500 recipes that make the most of summer's bounty / America's Test Kitchen.
Description: Boston, MA : America's Test Kitchen, 2020. | Includes index.
Identifiers: LCCN 2020003678 (print) | LCCN 2020003679 (ebook) | ISBN 9781948703147 (paperback) | ISBN 9781948703154 (ebook)
Subjects: LCSH: Cooking, American. | Seasonal cooking.
Classification: LCC TX715 .A5492 2020 (print) | LCC TX715 (ebook) | DDC 641.5/64--dc23
LC record available at https://lccn.loc.gov/2020003678
LC ebook record available at https://lccn.loc.gov/2020003679

AMERICA'S TEST KITCHEN
21 Drydock Avenue, Boston, MA 02210

Manufactured in the United States of America
10 9 8 7 6 5 4 3 2 1

Distributed by Penguin Random House Publisher Services
Tel: 800.733.3000

FRONT COVER
Pictured on Front Cover Mint Iced Tea (page 270), Watermelon-Tomato Salad (page 313), Brined Grilled Zucchini with Mint Salsa Verde (page 229), and Grilled Chicken Kebabs with Garlic and Herb Marinade (page 177)

BACK COVER
Pictured on Back Cover Icebox Margarita Cheesecake (page 387)
Photography Carl Tremblay
Food Styling Catrine Kelty

Editorial Director, Books Adam Kowit

Executive Food Editor Dan Zuccarello

Deputy Food Editor Stephanie Pixley

Executive Managing Editor Debra Hudak

Senior Editor Sara Mayer

Associate Editor Nina Denison

Assistant Editors Kelly Cormier and Brenna Donovan

Editorial Assistants Emily Rahravan and Sara Zatopek

Art Director, Books Lindsey Timko Chandler

Deputy Art Director Allison Boales

Associate Art Director Katie Barranger

Photography Director Julie Bozzo Cote

Photography Producer Meredith Mulcahy

Senior Staff Photographers Steve Klise and Daniel J. van Ackere

Staff Photographer Kevin White

Additional Photography Keller + Keller and Carl Tremblay

Food Styling Catrine Kelty, Chantal Lambeth, Ashley Moore, Marie Piraino, Elle Simone Scott, and Kendra Smith

Photoshoot Kitchen Team

  Photo Team Manager Timothy McQuinn

  Lead Test Cook Eric Haessler

  Assistant Test Cooks Sarah Ewald, Hannah Fenton, and Jacqueline Gochenouer

Senior Manager, Publishing Operations Taylor Argenzio

Imaging Manager Lauren Robbins

Production and Imaging Specialists Tricia Neumyer, Dennis Noble, and Amanda Yong

Copy Editor Cheryl Redmond

Proofreader Pat Jalbert-Levine

Indexer Elizabeth Parson

Chief Creative Officer Jack Bishop

Executive Editorial Directors Julia Collin Davison and Bridget Lancaster

Contents

WELCOME TO
America's Test Kitchen

This book has been tested, written, and edited by the folks at America's Test Kitchen. Located in Boston's Seaport District in the historic Innovation and Design Building, it features 15,000 square feet of kitchen space, including multiple photography and video studios. It is the home of *Cook's Illustrated* magazine and *Cook's Country* magazine and is the workday destination for more than 60 test cooks, editors, and cookware specialists. Our mission is to test recipes over and over again until we understand how and why they work and until we arrive at the best version.

We start the process of testing a recipe with a complete lack of preconceptions, which means that we accept no claim, no technique, and no recipe at face value. We simply assemble as many variations as possible, test a half-dozen of the most promising, and taste the results blind. We then construct our own recipe and continue to test it, varying ingredients, techniques, and cooking times until we reach a consensus. As we like to say in the test kitchen, "We make the mistakes so you don't have to." The result, we hope, is the best version of a particular recipe, but we realize that only you can be the final judge of our success (or failure). We use the same rigorous approach when we test equipment and taste ingredients.

All of this would not be possible without a belief that good cooking, much like good music, is based on a foundation of objective technique. Some people like spicy foods and others don't, but there is a right way to sauté, there is a best way to cook a pot roast, and there are measurable scientific principles involved in producing perfectly beaten, stable egg whites. Our ultimate goal is to investigate the fundamental principles of cooking to give you the techniques, tools, and ingredients you need to become a better cook. It is as simple as that.

To see what goes on behind the scenes at America's Test Kitchen, check out our social media channels for kitchen snapshots, exclusive content, video tips, and much more. You can watch us work (in our actual test kitchen) by tuning in to *America's Test Kitchen* or *Cook's Country* on public television or on our websites. Download our award-winning podcast *Proof*, which goes beyond recipes to solve food mysteries (AmericasTestKitchen.com/proof), or listen in to test kitchen experts on public radio (SplendidTable.org) to hear insights that illuminate the truth about real home cooking. Want to hone your cooking skills or finally learn how to bake—with an America's Test Kitchen test cook? Enroll in one of our online cooking classes. And you can engage the next generation of home cooks with kid-tested recipes from America's Test Kitchen Kids.

However you choose to visit us, we welcome you into our kitchen, where you can stand by our side as we test our way to the best recipes in America.

facebook.com/AmericasTestKitchen
twitter.com/TestKitchen
youtube.com/AmericasTestKitchen
instagram.com/TestKitchen
pinterest.com/TestKitchen

AmericasTestKitchen.com
CooksIllustrated.com
CooksCountry.com
OnlineCookingSchool.com
AmericasTestKitchen.com/kids

Introduction

Tomatoes and beans in every shape, color, and size. Bountiful yellow squash and green zucchini. Sweet corn on the cob. Vibrant, juicy berries. The ripe, flavorful summer harvest has an abundant array of colorful vegetables and fruits. With so much gorgeous seasonal produce, the culinary possibilities are inviting and seemingly endless.

But as the temperature outside rises, so does the challenge of putting together a meal without overtaxing yourself or overheating the kitchen. During the summer months, we like to focus on keeping things looser and easier. *The Complete Summer Cookbook* is full of inspired recipes that will help you settle into a more relaxed kind of cooking designed to keep you and your kitchen cool. You'll find recipes ready in 30 minutes or less, dinner-size salads, make-ahead meals, dishes that can be served cold or at room temperature, and so much more.

No-cook recipes are the ultimate in summer ease and are included throughout the book. You can make Thai-Style Chicken Salad Lettuce Wraps; Chopped Carrot Salad with Mint, Pistachios, and Pomegranate Seeds; or Blackberry–Key Lime Trifle without ever turning on the oven. Or, try out what we call countertop cooking with recipes that show you how to use your slow cooker or pressure cooker for fuss-free, hands-off weeknight fare like Slow-Cooker Lemony Chicken and Rice with Spinach and Feta or Pressure-Cooker Braised Striped Bass with Zucchini and Tomatoes. And, of course, our favorite part of summertime cooking is dinner off the grill. With recipes for all kinds of burgers as well as Paprika-and-Lime-Rubbed Chicken with Grilled Vegetable Succotash, Sweet and Tangy Grilled Country-Style Pork Ribs, and Grilled Jalapeño and Lime Shrimp Skewers, you can avoid the kitchen entirely and cook your whole meal outdoors.

One of the best parts of summer is cooking for friends. From backyard barbecues to beach picnics to patio parties, socializing outside on a beautiful summer day is best with food. For those days when you want a dish that keeps or travels well, look for our picnic-table favorites such as Fresh Corn and Tomato Salad, Picnic Fried Chicken, and Barbecued Pulled Pork. Hundreds more recipes cover all of your other summer meal needs. You'll also find chapters of small bites and finger foods to pair with refreshing summertime drinks. For stress-free entertaining, consult one of our menu suggestions (see pages 6–9).

The true star of any summer meal is fresh seasonal produce. With a simple side like Sautéed Radishes, a vegetable-filled main course such as Penne with Garden Vegetable Sauce, a fresh fruit dessert like Summer Berry Pie, or any of our summer-ready recipes, you're sure to impress. Much of the best produce can be found at a local farmers' market or farm stand, but it makes its way into grocery stores, too. To highlight this peak produce, we've included Farmers' Market Finds in each chapter with key shopping and storage information.

So, whether you're looking for a quick weeknight dinner, planning a make-ahead meal for a crowd, or taking the party outside, with *The Complete Summer Cookbook* in hand you'll be ready.

Top 10 Test Kitchen Tips for Summertime Cooking and Eating

Cooking during the summer months needn't make you and your kitchen any hotter. From assembling substantial salads of the freshest produce to grilling burgers and steaks outside to preparing no-cook dishes, summer cooking can be easy and still create great food. Here are some of our favorite ways to help you save time, keep cool, and get inspired as you cook your way through the season.

1 COOK MORE VEGETABLES AND EAT MORE FRUIT

Buy local summer produce whenever you can. The vegetables and fruits are fresher and more flavorful, and the colorful and unusual varieties available provide endless inspiration. And with our recipes at hand, it's easy to test-drive a new vegetable and enjoy all of your farm-stand finds. Tired of plain boiled corn on the cob? Try Mexican-Style Grilled Corn (page 223), Chorizo, Corn, and Tomato Tostadas with Lime Crema (page 112), and Creamy Corn Bucatini with Ricotta and Basil (page 112). Break out of your comfort zone and cook Whole Romanesco with Berbere and Tahini-Yogurt Sauce (page 108), Teriyaki Stir-Fried Garlic Scapes with Chicken (page 120), or Nettle Soup (page 124). You can serve ripe and flavorful fruit as a healthy no-cook ending to a meal or turn it into gratins, shortcakes, trifles, cobblers, crisps, and sonkers as well as tarts and pies.

2 LIGHTEN UP

In the summer months, we lean toward dishes that are lighter but still satisfying, such as cold soups, main-dish salads, grain-stuffed vegetables, pasta packed with vegetables, or poached salmon. When the heat stifles your appetite or your will to cook, meals that focus on lighter ingredients and fresher flavors—such as Marinated Eggplant with Capers and Mint (page 298) or Watermelon-Tomato Salad (page 313)—hold greater appeal. Incorporate fresh herbs, bright citrus, and complex spices to add deep flavor to dishes without loading down your plate. Make a flavorful lightened-up favorite like our satisfying Quinoa Taco Salad (page 63) or Pan-Seared Shrimp with Tomatoes and Avocado (page 132).

3 STEP AWAY FROM THE STOVE

When it's sweltering out, the last thing you want to do is turn on the oven. With our low-heat and no-heat recipes, you can still put together a flavorful and satisfying meal. We cut down on time and heat generation with tricks like cooking beets in the microwave rather than in the oven; skillet roasting cauliflower on the stovetop; and making fillings for tacos and sandwiches in our slow or pressure cooker. A No Cook icon identifies recipes that don't require any heat to prepare.

You can beat the heat and still prepare a hot meal with our slow- or pressure-cooked dishes. Avoid standing over a hot stove with countertop cooking that lets you prep and walk away. Using your slow/pressure cooker is a foolproof way to take the fuss out of dinner while still enjoying all the best flavors of the season in meals such as Slow-Cooker Garden Minestrone (page 155) or Pressure-Cooker Ratatouille (page 172).

4 IT'S OK TO BUY A COOKED CHICKEN

We understand the desire to minimize prep work in the summer and buy already-cooked proteins. Our recipes indicate when you can sub in rotisserie chicken to make a dinner-worthy cold salad like Chicken Salad with Pickled Fennel, Watercress, and Macadamia Nuts (page 40), or use store-bought smoked salmon in Smoked Salmon Niçoise Salad (page 54). Just as simple, you can use pantry items like canned tuna or chickpeas to add heft to greens and vegetables as in our supereasy Chickpea Salad with Carrots, Arugula, and Olives (page 260). You can also cook our easy poached chicken breasts (page 41) and store them for up to five days, to use in last-minute meals.

5 MAKE IT AHEAD

Planning and prepping meals ahead when it's cooler gives you a serious jump-start on another night's dinner. We provide recipes you can fully assemble ahead of time like Vietnamese Summer Rolls (page 35), easy one-dish meals, and recipes whose main ingredient can be cooked ahead of time like Farro Salad with Sugar Snap Peas and White Beans (page 63), where the farro can be cooked ahead and stored for up to three days, and many side dishes and desserts. All of these recipes are identified by a Make Ahead icon.

6 TAKE IT OUTSIDE

Everyone loves the smoky flavor of grilled foods, and summer is the perfect time to make them. You can prepare a main dish, sides, or your whole meal on the grill. Try Classic Barbecued Chicken (page 182), Grilled Caesar Salad (page 225), or Swordfish Kebabs with Zucchini Ribbon Salad (page 209). For recipes to make and take, such as 24-Hour Picnic Salad (page 251), or to simply eat outside at home, check out our 40-plus recipes of picnic-table favorites.

7 MAKE MEZZE YOUR MEAL

Not every meal has to be a main course and two sides. We often like to turn small bites and appetizers into dinner, an especially appealing proposition in the warmer summer months. For dinner any night, try putting together a spread of mezze dishes and shareable plates from our Small Bites chapter—the recipes are not just for entertaining. Also check out our Mediterranean-inspired menu on page 9.

8 CAN IT

The only thing we don't like about summer is when it ends. By canning and pickling summer's abundant fruits and vegetables, you can enjoy the season's freshest flavors year-round. Whether you have a surplus from your home garden or a haul from the farmers' market, our foolproof recipes show you to how to preserve with ease—from refrigerator jams to pickles to a big batch of tomato sauce (see the chapter Preserve the Season).

9 TRY COLD AND FROZEN TREATS

There's no better way to cool down than with a cold treat. When most of us think dessert, we think baking, but not all sweets require turning on the oven. We love baked summer fruit pies like Sweet Cherry Pie (page 370), but we also appreciate sweet cherries in our No-Bake Cherry Crisp (page 360). On a superhot day, make an icebox cake like our Frozen Lemonade Cake (page 392) or pull out your ice cream maker or ice pop molds to make gelato and Coconut Paletas (page 380).

10 DRINK IN SUMMER'S FLAVORS

Enjoy drinking as well as eating all that summer has to offer and use summer fruits, flavors, and even fresh herbs in cocktails and other ice-cold beverages. For a refreshing nonalcoholic cocktail, try Hibiscus-Guava Agua Fresca (page 272) or Switchel (page 273). Muddle berries to flavor a fruity drink, jazz up your lemonade with garden-fresh mint, or make herb-infused ice cubes to add excitement to everything from sparkling water to craft cocktails.

Tips for Storing Produce

Here are some guidelines for where to store your summer produce until you have the chance to use it all.

IN THE PANTRY
The following produce should be kept at cool room temperature away from light to prolong shelf life:

- Garlic
- Onions
- Shallots
- Potatoes

(Note: Onions give off gases that will hasten sprouting in potatoes, so keep the two separate.)

ON THE COUNTER
These items are very sensitive to chilling injury and are subject to dehydration, internal browning, and/or pitting if stored in the refrigerator:

- Avocados*
- Eggplant
- Tomatoes*
- Apricots
- Bananas*
- Kiwis*
- Mangos
- Nectarines
- Papayas
- Peaches
- Pears
- Pineapples
- Plums

*Once they've reached their peak ripeness, these fruits can be stored in the refrigerator to prevent overripening, but some discoloration may occur. You can also allow avocados to ripen in the refrigerator near the front of the middle to bottom shelves.

(Note: Placing tomatoes stem side down will prolong their shelf life. And so will refrigeration. We tested this and found that the shelf life for refrigerated ripe whole tomatoes was prolonged for five days. Cut tomatoes, stored in an airtight container, held up well for two days. Their flavor was unaffected.)

IN THE FRONT OF THE FRIDGE
These items are sensitive to chilling injury and should be placed in the front of the fridge, where the temperatures tend to be higher:

- Corn on the cob
- Peas
- Berries
- Melons
- Oranges

ANYWHERE IN THE FRIDGE
These items are not prone to chilling injury and can be stored anywhere in the fridge (including its coldest zones), provided the temperature doesn't freeze them:

- Asparagus
- Apples
- Cherries
- Grapes

IN THE CRISPER DRAWER
These items do best in the humid environment of the crisper:

- Artichokes
- Beets
- Broccoli
- Cabbages
- Carrots
- Cauliflower
- Celery
- Chiles
- Cucumbers
- Green beans
- Hearty greens
- Leafy greens
- Fresh herbs*
- Leeks
- Lettuce
- Okra
- Radishes
- Scallions
- Tomatillos
- Yellow summer squash
- Zucchini
- Lemons
- Limes

*To store fresh herbs, gently rinse and dry (a salad spinner works perfectly), then loosely roll in a few sheets of paper towel. Seal in a zipper-lock bag. Herbs will stay fresh for a week or longer.

Summertime Menus

Whether you're having a small summer dinner party or a backyard barbecue for a crowd, planning a menu can feel like a daunting task. To take the guesswork out of hosting a meal, and to ensure everyone leaves satisfied, we've created menus for different occasions that take serving size, cooking time, and equipment into account to help you confidently host summer get-togethers. Of course, these menus are only a glimpse of the endless menu combinations you can create with this book.

Garden Party

Pimm's Cups (page 274)
Prosciutto-Wrapped Figs with Gorgonzola (page 26)
Baguette with Radishes, Butter, and Herbs (page 29)
Smoked Salmon Rolls (page 32)
Serrano and Manchego Crostini with Orange Honey (page 28)
Chocolate Pots de Crème (page 383)

Dinner on the Patio for 8

Serve the roast beef hot or cold. Or swap the beef for Roasted Butterflied Leg of Lamb (page 245).

Summer Cheese Board (page 24)
Slow Roast Beef with Horseradish Sour Cream Sauce (page 243)
Mediterranean Chopped Salad (page 58)
Lemon and Herb Red Potato Salad (page 254)
Vanilla No-Churn Ice Cream (page 403)
Ice Cream Sundae Bar (page 406)

Summer Dinner for 6

Aperol Spritz (page 273)
Chilled Cucumber and Yogurt Soup (page 36)
One-Pan Pork Tenderloin and Panzanella Salad (page 134)
Pan-Steamed Asparagus with Lemon and Parmesan (page 284)
Fresh Fruit Tart (page 365)

Make-Ahead Dinner Party for 8

Rosé Sangria (page 275)
Gazpacho (page 37)
Poached Side of Salmon (page 246)
Roasted Tomatillo Salsa (page 236)
Green Bean Salad with Cilantro Sauce (page 287)
Summer Berry Trifle (page 357)

Kebabs on the Grill

Sweet Iced Tea (page 270)
Brined Grilled Zucchini with Mint Salsa Verde (page 229)
Grilled Chicken Kebabs with Garlic and Herb Marinade (page 177)
Watermelon-Tomato Salad (page 313)
Lemon Ice (page 401)

Backyard Barbecue for a Crowd

Margaritas (page 276)
Pimento Cheese Spread (page 238)
Seven-Layer Dip (page 238)
Texas Barbecue Brisket (page 195)
Buttermilk Coleslaw (page 249)
Spicy Salad with Mustard and Balsamic Vinaigrette (page 287)
Pressure-Cooker Boston Baked Beans (page 173)
Skillet Cornbread (page 244)
Texas Sheet Cake (page 264)

more summertime menus ahead!

Seafood Feast

Mint Iced Tea (page 270)
Bruschetta with Arugula Pesto and Goat Cheese
  Topping (page 28)
New England Clambake (page 216)
Simple Tomato Salad (page 307)
Lemon Icebox Pie (page 395)

Mediterranean Mezze Meal

Pita Chips (page 22)
Hummus (page 16) and Crudités (page 23)
Beet Muhammara (page 18)
Tzatziki (page 20)
Marinated Eggplant with Capers and Mint (page 298)
Tabbouleh (page 20)
Country-Style Greek Salad (page 297)
Nectarines and Berries in Prosecco (page 351)

No-Cook Light Dinner

Chilled Cucumber and Yogurt Soup (page 36)
Baguette with Radishes, Butter, and Herbs (page 29)
Chicken Salad with Whole-Grain Mustard Vinaigrette
  (page 44)
Melon, Plums, and Cherries with Mint and Vanilla
  (page 350)

4th of July Cookout

To feed a larger crowd, double the burger recipes.

Lemonade (page 271)
Classic Beef Burgers (page 72)
Southwestern Black Bean Burgers (page 80)
North Carolina–Style Pulled Pork (page 164)
24-Hour Picnic Salad (page 251)
Classic Potato Salad (page 253)
Cool and Creamy Macaroni Salad (page 254)
Patriotic Poke Cake (page 265)
Striped Fruit Ice Pops (page 381)

Picnic in the Park

Watermelon Lemonade (page 271)
Picnic Fried Chicken (page 241)
Quinoa, Black Bean, and Mango Salad (page 258)
Buttermilk Coleslaw (page 249)
Best Lemon Bars (page 261)

Early Summer Celebration

Grilled Salmon Steaks with Lime-Cilantro Sauce
  (page 211)
Grilled Asparagus (page 221)
Pearl Couscous Salad with Radishes and
  Watercress (page 65)
Strawberry Shortcakes (page 356)

End-of-Summer Farmers' Market Meal

Grilled Pork Chops with Plums (page 197)
Grilled Radicchio (page 228)
Fresh Corn and Tomato Salad (page 252)
Easy Apricot and Blueberry Tart (page 364)

Taco Tuesday

Easy Chipotle Chicken Tacos (page 96)
Fresh Corn Salsa with Tomato (page 237)
Classic Three-Bean Salad (page 259)
Coconut Paletas (page 380)

Canning Party

Sangria (page 275)
Whipped Feta Dip (page 21)
Broiled Coriander-Lemon Shrimp (page 33)
Chicken Satay with Spicy Peanut Dipping Sauce
  (page 30)
Watermelon Salad with Basil and Feta (page 253)
Egyptian Barley Salad (page 67)
Coconut-Raspberry Gelato Pie (page 400)

Our Favorite Summer Equipment

Especially when you want to keep cooking to a minimum, there are several pieces of equipment that make life in the kitchen or backyard easier and more productive during the summer months (and year-round). Our buying recommendations for larger kitchen appliances appear in their individual chapters: slow cookers (see page 148), electric pressure cookers (see page 163), canning equipment (see page 325), and ice cream makers (see page 409).

In the Kitchen

Salad Spinner

Farmers' market fresh greens and herbs need to be properly cleaned, and our preferred tool for the job is the **OXO Good Grips Salad Spinner**. It works easily—with just one hand—and effectively removes water from a variety of greens and other vegetables like cabbage for the crispest salads. It's easy to clean and dry, and it's dishwasher-safe.

Spiralizer

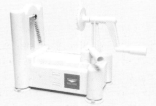

Fresh vegetables are beautiful, colorful, and delicious when spiralized. The **Paderno World Cuisine Tri-Blade Plastic Spiral Vegetable Slicer** easily spiralizes beets, potatoes, and zucchini with relatively little waste, and it's simple, intuitive, inexpensive, and stable. Better yet, the Paderno Tri-Blade can turn almost all of these vegetables into even, consistent noodles and ribbons.

Citrus Juicer

Fresh citrus juice adds bright summery flavor to any recipe, but getting the most out of each fruit is key. Our favorite citrus juicer, the **Chef'n FreshForce Citrus Juicer**, is distinct from citrus presses that use small holes, as it features a star-like arrangement of large draining slots, which direct the juice in a steady stream with no splattering or overflowing. Its large, rounded handles are easy to squeeze, which helps this press quickly extract far more juice than other models.

Rasp-Style Grater

Rasp-style graters make quick work of zesting citrus fruits and grating hard cheeses, ginger, shallots, garlic, nutmeg, and more. This **Microplane Premium Classic Zester/Grater** has a soft, grippy rubber handle and a grating surface that shreds cheese and grated nutmeg, garlic, and ginger with ease. The Premium Classic came sharp, stayed sharp, and looked as good as new after testing.

Tomato Corer

A knife works well to core a tomato, but our favorite corer is inexpensive and cuts prep time in half—handy when you're working with large quantities for stuffing, canning, or sauce. The **Norpro Tomato Core It** is lightweight and has the best head-handle combination for comfort and sharp, neat scooping. It makes tiny cuts and goes through tomatoes twice as fast as a knife does.

Strawberry Huller

Hulling strawberries with a paring knife can be tedious. Our winning **StemGem Strawberry Hull Remover** by Chef'n is a compact stainless steel–tipped huller that removes the stem and core from a strawberry with just a simple push of a button and twist of the wrist. It can also core tomatoes.

Cherry Pitter

De-stoning cherries is the pits—unless you have the right tool. The **Chef'n QuickPit Cherry Pitter** is compact and simple to operate. It resembles a plastic toy gun: Just pull the trigger to plunge the straight, moderately thick dowel into the cherry pit.

Nonstick Skillet

Stuck food can quickly ruin a summer meal, but the **OXO Good Grips Non-Stick 12-inch Open Frypan** cooks and releases food perfectly, thanks to its dark finish and excellent nonstick coating. We especially like its gently flared sides, broad cooking surface, and wide, comfortable handle. Its lightweight design makes it easy to maneuver.

Pie Plate

Creating a great summer pie starts with a great pie plate. The **Williams-Sonoma Goldtouch Nonstick Pie Dish** is a golden-hued metal plate that bakes crusts beautifully without overbrowning; even bottom crusts emerge crisp and flaky. Additionally, we love this plate's nonfluted lip, which allows for maximum crust-crimping flexibility.

Tart Pan

Summer fruits and vegetables make for stunning tarts. Our favorite tart pan, the **Matfer Steel Non-stick Fluted Tart Mold with Removable Bottom 9½"**, produces perfectly even golden-brown tarts with crisp, professional-looking edges. Its nonstick coating makes the transfer from pan to plate a cinch.

Blender

The **Breville Fresh & Furious** completely blends fibrous ingredients into silky smooth drinks. It's reasonably quiet and reasonably compact, and combined ingredients efficiently with minimal pauses to scrape down the sides. Its timer makes tracking recipe stages very easy. A good blender comes in handy during the summer for making cold soups and frosty drinks like our Bourbon Cherry Slush (page 279) or Piña Coladas (page 280).

In the Backyard

Charcoal Grill

The **Weber Original Kettle Premium Charcoal Grill, 22-inch** is our highly recommended Best Buy for its great construction and design; it is also fast and easy to assemble and move. Its versatile classic kettle is an expert griller and maintains heat well and its well-positioned vents allow for excellent air control. The ash catcher makes cleanup a breeze.

Gas Grill

The **Weber Spirit II E-310 Gas Grill** is our favorite grill under $500 because its burner design allows for evenness of heating front to back, varying heat levels, and the most cooking control. The heavy-duty cookbox of thick cast aluminum and enameled steel with just one narrow vent across the back makes it easy to maintain steady heat and distribute smoke. The angle of the lid when open helps to channel smoke away from your face.

Chimney Starter

If you grill with charcoal, you need a chimney starter. We love the **Weber Rapidfire Chimney Starter** for its sturdy construction, generous capacity, heat-resistant handle, and second handle for pouring control. With more ventilation holes than other models, the canister ignites coals quickly.

Grill Brush

A good grill brush should allow you to scrub the entire cooking grate, even the hard-to-reach grate ends, and remove debris with minimal effort. It should also be durable enough to use repeatedly without falling apart. The short metal bristles and triangular head shape of the **Weber 12-inch Grill Brush** made for a winning combination.

Grill Tongs

The best tool for grilling is a great pair of tongs. Grill tongs let you deftly grab, lift, and turn food without piercing it, and because they have long handles, they keep your hands far from the heat. Comfortable, lightweight, and sturdy, **OXO Good Grips 16-inch Locking Tongs** took top honors in our tests.

Grill Spatula

Testers really liked the **Weber Original Stainless Steel Spatula**'s slim handle, remarking on the agility, sense of control, and confidence that it inspired.

Grill Gloves

Our favorite gloves are the **Steven Raichlen Ultimate Suede Grilling Gloves**. Their pliant leather give great control when manipulating tongs and grabbing hot grill grates. Their long, wide cuffs protect your forearms and let air circulate to keep you cool.

Skewers

The **Norpro 12-inch Stainless Steel Skewers** are the test kitchen favorites.

Plastic Food Storage Container Set

The **Rubbermaid Brilliance Food Storage Container Set, 10-Piece** has everything you need for on-the-go picnic and barbecue fare. The set comes with two 1.3-cup containers with lids, two 3.2-cup containers with lids, and one 9.6-cup container with lid. Each container is made of lightweight Tritan plastic and stays as clear and stain-free as glass, and its audibly snug seal won't leak, even upside down. Its flat top makes for secure, compact stacking. If you need extras, the containers are also available individually.

Glass Food Storage Container

One of the most convenient aspects of summer cooking is making food ahead, and exceptional storage containers make it easy to prep in advance. With a plastic lid that latches easily and securely and an airtight, leakproof seal that won't drip or let moisture in, the **OXO Good Grips 8 Cup Smart Seal Rectangle Container** is our top choice for glass storage.

Wine Travel Bag

Dressing up your picnic with a bottle of wine? The **VinniBag** is an inflatable carrier that blows up and surrounds its bottle with cushioning air. It's made of thick plastic that closes by rolling over itself like a boating dry bag. It fits taller and wider bottles, is reusable and washable, and folds up for easy transport.

Insulated Shopping Tote

In a 90-degree room, the **Rachael Ray ChillOut Thermal Tote** can keep orange juice safely below 40 degrees for 2 hours. This tote's moderate size, thick layer of insulating foam, and additional gauze-like filler are designed to maintain the bag's interior temperature. Its square, flat design and wide woven shoulder strap make it comfortable for transporting.

Ice Pack

Ice packs are ideal for keeping smaller, more portable food cold—if they work well. The **Arctic Ice Alaskan Series, X-Large** is a hard-sided pack containing a large amount of liquid, has a convenient handle for easy transporting, and doesn't form bulges as it freezes.

Large Cooler

A cooler that successfully keeps food and drinks cold can simplify any outdoor picnic or barbecue. Our favorite cooler is the **Yeti Tundra 45**, an ultradurable cooler in which ice can last a whole week and beverages packed with ice packs can keep below 50 degrees for more than five days. We also love its rubber latches, which were easy to close, and its durable rope handles. Our Best Buy is the more budget-friendly **Coleman 50 QT Xtreme Wheeled Cooler**.

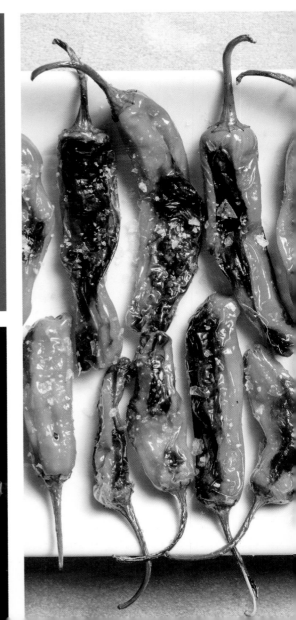

CHAPTER 1

Small Bites

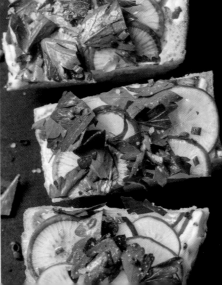

■ FAST (30 minutes or less total time)   ■ NO COOK   ■ MAKE AHEAD
Photos (clockwise from top left): Baba Ghanoush; Vietnamese Summer Rolls; Blistered Shishito Peppers; Baguette with Radishes, Butter, and Herbs; Caprese Skewers

Hummus

Serves 8 (Makes about 2 cups)

`NO COOK` `MAKE AHEAD`

Why This Recipe Works Paired with fresh summer vegetables, whole-grain crackers, or crispy pita chips, hummus is a delicious dip to add to your patio party spread or to pack for a picnic—but you can also just eat it for dinner on a hot night. Classic hummus is composed of simple ingredients: chickpeas, tahini, olive oil, garlic, and lemon juice. But many traditional recipes are surprisingly complex. We wanted a streamlined recipe for hummus with a light, silky-smooth texture and balanced flavor profile. We used convenient canned chickpeas and our food processor to quickly turn them into a smooth puree. But when we pureed the chickpeas alone, the hummus turned out grainy. The key to the best texture was to create an emulsion. We ground the chickpeas and then slowly added a mixture of water and lemon juice. We whisked the olive oil and tahini together and drizzled the mixture into the chickpeas while processing; this created a lush, light puree. Earthy cumin, garlic, and a pinch of cayenne kept the flavors balanced. If desired, garnish the hummus with 1 tablespoon of minced fresh cilantro or parsley and/or 2 tablespoons of reserved whole chickpeas. Serve with Pita Chips (page 22) or Crudités (page 23).

- ¼ cup water, plus extra as needed
- 3 tablespoons lemon juice
- 6 tablespoons tahini
- 2 tablespoons extra-virgin olive oil
- 1 (15-ounce) can chickpeas, rinsed
- 1 small garlic clove, minced
- ½ teaspoon table salt
- ¼ teaspoon ground cumin
  Pinch cayenne pepper

1. Combine water and lemon juice in small bowl. In separate bowl, whisk tahini and oil together.

2. Process chickpeas, garlic, salt, cumin, and cayenne in food processor until almost fully ground, about 15 seconds. Scrape down sides of bowl with rubber spatula. With machine running, add lemon juice mixture in steady stream. Scrape down sides of bowl and continue to process for 1 minute. With machine running, add tahini mixture in steady stream and process until hummus is smooth and creamy, about 15 seconds, scraping down sides of bowl as needed.

3. Transfer hummus to serving bowl, cover with plastic wrap, and let sit at room temperature until flavors meld, about 30 minutes. (Hummus can be refrigerated for up to 5 days; adjust consistency with up to 1 tablespoon warm water as needed.) Serve.

VARIATIONS

Artichoke-Lemon Hummus

While we prefer the flavor and texture of jarred whole baby artichokes, you can substitute 4½ ounces frozen artichoke hearts, thawed and patted dry, for the jarred.

Omit cumin and increase lemon juice to ¼ cup (2 lemons). Add ¾ cup drained jarred whole artichoke hearts, patted dry, and ¼ teaspoon grated lemon zest to food processor with chickpeas. Garnish hummus with additional ¼ cup drained jarred whole artichoke hearts, patted dry and chopped, and 2 teaspoons minced fresh parsley or mint.

Roasted Garlic Hummus

Remove outer papery skins from 2 heads garlic; cut top quarters off heads and discard. Wrap garlic in aluminum foil and roast in 350-degree oven until browned and very tender, about 1 hour; let cool, then squeeze out cloves from skins (you should have about ¼ cup). Meanwhile, heat 2 tablespoons extra-virgin olive oil and 2 thinly sliced garlic cloves in 8-inch skillet over medium-low heat. Cook, stirring occasionally, until garlic is golden brown, about 15 minutes; transfer garlic slices to paper towel–lined plate and reserve oil. Substitute garlic cooking oil for olive oil in step 1. Add roasted garlic to food processor with chickpeas. Garnish hummus with toasted garlic slices and 2 teaspoons minced fresh parsley.

Roasted Red Pepper Hummus

Omit water and cumin. Add ¼ cup jarred roasted red peppers, rinsed and patted dry, to food processor with chickpeas. Garnish hummus with 2 tablespoons toasted sliced almonds and 2 teaspoons minced fresh parsley.

INGREDIENT SPOTLIGHT

CANNED CHICKPEAS

Chickpeas are incredibly versatile, and the canned variety requires no soaking or involved prep, making them an ideal key player in quick summer salads, soups, dips, and more. We use them all the time to impart dishes with added protein, substance, and texture. Our favorite canned chickpeas are **Goya Chickpeas/Garbanzos** for their nicely seasoned, slight nutty flavor and firm-tender texture.

Butterbean and Pea Dip with Mint

Serves 8 (Makes about 2 cups)

`NO COOK`   `MAKE AHEAD`

Why This Recipe Works A creamy bean dip packed with garden-fresh flavor is a perfect summertime appetizer, but many bean dips turn out gluey rather than creamy. We sought lower-starch peas to balance high-starch butter beans (also known as lima beans). This addition turned the dip an appealing green, and we decided to play up the fresh flavors with scallion and mint for a flavorful dip that is a pleasant change from the typical drab version. Greek yogurt also helped round out the texture of our dip, while garlic and lemon zest and juice added complex flavors. We like whole Greek yogurt here, but you can use 2 percent or 0 percent. Serve with Pita Chips (page 22) or Crudités (page 23).

1 small garlic clove, minced
¼ teaspoon grated lemon zest plus 2 tablespoons juice, divided
1 cup frozen baby peas, thawed and patted dry, divided
1 (15-ounce) can butter beans, 2 tablespoons liquid reserved, beans rinsed
1 scallion, white and light-green parts cut into ½-inch pieces, green part sliced thin on bias
¼ cup fresh mint leaves
¾ teaspoon table salt
¼ teaspoon ground coriander
  Pinch cayenne pepper
¼ cup plain Greek yogurt
  Extra-virgin olive oil, for drizzling

1. Combine garlic and lemon zest and juice in small bowl; set aside for at least 15 minutes. Set aside 2 tablespoons peas for garnish.

2. Pulse butter beans, reserved liquid, scallion whites and light greens, mint, salt, coriander, cayenne, lemon juice mixture, and remaining peas in food processor until fully ground, 5 to 10 pulses. Scrape down bowl with rubber spatula. Continue to process until uniform paste forms, about 1 minute, scraping down bowl twice. Add yogurt and continue to process until smooth and homogeneous, about 15 seconds, scraping down bowl as needed. Transfer to serving bowl, cover, and let stand at room temperature for at least 30 minutes. (Dip can be refrigerated for up to 1 day. Let refrigerated dip stand at room temperature for 30 minutes before serving.)

3. Season with salt to taste. Sprinkle with reserved peas and scallion greens. Drizzle with oil and serve.

Roasted Garlic Hummus

Butterbean and Pea Dip with Mint

Beet Muhammara

Beet Muhammara
Serves 8 (Makes about 2 cups) `FAST` `MAKE AHEAD`

Why This Recipe Works Traditional muhammara is a sweet-smoky blend of roasted red peppers, toasted walnuts, pomegranate molasses, and spices popular in Turkish and Syrian cuisine. A true multiuse recipe bursting with flavor, it makes a perfect chilled condiment in the summer, upgrading all kinds of meals from grilled fish to sandwiches. It also makes a great dip for crudités or crackers. Our simple version incorporates shredded beets, which gives the mixture a splendid eye-catching color that's right at home on a lively summer table. Many beet recipes require long oven roasting, but here we simply used the microwave to soften the shredded beets before processing them with some walnuts, which helped thicken the mixture. Jarred roasted peppers added smokiness without any hassle, and some pomegranate molasses gave the dip its hallmark sweet yet slightly bitter flavor. Pomegranate molasses can be found in the international aisle of well-stocked supermarkets; if you can't find it, substitute 1 tablespoon lemon juice plus 1 tablespoon mild molasses for the 2 tablespoons of pomegranate molasses. You can use the large holes of a box grater or a food processor fitted with a shredding disk to shred the beets. Serve with Pita Chips (page 22) or Crudités (page 23).

8 ounces beets, trimmed, peeled, and shredded
1 cup jarred roasted red peppers, rinsed and patted dry
1 cup walnuts, toasted
1 scallion, sliced thin
2 tablespoons extra-virgin olive oil, plus extra for drizzling
2 tablespoons pomegranate molasses
2 teaspoons lemon juice
¾ teaspoon table salt
½ teaspoon ground cumin
⅛ teaspoon cayenne pepper
2 tablespoons minced fresh parsley

1. Microwave beets in covered bowl, stirring often, until beets are tender, about 4 minutes. Transfer beets to fine-mesh strainer set over bowl and let drain for 10 minutes.

2. Process drained beets, peppers, walnuts, scallion, oil, pomegranate molasses, lemon juice, salt, cumin, and cayenne in food processor until smooth, about 1 minute, scraping down sides of bowl as needed.

3. Transfer mixture to serving bowl. Season with salt to taste. (Muhammara can be refrigerated for up to 3 days; bring to room temperature before serving.) Drizzle with extra oil and sprinkle with parsley before serving.

Caponata

Baba Ghanoush
Serves 8 (Makes about 2 cups) `MAKE AHEAD`

Why This Recipe Works Baba ghanoush is a meze staple across Israel, Lebanon, Palestine, and beyond. We love it in the summer as a chilled or room-temperature dip that can be made in advance to have on hand for a hot-day snack. It's typically made by concentrating the rich flavors of eggplant over an open flame before scraping and mashing the pulp into a dip seasoned with any number of regional spices and oils, but we decided to prepare it in the oven for the sake of convenience. We pricked the eggplants' skin to help moisture evaporate during cooking and then roasted them whole until the flesh was very soft and tender. To avoid a watery texture in the finished dish, we scooped the hot pulp into a colander to drain before processing it. We kept the flavorings simple, choosing lemon juice, olive oil, garlic, and tahini. Look for eggplants with shiny, taut, and unbruised skins and an even shape (eggplants with a bulbous shape won't cook evenly). We prefer to serve baba ghanoush only lightly chilled; if cold, let it stand at room temperature for about 20 minutes before serving. Serve with Pita Chips (page 22), fresh warm pita, or Crudités (page 23).

- 2 eggplants (1 pound each), pricked all over with fork
- 2 tablespoons tahini
- 2 tablespoons extra-virgin olive oil, plus extra for drizzling
- 4 teaspoons lemon juice
- 1 small garlic clove, minced
- ¾ teaspoon table salt
- ¼ teaspoon pepper
- 2 teaspoons chopped fresh parsley

1. Adjust oven rack to middle position and heat oven to 500 degrees. Place eggplants on aluminum foil–lined rimmed baking sheet and roast, turning eggplants every 15 minutes, until uniformly soft when pressed with tongs, 40 minutes to 1 hour. Let eggplants cool for 5 minutes on sheet.

2. Set colander over bowl. Trim top and bottom off each eggplant and slit eggplants lengthwise. Using spoon, scoop hot pulp into colander (you should have about 2 cups pulp); discard skins. Let pulp drain for 3 minutes.

3. Transfer drained eggplant to food processor. Add tahini, oil, lemon juice, garlic, salt, and pepper. Pulse mixture to coarse puree, about 8 pulses. Season with salt and pepper to taste.

4. Transfer to serving bowl, cover tightly with plastic wrap, and refrigerate until chilled, about 1 hour. (Dip can be refrigerated for up to 24 hours; bring to room temperature before serving.) Season with salt and pepper to taste, drizzle with extra oil to taste, and sprinkle with parsley before serving.

Caponata
Serves 6 (Makes about 3 cups) `MAKE AHEAD`

Why This Recipe Works There's no shortage of preparations for farm-fresh eggplant in the height of summer, but caponata—a boldly flavored eggplant relish with sweet and sour notes—is a perfect addition to a picnic or summer soiree. To make sure the eggplant didn't turn to oil-soaked mush, we salted and microwaved it to eliminate excess moisture. Starting with bright tomatoey V8 juice added concentrated tomato flavor, and brown sugar and red wine vinegar gave us the traditional sweet-and-sour profile. Raisins brought additional sweetness, minced anchovies added a rich umami boost, and briny black olives offered balance. Simmering everything together allowed the mixture to thicken and the flavors to meld. Although we prefer the complex flavor of V8 juice, tomato juice can be substituted. If coffee filters are not available, food-safe, undyed paper towels can be substituted when microwaving the eggplant. Be sure to remove the eggplant from the microwave immediately so that the steam can escape. Serve caponata with slices of toasted baguette, alongside grilled meat or fish, mixed into pasta, or spooned over polenta.

- 1½ pounds eggplant, cut into ½-inch pieces
- ½ teaspoon table salt
- ¾ cup V8 juice
- ¼ cup red wine vinegar, plus extra for seasoning
- ¼ cup chopped fresh parsley
- 2 tablespoons packed brown sugar
- 1½ teaspoons minced anchovy fillets (2 to 3 fillets)
- 1 large tomato, cored, seeded, and chopped
- ¼ cup raisins
- 2 tablespoons minced black olives
- 2 tablespoons extra-virgin olive oil, divided
- 1 celery rib, chopped fine
- 1 red bell pepper, stemmed, seeded, and chopped fine
- 1 small onion, chopped fine
- ¼ cup pine nuts, toasted

1. Toss eggplant with salt in bowl. Line entire surface of large microwave-safe plate with double layer of coffee filters and lightly spray with vegetable oil spray. Spread eggplant in even layer on coffee filters. Microwave until eggplant is dry and shriveled to one-third of its original size, 8 to 15 minutes (eggplant should not brown). Transfer eggplant immediately to paper towel–lined plate.

2. Meanwhile, whisk V8 juice, vinegar, parsley, sugar, and anchovies together in medium bowl. Stir in tomato, raisins, and olives.

3. Heat 1 tablespoon oil in 12-inch nonstick skillet over medium-high heat until shimmering. Add eggplant and cook, stirring occasionally, until edges are browned, 4 to 8 minutes, adding 1 teaspoon more oil if pan appears dry; transfer to bowl.

4. Add remaining 2 teaspoons oil to now-empty skillet and heat over medium-high heat until shimmering. Add celery, bell pepper, and onion and cook, stirring occasionally, until softened and edges are spotty brown, 6 to 8 minutes.

5. Reduce heat to medium-low and stir in eggplant and V8 juice mixture. Bring to simmer and cook until V8 juice is thickened and coats vegetables, 4 to 7 minutes. Transfer to serving bowl and let cool to room temperature. (Caponata can be refrigerated for up to 1 week; let come to room temperature before serving.) Season with extra vinegar to taste, and sprinkle with pine nuts before serving.

Tzatziki
Serves 8 (Makes about 2 cups)
`NO COOK` `MAKE AHEAD`

Why This Recipe Works Tzatziki is a traditional Greek sauce made from strained yogurt and cucumber, as delicious eaten as a dip for raw vegetables as it is dolloped over some of our favorite summer mains like grilled chicken or lamb. To make our own classic version of this light, super fresh sauce, we started by shredding a cucumber on a coarse grater, salting it, and letting it drain to keep any excess liquid from watering down the dip. Greek yogurt gives tzatziki its pleasant tang and richness, but before stirring in our drained cucumber, we enhanced its flavor with minced fresh herbs and garlic. Using Greek yogurt here is key; do not substitute regular plain yogurt or the sauce will be very watery. Serve with Pita Chips (page 22), fresh warm pita, or Crudités (page 23).

- 1 (12-ounce) cucumber, peeled, halved lengthwise, seeded, and shredded
- ½ teaspoon table salt
- 1 cup whole-milk Greek yogurt
- 2 tablespoons extra-virgin olive oil
- 2 tablespoons minced fresh mint and/or dill
- 1 small garlic clove, minced

1. Toss cucumber with salt in colander and let drain for 15 minutes.

2. Whisk yogurt, oil, mint, and garlic together in bowl, then stir in drained cucumber. Cover and refrigerate until chilled, at least 1 hour or up to 2 days. Season with salt and pepper to taste and serve.

VARIATION
Beet Tzatziki
Reduce amount of cucumber to 6 ounces and add 6 ounces raw beets, peeled and grated, to cucumber and salt in step 1.

Tabbouleh
Serves 4 to 6 `NO COOK`

Why This Recipe Works Tabbouleh is a picnic-perfect salad bursting with some of summer's most ubiquitous flavors. Made of bulgur, parsley, tomato, and onion steeped in a penetrating mint and lemon dressing, it's a lively companion to grilled meats, vegetable-packed sandwiches, entertaining spreads, and more. We started by salting the tomatoes to rid them of excess moisture that otherwise made our salad soggy. Soaking the bulgur in lemon juice and some of the drained tomato liquid, rather than in water, allowed it to absorb lots of flavor as it softened. Chopped onion overwhelmed the salad; two mild scallions added just the right amount of oniony flavor. Parsley, mint, and a bit of cayenne pepper rounded out the dish. Adding the herbs and vegetables while the bulgur was still soaking gave the components time to mingle, resulting in a cohesive dish. Don't confuse bulgur with cracked wheat, which has a much longer cooking time and will not work in this recipe. Serve with crisp romaine lettuce and warm pita.

- 3 tomatoes, cored and cut into ½-inch pieces
- ½ teaspoon table salt, divided
- ½ cup medium-grind bulgur, rinsed
- ¼ cup lemon juice (2 lemons), divided
- 6 tablespoons extra-virgin olive oil
- ⅛ teaspoon cayenne pepper
- 1½ cups minced fresh parsley
- ½ cup minced fresh mint
- 2 scallions, sliced thin

1. Toss tomatoes with ¼ teaspoon salt in fine-mesh strainer set over bowl and let drain, tossing occasionally, for 30 minutes; reserve 2 tablespoons drained tomato juice. Toss bulgur with 2 tablespoons lemon juice and reserved tomato juice in bowl and let sit until grains begin to soften, 30 to 40 minutes.

2. Whisk remaining 2 tablespoons lemon juice, oil, cayenne, and remaining ¼ teaspoon salt together in large bowl. Add tomatoes, bulgur, parsley, mint, and scallions and toss gently to combine. Cover and let sit at room temperature until flavors have blended and bulgur is tender, about 1 hour. Before serving, toss salad to recombine and season with salt and pepper to taste.

VARIATION
Spiced Tabbouleh
Add ¼ teaspoon ground cinnamon and ¼ teaspoon ground allspice to dressing with cayenne.

Whipped Feta Dip
Serves 8 (Makes about 2 cups)

`FAST` `NO COOK` `MAKE AHEAD`

Why This Recipe Works Everyone loves a rich, cheesy dip to serve with crackers, chips, or bread. But in the heat of summer, so much richness can be unappealing. That's why we love this salty feta dip with a whipped, light texture. To ensure that our dip that was loose enough to easily scoop up with soft pita, we processed the cheese with a few tablespoons of milk in addition to extra-virgin olive oil. We also rinsed the feta in water before processing to avoid an overly salty dip. A little garlic and lemon juice, along with 2 teaspoons of oregano, rounded out the flavors with freshness and savory herbal notes. Cow's-milk feta makes a firmer dip that holds up well at room temperature; do not substitute sheep's-milk feta, which is softer. Because feta is quite salty, avoid serving this dip with salted chips; Crudités (page 23) and pita bread make great accompaniments.

- 1½ teaspoons lemon juice
- ¼ teaspoon minced garlic
- 8 ounces cow's-milk feta cheese
- 3 tablespoons milk
- 2 tablespoons plus 2 teaspoons extra-virgin olive oil, divided
- 2 teaspoons minced fresh oregano

1. Combine lemon juice and garlic in small bowl and set aside. Break feta into rough ½-inch pieces and place in medium bowl. Add water to cover, then swish briefly to rinse. Transfer to fine-mesh strainer and drain well.

Whipped Feta Dips

2. Transfer feta to food processor. Add milk and reserved lemon juice mixture and process until feta mixture resembles ricotta cheese, about 15 seconds. With processor running, slowly drizzle in 2 tablespoons oil. Continue to process until mixture has Greek yogurt–like consistency (some small lumps will remain), 1½ to 2 minutes, stopping once to scrape down bottom and sides of bowl. Add oregano and pulse to combine. Transfer dip to bowl. (Dip can be refrigerated for up to 3 days. Let sit at room temperature for 30 minutes before serving.) Drizzle with remaining 2 teaspoons oil and serve.

VARIATIONS
Whipped Feta Dip with Dill and Parsley
Substitute 1 tablespoon minced fresh dill (or mint, if desired) and 1 tablespoon minced fresh parsley for oregano.

Whipped Feta and Roasted Red Pepper Dip
Substitute red wine vinegar for lemon juice. Reduce milk to 2 tablespoons. Add ¼ cup jarred roasted red peppers, chopped; ½ teaspoon smoked paprika; and pinch cayenne pepper with milk. Omit oregano.

Pita Chips
Serves 8 `FAST` `MAKE AHEAD`

Why This Recipe Works There's no easier way to throw together an al fresco snack spread than serving up hummus, bean dips, vegetable dips, and salsas, and pita chips make for the perfect crispy, salty dippers. Store-bought pita chips are fine, but the homemade version is even better, and surprisingly easy. First, we separated each 8-inch pita into its two component layers. We seasoned the split rounds with olive oil and salt before stacking them and cutting them into wedges—much easier than seasoning each individual chip. They were perfectly cooked after only about 15 minutes in the oven, and luckily, we found that flipping the chips was unnecessary—they baked up evenly crisp and flavorful. Both white and whole-wheat pita breads will work well here. We prefer the larger crystal size of sea salt or kosher salt here; if using table salt, reduce the amount of salt by half.

4 (8-inch) pita breads
½ cup extra-virgin olive oil
1 teaspoon sea salt or kosher salt

1. Adjust oven racks to upper-middle and lower-middle positions and heat oven to 350 degrees. Using kitchen shears, cut around perimeter of each pita and separate into 2 thin rounds.

2. Working with 1 round at a time, brush rough side generously with oil and sprinkle with salt. Stack rounds on top of one another, rough sides up, as you go. Using chef's knife, cut pita stack into 8 wedges. Spread wedges, rough sides up and in single layer, on 2 rimmed baking sheets.

3. Bake until wedges are golden brown and crisp, about 15 minutes, switching and rotating sheets halfway through baking. Let cool before serving. (Pita chips can be stored at room temperature for up to 3 days.)

VARIATION
Rosemary-Parmesan Pita Chips
Reduce amount of salt to ½ teaspoon. Toss salt with ½ cup grated Parmesan and 2 tablespoons minced fresh rosemary before sprinkling over pitas.

Pita Chips

PREPARING PITA FOR CHIPS

1. Using kitchen shears or scissors, cut around perimeter of each pita to yield 2 thin rounds.

2. Brush rough sides of each round with oil, season with salt, and stack them. Using chef's knife, cut stack into 8 wedges.

Crudités

When done right, a platter of crudités can be a beautiful and versatile centerpiece for entertaining. For perfect crudités, you simply need to prep fresh vegetables properly: Some vegetables must first be blanched and then shocked in ice water; others benefit from being cut in a particular manner. To store crudités, refrigerate raw vegetables wrapped in damp paper towels in a zipper-lock bag and blanched vegetables in an airtight container for up to 2 days.

Asparagus To remove the tough, fibrous ends of the asparagus, bend the thick end of each stalk until it snaps off. Blanch the asparagus for 30 to 60 seconds.

Broccoli and Cauliflower Cut broccoli and cauliflower florets into bite-size pieces by slicing down through stem. Blanch broccoli and cauliflower (separately) for 1 to 1½ minutes.

Carrots and Celery Slice both celery and peeled carrots lengthwise into long, elegant lengths rather than short, stumpy pieces.

Endive Gently pull off leaves one at a time, continuing to trim root end as you work your way toward heart of endive.

Green Beans Line beans up in a row and trim off inedible stem ends with just 1 cut. Blanch beans for 1 minute.

Peppers Slice off top and bottom of pepper and remove seeds and stem. Slice down through side of pepper, unroll it so that it lies flat, then slice into ½-inch-wide strips.

Radishes Choose radishes with green tops still attached so that each half has a leafy handle for grasping and dipping. Slice each radish in half through stem.

BLANCHING DIRECTIONS
Bring 6 quarts water and 2 tablespoons table salt to boil in large pot over high heat. Cook vegetables, 1 variety at a time, until slightly softened but still crunchy at core, following times given for individual vegetables above. Transfer blanched vegetables immediately to bowl of ice water until completely cool, then drain and pat dry.

Summer Cheese Board

BUILDING THE PERFECT PLATE

A cheese board is an uncontested winner when it comes to easy, elegant entertaining, and makes an especially appealing no-cook option in the summer months. For much of the year, we dress up our board with fruit like apples and pears, jams, and other accompaniments. For a summery take, we opt for lighter additions and in-season fruit like berries and cherries. Choosing the right cheeses and pairing them with complementary crackers, spreads, and other bite-sized goodies is a simple formula to putting together a party centerpiece that everyone is sure to enjoy. But striking the perfect balance of flavors, textures, and aesthetic appeal is something of an art, especially when time is of the essence.

Think about cheeses Start by choosing three to five cheeses with different textures (soft, semisoft, semifirm, hard) and flavors (mild to strong). Include cow's-milk, goat's-milk, and sheep's-milk cheeses, or go with all of one type. Plan on 2 to 3 ounces of cheese per person and let the cheese sit at room temperature, covered, for 1 to 2 hours before serving.

Think about breads Mild-flavored bread such as a baguette and neutral-tasting chips like Pita Chips (page 22) or wheat crackers won't overshadow the cheeses.

Think about texture Crisp vegetables like Quick Pickled Carrots can add contrast to soft cheeses. The texture of soft fresh berries and chewy dried fruits works with hard cheeses. Crunchy nuts also add texture.

Think about flavor Select cheese accompaniments that are either complementary, like a mellow caramelized onion relish with a mild fresh cheese, or contrasting, like fruity Fig-Balsamic Jam with a salty, sharp aged cheese.

Think about appearance Fresh cherries and grapes, dried fruits, pickled vegetables, and olives add color as well as texture and flavor.

Marinated Olives

Serves 8

You can buy a wide variety of prepared olive products, but with just a little effort you can put together marinated olives with a lot more flavor and freshness. Make sure to bring the mixture to room temperature before serving or the oil will look cloudy and congealed.

- 1 cup brine-cured green olives with pits
- 1 cup brine-cured black olives with pits
- ¾ cup extra-virgin olive oil
- 1 shallot, minced
- 2 teaspoons grated lemon zest
- 2 teaspoons minced fresh thyme
- 2 teaspoons minced fresh oregano
- 1 garlic clove, minced
- ½ teaspoon red pepper flakes
- ½ teaspoon table salt

Pat olives dry with paper towels. Toss with oil, shallot, lemon zest, thyme, oregano, garlic, pepper flakes, and salt in bowl. Cover and refrigerate for at least 4 hours or up to 4 days. Let sit at room temperature for at least 30 minutes before serving.

Quick Pickled Carrots

Serves 6 to 8 (Makes one 1-pint jar)

These quick-pickled carrot sticks are a cinch to put together and are ready to enjoy in just 3 hours, making them a great introduction to pickling for anyone new to the craft. We love them as a touch of bright color on a cheese board, perfect for popping into your mouth between bites of cheese for a briny, tangy burst of flavor. If possible, choose carrots that are uniform in length. These pickled carrots cannot be processed for long-term storage.

- ¾ cup seasoned rice vinegar
- ¼ cup water
- 1 garlic clove, peeled and halved
- ⅛ teaspoon black peppercorns
- ⅛ teaspoon yellow mustard seeds
- 8 ounces carrots, peeled and cut into ½-inch-thick sticks
- 2 sprigs fresh tarragon

1. Bring vinegar, water, garlic, peppercorns, and mustard seeds to boil in medium saucepan over medium-high heat.

2. Place one 1-pint jar under hot running water until heated through, about 1 minute; shake dry. Pack carrots and tarragon sprigs into hot jar. Using funnel and ladle, pour hot brine over carrots to cover. Let jar cool completely, about 30 minutes.

3. Cover jar with lid and refrigerate for at least 2½ hours before serving. (Pickled carrots can be refrigerated for up to 6 weeks; tarragon will begin to taste funky after 6 weeks.)

Fig-Balsamic Jam

Serves 8 to 10 (Makes about 1 cup)

Combining fresh figs with balsamic vinegar and spices makes a sweet-savory jam perfect for cheese and delicious with canapés.

- 12 ounces fresh figs, stemmed and quartered
- ½ cup sugar
- ¼ cup balsamic vinegar
- ¼ cup water
- 1 tablespoon lemon juice
- 1 teaspoon yellow mustard seeds
- ¾ teaspoon minced fresh rosemary
  Pinch table salt
  Pinch pepper

1. Bring all ingredients to simmer in 10-inch nonstick skillet over medium-high heat. Reduce heat to medium-low and cook, stirring occasionally, until rubber spatula leaves distinct trail when dragged across bottom of skillet, 25 to 30 minutes.

2. Transfer jam to food processor and pulse until uniformly chunky, 4 to 6 pulses. Let jam cool to room temperature, about 1 hour, before serving. (Jam can be refrigerated for up to 2 months.)

Cheese Straws

Serves 4 to 6

Homemade cheese straws are quick to disappear from a party platter. To thaw frozen puff pastry, let it sit in the refrigerator for 24 hours or on the counter for 30 minutes to 1 hour.

- 1 (9½ by 9-inch) sheet puff pastry, thawed
- 2 ounces Parmesan or aged Asiago cheese, grated (1 cup)
- 1 tablespoon minced fresh parsley
- ¼ teaspoon table salt
- ⅛ teaspoon pepper

1. Adjust oven rack to middle position and heat oven to 425 degrees. Line rimmed baking sheet with parchment paper.

2. Lay puff pastry on second sheet of parchment and sprinkle with Parmesan, parsley, salt, and pepper. Top with third sheet of parchment. Using rolling pin, press cheese mixture into pastry, then roll pastry into 10-inch square.

3. Remove top sheet of parchment and cut pastry into thirteen ¾-inch-wide strips with sharp knife or pizza wheel. Gently twist each strip of pastry and space about ½ inch apart on prepared baking sheet.

4. Bake until cheese straws are fully puffed and golden brown, 10 to 15 minutes. Let cheese straws cool completely on baking sheet. (Cheese straws can be wrapped in plastic wrap and stored at room temperature for up to 24 hours before serving.)

Prosciutto-Wrapped Figs with Gorgonzola

Serves 8 to 10 `FAST` `NO COOK` `MAKE AHEAD`

Why This Recipe Works Few food pairings are more perfect than savory, salty prosciutto and sweet fresh figs. Even better? These crowd-pleasing bites require no cooking—they're last-minute hors d'oeuvres that you can throw together without heating up the kitchen. To add another level of sweet-salty complexity and textural interest to this appetizer, we incorporated bold, pungent blue cheese and golden honey into the mix. We started by halving the figs to make them easier to eat. Tasters preferred creamy, assertive Gorgonzola. Small mounds of the cheese, placed in the center of each fig before adding the honey, offered a rich, bold counterpoint to the figs' tender flesh and sweet flavor. Briefly microwaving the honey ensured that it was easy to drizzle over the cheese-stuffed figs. Finally, we wrapped the whole thing in thin slices of prosciutto. To guarantee that the ham would stay put, we stuck a toothpick through the center of each fig. Be sure to choose ripe figs for this recipe. They not only taste best, but they also yield easily when mounding the blue cheese gently into the centers.

- 2 ounces Gorgonzola cheese
- 16 fresh figs, stemmed and halved lengthwise
- 1 tablespoon honey
- 16 thin slices prosciutto, halved lengthwise

Mound 1 teaspoon Gorgonzola into center of each fig half. Microwave honey in bowl to loosen, about 10 seconds, then drizzle over cheese. Wrap prosciutto securely around figs, leaving fig ends uncovered. Secure prosciutto with toothpick and serve. (Wrapped figs can be refrigerated for up to 8 hours. Let come to room temperature before serving.)

Caprese Skewers

Serves 10 `FAST` `NO COOK`

Why This Recipe Works There's nothing that says summer more than the classic combination of bright tomatoes, fresh basil, and creamy mozzarella. For an appetizer take on the caprese salad, we used toothpicks to stand bite-size portions of the components upright on a halved grape tomato pedestal. We found that a quick garlic-infused oil, which we made by mincing garlic into a paste and stirring it into fruity extra-virgin olive oil, boosted the flavor of the tomatoes and fresh baby mozzarella balls, as did a bit of salt and pepper. Basil leaves, skewered onto our toothpicks whole, completed the caprese flavor profile and added a fresh-from-the-garden touch. You will need about 40 sturdy wooden toothpicks for this recipe; avoid using very thin, flimsy toothpicks. Placing a halved grape tomato, with its flat side facing down, on the bottom of the toothpick makes it easy to stand the skewers upright on a serving platter. You can use larger fresh mozzarella balls, but they should be cut into ¾- to 1-inch pieces.

- ¼ cup extra-virgin olive oil
- 1 garlic clove, minced
- ¼ teaspoon table salt
- ⅛ teaspoon pepper
- 10 ounces grape or cherry tomatoes, halved
- 8 ounces baby mozzarella balls, halved
- 1 cup fresh basil leaves

1. Combine oil, garlic, salt, and pepper in small bowl. Toss tomatoes and mozzarella with 2 tablespoons of garlic oil in separate bowl.

2. Skewer tomatoes, mozzarella, and basil leaves on sturdy wooden toothpicks in following order from top to bottom: tomato half, basil leaf (folded if large), mozzarella half, and tomato half with flat side facing down. (You should have about 40 skewers.) Stand skewers upright on serving platter. Drizzle remaining garlic oil over skewers and serve.

Blistered Shishito Peppers

Serves 4 to 6 `FAST`

Why This Recipe Works Fried blistered little chile peppers that you pick up by the stems and pop into your mouth whole are a trendy bar snack, but we thought they'd be just as at home as one-bite vegetable hors d'oeuvres. Shishitos are the Japanese cousin to Spain's Padrón chiles, which are prevalent at tapas restaurants. You'll find them cropping up at farm stands in the summer months, and they're also easy to grow yourself in your home garden—you just need good-quality soil and a sunny location. These bright-tasting, citrusy, mild green chiles are thin-skinned and crisp-textured and altogether addictive. Restaurants often deep-fry the whole shishitos, but we found that cooking them in a small amount of oil worked just as well and was much less messy. The larger granules of kosher salt sprinkled on top add a wonderful crunch, but you can use regular table salt instead, if you prefer. It's said that only one in 10 shishito peppers is truly spicy, so happy hunting!

2 tablespoons vegetable oil
8 ounces shishito peppers
    Kosher salt

Heat oil in 12-inch skillet over medium-high heat until just smoking. Add shishito peppers and cook, without stirring, until skins are blistered, 3 to 5 minutes. Using tongs, flip peppers and continue to cook until blistered on second side, 3 to 5 minutes. Transfer to serving bowl, season with salt to taste, and serve immediately.

Bruschetta with Arugula Pesto and Goat Cheese Topping

Serves 8 to 10 `FAST`

Why This Recipe Works Bruschetta might seem too simple to be the star of the show, but with the right toppings and presentation, this classic Italian antipasto can go way beyond chopped tomatoes and basil and bring a huge spectrum of summer flavors to the table. Classic bruschetta starts with wide slices of simple toasted garlic bread, usually from a rustic Italian or similar loaf. Many bruschetta recipes result in soggy bread, especially once substantial toppings are added. Bread choice is key to fixing this—we used a crusty loaf of country-style bread with a tight crumb so the toppings wouldn't fall through and we cut the bread into thick slices for maximum support. Presented here are a few of our favorite bright, flavorful toppings for this infinitely customizable appetizer. Toast the bread just before assembling the bruschetta.

Toasts
1 loaf country bread, ends discarded, sliced crosswise into ¾-inch-thick pieces
½ garlic clove, peeled
    Extra-virgin olive oil, for brushing

Arugula Pesto and Goat Cheese Topping
5 ounces (5 cups) baby arugula
¼ cup extra-virgin olive oil, plus extra for drizzling
¼ cup pine nuts, toasted
1 tablespoon minced shallot
1 teaspoon grated lemon zest plus 1 teaspoon juice
½ teaspoon table salt
¼ teaspoon pepper
2 ounces goat cheese, crumbled

Prosciutto-Wrapped Figs with Gorgonzola

1. For the toasts Adjust oven rack 4 inches from broiler element and heat broiler. Place bread on aluminum foil–lined baking sheet. Broil until bread is deep golden on both sides, 1 to 2 minutes per side. Lightly rub 1 side of each slice with garlic and brush with oil. Season with salt to taste.

2. For the arugula pesto and goat cheese topping Pulse arugula, oil, pine nuts, shallot, lemon zest and juice, salt, and pepper in food processor until mostly smooth, about 8 pulses, scraping down sides of bowl as needed. Spread arugula mixture evenly on toasts, top with goat cheese, and drizzle with extra oil. Serve.

VARIATIONS
Bruschetta with Whipped Feta and Roasted Red Pepper Topping
Omit arugula pesto and goat cheese topping. Combine 24 ounces rinsed jarred roasted peppers, cut into ½ inch pieces, 1 minced garlic clove, 2 tablespoons red wine vinegar, 2 tablespoons sugar, ¼ teaspoon red pepper flakes, and ¼ teaspoon table salt in medium bowl; set aside.

Process 8 ounces crumbled feta, 2 teaspoons lemon juice, 2 tablespoons extra-virgin olive oil, and ¼ teaspoon pepper in food processor until smooth, about 10 seconds, scraping down bowl once during processing. Substitute feta mixture for arugula mixture and pepper mixture for goat cheese.

Bruschetta with Ricotta, Tomato, and Basil Topping

We prefer the rich flavor of whole-milk ricotta; however, part-skim ricotta can be substituted. Do not use fat-free ricotta.

Omit arugula pesto and goat cheese topping. Toss 1 pound quartered cherry tomatoes with 1 teaspoon table salt in colander and let drain for 15 minutes. Transfer drained tomatoes to bowl and toss with 1 tablespoon extra-virgin olive oil, ¼ cup shredded fresh basil, and season with salt and pepper to taste. In separate bowl, combine 10 ounces whole-milk ricotta cheese and 1 tablespoon shredded fresh basil; season with salt and pepper to taste. Substitute ricotta mixture for arugula mixture and substitute tomato mixture for goat cheese.

Serrano and Manchego Crostini with Orange Honey

Serves 8 FAST

Why This Recipe Works Smaller than bruschetta, crostini are an easy-yet-elegant appetizer that will impress your guests but that won't take more than a few minutes away from setting the perfect summer table and mixing up some refreshing cocktails. There's more to making great crostini than just putting cheese on toast. The right combination of ingredients can take this deceptively simple appetizer to a whole other level. In our version, Serrano ham, Manchego cheese, and artisanal bread come together to form an elegant yet stress-free Spanish-inspired starter. For the bread, we preferred a nutty artisanal loaf such as walnut or pecan with dried fruit to complement the cheese. Toasting the bread intensified its nutty flavor. Assembling the crostini was as easy as topping the bread with the ham and cheese and drizzling each toast with a mixture of honey, orange marmalade, and fresh thyme for a sweet-salty flavor contrast. The key to this recipe is using high-quality ingredients; be sure to use authentic Spanish Serrano ham and Manchego cheese. If you can't find walnut or pecan bread, any variety of hearty artisanal-style nut and fruit bread would work here.

Serrano and Manchego Crostini with Orange Honey

1	loaf artisanal-style walnut or pecan bread
¼	cup honey
1	tablespoon orange marmalade
½	teaspoon minced fresh thyme
8	ounces thinly sliced Serrano ham
4	ounces thinly sliced Manchego cheese

1. Adjust oven rack 6 inches from broiler element and heat broiler. Slice bread into ¼-inch-thick pieces; cut larger pieces in half if necessary. Lay bread on 2 rimmed baking sheets. Broil bread, 1 baking sheet at a time, until golden brown on both sides, about 2 minutes per side.

2. Combine honey, marmalade, and thyme. Top toasts with ham and Manchego, then drizzle with honey mixture. Serve.

Baguette with Radishes, Butter, and Herbs

Serves 8 to 12 `FAST` `NO COOK`

Why This Recipe Works Leave it to the French to come up with one of the most indulgent, rustic-chic snacks of all time. Crusty baguette, farm-fresh radishes, and butter are a time-tested combination, and demand zero cooking and little time to prepare. We wanted to really highlight the vegetable in our version to take advantage of its peak season. We started by halving our loaf lengthwise and laying down just enough butter on top to coat both halves. Leaving the baguette whole allowed us to place more radishes on the bread and made for an impressive presentation. (Easter egg and watermelon radishes are especially pretty.) We shingled thinly sliced radishes all over in a fish-scale pattern, ensuring that each bite was packed with radish flavor. To coax even more flavor out of this dish, we made a simple compound butter with chives and cultured butter. And to complement the pepperiness of the radishes, we topped the baguette with a parsley salad for visual contrast and welcome brightness. Of course, this snack wouldn't be complete without a generous sprinkle of sea salt. The success of this recipe depends on high-quality ingredients, including European-style butter, fresh baguette, and in-season radishes.

10 tablespoons European-style unsalted butter, softened
6 tablespoons minced fresh chives, divided
¼ teaspoon table salt
¼ teaspoon pepper
1 teaspoon lemon juice
1 teaspoon extra-virgin olive oil
1 cup coarsely chopped fresh parsley
1 (18-inch) baguette, halved lengthwise
8 ounces radishes, trimmed and sliced thin
Flake sea salt

1. Combine butter, ¼ cup chives, salt, and pepper in bowl. Whisk remaining 2 tablespoons chives, lemon juice, and oil in second bowl. Add parsley and toss to coat. Season with salt and pepper to taste.

2. Spread butter mixture over cut sides of baguette. Shingle radishes evenly over butter and top with parsley salad. Sprinkle with sea salt to taste. Cut baguette crosswise into 12 pieces. Serve.

Farmers' Market Find Radishes

Radishes belong to the broccoli and kale family, and their strong flavor comes from the same compound that gives mustard and horseradish their pungency. Many varieties of radishes are available year-round in supermarkets but their best seasons are typically late spring into the fall. Try to buy radishes with crisp greens attached, a sign that the radishes are fresh. If they don't have greens attached (often the case in stores), make sure the radishes are firm and their skin is smooth and not cracked. Avoid very large radishes, which can have a woody texture. Store radishes wrapped in paper towels in a loosely closed plastic produce bag in the refrigerator for about a week. Remove and store greens separately, wrapped in paper towels in a plastic produce bag.

Round Red is the most commonly seen color, but they also appear in s-hades of white, pink, and purple. The different colors are sometimes sold in a bunch and labeled as "Easter egg radishes." Their flavor is sharp and bright and they have a juicy crunch.

French Breakfast These red-and-white radishes are an elongated version of regular round radishes. They are harvested primarily in the springtime and tend to have the mildest flavor of the various varieties.

Watermelon These magical-looking radishes have a pale green skin and a bright watermelon-pink interior, with a mildly spicy-sweet flavor. They are gorgeous raw—it's a waste to cook these, since their striking coloring will fade.

Daikon Long and white, daikon is the most commonly available large radish variety. They are more typically served cooked, but they can also be eaten raw and have a mildly peppery flavor. Daikon radishes with their greens attached are freshly harvested and will have a more mellow flavor, and the greens are edible.

White Icicle This heirloom variety is long and slender, like its namesake, and has a sinus-clearing peppery quality and slow-burning heat.

**Chicken Satay with Spicy
Peanut Dipping Sauce**

**Peruvian Fish
Ceviche with
Radishes and
Orange**

Chicken Satay with
Spicy Peanut Dipping Sauce

Serves 10 to 15

Why This Recipe Works Any dish that comes with its own handle is bound to be an appetizer favorite, and this Southeast Asian dish of marinated, broiled chicken has deep flavor to match its convenient form. We set out to create a recipe for a simple but satisfying appetizer perfect for eating with your hands at a breezy summer gathering. For the marinade, we made a mixture of brown sugar, soy sauce, ketchup, and hot sauce that guaranteed moist, full-flavored meat. We chilled boneless chicken breasts, sliced into skewer-ready strips, in the marinade for about a half-hour before broiling them. The intense, direct heat of the broiler cooked the chicken strips through perfectly in under 10 minutes. A peanut dipping sauce with sweet, tart, and spicy elements echoed the marinade for a fresh, bright finish. Covering the exposed ends of the skewers with aluminum foil protects them from burning. Freezing the chicken for 30 minutes will make it easier to slice into strips. You will need thirty 6-inch wooden skewers for this recipe.

Skewers
- ¼ cup soy sauce
- ¼ cup vegetable oil
- ¼ cup packed dark brown sugar
- ¼ cup minced fresh cilantro
- 4 scallions, sliced thin
- 3 tablespoons ketchup
- 2 garlic cloves, minced
- 1 teaspoon hot sauce
- 2 pounds boneless, skinless chicken breasts, trimmed and sliced diagonally into ¼-inch-thick strips
- 30 (6-inch) wooden skewers

Spicy Peanut Dipping Sauce
- ½ cup peanut butter, creamy or chunky
- ¼ cup hot water
- 3 tablespoons lime juice (2 limes)
- 2 scallions, sliced thin
- 2 tablespoons ketchup
- 1 tablespoon soy sauce
- 1 tablespoon packed dark brown sugar
- 1 tablespoon minced fresh cilantro
- 1½ teaspoons hot sauce
- 1 garlic clove, minced

1. For the skewers Combine soy sauce, oil, sugar, cilantro, scallions, ketchup, garlic, and hot sauce in medium bowl, add chicken, and toss to combine. Cover and refrigerate for at least 30 minutes. Weave chicken onto skewers.

2. For the spicy peanut dipping sauce Whisk peanut butter and hot water together in medium bowl. Stir in lime juice, scallions, ketchup, soy sauce, sugar, cilantro, hot sauce, and garlic. Transfer to serving bowl.

3. Adjust oven rack 6 inches from broiler element and heat broiler. Set wire rack in aluminum foil–lined rimmed baking sheet. Lay skewers on prepared rack and cover skewer ends with foil. Broil until fully cooked, about 8 minutes, flipping skewers halfway through broiling. Serve with peanut sauce.

Peruvian Fish Ceviche with Radishes and Orange

Serves 6 to 8   `NO COOK`

Why This Recipe Works Ceviche—a South American dish of raw seafood marinated in citrus juice until effectively "cooked"—is uniquely suited to hot summer nights; it's a supereasy, incredibly light preparation of fish that requires no heat and is served chilled for a refreshing, cooling option. To create a flavorful yet balanced "cooking" liquid for our Peruvian fish ceviche, we made what's known as a *leche de tigre* by blending lime juice, aji amarillo chile paste, garlic, extra-virgin olive oil, and a small amount of fish to add savory depth to the marinade. Once strained, the liquid was an intensely flavorful and silky-textured emulsion. We then soaked thinly sliced and briefly salted fish (red snapper, sea bass, halibut, and grouper were all good options) in the leche for 30 to 40 minutes until it was just opaque and slightly firm. To complete the dish, we added sweet oranges; crisp, peppery radishes; and chopped cilantro. We served the ceviche with corn nuts and popcorn, which provided salty crunch. It is imperative that you use the freshest fish possible in this recipe. Do not use frozen fish. Sea bass, halibut, or grouper can be substituted for the snapper, if desired. Aji amarillo chile paste can be found in the Latin section of grocery stores; if you can't find it, you can substitute 1 stemmed and seeded habanero chile. Serving the popcorn and corn nuts separately allows diners to customize their ceviche to suit their taste.

1 pound skinless red snapper fillets, ½ inch thick
3½ teaspoons kosher salt, divided
¾ cup lime juice (6 limes)
3 tablespoons extra-virgin olive oil, divided
1 tablespoon aji amarillo chile paste
2 garlic cloves, peeled
3 oranges
8 ounces radishes, trimmed, halved, and sliced thin
¼ cup coarsely chopped fresh cilantro
1 cup corn nuts
1 cup lightly salted popcorn

1. Using sharp knife, cut fish lengthwise into ½-inch-wide strips. Slice each strip crosswise ⅛ inch thick. Set aside ⅓ cup (2½ ounces) fish pieces. Toss remaining fish with 1 teaspoon salt and refrigerate for at least 10 minutes or up to 30 minutes.

2. Meanwhile, process reserved fish pieces, remaining 2½ teaspoons salt, lime juice, 2 tablespoons oil, chile paste, and garlic in blender until smooth, 30 to 60 seconds. Strain mixture through fine-mesh strainer set over large bowl, pressing on solids to extract as much liquid as possible. Discard solids. (Sauce can be refrigerated for up to 24 hours. It will separate slightly; whisk to recombine before proceeding with recipe.)

3. Cut away peel and pith from oranges. Holding fruit over bowl, use paring knife to slice between membranes to release segments. Cut orange segments into ¼-inch pieces. Add oranges, salted fish, and radishes to bowl with sauce and toss to combine. Refrigerate for 30 to 40 minutes (for more-opaque fish, refrigerate for 45 minutes to 1 hour).

4. Add cilantro to ceviche and toss to combine. Portion ceviche into individual bowls and drizzle with remaining 1 tablespoon oil. Serve, passing corn nuts and popcorn separately.

NOTES FROM THE TEST KITCHEN

HOW TO BUY THE FRESHEST FISH
When making ceviche (or any dish in which the fish is not fully cooked), using the freshest seafood possible is imperative for both flavor and food safety reasons. Here's what to look for:

Clean Smell The seafood (and the store or counter) should smell like the sea, not fishy or sour.

Shiny Surface Fillets should look bright and shiny; whole fish should have bright, clear eyes.

Firm Texture Fresh fish is firm. Ask your fishmonger to press the flesh with their finger; it should spring back.

Advice Ask your fishmonger what's freshest that day, even if it's not what you originally had in mind. Ceviche works with many different varieties of fish.

Grilled Clams, Mussels, or Oysters with Mignonette Sauce

Serves 4 to 6

Why This Recipe Works While steaming is an easy way to cook clams and mussels (oysters are often eaten raw on the half shell), grilling these bivalves is an appealing option, especially for summer entertaining. It's also an incredibly simple preparation. Before we got to cooking, carefully scrubbing our shellfish was an important step for ridding them of any grit. The key to great bivalves on the grill was to not move the shellfish around too much and to handle them carefully once they open. You want to preserve the natural juices, so when the clams or mussels open, transfer them with tongs to a platter, holding them steady so as not to spill any of the liquid. Always look for tightly closed clams, mussels, and oysters (avoid any that are gaping; they may be dying or dead). The clams may take slightly longer to cook on a gas grill than they do on a charcoal grill. If you like, serve the clams with lemon wedges, hot sauce, and tomato salsa.

- ½ cup red wine vinegar
- 2 shallots, chopped fine, or ¼ cup finely chopped red onion
- 2 tablespoons lemon juice, plus lemon wedges for serving
- 1½ tablespoons minced fresh parsley
- 24 clams or oysters, or 30 to 35 mussels (about 2 pounds), scrubbed and debearded if cooking mussels

1. Mix together vinegar, shallots, lemon juice, and parsley in small serving bowl; set aside for serving.

2A. For a charcoal grill Open bottom vent completely. Light large chimney starter filled with charcoal briquettes (6 quarts). When top coals are partially covered with ash, pour evenly over grill. Set cooking grate in place, cover, and open lid vent completely. Heat grill until hot, about 5 minutes.

2B. For a gas grill Turn all burners to high, cover, and heat grill until hot, about 15 minutes. Leave all burners on high.

3. Clean and oil cooking grate. Place shellfish directly on cooking grate. Grill (covered if using gas) without turning, until shellfish open, 3 to 5 minutes for mussels and oysters or 6 to 10 minutes for clams.

4. With tongs, carefully transfer opened shellfish to flat serving platter, trying to preserve juices. Discard top shells and loosen meat in bottom shells before serving, if desired. Serve with mignonette sauce and lemon wedges.

Smoked Salmon Rolls

Makes about 18 rolls `NO COOK` `MAKE AHEAD`

Why This Recipe Works Smoked salmon is a tried-and-true choice for many a cocktail party, garden party, or patio soiree spread. We wanted to try our hand at coming up with a smoked salmon roll recipe that would be a light, visually appealing, and easy starter. A modest schmear of cream-cheese-and-sour-cream spread held the rolls together without weighing them down. We found that letting the cream cheese soften at room temperature before mixing the spread allowed it to blend easily with the other ingredients. To liven up the spread, we flavored it with lemon, shallot, capers, and chives or dill. Once the rolls were assembled, we garnished the top of each one with a single leaf of baby arugula; its peppery bite lent a welcome freshness.

- 1 tablespoon cream cheese, softened
- 1 tablespoon sour cream
- ½ teaspoon lemon juice
- Pinch table salt
- Pinch pepper
- 1 teaspoon minced shallot
- 1 teaspoon capers, rinsed and minced
- 1 teaspoon minced fresh chives or dill
- 9 thin slices smoked salmon
- 18 small leaves baby arugula

1. Mix cream cheese, sour cream, lemon juice, salt, and pepper in bowl until uniform, then stir in shallot, capers, and chives.

2. Spread cream cheese mixture evenly over slices of salmon. Roll salmon around cream cheese mixture. Transfer salmon rolls to airtight container and refrigerate for up to 4 hours.

3. When ready to serve, slice each salmon roll in half with sharp knife. Stand each roll on its cut end, garnish with arugula leaf, and serve.

INGREDIENT SPOTLIGHT

SMOKED SALMON
Nova, Nova Scotia salmon, and lox are all generic terms for cold-smoked salmon, which is mostly what you find at the grocery store. Our favorite is **Spence & Co. Traditional Scottish Style Smoked Salmon.** Gravlax, not to be confused with lox, is salmon that has been cured under pressure.

Broiled Coriander-Lemon Shrimp
Serves 8 to 10

Why This Recipe Works For the easiest-ever version of shrimp cocktail that serves a crowd, we bypassed the traditional method of poaching and instead used the high heat of the broiler and a spice rub to give the shrimp great flavor. The little bit of sugar in our simple rub caramelized quickly under the broiler, adding good color to the outside of the shrimp and helping to bring out the fresh, sweet shrimp flavor. Instead of a traditional horseradish cocktail sauce, we paired the broiled shrimp with a creamy and lemony tarragon sauce. Other fresh herbs, such as dill, basil, cilantro, or mint, can be substituted for the tarragon. It's important to dry the shrimp thoroughly before tossing with the oil. We prefer to use jumbo shrimp here, but extra-large shrimp (21 to 25 per pound) can be substituted; if using smaller shrimp, reduce the broiling time by 1 to 2 minutes.

Creamy Tarragon Sauce
- ¾ cup mayonnaise
- 3 tablespoons lemon juice
- 2 scallions, minced
- 2 tablespoons minced fresh tarragon
- ¼ teaspoon table salt
- ⅛ teaspoon pepper

Shrimp
- ¾ teaspoon table salt
- ¾ teaspoon ground coriander
- ¼ teaspoon pepper
- ¼ teaspoon sugar
  Pinch cayenne pepper
- 2 pounds jumbo shrimp (16 to 20 per pound), peeled and deveined
- 2 tablespoons extra-virgin olive oil

1. For the creamy tarragon sauce Stir all ingredients together in serving bowl. Cover and refrigerate until flavors have blended, at least 30 minutes.

2. For the shrimp Adjust oven rack 3 inches from broiler element and heat broiler. Combine salt, coriander, pepper, sugar, and cayenne in small bowl. Pat shrimp dry with paper towels, then toss with oil and spice mixture in large bowl.

3. Spread shrimp in single layer on rimmed baking sheet. Broil shrimp until opaque and light golden in spots, 4 to 6 minutes. Transfer shrimp to serving platter and serve with sauce.

Smoked Salmon Rolls

Broiled Coriander-Lemon Shrimp

Mexican Shrimp Cocktail

Mexican Shrimp Cocktail (Cóctel de Camarón)

Serves 6 FAST

Why This Recipe Works Shrimp cocktail is a timeless chilled appetizer perfect for passing around a summer gathering. But when we want something a little more exciting than the shrimp and standard cocktail sauce, we look to this popular Mexican version, which consists of cooked shrimp tossed with chopped vegetables in a bright tomato sauce. For tender, not rubbery, shrimp, we brought water to a boil before adding the shrimp so there'd be enough heat in the saucepan to cook them through. Cutting the shrimp into bite-size pieces made them easier to eat. For a well-balanced sauce with concentrated tomato flavor, we used V8, which was equal parts sweet and savory with a bit of tartness. Along with ketchup, lime juice, and hot sauce, the viscosity of the V8 gave the sauce body to nicely coat the shrimp. Cucumber and red onion added crunch, avocado added creaminess, and cilantro added freshness. The balanced flavor of Valentina, Cholula, or Tapatío hot sauce works best here. If using a spicier, vinegary hot sauce such as Tabasco, start with half the amount called for and adjust to your taste after mixing. Saltines are a traditional accompaniment, but tortilla chips or thick-cut potato chips are also good.

1¼ pounds large shrimp (26 to 30 per pound), peeled, deveined, and tails removed
¼ teaspoon table salt, plus salt for cooking shrimp
1 cup V8 juice, chilled
½ cup ketchup
3 tablespoons lime juice (2 limes), plus lime wedges for serving
2 teaspoons hot sauce, plus extra for serving
½ English cucumber, cut into ½-inch pieces
1 cup finely chopped red onion
1 avocado, halved, pitted, and cut into ½-inch pieces
¼ cup chopped fresh cilantro
Saltines

1. Bring 3 cups water to boil in large saucepan over high heat. Stir in shrimp and 1 tablespoon salt. Cover and let stand off heat until shrimp are opaque, about 5 minutes, shaking saucepan halfway through. Fill large bowl halfway with ice and water. Transfer shrimp to ice bath and let cool for 3 to 5 minutes. Once cool, cut each shrimp crosswise into 3 pieces.

2. Combine V8 juice, ketchup, lime juice, hot sauce, and salt in medium bowl. Add cucumber, onion, and shrimp and stir until evenly coated. Stir in avocado and cilantro. Portion cocktail into individual bowls or glasses and serve immediately, passing saltines, lime wedges, and extra hot sauce separately.

Vietnamese Summer Rolls

Vietnamese Summer Rolls

Serves 8 (Makes 12 rolls) `MAKE AHEAD`

Why This Recipe Works Springy noodles, crisp lettuce, fresh herbs, and some protein make Vietnamese summer rolls perfect for a satisfying chilled appetizer or light meal. We wanted a streamlined process for flavorful rolls at home. Using indirect heat kept the shrimp tender, and a quick dunk in cold water made the wrappers easy to work with. Three different herbs, a spicy peanut sauce, and a fish sauce and lime mixture (*nuoc cham*) rounded out the delicate flavors. You can omit the pork; double the amount of shrimp (use the same timing and amounts of water and salt), and place three shrimp halves on top of the scallions. If Thai basil is unavailable, increase the mint and cilantro to 1½ cups each. A wooden surface will draw moisture away from the wrappers, so assemble the rolls on your counter or a plastic cutting board. If the wrapper dries out while you are forming the rolls, moisten it with your dampened fingers. We like to alternate between dipping these rolls in Peanut-Hoisin Sauce and Vietnamese Dipping Sauce (recipe follows).

Peanut-Hoisin Sauce

- 1 Thai chile, stemmed and sliced thin
- 1 garlic clove, minced
- 1 teaspoon kosher salt
- ⅔ cup water
- ⅓ cup creamy peanut butter
- 3 tablespoons hoisin sauce
- 2 tablespoons tomato paste
- 1 tablespoon distilled white vinegar

Summer Rolls

- 6 ounces rice vermicelli
- 10 ounces boneless country-style pork ribs, trimmed
- 2 teaspoons kosher salt
- 18 medium-large shrimp (31 to 40 per pound), peeled, deveined, and tails removed
- 1 cup fresh mint leaves
- 1 cup fresh cilantro leaves and thin stems
- 1 cup Thai basil leaves
- 12 (8½-inch) round rice paper wrappers
- 12 leaves red or green leaf lettuce, thick ribs removed
- 2 scallions, sliced thin on bias

1. For the peanut-hoisin sauce Using mortar and pestle (or on cutting board using flat side of chef's knife), mash Thai chile, garlic, and salt to fine paste. Transfer to medium bowl. Add water, peanut butter, hoisin, tomato paste, and vinegar and whisk until smooth.

2. For the summer rolls Bring 2 quarts water to boil in medium saucepan. Stir in noodles. Cook until noodles are tender but not mushy, 3 to 4 minutes. Drain noodles and rinse with cold water until cool. Drain noodles again, then spread on large plate to dry.

3. Bring 2 quarts water to boil in now-empty saucepan. Add pork and salt. Reduce heat, cover, and simmer until thickest part of pork registers 150 degrees, 8 to 12 minutes. Transfer pork to cutting board, reserving water.

4. Return water to boil. Add shrimp and cover. Let stand off heat until shrimp are opaque throughout, about 3 minutes. Drain shrimp and rinse with cold water until cool. Transfer to cutting board. Pat shrimp dry and halve lengthwise. Transfer to second plate.

HOW TO ROLL A SUMMER ROLL

1. Bring lower edge of wrapper up and over herbs.

2. Roll snugly but gently until greens and noodles are enclosed.

3. Fold in sides to enclose ends.

4. Arrange 3 shrimp halves, cut side up, on remaining wrapper. Continue to roll until filling is completely enclosed in neat cylinder.

5. When pork is cool enough to handle, cut each rib crosswise into 2-inch lengths. Slice each 2-inch piece lengthwise ⅛ inch thick (you should have at least 24 slices) and transfer to plate with shrimp. Tear mint, cilantro, and Thai basil into 1-inch pieces and combine in bowl.

6. Fill large bowl with cold water. Submerge 1 wrapper in water until wet on both sides, no longer than 2 seconds. Shake gently over bowl to remove excess water, then lay wrapper flat on counter (wrapper will be fairly stiff but will continue to soften as you assemble roll). Repeat with second wrapper and place next to first wrapper. Fold 1 lettuce leaf and place on lower third of first wrapper, leaving about ½-inch margin on each side. Spread ⅓ cup noodles on top of lettuce, then sprinkle with 1 teaspoon scallions. Top scallions with 2 slices pork. Spread ¼ cup herb mixture over pork.

7. Bring lower edge of wrapper up and over herbs. Roll snugly but gently until long sides of greens and noodles are enclosed. Fold in sides to enclose ends. Arrange 3 shrimp halves, cut side up, on remaining section of wrapper. Continue to roll until filling is completely enclosed in neat cylinder. Transfer roll to serving platter, shrimp side up, and cover with plastic wrap. Repeat with second moistened wrapper. Repeat with remaining wrappers and filling, keeping completed rolls covered with plastic. Uncover, cut in half using a sharp, wet knife, and serve with sauce. (Leftovers can be wrapped tightly and refrigerated for up to 24 hours, but wrappers will become chewier and may break in places.)

Vietnamese Dipping Sauce (Nuoc Cham)
Serves 8 (Makes 1 cup)
Hot water helps the sugar dissolve into the sauce.

  3 tablespoons sugar, divided
  1 small Thai chile, stemmed and minced
  1 garlic clove, minced
  ⅔ cup hot water
  5 tablespoons fish sauce
  ¼ cup lime juice (2 limes)

Using mortar and pestle (or on cutting board using flat side of chef's knife), mash 1 tablespoon sugar, Thai chile, and garlic to fine paste. Transfer to medium bowl and add hot water and remaining 2 tablespoons sugar. Stir until sugar is dissolved. Stir in fish sauce and lime juice.

Chilled Cucumber and Yogurt Soup
Serves 6 `NO COOK` `MAKE AHEAD`

Why This Recipe Works Both refreshing and elegant, this chilled soup is the perfect antidote for a swelteringly hot summer's evening. But because it has so few ingredients, we knew that balance and finesse would be key, especially if the subtle vegetal flavor of the cucumbers was to shine through. A food processor turned our soup mushy, and hand-chopping all of the cucumber gave us something watery and inconsistent. We found that blending some of the cucumbers and reserving a final chopped handful as a garnish gave us the smooth consistency we wanted with texture to boot. Peeling and seeding the cucumbers removed any unpleasantly bitter flavors. We tried garlic, shallots, red onion, and scallions in the soup, but they were all too astringent; it was only after we left in just the scallion greens that we found the right balance. Tasters preferred dill and mint to other herb combinations, as they brought out the freshest aspect of this appealing soup. Serve in chilled bowls, if desired.

  5 pounds cucumbers, peeled and seeded (1 cucumber cut into ½-inch pieces, remaining cucumbers cut into 2-inch pieces), divided
  4 scallions, green parts only, chopped
  2 cups water
  2 cups plain Greek yogurt
  1 tablespoon lemon juice
  1½ teaspoons table salt
  ¼ teaspoon sugar
     Pinch pepper
  1½ tablespoons minced fresh dill
  1½ tablespoons minced fresh mint
     Extra-virgin olive oil

1. Toss 2-inch pieces of cucumber with scallions. Working in 2 batches, process cucumber-scallion mixture in blender with water until completely smooth, about 2 minutes; transfer to large bowl. Whisk in yogurt, lemon juice, salt, sugar, and pepper. Cover and refrigerate to meld flavors, at least 1 hour or up to 12 hours.

2. Stir in dill and mint and season with salt and pepper to taste. Serve cold, topping individual portions with remaining ½-inch pieces of cucumber and drizzling with oil.

Gazpacho

Serves 8 to 10 `NO COOK` `MAKE AHEAD`

Why This Recipe Works Gazpacho—a chilled mixture of hand-cut vegetables marinated in seasoned vinegar—is perhaps the ultimate summer soup: fresh, light, and perfectly suited for leftovers to have on hand for lunch on a hot afternoon. Letting the diced vegetables sit briefly in a sherry vinegar marinade seasoned them thoroughly. A combination of tomato juice and ice cubes provided the right amount of liquid for the soup. A 4-hour chill was critical to allow the flavors of the soup to develop and meld. Luckily, this meant we could make the soup well in advance of a meal. Use a Vidalia, Maui, or Walla Walla onion here. This recipe makes enough for leftovers, but it can be halved if you prefer. Traditionally, diners garnish their gazpacho with more of the same diced vegetables that are in the soup, so cut some extra vegetables when preparing those in the recipe. Serve with Herbed Croutons, chopped pitted black olives, chopped Easy-Peel Hard-Cooked Eggs (page 54), and finely diced avocados. Serve in chilled bowls, if desired.

Gazpacho

1½ pounds tomatoes, cored and cut into ¼-inch dice
 2 red bell peppers, stemmed, seeded, and cut into ¼-inch dice
 2 small cucumbers (1 peeled, 1 unpeeled), sliced lengthwise, seeded, and cut into ¼-inch dice
 ½ small sweet onion or 2 large shallots, minced
 ⅓ cup sherry vinegar
 2 garlic cloves, minced
 2 teaspoons table salt
 5 cups tomato juice
 8 ice cubes
 1 teaspoon hot sauce (optional)
   Extra-virgin olive oil

1. Combine tomatoes, bell peppers, cucumbers, onion, vinegar, garlic, and salt in large (at least 4-quart) bowl and season with pepper to taste. Let sit until vegetables just begin to release their juices, about 5 minutes. Stir in tomato juice, ice cubes, and hot sauce, if using. Cover and refrigerate to meld flavors, at least 4 hours or up to 2 days.

2. Discard any unmelted ice cubes and season soup with salt and pepper to taste. Divide into individual bowls, drizzling individual portions with oil. Serve cold.

VARIATION
Gazpacho with Avocado and Crab
Add 1 pound lump crab meat, picked over for shells, and 1 pitted, skinned, and diced avocado to bowls before serving.

Herbed Croutons
Makes about 2½ cups
Either fresh or stale bread can be used in this recipe.

 1 tablespoon butter
 1 teaspoon minced fresh parsley
 ½ teaspoon minced fresh thyme
 4 slices hearty white sandwich bread, crusts removed, cut into ½-inch pieces

Melt butter in 10-inch skillet over medium heat. Add parsley and thyme; cook, stirring constantly, for 20 seconds. Add bread pieces and cook, stirring frequently, until light golden brown, 5 to 10 minutes. Transfer croutons to paper towel–lined plate and season with salt and pepper to taste.

CHAPTER 2

Dinner-Size Salads

■ FAST (30 minutes or less total time)   ■ NO COOK   ■ MAKE AHEAD

Photos (clockwise from top left): Grilled Thai Beef Salad; Farro Salad with Sugar Snap Peas and White Beans; Moroccan Chicken Salad with Apricots and Almonds; Chilled Soba Noodle Salad with Cucumber, Snow Peas, and Radishes; Smoked Salmon Niçoise Salad

Chicken Salad with Pickled Fennel, Watercress, and Macadamia Nuts

Chicken and Arugula Salad with Figs and Warm Spices

Chicken Salad with Pickled Fennel, Watercress, and Macadamia Nuts

Serves 4 to 6 MAKE AHEAD

Why This Recipe Works For a dinner salad with plenty of fresh summer flavor, contrasting textures, and satisfying heft, we combined spicy watercress with pickled fennel, crunchy macadamia nuts, and mildly flavored poached chicken. Pickling is a perfect technique to imbue fresh summery vegetables with complexity and nuance, tenderize raw textures, and introduce punchy flavor into a salad. A quick stint in a spiced hot brine rounded out the fresh, vegetal flavor of the fennel with the more floral notes of fennel seeds. While the pickles were steeping, we prepared the rest of the light meal. We gently poached some chicken breasts to add protein to the salad and then made further use of the flavorful pickling liquid by incorporating it into our vinaigrette. Then it was just a matter of tossing the watercress, macadamia nuts, and pickled fennel with our perfectly cooked chicken. Not wanting to waste anything, we used some of the fennel fronds to add another fresh element. If your fennel comes without fronds, they can be omitted. You can substitute rotisserie chicken for the cooked chicken in this recipe.

Pickled Fennel
- ¾ cup seasoned rice vinegar
- ¼ cup water
- 1 garlic clove, peeled and smashed
- 1 (3-inch) strip orange zest
- ¼ teaspoon fennel seeds
- ⅛ teaspoon black peppercorns
- ⅛ teaspoon mustard seeds
- 1 fennel bulb, 2 tablespoons fronds minced, stalks discarded, bulb halved, cored, and sliced thin

Salad
- 2 tablespoons extra-virgin olive oil
- ¼ teaspoon table salt
- 1 recipe Shredded Cooked Chicken (page 41)
- 10 ounces (10 cups) watercress, torn into bite-size pieces
- ½ cup macadamia nuts or cashews, toasted and chopped

1. For the pickled fennel Combine vinegar, water, garlic, orange zest, fennel seeds, peppercorns, and mustard seeds in 2-cup liquid measuring cup and microwave until boiling, about 5 minutes. Stir in sliced fennel bulb until completely submerged and let cool completely, about 30 minutes. (Pickled fennel can be refrigerated for up to 6 weeks.)

2. For the salad Drain fennel, reserving ⅓ cup brine; discard solids. Whisk reserved brine, oil, and salt in large bowl. Add pickled fennel, chicken, watercress, and fennel fronds and toss to combine. Season with salt and pepper to taste. Sprinkle with macadamia nuts and serve.

Chicken and Arugula Salad with Figs and Warm Spices

Serves 6 FAST

Why This Recipe Works To create an easy layered dinner salad perfect for a hot summer evening, we added beautiful, deep purple figs to refreshing greens to transform simple into special. Fresh figs have a subtle floral sweetness, which we wanted to enhance with a dressing seasoned with warm spices. We tried a variety of spice blends and homed in on coriander for its light citrus note, along with smoked paprika and cinnamon for depth. We microwaved the spices to bloom their flavor for a bolder dressing and then whisked in lemon juice and a teaspoon of honey to balance the spice. To make the salad substantial enough to serve for dinner, we added shredded chicken for some protein, along with chickpeas to bring more heartiness and texture. A bed of peppery baby arugula complemented our dressing well. Our salad was now full of warm, bright flavors, but needed a bit of crunch to play against the soft figs. Toasted and chopped almonds made the perfect topping. You can substitute dried figs for fresh and rotisserie chicken for the cooked chicken in this recipe.

- 6 tablespoons extra-virgin olive oil, divided
- 1 teaspoon ground coriander
- ½ teaspoon smoked paprika
- ¼ teaspoon ground cinnamon
- 3 tablespoons lemon juice
- 1 teaspoon honey
- ½ teaspoon table salt
- ¼ teaspoon pepper
- 1 recipe Shredded Cooked Chicken
- 1 (15-ounce) can chickpeas, rinsed
- 5 ounces (5 cups) baby arugula
- ½ cup fresh parsley leaves
- 1 shallot, sliced thin
- 8 fresh figs, stemmed and quartered
- ½ cup whole almonds, toasted and chopped

1. Microwave 1 tablespoon oil, coriander, paprika, and cinnamon in large bowl until fragrant, about 30 seconds. Whisk lemon juice, honey, salt, and pepper into spice mixture. Whisking constantly, slowly drizzle in remaining 5 tablespoons oil.

2. Add chicken, chickpeas, arugula, parsley, and shallot to dressing in bowl and gently toss to combine. Transfer salad to serving platter, arrange figs over top, and sprinkle with almonds. Serve.

Shredded Cooked Chicken
Makes about 4 cups
This easy poached chicken tastes great served at room temperature or chilled and makes a great protein to add to a wide variety of main-dish salads.

- 4 (6- to 8-ounce) boneless, skinless chicken breasts
- 2 tablespoons table salt

1. Cover chicken breasts with plastic wrap and pound thick ends gently until ¾ inch thick. Whisk salt into 4 quarts cool water in Dutch oven.

2. Arrange chicken breasts in steamer basket without overlapping. Submerge in pot. Heat over medium heat, stirring occasionally, until water registers 175 degrees, 15 to 20 minutes.

3. Turn off heat, cover pot, remove from burner, and let stand until chicken registers 160 degrees, 17 to 22 minutes. Transfer chicken to cutting board and let cool for 10 to 15 minutes.

4. Using 2 forks, shred chicken into bite-size pieces. (Chicken can be stored in refrigerator for up to 5 days.)

SHREDDING CHICKEN

Using 2 forks, shred chicken into bite-size pieces.

Foolproof Vinaigrettes and Bold Salad Dressings

A good salad dressing makes all the difference between a salad that is just OK and one you really enjoy. The vinaigrettes here include a little bit of mayonnaise, whisked with the oil and vinegar, as an emulsifier to keep the vinaigrette from separating. All of these salad dressings keep for a few days or longer, so you can save extra dressing to have on hand and use in a salad later in the week. It is important to use high-quality vinegars and olive oils to make a really great salad dressing.

Classic Vinaigrette

Makes ¼ cup (enough for 4 to 5 cups greens)

This vinaigrette works well with all types of greens. To make an herb vinaigrette, whisk in 1 tablespoon minced fresh parsley or chives and ½ teaspoon minced fresh thyme, tarragon, marjoram, or oregano before serving. You can use red wine vinegar, white wine vinegar, or champagne vinegar here.

- 1 tablespoon wine vinegar
- 1½ teaspoons minced shallot
- ½ teaspoon mayonnaise
- ½ teaspoon Dijon mustard
- ⅛ teaspoon table salt
  Pinch pepper
- 3 tablespoons extra-virgin olive oil

Whisk vinegar, shallot, mayonnaise, mustard, salt, and pepper together in bowl. Whisking constantly, drizzle in oil until completely emulsified. (Vinaigrette can be refrigerated for up to 1 week; whisk to recombine.)

Lemon Vinaigrette

Makes ¼ cup (enough for 4 to 5 cups greens)

This vinaigrette is best for dressing mild greens.

- ½ teaspoon mayonnaise
- ½ teaspoon Dijon mustard
- ¼ teaspoon grated lemon zest plus 1 tablespoon juice
- ⅛ teaspoon table salt
- Pinch pepper
- 3 tablespoons extra-virgin olive oil

Whisk mayonnaise, mustard, lemon zest and juice, salt, and pepper together in bowl. Whisking constantly, drizzle in oil until completely emulsified. (Vinaigrette can be refrigerated for up to 1 week; whisk to recombine.)

Balsamic-Mustard Vinaigrette

Makes ¼ cup (enough for 4 to 5 cups greens)

This vinaigrette is best for dressing assertive greens.

- 1 tablespoon balsamic vinegar
- 2 teaspoons Dijon mustard
- 1½ teaspoons minced shallot
- ½ teaspoon mayonnaise
- ½ teaspoon minced fresh thyme
- ⅛ teaspoon table salt
- Pinch pepper
- 3 tablespoons extra-virgin olive oil

Whisk vinegar, mustard, shallot, mayonnaise, thyme, salt, and pepper together in bowl. Whisking constantly, drizzle in oil until completely emulsified. (Vinaigrette can be refrigerated for up to 1 week; whisk to recombine.)

Tahini-Lemon Dressing

Makes ½ cup (enough for 6 to 7 cups greens)

This dressing is best for dressing mild greens.

- 2½ tablespoons lemon juice
- 2 tablespoons tahini
- 1 tablespoon water
- 1 garlic clove, minced
- ½ teaspoon table salt
- ⅛ teaspoon pepper
- ¼ cup extra-virgin olive oil

Whisk lemon juice, tahini, water, garlic, salt, and pepper together in bowl. Whisking constantly, drizzle in oil until completely emulsified. (Dressing can be refrigerated for up to 1 week; whisk to recombine.)

Green Goddess Dressing

Makes about 1¼ cups (enough for 10 to 12 cups greens)

Pair this creamy, herbaceous dressing with crisp romaine, or toss with potatoes and cubed cooked chicken for a vibrant salad.

- 1 tablespoon lemon juice
- 1 tablespoon water
- 2 teaspoons dried tarragon
- ¾ cup mayonnaise
- ¼ cup sour cream
- ¼ cup minced fresh parsley
- 1 garlic clove, minced
- 1 anchovy fillet, rinsed
- ¼ cup minced fresh chives

Combine lemon juice, water, and tarragon in small bowl and let sit for 15 minutes. Process tarragon mixture, mayonnaise, sour cream, parsley, garlic, and anchovy in blender until smooth, scraping down sides of blender jar as needed; transfer dressing to clean bowl. Stir in chives and season with salt and pepper to taste. Refrigerate until flavors meld, about 1 hour. (Dressing can be refrigerated for up to 4 days; whisk to recombine before using.)

Parmesan-Peppercorn Dressing

Makes ½ cup (enough for 8 to 10 cups greens)

This dressing works well with all types of greens.

- 2 tablespoons buttermilk
- 2 tablespoons mayonnaise
- 2 tablespoons low-fat sour cream
- 2 tablespoons grated Parmesan cheese
- 1 tablespoon water
- 1½ teaspoons lemon juice
- ½ teaspoon Dijon mustard
- ½ teaspoon minced shallot
- ¼ teaspoon pepper
- ¼ teaspoon garlic powder

Whisk all ingredients in bowl until smooth. (Dressing can be refrigerated for up to 1 week; whisk to recombine.)

Chicken Salad with Whole-Grain Mustard Vinaigrette

Serves 4 FAST

Why This Recipe Works Fresh lemon juice brightens this light and summery dinner salad, while sugar snap peas and red grapes add a juicy crunch. Shredded chicken is the perfect protein to make this refreshing salad a light but satisfying meal. Whole-grain mustard helps make a thick, hearty vinaigrette for this salad. You can substitute rotisserie chicken for the cooked chicken in this recipe. You can substitute more delicate Bibb lettuce for the red leaf lettuce if you prefer.

⅓ cup whole-grain mustard
3 tablespoons lemon juice
¼ teaspoon pepper
⅛ teaspoon table salt
3 tablespoons extra-virgin olive oil
1 recipe Shredded Cooked Chicken (page 41)
1 small head red leaf lettuce (8 ounces), torn into bite-size pieces
8 ounces sugar snap peas, trimmed and halved lengthwise
1 cup red grapes, halved
3 tablespoons minced fresh chives

1. Whisk mustard, lemon juice, pepper, and salt together in large bowl. Whisking constantly, slowly drizzle in oil until incorporated.

2. Measure ¼ of vinaigrette and transfer to medium bowl. Add chicken and toss until well coated with vinaigrette.

3. Add lettuce, snap peas, grapes, and chives to remaining vinaigrette in large bowl and toss until combined. Season with salt and pepper to taste.

4. Divide salad among individual serving plates and top with chicken. Serve.

INGREDIENT SPOTLIGHT

PREMIUM EXTRA-VIRGIN OLIVE OIL
High-end extra-virgin olive oils offer a world of flavor beyond supermarket options and are great for making a superior salad dressing or for drizzling over a chilled soup. Our favorite, **Gaea Fresh Extra Virgin Olive Oil** is a "medium" on the mild-to-robust spectrum and has buttery, smooth notes, a sweet olive fruitiness, and a peppery aftertaste.

Moroccan Chicken Salad with Apricots and Almonds

Serves 4 to 6 MAKE AHEAD

Why This Recipe Works For a creative chicken salad, we were inspired by the vibrant flavors of Morocco: apricots, lemon, and warm spices. To give our dressing complex flavor, we reached for garam masala, a traditional spice blend of coriander, cumin, ginger, cinnamon, and black pepper. We also added a little more coriander, honey, and smoked paprika for depth. Blooming the spices in the microwave deepened their flavors for an even bolder dressing. Chickpeas further echoed the Moroccan theme and lent heartiness, and crisp romaine combined with slightly bitter watercress made the perfect bed of greens for our toppings. Reserving a bit of the dressing to drizzle on just before serving made the flavors pop.

1½ pounds boneless, skinless chicken breasts, trimmed
¾ teaspoon table salt, divided
½ teaspoon pepper, divided
¾ cup extra-virgin olive oil, divided
1 teaspoon garam masala
½ teaspoon ground coriander
    Pinch smoked paprika
¼ cup lemon juice (2 lemons), divided
1 tablespoon honey
1 (15-ounce) can chickpeas, rinsed
¾ cup dried apricots, chopped
1 shallot, sliced thin
2 tablespoons minced fresh parsley
2 romaine lettuce hearts (12 ounces), cut into 1-inch pieces
4 ounces (4 cups) watercress
½ cup whole almonds, toasted and chopped

1. Pat chicken dry with paper towels and sprinkle with ½ teaspoon salt and ¼ teaspoon pepper. Heat 1 tablespoon oil in 12-inch skillet over medium-high heat until just smoking. Brown chicken well on first side, 6 to 8 minutes. Flip chicken, add ½ cup water, and cover. Reduce heat to medium-low and continue to cook until chicken registers 160 degrees, 5 to 7 minutes. Transfer chicken to cutting board and let cool for 10 to 15 minutes, then slice ½ inch thick on bias.

2. Meanwhile, microwave 1 tablespoon oil, garam masala, coriander, and paprika in medium bowl until oil is hot and fragrant, about 30 seconds. Whisk 3 tablespoons lemon juice, honey, remaining ¼ teaspoon salt, and remaining ¼ teaspoon pepper into spice mixture. Whisking constantly, drizzle in remaining oil.

3. In large bowl, combine cooled chicken, chickpeas, apricots, shallot, parsley, and half of dressing and toss to coat. Let mixture sit for 15 to 30 minutes. Whisk remaining 1 tablespoon lemon juice into remaining dressing. (Dressed chicken mixture and remaining vinaigrette can be refrigerated for up to 2 days. Bring to room temperature before continuing with step 4.)

4. Toss romaine, watercress, and almonds together in serving bowl, drizzle remaining dressing over top, and toss to combine. Season with salt and pepper to taste. Top with chicken mixture and serve.

Kale Caesar Salad with Chicken
Serves 4   `MAKE AHEAD`

Why This Recipe Works A Caesar salad topped with chicken is a superpopular dinner option for those summer nights when you want to feel satiated without weighing yourself down with a heavy meal. This play on a traditional chicken Caesar uses hearty, healthy kale rather than romaine for a bit more heft, but otherwise keeps all the savory punch of the classic salad. To stand up to the assertive flavor of the kale, we made our dressing extra-potent, with a stronger dose of lemon juice and anchovies than is typical in Caesar salad. We also made some easy, well-seasoned croutons, which could bake in the oven while we were preparing the salad. Parmesan cheese was the finishing touch, adding a rich, salty note.

Kale Caesar Salad with Chicken

½	cup extra-virgin olive oil, divided
2	garlic cloves, minced, divided
½–¾	loaf ciabatta, cut into ¾-inch cubes (5 cups)
½	teaspoon plus ⅛ teaspoon table salt, divided
½	teaspoon pepper, divided
12	ounces curly kale, stemmed and cut into 1-inch pieces
1	ounce Parmesan cheese, grated (½ cup), divided
⅓	cup mayonnaise
1	tablespoon lemon juice
2	teaspoons white wine vinegar
2	teaspoons Worcestershire sauce
2	teaspoons Dijon mustard
3	anchovy fillets, rinsed
4	(3- to 4-ounce) chicken cutlets, ½ inch thick, trimmed

1. Combine 1 tablespoon oil and half of garlic in small bowl. Place bread in large bowl, sprinkle with water and ¼ teaspoon salt, and squeeze bread gently to absorb water. Heat ¼ cup oil in 12-inch nonstick skillet over medium-high heat; add bread and cook, stirring often, until browned and crisp, 7 to 10 minutes.

2. Off heat, push bread to sides of skillet. Add garlic mixture and cook using residual heat of skillet, mashing mixture into skillet, for 10 seconds. Mix together with bread. Transfer croutons to bowl and let cool slightly; set aside for serving.

3. Place kale in large bowl and cover with warm tap water (110 to 115 degrees). Swish kale around to remove grit. Let kale sit in warm water bath for 10 minutes. Remove kale from water and spin dry in salad spinner in multiple batches. Pat leaves dry with paper towels if still wet.

4. Process ¼ cup Parmesan, mayonnaise, lemon juice, vinegar, Worcestershire, mustard, anchovies, remaining garlic, ¼ teaspoon salt, and ¼ teaspoon pepper in blender until smooth, about 30 seconds. With blender running, slowly add 2 tablespoons oil until incorporated. Toss kale with dressing and refrigerate for at least 20 minutes or up to 6 hours.

5. Pat chicken dry with paper towels and sprinkle with remaining ⅛ teaspoon salt and remaining ¼ teaspoon pepper. Heat remaining 1 tablespoon oil in 12-inch nonstick skillet over medium-high heat until just smoking. Add chicken and cook until golden brown and registers 160 degrees, about 3 minutes per side. Transfer chicken to cutting board and let cool, 10 to 15 minutes.

6. Toss dressed kale with croutons and remaining ¼ cup Parmesan. Divide salad among individual serving plates. Slice chicken thin and arrange over salads. Serve at room temperature or cold.

Beet and Carrot Noodle Salad with Chicken

Serves 4

Why This Recipe Works This colorful dish uses homemade beet and carrot noodles for the appeal of pasta salad with the freshness and lightness of raw vegetables. With their dense texture, beets make excellent vegetable "noodles," as spiralizing renders them delicate enough to eat raw. Pairing them with carrot noodles made for a visually stunning salad. The noodles' crisp-tender texture was a perfect foil for the creamy sweet-and-savory dressing. Topping the salad with pan-seared chicken cutlets was a quick and fuss-free way to make this dish a meal. You will need a spiralizer to make the beet and carrot noodles; if you don't have one, use precut store-bought vegetable noodles. You'll need about 12 ounces of each. Generously sized vegetables spiralize more easily, so use beets that are at least 1½ inches in diameter and carrots that are at least ¾ inch across at the thinnest end and 1½ inches across at the thickest end. You can use smooth or chunky peanut butter in the dressing for this recipe.

¼ cup smooth or chunky peanut butter
3 tablespoons tahini
2 tablespoons lime juice, plus lime wedges for serving
1 tablespoon soy sauce
1 tablespoon honey
1 tablespoon grated fresh ginger
2 garlic cloves, minced
½ teaspoon toasted sesame oil

Beet and Carrot Noodle
Salad with Chicken

½ teaspoon plus ⅛ teaspoon table salt, divided
1 to 6 tablespoons hot water
1 pound beets, trimmed and peeled
1 pound carrots, trimmed and peeled
5 scallions, sliced thin on the bias
4 (3- to 4-ounce) chicken cutlets, ½ inch thick, trimmed
¼ teaspoon pepper
1 tablespoon vegetable oil
¼ cup fresh cilantro leaves

1. Whisk peanut butter, tahini, lime juice, soy sauce, honey, ginger, garlic, sesame oil, and ½ teaspoon salt in large bowl until well combined. Whisking constantly, add hot water, 1 tablespoon at a time (up to 6 tablespoons), until dressing has consistency of heavy cream.

2. Using spiralizer, cut beets and carrots into ⅛-inch-thick noodles, cutting noodles into 6- to 8-inch lengths with kitchen shears as you spiralize (about every 2 to 3 revolutions).

3. Add beet and carrot noodles and scallions to dressing and toss well to combine.

4. Pat chicken dry with paper towels and sprinkle with remaining ⅛ teaspoon salt and pepper. Heat oil in 12-inch nonstick skillet over medium-high heat until just smoking. Add chicken and cook until golden brown and registers 160 degrees, about 3 minutes per side. Transfer chicken to cutting board and let cool for 10 to 15 minutes.

5. Divide noodles among individual serving plates. Slice chicken thin and arrange over salads. Sprinkle with cilantro and serve with lime wedges.

SPIRALIZING CARROTS

1. Trim carrot so it will fit on prongs. Secure vegetable between prongs and blade surface.

2. Spiralize by turning crank. Pull noodles straight and cut into correct lengths as directed in recipe.

INGREDIENT SPOTLIGHT

TAHINI

Tahini is a thick paste made from ground sesame seeds. It is often used to flavor eastern Mediterranean dishes such as hummus. It is also a popular condiment for falafel and can act as a base for creamy vinaigrettes. You can make your own tahini by grinding sesame seeds in a blender with just enough toasted sesame oil to make a smooth paste. Our favorite store-bought brand is **Ziyad Sesame Tahini Paste**, which has an intense sesame flavor and a smooth and fluid consistency.

Asian Chicken and Cellophane Noodle Salad

Serves 4   `FAST`

Why This Recipe Works Cellophane noodles, also known as glass noodles, are thin, transparent Asian noodles usually made from mung bean starch and water. They're great in soups and stir-fries, but we also love them as an interesting base of a chilled, hearty, summery dinner salad. To keep this salad easy without sacrificing flavor or visual appeal, we loaded it up with color and flavorful bite by adding quick-pickled carrots and cucumbers, which were easy to prepare while the noodles cooked. Inspired by the cellophane noodles, we chose an Asian-flavored dressing for this salad, using rice vinegar, toasted sesame oil, fresh ginger, and minced garlic to build a rounded vinaigrette. Our Shredded Cooked Chicken was the perfect choice for the protein component of this salad, as its mild flavor perfectly picked up the savory dressing. You can substitute rotisserie chicken for the cooked chicken in this recipe.

8	ounces cellophane noodles
3	carrots, peeled and cut into 2-inch-long matchsticks
2	English cucumbers, peeled and cut into 2-inch-long matchsticks
6	tablespoons rice vinegar, divided
⅓	cup soy sauce
2	tablespoons vegetable oil
1	tablespoon toasted sesame oil
1	tablespoon grated fresh ginger
1	garlic clove, minced
2	cups Shredded Cooked Chicken (page 41)

1. Bring 4 quarts water to boil in large pot. Add noodles and cook until tender. Drain, rinse with cold water, and drain again to remove as much water as possible.

2. Meanwhile, toss carrots and cucumbers with 2 tablespoons vinegar in large bowl; set aside to marinate for 10 minutes. Whisk soy sauce, remaining ¼ cup vinegar, vegetable oil, sesame oil, ginger, and garlic together in bowl.

3. Drain and discard vinegar from marinating vegetables. Add noodles, chicken, and dressing to bowl with vegetables and toss to thoroughly combine. Serve.

Wedge Salad with Steak Tips

Wedge Salad with Steak Tips
Serves 4 `FAST`

Why This Recipe Works Crunchy iceberg lettuce, tangy blue cheese, and crispy bacon: these are the makings of the ever-popular steakhouse salad. In the summer, we love this salad as a light counterpoint to richer, meaty steak tips—a nod to the salad's steakhouse roots—as the refreshing iceberg provides pleasant crunch and volume while serving as a cool, refreshing base of a complete meal. We prefer Stilton in this salad, but you can substitute any high-quality blue cheese. Sirloin steak tips, also known as flap meat, can be sold as whole steaks, cubes, and strips; to ensure uniform pieces, we prefer to purchase whole steaks and cut them ourselves. This salad is best when the iceberg wedges are cold, so leave the lettuce in the refrigerator until the steak is done cooking.

- 4 slices bacon, cut into ½-inch pieces
- ¾ cup plain yogurt
- 3 ounces Stilton cheese, crumbled (¾ cup), divided
- 1 teaspoon red wine vinegar
- 1 garlic clove, minced
- ¾ teaspoon table salt, divided
- ½ teaspoon pepper, divided
- 1½ pounds sirloin steak tips, trimmed and cut into 2-inch pieces
- 1 head iceberg lettuce (9 ounces), cored and cut into 8 wedges
- 10 ounces cherry tomatoes, halved
- 2 tablespoons minced fresh chives

1. Cook bacon in 12-inch skillet over medium heat until crispy, 5 to 7 minutes. Using slotted spoon, transfer bacon to paper towel–lined plate and remove skillet from heat (do not wipe out skillet).

2. Whisk yogurt, ½ cup Stilton, vinegar, garlic, ¼ teaspoon salt, and ¼ teaspoon pepper in bowl until combined.

3. Pat steak dry with paper towels and sprinkle with remaining ½ teaspoon salt and remaining ¼ teaspoon pepper. Heat bacon fat in skillet over medium-high heat until just smoking. Add steak and cook until well browned on all sides and meat registers 125 degrees (for medium-rare), about 7 minutes. Transfer to plate, tent with aluminum foil, and let rest.

4. Arrange lettuce wedges and steak tips on individual serving plates and drizzle with dressing. Top with tomatoes, bacon, and remaining ¼ cup Stilton. Sprinkle with chives and season with salt and pepper to taste. Serve.

Arugula Salad with Steak Tips and Gorgonzola

Arugula Salad with Steak Tips and Gorgonzola

Serves 4 `FAST`

Why This Recipe Works Dressing peppery arugula with a simple vinaigrette and fortifying it with tender steak tips and blue cheese makes for a quick and elegant dinner salad when you don't want to spend your whole summer evening in the kitchen. Adding Dijon mustard to the vinaigrette amped up the spiciness of the arugula, and cider vinegar and honey added a complementary fruity, sweet touch to the assertive greens. Sirloin steak tips, also known as flap meat, can be sold as whole steaks, cubes, and strips. To ensure uniform pieces, we prefer to purchase whole steaks and cut them ourselves after cooking. For optimal tenderness, make sure to slice the cooked steak against the grain (perpendicular to the fibers). You can substitute any blue cheese for the Gorgonzola.

- 1 pound sirloin steak tips, trimmed
- ½ teaspoon table salt, divided
- ½ teaspoon pepper, divided
- 6 tablespoons extra-virgin olive oil, divided
- 1 shallot, minced
- 2 tablespoons cider vinegar
- 2 garlic cloves, minced
- 1 teaspoon Dijon mustard
- 1 teaspoon honey
- 12 ounces (12 cups) baby arugula
- 6 ounces Gorgonzola cheese, crumbled (1½ cups)

1. Pat steak dry with paper towels and sprinkle with ¼ teaspoon salt and ¼ teaspoon pepper. Heat 2 tablespoons oil in 12-inch nonstick skillet over medium-high heat until just smoking. Add steak and cook until well browned all over and beef registers 125 degrees, 8 to 10 minutes. Transfer to plate, tent with aluminum foil, and let rest for 5 to 10 minutes.

2. Whisk shallot, vinegar, garlic, mustard, honey, remaining ¼ teaspoon salt, and remaining ¼ teaspoon pepper together in large bowl. While whisking constantly, slowly drizzle in remaining ¼ cup oil until combined. Add arugula and Gorgonzola to vinaigrette and toss to combine. Season with salt and pepper to taste. Slice steak against grain ¼ inch thick. Divide salad among individual plates and top with sliced steak. Serve.

ALL ABOUT VINEGARS
Bright, acidic vinegar is essential to making many salad dressings. We also frequently reach for vinegar to add flavor to sauces, stews, soups, and bean dishes. Because different vinegars have distinctly different flavors, you will want to stock several varieties in your pantry.

Balsamic Vinegar Traditional Italian balsamic vinegars are aged for years to develop complex flavor—but they're very pricey. They're best saved to drizzle over finished dishes. Our recommended best buy for high-end balsamic is **Oliviers & Co. Premium Balsamic Vinegar of Modena**. For vinaigrettes and glazes, we use commercial balsamic vinegars, which are younger wine vinegars with added sugar and coloring. Our favorite everyday balsamic is **Bertolli Balsamic Vinegar of Modena**.

Red Wine Vinegar Use this slightly sweet, sharp vinegar for bold vinaigrettes. With its high acidity level, it works well with potent flavors. We prefer red wine vinegars made from a blend of wine and Concord grapes; our favorite brand is **Laurent du Clos**.

White Wine Vinegar This vinegar's refined, fruity bite is perfect for light vinaigrettes. We also use it in dishes like potato salad where the color of red wine vinegar would detract from the presentation. **Spectrum Naturals Organic White Wine Vinegar** is our favorite.

Sherry Vinegar Sherry vinegar is a Spanish condiment with complex savory flavors. It adds fruity depth to vegetable salads as well as gazpachos. Our favorite is **Napa Valley Naturals Reserve**.

Cider Vinegar This vinegar has a bite and a fruity sweetness perfect for vinaigrettes; it works well in salads tossed with apple or dried fruits. Our favorite is **Spectrum Naturals Organic Apple Cider Vinegar.**

Steak Taco Salad
Serves 4

Why This Recipe Works Steak tacos are a fan-favorite summer food, but for a different spin on the classic, we worked the traditional components of steak tacos into a vibrant salad. We were after a fresher take on a taco salad, one featuring sliced steak, beans, and avocado heaped over shredded lettuce. For the greens, we tried versions with chopped romaine, iceberg, and Bibb lettuces and eventually chose romaine for its pronounced flavor and superior crunch. We settled on skirt steak for its meaty flavor and its textured exterior, which held on to plenty of seasonings. Searing the skirt steak in our nonstick skillet to medium and slicing it against the grain kept it pink in the center and minimized chewiness. An avocado did double duty as a salad topping and as the base of an ultracreamy, vibrantly fresh dressing. To make it a taco salad, we needed chips, but cutting fresh corn tortillas into strips and frying them was a little too much work for a simple salad. Store-bought tortilla chips added a salty crunch but lacked richness. Even better was another chip-aisle staple: Fritos, which brought a huge crunch and loads of corn flavor. We cook the skirt steak to medium so that it's less chewy than it would be at medium-rare. You can substitute 1 cup of store-bought pico de gallo for the homemade version if you prefer.

Pico de Gallo
- 1 tomato, cored and chopped
- 2 tablespoons finely chopped red onion
- 2 tablespoons chopped fresh cilantro
- 2 teaspoons minced jalapeño chile
- 1½ teaspoons lime juice
- ¼ teaspoon table salt

Dressing
- ½ ripe avocado
- ½ cup buttermilk
- 2 tablespoons chopped fresh cilantro
- 1½ tablespoons lime juice
- 1 garlic clove, minced
- 1 teaspoon table salt
- ¼ teaspoon pepper

Steak
- ¾ teaspoon chili powder
- ½ teaspoon ground cumin
- ½ teaspoon table salt
- ½ teaspoon pepper
- 1 (1-pound) skirt steak, trimmed and cut crosswise into 4 equal pieces
- 1 tablespoon vegetable oil

Salad
- 1 (15-ounce) can pinto beans, rinsed
- 2 romaine lettuce hearts (12 ounces), cut into 1-inch pieces
- 4 ounces Monterey Jack cheese, shredded (1 cup), divided
- ½ ripe avocado, cut into ½-inch pieces
- 1 cup Fritos corn chips

1. For the pico de gallo Combine all ingredients in bowl and set aside.

2. For the dressing Process all ingredients in blender until smooth, about 60 seconds.

3. For the steak Combine chili powder, cumin, salt, and pepper in bowl. Sprinkle steaks with spice mixture. Heat oil in 12-inch nonstick skillet over medium-high heat until just smoking. Cook steaks until well browned and meat registers 135 degrees (for medium), 2 to 4 minutes per side. Transfer steaks to carving board, tent with aluminum foil, and let rest for 5 minutes.

4. For the salad Toss beans, lettuce, and ½ cup Monterey Jack with dressing in large bowl. Season with salt and pepper to taste. Transfer to large serving platter. Slice steaks thin against grain. Layer avocado, pico de gallo, steak, and remaining ½ cup Monterey Jack on top of lettuce mixture. Scatter chips around salad. Serve.

Grilled Steak and Vegetable Salad
Serves 4

Why This Recipe Works In the summertime, grilled steak and vegetables is a go-to combination for dinner, as the grill offers smoky flavors, outdoor appeal, and the convenience of using one cooking method for the whole meal. We were inspired to take these components and turn them into a dinner-worthy grilled salad. For the vegetables, we chose some of the season's finest: zucchini, red bell peppers, and tomatoes. Before grilling the sturdier zucchini and peppers, we brushed them with a garlic-and-herb vinaigrette. We cooked them on the grill simultaneously with a couple of boneless strip steaks. Once they were grilled, we tossed the vegetables with more of the vinaigrette and the tomatoes, which we'd cut into wedges. Finally, we sliced the steak and arranged the slices on top of the vegetable mixture for a vibrant, colorful, and supersimple summery grilled salad.

Grilled Steak and Vegetable Salad

2B. For a gas grill Turn all burners to high, cover, and heat grill until hot, about 15 minutes. Leave primary burner on high and turn off other burner(s).

3. Clean and oil cooking grate. Pat steaks dry with paper towels and sprinkle with remaining ½ teaspoon salt and remaining ¼ teaspoon pepper. Place steaks, zucchini, and bell peppers on grill and cook until meat registers 125 degrees (for medium-rare), 4 to 8 minutes per side, and vegetables are well browned, about 4 minutes per side. Transfer vegetables and steaks to carving board, tent steaks with foil, and let rest for 5 minutes.

4. Cut vegetables into 1-inch pieces. Add vegetables and tomatoes to reserved vinaigrette and toss gently to combine; divide vegetables evenly among plates. Slice steaks ¼ inch thick and arrange on top of vegetables. Drizzle with extra oil. Serve.

Grilled Thai Beef Salad
Serves 4 to 6

Why This Recipe Works In the best versions of Thai grilled beef salad, known as *nam tok*, the cuisine's five signature flavor elements—hot, sour, salty, sweet, and bitter—come into balance, making for a light but satisfying dish perfectly suited for a weeknight or special-occasion summer dinner. We prepared a standard half-grill fire for grilling the meat, starting the meat over high heat to sear the exterior and then moving it to the cooler side to finish cooking for a perfect medium-rare steak with a nicely charred crust. The dressing for this dish should have a good balance of flavor elements to provide a counterpoint to the subtle bitter char of the meat. Fish sauce, lime juice, sugar, and a mix of hot spices provided these elements and the final addition—toasted rice powder made in a food processor—added extra body to the dressing. Serve with rice, if desired. If fresh Thai chiles are unavailable, substitute half of a serrano chile. Don't skip the toasted rice; it's integral to the texture and flavor of the dish. Any variety of white rice can be used. Toasted rice powder (*kao kua*) can also be found in many Asian markets; substitute 1 tablespoon rice powder for the white rice.

¼ cup extra-virgin olive oil, plus extra for drizzling
¼ cup red wine vinegar
2 garlic cloves, minced
2 teaspoons minced fresh thyme
1 teaspoon Dijon mustard
1 teaspoon table salt, divided
¾ teaspoon pepper, divided
2 zucchini, sliced lengthwise into ½-inch-thick planks
2 red bell peppers, halved, stemmed, and seeded
2 (12-ounce) boneless strip steaks, about 1 inch thick
2 tomatoes, cored and cut into ½-inch wedges

1. Whisk oil, vinegar, garlic, thyme, mustard, ¾ teaspoon salt, and ½ teaspoon pepper together in large bowl. Brush zucchini and bell peppers with 2 tablespoons vinaigrette; set aside remaining vinaigrette.

2A. For a charcoal grill Open bottom vent completely. Light large chimney starter filled with charcoal briquettes (6 quarts). When top coals are partially covered with ash, pour in even layer over half of grill. Set cooking grate in place, cover, and open lid vent completely. Heat grill until hot, about 5 minutes.

1 teaspoon paprika
1 teaspoon cayenne pepper
1 tablespoon white rice
3 tablespoons lime juice (2 limes)
2 tablespoons fish sauce
2 tablespoons water
½ teaspoon sugar
1 (1½-pound) flank steak, trimmed
½ teaspoon table salt
¼ teaspoon white pepper
1 English cucumber, sliced ¼ inch thick on bias
1½ cups fresh mint leaves, torn
1½ cups fresh cilantro leaves
4 shallots, sliced thin
1 Thai chile, stemmed, seeded, and sliced thin into rounds

1. Heat paprika and cayenne in 8-inch skillet over medium heat; cook, shaking pan, until fragrant, about 1 minute. Transfer to small bowl. Return skillet to medium-high heat; add rice and toast, stirring constantly, until deep golden brown, about 5 minutes. Transfer to a second small bowl and let cool for 5 minutes. Grind rice with spice grinder, mini food processor, or mortar and pestle until it resembles fine meal, 10 to 30 seconds (you should have about 1 tablespoon rice powder).

2. Whisk lime juice, fish sauce, water, sugar, and ¼ teaspoon toasted paprika mixture in large bowl and set aside.

3A. For a charcoal grill Open bottom vent completely. Light large chimney starter filled with charcoal briquettes (6 quarts). When top coals are partially covered with ash, pour in even layer over half of grill. Set cooking grate in place, cover, and open lid vent completely. Heat grill until hot, about 5 minutes.

3B. For a gas grill Turn all burners to high, cover, and heat grill until hot, about 15 minutes. Leave primary burner on high and turn off other burner(s).

4. Clean and oil cooking grate. Pat steak dry and sprinkle with salt and white pepper. Place steak on hotter part of grill and cook until beginning to char and beads of moisture appear on outer edges of meat, 5 to 6 minutes. Flip steak, and continue to cook on second side until meat registers 125 degrees (for medium-rare), about 5 minutes. Transfer to carving board, tent with aluminum foil, and let rest for 10 minutes (or let cool to room temperature, about 1 hour).

5. Line large platter with cucumber slices. Slice steak ¼ inch thick against grain on bias. Transfer sliced steak to bowl with fish sauce mixture. Add mint, cilantro, shallots, Thai chile, and half of rice powder, and toss to combine. Arrange steak over cucumber-lined platter. Serve, passing remaining rice powder and remaining toasted paprika mixture separately.

Bistro Salad with Fried Egg
Serves 4 `FAST`

Why This Recipe Works A traditional French bistro salad normally consists of light, curly frisée and crunchy romaine dressed with a mustard vinaigrette and topped with chopped salty bacon and perfectly cooked eggs. To take this classic appetizer salad and turn it into a satisfying and richly flavored meal, we added some savory sautéed mushrooms to the mix for more substance. Along with the mushrooms, the thick-cut bacon and the standard fried egg now amounted to enough heft to serve our version of this salad as a light but deeply flavored dinner salad. The eggs' runny yolks coated the delicate greens and mingled with the other ingredients to enrich and balance the acidic red wine vinaigrette. If you like your fried eggs less runny, use the following resting times in step 4: Let sit 45 to 60 seconds for soft but set yolks, or about 2 minutes for medium-set yolks. Sautéing the mushrooms in reserved bacon fat helps deepen the flavors of the dish. You can substitute 8 cups of mixed greens for the frisée and romaine, if you like.

2 tablespoons red wine vinegar
1½ teaspoons Dijon mustard
1 small shallot, minced
⅛ teaspoon plus ½ teaspoon table salt, divided
¼ teaspoon pepper, divided
3 tablespoons extra-virgin olive oil
6 slices thick-cut bacon, cut into 1-inch pieces
8 ounces cremini mushrooms, trimmed and halved if small, quartered if large
4 large eggs
1 head frisée (6 ounces), trimmed and cut into 1-inch pieces
1 romaine lettuce heart (6 ounces), trimmed and cut into 1-inch pieces

1. Whisk vinegar, mustard, shallot, ⅛ teaspoon salt, and ⅛ teaspoon pepper together in large bowl. Whisking constantly, slowly drizzle in oil until incorporated.

2. Cook bacon in 12-inch nonstick skillet over medium heat until crispy, about 8 minutes. Using slotted spoon, transfer bacon to paper towel–lined plate. Pour off and reserve 5 teaspoons fat from skillet; discard any remaining fat.

3. Add 1 tablespoon reserved fat back to skillet and heat over medium-high heat until shimmering. Add mushrooms and ¼ teaspoon salt and cook, stirring occasionally, until liquid has released, about 3 minutes. Increase heat to high and continue to cook until liquid has evaporated and mushrooms begin to brown, about 5 minutes. Transfer mushrooms to bowl and cover to keep warm.

4. Crack eggs into 2 small bowls (2 eggs per bowl) and sprinkle with remaining ¼ teaspoon salt and remaining ⅛ teaspoon pepper. Add remaining 2 teaspoons reserved fat to now-empty skillet and heat over medium-high heat until shimmering. Pour 1 bowl of eggs in 1 side of pan and second bowl in other side. Cover and cook for 1 minute. Remove skillet from heat. Let sit, covered, 15 to 45 seconds for runny yolks (white around edge of yolk will be barely opaque).

5. Toss frisée and romaine in bowl with dressing and season with salt and pepper to taste. Divide salad among individual serving plates. Top with mushrooms, bacon, and fried eggs. Serve.

Bitter Greens and Fig Salad with Warm Shallot Dressing

Serves 4

Why This Recipe Works Fresh figs and salty prosciutto are a perfect pair around which to build a hearty main-dish salad. To match their strong flavors with a sturdy salad base, we chose to create a wilted green salad with a rich warm dressing. Spinach is the typical choice for tossing with a warm vinaigrette, but we wanted to feature greens that don't get as much attention: curly frisée, ruffled escarole, and frilly chicory. We hoped that each (or a combination thereof) would soften under a hot dressing and provide a robust canvas for our bold ingredients. Drizzling a hot vinaigrette over the greens wasn't enough to wilt them, so we thought of warming the greens while warming the dressing. We tried heating the dressing in a roomy Dutch oven, but by the time we'd tossed in all the greens, some leaves were not just wilted but cooked. Instead, we sautéed the mix-ins in the Dutch oven to warm the pot, let them cool briefly, and added the greens and vinaigrette off the heat. After a few turns of the tongs, the greens had just the right slightly softened texture. All that was left was to add some contrasting yet complementary tastes and textures to balance out the sweet figs and savory prosciutto: pine nuts for crunch and Parmesan cheese for salty richness. The volume measurement of the greens may vary depending on the variety or combination used.

Vinaigrette

- ¼ cup sherry vinegar
- 2 tablespoons extra-virgin olive oil
- 1 tablespoon Dijon mustard
- 1 tablespoon minced shallot
- 1 teaspoon minced fresh thyme
- ¼ teaspoon table salt
- ¼ teaspoon pepper

Bistro Salad with Fried Egg

Bitter Greens and Fig Salad with Warm Shallot Dressing

Salad

- 3 ounces thinly sliced prosciutto
- 2 tablespoons extra-virgin olive oil
- 8 shallots, peeled and quartered lengthwise
  Pinch table salt
- 8 fresh figs, halved and sliced thin
- ⅓ cup pine nuts
- 12 ounces (10–12 cups) bitter greens, such as escarole, chicory, and/or frisée, torn into bite-size pieces
- 1½ ounces Parmesan cheese, shaved

1. For the vinaigrette Whisk all ingredients in bowl until emulsified.

2. For the salad Place prosciutto between 2 layers of paper towels on plate and microwave until rendered and beginning to crisp, 2 to 3 minutes. Transfer prosciutto to cutting board. Let cool slightly, then chop coarse.

3. Heat oil in Dutch oven over medium heat until shimmering. Add shallots and salt and cook, stirring frequently, until browned and softened, 12 to 15 minutes. Add figs and pine nuts and continue to cook, stirring occasionally, until pine nuts are golden, 3 to 4 minutes. Remove pot from heat and let cool for 5 minutes.

4. Add half of vinaigrette to pot, then add half of greens and toss for 1 minute to warm and wilt. Add remaining greens followed by remaining vinaigrette and continue to toss until greens are evenly coated and warmed through, about 2 minutes longer. Season with salt and pepper to taste. Transfer greens to serving platter, top with prosciutto and Parmesan, and serve.

Smoked Salmon Niçoise Salad
Serves 4

Why This Recipe Works French *salade Niçoise* is a satisfying composed salad of individually prepared vegetables, hard-cooked eggs, olives, and canned tuna. For an unexpected twist on the classic, we swapped in smoked salmon, a convenient no-cook protein that packs a flavorful punch different from traditional tuna. Instead of the standard vinaigrette, we opted for a simple creamy dressing. Since they'd be adorned with the flavorful dressing, the potatoes and green beans needed nothing more than a boil in salted water. Starting the potatoes first and adding the green beans later ensured that both vegetables finished cooking at the same time and that the green beans remained bright and vibrant. A simple dressing of sour cream, lemon, and dill was a fitting pairing for smoked salmon and brought this new niçoise together; we tossed a small

amount with the greens for even distribution and served the rest for drizzling on top of the other components. Use red potatoes measuring 1 to 2 inches in diameter. If you don't have a steamer basket, use a spoon or tongs to gently place the eggs directly in the boiling water.

- 1 pound small red potatoes, unpeeled, halved
- ¼ teaspoon table salt, plus salt for cooking potatoes and green beans
- 8 ounces green beans, trimmed
- ⅔ cup sour cream
- 2 tablespoons lemon juice
- 1 tablespoon chopped fresh dill
- ⅛ teaspoon pepper
- 10 ounces (10 cups) mesclun
- 4 Easy-Peel Hard-Cooked Eggs, halved
- ½ cup pitted kalamata olives, halved
- 8 ounces sliced cold-smoked salmon

1. Bring 4 quarts water to boil in large saucepan. Add potatoes and 1½ tablespoons salt, return to boil, and cook for 10 minutes. Add green beans and continue to cook until both vegetables are tender, about 4 minutes. Drain vegetables well and set aside to cool slightly.

2. Whisk sour cream, 2 tablespoons water, lemon juice, dill, salt, and pepper in large bowl until incorporated; measure out and reserve all but ¼ cup. Add mesclun to ¼ cup dressing in bowl and toss to coat, then divide among individual serving dishes. Top with potatoes, green beans, eggs, olives, and salmon and drizzle with reserved dressing. Serve.

Easy-Peel Hard-Cooked Eggs
Makes 4 eggs
Be sure to use large eggs that have no cracks and are cold from the refrigerator. This recipe can be doubled.

- 4 large eggs

1. Bring 1 inch water to rolling boil in medium saucepan over high heat. Place eggs in steamer basket. Transfer basket to saucepan. Cover, reduce heat to medium-low, and cook eggs for 13 minutes.

2. When eggs are almost finished cooking, combine 2 cups ice cubes and 2 cups cold water in medium bowl. Using tongs or spoon, transfer eggs to ice bath; let sit for 15 minutes. (Eggs can be refrigerated for up to 5 days.) Peel before using.

Mediterranean Couscous Salad with Smoked Trout

Serves 4 to 6 `FAST`

Why This Recipe Works We love eating a lot of green salads in the summer, but for a change of pace, couscous makes a fantastic base, particularly as a mild canvas for smoked fish. We flaked richly flavored smoked trout into quick-cooking couscous for a Mediterranean-inspired salad. Pepperoncini and cherry tomatoes added spiciness and freshness for a simple salad with incredible complexity. We thought a tangy vinaigrette would soak into and liven up the grains and provide a refreshing pairing to the smoky richness of the trout. For the acid in our dressing, we used brine from the pepperoncini, an ingredient that often goes to waste. Tossing the cooked couscous with the dressing while it was still warm helped it absorb the dressing as it cooled in the refrigerator. As this is a dinner-worthy salad, we like to individually plate it and serve it with lemon wedges for a final squeeze of freshness. You can heat the water in a kettle and pour it over the couscous in a bowl instead of boiling it in a saucepan, if desired.

  2 cups water
1½ cups couscous
  ¾ teaspoon table salt
  ⅓ cup extra-virgin olive oil, plus extra for drizzling
  1 cup pepperoncini, stemmed and sliced into thin rings, plus 3 tablespoons brine
  1 garlic clove, minced
  8 ounces cherry tomatoes, halved
  ½ cup fresh parsley leaves
  3 scallions, sliced thin
  6 ounces hot-smoked trout, skin and pin bones removed, flaked
      Lemon wedges

1. Bring water to boil in medium saucepan. Remove pot from heat, then stir in couscous and salt. Cover and let sit for 10 minutes. Fluff couscous with fork.

2. Whisk oil, brine, and garlic together in large bowl. Transfer couscous to bowl with dressing and toss to combine. Let sit until cooled completely, about 20 minutes.

3. Add cherry tomatoes, parsley, scallions, and pepperoncini rings to cooled couscous and gently toss to combine. Season with salt and pepper to taste, and drizzle with extra oil to taste. Divide salad among individual serving plates and top with smoked trout. Serve with lemon wedges.

Mediterranean Couscous Salad with Smoked Trout

Smoked Salmon Niçoise Salad

Seared Tuna Salad with Olive Dressing

Fennel and Bibb Salad with Scallops and Hazelnuts

Seared Tuna Salad with Olive Dressing

Serves 4 to 6 `FAST`

Why This Recipe Works Fresh, quick-cooking tuna steaks are a perfect base for a hearty but lean dinner salad in the summer. To make sure we didn't overcook the fish, we patted it dry before searing it in a very hot pan. Slicing it right away ensured that it didn't overcook as it rested. A potent vinaigrette made with chopped green olives, parsley, garlic, and lemon juice stood up to the meaty flavor of the tuna. Cherry tomatoes provided pops of freshness, and cannellini beans added an appealing texture. Peppery arugula provided a perfect vehicle for the rest of our flavorful ingredients. Tuna steaks can be pricey. To get your money's worth, only purchase tuna steaks that are deep purplish red, firm to the touch, and devoid of any "fishy" odor.

½ cup pimento-stuffed green olives, chopped
3 tablespoons lemon juice
1 tablespoon chopped fresh parsley
1 garlic clove, minced
6 tablespoons extra-virgin olive oil, divided
½ teaspoon table salt
¼ teaspoon pepper
2 (12-ounce) tuna steaks, 1 to 1¼ inches thick
5 ounces (5 cups) baby arugula
12 ounces cherry tomatoes, halved
1 (15-ounce) can cannellini beans, rinsed

1. Whisk olives, lemon juice, parsley, and garlic together in large bowl. Whisking constantly, slowly drizzle in 5 tablespoons oil. Season with salt and pepper to taste.

2. Pat tuna dry with paper towels and sprinkle with salt and pepper. Heat remaining 1 tablespoon oil in 12-inch nonstick skillet over medium-high heat until just smoking. Cook tuna until well browned and translucent red at center when checked with tip of paring knife and registers 110 degrees (for rare), about 2 minutes per side. Transfer to cutting board and slice into ½-inch-thick slices.

3. Whisk dressing to re-emulsify, then drizzle 1 tablespoon dressing over tuna. Add arugula, tomatoes, and beans to bowl with remaining dressing and gently toss to combine. Season with salt and pepper to taste. Divide salad among plates and top with tuna. Serve.

Fennel and Bibb Salad with Scallops and Hazelnuts

Serves 4 FAST

Why This Recipe Works Scallops can come off as a little fancy: Their pristinely smooth flesh and superlative sweetness seem to call for an extra-special occasion. But scallops don't have to be finished with luxurious sauces at a special dinner; they're an ideal weeknight meal because they're super-quick-cooking and they're right at home simply paired with greens. After quickly searing scallops to browned perfection, we made a salad of delicate Bibb lettuce, crisp sliced fennel, and radishes. We tossed the vegetables with a lemon vinaigrette and topped individual portions with warm scallops. Chopped toasted hazelnuts brought out the natural sweet nuttiness of the scallops and tarragon emphasized the anise flavor of the fennel.

1½ pounds large sea scallops, tendons removed
¾ teaspoon table salt, divided
½ teaspoon pepper, divided
7 tablespoons extra-virgin olive oil, divided
1 small shallot, minced
1 teaspoon Dijon mustard
½ teaspoon grated lemon zest plus 1½ tablespoons juice
2 heads Bibb lettuce (1 pound), torn into bite-size pieces
1 fennel bulb, 1 tablespoon fronds minced, stalk discarded, bulb halved, cored and sliced thin
4 radishes, trimmed and sliced thin
¼ cup hazelnuts, toasted, skinned, and chopped
2 tablespoons minced fresh tarragon

1. Pat scallops dry with paper towels and sprinkle with ½ teaspoon salt and ¼ teaspoon pepper. Heat 1 tablespoon oil over high heat until just smoking. Add half of scallops in single layer and cook, without moving, until well browned, 1½ to 2 minutes. Flip and cook until sides are firm and centers are opaque, 30 to 90 seconds (remove scallops as they finish cooking). Transfer scallops to plate and tent with aluminum foil. Wipe out skillet with paper towels and repeat with 1 tablespoon oil and remaining scallops.

2. Whisk shallot, mustard, lemon zest and juice, remaining ¼ teaspoon salt, and remaining ¼ teaspoon pepper together in large bowl. Whisking constantly, slowly drizzle in remaining 5 tablespoons oil until combined. Add lettuce, fennel, and radishes and toss to combine. Season with salt and pepper to taste. Divide salad among individual serving plates, then top with scallops and sprinkle with hazelnuts, tarragon, and fennel fronds. Serve.

PREPPING SCALLOPS

Use your fingers to peel away small, crescent-shaped tendon that is sometimes attached to scallops, as it is incredibly tough when cooked.

NOTES FROM THE TEST KITCHEN

BUYING SCALLOPS
In general, most recipes use only one type of scallop—sea scallops. The other scallop varieties, bay and Calico (the latter often mislabeled as bay), are much smaller and often too rare and expensive or very cheap and rubbery.

Dry Versus Wet Scallops Wet scallops are dipped in preservatives (a solution of water and sodium tripolyphosphate, known as STP) to extend their shelf life. Unfortunately, these watery preservatives dull the scallops' flavor and ruin their texture. Unprocessed, or dry, scallops have much more flavor and a creamy, smooth texture; plus, they brown very nicely. Dry scallops look ivory or pinkish; wet scallops are bright white.

Distinguishing Dry from Wet If your scallops are not labeled, you can find out if they are wet or dry with this quick microwave test: Place one scallop on a paper towel–lined plate and microwave for 15 seconds. A dry scallop will exude very little water, but a wet scallop will leave a sizable ring of moisture on the paper towel. (The microwaved scallop can be cooked as is.)

Treating Wet Scallops When you can find only wet scallops, you can hide the off-putting taste of the preservative by soaking the scallops in a solution of 1 quart of cold water, ¼ cup of lemon juice, and 2 tablespoons of salt for 30 minutes. Be sure to pat the scallops very dry after soaking them. Even after this treatment, these scallops will be harder to brown than untreated dry scallops.

Shrimp and White Bean Salad with Garlic Toasts

Serves 4

Why This Recipe Works Quick-cooking shrimp are a great ingredient to use for last-minute weeknight dinners, especially in the summer when less is more as far as time spent over the stove is concerned. For this dinner salad, the secret was in making sure that the shrimp were perfectly cooked—seared on the outside and moist on the inside. The sweetness of mild, creamy cannellini beans was a perfect foil to the briny shrimp, so we chose these beans to make up the base of the salad and added color, texture, and vibrancy with bell pepper and red onion. Assertive arugula brought some green freshness to the bean salad, and the greens also stood up well to the flavor of the shrimp without being drowned out. Finally, toasted bread rubbed with garlic gave the meal some more heft. Keeping frozen shrimp in your freezer is a great shortcut to a quick meal. If you're using frozen shrimp, make sure to thaw them before starting the recipe.

- 4 (¾-inch) slices rustic bread
- 3 garlic cloves (2 minced, 1 peeled and left whole)
- 5 tablespoons extra-virgin olive oil, divided
- 1 red bell pepper, stemmed, seeded, and chopped fine
- 1 small red onion, chopped fine
- ½ teaspoon table salt, divided
- ¼ teaspoon red pepper flakes
- 2 (15-ounce) cans cannellini beans, rinsed
- ¼ cup water
- 1 pound extra-large shrimp (21 to 25 per pound), peeled and deveined
- ⅛ teaspoon pepper
- 2 ounces (2 cups) baby arugula
- 2 tablespoons lemon juice

1. Adjust oven rack 6 inches from broiler element and heat broiler. Spread bread out evenly over rimmed baking sheet. Broil, flipping as needed, until well toasted on both sides, about 4 minutes. Rub 1 side of each toast with whole garlic clove, then drizzle with 1 tablespoon oil and season with salt and pepper to taste.

2. Heat 3 tablespoons oil in 12-inch nonstick skillet over medium heat until shimmering. Add bell pepper, onion, and ¼ teaspoon salt. Cook until softened, about 5 minutes. Stir in pepper flakes and minced garlic. Cook until fragrant, about 30 seconds. Add beans and water and cook until heated through, about 5 minutes. Transfer mixture to serving bowl and cover to keep warm.

3. Pat shrimp dry with paper towels and sprinkle with remaining ¼ teaspoon salt and pepper. Wipe skillet clean with paper towels. Heat remaining 1 tablespoon oil in now-empty skillet over high heat until just smoking. Add shrimp to skillet in single layer and cook, without stirring, until spotty brown and edges turn pink on first side, about 1 minute. Off heat, flip shrimp and let sit until opaque throughout, about 30 seconds.

4. Add shrimp, arugula, and lemon juice to beans and gently toss to combine. Season with salt and pepper to taste, and drizzle with extra oil to taste. Serve with garlic toasts.

Mediterranean Chopped Salad

Serves 6 FAST NO COOK

Why This Recipe Works The appeal of a chopped salad is that all the ingredients are cut to a uniform size and tossed together, permitting a taste of everything in each bite. Virtually any ingredients may be used, yet most chopped salads are uninspired, laden with deli meats and cheeses and drowned in dressing. With a world of options at our disposal, we steered our salad in a Mediterranean direction, starting with escarole. A member of the chicory family, this underutilized leafy green is loaded with vitamins and has a mild bitterness that pairs well with bold flavors. Next we added chopped cucumbers and grape tomatoes, salting them to remove excess moisture, and red onion. To make our salad hearty, instead of deli meat we incorporated nutty chickpeas. Kalamata olives added richness, and walnuts brought crunch and healthy fats. We tossed everything with a simple red wine vinaigrette to let the salad's flavors shine through. Finally, not wanting to completely eliminate cheese from our salad, we sprinkled on ½ cup of briny feta to round out the flavors. Cherry tomatoes can be substituted for the grape tomatoes.

- 1 cucumber, halved lengthwise, seeded, and cut into ½-inch pieces
- 10 ounces grape tomatoes, quartered
- 1 teaspoon table salt
- 3 tablespoons red wine vinegar
- 1 garlic clove, minced
- 3 tablespoons extra-virgin olive oil
- 1 (15-ounce) can chickpeas, rinsed
- ½ cup pitted kalamata olives, chopped
- ½ small red onion, chopped fine
- ½ cup chopped fresh parsley
- 1 head escarole (1 pound), trimmed and cut into ½-inch pieces
- 2 ounces feta cheese, crumbled (½ cup)
- ½ cup walnuts, toasted and chopped

1. Toss cucumber and tomatoes with salt and let drain in colander for 15 minutes.

2. Whisk vinegar and garlic together in large bowl. Whisking constantly, drizzle in oil. Add drained cucumber-tomato mixture, chickpeas, olives, onion, and parsley and toss to coat. Let sit for at least 5 minutes or up to 20 minutes.

3. Add escarole, feta, and walnuts and toss gently to combine. Season with salt and pepper to taste. Serve.

Vegetarian Cobb Salad
Serves 4 `FAST`

Why This Recipe Works For a meatless take on this classic hearty dinner salad, we tossed mixed greens and chickpeas in a creamy dressing of yogurt, whole-grain mustard, and fresh dill and topped the greens with soft-boiled eggs, croutons, and avocado. To give the salad a little heft and pleasant layer of crunch, we toasted cubes of sandwich bread in a nonstick skillet until crisp and perfectly browned and used them to top off the salad. For ripe avocados at their creamy best, look for purple-black (not green) fruit that yields slightly when gently squeezed.

    8 large eggs
    ¼ cup extra-virgin olive oil, divided
    3 slices hearty white sandwich bread,
       cut into ½-inch cubes
    ½ teaspoon table salt, divided
    ½ teaspoon pepper, divided
    ⅔ cup plain whole-milk yogurt
    ¼ cup chopped fresh dill
    3 tablespoons whole-grain mustard
    7 ounces (7 cups) mixed greens
    1 (15-ounce) can chickpeas, rinsed
    1 avocado, pitted and quartered

1. Bring 3 quarts water to boil in large saucepan over high heat. Gently lower eggs into boiling water and cook for 6 minutes. Transfer eggs to medium bowl filled with ice water and let sit until cool, about 3 minutes. Peel eggs and set aside.

2. Heat 2 tablespoons oil in 12-inch nonstick skillet over medium heat until shimmering. Add bread, ¼ teaspoon salt, and ¼ teaspoon pepper and cook, stirring frequently, until golden brown and crisp, about 10 minutes.

3. Whisk yogurt, dill, mustard, remaining 2 tablespoons oil, remaining ¼ teaspoon salt, and remaining ¼ teaspoon pepper together in large bowl. Add greens and chickpeas and toss to combine. Divide salad among plates. Divide avocado, croutons, and eggs among salads. Serve.

Shrimp and White Bean Salad with Garlic Toasts

Vegetarian Cobb Salad

Marinated Tofu and Vegetable Salad

Serves 4 FAST NO COOK

Why This Recipe Works For an Asian-inspired, no-cook dinner salad, we combined marinated tofu with a bright dressing and crunchy cabbage, snow peas, and bell pepper. Marinating is a great way to imbue raw tofu with flavor without having to cook it; here, a sriracha-based salad dressing did double-duty as the marinade, bringing in a touch of heat and tons of flavor. Firm tofu is tender and supple when eaten raw, but still sturdy. Do not substitute other varieties in this recipe.

- 28 ounces firm tofu, cut into ¾ inch cubes
- ¼ cup rice vinegar
- 3 tablespoons toasted sesame oil
- 2 tablespoons sriracha
- 2 teaspoons honey
- ¼ teaspoon table salt
- ½ small head napa cabbage, cored and sliced thin (4 cups)
- 6 ounces snow peas, strings removed, cut in half crosswise
- 1 red bell pepper, stemmed, seeded, and cut into ½ inch pieces
- 2 scallions, sliced thin on bias
- 2 tablespoons toasted sesame seeds

1. Gently press tofu cubes dry with paper towels. Whisk vinegar, oil, sriracha, honey, and salt in large bowl until combined.

2. Gently toss tofu in dressing until evenly coated, then cover and refrigerate for 20 minutes.

3. Add cabbage, snow peas, and bell pepper to bowl with tofu and gently toss to combine. Season with salt and pepper to taste, sprinkle with scallions and sesame seeds, and serve.

NOTES FROM THE TEST KITCHEN

CHOOSING THE RIGHT TOFU
Tofu is available in a variety of textures: extra-firm, firm, medium-firm, soft, and silken. We prefer extra-firm or firm tofu for stir-fries as they hold their shape in high-heat cooking applications; they're also great marinated or tossed raw into salads. Medium and soft tofu's creamy texture is perfect for pan-frying for a crispy exterior and a silky interior. Ultracreamy silken tofu is often used as a base for smoothies and dips or in desserts.

Fattoush

Serves 4 to 6

Why This Recipe Works Fattoush is an eastern Mediterranean salad that combines fresh produce and herbs, toasted pita bread, and bright, tangy sumac. Sumac is a commonly used spice across the region—where it's often used on its own as a finishing spice—and it traditionally lends its citrusy punch to this salad. We opted to use an ample amount of sumac in the dressing to intensify the flavor, and also used it as a garnish for the finished salad. To prevent the bread from becoming soggy, many recipes call for eliminating excess moisture by seeding and salting the cucumbers and tomatoes. We skipped these steps in order to preserve the crisp texture of the cucumber and the flavorful seeds and juice of the tomatoes. Instead, we made the pita pieces moisture-repellent by brushing their craggy sides with plenty of olive oil before baking them. The oil prevented the pita from absorbing moisture from the salad and becoming soggy while still allowing it to pick up flavor from the lemony dressing. The success of this recipe depends on using ripe, in-season tomatoes.

- 2 (8-inch) pita breads
- 7 tablespoons extra-virgin olive oil, divided
- 3 tablespoons lemon juice
- 4 teaspoons ground sumac, plus extra for sprinkling
- ¼ teaspoon minced garlic
- ¼ teaspoon table salt
- 1 pound ripe tomatoes, cored and cut into ¾-inch pieces
- 1 English cucumber, peeled and sliced ⅛ inch thick
- 1 cup arugula, chopped
- ½ cup chopped fresh cilantro
- ½ cup chopped fresh mint
- 4 scallions, sliced thin

1. Adjust oven rack to middle position and heat oven to 375 degrees. Using kitchen shears, cut around perimeter of each pita and separate into 2 thin rounds. Cut each round in half. Place pitas smooth side down on wire rack set in rimmed baking sheet. Brush 3 tablespoons oil on surface of pitas. (Pitas do not need to be uniformly coated; oil will spread during baking.) Season with salt and pepper to taste. Bake until pitas are crisp and light golden brown, 10 to 14 minutes. Let cool completely.

2. Whisk lemon juice, sumac, garlic, and salt together in large bowl and let sit for 10 minutes. Whisking constantly, slowly drizzle in remaining ¼ cup oil. Add tomatoes, cucumber, arugula, cilantro, mint, and scallions. Break pitas into ½-inch pieces and add to bowl; gently toss to coat. Season with salt and pepper to taste. Serve, sprinkling individual portions with extra sumac.

Tomato and Burrata Salad with Pangrattato and Basil

Serves 4

Why This Recipe Works Burrata is a deluxe version of fresh mozzarella in which supple cheese is bound around a filling of cream and bits of cheese. We wanted to create a Caprese-inspired salad in which summer's best tomatoes could star alongside this decadent cheese. To concentrate the tomato flavor, we combined standard tomatoes and cherry tomatoes and salted them to help draw out their watery juices. Minced shallot and white balsamic vinegar made a bold vinaigrette. A topping of Italian pangrattato (rustic garlicky bread crumbs) brought the dish together, soaking up the tomato juices and the burrata cream. The success of this dish depends on using ripe, in-season tomatoes and very fresh, high-quality burrata.

- 1½ pounds ripe tomatoes, cored and cut into 1-inch pieces
- 8 ounces ripe cherry tomatoes, halved
- ½ teaspoon plus pinch table salt, divided
- 3 ounces rustic Italian bread, cut into 1-inch pieces (1 cup)
- 6 tablespoons extra-virgin olive oil, divided
  Pinch pepper
- 1 garlic clove, minced
- 1 shallot, halved and sliced thin
- 1½ tablespoons white balsamic vinegar
- ½ cup chopped fresh basil
- 8 ounces burrata cheese, room temperature

1. Toss tomatoes with ¼ teaspoon salt and let drain in colander for 30 minutes.

2. Pulse bread in food processor into large crumbs measuring between ⅛ and ¼ inch, about 10 pulses. Combine crumbs, 2 tablespoons oil, pinch salt, and pepper in 12-inch nonstick skillet. Cook over medium heat, stirring often, until crumbs are crisp and golden, about 10 minutes. Clear center of skillet, add garlic, and cook, mashing it into skillet, until fragrant, about 30 seconds. Stir garlic into crumbs. Transfer to plate and let cool slightly.

3. Whisk shallot, vinegar, and remaining ¼ teaspoon salt together in large bowl. Whisking constantly, slowly drizzle in remaining ¼ cup oil. Add tomatoes and basil and gently toss to combine. Season with salt and pepper to taste, and arrange on serving platter. Cut burrata into 1-inch pieces, collecting creamy liquid. Sprinkle burrata over tomatoes and drizzle with creamy liquid. Sprinkle with bread crumbs and serve immediately.

Fattoush

Tomato and Burrata Salad with Pangrattato and Basil

Tomatillos are husk-encased green spheres that look much like small green tomatoes when out of their papery husks. In many regions in the United States, tomatillos are in season in the summer and fall. When shopping for tomatillos, choose those of a similar size so they will cook evenly. Look for firm specimens that boast bright green skin—a yellow color indicates that the flesh is overripe and will taste sweet, not tangy. A light green, flexible, unblemished husk is also desirable; a brown hue and a dry, papery texture indicate overripeness. Finally, the tomatillo should completely fill out its husk (the husk should not balloon away from the fruit). Don't remove the husks or rinse off the sticky coating (which protects the fruit from bugs) until you are ready to cook the tomatillos. Store tomatillos in an open plastic produce bag in the refrigerator for a couple of weeks.

Salad with Pickled
Tomatillos, Sun-Dried
Tomatoes, and
Goat Cheese

Salad with Pickled Tomatillos, Sun-Dried Tomatoes, and Goat Cheese
Serves 4

Why This Recipe Works Tomatillos are most often used in sauces and salsas to be served alongside any number of main dishes, but we thought these green summer gems deserved more of a starring role. To show them off in a new light, we built a salad with an unexpected flavor profile around the focal point of pickled tomatillos. Tomatillos' crunchy skin holds up well to the pickling process and their tart flavor is enhanced by a balanced sweet and vinegary brine. We boiled the tomatillo wedges in a simple brine of cider vinegar, sugar, water, and salt for just 1 minute to infuse flavor before transferring the mixture to a bowl to cool to room temperature. While the tomatillo pickles were cooling, we built our salad. Oil-packed sun-dried tomatoes were an unexpected flavor complement, their assertively bright flavor pairing perfectly with the pickled tomatillos. Refreshing leaf lettuce made a sturdy base for our salad. For a zippy, punchy dressing, we used the sun-dried tomato packing oil and the tomatillo pickle brine. To finish the salad, creamy goat cheese balanced the acidity of the tomatillos and dressing, and toasted walnuts added a crunchy final touch.

½ cup cider vinegar
¼ cup sugar
2¼ teaspoons table salt, divided
12 ounces tomatillos, husks and stems removed, rinsed well and dried, and cut into eighths
⅓ cup oil-packed sun-dried tomatoes, patted dry and sliced thin, plus 2 tablespoons packing oil, divided
¼ cup chopped fresh basil
1 garlic clove, minced
¼ teaspoon red pepper flakes
1 head red or green leaf lettuce (8 ounces), torn into bite-size pieces
2 ounces goat cheese, crumbled (½ cup)
¼ cup walnuts, toasted and chopped

1. Bring vinegar, sugar, 2 tablespoons water, and 2 teaspoons salt to boil in medium saucepan over medium-high heat. Add tomatillos and boil for 1 minute. Transfer mixture to bowl and let cool to room temperature, about 30 minutes. Drain tomatillos, reserving 2 tablespoons brine.

2. Whisk reserved brine, sun-dried tomato oil, basil, garlic, pepper flakes, and remaining ¼ teaspoon salt together in large serving bowl. Add pickled tomatillos, red leaf lettuce, and sun-dried tomatoes and toss to combine. Season with salt and pepper to taste. Sprinkle with goat cheese and walnuts. Serve.

HUSKING AND RINSING TOMATILLOS

1. Pull papery husks and stems off of tomatillos; discard.

2. Rinse tomatillos in colander to rid them of sticky residue from husks. Dry tomatillos thoroughly.

Farro Salad with Sugar Snap Peas and White Beans

Serves 4 to 6 MAKE AHEAD

Why This Recipe Works While often relegated to simple side-dish status, farro works just as well as the base of a hearty grain salad to serve as a main course. We wanted a farro salad featuring some summer farmers' market vegetables that was substantial enough for a main course. Boiling the farro and then draining it yielded nicely firm but tender farro. We let the grains cool and then tossed them with fresh, crunchy snap peas that we had cooked first in the boiling water to bring out their vibrant color and crisp-tender bite. A lemon-dill dressing served as a citrusy, herbal complement to the earthy farro and fresh-tasting peas. For a full-flavored finish, we added in some cherry tomatoes and meaty kalamata olives, and we stirred in creamy cannellini beans to make this salad even more of a hearty meal. We prefer the flavor and texture of whole-grain farro; pearled farro can be used in this dish, but the texture may be softer. We found a wide range of cooking times among various brands of farro, so start checking for doneness after 10 minutes. Be sure not to use quick-cooking farro here.

12 ounces sugar snap peas, strings removed, cut into 1-inch lengths
¼ teaspoon table salt, plus salt for cooking snap peas and farro
1½ cups whole farro
3 tablespoons extra-virgin olive oil
2 tablespoons lemon juice
2 tablespoons minced shallot
1 teaspoon Dijon mustard
¼ teaspoon pepper
1 (15-ounce) can cannellini beans, rinsed
6 ounces cherry tomatoes, halved
⅓ cup chopped pitted kalamata olives
2 tablespoons chopped fresh dill

1. Bring 4 quarts water to boil in large pot. Add snap peas and 1 tablespoon salt and cook until crisp-tender, about 2 minutes. Using slotted spoon, transfer snap peas to large plate and let cool completely, about 15 minutes.

2. Add farro to water, return to boil, and cook until grains are tender with slight chew, 15 to 30 minutes. Drain farro, spread on rimmed baking sheet, and let cool completely, about 15 minutes. (Cooled farro can be refrigerated for up to 3 days.)

3. Whisk oil, lemon juice, shallot, mustard, pepper, and salt together in large bowl. Add cooled snap peas, cooled farro, beans, tomatoes, olives, and dill and toss to combine. Season with salt and pepper to taste, and serve.

Quinoa Taco Salad
Serves 4

Why This Recipe Works Taco salad hits a home run with any crowd. While we love a traditional beef taco variety, here we wanted a substantial grain-based taco salad that retained all of the components that make taco salad a crowdpleaser, so we replaced the beef with quinoa. Some tasters had doubts, but this high-protein grain—with its chewy texture and ability to absorb flavors—made a good stand-in for ground beef. Toasted and simmered in chicken broth with chipotles in adobo, tomato paste, anchovy paste, and cumin, it acquired a rich, spiced, meaty flavor. We substituted escarole for lettuce, cut back on cheese, opting for queso fresco, and added an extra-hefty amount of cilantro. Black beans, avocado, cherry tomatoes, and scallions completed the picture. Tasters found the salad so hearty it didn't need tortilla chips, but if you prefer, serve with your favorite multigrain chip. We like the convenience of prewashed quinoa; rinsing removes the quinoa's bitter protective coating (called saponin). If you buy unwashed quinoa, rinse it and then spread it out on a clean dish towel to dry for 15 minutes.

- ¾ cup prewashed white quinoa, rinsed
- 3 tablespoons extra-virgin olive oil, divided
- 1 small onion, chopped fine
- ½ teaspoon table salt, divided
- 2 teaspoons minced canned chipotle chile in adobo sauce
- 2 teaspoons tomato paste
- 1 teaspoon anchovy paste (optional)
- ½ teaspoon ground cumin
- 1 cup chicken or vegetable broth
- 2 tablespoons lime juice
- ¼ teaspoon pepper
- 1 head escarole (1 pound), trimmed and sliced thin
- 2 scallions, sliced thin
- ½ cup chopped fresh cilantro, divided
- 1 (15-ounce) can black beans, rinsed
- 8 ounces cherry or grape tomatoes, quartered
- 1 ripe avocado, halved, pitted, and chopped
- 2 ounces queso fresco, crumbled (½ cup)

1. Toast quinoa in medium saucepan over medium-high heat, stirring frequently, until quinoa is very fragrant and makes continuous popping sound, 5 to 7 minutes; transfer to bowl.

2. Heat 1 tablespoon oil in now-empty saucepan over medium heat until shimmering. Add onion and ¼ teaspoon salt and cook until onion is softened and lightly browned, 5 to 7 minutes.

3. Stir in chipotle; tomato paste; anchovy paste, if using; and cumin and cook until fragrant, about 30 seconds. Stir in broth and toasted quinoa, increase heat to medium-high, and bring to simmer. Cover, reduce heat to low, and simmer until quinoa is tender and liquid has been absorbed, 18 to 22 minutes, stirring once halfway through cooking. Remove pan from heat and let sit, covered, for 10 minutes. Spread quinoa onto rimmed baking sheet and let cool for 20 minutes.

4. Whisk remaining 2 tablespoons oil, lime juice, remaining ¼ teaspoon salt, and pepper together in large bowl. Add escarole, scallions, and ¼ cup cilantro and toss to combine. Gently fold in beans, tomatoes, and avocado. Transfer to serving platter and top with quinoa, queso fresco, and remaining ¼ cup cilantro. Serve.

Bulgur Salad with Chickpeas, Spinach, and Za'atar

Serves 4 to 6

Why This Recipe Works This hearty salad combines creamy, nutty chickpeas and hearty bulgur with the clean, vegetal punch of fresh spinach. To boost the flavor of this dish, we decided to add the aromatic eastern Mediterranean spice blend za'atar, with its fragrant wild herbs, toasted sesame seeds, and tangy sumac. We found that incorporating the za'atar at two distinct points in the cooking process brought out its most complex flavor. First, to release its deep, earthy flavors, we bloomed half of the za'atar in an aromatic base of onion and garlic before adding the bulgur, chickpeas, and cooking liquid. We added the remainder of the za'atar along with the fresh spinach, off the heat; the residual heat in the bulgur was enough to perfectly soften the spinach and to highlight the za'atar's more delicate aromas. The finished salad was robust enough to serve as a satisfying main dish. When shopping, don't confuse bulgur with cracked wheat, which has a much longer cooking time and will not work in this recipe.

- 3 tablespoons extra-virgin olive oil, divided
- 1 onion, chopped fine
- ½ teaspoon table salt
- 3 garlic cloves, minced
- 2 tablespoons za'atar, divided
- 1 cup medium-grind bulgur, rinsed
- 1 (15-ounce) can chickpeas, rinsed
- ¾ cup chicken or vegetable broth
- ¾ cup water
- 3 ounces (3 cups) baby spinach, chopped
- 1 tablespoon lemon juice

1. Heat 2 tablespoons oil in large saucepan over medium heat until shimmering. Add onion and salt and cook until softened, about 5 minutes. Stir in garlic and 1 tablespoon za'atar and cook until fragrant, about 30 seconds.

2. Stir in bulgur, chickpeas, broth, and water and bring to simmer. Reduce heat to low, cover, and simmer gently until bulgur is tender, 16 to 18 minutes.

3. Off heat, lay clean dish towel underneath lid and let bulgur sit for 10 minutes. Add spinach, lemon juice, remaining 1 tablespoon za'atar, and remaining 1 tablespoon oil and fluff gently with fork to combine. Season with salt and pepper to taste. Serve.

Pearl Couscous Salad with Radishes and Watercress

Serves 6 `MAKE AHEAD`

Why This Recipe Works Pearl couscous, also known as Israeli couscous, has a chewy texture and toasty flavor. We wanted a foolproof method for cooking pearl couscous to serve as the base for a main-course salad featuring crisp radishes. To give the couscous spheres maximum flavor, we toasted them in oil to bring out their nuttiness. Once they turned golden brown, we added a measured amount of water that the pearls soaked up. This absorption method helped produce more evenly cooked results than boiling the couscous like regular pasta. Plus, the covered pot required little attention. When the water was absorbed, we spread the warm couscous out to cool quickly. Along with the crunchy, peppery radishes, we added watercress, fresh herbs, toasted walnuts, and tangy goat cheese just before serving. This kept the salad bright, light, and moist. Do not substitute regular couscous in this dish, as it requires a different cooking method and will not work.

- ¼ cup extra-virgin olive oil, divided
- 2 cups pearl couscous
- 2½ cups water
- ½ teaspoon plus ⅛ teaspoon table salt, divided
- 3 tablespoons sherry vinegar, plus extra for seasoning
- 1 teaspoon Dijon mustard
- 1 teaspoon smoked paprika
- ¼ teaspoon sugar
- 2 ounces (2 cups) watercress, torn into bite-size pieces
- 6 scallions, sliced thin
- 6 radishes, trimmed and cut into matchsticks
- 1½ cups chopped fresh parsley
- ½ cup walnuts, toasted and chopped
- 4 ounces goat cheese, crumbled (1 cup)

1. Cook 1 tablespoon oil and couscous in medium saucepan over medium heat, stirring frequently, until half of grains are golden brown, about 5 minutes. Stir in water and ½ teaspoon salt, increase heat to high, and bring to boil. Reduce heat to medium-low, cover, and simmer, stirring occasionally, until water is absorbed and couscous is tender, 9 to 12 minutes.

2. Off heat, let couscous sit, covered, for 3 minutes. Transfer couscous to rimmed baking sheet and let cool completely, about 15 minutes. (Couscous can be refrigerated for up to 3 days, bring to room temperature before continuing with recipe.)

Bulgur Salad with Chickpeas, Spinach, and Za'atar

Pearl Couscous Salad with Radishes and Watercress

Wheat Berry and Endive Salad with Blueberries and Goat Cheese

3. Whisk vinegar, mustard, paprika, sugar, and remaining ⅛ teaspoon salt together in large bowl. Whisking constantly, drizzle in remaining 3 tablespoons oil. (Dressing can be refrigerated for up to 3 days)

4. Add couscous, watercress, scallions, radishes, parsley, and walnuts to vinaigrette and toss to combine. Season with salt, pepper, and extra vinegar to taste. Let sit for 5 minutes. Sprinkle with goat cheese and serve. (Salad can be refrigerated for up to 2 hours)

VARIATION

Pearl Couscous Salad with Tomatoes, Olives, and Ricotta Salata

Do not substitute regular couscous in this dish, as it requires a different cooking method and will not work in this recipe. Crumbled feta cheese can be substituted for the ricotta salata.

Substitute red wine vinegar for sherry vinegar, baby spinach for watercress, and basil for parsley. Omit smoked paprika, sugar, scallions, radishes, walnuts, and goat cheese. Add couscous, 12 ounces quartered grape tomatoes, spinach, basil, ½ cup crumbled ricotta salata, ⅔ cup pitted, sliced kalamata olives, 6 tablespoons toasted pine nuts, and ¼ cup minced fresh chives to bowl with vinaigrette and gently toss to combine. Season with salt and pepper to taste, and transfer to serving bowl. Let sit for 5 minutes. Sprinkle with ¼ cup crumbled ricotta salata and 2 tablespoons toasted pine nuts and serve.

Wheat Berry and Endive Salad with Blueberries and Goat Cheese

Serves 4 to 6   `MAKE AHEAD`

Why This Recipe Works Nutty, chewy wheat berries (unprocessed kernels of wheat) retain their natural bran and germ, making them whole grains that serve as a hearty, substantive base of a grain salad. We cooked the wheat berries like we do pasta, simply simmering them in a large pot of water until they were tender but still had some nice chew. We used less salt than we do for other grains; too much, and the grains didn't absorb enough water and remained hard. To round out the grains with pleasing textures and complex flavors, we started with assertive endive, which we found added bitter contrast to sweet fresh blueberries and tangy, creamy goat cheese. A bright vinaigrette made with champagne vinegar, shallot, chives, and mustard brought all the ingredients together harmoniously. If using quick-cooking or presteamed wheat berries (read the package carefully to determine this), you will need to decrease the wheat berry cooking time in step 1.

Egyptian Barley Salad

1½ cups wheat berries
½ teaspoon table salt, plus salt for cooking wheat berries
2 tablespoons champagne vinegar
1 tablespoon minced shallot
1 tablespoon minced fresh chives
1 teaspoon Dijon mustard
¼ teaspoon pepper
6 tablespoons extra-virgin olive oil
2 heads Belgian endive (4 ounces each), halved, cored, and sliced crosswise ¼ inch thick
7½ ounces (1½ cups) blueberries
¾ cup pecans, toasted and chopped
4 ounces goat cheese, crumbled (1 cup)

1. Bring 4 quarts water to boil in large pot. Add wheat berries and ¼ teaspoon salt, return to boil, and cook until tender but still chewy, 50 minutes to 1 hour 10 minutes. Drain and rinse under cold running water until cool; drain well. (Wheat berries can be refrigerated for up to 3 days. Bring to room temperature before continuing with recipe.)

2. Whisk vinegar, shallot, chives, mustard, ½ teaspoon salt, and pepper together in large bowl. Whisking constantly, slowly drizzle in oil until combined. Add drained wheat berries, endive, blueberries, and pecans and toss to combine. Season with salt and pepper to taste, sprinkle with goat cheese, and serve.

VARIATION

Wheat Berry Salad with Figs, Pine Nuts, and Goat Cheese

Omit chives. Add 1 teaspoon honey to vinegar mixture. Decrease oil to 3 tablespoons. Omit endive, blueberries, and pecans. Add 8 ounces chopped figs, ½ cup fresh parsley leaves and ¼ cup toasted pine nuts to wheat berries. Reduce goat cheese to 2 ounces.

INGREDIENT SPOTLIGHT

GOAT CHEESE

Goat cheese (sometimes labeled chèvre) can be aged or fresh, soft or firm, musky or mild. That said, most of what you can buy in American supermarkets is young cheese packaged in a log shape; it has a creamy, grainy texture and a tangy, milky flavor. Avoid precrumbled cheeses—they tend to be dry and chalky. Our favorite goat cheese is **Laura Chenel's Pure Goat Milk Cheese Original Log.**

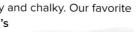

Egyptian Barley Salad
Serves 6 to 8 MAKE AHEAD

Why This Recipe Works We set out to create a vibrantly spiced pearl barley salad with the right balance of sweetness, tang, and nuttiness that was just as aesthetically stunning as it was flavorful. Inspired by the flavors of Egypt, where barley is a staple and is featured in a range of dishes, we incorporated toasty pistachios and bright cilantro and balanced their flavors with warm, earthy spices and sweet golden raisins. Salty feta cheese, pungent scallions, and pomegranate seeds adorned the dish for a colorful composed salad with dynamic flavors and textures. For the dressing, we used pomegranate molasses—another prominent ingredient in Egyptian cuisine—combined with olive oil, bright lemon, and warm cumin and cinnamon. If you can't find pomegranate molasses, substitute 2 tablespoons of lemon juice, 2 teaspoons of mild molasses, and 1 teaspoon of honey. Do not substitute hulled barley or hull-less barley in this recipe. If using quick-cooking or presteamed barley (read the ingredient list on the package to determine this), you will need to decrease the barley cooking time in step 1.

1½ cups pearl barley
½ teaspoon table salt, plus salt for cooking barley
3 tablespoons extra-virgin olive oil, plus extra for serving
2 tablespoons pomegranate molasses
1 teaspoon lemon juice
½ teaspoon ground cinnamon
¼ teaspoon ground cumin
½ cup chopped fresh cilantro
⅓ cup golden raisins
¼ cup shelled pistachios, toasted and chopped
3 ounces feta cheese, cut into ½-inch cubes (¾ cup)
6 scallions, green parts only, sliced thin
½ cup pomegranate seeds

1. Bring 4 quarts water to boil in Dutch oven. Add barley and 1 tablespoon salt, return to boil, and cook until tender, 20 to 40 minutes. Drain barley, spread in rimmed baking sheet, and let cool for 15 minutes. (Barley can be refrigerated for up to 2 days; bring to room temperature before proceeding with recipe.)

2. Whisk oil, pomegranate molasses, lemon juice, cinnamon, cumin, and ½ teaspoon salt together in large bowl. (Dressing can be refrigerated for up to 2 days.)

3. Add barley, cilantro, raisins, and pistachios and gently toss to combine. Season with salt and pepper to taste. Spread barley salad evenly on serving platter and arrange feta, scallions, and pomegranate seeds in separate diagonal rows on top. Drizzle with extra oil and serve. (Salad can be refrigerated for up to 2 hours.)

Brown Rice Salad with Jalapeños, Tomatoes, and Avocado

Chilled Soba Noodle Salad with Cucumber, Snow Peas, and Radishes

Brown Rice Salad with Jalapeños, Tomatoes, and Avocado

Serves 4 to 6

Why This Recipe Works Nutty, pleasantly chewy brown rice works perfectly in a hearty and vibrantly flavored salad. Baking the brown rice didn't work here. In an early test, we discovered that once it was cooled and drizzled with dressing, the baked rice turned gummy. Instead, we cooked the rice by boiling it in a large pot of water, which washed away its excess starches. Then we spread it out on a baking sheet to cool rapidly, preventing it from overcooking as it sat. To give the rice some bright flavor, we drizzled it with tangy lime juice while it was still warm. We then added some bold summery mix-ins for contrasting flavors and textures: bright tomatoes, creamy and mild avocado, fiery minced jalapeño, crunchy scallions, and fresh cilantro. To make this salad spicier, add the chile seeds.

1½ cups long-grain brown rice
½ teaspoon table salt, plus salt for cooking rice
1 teaspoon grated lime zest plus 3 tablespoons juice (2 limes), divided
2½ tablespoons extra-virgin olive oil
2 teaspoons honey
2 garlic cloves, minced
½ teaspoon ground cumin
½ teaspoon pepper
10 ounces cherry tomatoes, halved
1 avocado, halved, pitted, and cut into ½-inch pieces
1 jalapeño chile, stemmed, seeded, and minced
5 scallions, sliced thin, divided
¼ cup minced fresh cilantro

1. Bring 3 quarts water to boil in large pot. Add rice and 2 teaspoons salt and cook, stirring occasionally, until rice is tender, 22 to 25 minutes. Drain rice, spread onto rimmed baking sheet, and drizzle with 1 tablespoon lime juice. Let rice cool completely, about 10 minutes; transfer to large bowl.

2. Whisk oil, honey, garlic, cumin, pepper, salt, and lime zest and remaining 2 tablespoons juice together in small bowl, then drizzle over cooled rice. Add tomatoes, avocado, and jalapeño and toss to combine. Let sit for 10 minutes.

3. Add ¼ cup scallions and cilantro and toss to combine. Season with salt and pepper to taste. Sprinkle with remaining scallions and serve.

Chilled Soba Noodle Salad with Cucumber, Snow Peas, and Radishes
Serves 4 to 6

Why This Recipe Works Soba noodles, made from buckwheat flour or a buckwheat-wheat flour blend, have a chewy texture and nutty flavor and are often enjoyed chilled. For a refreshing cold noodle salad to serve on a hot summer evening, we cooked soba noodles in unsalted boiling water until tender but still resilient and rinsed them under cold running water to remove excess starch and prevent sticking. We then tossed the soba with a miso-based dressing, which clung to and flavored the noodles without overpowering their distinct taste. We also cut a mix of vegetables into varying sizes so they'd incorporate nicely into the noodles while adding crunch and color. Sprinkling strips of toasted nori over the top added more texture and a subtle briny taste. Sheets of nori, a dried seaweed that adds umami flavor and crisp texture to this salad, can be found in packets at Asian markets or in the Asian section of the supermarket. Plain pretoasted seaweed snacks can be substituted for the toasted nori, and yellow, red, or brown miso can be substituted for the white miso, if desired. This dish isn't meant to be overtly spicy, but if you prefer more heat, use the full ½ teaspoon of red pepper flakes.

> 8 ounces dried soba noodles
> 1 (8-inch square) sheet nori (optional)
> 3 tablespoons white miso
> 3 tablespoons mirin
> 2 tablespoons toasted sesame oil
> 1 tablespoon sesame seeds
> 1 teaspoon grated fresh ginger
> ¼–½ teaspoon red pepper flakes
> ⅓ English cucumber, quartered lengthwise, seeded, and sliced thin on bias
> 4 ounces snow peas, strings removed, cut lengthwise into matchsticks
> 4 radishes, trimmed, halved, and sliced into thin half-moons
> 3 scallions, sliced thin on bias

1. Bring 4 quarts water to boil in large pot. Stir in noodles and cook according to package directions, stirring occasionally, until noodles are cooked through but still retain some chew. Drain noodles and rinse under cold water until chilled. Drain well and transfer to large bowl.

2. Grip nori sheet, if using, with tongs and hold about 2 inches above low flame on gas burner. Toast nori, flipping every 3 to 5 seconds, until nori is aromatic and shrinks slightly, about 20 seconds. If you do not have a gas stove, toast nori on rimmed baking sheet in 275-degree oven until it is aromatic and shrinks slightly, 20 to 25 minutes, flipping nori halfway through toasting. Using scissors, cut nori into four 2-inch strips. Stack strips and cut crosswise into thin strips.

3. Whisk miso, mirin, oil, 1 tablespoon water, sesame seeds, ginger, and pepper flakes in small bowl until smooth. Add dressing to noodles and toss to combine. Add cucumber, snow peas, radishes, scallions, and nori, if using, and toss well to evenly distribute. Season with salt to taste, and serve.

TRIMMING SNOW AND SNAP PEAS

Use paring knife to snip off stem end of pod. Then, use your thumb to pull stem end along flat side of pod to remove string.

INGREDIENT SPOTLIGHT

MISO
Miso is the Japanese word for bean paste. An ingredient commonly found in Asian (most notably Japanese) cuisines, miso is a fermented paste of soy beans and rice, barley, or rye. It is salty and ranges in strength and color from mild, pale yellow (referred to as white) miso to stronger-flavored red or brownish-black miso. The color of miso depends on its fermentation method and ingredients. Miso paste is an incredibly versatile ingredient; it can be used in soups, braises, dressings, and sauces and as a topping for grilled foods. The lighter misos are typically used in more delicate dishes such as soups and salads; the darker misos are best used in heavier recipes. Miso can be found in most supermarkets as well as Japanese and Asian markets. It will keep for up to a year in the refrigerator. We like **Hikari Organic White Miso** for its intense umami flavor with sweet and subtly tart notes.

CHAPTER 3

Burgers, Sandwiches, and Tacos

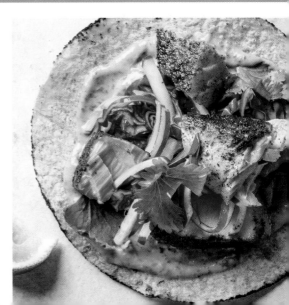

For more sandwiches, see Keep Cool with Countertop Cooking (pages 142–173), Dinner Off the Grill (pages 174–231), and Picnic-Table Favorites (pages 232–267).

■ FAST (30 minutes or less total time)   ■ NO COOK   ■ MAKE AHEAD
Photos (left to right): Grilled Bacon Burgers with Caramelized Onions and Blue Cheese; Tofu Banh Mi; Salmon Tacos with Avocado Crema

Classic Beef Burgers

Well-Done Burgers

Classic Beef Burgers
Serves 4 FAST

Why This Recipe Works Nothing says summer like a juicy burger. For quick weeknight burgers or a backyard barbecue, choosing the right store-bought ground beef was a necessity to produce tender patties. Generically labeled "ground beef" can be a combination of different cuts that yields fatty, greasy, or mushy burgers, but 85 percent lean ground chuck gave us burgers with rich, beefy flavor and a tender, moist texture. Our first few batches puffed up like tennis balls, but we quickly figured out that slightly indenting the center of each burger helped them cook evenly. For the ultimate versatility, we devised methods to cook up these burgers both in a skillet and on the grill, so perfect patties are possible whether you're cooking inside or outdoors. Serve with classic condiments, lettuce, and sliced ripe tomatoes, or try one of our homemade toppings on page 82.

1½ pounds 85 percent lean ground beef
½ teaspoon table salt
¼ teaspoon pepper
1 teaspoon vegetable oil, if using skillet
4 slices cheese (4 ounces) (optional)
4 hamburger buns, toasted if desired

1. Divide ground beef into 4 equal portions, then gently shape each portion into ¾-inch-thick patty. Using your fingertips, press center of each patty down until about ½ inch thick, creating slight divot.

2A. For a skillet Sprinkle patties with salt and pepper. Heat oil in 12-inch skillet over medium heat until just smoking. Transfer patties to skillet, divot side up, and cook until well browned on first side, 2 to 4 minutes. Flip patties, top with cheese, if using, and continue to cook until browned on second side and meat registers 120 to 125 degrees (for medium-rare), 3 to 5 minutes. Transfer burgers to platter and let rest for 5 minutes. Serve burgers on buns.

2B. For a charcoal grill Open bottom vent completely. Light large chimney starter filled with charcoal briquettes (6 quarts). When top coals are partially covered with ash, pour evenly over grill. Set cooking grate in place, cover, and open lid vent completely. Heat grill until hot, about 5 minutes. Clean and oil cooking grate. Sprinkle patties with salt and pepper. Place patties on grill, divot side up, and cook until well browned on first side, 2 to 4 minutes. Flip patties, top with cheese, if using, and continue to cook until browned on second side and meat registers 120 to 125 degrees (for medium-rare), 3 to 5 minutes. Transfer burgers to platter and let rest for 5 minutes. Serve burgers on buns.

2C. For a gas grill Turn all burners to high, cover, and heat grill until hot, about 15 minutes. Leave all burners on high. Clean and oil cooking grate. Sprinkle patties with salt and pepper. Place patties on grill, divot side up, and cook until well browned on first side, 2 to 4 minutes. Flip patties, top with cheese, if using, and continue to cook until browned on second side and meat registers 120 to 125 degrees (for medium-rare), 3 to 5 minutes. Transfer burgers to platter and let rest for 5 minutes. Serve burgers on buns.

Well-Done Burgers
Serves 4

Why This Recipe Works There's nothing worse than rushing to the grill to check your burger and finding it has passed medium and hit the dreaded well-done stage—at least, that's what we believed before we perfected the well-done burger. There are plenty of reasons to opt for well-done: It makes the cooking more hands-off and it requires less precise timing than rarer patties. Taste tests proved that well-done burgers made from 80 percent lean ground chuck were noticeably moister than burgers made from leaner beef, but they still weren't juicy enough; adding a panade—a paste of bread and milk—stemmed moisture loss and ensured the burgers were mouthwateringly tender. To punch up the flavor, we added minced garlic and tangy steak sauce. Make sure to use 80 percent lean ground beef; leaner ground beef will result in a drier burger. Serve with classic condiments, lettuce, and sliced ripe tomatoes, or try one of our homemade toppings on page 82.

- 1 slice hearty white sandwich bread, crust removed, torn into 1-inch pieces
- 2 tablespoons milk
- 2 teaspoons steak sauce
- 1 garlic clove, minced
- 1½ pounds 80 percent lean ground beef
- ½ teaspoon table salt
- ¼ teaspoon pepper
- 2 teaspoons vegetable oil, if using skillet
- 4 slices American cheese (4 ounces) (optional)
- 4 hamburger buns, toasted if desired

1. Using fork, mash bread, milk, steak sauce, and garlic to paste in large bowl. Break ground beef into small pieces and add to bowl with bread mixture. Gently knead with your hands until well combined. Divide beef mixture into 4 equal portions, then gently shape each portion into ¾-inch-thick patty. Using your fingertips, press center of each patty down until about ½ inch thick, creating slight divot.

2A. For a skillet Sprinkle patties with salt and pepper. Heat oil in 12-inch nonstick skillet over medium heat until just smoking. Transfer patties to skillet, divot side up, and cook until well browned on first side, about 5 minutes. Flip patties, top with cheese, if using, and continue to cook until browned on second side and meat registers 140 to 145 degrees (for medium-well) or 150 to 155 degrees (for well-done), 4 to 6 minutes. Transfer burgers to platter and let rest for 5 minutes. Serve burgers on buns.

2B. For a charcoal grill Open bottom vent completely. Light large chimney starter filled with charcoal briquettes (6 quarts). When top coals are partially covered with ash, pour evenly over grill. Set cooking grate in place, cover, and open lid vent completely. Heat grill until hot, about 5 minutes. Clean and oil cooking grate. Sprinkle patties with salt and pepper. Place patties on grill, divot side up, and cook until well browned on first side, 2 to 4 minutes. Flip patties, top with cheese, if using, and continue to cook until browned on second side and meat registers 140 to 145 degrees (for medium-well) or 150 to 155 degrees (for well-done), 4 to 6 minutes. Transfer burgers to platter and let rest for 5 minutes. Serve burgers on buns.

2C. For a gas grill Turn all burners to high, cover, and heat grill until hot, about 15 minutes. Leave all burners on high. Clean and oil cooking grate. Sprinkle patties with salt and pepper. Place patties on grill, divot side up, and cook, covered, until well browned on first side, 2 to 4 minutes. Flip patties, top with cheese, if using, and continue to cook until browned on second side and meat registers 140 to 145 degrees (for medium-well) or 150 to 155 degrees (for well-done), 4 to 6 minutes. Transfer burgers to platter and let rest for 5 minutes. Serve burgers on buns.

INGREDIENT SPOTLIGHT

KETCHUP
We tasted a lineup of eight classic tomato ketchups plain and with fries. In the end, we found that we preferred Heinz Organic Tomato Ketchup. Tasters deemed it "bright and fresh," with "well-rounded ketchup-y flavor." Its bold, harmonious punch of saltiness, sweetness, tang, and tomato flavor nudged it into first place. Overall, tasters praised this ketchup as being "like ketchup should be."

Onions, shallots, scallions, and leeks all belong to the allium family and are available year-round. Onions from the farmers' market sometimes come with their long, green stalks still attached to the bulb. Sweet onions, in particular, are best when fresh from the farmers' market, because their natural flavor is much more pronounced. Purchase rock-hard onions covered with smooth, papery skin. Avoid any with soft or dark powdery spots or green sprouts. Stored in a cool, well-ventilated spot, onions will keep for several weeks. When buying scallions and leeks, look for firm stalks, with crisp dark-green leaves and healthy-looking attached roots. Avoid leeks that have had their greens trimmed. Refrigerate them in an open plastic produce bag for a week.

Yellow Onions These all-purpose gold standards of the onion world are sweet and rich when cooked. Spanish onions are a larger, milder, firmer variety.

Red Onions Crisply pungent when raw (they're great on burgers), red onions are jammier than yellow onions when cooked.

White Onions White onions have a simpler, less complex flavor than yellow onions and break down more quickly when cooked.

Sweet Onions Vidalia, Maui, Walla Walla, and other sweet onions are best when they are the star of the dish.

Pearl Onions Pearl onions and Italian cipollini onions are intensely sweet when cooked.

Shallots Like garlic, shallots comprise a head with multiple cloves. Raw or cooked, they have a mellow oniony-garlicky flavor.

Scallions The earthy flavor and delicate crunch of scallions work well in dishes that involve little or no cooking.

Leeks The edible portions of leeks are found in their long, leafy stalks; there is no bulb. Their flavor is the mildest of all.

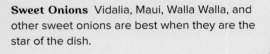

Grilled Bacon Burgers with Caramelized Onions and Blue Cheese
Serves 4

Why This Recipe Works Smoky, salty bacon can take any burger to the next level, but burgers with just a few strips on top fail to deliver bold bacon flavor. Our version nixes the strips and mixes bacon directly into the burger for bacony bliss in every bite. Mixing raw bacon with raw ground beef overworked and compressed the patties so that they cooked up tough and dry, and cooked crumbled bacon—though it mixed in better—was too crunchy. For the perfect balance of bacon flavor and juicy texture, we processed raw bacon in the food processor and then cooked it briefly in a skillet. The parcooked pieces incorporated easily into the ground beef and dispersed bacon flavor more evenly throughout while the burgers stayed moist and juicy. Instead of tossing the leftover bacon fat, we used it to sauté some onions, which provided salty balance to their sweet flavor. To turn these burgers into a savory showstopper, we topped them with rich and creamy crumbled blue cheese.

    8 slices bacon
    1 large onion, halved and sliced thin
  ¼ teaspoon table salt
1½ pounds 85 percent lean ground beef
  ¼ teaspoon pepper
    4 ounces blue cheese, crumbled and chilled (1 cup)
    4 hamburger buns, toasted if desired

1. Process bacon in food processor to smooth paste, about 1 minute, scraping down sides of bowl as needed. Cook bacon in 12-inch nonstick skillet over medium heat, breaking up pieces with wooden spoon, until lightly browned in spots but still pink (do not cook until crisp), about 5 minutes. Drain bacon in fine-mesh strainer set over bowl. Transfer bacon to paper towel–lined plate and let cool completely. Reserve bacon fat.

2. Add 2 tablespoons reserved fat to now-empty skillet and heat over medium heat until shimmering. Add onion and salt and cook until well browned, about 20 minutes. Transfer to bowl and set aside.

3. Break ground beef into small pieces and spread into even layer on rimmed baking sheet. Sprinkle with bacon and gently toss to combine using 2 forks. Divide beef mixture into 4 equal portions, then gently shape each portion into ¾-inch-thick patty. Using your fingertips, press center of each patty down until about ½ inch thick, creating slight divot.

4A. For a charcoal grill Open bottom vent completely. Light large chimney starter filled with charcoal briquettes (6 quarts). When top coals are partially covered with ash, pour evenly over grill. Set cooking grate in place, cover, and open lid vent completely. Heat grill until hot, about 5 minutes.

4B. For a gas grill Turn all burners to high, cover, and heat grill until hot, about 15 minutes. Leave all burners on high.

5. Clean and oil cooking grate. Sprinkle patties with pepper. Place patties on grill, divot side up, and cook until well browned on first side, 2 to 4 minutes. Flip patties, top with blue cheese, and continue to cook until well browned on second side and meat registers 120 to 125 degrees (for medium rare) or 130 to 135 degrees (for medium), 3 to 5 minutes. Transfer burgers to platter and let rest for 5 minutes. Serve burgers on buns, topped with onions.

Classic Turkey Burgers
Serves 4 `FAST`

Why This Recipe Works A lean, flavorful turkey burger is a delicious alternative to the classic beef burger, and we wanted to create a simple and satisfying patty that would be the perfect base for a variety of bold and flavorful summery toppings. To start, we took a close look at the ground turkey sold in supermarkets and found a few kinds: ground white meat, ground dark meat, and 93 percent lean ground turkey. Our tasters preferred the flavor of 93 percent lean ground turkey. For extra richness, we added melted butter, which kept the burgers moist and juicy. A little bit of Worcestershire and Dijon mustard added plenty of flavor and a pleasant tang to the mild meat. Be sure to use ground turkey, not ground turkey breast (also labeled 99 percent fat-free), in this recipe. Serve with classic condiments, lettuce, and sliced ripe tomatoes, or try one of our homemade toppings on page 82.

1½ pounds ground turkey
2 tablespoons unsalted butter, melted and cooled
2 teaspoons Worcestershire sauce
2 teaspoons Dijon mustard
½ teaspoon table salt
¼ teaspoon pepper
2 teaspoons vegetable oil, if using skillet
4 slices cheese (4 ounces) (optional)
4 hamburger buns, toasted if desired

Classic Turkey Burgers

1. Break ground turkey into small pieces in large bowl. Add melted butter, Worcestershire, and mustard and gently knead with your hands until well combined. Divide turkey mixture into 4 equal portions, then gently shape each portion into ¾-inch-thick patty. Using your fingertips, press center of each patty down until about ½ inch thick, creating slight divot.

2A. For a skillet Sprinkle patties with salt and pepper. Heat oil in 12-inch skillet over medium heat until just smoking. Transfer patties to skillet, divot side up, and cook until well browned on first side, 4 to 6 minutes. Flip patties, top with cheese, if using, and continue to cook until browned on second side and meat registers 160 degrees, 5 to 7 minutes. Transfer burgers to platter and let rest for 5 minutes. Serve burgers on buns.

2B. For a charcoal grill Open bottom vent completely. Light large chimney starter filled with charcoal briquettes (6 quarts). When top coals are partially covered with ash, pour evenly over grill. Set cooking grate in place, cover, and open lid vent completely. Heat grill until hot, about 5 minutes. Clean and oil cooking grate. Sprinkle patties with salt and pepper.

Place patties on grill, divot side up, and cook until well browned on first side and meat easily releases from grill, 4 to 6 minutes. Flip patties, top with cheese, if using, and continue to cook until browned on second side and meat registers 160 degrees, 5 to 7 minutes. Transfer burgers to platter and let rest for 5 minutes. Serve burgers on buns.

2C. For a gas grill Turn all burners to high, cover, and heat grill until hot, about 15 minutes. Turn all burners to medium. Clean and oil cooking grate. Sprinkle patties with salt and pepper. Place patties on grill, divot side up, and cook until well browned on first side and meat easily releases from grill, 4 to 6 minutes. Flip patties, top with cheese, if using, and continue to cook until browned on second side and meat registers 160 degrees, 5 to 7 minutes. Transfer burgers to platter and let rest for 5 minutes. Serve burgers on buns.

Buffalo Chicken Burgers
Serves 4 `FAST`

Why This Recipe Works To translate the popular combination of chicken, buffalo sauce, and celery into a spicy burger made for a hot summer day, we started off with ground chicken and then added some Worcestershire and shallot for umami. We learned from our Classic Turkey Burgers that melted butter helped keep the patties moist during cooking. For a bold buffalo sauce to top our burgers that would be cohesive enough to cling to the patties, we added cornstarch and molasses to the traditional hot sauce and butter. Piling on blue cheese before serving added a pungent counterpoint to the hot sauce. In a nod to the classic buffalo accompaniment, we topped our burgers with thinly sliced celery along with the leaves, which brought pleasing crispness and refreshing contrast. If the delicate leaves attached to the celery stalks are not available, you can omit them. We prefer a mild blue cheese, such as Gorgonzola, for this recipe. Be sure to use ground chicken, not ground chicken breast (also labeled 99 percent fat free), or the burgers will be tough.

- 4 tablespoons unsalted butter, plus 2 tablespoons melted and cooled, divided
- 6 tablespoons hot sauce
- 1 tablespoon molasses
- ½ teaspoon cornstarch
- 1½ pounds ground chicken
- 1 large shallot, minced
- 2 teaspoons Worcestershire sauce
- ¼ teaspoon pepper
- ½ teaspoon table salt
- 2 teaspoons vegetable oil
- 4 Bibb lettuce leaves
- 4 hamburger buns, toasted if desired
- 2 ounces mild blue cheese, crumbled (½ cup), room temperature
- 1 celery rib, sliced thin on bias, plus ¼ cup celery leaves

1. Microwave 4 tablespoons butter, hot sauce, molasses, and cornstarch in bowl, whisking occasionally, until butter is melted and mixture has thickened slightly, 2 to 3 minutes; cover to keep warm and set aside.

2. Break ground chicken into small pieces in large bowl. Add remaining 2 tablespoons melted butter, shallot, Worcestershire, and pepper and gently knead with your hands until well combined. Divide chicken mixture into 4 equal portions, then gently shape each portion into ¾-inch-thick patty. Using your fingertips, press center of each patty down until about ½ inch thick, creating slight divot.

3. Sprinkle patties with salt. Heat oil in 12-inch nonstick skillet over medium heat until just smoking. Transfer patties to skillet, divot side up, and cook until well browned on first side, 4 to 6 minutes. Flip patties, reduce heat to medium-low, and continue to cook until browned on second side and meat registers 160 degrees, 5 to 7 minutes. Transfer burgers to platter, brush with half of buffalo sauce, and let rest for 5 minutes.

4. Arrange lettuce on bun bottoms. Serve burgers on buns, topped with blue cheese, celery, and celery leaves, passing remaining buffalo sauce separately.

> **INGREDIENT SPOTLIGHT**
>
> **BURGER BUNS**
> Juicy burgers require top-notch buns. Our favorites are **Martin's Sandwich Potato Rolls**; they boast a mild sweetness that pairs well with a rich burger. They also have a particularly light, tender, moist texture. That's because instead of hydrating the dough with water, Martin's uses a mixture of potato flakes, milk, and butter (essentially mashed potatoes). Mashed potatoes are hefty and substantial, but in potato rolls, the milk protein and butterfat weaken the structure of the dough, leaving the rolls softer, moister, and more tender.

Grilled Harissa Lamb Burgers
Serves 4

Why This Recipe Works Lamb might not be your first thought when it comes to burgers, but with its earthy flavor and tender texture—and with a charred onion topping that grills right alongside the patty—this easy, flavor-packed burger is sure to become your new barbecue favorite. Lamb's distinctive taste pairs perfectly with the bold flavor of harissa, a traditional North African condiment with irresistibly complex chile flavor. Cool, creamy mayonnaise provides a rich base for our spicy harissa-spiked sauce, and a blast of fresh mint and lemon zest balances out the harissa's heat. Harissa, a chile paste, can be found in the international aisle of your supermarket, usually with Middle Eastern or Indian ingredients. The red color of the harissa makes these burgers look more rare than they actually are—use an instant-read thermometer to accurately check doneness.

- 3 tablespoons mayonnaise
- 2 tablespoons harissa, divided
- 1 tablespoon minced fresh mint
- 1½ teaspoons grated lemon zest, divided
- 1½ pounds ground lamb
- ½ teaspoon pepper, divided
- 1 red onion, sliced into ½-inch-thick rounds
- 1 tablespoon vegetable oil
- ½ teaspoon table salt
- 4 hamburger buns, toasted if desired
- 1 cup baby arugula

1. Combine mayonnaise, 1 tablespoon harissa, mint, and ½ teaspoon lemon zest in bowl and season with salt and pepper to taste; cover and refrigerate until ready to serve.

2. Break ground lamb into small pieces in large bowl. Add remaining 1 tablespoon harissa, remaining 1 teaspoon lemon zest, and ¼ teaspoon pepper and gently knead with your hands until well combined. Divide lamb mixture into 4 equal portions, then gently shape each portion into ¾-inch-thick patty. Using your fingertips, press center of each patty down until about ½ inch thick, creating slight divot.

3. Push toothpick horizontally through each onion round to keep rings intact while grilling. Brush onion rounds with oil.

4A. For a charcoal grill Open bottom vent completely. Light large chimney starter filled with charcoal briquettes (6 quarts). When top coals are partially covered with ash, pour evenly over grill. Set cooking grate in place, cover, and open lid vent completely. Heat grill until hot, about 5 minutes.

4B. For a gas grill Turn all burners to high, cover, and heat grill until hot, about 15 minutes. Leave all burners on high.

Buffalo Chicken Burgers

Grilled Harissa Lamb Burgers

Crispy Salmon Burgers with Tomato Chutney

5. Clean and oil cooking grate. Place onion rounds on grill and cook (covered if using gas) until softened and lightly charred, 3 to 6 minutes per side. As they finish cooking, transfer onion rounds to bowl and cover to keep warm.

6. Meanwhile, sprinkle patties with salt and remaining ¼ teaspoon pepper. Place patties on grill, divot side up, and cook until well browned on first side, 2 to 4 minutes. Flip patties and continue to cook until browned on second side and meat registers 120 to 125 degrees (for medium-rare) or 130 to 135 (for medium), 3 to 5 minutes. Transfer burgers to platter and let rest for 5 minutes.

7. Remove toothpicks from onion rounds and separate into rings. Spread mayonnaise mixture on bun tops. Serve burgers on buns, topped with onion and arugula.

Crispy Salmon Burgers with Tomato Chutney

Serves 4 MAKE AHEAD

Why This Recipe Works Rich, flavorful salmon should make for exceptional burgers, but too often the fish overcooks and dries out or the patties turn into a textureless mess. For delicious burgers with meaty flavor and tender texture, we coarsely chopped chunks of fish in a food processor in three batches. Briefly refrigerating the patties helped them hold their shape when cooked. To build a crispy crust without overcooking the fish, we opted to sear the patties in a skillet. We wanted a chutney topping that would highlight the flavor of tomatoes without overpowering it, so we kept the flavorings minimal—Asian sweet chili sauce, bright lemon juice, and fresh cilantro—and cooked the mixture until it had thickened into a sweet-yet-spicy topping. If using wild salmon, which contains less fat, cook the burgers to 120 degrees (for medium-rare).

1¼ pounds skinless salmon, cut into 1-inch pieces
½ cup panko bread crumbs
½ cup chopped fresh cilantro, divided
8 scallions, minced, divided
3 tablespoons lemon juice, divided
2 tablespoons mayonnaise
½ teaspoon pepper, divided
2 tablespoons vegetable oil, divided
1 tablespoon grated fresh ginger
2 tomatoes, cored, seeded, and chopped
3 tablespoons Asian sweet chili sauce
½ teaspoon table salt
4 Bibb lettuce leaves
4 hamburger buns, toasted if desired

Grilled Tuna Burgers with Wasabi and Pickled Ginger

1. Working in 3 batches, pulse salmon in food processor until coarsely chopped into ¼-inch pieces, about 2 pulses, transferring each batch to large bowl.

2. Add panko, 6 tablespoons cilantro, 3 tablespoons scallions, 1 tablespoon lemon juice, mayonnaise, and ¼ teaspoon pepper to chopped salmon and gently knead with hands until well combined. Using your lightly moistened hands, divide salmon mixture into 4 equal portions, then gently shape each portion into 1-inch-thick patty. Place patties on parchment paper–lined rimmed baking sheet and refrigerate for at least 15 minutes or up to 24 hours.

3. Heat 1 tablespoon oil in 12-inch nonstick skillet over medium-high heat until shimmering. Add ginger and remaining scallions and cook until fragrant, about 1 minute. Add tomatoes, chili sauce, and remaining 2 tablespoons lemon juice and cook until mixture is very thick, about 6 minutes. Stir in remaining 2 tablespoons cilantro and season with salt and pepper to taste. Transfer chutney to bowl and wipe out skillet with paper towels.

4. Sprinkle patties with salt and remaining ¼ teaspoon pepper. Heat remaining 1 tablespoon oil in now-empty skillet over medium heat until shimmering. Cook patties until browned, centers are still translucent when checked with tip of paring knife, and burgers register 125 degrees (for medium-rare), about 4 minutes per side. Arrange lettuce on bun bottoms. Serve burgers on buns, topped with chutney.

Grilled Tuna Burgers with Wasabi and Pickled Ginger

Serves 4 MAKE AHEAD

Why This Recipe Works Tuna's rich, meaty texture makes for an outstanding burger patty, but because the fish is so lean, tuna burgers are prone to cooking up dry and disappointing. To ensure that our burgers would retain good texture and flavor, we hand-chopped the fish and then combined it with a little garlic and pickled ginger, which paired well with the tuna's distinctive flavor without overpowering it. The fragile nature of the patties made them prone to sticking, but wiping the grill grate with well-oiled paper towels multiple times to build up a stick-resistant coating solved this problem. Coating the spatula with vegetable oil spray also helped loosen the burgers from the cooking grate. To avoid dry burgers we made sure we didn't overcook the tuna, taking the patties off the grill when they reached medium-rare. A simple wasabi mayonnaise paired wonderfully with the tuna, and in place of the traditional bun we served these delicate burgers in crisp lettuce wraps along with a few crunchy vegetables. Extra pickled

ginger on top lent additional tangy flavor. Do not let these burgers overcook; tuna tends to get very dry when cooked for too long. You can serve this burger with a simple salad on the side instead of the lettuce wraps.

- ½ cup mayonnaise
- 1½ tablespoons wasabi powder
- 1 teaspoon soy sauce
- ½ teaspoon water
- 1¼ pounds skinless tuna steaks
- 2 teaspoons minced pickled ginger, plus 2 tablespoons pickled ginger
- 1 garlic clove, minced
- ½ teaspoon table salt
- ¼ teaspoon pepper
- 8 large iceberg lettuce leaves
- 6 radishes, trimmed and sliced thin
- 2 scallions, sliced thin on bias

1. Whisk mayonnaise, wasabi, soy sauce, and water together in bowl. Cover and refrigerate for at least 15 minutes or up to 3 days.

2. Chop tuna into ¼-inch pieces. Using rocking motion, continue to chop tuna until it is coarsely chopped into pieces roughly ⅛ inch each; transfer to bowl. Add minced pickled ginger and garlic and gently knead with your hands until well combined. Using your lightly moistened hands, divide tuna mixture into 4 equal portions, then gently shape each portion into 1-inch-thick patty. Place patties on parchment paper–lined rimmed baking sheet and refrigerate for at least 15 minutes or up to 24 hours.

3A. For a charcoal grill Open bottom vent completely. Light large chimney starter filled with charcoal briquettes (6 quarts). When top coals are partially covered with ash, pour evenly over grill. Set cooking grate in place, cover, and open lid vent completely. Heat grill until hot, about 5 minutes.

3B. For a gas grill Turn all burners to high, cover, and heat grill until hot, about 15 minutes. Leave burners on high.

4. Clean cooking grate, then repeatedly brush grate with well-oiled paper towels until black and glossy, 5 to 10 times. Sprinkle patties with salt and pepper.

5. Using greased spatula, place patties on grill and cook until well browned on first side and patties easily release from grill, about 3 minutes. Gently flip patties and continue to cook until well browned on second side, centers are still reddish pink when checked with tip of paring knife, and burgers register 125 degrees (for medium-rare), 2 to 3 minutes.

6. Stack lettuce leaves together to create 4 lettuce wraps. Serve burgers on lettuce wraps, topped with wasabi mayonnaise, radishes, scallions, and remaining 2 tablespoons pickled ginger.

South Carolina Shrimp Burgers
Serves 4 `FAST`

Why This Recipe Works Shrimp may seem like an unconventional choice for a burger, but our version of this Southern fisherman's summertime special combines the sweet taste of shrimp with a bread-crumb coating that mimics the taste and crunch of golden fried seafood. Most shrimp burger recipes call for cooked shrimp, but we were disappointed by how dry and rubbery this made our burgers. Instead, we opted to start with raw shrimp so that we could control the cooking. Pulsing a small amount of shrimp in the food processor with mayonnaise gave us a sticky paste that was the perfect binder for our burgers, and leaving the remaining shrimp coarse ensured meaty bites. Grinding the panko to a fine powder helped our coating to thoroughly cover and stick to our burgers while they cooked. Served with a simple tartar sauce, this burger is certainly seaworthy. If you're purchasing peeled and deveined shrimp, you should buy about 1¼ pounds.

- 1 cup panko bread crumbs
- 1½ pounds large shrimp (26 to 30 per pound), peeled, deveined, and tails removed, divided
- 2 tablespoons mayonnaise
- ½ teaspoon table salt
- ¼ teaspoon pepper
- ⅛ teaspoon cayenne pepper
- 3 scallions, chopped fine
- 3 tablespoons vegetable oil
- 4 Bibb lettuce leaves
- 4 hamburger buns, toasted if desired
- 1 recipe Tartar Sauce

1. Pulse panko in food processor until finely ground, about 15 pulses; transfer to shallow dish. Place one-third of shrimp (1 cup), mayonnaise, salt, pepper, and cayenne in now-empty processor and pulse until shrimp are finely chopped, about 8 pulses. Add remaining shrimp to shrimp mixture in processor and pulse until coarsely chopped, about 4 pulses, scraping down sides of bowl as needed. Transfer shrimp mixture to bowl and stir in scallions.

2. Using your lightly moistened hands, divide shrimp mixture into 4 equal portions, then gently shape each portion into ¾-inch-thick patty. Working with 1 patty at a time, dredge both sides in panko, pressing lightly to adhere, and transfer to plate.

3. Heat oil in 12-inch nonstick skillet over medium heat until shimmering. Cook patties until golden brown and register 140 to 145 degrees, 3 to 5 minutes per side. Transfer burgers to paper towel–lined plate and let drain, about 30 seconds per side. Arrange lettuce on bun bottoms. Serve burgers on buns, topped with tartar sauce.

Tartar Sauce
Makes about 1 cup

- ¾ cup mayonnaise
- 3 tablespoons finely chopped dill pickles plus 1 teaspoon brine
- 1 small shallot, minced
- 1 tablespoon capers, rinsed and chopped fine
- ¼ teaspoon pepper

Combine all ingredients in bowl and refrigerate until flavors meld, about 15 minutes. (Sauce can be refrigerated for up to 3 days.)

Southwestern Black Bean Burgers
Serves 6 `MAKE AHEAD`

Why This Recipe Works As with many meatless patties, black bean burgers often get their structure from fillers that turn the burgers into a gluey mess and rob them of their black bean flavor. We wanted burgers that featured earthy bean flavor at their heart with just enough seasoning and mix-ins to give them a little zest and intrigue. For convenient and reliable beans, we turned to canned. Thoroughly drying the beans and grinding them coarse helped prevent pasty, soggy patties. Scallions and cilantro added fresh bite, while garlic, hot sauce, cumin, and coriander amped up the Southwestern-inspired flavor of the bean mixture. To avoid an overly soft, mealy patty, we used a combination of flour and ground tortilla chips, which added pleasant texture, to bind our spice-infused burgers. Refrigerating the mixture for at least an hour before forming patties allowed it to firm up so the patties would better hold their shape when cooked. For easy veggie burgers on a busy weeknight, make the patties in advance and freeze them. When forming the patties, it's important to pack them together firmly.

- 2 (15-ounce) cans black beans, rinsed
- 2 large eggs
- 2 tablespoons all-purpose flour
- 4 scallions, minced
- 3 tablespoons minced fresh cilantro, plus 1 cup leaves, divided
- 2 garlic cloves, minced
- 1 teaspoon hot sauce
- 1 teaspoon ground cumin
- ½ teaspoon ground coriander
- ¼ teaspoon table salt

1 ounce tortilla chips, crushed coarse (½ cup)
8 teaspoons vegetable oil, divided
1 recipe Chipotle Sauce (page 82)
6 hamburger buns, toasted if desired
2 avocados, halved, pitted, and sliced thin
½ cup Quick Pickled Red Onions (page 100)

1. Spread beans onto rimmed baking sheet lined with triple layer of paper towels and let drain for 15 minutes. In large bowl, whisk eggs and flour into uniform paste, then stir in scallions, minced cilantro, garlic, hot sauce, cumin, coriander, and salt.

2. Process tortilla chips in food processor until finely ground, about 30 seconds. Add black beans and pulse until beans are roughly broken down, about 5 pulses. Stir processed bean mixture into egg mixture until well combined. Cover and refrigerate for at least 1 hour or up to 24 hours.

3. Divide bean mixture into 6 equal portions. Using your lightly moistened hands, tightly pack each portion into ½-inch-thick patty. (Patties can be frozen for up to 1 month. To freeze, transfer patties to parchment paper–lined rimmed baking sheet, cover with plastic wrap, and freeze until firm, about 1 hour. Stack patties, separated by parchment paper; wrap in plastic wrap; and place in zipper-lock freezer bag. Thaw patties completely before cooking.)

4. Adjust oven rack to middle position and heat oven to 200 degrees. Set wire rack in rimmed baking sheet. Heat 2 teaspoons oil in 12-inch nonstick skillet over medium heat until shimmering. Place 3 patties in skillet and cook until well browned and crisp on first side, about 5 minutes. Using 2 spatulas, gently flip patties, add 2 teaspoons oil to skillet, and cook until well browned and crisp on second side, 3 to 5 minutes. Transfer burgers to prepared rack and keep warm in oven. Repeat with remaining 4 teaspoons oil and remaining 3 patties. Spread chipotle sauce over bun bottoms. Serve burgers on buns, topped with avocados, pickled onions, and remaining 1 cup cilantro leaves.

NOTES FROM THE TEST KITCHEN

FREEZING BURGERS

When patties are frozen, water vapor escapes from the surface, migrates through an air space in the package, and condenses on the inner surface of the package. The result is a burger patty covered with ice crystals—what's commonly known as freezer burn. Freezer burn indicates a loss of moisture in the food and should be avoided. The food is still safe to eat, but the quality has suffered. To prevent freezer burn, stack patties, separated by parchment paper, wrap in plastic wrap, and place in a zipper-lock freezer bag.

South Carolina Shrimp Burgers

Southwestern Black Bean Burgers

Burger Sauces and Toppings

No burger would be complete without sauces and toppings to add richness, moisture, flavor, and texture. You can't go wrong with the standard ketchup and mustard or lettuce and tomato, but for a quick burger boost consider one of these easy upgrades.

Classic Burger Sauce
Makes about 1 cup

- ½ cup mayonnaise
- ¼ cup ketchup
- 2 teaspoons sweet pickle relish
- 2 teaspoons sugar
- 2 teaspoons distilled white vinegar
- 1 teaspoon pepper

Whisk all ingredients together in bowl. (Sauce can be refrigerated in airtight container for up to 4 days; bring to room temperature before serving.)

Pub-Style Burger Sauce
Makes about 1 cup
This sauce can be made vegan by substituting vegan mayonnaise and vegan Worcestershire sauce.

- ¾ cup mayonnaise
- 2 tablespoons soy sauce
- 1 tablespoon packed dark brown sugar
- 1 tablespoon Worcestershire sauce
- 1 tablespoon minced chives
- 1 garlic clove, minced
- ¾ teaspoon pepper

Whisk all ingredients together in bowl. (Sauce can be refrigerated in airtight container for up to 4 days; bring to room temperature before serving.)

Chipotle Sauce
Makes about 1 cup

- ½ cup mayonnaise
- ½ cup sour cream
- 2 tablespoons lime juice
- 2 tablespoons minced canned chipotle chile in adobo sauce
- 2 garlic cloves, minced

Combine all ingredients in bowl; refrigerate until ready to serve. (Sauce can be refrigerated in airtight container for up to 4 days; bring to room temperature before serving.)

Sautéed Mushroom Topping
Makes about 1½ cups

- 3 tablespoons unsalted butter, divided
- 1 onion, chopped
- 1¼ pounds cremini or white mushrooms, trimmed and sliced thin
- ¼ teaspoon table salt
- 1 teaspoon minced fresh thyme
- 2 garlic cloves, minced
- ¼ cup dry white wine

1. Melt 2 tablespoons butter in 12-inch skillet over medium heat. Add onion and cook until softened, about 5 minutes. Stir in mushrooms and salt and increase heat to medium-high. Cover and cook, stirring occasionally, until mushrooms have released their moisture, 8 to 10 minutes.

2. Remove lid, add remaining 1 tablespoon butter, and cook, stirring occasionally, until mushrooms are deep golden brown and tender, 8 to 10 minutes. Stir in thyme and garlic and cook until fragrant, about 30 seconds. Stir in wine and cook, scraping up any browned bits, until liquid is nearly evaporated, about 1 minute. Season with salt and pepper to taste.

Crispy Bacon
Serves 4

- 6 slices bacon, halved crosswise

Place bacon in 12-inch skillet and add just enough water to cover (about ½ cup). Bring to simmer over medium-high heat and cook until water has evaporated, about 8 minutes. Lower heat to medium-low and cook bacon until crisp and well browned, 5 to 8 minutes. Transfer bacon to paper towel–lined plate to drain.

Vegan Pinto Bean and Beet Burgers

Serves 8 `MAKE AHEAD`

Why This Recipe Works To create a veggie burger as hearty as any meat burger, we combined starchy pinto beans, vibrant beet, and wholesome bulgur in a patty rich with both protein and flavor. Meatless burgers are prone to crumbling, and although bread crumbs helped to keep the patties from falling apart, they weren't enough alone. We discovered a surprisingly perfect vegan binder—carrot baby food, which added tackiness to help the burgers hold their shape and a subtle sweetness that heightened the flavor of the beet. Ground nuts lent extra meaty flavor, and a generous amount of basil added bright, aromatic notes. As a bonus, these patties are perfect to make ahead and freeze for superfast weeknight burgers. Use a coarse grater or the shredding disk of a food processor to shred the beet.

1½ teaspoons table salt, plus salt for cooking bulgur
⅔ cup medium-grind bulgur, rinsed
1 large beet (9 ounces), peeled and shredded
¾ cup walnuts
½ cup fresh basil leaves
2 garlic cloves, minced
1 (15-ounce) can pinto beans, rinsed
1 (4-ounce) jar carrot baby food
1 tablespoon whole-grain mustard
½ teaspoon pepper
1½ cups panko bread crumbs
6 tablespoons vegetable oil, divided, plus extra as needed
8 hamburger buns, toasted if desired

1. Bring 1½ cups water and ½ teaspoon salt to boil in small saucepan. Off heat, stir in bulgur, cover, and let sit until tender, 15 to 20 minutes. Drain bulgur, spread onto rimmed baking sheet, and let cool slightly.

2. Pulse beet, walnuts, basil, and garlic in food processor until finely chopped, about 12 pulses, scraping down sides of bowl as needed. Add beans, carrot baby food, 2 tablespoons water, mustard, salt, and pepper and pulse until well combined, about 8 pulses. Transfer mixture to large bowl and stir in panko and cooled bulgur.

3. Divide beet-bulgur mixture into 8 equal portions, then tightly pack each portion into ¾-inch-thick patty. (Patties can be refrigerated for up to 3 days. To freeze, transfer patties to parchment paper–lined rimmed baking sheet, cover with plastic wrap, and freeze until firm, about 1 hour. Stack patties, separated by parchment paper, wrap in plastic wrap, and place in zipper-lock freezer bag. Do not thaw patties before cooking.)

Vegan Pinto Bean and Beet Burgers

4. Adjust oven rack to middle position and heat oven to 200 degrees. Set wire rack in rimmed baking sheet. Heat 3 tablespoons oil in 12-inch nonstick skillet over medium-high heat until shimmering. Place 4 patties in skillet and cook until well browned and crisp on first side, about 4 minutes. Using 2 spatulas, gently flip patties and continue to cook until well browned and crisp on second side, about 4 minutes, adding extra oil as needed if skillet looks dry. Transfer burgers to prepared rack and keep warm in oven. Wipe skillet clean with paper towels and repeat with remaining 3 tablespoons oil and remaining 4 patties. Serve burgers on buns.

FLIPPING A DELICATE BURGER

To flip delicate burger, slide 1 spatula under patty and use second spatula to support and guide patty as you flip it.

Grilled Portobello Burgers with Goat Cheese and Arugula

Serves 4

Why This Recipe Works When the king of mushrooms meets the heat of the grill, magic happens as its texture softens and its earthy, rich flavor deepens. Layer this portobello burger with melty goat cheese and peppery arugula, top it off with a tomato slice and smoky grilled onion, and you have a meatless burger featuring an irresistible combination of flavors and textures. Portobello mushroom gills can have an off-flavor, so we scraped them out to avoid a muddy taste. Before cooking, we lightly scored the smooth side of the mushroom with a crosshatch pattern to expedite the release of moisture and give the caps a more tender texture.

    4   portobello mushroom caps (4 to 5 inches in diameter),
        gills removed
    1   large red onion, sliced into ½-inch-thick rounds
        (do not separate rings)
    3   tablespoons plus 1 teaspoon extra-virgin olive oil,
        divided
    2   garlic cloves, minced
    2   teaspoons minced fresh thyme
    ¼   teaspoon table salt
    ¼   teaspoon pepper
    2   ounces goat cheese, crumbled (½ cup)
    1   cup baby arugula
    ¼   teaspoon balsamic vinegar
    4   hamburger buns, toasted if desired
    1   tomato, cored and sliced thin

1. Cut ¹⁄₁₆-inch-deep slits on top side of mushroom caps, spaced ½ inch apart, in crosshatch pattern. Brush onion with 1 tablespoon oil and season with salt and pepper to taste. Combine garlic, thyme, salt, pepper, and 2 tablespoons oil in bowl.

2A. For a charcoal grill Open bottom vent completely. Light large chimney starter three-quarters filled with charcoal briquettes (4½ quarts). When top coals are partially covered with ash, pour evenly over grill. Set cooking grate in place, cover, and open lid vent completely. Heat grill until hot, about 5 minutes.

2B. For a gas grill Turn all burners to high, cover, and heat grill until hot, about 15 minutes. Turn all burners to medium-high.

3. Clean and oil cooking grate. Place mushrooms, gill side down, and onion on grill. Cook mushrooms (covered if using gas) until lightly charred and beginning to soften on gill side, 4 to 6 minutes. Flip mushrooms, brush with oil-garlic mixture, and cook until tender and browned on second side, 4 to 6 minutes. Sprinkle with goat cheese and let cheese melt, about 2 minutes.

4. Meanwhile, cook onion, turning as needed, until lightly charred on both sides, 8 to 12 minutes. As they finish cooking, transfer mushrooms and onion to platter and tent with aluminum foil.

5. Toss arugula with vinegar and remaining 1 teaspoon oil in bowl and season with salt and pepper to taste. Separate onion rings. Place arugula and mushroom caps on buns. Top with tomato and onion. Serve.

Chicken Avocado Salad Sandwiches

Serve 4 FAST NO COOK

Why This Recipe Works A rich chicken salad sandwich is a summer lunchtime staple that comes together in seconds, but we wanted a version that wasn't laden with heavy mayonnaise. Instead, we found that we could achieve the same tangy flavor from a combination of buttermilk and a bright lime vinaigrette. For a lighter add-in that would lend the creamy texture we were after, we turned to avocado. Mashing the ripe avocado into the dressing gave us exactly the right consistency for our summery chicken salad. For best results, be sure to use a very ripe avocado. You can substitute rotisserie chicken for the cooked chicken in this recipe.

    ¼   cup buttermilk
    2   tablespoons lime juice
    1   tablespoon extra-virgin olive oil
    1   teaspoon sugar
    ½   teaspoon table salt
    ½   teaspoon pepper
    1   ripe avocado, halved, pitted, and chopped
    3   cups Shredded Cooked Chicken (page 41)
    8   slices hearty sandwich bread, toasted
    1   head Bibb lettuce (8 ounces), leaves separated
    2   tomatoes, cored and sliced thin

1. Combine buttermilk, lime juice, oil, sugar, salt, and pepper in medium bowl. Add avocado and mash into dressing with fork. Stir in chicken until fully combined. Season with salt and pepper to taste.

2. Place heaping ½ cup chicken salad on each of 4 bread slices. Divide and arrange lettuce and tomatoes over chicken salad, then top with remaining bread slices. Serve at room temperature or cold.

Curried Chicken Salad with Cashews

Serves 4 to 6 `FAST` `NO COOK`

Why This Recipe Works With just a few ingredients, this chicken salad quickly packs in boldly spiced flavor to upgrade the traditional cool, tangy mayo. Curry powder, cayenne, lime juice, and ginger mixed in with the mayonnaise transformed the standard chicken salad dressing into a flavor-packed sauce with bright heat. For crunch, celery was a must, and chopped cashews added extra texture and toasted flavor. To balance out the textures, lightly sweet raisins added chewy bite. Shallots and cilantro lent bright freshness to finish off this elevated and elegant chicken salad. This salad can be served in a sandwich or spooned over leafy greens. You can substitute rotisserie chicken for the cooked chicken in this recipe.

- 1 teaspoon vegetable oil
- 1 teaspoon curry powder
- ⅛ teaspoon cayenne pepper
- ½ cup mayonnaise
- 2 tablespoons lime juice
- 1 teaspoon grated fresh ginger
- 3 cups Shredded Cooked Chicken (page 41)
- 2 celery ribs, minced
- 1 shallot, minced
- ½ cup raw cashews, toasted and chopped coarse
- ⅓ cup golden raisins
- 2 tablespoons minced fresh cilantro

1. Microwave oil, curry powder, and cayenne in bowl until oil is hot, about 30 seconds. Whisk mayonnaise, lime juice, ginger, and curry mixture together in large bowl.

2. Add chicken, celery, shallot, cashews, raisins, and cilantro to mayonnaise mixture and toss to combine. Season with salt and pepper to taste. Serve at room temperature or cold.

Chicken Caesar Salad Wraps

Serves 4 `FAST` `NO COOK`

Why This Recipe Works Caesar salad with chicken is a classic combination, but to easily make the ubiquitous flavors transportable, we wrapped them up for a delicious handheld meal. The Caesar-inspired dressing does double duty, flavoring the salad greens as well as the chicken. Mayonnaise and umami-rich Parmesan were a must as the base for the traditional dressing. For extra tanginess, we added Worcestershire sauce, Dijon mustard, and garlic. Olive oil helped thin the dressing

Grilled Portobello Burgers with Goat Cheese and Arugula

Curried Chicken Salad with Cashews

Grilled Steak Sandwiches

Crispy Fish Sandwiches

to the perfect creamy consistency to thoroughly coat our lettuce and chicken. For convenience and speed, we turned to pre-cooked chicken. Tearing the lettuce into bite-size pieces ensured that the wrap was easy to eat without making a mess. You can substitute rotisserie chicken for the cooked chicken in this recipe.

¼ cup mayonnaise
¼ cup grated Parmesan cheese
2 tablespoons lemon juice
1 tablespoon Worcestershire sauce
1 tablespoon Dijon mustard
1 garlic clove, minced
¼ cup olive oil
3 cups Shredded Cooked Chicken (page 41)
1 romaine lettuce heart (6 ounces), torn into bite-size pieces
4 (10-inch) flour tortillas

1. Whisk mayonnaise, Parmesan, lemon juice, Worcestershire, mustard, and garlic in bowl until combined. Whisk in oil slowly until thoroughly incorporated.

2. Toss chicken with half of dressing and toss romaine with remaining dressing. Lay tortillas on counter. Divide chicken equally among tortillas. Top chicken on each tortilla with 1 cup dressed lettuce mixture and roll into wraps. Serve.

Grilled Steak Sandwiches
Serves 4 FAST

Why This Recipe Works For a fast and easy summer sandwich with tons of beefy, char-grilled flavor, skirt steak—which takes only about 5 minutes to grill to doneness—was the perfect choice. A bold blue cheese spread that comes together in seconds with mayonnaise, vinegar, and Dijon mustard made for a creamy, tangy addition to the rich steak. Thick, hearty ciabatta rolls slathered in the cheesy spread were a sturdy base for our juicy, tender steak. Quickly grilling the rolls added an extra hit of charred flavor, and a final topping of peppery arugula and crunchy red onion finished off these simple steak sandwiches.

¾ cup mayonnaise
3 ounces blue cheese, crumbled (¾ cup)
1 tablespoon balsamic vinegar
1 tablespoon Dijon mustard
½ teaspoon pepper, divided

1 (1-pound) skirt steak, cut crosswise into
　4 equal pieces and trimmed
½ teaspoon table salt
4 ciabatta sandwich rolls, halved lengthwise
¼ cup extra-virgin olive oil
2 ounces (2 cups) baby arugula
1 small red onion, halved and sliced thin

1. Process mayonnaise, blue cheese, vinegar, mustard, and ¼ teaspoon pepper in food processor until smooth, about 30 seconds. Set aside blue cheese sauce.

2A. For a charcoal grill Open bottom vent completely. Light large chimney starter filled with charcoal briquettes (6 quarts). When top coals are partially covered with ash, pour evenly over grill. Set cooking grate in place, cover, and open lid vent completely. Heat grill until hot, about 5 minutes.

2B. For a gas grill Turn all burners to high, cover, and heat grill until hot, about 15 minutes. Leave all burners on high.

3. Clean and oil cooking grate. Pat steak dry with paper towels and sprinkle with salt and remaining ¼ teaspoon pepper. Brush cut sides of rolls with oil. Grill steak until meat registers 125 degrees (for medium-rare), 2 to 3 minutes per side. Transfer steak to carving board and tent with foil. Grill rolls, cut side down, until lightly toasted, 1 to 2 minutes.

4. Slice steak thin against grain. Spread blue cheese sauce on rolls. Divide steak, arugula, and onion evenly among rolls. Serve at room temperature or cold.

Tuna Niçoise Salad Sandwiches
Serves 4 FAST NO COOK

Why This Recipe Works To transform a French classic—the venerable niçoise salad—into a hearty summer sandwich that's perfect for a picnic, we traded the usual garnish of briny niçoise olives for jarred black olive tapenade, which packs all the quintessential flavors of Provence—garlic, olives, anchovies, capers, and olive oil—into a single handy spread. We then coated the tuna in a light dressing and piled it on a hollowed-out baguette with lettuce, hard-cooked eggs, and radishes. If you can't find tuna packed in olive oil, substitute water-packed solid white tuna (do not use tuna packed in vegetable oil). Olive tapenade, which is sometimes sold as olive spread, is a robustly flavored condiment made from olives, garlic, olive oil, and sometimes capers and anchovies. We recommend using a baguette that is about 3½ inches thick at its thickest point for this packed sandwich.

1 large shallot, minced
3 tablespoons extra-virgin olive oil
2 tablespoons chopped fresh parsley
1 tablespoon red wine vinegar
1 teaspoon Dijon mustard
2 (6-ounce) cans solid white tuna in olive oil,
　drained and flaked
1 (24-inch) baguette, halved lengthwise
¼ cup black olive tapenade
8 Bibb lettuce leaves
2 Easy-Peel Hard-Cooked Eggs (page 54), sliced thin
4 radishes, trimmed and sliced thin

1. Whisk shallot, oil, parsley, vinegar, and mustard together in medium bowl. Add tuna and toss to coat. Season with pepper to taste.

2. Using your fingers, remove soft interior bread from top and bottom halves of baguette. Discard interior bread.

3. Spread tapenade on baguette bottom. Top with lettuce, tuna, eggs, and radishes. Season with salt and pepper to taste. Place baguette top over radish layer and press with your hand to flatten. Slice into 4 equal portions and serve at room temperature or cold.

Crispy Fish Sandwiches
Serves 4

Why This Recipe Works A deliciously golden fried fish sandwich is undoubtedly a summertime staple in New England. When making our own crispy fish sandwich, we were swayed by the style of sandwiches made in our seaside backyard. In New England, you'll most often get your fish—usually a generous piece of haddock—topped with coleslaw and creamy tartar sauce for the perfect bite of moist, crispy fish; rich, creamy sauce; a fresh, crunchy component; and a bun to soak it all up. To enhance the slaw's freshness even more, we preferred a vinegar-based dressing to a traditional creamy one for extra acidity to counterbalance the fish, which we fried dunked in a seltzer-based batter. Store-bought coleslaw mix can be substituted for the cabbage, carrot, and parsley in the slaw. Use a Dutch oven that holds 6 quarts or more for this recipe. You can substitute black sea bass, cod, hake, or pollock for the haddock in this recipe.

Fish

½ cup all-purpose flour
½ cup cornstarch
½ teaspoon table salt
½ teaspoon baking powder
¾ cup plain seltzer
2 quarts peanut or vegetable oil for frying
4 (4- to 6-ounce) skinless haddock fillets, 1 inch thick

Slaw

1 tablespoon cider vinegar
1½ teaspoons vegetable oil
1½ teaspoons sugar
¼ teaspoon table salt
¼ teaspoon pepper
1½ cups shredded red or green cabbage
1 carrot, peeled and shredded
1 tablespoon minced fresh parsley or cilantro

⅓ cup Tartar Sauce (page 80)
4 brioche buns, toasted

1. For the fish Whisk flour, cornstarch, salt, and baking powder together in large bowl. Whisk in seltzer until smooth. Cover and refrigerate for 20 minutes.

2. Set wire rack in rimmed baking sheet. Add oil to Dutch oven until it measures about 1½ inches deep and heat over medium-high heat to 375 degrees. Pat haddock dry with paper towels and transfer to batter, tossing gently to evenly coat. Using fork, remove fish from batter, allowing excess batter to drip back into bowl, and add to hot oil, briefly dragging haddock along surface of oil to prevent sticking before gently dropping into oil. Adjust burner, if necessary, to maintain oil temperature between 350 and 375 degrees.

3. Cook, stirring gently to prevent pieces from sticking together, until deep golden brown and crisp, about 4 minutes per side. Using spider skimmer or slotted spoon, transfer haddock to prepared rack.

4. For the slaw Whisk vinegar, oil, sugar, salt, and pepper together in large bowl. Add cabbage, carrot, and parsley and toss to combine; season with salt and pepper to taste. Divide tartar sauce evenly among bun bottoms, then top with fish and slaw. Cover with bun tops. Serve immediately.

VARIATION

Spicy Crispy Fish Sandwiches

Combine ¼ cup mayonnaise, 1 to 2 tablespoons sriracha, ½ teaspoon grated lime zest, and 1 teaspoon lime juice in bowl. Substitute for tartar sauce.

Shrimp Po' Boys
Serves 4

Why This Recipe Works Nothing says Louisiana summer like a fried shrimp po' boy, with deliciously crispy, golden-brown shrimp nestled into a roll with a fluffy interior and crisp exterior. The key to recreating these sandwiches at home was perfecting the shrimp's crunchy coating, so we turned to a foolproof three-step process. First, we tossed them in a dry mixture of flour, cornmeal, and Creole seasoning for a subtly spicy kick. Next, we dipped them in beaten eggs with a bit of the dry mixture added. Finally, we again dredged them in the flour mixture. This breading process allowed more batter to stick to the shrimp, maximizing crunchiness. We let the coated shrimp rest in the refrigerator before frying to ensure that the batter didn't slough off during cooking. Lightly toasting the sub rolls gave them the traditional crunch of New Orleans–style French bread. Use refrigerated prepared horseradish, not the shelf-stable kind, which contains preservatives and additives. Use a Dutch oven that holds 6 quarts or more. Do not refrigerate the breaded shrimp for longer than 30 minutes, or the coating will be too wet.

Rémoulade

⅔ cup mayonnaise
2 tablespoons prepared horseradish
1 tablespoon Worcestershire sauce
1 tablespoon hot sauce
¼ teaspoon pepper

Shrimp

2 cups all-purpose flour
¼ cup cornmeal
2 tablespoons Creole seasoning
4 large eggs
1 pound medium-large shrimp (31 to 40 per pound), peeled, deveined, and tails removed, divided
2 quarts peanut or vegetable oil
4 (8-inch) Italian sub rolls, split lengthwise and toasted
2 cups shredded iceberg lettuce
2 large tomatoes, cored and sliced thin
1 cup dill pickle chips

1. For the rémoulade Whisk all ingredients together in bowl. Set aside.

2. For the shrimp Set wire rack in rimmed baking sheet. Whisk flour, cornmeal, and Creole seasoning together in shallow dish. Whisk eggs and ½ cup flour mixture together in second shallow dish.

3. Place half of shrimp in flour mixture and toss to thoroughly coat. Shake off excess flour mixture, dip shrimp into egg mixture, then return to flour mixture, pressing gently to adhere. Transfer shrimp to prepared wire rack. Repeat with remaining half of shrimp. Refrigerate shrimp for at least 15 minutes or up to 30 minutes.

4. Line large plate with triple layer of paper towels. Add oil to Dutch oven until it measures about 1½ inches deep and heat over medium-high heat to 375 degrees. Carefully add half of shrimp to oil. Cook, stirring occasionally, until golden brown, about 4 minutes. Using slotted spoon or spider skimmer, transfer shrimp to prepared plate. Return oil to 375 degrees and repeat with remaining shrimp.

5. Spread rémoulade evenly on both cut sides of each roll. Divide lettuce, tomatoes, pickle chips, and shrimp evenly among rolls. Serve.

New England Lobster Rolls
Serves 6 `FAST`

Why This Recipe Works A lobster roll is the quintessential New England summer sandwich, but to capture the luxurious, decadent balance of dressing and meat without taking a road trip we knew we needed to let the natural flavor of the lobster shine. For our dressing, we used just 2 tablespoons of mayonnaise and added lemon juice, cayenne, and chives for complementary brightness. To assemble our lobster roll, we mostly adhered to tradition—top-loading supermarket hot dog bun and lots of lobster—but we added a hint of crunch in the form of small amounts of lettuce and celery (a contentious addition). This recipe is best when made with lobster you've cooked yourself. Use a very small pinch of cayenne pepper, as it should not make the dressing spicy. We prefer New England–style top-loading hot dog buns, as they provide maximum surface on the sides for toasting. If using other buns, butter, salt, and toast the interior of each bun instead of the exterior.

  2 tablespoons mayonnaise
  2 tablespoons minced celery
1½ teaspoons lemon juice
  1 teaspoon minced fresh chives
⅛ teaspoon table salt
     Pinch cayenne pepper
  1 pound lobster meat, tail meat cut into ½-inch pieces
     and claw meat cut into 1-inch pieces (see page 247)
  2 tablespoons unsalted butter, softened
  6 New England–style hot dog buns
  6 Bibb lettuce leaves

Shrimp Po' Boys

New England Lobster Rolls

Tomato Sandwiches

1. Whisk mayonnaise, celery, lemon juice, chives, salt, and cayenne together in large bowl. Add lobster and gently toss to combine.

2. Place 12-inch nonstick skillet over low heat. Butter both sides of buns and season lightly with salt to taste. Place buns in skillet, 1 buttered side down; increase heat to medium-low; and cook until crisp and brown, 2 to 3 minutes. Flip and cook second side until crisp and brown, 2 to 3 minutes. Transfer buns to large platter. Line each bun with 1 lettuce leaf. Spoon lobster salad into buns and serve immediately.

Tomato Sandwiches
Serves 4 `FAST` `NO COOK`

Why This Recipe Works There's no better way to highlight juicy, ripe tomatoes than in a flavorful, but dead-simple, sandwich. For bold, intense tomato flavor, we marinated them in a mixture of extra-virgin olive oil, red wine vinegar, and salt, which enhanced and amplified their bright, complex flavor. We then used some of the leftover tangy, tomato-juice-infused marinade liquid to liven up the mayonnaise. After spreading it on each slice of toast, we topped the zesty mayo with shingled tomato slices and black pepper. Choose tomatoes that measure no more than 2 inches in diameter. You can use any medium-size round, ripe tomatoes (do not use plum tomatoes). The tomatoes may break if you toss them with the marinade in a bowl; combining them in a zipper-lock bag is gentler.

- 3 tablespoons extra-virgin olive oil
- 1 tablespoon red wine vinegar
- ¾ teaspoon table salt
- 1 pound mixed ripe tomatoes, cored and sliced ¼ inch thick
- ½ cup mayonnaise
- 8 slices hearty white sandwich bread, toasted

1. Whisk oil, vinegar, and salt together in medium bowl; transfer marinade to 1-gallon zipper-lock bag. Add tomatoes to bag, press out air, seal bag, and gently turn to coat tomatoes with marinade. Lay bag flat on counter and let sit for 10 minutes.

2. Transfer tomato slices to now-empty bowl, leaving marinade in bag. Combine 1½ tablespoons marinade with mayonnaise in small bowl. Discard remaining marinade.

3. Place toast on cutting board. Spread 1 tablespoon mayonnaise mixture on 1 side of toast. Shingle tomatoes evenly on 4 slices of toast, covering as much of toast as possible. Season tomatoes with pepper to taste. Top tomatoes with remaining 4 slices of toast, mayonnaise side down. Cut sandwiches in half. Serve.

Avocado Toast

Avocado Toast

Serves 4 FAST NO COOK

Why This Recipe Works Avocado toast is the perfect fuss-free summer meal; it's healthy and delicious, and it's one of the simplest things to make for a quick breakfast or lunch without heating up the whole house. A quick stint under the broiler rendered our bread perfectly—and evenly—toasted. We took our toast up a notch by whisking together a lemony vinaigrette and mixing it in as we mashed one of the avocados, giving our dish a distinct citrusy punch. Smeared on toasted rustic country bread, topped with sliced avocado, then sprinkled with a little coarse sea salt and red pepper flakes, our version of this dish is spectacularly tasty. Topping it with a fried egg just takes it over the top.

- 2 tablespoons extra-virgin olive oil
- 1 teaspoon finely grated lemon zest plus 1 tablespoon juice
- ½ teaspoon coarse sea salt, divided
- ⅛ teaspoon pepper
- 2 ripe avocados, halved and pitted (1 chopped, 1 sliced thin)
- 4 (½-inch-thick) slices crusty bread, toasted
- ¼ teaspoon red pepper flakes (optional)

1. Whisk oil, lemon zest and juice, ¼ teaspoon salt, and pepper together in small bowl. Add chopped avocado and mash into dressing with fork.

2. Spread mashed avocado mixture evenly on toasts. Arrange avocado slices evenly over top. Sprinkle with remaining ¼ teaspoon salt and pepper flakes, if using, and serve.

VARIATION

Avocado Toast with Fried Eggs

Cut 2 teaspoons unsalted butter into 4 pieces; keep chilled. Crack 4 eggs into 2 small bowls (2 eggs per bowl) and season with salt and pepper. Heat 2 teaspoons vegetable oil in 12-inch nonstick skillet over low heat for 5 minutes. Increase heat to medium-high and heat until oil is shimmering. Add butter and swirl to coat pan. Working quickly, add eggs to pan from opposite sides, cover, and cook for 1 minute. Remove skillet from burner and let sit, covered, for 15 to 45 seconds for runny yolks (white around edge of yolk will be barely opaque), 45 to 60 seconds for soft but set yolks, and about 2 minutes for medium-set yolks. Top avocado toasts with fried eggs and serve.

Israeli Eggplant and Egg Sandwiches

Serves 4

Why This Recipe Works *Sabich*, a popular Israeli street food, combines creamy fried eggplant, hard-cooked eggs, savory hummus, and crunchy pickles in a soft pita. To create an appealing version that could be made at home, we started with the eggplant. Although it's traditionally fried, we found that we liked the flavor (and simplicity) of broiled eggplant as much as fried. Salting the eggplant for 30 minutes before broiling helped to eliminate excess moisture and encourage deep, flavorful browning. Chopped dill pickles offered great briny flavor, and cherry tomatoes, red onion, and parsley provided bright, fresh notes. Sabich is often eaten as a sandwich, but we decided to lay the pitas flat and pile everything on top to create a beautiful presentation and make the dish easier to eat. Cutting our hard-cooked eggs into thin slices (as opposed to wedges) worked best, since the flat slices could easily be layered with the other ingredients. Finishing our open-faced sandwiches with a drizzle of our tangy Tahini-Yogurt Sauce brought all the elements together. We prefer to use our homemade Hummus (page 16) but you can substitute store-bought if desired. If you can't find Aleppo pepper, you can substitute ¼ teaspoon paprika and ¼ teaspoon finely chopped red pepper flakes.

- 1 pound eggplant, sliced into ½-inch-thick rounds
- 2 teaspoons table salt
- ¼ cup extra-virgin olive oil, divided
- 8 ounces cherry tomatoes, quartered
- ½ cup finely chopped dill pickles
- ¼ cup finely chopped red onion
- ¼ cup fresh parsley leaves
- 1 tablespoon lemon juice
- 1 garlic clove, minced
- 4 (8-inch) pita breads
- 1 cup Hummus (page 16)
- 6 Easy-Peel Hard-Cooked Eggs (page 54), sliced thin
- ½ cup Tahini-Yogurt Sauce (page 92)
- 1 teaspoon ground dried Aleppo pepper

1. Spread eggplant on baking sheet lined with paper towels, sprinkle both sides with salt, and let sit for 30 minutes.

2. Adjust oven rack 4 inches from broiler element and heat broiler. Thoroughly pat eggplant dry with paper towels, arrange on aluminum foil–lined rimmed baking sheet in single layer, and lightly brush both sides with 2 tablespoons oil. Broil eggplant until spotty brown, about 5 minutes per side.

3. Combine tomatoes, pickles, onion, parsley, lemon juice, garlic, and remaining 2 tablespoons oil in bowl and season with salt and pepper to taste. Lay each pita on individual plate, spread with ¼ cup hummus, and top evenly with eggplant, tomato salad, and eggs. Drizzle with tahini-yogurt sauce and sprinkle with Aleppo. Serve immediately.

Tahini-Yogurt Sauce
Makes about 1 cup

⅓ cup tahini
⅓ cup plain Greek yogurt
¼ cup water
3 tablespoons lemon juice
1 garlic clove, minced
¾ teaspoon table salt

Whisk all ingredients in bowl until combined. Season with salt and pepper to taste. Let sit until flavors meld, about 30 minutes. (Sauce can be refrigerated for up to 4 days.)

Roasted Eggplant and Mozzarella Panini

Serve 4

Why This Recipe Works With a simple ingredient list that highlights fresh eggplant and tomatoes, melty mozzarella, and flavorful basil, these sandwiches are sure to become a summertime favorite. Pan-frying the eggplant turned it greasy, so we opted to broil it instead. Tomato, mozzarella, and basil are traditional toppings, but since we were already broiling the eggplant, we opted to broil our grape tomatoes as well, along with some garlic, deepening and rounding out their flavors. Once the tomatoes were nicely charred and had split open, we mashed them together with the roasted garlic and some red wine vinegar to make a chunky, bright tomato sauce. We layered the broiled eggplant with the tomato sauce, shredded mozzarella, and chopped fresh basil to make a bold, balanced eggplant panini that's even better than the classic. To weigh down our panini we found that a common kitchen tool, the Dutch oven, was surprisingly perfect. We like the attractive grill marks that a grill pan gives the panini, but you can substitute a 12-inch nonstick skillet.

1 pound eggplant, sliced into ½-inch-thick rounds
10 ounces grape tomatoes
2 garlic cloves, peeled
5 tablespoons extra-virgin olive oil, divided
1 teaspoon table salt, divided
½ teaspoon pepper, divided
1 tablespoon red wine vinegar
8 (½-inch-thick) slices crusty bread
6 ounces mozzarella cheese, shredded (1½ cups)
½ cup chopped fresh basil

1. Adjust 1 oven rack 4 inches from broiler element and second rack to middle position, and heat broiler. Line rimmed baking sheet with aluminum foil and spray with vegetable oil spray. Spread eggplant, tomatoes, and garlic evenly over baking sheet and drizzle with 3 tablespoons oil. Sprinkle with ½ teaspoon salt and ¼ teaspoon pepper. Broil until vegetables are browned and tomatoes have split open, 8 to 10 minutes, flipping eggplant once during broiling.

2. Transfer tomatoes to small bowl and mash with fork. Mince roasted garlic and stir into tomatoes. Stir in vinegar, remaining ½ teaspoon salt, and remaining ¼ teaspoon pepper.

3. Reduce oven temperature to 200 degrees. Set wire rack in clean rimmed baking sheet. Brush remaining 2 tablespoons oil evenly over 1 side of each slice of bread. Assemble 4 sandwiches by layering ingredients as follows between prepared bread (with oiled sides outside sandwich): half of mozzarella, tomato sauce, eggplant, basil, and remaining mozzarella. Press gently on sandwiches to set.

4. Heat 12-inch nonstick grill pan over medium heat for 1 minute. Place 2 sandwiches in pan, place Dutch oven on top, and cook until bread is golden and crisp on first side, about 4 minutes. Flip sandwiches, replace Dutch oven, and cook until second side is crisp and cheese is melted, about 4 minutes.

5. Transfer sandwiches to prepared wire rack and keep warm in oven. Wipe out grill pan with paper towels and cook remaining 2 sandwiches. Serve.

COOKING PANINI IN A GRILL PAN

Place sandwiches in grill pan, place Dutch oven on top, and cook until bread is golden and crisp on first side, about 4 minutes. Flip sandwiches and cook until second side is crisp and cheese is melted, about 4 minutes.

French Summer Sandwiches with Zucchini and Olive Tapenade

Serves 4 `FAST`

Why This Recipe Works Packed with ripe summer zucchini, tender mesclun, and refreshing mint, this quick and easy sandwich is picnic-ready. We tried simply adding the zucchini to the sandwich without cooking it, but no matter how thin we shaved it, it tasted raw, so we decided to roast it for just 15 minutes to get it softened and nicely caramelized. While the zucchini roasted, we made the fastest-ever olive tapenade by pulsing fruity green olives, lemon juice, shallot, garlic, and capers in the food processor. We spread some rich, creamy goat cheese over the baguette pieces, drizzled them with our incredibly flavorful tapenade, and layered in the thin slices of roasted zucchini. Finally, we tossed the mesclun and mint with oil and lemon juice and topped our sandwich with the crisp greens. The end result was a nuanced but simple sandwich celebrating summer vegetables.

- 2 zucchini, cut in half crosswise, then sliced lengthwise into ¼-inch-thick planks
- 5 tablespoons extra-virgin olive oil, divided
- ½ teaspoon table salt
- ¼ teaspoon pepper
- 10 pitted green olives
- 1 tablespoon minced shallot
- 1 tablespoon lemon juice, divided
- 1 teaspoon capers, rinsed
- 1 small garlic clove, minced
- 1½ ounces (1½ cups) mesclun
- ⅓ cup minced fresh mint
- 4 ounces goat cheese, softened
- 1 (24-inch) baguette, cut crosswise into 4 equal lengths and sliced in half lengthwise

1. Adjust oven rack to middle position and heat oven to 425 degrees. Toss zucchini with 2 tablespoons oil, salt, and pepper, then spread in single layer on aluminum foil–lined rimmed baking sheet. Bake until zucchini are spotty brown on both sides, about 15 minutes, flipping halfway through baking.

2. Meanwhile, pulse 2 tablespoons oil, olives, shallot, 1 teaspoon lemon juice, capers, and garlic in food processor until mixture forms slightly chunky paste, about 10 pulses (do not overprocess). Whisk remaining 1 tablespoon oil and remaining 2 teaspoons lemon juice together in medium bowl. Add mesclun and mint and toss to coat. Season with salt and pepper to taste.

Roasted Eggplant and Mozzarella Panini

French Summer Sandwich with Zucchini and Olive Tapenade

Philly-Style Broccoli Rabe, Portobello, and Cheese Sandwiches

3. Spread goat cheese evenly over cut sides of each baguette piece. Assemble 4 sandwiches by layering ingredients as follows between prepared baguette pieces: olive tapenade, zucchini, then mesclun mixture. Press gently on sandwiches to set. Serve at room temperature or cold.

VARIATION
French Summer Sandwiches with Roasted Tomatoes and Olive Tapenade
Substitute 4 plum tomatoes, cored and halved lengthwise, for zucchini and basil for mint.

Philly-Style Broccoli Rabe, Portobello, and Cheese Sandwiches
Serves 4

Why This Recipe Works Philly's famous cheesesteak is an undeniable classic, but we wanted to make a vegetable-forward version that was more suited to the summer months without sacrificing on meaty flavor. First we swapped out the steak for hearty, umami-rich portobellos. To give the sandwiches complex and satisfying texture, we added subtly bitter, hearty broccoli rabe. The stovetop provided quick cooking, so we sautéed the broccoli rabe with some garlic and pepper flakes for heat and then tossed it with vinegar before letting it sit while we cooked the mushrooms. To mimic the traditional thinly shaved steak, we cut the mushrooms into thin slices and sautéed them until they were nicely browned and flavorful. Once the mushrooms were cooked, we stirred in the broccoli rabe. To bind it all together, we let slices of American cheese melt into the vegetables to make a rich, cohesive filling that we piled high on toasted sub rolls.

- 3 tablespoons vegetable oil, divided
- 2 garlic cloves, sliced thin
- ⅛ teaspoon red pepper flakes
- 12 ounces broccoli rabe, trimmed and cut into ½-inch pieces
- 2 tablespoons water
- ½ teaspoon table salt
- 2 tablespoons balsamic vinegar
- 6 portobello mushroom caps, gills removed, caps halved and sliced thin
- 10 slices (10 ounces) American cheese
- 4 (8-inch) Italian sub rolls, split lengthwise and toasted

Farmers' Market Find   Broccoli

Though you've likely often found broccoli at the supermarket, you might be surprised to learn that the freshest, most vibrant broccoli can be found at your local farmers' market. Choose broccoli heads with firm florets that are tightly closed and are dark green or purplish-green. Avoid broccoli heads where the green buds are starting to turn yellow or tiny flowers are emerging; this is a sign it's past its prime and will be bitter. **Broccoli rabe** is a sturdy, strongly flavored variety that's sometimes called rapini or broccoli raab. As with regular broccoli, avoid bunches with yellowing leaves and flowers in favor of dark green foliage and florets. **Broccolini** is a slender, crunchy variety with a sweeter, milder flavor than broccoli. Unlike with regular broccoli, the tiny yellow flowers that often appear on broccolini are tasty and perfectly edible. Store all of these types of broccoli wrapped in paper towels in a loosely closed plastic produce bag for up to a week.

1. Heat 1 tablespoon oil in 12-inch nonstick skillet over medium heat until shimmering. Add garlic and pepper flakes and cook for 1 minute. Stir in broccoli rabe, water, and salt. Cover and cook until broccoli rabe is bright green and crisp-tender, 3 to 4 minutes. Off heat, stir in vinegar, then transfer to bowl.

2. Heat remaining 2 tablespoons oil in now-empty skillet over medium-high heat until shimmering. Add mushrooms (skillet will be very full), cover, and cook, stirring occasionally, until mushrooms release their liquid, 6 to 8 minutes. Uncover and continue to cook until moisture has evaporated and mushrooms begin to brown, 6 to 8 minutes.

3. Stir broccoli rabe back into skillet and season with salt and pepper to taste. Reduce heat to low and shingle cheese over vegetables. Cook until cheese is melted, about 2 minutes. Fold melted cheese thoroughly into mushroom mixture. Divide mixture evenly among toasted rolls. Serve.

Tofu Banh Mi
Serves 4

Why This Recipe Works In Vietnam, *banh mi* is simply a term for all kinds of bread, but in the United States most people recognize it as a Vietnamese-style sandwich featuring chicken, pork, or tofu and crunchy pickled vegetables. For our own version, we started by making crispy, flavorful tofu. We sliced the tofu into sandwich-size slabs and drained them on paper towels to make it easier to get a crispy crust. Then we dredged the slabs in cornstarch and seared them in a hot skillet until they were nicely browned. For the vegetables, we quick-pickled cucumber slices and shredded carrot in lime juice and fish sauce. Sriracha-spiked mayonnaise gave the sandwich a spicy kick, while a sprinkling of fresh cilantro added an authentic garnish.

14 ounces firm tofu, sliced crosswise into ½-inch-thick slabs
¼ teaspoon table salt
⅛ teaspoon pepper
⅓ cup cornstarch
2 carrots, peeled and shredded
½ cucumber, peeled, halved lengthwise, seeded, and sliced thin
1 teaspoon grated lime zest plus 1 tablespoon juice
1 tablespoon fish sauce
¼ cup mayonnaise
1 tablespoon sriracha
3 tablespoons vegetable oil
4 (8-inch) Italian sub rolls, split lengthwise and toasted
⅓ cup fresh cilantro leaves

1. Spread tofu over paper towel–lined baking sheet, let drain for 20 minutes, then gently press dry with paper towels and sprinkle with salt and pepper. Spread cornstarch in shallow dish. Dredge tofu in cornstarch and transfer to plate.

2. Meanwhile, combine carrots, cucumber, lime juice, and fish sauce in bowl and let sit for 15 minutes. Whisk mayonnaise, sriracha, and lime zest together in separate bowl.

3. Heat oil in 12-inch nonstick skillet over medium-high heat until just smoking. Add tofu and cook until both sides are crisp and browned, about 4 minutes per side. Transfer to paper towel–lined plate.

4. Spread mayonnaise mixture evenly over cut sides of each roll. Assemble 4 sandwiches by layering ingredients as follows between prepared rolls: tofu, pickled vegetables (leaving liquid in bowl), and cilantro. Press gently on sandwiches to set. Serve at room temperature or cold.

Chickpea Salad Sandwiches
Serves 6 `FAST` `NO COOK`

Why This Recipe Works Chicken, egg, and tuna salads are classics, but using protein-packed chickpeas as the salad base makes for a surprisingly delicious, and conveniently vegan-friendly, sandwich that requires zero cooking. When we simply mashed our chickpeas and stirred our ingredients together, however, our salads turned out dry, crumbly, and pasty. We wanted the richness and almost saucy texture of a traditional deli salad. Vegan mayonnaise helped the cause, lending a rich smoothness, but too much of it masked the savory chickpea flavor. Since we were already opening cans of chickpeas, why not make a hummus-style puree for creaminess? We buzzed a portion of the chickpeas with vegan mayo, water, and lemon juice in the food processor for the perfect creamy binder. Then we added the remaining chickpeas to the mixture and briefly pulsed them to give us just the right textural contrast. To round things out, we turned to classic flavors: Chopped celery provided crunch, dill pickle brought a salty brininess, and scallions and herbs finished the salad with bright, fresh flavor. Served on toasted bread, this salad makes a creamy, luscious sandwich sure to satisfy any lunchtime craving. This salad is also delicious served in lettuce wraps. We strongly prefer our favorite vegan mayonnaise, Just Mayo.

2   (15-ounce) cans chickpeas, rinsed, divided
½   cup vegan mayonnaise
¼   cup water
1   tablespoon lemon juice
½   teaspoon table salt
2   celery ribs, finely chopped
⅓   cup dill pickles, finely chopped
2   scallions, sliced thin
2   tablespoons minced fresh parsley, dill, or tarragon
12 slices hearty multigrain bread, toasted

1. Process ¾ cup chickpeas, mayonnaise, water, lemon juice, and salt in food processor until smooth, about 30 seconds, scraping down sides of bowl as needed.

2. Add remaining chickpeas to food processor and pulse until coarsely chopped with some larger pieces remaining, about 4 pulses.

3. Combine chickpea mixture, celery, pickles, scallions, and parsley in large bowl and season with salt and pepper to taste. Spread chickpea salad evenly over 6 bread slices. Top with remaining bread slices and serve.

Crispy Falafel Pitas
Serves 4   FAST

Why This Recipe Works To bring crispy, well-spiced falafel from Mediterranean street carts to the home kitchen, we turned to convenient canned chickpeas and the food processor instead of traditional dried chickpeas, which need to be soaked before starting the falafel. Pita bread plays a double role in this recipe; not only does it serve as the portable, pocket-shaped sandwich base for the finished falafel, but we also ground up some extra pita and used it as a starchy binder to hold the falafel patties together and help prevent the canned chickpeas from making the falafel too mushy. Bright, summery tomatoes and a cool, creamy yogurt sauce added a burst of freshness to the crispy fried falafel patties.

2½ (8-inch) pita breads
1   (15-ounce) can chickpeas, rinsed
¼   cup chopped fresh parsley, divided
1   large egg
1½ teaspoons ground cumin, divided
1¼ teaspoons table salt, divided
1   teaspoon pepper, divided
1   cup plain whole-milk yogurt
1   tablespoon lemon juice
2   ripe tomatoes, cored and chopped (1 cup)
½   cup vegetable oil

1. Tear ½ pita into small pieces and process in food processor until finely ground, about 15 seconds. Add chickpeas, 2 tablespoons parsley, egg, 1 teaspoon cumin, ¾ teaspoon salt, and ½ teaspoon pepper and pulse until chickpeas are coarsely chopped and mixture is cohesive, about 10 pulses. Divide mixture into 16 patties, about 2 inches in diameter.

2. Whisk yogurt, lemon juice, remaining 2 tablespoons parsley, remaining ½ teaspoon cumin, remaining ½ teaspoon salt, and remaining ½ teaspoon pepper together in bowl. Season tomatoes with salt and pepper to taste.

3. Heat oil in 12-inch nonstick skillet over medium-high heat until just smoking. Fry patties until golden brown, about 2 minutes per side. Cut remaining 2 pitas in half and stuff each pocket with ¼ cup tomatoes, 4 falafel, and ¼ cup yogurt sauce. Serve warm or at room temperature.

Easy Chipotle Chicken Tacos
Serves 4   FAST

Why This Recipe Works Much of the appeal of tacos for a weeknight dinner is their essential simplicity. For easy chicken tacos, we found that boneless, skinless breasts were a convenient place to start, and poaching proved to be the easiest way to cook them while imbuing them with flavor. To build our poaching liquid, we started by sautéing chipotle chile in adobo and garlic for a smoky, savory flavor base. Sautéing our aromatic ingredients in butter instead of oil added richness to the lean breast meat. We then added orange juice for citrusy freshness, cilantro for a pleasant herbal note, and Worcestershire sauce for savory depth. Once the chicken was done cooking, our poaching liquid pulled double duty: We reduced it to a sauce. A bit of yellow mustard thickened the sauce and provided a sharp counterpoint to the sweet orange juice. Finally, we shredded and sauced the chicken. Warm tortillas, a squeeze of lime, and a few basic toppings completed our tacos. Serve with Mexican Crema (page 100), sour cream, and one of our homemade taco toppings (page 100).

3   tablespoons unsalted butter
4   garlic cloves, minced
2   teaspoons minced canned chipotle chile in adobo sauce
¾   cup chopped fresh cilantro, divided
½   cup orange juice
1   tablespoon Worcestershire sauce
1½ pounds boneless, skinless chicken breasts, trimmed
1   teaspoon yellow mustard
12 (6-inch) corn tortillas, warmed
    Lime wedges

1. Melt butter in 12-inch skillet over medium-high heat. Add garlic and chipotle and cook until fragrant, about 30 seconds. Stir in ½ cup cilantro, orange juice, and Worcestershire and bring to simmer. Nestle chicken into sauce. Cover, reduce heat to medium-low, and cook until chicken registers 160 degrees, 10 to 15 minutes, flipping chicken halfway through cooking. Transfer chicken to plate and cover.

2. Increase heat to medium-high and cook liquid left in skillet until reduced to ¼ cup, about 5 minutes. Off heat, whisk in mustard. Using 2 forks, shred chicken into bite-size pieces and return to skillet. Add remaining ¼ cup cilantro and toss until well combined. Season with salt and pepper to taste. Serve chicken with tortillas and lime wedges.

Easy Chipotle Chicken Tacos

Grilled Chicken Tacos with Salsa Verde

Serves 4

Why This Recipe Works For weeknight tacos we could make entirely on the grill on a hot summer evening, we paired chicken with a charred tomatillo salsa and perfectly toasted tortillas. Since it would be topped with other flavorful elements, we found that our chicken needed only a brief stint in a garlic-lime marinade. A bit of salt and sugar in our marinade kept the chicken moist as it grilled and rounded out its flavor. To complement the smoky, charred chicken, we grilled some of the salsa ingredients; sliced onion, jalapeño, and half the tomatillos cooked at the same rate as the chicken. We pulsed our grilled vegetables with additional raw tomatillos and added cilantro, lime juice, and garlic for fresh bite. As a final touch, we grilled our tortillas briefly to warm and lightly char them.

- ¼ cup vegetable oil, divided
- 3 tablespoons lime juice (2 limes), divided, plus lime wedges for serving
- 2 tablespoons water
- 5 garlic cloves, minced, divided
- 1 teaspoon plus pinch sugar, divided
- 2 teaspoons table salt, divided
- ½ teaspoon pepper
- 1½ pounds boneless, skinless chicken breasts, trimmed
- 1 onion, peeled and cut into ½-inch-thick rounds
- 1 jalapeño chile, stemmed, halved, and seeded
- 1 pound tomatillos, husks and stems removed, rinsed well and dried, divided
- 12 (6-inch) corn tortillas
- ½ cup chopped fresh cilantro

Grilled Chicken Tacos with Salsa Verde

1. Whisk 3 tablespoons oil, 1 tablespoon lime juice, water, half of garlic, 1 teaspoon sugar, 1½ teaspoons salt, and pepper together in medium bowl. Add chicken, cover, and refrigerate, turning occasionally, for 30 minutes. Brush onion, jalapeño, and half of tomatillos with remaining 1 tablespoon oil and season with salt to taste. Halve remaining tomatillos; set aside.

2A. For a charcoal grill Open bottom vent completely. Light large chimney starter filled with charcoal briquettes (6 quarts). When top coals are partially covered with ash, pour evenly over grill. Set cooking grate in place, cover, and open lid vent completely. Heat grill until hot, about 5 minutes.

2B. For a gas grill Turn all burners to high, cover, and heat grill until hot, about 15 minutes. Leave all burners on high.

3. Clean and oil cooking grate. Place chicken and oiled vegetables on grill. Cook (covered if using gas), turning as needed, until chicken registers 160 degrees and vegetables are lightly charred and tender, 10 to 15 minutes. Transfer chicken and vegetables to cutting board and tent with aluminum foil.

4. Working in batches, grill tortillas, turning as needed, until warm and soft, about 30 seconds; wrap tightly in foil to keep soft.

5. Chop grilled vegetables, then pulse with cilantro, remaining tomatillos, remaining 2 tablespoons lime juice, remaining garlic, remaining ½ teaspoon salt, and remaining pinch sugar in food processor until slightly chunky, 16 to 18 pulses. Slice chicken thin on bias and serve with tortillas, tomatillo salsa, and lime wedges.

Grilled Skirt Steak and Poblano Tacos

Serves 6

Why This Recipe Works In this popular northern Mexican taco, rich, smoky beef is perfectly complemented by sweet-hot poblano chiles and piquant onions. We wanted an authentic version that could be made on a home grill. First, we tackled the chiles. When roasted, peeled, seeded, and cut into strips, poblano chiles are called *rajas*, and they're used not only in tacos but also on tostadas or grilled seafood. We grilled the poblanos over a very hot fire; this left the skins charred and blistered while the flesh remained relatively unscathed. Putting the peppers in a covered bowl when they came off the grill made the bitter skins easy to peel off later. The onions needed only a quick stint over the fire to develop good grill marks. We found that marinating our skirt steak was unnecessary; instead, while the cooked steak rested we covered it with a flavorful puree of onion, lime juice, garlic, cumin, and salt. If you can't find skirt steak, substitute flank steak, although the meat will be a bit more chewy. Serve with chopped cilantro and Mexican Crema (page 100) or sour cream.

4 onions (3 sliced crosswise into ½-inch-thick rounds, 1 chopped)
6 tablespoons lime juice (3 limes), plus lime wedges for serving
3 garlic cloves, minced
½ teaspoon ground cumin
2 teaspoons table salt, divided
1½ pounds poblano chiles
1 tablespoon vegetable oil
2 pounds skirt steak, trimmed
½ teaspoon pepper
18 (6-inch) corn tortillas

1. Process chopped onion, lime juice, garlic, cumin, and 1 teaspoon salt in food processor until smooth. Brush onion rounds and poblanos with oil and season with salt and pepper to taste. Pat steak dry and sprinkle with remaining 1 teaspoon salt and pepper.

2A. For a charcoal grill Open bottom vent completely. Light large chimney starter filled with charcoal briquettes (6 quarts). When top coals are partially covered with ash, pour evenly over half of grill. Set cooking grate in place, cover, and open lid vent completely. Heat grill until hot, about 5 minutes.

2B. For a gas grill Turn all burners to high, cover, and heat grill until hot, about 15 minutes. Leave primary burner on high and turn other burner(s) off.

3. Clean and oil cooking grate. Place poblanos on hotter side of grill and onion rounds on cooler side of grill. Grill (covered if using gas), turning as needed, until poblanos are blistered and blackened and onions are softened and golden, 6 to 12 minutes. Transfer onions to platter and cover to keep warm. Transfer peppers to bowl, cover, and let steam while cooking steak and tortillas.

4. Place steak on hotter side of grill. Grill (covered if using gas), turning as needed, until well browned on both sides and meat registers 120 to 125 degrees (for medium-rare), 4 to 8 minutes. Transfer steak to 13 by 9-inch pan and poke all over with fork. Pour pureed onion mixture over top, cover, and let rest for 5 to 10 minutes.

5. Working in batches, grill tortillas, turning as needed, until warm and soft, about 30 seconds; wrap tightly in aluminum foil to keep soft.

6. Peel poblanos, then slice thin. Separate onions into rings and chop, then toss with poblanos. Remove steak from marinade, slice into 4- to 6-inch lengths, then slice thin against grain. Serve with warm tortillas, poblano-onion mixture, and lime wedges.

Baja Fish Tacos
Serves 6

Why This Recipe Works It's impossible to hear "Baja" without picturing warm, sandy beaches and clear blue skies, where battered and fried fish tacos are a common taco stand offering. These popular tacos are filled with tender white fish encased in a crisp coating with toppings such as crunchy shredded cabbage and cooling crema. An ultrathin beer batter made with flour, cornstarch, and baking powder proved to be ideal for getting a light, crispy coating on the fish. Light-bodied American lagers, such as Budweiser, work best here. Cut the fish on a slight bias if your fillets aren't quite 4 inches wide; you should end up with about 24 pieces of fish. Use a Dutch oven that holds 6 quarts or more.

- 2 pounds skinless white fish fillets such as cod, haddock, or halibut, cut crosswise into 4 by 1-inch strips
- 1½ teaspoons table salt, divided
- ¼ teaspoon pepper
- ¾ cup all-purpose flour
- ¼ cup cornstarch
- 1 teaspoon baking powder
- 1 cup beer
- 1 quart peanut or vegetable oil
- 18 (6-inch) corn tortillas, warmed
- 1 cup fresh cilantro leaves
- 1 cup Mexican Crema (page 100)
- 1 recipe Pickled Onion and Cabbage (page 100)
  Lime wedges

1. Adjust oven rack to middle position and heat oven to 200 degrees. Set wire rack in rimmed baking sheet. Pat fish dry with paper towels and sprinkle with ½ teaspoon salt and pepper. Whisk flour, cornstarch, baking powder, and remaining 1 teaspoon salt together in large bowl. Add beer and whisk until smooth. Add fish to batter and toss to coat evenly.

2. Add oil to large Dutch oven until it measures about ¾ inch deep and heat over medium-high heat to 350 degrees.

3. Remove 5 or 6 pieces of fish from batter, allowing excess to drip back into bowl, and add to hot oil, briefly dragging fish along surface of oil to prevent sticking. Adjust burner, if necessary, to maintain oil temperature between 325 and 350 degrees. Fry fish, stirring gently to prevent pieces from sticking together and turning as needed, until golden brown and crisp, about 8 minutes.

4. Transfer fish to prepared wire rack and place in oven to keep warm. Return oil to 350 degrees and repeat with remaining fish, working with 5 or 6 pieces at a time. Serve with warm tortillas, cilantro, crema, pickled onion and cabbage, and lime wedges.

Grilled Skirt Steak and Poblano Tacos

Baja Fish Tacos

Taco Sauces and Toppings

When topped well, tacos are the ultimate flavor and texture combination: tangy, spicy, creamy, and crunchy. These simple, but complexly flavorful, recipes make it easier than ever to customize your taco toppings.

Mexican Crema
Makes about 1¼ cups
The texture should be similar to that of crème fraîche.

- ½ cup mayonnaise
- ½ cup sour cream
- 2 tablespoons lime juice
- 2 tablespoons milk

Whisk all ingredients together in bowl. (Mexican crema can be refrigerated for up to 2 days.)

Avocado Crema
Makes about ½ cup
You can also serve with nachos or your favorite chili.

- ½ avocado, pitted and chopped
- ¼ cup chopped fresh cilantro
- 3 tablespoons water
- 1 tablespoon lime juice
- 1 tablespoon plain low-fat yogurt

Process all ingredients in food processor until completely smooth, about 1 minute, scraping down sides of bowl as needed. Season with salt and pepper to taste. (Crema can be refrigerated with plastic wrap pressed flush to surface for up to 2 days.)

Quick Pickled Shallot and Radishes
Makes about 1 cup

- 5 radishes, trimmed and sliced thin
- 1 shallot, sliced thin
- ¼ cup lime juice (2 limes)
- 1 teaspoon sugar
- ⅛ teaspoon table salt

Combine all ingredients in bowl. (Pickled shallot and radishes can be refrigerated in airtight container for up to 1 week.)

Quick Pickled Red Onions
Makes about 1 cup

- 1 cup red wine vinegar
- ⅓ cup sugar
- ¼ teaspoon table salt
- 1 red onion, halved and sliced thin through root end

Bring vinegar, sugar, and salt to simmer in small saucepan over medium-high heat, stirring occasionally, until sugar has dissolved. Off heat, stir in onion, cover, and let cool to room temperature, about 1 hour. (Pickled onions can be refrigerated in airtight container for up to 1 week.)

Pickled Onion and Cabbage
Makes about 4 cups

- 1 small red onion, halved and sliced thin
- 2 jalapeño chiles, stemmed and sliced into thin rings
- 1 cup white wine vinegar
- 2 tablespoons lime juice
- 1 tablespoon sugar
- ½ teaspoon table salt, plus salt for pickling liquid
- ½ teaspoon pepper
- 3 cups shredded green cabbage

Combine onion and jalapeños in medium bowl. Bring vinegar, lime juice, sugar, and 1 teaspoon salt to boil in small saucepan. Pour vinegar mixture over onion mixture and let sit for at least 30 minutes, or refrigerate for up to 2 days. Transfer ¼ cup pickling liquid to second medium bowl; add cabbage, salt, and pepper; and toss to combine.

Grilled Fish Tacos
Serves 6

Why This Recipe Works In the Yucatán Peninsula, far from the battered-and-fried-fish taco stands of Baja, another style of fish taco is popular: grilled fish tacos. Traditionally, a whole fish is split in half lengthwise, bathed in a chile-citrus marinade, and grilled. We wanted grilled fish tacos featuring a similarly bold flavor profile, but a simpler approach—no dealing with whole, skin-on fish. Although most recipes use whole snapper or grouper, we found that swordfish was easier to find, stood up well to flipping on the grill, and picked up plenty of flavorful char before the interior cooked through. We created a flavorful paste from ancho and chipotle chile powders, oregano, and ground coriander, which we bloomed in oil to bring out their flavors. Tomato paste provided a savory-sweet punch. To replicate the flavor of traditional sour oranges, we used a combination of lime and orange juices. A fresh pineapple salsa was the perfect accompaniment to our spicy, earthy fish. Halibut, mahi-mahi, red snapper, and striped bass are all suitable substitutes for the swordfish. The recipe for the pineapple salsa makes more than is needed for the tacos; leftovers can be refrigerated for up to two days. Serve with shredded lettuce and diced avocado.

- 3 tablespoons vegetable oil, divided
- 1 tablespoon ancho chile powder
- 2 teaspoons chipotle chile powder
- 2 garlic cloves, minced
- 1 teaspoon dried oregano
- 1 teaspoon ground coriander
- 1 teaspoon table salt
- 2 tablespoons tomato paste
- ½ cup orange juice
- 6 tablespoons lime juice (3 limes), divided, plus lime wedges for serving
- 2 pounds skinless swordfish steaks, 1 inch thick, cut lengthwise into 1-inch thick strips
- 1 pineapple, peeled, quartered lengthwise, cored, and each quarter halved lengthwise
- 1 jalapeño chile
- 18 (6-inch) corn tortillas
- 1 red bell pepper, stemmed, seeded, and cut into ¼-inch pieces
- 2 tablespoons minced fresh cilantro, plus extra for serving

Grilled Fish Tacos

1. Heat 2 tablespoons oil, ancho chile powder, and chipotle chile powder in 8-inch skillet over medium heat, stirring constantly, until fragrant and some bubbles form, 2 to 3 minutes. Add garlic, oregano, coriander, and salt and continue to cook until fragrant, about 30 seconds. Add tomato paste and, using spatula, mash tomato paste with spice mixture until combined, about 20 seconds. Stir in orange juice and 2 tablespoons lime juice. Cook, stirring constantly, until thoroughly mixed and reduced slightly, about 2 minutes. Transfer chile mixture to large bowl and let cool for 15 minutes.

2. Add swordfish to chile mixture and stir gently to coat. Cover and refrigerate for at least 30 minutes or up to 2 hours. Brush pineapple and jalapeño with remaining 1 tablespoon oil.

3A. For a charcoal grill Open bottom vent completely. Light large chimney starter mounded with charcoal briquettes (7 quarts). When top coals are partially covered with ash, pour evenly over grill. Set cooking grate in place, cover, and open lid vent completely. Heat grill until hot, about 5 minutes.

3B. For a gas grill Turn all burners to high, cover, and heat grill until hot, about 15 minutes. Turn all burners to medium-high.

4. Clean cooking grate, then repeatedly brush grate with well-oiled paper towels until black and glossy, 5 to 10 times. Place fish, pineapple, and jalapeño on grill. Cover and cook until fish, pineapple, and jalapeño have begun to brown, 3 to 5 minutes. Using thin spatula, turn fish, pineapple, and jalapeño. Cover and cook until pineapple and jalapeño are well browned and swordfish registers 140 degrees, 3 to 5 minutes; transfer to platter and cover with aluminum foil.

5. Working in batches, grill tortillas, turning as needed, until warm and soft, about 30 seconds; wrap tightly in foil to keep soft.

6. Chop pineapple and jalapeño fine and combine with bell pepper, cilantro, and remaining ¼ cup lime juice in bowl. Season with salt to taste. Using 2 forks, pull fish apart into large flakes and serve with pineapple salsa, tortillas, and lime wedges.

Salmon Tacos with Avocado Crema

Serves 4 FAST

Why This Recipe Works Like many fruits and vegetables, fresh, flavorful wild salmon is in season during the summer months. Rich wild salmon is both satisfying and quick-cooking, and paired with a flavorful spice rub and fresh, crunchy slaw, these tacos are sure to be the hit of taco night. For a slaw that would stand up to the salmon, we turned to dark, leafy collards. Though cooked collards are common, when thinly sliced, they conveniently require no precooking. Radishes, jícama, and red onion rounded out the slaw, and avocado crema lent creaminess. Skin-on salmon fillets hold together better during cooking, and the skin helps keep the fish moist. If your salmon is less than 1 inch thick, start checking for doneness early. If using wild-caught salmon, cook until thickest part of the fillet registers 120 degrees. You can substitute 2 cups of thinly sliced cabbage for the collards if desired.

- ¼ teaspoon grated lime zest plus 2 tablespoons juice
- 1 teaspoon table salt, divided
- 4 ounces collard greens, stemmed and sliced thin (2 cups)
- 4 ounces jícama, peeled and cut into 2-inch-long matchsticks
- 4 radishes, trimmed and cut into 1-inch-long matchsticks
- ½ small red onion, halved and sliced thin
- ¼ cup fresh cilantro leaves
- 1½ teaspoons chili powder

- ¼ teaspoon pepper
- 4 (6- to 8-ounce) skin-on salmon fillets, 1 inch thick
- 1 tablespoon vegetable oil
- 1 recipe Avocado Crema (page 100)
- 12 (6-inch) corn tortillas, warmed
  Hot sauce
  Lime wedges

1. Whisk lime zest and juice and ¼ teaspoon salt together in large bowl. Add collards, jícama, radishes, onion, and cilantro and toss to combine.

2. Combine chili powder, pepper, and remaining ¾ teaspoon salt in small bowl. Pat salmon dry with paper towels and sprinkle evenly with spice mixture. Heat oil in 12-inch nonstick skillet over medium-high heat until shimmering. Cook salmon, skin side up, until well browned, 3 to 5 minutes. Flip and continue to cook until salmon is still translucent when checked with tip of paring knife and registers 125 degrees (for medium-rare), 3 to 5 minutes. Transfer salmon to plate and let cool slightly, about 2 minutes. Using 2 forks, flake fish into 2-inch pieces, discarding skin.

3. Divide fish, collard slaw, and avocado crema evenly among tortillas and drizzle with hot sauce to taste. Serve with lime wedges.

Soft Corn Tacos with Sweet Potatoes, Poblano, and Corn

Serves 4

Why This Recipe Works In-season, late-summer corn has an unbeatable lightly sweet flavor that pairs perfectly with sweet potatoes and vegetal, mildly hot poblano peppers to create a vegetarian taco that's hearty and satisfying. To balance their sweet flavors, we seasoned the vegetables with plenty of garlic, cumin, coriander, and oregano. Then we spread all of the vegetables out on baking sheets and roasted them to get crunchy, caramelized exteriors and tender interiors. Finally, we piled the warm vegetables in soft tacos and topped them with crumbled *queso fresco* and a rich Mexican crema. Crumbled feta can be substituted for the queso fresco.

- 3 tablespoons extra-virgin olive oil
- 3 garlic cloves, minced
- 1½ teaspoons ground cumin
- 1½ teaspoons ground coriander
- 1 teaspoon minced fresh oregano or ¼ teaspoon dried

1 teaspoon table salt
½ teaspoon pepper
1 pound sweet potatoes, peeled and cut into ½-inch pieces
4 poblano chiles, stemmed, seeded, and cut into ½-inch-wide strips
3 ears corn, kernels cut from cobs
1 large onion, halved and sliced ½ inch thick
¼ cup minced fresh cilantro
12 (6-inch) corn tortillas, warmed
2 ounces queso fresco, crumbled (½ cup)
1 recipe Mexican Crema (page 100)

1. Adjust oven racks to upper-middle and lower-middle positions and heat oven to 450 degrees. Whisk oil, garlic, cumin, coriander, oregano, salt, and pepper together in large bowl. Add potatoes, poblanos, corn, and onion to bowl and toss to coat.

2. Spread vegetable mixture in even layer over 2 rimmed baking sheets. Bake vegetables until tender and golden brown, about 30 minutes, stirring vegetables and switching and rotating sheets halfway through baking.

3. Return vegetables to now-empty large bowl, add cilantro, and toss to combine. Divide vegetables evenly among tortillas and top with queso fresco and crema. Serve.

Salmon Tacos with Avocado Crema

NOTES FROM THE TEST KITCHEN

FOUR WAYS TO WARM TORTILLAS
Warming tortillas not only makes them more pliable but can also add flavorful toasty char, depending on the method. Wrap the tortillas in foil or clean dish towels to keep them warm until serving.

Gas Flame Using tongs, place tortilla directly over medium flame of gas burner until lightly charred, about 30 seconds per side.

Skillet Toast tortilla in dry nonstick skillet over medium-high heat until softened and spotty brown, 20 to 30 seconds per side.

Microwave Wrap up to 6 tortillas in damp, clean dish towel and microwave until warm, 30 to 45 seconds.

Grill Working in batches, grill tortillas, turning as needed, until warm and soft, about 30 seconds.

Soft Corn Tacos with Sweet Potatoes, Poblano, and Corn

Mains Inspired by the Farmers' Market

■ FAST (30 minutes or less total time) ■ NO COOK ■ MAKE AHEAD
Photos (clockwise from top): Braised Halibut with Leeks and Mustard; Cauliflower Steaks with Salsa Verde;
Pan-Seared Skirt Steak with Zucchini and Scallion Sauce; Vegetable and Orzo Tian

Asparagus and Goat Cheese Tart

Asparagus and Goat Cheese Tart
Serves 4

Why This Recipe Works Fresh asparagus shines as the main attraction of an impressive tart that takes just minutes to assemble. Rather than fuss with making a crust, we turned to store-bought puff pastry, which was buttery, flaky, and easy to prep. For a light filling predominantly flavored by the asparagus, we simply scattered the vegetable and other toppings over the pastry base. Cutting the asparagus spears into thin pieces made the tart easier to eat and ensured that the asparagus didn't need precooking to soften. We tossed the pieces with olive oil, garlic, lemon zest, scallions, and olives, which all enhanced the asparagus without overpowering it. For a creamy base, goat cheese nicely complemented the bright, grassy asparagus. Blending in some olive oil made it easier to spread. We dolloped more cheese on top of the asparagus and baked the tart to golden perfection. Serve with a green salad for a light lunch or dinner. To thaw frozen puff pastry, let it sit in the refrigerator for 24 hours or on the counter for 30 minutes to 1 hour. Look for asparagus spears no thicker than ½ inch.

- 6 ounces thin asparagus, trimmed and cut ¼ inch thick on bias (1 cup)
- 2 scallions, sliced thin
- 3 tablespoons extra-virgin olive oil, divided
- 2 tablespoons chopped pitted kalamata olives
- 1 garlic clove, minced
- ¼ teaspoon grated lemon zest
- ¼ teaspoon table salt
- ¼ teaspoon pepper
- 4 ounces (1 cup) goat cheese, softened, divided
- 1 (9½ by 9-inch) sheet puff pastry, thawed

1. Adjust oven rack to upper-middle position and heat oven to 425 degrees. Line rimmed baking sheet with parchment paper. Combine asparagus, scallions, 1 tablespoon oil, olives, garlic, zest, salt, and pepper in bowl. In separate bowl, mix ¾ cup goat cheese and 1 tablespoon oil until smooth; set aside.

2. Unfold pastry onto lightly floured counter and roll into 10-inch square; transfer to prepared sheet. Lightly brush outer ½ inch of pastry square with water to create border, then fold border toward center, pressing gently to seal.

3. Spread goat cheese mixture in even layer over center of pastry, avoiding folded border. Scatter asparagus mixture over goat cheese, then crumble remaining ¼ cup goat cheese over top of asparagus mixture.

4. Bake until pastry is puffed and golden and asparagus is crisp-tender, 15 to 20 minutes. Let cool for 15 minutes. Drizzle with remaining 1 tablespoon oil, cut into 4 equal pieces, and serve warm or at room temperature.

Stir-Fried Shrimp and Broccoli

Stir-Fried Shrimp and Broccoli
Serves 4

Why This Recipe Works Stir-frying is an ideal way to make broccoli part of a delicious stovetop meal, as the hearty vegetable readily picks up flavorful sauces. To keep our meal light, we paired broccoli with shrimp, tossing them with salt and sugar and letting them sit, which seasoned the shrimp and helped them retain moisture. To ensure that the broccoli cooked evenly, we started cooking both the florets and peeled stalks in a covered skillet along with a splash of our stir-fry sauce before removing the lid so it could brown up a bit. Because shrimp are so delicate, rather than cook them in a hot skillet, we poached them gently in the remaining sauce, which kept them moist. If your shrimp are treated with salt, skip step 1. If you can't find chili-garlic sauce, substitute 2 teaspoons sriracha. You will need a 12-inch nonstick skillet with a tight-fitting lid for this recipe. Serve with Everyday White Rice.

- 1 pound extra-large shrimp (21 to 25 per pound), peeled, deveined, and tails removed
- 1 teaspoon sugar
- ½ teaspoon table salt
- ⅓ cup plus 2 tablespoons dry sherry, divided
- 2 tablespoons oyster sauce
- 1 tablespoon soy sauce
- 1 tablespoon Asian chili-garlic sauce
- 1 teaspoon sherry vinegar
- 2 teaspoons cornstarch
- 2 tablespoons vegetable oil, divided
- 1 pound broccoli, florets cut into 1-inch pieces, stalks peeled and sliced ¼ inch thick
- 1 tablespoon grated fresh ginger
- 2 garlic cloves, minced

1. Combine shrimp, sugar, and salt in medium bowl. Let sit at room temperature for 30 minutes.

2. Whisk ⅓ cup sherry, oyster sauce, soy sauce, chili-garlic sauce, and vinegar together in bowl. Whisk cornstarch and remaining 2 tablespoons sherry together in second bowl.

3. Heat 1 tablespoon oil in 12-inch nonstick skillet over high heat until smoking. Add broccoli and 2 tablespoons sherry–oyster sauce mixture and toss to coat. Cover skillet and cook for 4 minutes, stirring halfway through cooking. Uncover and continue to cook until broccoli is crisp-tender and beginning to brown in spots, 2 to 3 minutes. Transfer broccoli to bowl.

4. Add remaining 1 tablespoon oil, ginger, and garlic to skillet and cook until fragrant, about 1 minute. Add remaining sherry–oyster sauce mixture and shrimp to skillet and bring to simmer. Reduce heat to medium-low, cover, and cook, stirring occasionally, until shrimp are just cooked through, 3 to 5 minutes.

5. Whisk sherry-cornstarch mixture to recombine and add to skillet; increase heat to high and cook, stirring constantly, until sauce is thickened, 1 to 2 minutes. Return broccoli to skillet and toss to combine. Transfer to serving platter and serve.

DEVEINING SHRIMP

1. After removing shell, use paring knife to make shallow cut along back of shrimp, exposing vein.

2. Use tip of knife to lift out vein. Discard vein by wiping blade against paper towel.

Everyday White Rice
Serves 6 (Makes 6 cups)
It's important to rinse the rice before cooking it to remove excess starch from the grains. Omit the salt if you're serving this rice with a salty dish such as a stir-fry. You can use any variety of long-grain white rice, such as basmati, jasmine, and Texmati.

- 2 cups long-grain white rice
- 3 cups water
- ½ teaspoon salt (optional)

1. Place rice in fine-mesh strainer and rinse under running water until water running through rice is almost clear, about 1½ minutes, agitating rice with your hand every so often.

2. Combine rice, water, and salt, if using, in large saucepan and bring to simmer over high heat. Stir rice with rubber spatula, dislodging any rice that sticks to bottom of saucepan.

3. Cover, reduce heat to low, and cook for 20 minutes. (Steam should steadily emit from sides of saucepan. If water bubbles out from under lid, reduce heat slightly.)

4. Remove from heat; do not uncover. Let sit, covered, for 10 minutes. Gently fluff rice with fork. Serve.

Roasted Salmon and Broccoli Rabe with Pistachio Gremolata

Serves 4 FAST

Why This Recipe Works Pairing the right fish with the right vegetable and cooking both in a single pan promises a quick summer dinner with endless flavor potential. The trick is ensuring that they finish cooking at the same time. Here, we chose rich salmon and broccoli rabe. We cut the broccoli rabe into pieces before roasting it alongside the salmon fillets on a sheet pan in a hot oven. Both were perfectly done in just 10 minutes. Roasting also tempered the broccoli rabe's characteristic bitterness into something more well-rounded. To accent the flavors of both components and elevate the simple meal into something a little more special, we sprinkled the broccoli rabe and fish with a quick, fresh-tasting gremolata, an Italian condiment made with parsley, lemon zest, garlic, and—in this case—pistachios. To ensure uniform pieces of fish that cooked at the same rate, we prefer to buy a whole center-cut fillet and cut it into four pieces ourselves. Arctic char and wild salmon are good substitutes for the salmon. If using, make sure to cook them to 120 degrees.

¼ cup shelled pistachios, toasted and chopped fine
2 tablespoons minced fresh parsley
1 teaspoon grated lemon zest
2 garlic cloves, minced, divided
1 pound broccoli rabe, trimmed and cut into 1½-inch pieces
2 tablespoons plus 2 teaspoons extra-virgin olive oil, divided
¾ teaspoon table salt, divided
¾ teaspoon pepper, divided
   Pinch red pepper flakes
1 (2-pound) skinless salmon fillet, 1 to 1½ inches thick

1. Adjust oven rack to middle position and heat oven to 450 degrees. Combine pistachios, parsley, lemon zest, and half of garlic in small bowl; set gremolata aside.

2. Toss broccoli rabe with 2 tablespoons oil, ¼ teaspoon salt, ¼ teaspoon pepper, pepper flakes, and remaining garlic in bowl. Arrange on 1 half of rimmed baking sheet. Cut salmon crosswise into 4 fillets. Pat salmon dry with paper towels, then rub with remaining 2 teaspoons oil and sprinkle with remaining ½ teaspoon salt and remaining ½ teaspoon pepper. Arrange salmon on empty half of sheet, skinned side down.

3. Roast until salmon registers 125 degrees (for medium-rare) and broccoli rabe is tender, about 10 minutes. Sprinkle individual portions with gremolata before serving.

Whole Romanesco with Berbere and Tahini-Yogurt Sauce

Serves 4 FAST

Why This Recipe Works Beautiful, fractal-looking romanesco is related to cauliflower and broccoli. It is perfect for cooking whole, and when served with a savory sauce it makes an inspired vegetarian dinner. To achieve a tender interior and nicely charred exterior, we started by microwaving the whole head for about 10 minutes, which saved us from roasting it for more than an hour in the oven. We then brushed it with melted butter and placed it under the broiler to develop some browning. To further enrich and deeply flavor the romanesco, we basted it with more butter that we'd enhanced with berbere, a warmly aromatic and highly flavorful Ethiopian spice blend. A bright, cooling tahini-yogurt sauce and a sprinkle of crunchy chopped pine nuts and fresh cilantro finished it off. If you can't find a 2-pound head of romanesco, purchase two 1-pound heads and reduce the microwaving time in step 1 to 5 to 7 minutes. You can substitute cauliflower for the romanesco.

1 head romanesco or cauliflower (2 pounds)
6 tablespoons unsalted butter, cut into 6 pieces, divided
¼ teaspoon table salt
½ teaspoon paprika
¼ teaspoon cayenne pepper
¼ teaspoon ground coriander
⅛ teaspoon ground allspice
⅛ teaspoon ground cardamom
⅛ teaspoon ground cumin
⅛ teaspoon pepper
2 tablespoons toasted and chopped pine nuts
1 tablespoon minced fresh cilantro
1 recipe Tahini-Yogurt Sauce (page 92)

1. Adjust oven rack 6 inches from broiler element and heat broiler. Trim outer leaves of romanesco and cut stem flush with bottom florets. Microwave romanesco and 3 tablespoons butter in covered large bowl until paring knife slips easily in and out of core, 8 to 12 minutes.

2. Transfer romanesco, stem side down, to 12-inch ovensafe skillet. Brush romanesco evenly with melted butter from bowl and sprinkle with salt. Transfer skillet to oven and broil until top of romanesco is spotty brown, 8 to 10 minutes. Meanwhile, microwave remaining 3 tablespoons butter, paprika, cayenne, coriander, allspice, cardamom, cumin, and pepper in now-empty bowl, stirring occasionally, until fragrant and bubbling, 1 to 2 minutes.

3. Using pot holder, remove skillet from oven, transfer to wire rack, and add melted butter to skillet. Being careful of hot skillet handle, gently tilt skillet so butter pools to 1 side. Using spoon, baste romanesco until butter is absorbed, about 30 seconds.

4. Cut romanesco into wedges and transfer to serving platter. Season with salt to taste and sprinkle pine nuts and cilantro over top. Serve with tahini-yogurt sauce.

MICROWAVING ROMANESCO

To jump-start cooking, microwave whole head of romanesco in large covered bowl until paring knife slips easily in and out of core.

Cauliflower Steaks with Salsa Verde

Serves 4

Why This Recipe Works When you cook thick slabs of cauliflower as vegetarian "steaks," they develop a substantial, meaty texture and become nutty, sweet, and caramelized. Recipes for cauliflower steaks abound, but many involve fussy transitions between stovetop and oven. To find a simple way to produce four perfectly cooked cauliflower steaks simultaneously, we opted for an oven-only method. Steaming the cauliflower briefly by covering the baking sheet with foil, followed by high-heat uncovered roasting on the lowest oven rack, produced dramatic-looking, caramelized seared steaks with tender interiors. To elevate the cauliflower to centerpiece status, we paired it with a vibrant Italian-style salsa verde—a blend of parsley, mint, capers, garlic, olive oil, and white wine vinegar. Brushing the hot steaks with the salsa verde ensured they'd soak up all of its robust flavor. Look for fresh, firm, bright white heads of cauliflower that feel heavy for their size and are free of blemishes or soft spots; florets are more likely to separate from older heads of cauliflower. You will have leftover cauliflower, which you can save for another use such as roasting or sautéing.

Roasted Salmon and Broccoli Rabe with Pistachio Gremolata

Whole Romanesco with Berbere and Tahini-Yogurt Sauce

1½ cups fresh parsley leaves
½ cup fresh mint leaves
½ cup extra-virgin olive oil, divided
2 tablespoons water
1½ tablespoons white wine vinegar
1 tablespoon capers, rinsed
1 garlic clove, minced
⅛ teaspoon plus ½ teaspoon table salt, divided
2 heads cauliflower (2 pounds each)
¼ teaspoon pepper, divided
Lemon wedges

1. Adjust oven rack to lowest position and heat oven to 500 degrees. Pulse parsley, mint, ¼ cup oil, water, vinegar, capers, garlic, and ⅛ teaspoon salt in food processor until mixture is finely chopped but not smooth, about 10 pulses, scraping down sides of bowl as needed. Transfer salsa verde to small bowl and set aside for serving.

2. Working with 1 head cauliflower at a time, discard outer leaves of cauliflower and trim stem flush with bottom florets. Halve cauliflower lengthwise through core. Cut 1½-inch-thick slab lengthwise from each half, trimming any florets not connected to core. (You should have 4 steaks; reserve remaining cauliflower for another use.) Place steaks on rimmed baking sheet and drizzle with 2 tablespoons oil. Sprinkle with ¼ teaspoon salt and ⅛ teaspoon pepper and rub to distribute. Flip steaks and repeat with remaining 2 tablespoons oil, remaining ¼ teaspoon salt, and remaining ⅛ teaspoon pepper.

3. Cover baking sheet tightly with aluminum foil and roast for 5 minutes. Remove foil and roast until bottoms of steaks are well browned, 8 to 10 minutes. Gently flip steaks and continue to roast until tender and second sides are well browned, 6 to 8 minutes.

4. Transfer steaks to platter and brush evenly with ¼ cup salsa verde. Serve with lemon wedges, passing remaining salsa verde separately.

CUTTING CAULIFLOWER STEAKS

1. Halve cauliflower lengthwise through core.

2. Cut one 1½-inch-thick slab from each cauliflower half.

Roast Chicken with Cauliflower and Tomatoes

Serves 4

Why This Recipe Works Cauliflower's mildness makes it a fantastic blank canvas for pairing with a wide variety of main dishes. Just as versatile are chicken leg quarters, which are cheap, easy to work with, flavorful, and hard to overcook. We wanted to pair these two components and cook them simultaneously for an easy summer weeknight dinner with great flavor and minimal cleanup. We whisked lemon, garlic, and chopped sage into olive oil and brushed it onto the chicken. To balance the meal between the chicken and the vegetables, we added some shallots to bulk up the vegetable component. Arranging the vegetables in the middle of the baking sheet and positioning the chicken legs around the edge ensured that everything cooked at the same rate. Tossing a handful of grape tomatoes into the pan and blasting the pan under the broiler at the end made for crispy chicken skin, browned cauliflower, and blistered tomatoes. Some leg quarters are sold with the backbone attached. Remove it before cooking to make serving easier. If you substitute cherry tomatoes, cut them in half before adding them to the baking sheet.

1 head cauliflower (2 pounds), cut into 8 equal wedges
6 shallots, peeled and halved
¼ cup extra-virgin olive oil, divided
2 tablespoons chopped fresh sage or 2 teaspoons dried, divided
1¾ teaspoons table salt, divided
1 teaspoon pepper, divided
4 (10-ounce) chicken leg quarters, trimmed
2 garlic cloves, minced
1 teaspoon grated lemon zest, plus lemon wedges for serving
8 ounces grape tomatoes
1 tablespoon chopped fresh parsley

1. Adjust 1 oven rack to lower-middle position and second rack 6 inches from broiler element. Heat oven to 475 degrees. Gently toss cauliflower wedges, shallots, 2 tablespoons oil, 1 tablespoon sage, ½ teaspoon salt, and ½ teaspoon pepper on rimmed baking sheet to combine. Position vegetables cut sides down in single layer in center of sheet.

2. Pat chicken dry with paper towels. Leaving drumsticks and thighs attached, make 4 parallel diagonal slashes in chicken: one across drumsticks, one across leg joints, and two across thighs (each slash should reach bone). Sprinkle chicken with remaining 1¼ teaspoons salt and remaining ½ teaspoon pepper. Place 1 piece of chicken, skin side up, in each corner of sheet (chicken should rest directly on sheet, not on vegetables).

3. Whisk garlic, lemon zest, remaining 2 tablespoons oil, and remaining 1 tablespoon sage together in bowl, then brush all over skin side of chicken. Transfer sheet to lower rack and bake until cauliflower is browned, shallots are tender, and chicken registers 175 degrees, 25 to 30 minutes.

4. Remove sheet from oven and heat broiler. Scatter tomatoes over vegetables and place sheet on upper rack. Broil until chicken skin is browned and crisp and tomatoes have started to wilt, 3 to 5 minutes.

5. Transfer sheet to wire rack and let rest for 5 minutes. Sprinkle with parsley and serve with lemon wedges.

Steak Tips with Spicy Cauliflower
Serves 4

Why This Recipe Works Tender, beefy, quick-cooking sirloin steak tips are a nice option when you want get dinner on the table without breaking a sweat. For a vegetable side, we bypassed starchy potatoes in favor of lighter cauliflower. To dress up the mild vegetable with some heat and zest we made an Italian-style relish of jarred roasted red peppers, cherry peppers, parsley, and capers all whisked with some olive oil. We cooked the cauliflower in the skillet until browned, keeping the pan covered so it would steam a bit and cook through evenly. We then cooked the steak tips in the same skillet until browned but still juicy and tender. Steak tips are often sold as flap meat. They can be packaged as whole steaks, cubes, or strips. We prefer to buy whole steaks so we can cut our own steak tips.

- ½ cup jarred roasted red peppers, patted dry and chopped
- 5 tablespoons extra-virgin olive oil, divided
- ¼ cup pickled cherry peppers, minced
- 2 tablespoons chopped fresh parsley
- 1 tablespoon capers, rinsed and minced
- 1¼ teaspoons table salt, divided
- ⅛ teaspoon plus ½ teaspoon pepper, divided
- 1 large head cauliflower (3 pounds), cored and cut into 1-inch pieces
- 2 pounds sirloin steak tips, trimmed and cut into 2-inch pieces

Roast Chicken with Cauliflower and Tomatoes

Farmers' Market Find Cauliflower

At farmers' markets, and some supermarkets, you will often find orange or purple cauliflower. Both of these varieties can be substituted for white cauliflower. The orange variety has more vitamin A than white cauliflower, and the purple variety is high in antioxidants. **Romanesco** is a beautiful cousin, Key-lime green in hue and fractal in appearance. When shopping for cauliflower, look for firm, bright white or deeply colored heads that are free of brown spots and soft spots and that feel heavy for their size, with tightly packed florets and firm leaves without any fading; florets are more likely to separate from older heads of cauliflower. Romanesco should be a bright chartreuse color and similarly free of blemishes. You can store cauliflower and romanesco in the packaging they come in, but for longer life, transfer them to a loosely closed plastic produce bag in the refrigerator with paper towels wrapped around them to absorb moisture. They should keep for a week or more.

1. Combine red peppers, 3 tablespoons oil, cherry peppers, parsley, capers, ¼ teaspoon salt, and ⅛ teaspoon pepper in large bowl; set relish aside.

2. Heat 1 tablespoon oil in 12-inch nonstick skillet over medium-high heat until shimmering. Add cauliflower and cook, covered, stirring occasionally, until browned and tender, about 10 minutes. Add cauliflower to relish and toss to combine. Season with salt and pepper to taste.

3. Pat steak dry with paper towels and sprinkle with remaining 1 teaspoon salt and remaining ½ teaspoon pepper. Add remaining 1 tablespoon oil to now-empty skillet and heat over medium-high heat until just smoking. Add steak and cook until browned on all sides and meat registers 125 degrees (for medium-rare), about 7 minutes. Serve steak with cauliflower.

Chorizo, Corn, and Tomato Tostadas with Lime Crema

Serves 4

Why This Recipe Works Tostadas are flat, crisped tortillas that serve as a crunchy base for flavorful toppings. We top ours with fresh corn, cherry tomatoes, and cabbage slaw along with chorizo sausage and canned black beans to make them hearty enough for a meal. To simplify this multi-component meal, we used a sheet pan to brown the chorizo and corn and warm the tostadas—spread with a flavorful black bean–jalapeño mixture—on another baking sheet at the same time. The brine from jarred jalapeños added zingy flavor to our quick cabbage slaw. Another hard, cured sausage (such as linguiça) can be substituted for the chorizo. Look for tostadas next to the taco kits at most supermarkets.

  1 (14-ounce) bag green coleslaw mix
  1 tablespoon chopped jarred jalapeños plus
    ¼ cup brine, divided
  ½ cup sour cream
  3 tablespoons lime juice (2 limes), divided
  1 tablespoon vegetable oil
  8 ounces Spanish-style chorizo sausage,
    halved and sliced ¼-inch thick
  4 ears corn, kernels cut from cobs (about 3 cups)
  1 (15-ounce) can black beans, rinsed
  ¼ cup chicken or vegetable broth
  12 (6-inch) corn tostadas
  6 ounces cherry tomatoes, quartered
  ¼ cup fresh cilantro leaves
  4 ounces queso fresco or feta cheese,
    crumbled (1 cup)

1. Adjust oven racks to upper-middle and lower-middle positions, place rimmed baking sheet on upper rack, and heat oven to 450 degrees.

2. Toss coleslaw mix with 3 tablespoons jalapeño brine in bowl and season with salt and pepper to taste. In second bowl, whisk sour cream and 2 tablespoons lime juice together, and season with salt and pepper to taste; set slaw and crema aside for serving.

3. Combine oil, chorizo, and corn in bowl. Remove sheet from oven and spread chorizo and corn in single layer on hot sheet. Cook until browned, about 15 minutes.

4. Meanwhile, combine beans, broth, chopped jalapeños, and remaining 1 tablespoon brine in clean bowl and microwave until warm, about 2 minutes. Mash beans with potato masher until spreadable, season with salt and pepper to taste, and spread evenly over tostadas. Arrange on clean rimmed baking sheet, overlapping as needed.

5. During final 5 minutes of roasting chorizo and corn, transfer sheet with tostadas to lower oven rack to warm through.

6. Remove tostadas from oven. Transfer chorizo-corn mixture to large bowl, and stir in remaining 1 tablespoon lime juice and tomatoes. Divide mixture evenly among tostadas. Top tostadas with slaw and crema. Crumble queso fresco over top and sprinkle with cilantro. Serve.

Creamy Corn Bucatini with Ricotta and Basil

Serves 4 to 6 FAST

Why This Recipe Works In this ingenious summer recipe, corn serves as the base for a simple, creamy pasta sauce that comes together in a flash. We started by bringing corn and milk to a simmer before blending the mixture to a smooth puree. Corn kernels naturally contain cornstarch, which thickens into a pasta-coating sauce if heated above 150 degrees. Heating also intensifies the characteristic aroma of corn, which is largely due to a compound that is also prominent in the aroma of milk. That means that our puree tasted more like corn, and it also tasted more like milk. Simmering our pasta in this sauce further thickened the sauce to a velvety consistency while ensuring a perfect al dente texture for the pasta. We even added a touch of red pepper flakes for a subtle kick. Finished with dollops of creamy ricotta and fresh basil, this is a satisfying dish that's great any day of the week. Although this is a fantastic use for in-season corn, you can substitute 18 ounces frozen corn for fresh. You can also use spaghetti in place of bucatini.

4 ears corn, kernels cut from cobs (about 3 cups)
1 cup whole milk
1 pound bucatini
¼ teaspoon table salt, plus salt for cooking pasta
¼ teaspoon red pepper flakes
6 ounces (¾ cup) whole-milk ricotta cheese
¼ cup fresh basil leaves, torn

1. Bring corn and milk to simmer in 12-inch skillet over medium heat. Carefully transfer corn and milk to blender and let cool slightly, about 5 minutes. Process until smooth, about 3 minutes, scraping down sides of blender jar as needed. Strain corn mixture through fine-mesh strainer into now-empty skillet, pressing on solids to extract as much liquid as possible.

2. Meanwhile, bring 4 quarts water to boil in large pot. Add pasta and 1 tablespoon salt and cook, stirring often, until pasta is flexible but still firm, about 5 minutes. Reserve 2 cups cooking water, then drain pasta.

3. Stir pasta, 1½ cups reserved cooking water, ¼ teaspoon salt, and pepper flakes into corn mixture in skillet. Cook over medium-high heat, stirring constantly, until pasta is al dente and well coated with sauce, 2 to 4 minutes. Adjust consistency with remaining reserved cooking water. Season with salt and pepper to taste.

4. Transfer pasta to serving dish, dollop with ricotta, and sprinkle with basil. Serve.

Spice-Rubbed Pork Chops with Corn, Summer Squash, and Poblano Sauté
Serves 4 `FAST`

Why This Recipe Works The combination of paprika and chili powder gives these stovetop pork chops a big hit of flavor, while the mixture of fresh corn, summer squash, and poblano chiles (a moderately hot variety) serves as a sweet, smoky, and slightly spicy side dish that complements the pork in this easy one-pan dinner. For this recipe, we cooked the pork over medium heat to prevent the spice rub from burning. If you can't find poblano chiles, you can substitute Anaheim chiles, though they are a bit milder and don't have the smoky flavor profile of the poblanos. Feel free to substitute zucchini for the summer squash or use a combination of the two. We prefer fresh corn in this recipe, but you can substitute 1½ cups of frozen corn for the fresh: Thaw it before using and add it to the vegetable mixture only for the last 2 minutes to heat through.

Chorizo, Corn, and Tomato Tostadas with Lime Crema

Creamy Corn Bucatini with Ricotta and Basil

Orecchiette with Baby
Dandelion Greens in
Lemony Cream Sauce

Classic
Stir-Fried
Eggplant

1 teaspoon paprika
1 teaspoon chili powder
½ teaspoon table salt
½ teaspoon pepper
4 (8- to 10-ounce) bone-in pork rib or center-cut chops, ¾ to 1 inch thick, trimmed
2 tablespoons vegetable oil, divided
1 pound yellow summer squash, cut into ½-inch pieces
2 ears corn, kernels cut from cob (about 1½ cups)
2 poblano chiles, stemmed, halved, seeded, and sliced into ¼-inch-wide strips
1 small onion, chopped fine
2 tablespoons chopped fresh cilantro
  Lime wedges

1. Combine paprika, chili powder, salt, and pepper in small bowl. Pat chops dry with paper towels and rub with spice mixture.

2. Heat 1 tablespoon oil in 12-inch nonstick skillet over medium heat until just smoking. Add chops and cook until well browned and meat registers 145 degrees, about 5 minutes per side. Transfer to serving platter and tent loosely with aluminum foil.

3. Add remaining 1 tablespoon oil, squash, corn, poblanos, and onion to skillet and cook until vegetables have softened, about 6 minutes. Stir in cilantro, season with salt and pepper to taste, and transfer to serving platter with chops. Serve with lime wedges.

Orecchiette with Baby Dandelion Greens in Lemony Cream Sauce

Serves 4 to 6

Why This Recipe Works Like their mature incarnation, baby dandelion greens pack strong, grassy flavors and a bitter punch. But unlike their grownup selves, the babies are very tender and require minimal cooking, making them the perfect addition to a range of dishes that cry out for wilted greens. We wanted to create a pasta dish in which baby dandelion greens were the main event but weren't too strongly bitter. Initially thinking a light and fresh dish would be appropriate for these greens, we started out with a wine and butter sauce. But tasters found that the acidic wine only compounded the greens' bitterness.

So we switched direction and made a rich, creamy Parmesan sauce instead. This sauce beautifully tamed the greens without overshadowing them, and the addition of fresh lemon juice and zest and basil finished the dish on a bright note. If you can't find baby dandelion greens, you can substitute 12 ounces of arugula. We chose orecchiette for its talent for scooping up pockets of sauce, but farfalle can be substituted.

  1 pound orecchiette
  ¾ teaspoon table salt, divided, plus salt for cooking pasta
  2 tablespoons extra-virgin olive oil
  1 shallot, halved and sliced thin
  ¼ teaspoon pepper
  2 garlic cloves, minced
  ¼ teaspoon red pepper flakes
  8 ounces baby dandelion greens, cut into 1-inch pieces
  1 cup heavy cream
  2 tablespoons unsalted butter
2½ ounces Parmesan cheese, grated (1¼ cups), divided
  ½ teaspoon lemon zest plus 1 tablespoon lemon juice
  ¼ cup chopped fresh basil

1. Bring 4 quarts water to boil in large pot. Add pasta and 1 tablespoon salt and cook, stirring occasionally, until al dente. Reserve 1 cup cooking water, then drain pasta and return it to pot.

2. Meanwhile, heat oil in 12-inch skillet over medium heat until shimmering. Add shallot, ¼ teaspoon salt, and pepper and cook until softened, about 3 minutes. Stir in garlic and pepper flakes and cook until fragrant, about 30 seconds. Add dandelion greens 1 handful at a time, and cook until greens are just wilted, 2 to 3 minutes; transfer to pot with pasta. Wipe skillet clean with paper towels.

3. Bring cream and butter to simmer in now-empty skillet over medium-high heat. Reduce heat to medium-low and simmer gently until reduced to ¾ cup, about 3 minutes. Reduce heat to low, whisk in ¾ cup Parmesan, lemon zest and juice, and remaining ½ teaspoon salt, and cook until Parmesan is fully incorporated and sauce is smooth, about 1 minute.

4. Add sauce and basil to pot with pasta and toss to combine. Adjust consistency with reserved cooking water as needed. Season with salt and pepper to taste. Serve, passing remaining ½ cup Parmesan separately.

Classic Stir-Fried Eggplant
Serves 4 FAST

Why This Recipe Works This stir-fry takes advantage of an abundance of summer eggplant and showcases the meaty vegetable as a main course. Eggplant absorbs the flavors of whatever it's cooked in, so we decided to highlight a classic stir-fry sauce, with savory, balanced flavor. We combined chicken broth, rice wine, hoisin, and soy sauce and thickened the mixture with cornstarch. Just a teaspoon of toasted sesame oil added an extra layer of umami flavor. Eggplant takes well to stir-frying; the high heat and shallow skillet allow the eggplant's moisture (a liability in many recipes) to evaporate quickly, leaving the eggplant browned and tender. Scallions and basil lent the dish some aromatic notes that played nicely off of the savory sauce. When shopping for Chinese rice wine, look for one that is amber in color; dry sherry may be substituted for rice wine. Serve with Everyday White Rice (page 107).

Stir-Fry Sauce
  ½ cup chicken broth
  ¼ cup Chinese rice wine
  3 tablespoons hoisin sauce
  1 tablespoon soy sauce
  2 teaspoons cornstarch
  1 teaspoon toasted sesame oil

Eggplant
  1 teaspoon plus 2 tablespoons vegetable oil, divided
  6 garlic cloves, minced
  1 tablespoon grated fresh ginger
1½ pounds eggplant, cut into ¾-inch pieces
  2 scallions, sliced ¼ inch thick on bias
  ½ cup fresh basil leaves, torn into rough ½-inch pieces
  1 tablespoon sesame seeds, toasted

1. For the stir-fry sauce Whisk all ingredients together in bowl, set aside. (Sauce can be refrigerated for up to 2 days; whisk to recombine before using.)

2. Combine 1 teaspoon oil, garlic, and ginger in bowl. Heat 1 tablespoon oil in 12-inch nonstick skillet over high heat until shimmering. Add half of eggplant and cook, stirring every 10 to 15 seconds, until browned and tender, 4 to 5 minutes; transfer to separate bowl. Repeat with remaining 1 tablespoon oil and eggplant; transfer to bowl.

3. Add garlic-ginger mixture to now-empty skillet and cook, mashing mixture into skillet, until fragrant, about 30 seconds. Stir in eggplant and any accumulated juices. Add stir-fry sauce and cook, stirring constantly, until eggplant is well coated and sauce is thickened, about 30 seconds. Stir in scallions and basil. Sprinkle with sesame seeds and serve.

Braised Eggplant with Paprika, Coriander, and Yogurt

Serves 4

Why This Recipe Works Braising eggplant produces a meltingly tender, creamy texture for an innovative vegetable-centric meal. We cut the eggplant into slim wedges, making sure that each piece had some skin attached to keep it from falling apart during cooking. We braised the eggplant in a mixture of water enhanced with flavor-packed tomato paste, warm Mediterranean spices, and aromatics. Once the eggplant was tender, we reduced the braising liquid to create a sauce. Drizzling some tangy yogurt on top added welcome richness to the light finished dish. Large globe and Italian eggplants disintegrate when braised, so do not substitute a single 1- to 1¼-pound eggplant here. You can substitute 1 to 1¼ pounds of long, slim Chinese or Japanese eggplants if they are available; cut them as directed. You will need a 12-inch nonstick skillet with a tight-fitting lid for this recipe.

- 2 (8- to 10-ounce) eggplants
- 3 tablespoons vegetable oil
- 2 garlic cloves, minced
- 1 tablespoon tomato paste
- 2 teaspoons paprika
- 1 teaspoon table salt
- 1 teaspoon ground coriander
- ½ teaspoon sugar
- ½ teaspoon ground cumin
- ½ teaspoon ground cinnamon
- ½ teaspoon ground nutmeg
- ½ teaspoon ground ginger
- 2¾ cups water
- ⅓ cup plain whole-milk yogurt
- 2 tablespoons minced fresh cilantro

1. Trim ½ inch from top of 1 eggplant. Halve eggplant crosswise. Cut each half lengthwise into 2 pieces. Cut each piece into ¾-inch-thick wedges. Repeat with remaining eggplant.

2. Heat oil in 12-inch nonstick skillet over medium heat until shimmering. Add garlic and cook, stirring constantly, until fragrant, about 30 seconds. Add tomato paste, paprika, salt, coriander, sugar, cumin, cinnamon, nutmeg, and ginger and cook, stirring constantly, until mixture starts to darken, 1 to 2 minutes.

Spread eggplant evenly in skillet (pieces will not form single layer). Pour water over eggplant. Increase heat to high and bring to boil. Reduce heat to maintain gentle boil. Cover and cook until eggplant is soft and has decreased in volume enough to form single layer on bottom of skillet, about 15 minutes, gently shaking skillet to settle eggplant halfway through cooking (some pieces will remain opaque).

3. Uncover and continue to cook, swirling skillet occasionally, until liquid is thickened and reduced to just a few tablespoons, 12 to 14 minutes. Off heat, season with salt and pepper to taste. Transfer to platter, drizzle with yogurt, sprinkle with cilantro, and serve.

PREPPING EGGPLANT FOR BRAISING

Peeled pieces of eggplant, as well as pieces that are too large, will disintegrate as they simmer. For intact pieces, it's important to choose a medium-size eggplant (if using a globe or Italian variety) and cut it so that each piece has some skin attached.

1. Cut trimmed eggplant in half crosswise.

2. Cut each half lengthwise to form 2 pieces.

3. Cut each piece into ¾-inch-thick wedges. Repeat with remaining eggplant.

Eggplant Involtini
Serves 4 `MAKE AHEAD`

Why This Recipe Works Eggplant *involtini* is like a lighter and more summery version of eggplant Parmesan, with the flavorful eggplant rolled around a creamy ricotta filling. For a streamlined take on these cheese-filled bundles that emphasized the eggplant, we skipped the breading and frying and instead brushed eggplant planks with oil, seasoned them with salt and pepper, and baked them. They emerged light brown and tender, with a compact texture that was neither mushy nor sodden. To lighten up the filling, we replaced part of the ricotta with bold Pecorino Romano cheese, which meant we could use less filling without sacrificing flavor, and we brightened it with a squeeze of lemon juice. While the eggplant baked, we made a simple tomato sauce, then added the eggplant rolls directly to the sauce. Using a skillet meant that we could easily transfer the whole operation to the oven. We crowned the skillet with an additional dusting of Pecorino and a sprinkling of basil before serving. Select shorter, wider eggplants for this recipe. Part-skim ricotta may be used, but do not use fat-free.

- 2 large eggplants (1½ pounds each), peeled
- 6 tablespoons vegetable oil, divided
- 1 teaspoon table salt, divided
- ½ teaspoon pepper, divided
- 2 garlic cloves, minced
- ¼ teaspoon dried oregano
  Pinch red pepper flakes
- 1 (28-ounce) can whole peeled tomatoes, drained with juice reserved, chopped
- 1 slice hearty white sandwich bread, torn into 1-inch pieces
- 8 ounces (1 cup) whole-milk ricotta cheese
- 1½ ounces Pecorino Romano cheese, grated (¾ cup), divided
- 5 tablespoons chopped fresh basil, divided
- 1 tablespoon lemon juice

1. Slice each eggplant lengthwise into ½-inch-thick planks (you should have 12 planks). Trim rounded surface from each end piece so it lies flat.

2. Adjust 1 oven rack to lower-middle position and second rack 8 inches from broiler element. Heat oven to 375 degrees. Line 2 rimmed baking sheets with parchment paper and spray with vegetable oil spray.

3. Arrange eggplant slices in single layer on prepared sheets. Brush 1 side of eggplant slices with 2½ tablespoons oil and sprinkle with ¼ teaspoon salt and ¼ teaspoon pepper. Flip eggplant slices and brush with 2½ tablespoons oil and sprinkle with ¼ teaspoon salt and remaining ¼ teaspoon pepper.

Braised Eggplant with Paprika, Coriander, and Yogurt

Eggplant Involtini

Bake until tender and lightly browned, 30 to 35 minutes, switching and rotating sheets halfway through baking. Let cool for 5 minutes. Using thin spatula, flip each slice. Heat broiler.

4. While eggplant cooks, heat remaining 1 tablespoon oil in 12-inch broiler-safe skillet over medium-low heat until just shimmering. Add garlic, oregano, pepper flakes, and ¼ teaspoon salt and cook, stirring occasionally, until fragrant, about 30 seconds. Stir in tomatoes and their juice. Increase heat to high and bring to simmer. Reduce heat to medium-low and simmer until thickened, about 15 minutes. Cover and set aside.

5. Pulse bread in food processor until finely ground, 10 to 15 pulses. Combine bread crumbs, ricotta, ½ cup Pecorino, ¼ cup basil, lemon juice, and remaining ¼ teaspoon salt in bowl. With widest ends of eggplant slices facing you, spoon about 3 tablespoons ricotta mixture on bottom third of each slice. Gently roll up each eggplant slice and place seam side down in tomato sauce. (Cooked sauce and stuffed eggplant can be refrigerated separately for up to 24 hours.)

6. Bring sauce to simmer over medium heat. Simmer for 5 minutes. Transfer skillet to oven and broil until eggplant is well browned and cheese is warmed through, 5 to 10 minutes. Sprinkle with remaining ¼ cup Pecorino and let sit for 5 minutes. Sprinkle with remaining 1 tablespoon basil and serve.

MAKING EGGPLANT INVOLTINI

1. Peel eggplant and slice lengthwise into ½-inch-thick planks.

2. Arrange eggplant slices in single layer on prepared baking sheets, brush with oil and season with salt and pepper, and bake until tender and lightly browned, 30 to 35 minutes.

3. Spoon about 3 tablespoons ricotta mixture over wide end of each eggplant slice and gently roll up each eggplant slice.

Stuffed Eggplant with Bulgur
Serves 4 `MAKE AHEAD`

Why This Recipe Works Stuffed eggplant is a fantastic dinner option when you crave a satisfying meal that's also appealingly light. The smaller-size Italian eggplants you often see at summer farmers' market are ideal for stuffing, making this dish all the more appealing this time of year. There are countless variations on stuffed eggplant, but we found ourselves enamored of a classic Turkish preparation known as *imam bayildi*. Most recipes for it are similar: Eggplant is cooked in olive oil and then stuffed with onions, garlic, and tomatoes. For our version, we wanted to make sure that the eggplants were rich and creamy and that the filling was hearty. Roasting small Italian eggplants prior to stuffing was the key to preventing them from turning watery and tasteless. The slight caramelizing effect of roasting them on a preheated baking sheet added depth of flavor. We let the eggplants drain briefly on paper towels (which got rid of excess liquid) before adding the stuffing. Nutty bulgur made a perfect filling base and added enough heft that this dish could serve as a satisfying main course. Plum tomatoes lent bright flavor and a bit of moisture, and Pecorino Romano and pine nuts provided richness. When shopping, do not confuse bulgur with cracked wheat, which has a much longer cooking time and will not work in this recipe.

- 4 (10-ounce) Italian eggplants, halved lengthwise
- 2 tablespoons extra-virgin olive oil, divided
- 1 teaspoon table salt, divided
- ¼ teaspoon pepper
- ½ cup medium-grind bulgur, rinsed
- ¼ cup water
- 1 onion, chopped fine
- 3 garlic cloves, minced
- 2 teaspoons minced fresh oregano or ½ teaspoon dried
- ¼ teaspoon ground cinnamon
  Pinch cayenne pepper
- 1 pound plum tomatoes, cored, seeded, and chopped
- 2 ounces Pecorino Romano cheese, grated (1 cup), divided
- 2 tablespoons toasted pine nuts
- 2 teaspoons red wine vinegar
- 2 tablespoons minced fresh parsley

1. Adjust oven racks to upper-middle and lowest positions, place parchment paper–lined rimmed baking sheet on lower rack, and heat oven to 400 degrees.

Stuffed Eggplant with Bulgur

2. Score flesh of each eggplant half in 1-inch diamond pattern, about 1 inch deep. Brush scored sides of eggplant with 1 tablespoon oil and sprinkle with ½ teaspoon salt and pepper. Lay eggplant cut side down on hot sheet and roast until flesh is tender, 40 to 50 minutes. Transfer eggplants cut side down to paper towel–lined baking sheet and let drain.

3. Toss bulgur with water in bowl and let sit until grains are softened and liquid is fully absorbed, 20 to 40 minutes.

4. Heat remaining 1 tablespoon oil in 12-inch skillet over medium heat until shimmering. Add onion and cook until softened, 5 minutes. Stir in garlic, oregano, cinnamon, cayenne, and remaining ½ teaspoon salt, and cook until fragrant, about 30 seconds. Off heat, stir in bulgur, tomatoes, ¾ cup Pecorino, pine nuts, and vinegar and let sit until heated through, about 1 minute. Season with salt and pepper to taste.

5. Return eggplant cut side up to rimmed baking sheet. Using 2 forks, gently push eggplant flesh to sides to make room for filling. Mound bulgur mixture into eggplant halves and pack lightly with back of spoon. Sprinkle with remaining ¼ cup Pecorino. (Stuffed eggplant can be refrigerated for up to 24 hours. To serve, increase cooking time to 10 to 12 minutes.) Bake on upper rack until cheese is melted, 5 to 10 minutes. Sprinkle with parsley and serve warm or at room temperature.

Whole-Wheat Pasta with Italian Sausage and Fennel

Serves 4 to 6   FAST

Why This Recipe Works This pasta dish puts fennel front and center and builds a whole meal around its unique flavor. Fennel is a traditional and classic flavoring for Italian sausage, usually in the form of fennel seeds in the sausage mixture. Here, we upped the ante by adding fresh fennel slices, which we sautéed with plenty of garlic and a not-shy amount of red pepper flakes in the fat left in the pan from cooking the sweet sausage. The sauce had such bold flavor that we decided to put it over whole-wheat pasta, which has a distinctively full, nutty flavor and a firmer texture than regular spaghetti. Starch from the pasta cooking water thickened the sauce nicely and helped it cling to the spaghetti. Pine nuts contributed nutty crunch to the dish, and a sprinkling of freshly grated Pecorino Romano at the end added a salty tang to this hearty pasta dish that's quick enough for any weeknight.

8 ounces sweet Italian sausage, casings removed
1 fennel bulb, stalks discarded, bulb halved, cored, and sliced thin
¾ teaspoon table salt, divided, plus salt for cooking pasta
¼ cup extra-virgin olive oil
6 garlic cloves, minced
½ teaspoon red pepper flakes
½ cup pine nuts, toasted and chopped
½ cup chopped fresh basil
2 tablespoons lemon juice
1 pound whole-wheat spaghetti
Grated Pecorino Romano cheese

1. Cook sausage in 12-inch nonstick skillet over medium-high heat, breaking up any large pieces with wooden spoon, until well browned, about 5 minutes. Using slotted spoon, transfer sausage to paper towel–lined plate.

2. Add fennel and ¼ teaspoon salt to fat left in skillet and cook over medium heat until softened, about 5 minutes. Add oil, garlic, pepper flakes, and remaining ½ teaspoon salt to skillet and cook until fragrant, about 30 seconds. Off heat, stir in pine nuts, basil, lemon juice, and browned sausage.

3. Meanwhile, bring 4 quarts water to boil in large pot. Add pasta and 1 tablespoon salt and cook, stirring often, until tender. Reserve ¾ cup cooking water, then drain pasta and return it to pot. Add sausage mixture and reserved cooking water and toss to combine. Season with salt to taste. Serve with Pecorino.

Braised Halibut with Fennel and Tarragon

Serves 4 `FAST`

Why This Recipe Works The sweet flavor of fennel is a perfect complement to mild, perfectly cooked fish. Fennel is especially delicious when braised because it takes on a silky texture and deeper anise flavor, so we decided to pair it with braised halibut, as it would be easy enough to cook the vegetables with the fish to create a simple one-pan meal. To avoid overcooking the side of the halibut fillets that would be submerged in liquid, we precooked one side of the fillets in butter, intending to flip them over for braising. Shallots were a natural partner for the fennel and also complemented the mild fish; we softened the vegetables in the skillet before pouring in white wine. With the vegetables buffering the skillet's direct heat, we returned the fish to the skillet raw side down, covered the skillet, and let the fish and vegetables cook gradually and take on the braising liquid's bright flavors. Preparing a lush sauce was as easy as reducing the cooking liquid (and adding some lemon for zing). A sprinkling of fresh tarragon made for a lively presentation. We prefer halibut for this recipe, but a similar firm-fleshed white fish, such as striped bass or sea bass, that is between ¾ and 1 inch thick can be substituted. To ensure that your fish cooks evenly, purchase fillets that are similarly shaped and uniformly thick. You will need a 12-inch skillet with a tight-fitting lid for this recipe.

- 4 (6- to 8-ounce) skinless halibut fillets, ¾ to 1 inch thick
- 1 teaspoon table salt, divided
- 6 tablespoons unsalted butter
- 2 fennel bulbs, stalks discarded, bulbs halved, cored, and sliced thin
- 4 shallots, halved and sliced thin
- ¾ cup dry white wine
- 1 teaspoon lemon juice, plus lemon wedges for serving
- 1 tablespoon minced fresh tarragon

1. Sprinkle halibut with ½ teaspoon salt. Melt butter in 12-inch skillet over low heat. Place halibut in skillet skinned side up, increase heat to medium, and cook, shaking skillet occasionally, until butter begins to brown (fish should not brown), 3 to 4 minutes. Using spatula, carefully transfer halibut to large plate, raw side down.

2. Add fennel, shallots, and remaining ½ teaspoon salt to skillet and cook, stirring frequently, until vegetables begin to soften, 2 to 4 minutes. Add wine and bring to gentle simmer. Place halibut, raw side down, on top of vegetables. Cover skillet and cook, adjusting heat to maintain gentle simmer, until halibut registers 135 to 140 degrees, 10 to 14 minutes. Remove skillet from heat and, using 2 spatulas, transfer halibut and vegetables to serving platter or individual plates. Tent with aluminum foil.

3. Cook liquid left in skillet over high heat until thickened, 2 to 3 minutes. Off heat, stir in lemon juice and season with salt and pepper to taste. Spoon sauce over halibut and sprinkle with tarragon. Serve immediately, passing lemon wedges separately.

VARIATIONS

Braised Halibut with Carrots and Cilantro
Substitute 1 pound carrots, peeled and shaved with vegetable peeler lengthwise into ribbons, for fennel. Add ½ teaspoon ground coriander with shallots. Increase lemon juice to 1½ teaspoons. Substitute cilantro for tarragon.

Braised Halibut with Leeks and Mustard
Substitute 1 pound leeks, white and light green parts only, halved lengthwise, sliced thin, and washed thoroughly, for fennel and shallots. Add 1 teaspoon Dijon mustard with leeks. Substitute parsley for tarragon.

Teriyaki Stir-Fried Garlic Scapes with Chicken

Serves 4

Why This Recipe Works The sinuous green stems that grow from the neck of garlic, garlic scapes can be found in early summer farmers' markets and even some supermarkets. You can grill the scapes or blend them into pesto, but we wanted a dish that showcased their grassy, mild garlic flavor and crisp-tender texture. A stir-fry proved ideal for this. We paired the scapes with chicken and earthy cremini mushrooms. A teriyaki stir-fry sauce beautifully tied together all the components. For a sauce with the right balance of sweet, savory, and acidic notes, we combined soy sauce, oyster sauce, dry sherry, and sugar, with red pepper flakes for some subtle heat. "Velveting" the chicken with a mixture of cornstarch, flour, toasted sesame oil, and soy sauce encouraged the sauce to cling to the chicken. To promote browning, we sautéed the chicken in batches. Then we gave the mushrooms a head start in the pan and added the scapes, letting them develop some char before adding a healthy amount of fresh ginger. Finally, we added everything back to the skillet and poured in our sauce, which thickened and evenly cloaked the vegetables and chicken.

Sauce

- ⅓ cup water
- ¼ cup chicken broth
- 1 tablespoon soy sauce
- 1 tablespoon dry sherry
- 1 tablespoon oyster sauce
- 1 teaspoon sugar
- 1 teaspoon cornstarch
- ¼ teaspoon red pepper flakes

Stir-Fry

- 2 tablespoons toasted sesame oil
- 1 tablespoon cornstarch
- 1 tablespoon all-purpose flour
- 1 tablespoon soy sauce
- 1 pound boneless, skinless chicken breasts, trimmed, halved lengthwise, and sliced ¼ inch thick
- 1 teaspoon plus 2 tablespoons vegetable oil, divided
- 1 tablespoon grated fresh ginger
- 8 ounces cremini mushrooms, trimmed and sliced thin
- 12 ounces garlic scapes, trimmed and cut into 2-inch lengths
- 2 tablespoons chopped fresh basil

1. For the sauce Whisk all ingredients together in bowl; set aside.

2. For the stir-fry Whisk sesame oil, cornstarch, flour, and soy sauce in medium bowl until smooth, then stir in chicken. In separate bowl, combine 1 teaspoon vegetable oil and ginger.

3. Heat 2 teaspoons vegetable oil in 12-inch nonstick skillet over high heat until just smoking. Add half of chicken mixture, breaking up any clumps, and cook, without stirring, for 1 minute. Stir chicken and continue to cook until lightly browned, about 30 seconds; transfer to clean bowl. Repeat with 2 teaspoons vegetable oil and remaining chicken mixture; transfer to bowl.

4. Heat remaining 2 teaspoons vegetable oil in now-empty skillet over high heat until just smoking. Add mushrooms and cook, stirring frequently, until tender and well browned, about 5 minutes. Add garlic scapes and cook until well charred, 2 to 4 minutes.

5. Push vegetables to sides of skillet. Add ginger-oil mixture to center and cook, mashing mixture into skillet, until fragrant, about 30 seconds. Stir ginger-oil mixture into vegetables.

6. Return chicken and any accumulated juices to skillet and toss to combine. Add sauce and cook, stirring constantly, until chicken and vegetables are evenly coated and sauce is thickened, about 30 seconds. Off heat, sprinkle with basil. Serve.

Farmers' Market Find Garlic

Garlic falls into two primary categories: soft-neck and hard-neck. Soft-neck garlic is prolific, more heat-tolerant, and stores well, so it's the favored commercially available garlic. But hard-neck garlic, which is the original cultivated type, is considered superior in flavor. You may find multiple cultivars at farmers' markets. **Green garlic**, which can take the place of scallions or spring onions in many recipes, is young garlic with tender green leaves that is available early in the season before the bulbs have fully formed. **Garlic scapes** are the long, slim flower stems that grow from the tops of hard-neck garlic; farmers remove them to encourage the plant to direct its energy toward growing a plump bulb. Raw scapes have a mild flavor that's grassier and less fiery than that of raw cloves. They can be pureed to make pesto, grilled, or stir-fried; their flavor becomes muted and sweet and their texture grows dense and meaty. Garlic scapes can be wrapped in paper towels in a plastic produce bag and refrigerated for up to three weeks.

Teriyaki Stir-Fried Garlic Scapes with Chicken

Stir-Fried Sichuan Green Beans

Serves 4 `FAST`

Why This Recipe Works The flavors of Sichuan-style green beans are irresistible: wrinkled, sweet beans seasoned with a small amount of flavorful pork and coated in a pungent sauce. The dish is spicy, aromatic, and tangy all at the same time, and it places the beans center-stage in tandem with the pork. In Chinese restaurants, the beans are usually deep-fried in a wok filled with oil, which produces their wrinkled appearance, slightly chewy texture, and intense flavor. To make this dish at home, we opted instead to stir-fry the beans until the skins began to shrivel. The time spent in the pan produced spotty charring, which resulted in a nice chewy texture and a deeper flavor that more than compensated for their not being deep-fried. To achieve the desired characteristic tanginess and modest heat in the sauce, we used dry mustard and sherry for their subtle tang and red pepper flakes and white pepper for their aromatic warmth and complex muskiness. The ground pork, already stir-fried with lots of garlic and ginger, absorbed the sauce perfectly, adding meaty richness. Some chopped scallions and a drizzle of sesame oil were the perfect finishing touches.

- 2 tablespoons soy sauce
- 2 tablespoons water
- 1 tablespoon dry sherry
- 1 teaspoon sugar
- ½ teaspoon cornstarch
- ¼ teaspoon white pepper
- ¼ teaspoon red pepper flakes
- ¼ teaspoon dry mustard
- 2 tablespoons vegetable oil
- 1 pound green beans, trimmed and cut into 2-inch lengths
- 4 ounces ground pork
- 3 garlic cloves, minced
- 1 tablespoon grated fresh ginger
- 3 scallions, white and light green parts only, sliced thin
- 1 teaspoon toasted sesame oil

1. Whisk soy sauce, water, sherry, sugar, cornstarch, pepper, pepper flakes, and mustard in small bowl until sugar dissolves; set aside.

2. Heat vegetable oil in 12-inch nonstick skillet over high heat until just smoking. Add green beans and cook, stirring frequently, until crisp-tender and skins are shriveled and blackened in spots, 5 to 8 minutes (reduce heat to medium-high if green beans begin to darken too quickly). Transfer green beans to large plate and cover loosely with aluminum foil to keep warm.

3. Reduce heat to medium-high and add pork to now-empty skillet. Cook, breaking pork into small pieces with wooden spoon, until no longer pink, about 2 minutes. Push pork to sides of skillet. Add garlic and ginger to center and cook, mashing mixture into skillet, until fragrant, 30 seconds. Stir mixture into pork; transfer to bowl.

4. Whisk sauce to recombine, then add to now-empty skillet. Cook over high heat until sauce is thickened and reduced slightly, about 15 seconds. Return green beans and pork to skillet and gently toss to coat with sauce. Off heat, stir in scallions and sesame oil. Serve immediately.

Pearl Couscous with Clams, Leeks, and Tomatoes

Serves 4

Why This Recipe Works A brothy bowl of clams, vegetables, and tiny pasta is ideal seaside comfort food. Mild, sweet leeks made the perfect base that would complement the briny flavor of the clams. For pasta, pearl couscous offered an appealing shape and texture and was easy to prepare. To avoid overpowering the flavor of the clams and leeks, we kept our remaining ingredients simple. We built a base by sautéing the leeks with garlic and fragrant tarragon, then added plenty of white wine to produce a fragrant cooking liquid. As a next step, we tried cooking our couscous and steaming the clams on top. But by the time the shells opened, the couscous had turned to mush and we couldn't access the pearls of pasta to fluff before serving. Our solution was to reverse the cooking order, first steaming the clams in the aromatic broth until they just opened, and then setting them aside so they wouldn't become rubbery. This freed up the pot to cook the couscous in our liquid—now flavored with the clam's juices—which we stretched with chicken broth. The couscous pearls came out perfectly, and their starch helped subtly thicken the broth. Fresh tomatoes and bright lemon zest enhanced the briny flavor and added more summertime appeal. We returned the clams to the pot, along with their juices, to let everything warm through before serving. A sprinkling of lightly licorice-flavored tarragon was the perfect finish to the dish. Serve with crusty bread.

- 2 tablespoons unsalted butter
- 1½ pounds leeks, white and light green parts only, halved lengthwise, sliced thin, and washed thoroughly
- 3 garlic cloves, minced
- 2 tablespoons minced fresh tarragon, divided
- 1 cup dry white wine

    4 pounds littleneck clams, scrubbed
2½ cups chicken broth
    2 cups pearl couscous
    3 tomatoes, cored, seeded, and chopped
    1 teaspoon grated lemon zest

1. Melt butter in Dutch oven over medium heat. Add leeks and cook until softened, about 4 minutes. Stir in garlic and 1 tablespoon tarragon and cook until fragrant, about 30 seconds. Stir in wine, increase heat to high, and bring to boil. Add clams, cover, and cook, stirring occasionally, until clams have opened, 5 to 7 minutes.

2. Using slotted spoon, transfer clams to large bowl and tent with aluminum foil; discard any clams that refuse to open. Reduce heat to medium, add chicken broth and couscous to pot, and bring to simmer. Cover and cook until couscous is nearly tender and some broth remains, 8 to 10 minutes.

3. Off heat, stir in tomatoes and lemon zest and season with salt and pepper to taste. Nestle clams and any accumulated juices into couscous mixture. Cover and let sit until heated through, about 5 minutes. Sprinkle with remaining 1 tablespoon tarragon and serve.

Thai-Style Chicken Salad Lettuce Wraps

Serves 4 to 6 `FAST` `NO COOK`

Why This Recipe Works Delicate heads of just-picked lettuce can be irresistible at the farmers' market and have uses beyond salads. Large, soft lettuce leaves can serve as wrappers for a light chicken salad, a perfect meal for a sweltering day. While a creamy chicken salad is always nice, we were drawn to the pungent flavors of a Thai-style salad with a classic balance of sour, salty, sweet, and hot flavors in the form of lime juice, fish sauce, brown sugar, and Thai chiles. Starting with our make-ahead Shredded Cooked Chicken (page 41) meant we didn't have to turn on the stove. Fresh mango added delightful juiciness and color, and multiple handfuls of herbs (mint, cilantro, and Thai basil) added incredible freshness. We then spooned the chicken salad into our lettuce cups to serve. If fresh Thai chiles are unavailable, substitute two serranos or one jalapeño. We like to serve this salad in leaves of Bibb lettuce to form lettuce cups, but it can also be served in leaves of green or red leaf lettuce or on a bed of greens. You can substitute rotisserie chicken for the poached chicken in this recipe.

Pearl Couscous with Clams, Leeks, and Tomatoes

Thai-Style Chicken Salad Lettuce Wraps

Dressing

- 3 tablespoons lime juice (2 limes)
- 1 shallot, minced
- 2 tablespoons fish sauce, plus extra for serving
- 1 tablespoon packed brown sugar
- 1 garlic clove, minced
- ¼ teaspoon red pepper flakes

Salad

- 1 recipe Shredded Cooked Chicken (page 41)
- 1 ripe mango, peeled, pitted, and cut into ¼-inch pieces
- ½ cup chopped fresh mint
- ½ cup chopped fresh cilantro
- ½ cup chopped fresh Thai basil
- 1 head Bibb, red leaf, or green leaf lettuce (8 ounces), leaves separated
- 2 Thai chilies, sliced thin

1. For the dressing Whisk all ingredients together in large bowl.

2. For the salad Add chicken to bowl with dressing and toss to coat. Add mango, mint, cilantro, and basil to bowl with chicken and toss to coat. Season with salt to taste. Serve salad at room temperature or cold in lettuce cups, passing Thai chiles and extra fish sauce separately.

Korean Sizzling Beef Lettuce Wraps

Serves 4 `FAST`

Why This Recipe Works This lighter take on ground beef tacos uses farm-fresh lettuce leaves to hold a satisfying filling. Our simple and fast riff is made on the stovetop, helping to keep the kitchen cool. To punch up the filling, we took inspiration from the sweet and savory flavor of Korean barbecue. We tossed browned ground beef with a quickly made umami-filled barbecue sauce of soy sauce, brown sugar, garlic, and toasted sesame oil. Quickly pickled cucumber added a refreshing crunchy topping and a superquick sriracha mayo added a little heat. Rice also makes a great accompanying filling for these lettuce wraps.

- 1 English cucumber, halved and sliced thin
- ¼ cup seasoned rice vinegar
- ¼ cup mayonnaise
- 2 tablespoons sriracha
- 3 tablespoons soy sauce
- 2 tablespoons packed brown sugar
- 4 garlic cloves, minced
- 1 tablespoon toasted sesame oil
- 1½ pounds 85 percent lean ground beef
- 1 head Bibb, green leaf, or red leaf lettuce (8 ounces), leaves separated

1. Combine cucumber and vinegar in bowl; set aside. Combine mayonnaise and sriracha in second bowl; set aside. Combine soy sauce, sugar, garlic, and oil in third bowl.

2. Cook beef in 12-inch nonstick skillet over high heat until any juices have evaporated and beef begins to fry in its own fat, 8 to 10 minutes. Add soy sauce mixture to skillet and cook until nearly evaporated, about 2 minutes. To serve, fill lettuce leaves with beef mixture and top with pickled cucumbers and sriracha mayonnaise.

Nettle Soup

Serves 4 to 6

Why This Recipe Works The nettle, sometimes called the "stinging nettle," is an herbaceous flowering plant that blooms in the spring but is available into the summer months. The prickly leaves from the nettle plant can be cooked and treated much like spinach. Cream of nettle soup is often the first recipe a new nettle forager (or farmers' market explorer) will try out. We wanted to create a soup that coaxed out and highlighted the unique, subtle character of the nettles. We started by blanching the nettles quickly and shocking them in ice water to preserve their green color. For the base, we landed on a mix of broth and water, which we infused with nettle flavor by using it as our blanching liquid. A small amount of Arborio rice, cooked in the broth, thickened the soup but had a neutral flavor. We loved the delicacy of the soup but had one qualm: The soup could cause a "stinging" sensation. We learned that while the stinging chemicals were completely deactivated, the sharp hairs had avoided full pulverization and could be irritating; this was easily fixed by straining the soup after we pureed it. We drizzled a bit of tangy crème fraîche over the top, sprinkled on crunchy pepitas, and ended up with a beautiful green soup with the essence of nettles. Always use thick kitchen gloves when handling fresh nettles, as their fine hairs can sting you or cause redness or itching. Be sure to set up the ice water bath before cooking the nettles; plunging them into the water after blanching ensures a brightly colored soup.

6	tablespoons crème fraîche
4	cups chicken or vegetable broth
6	ounces (12 packed cups) stinging nettles leaves
4	tablespoons unsalted butter
3	shallots, chopped
¼	teaspoon table salt
⅓	cup Arborio rice
3	sprigs fresh thyme
1	bay leaf
1½	tablespoons lemon juice
⅓	cup roasted, salted pepitas

1. Combine crème fraîche and 1 tablespoon water in bowl; set aside until ready to serve. Bring broth and 3 cups water to boil in Dutch oven over high heat. Meanwhile, fill large bowl halfway with ice and water.

2. Add nettles to boiling broth mixture and cook until nettles are wilted and tender, about 3 minutes. Drain nettles in fine-mesh strainer set over large bowl. Using rubber spatula, press nettles to release excess liquid; reserve blanching liquid. Transfer nettles to ice water and let sit until cool, about 3 minutes. Drain nettles and set aside.

3. Melt butter in now-empty pot over medium heat. Add shallots and salt and cook, stirring occasionally, until shallots are softened, about 3 minutes. Stir in reserved blanching liquid, rice, thyme sprigs, and bay leaf and bring to simmer. Cover, reduce heat to low, and cook until rice is very soft, about 30 minutes.

4. Discard thyme sprigs and bay leaf. Working in batches, process broth mixture and nettles in blender until smooth, about 2 minutes. Strain soup through fine-mesh strainer into clean pot and bring soup to simmer over medium heat. Adjust consistency of soup with additional water as needed. Stir in lemon juice and season with salt and pepper to taste. Drizzle individual portions with crème fraîche mixture and sprinkle with pepitas before serving.

HANDLING NETTLES

Always wear food-handling gloves (we recommend a double layer) and wash your hands well with warm soapy water afterward. If any of the little hairs cling to your skin, remove them with duct tape.

Korean Sizzling Beef Lettuce Wraps

Nettle Soup

Okra is a quintessential vegetable of the American South, where, evocatively, it is sometimes called "ladies' fingers." Native okra is becoming more and more available throughout the country, mainly in the late summer and early fall. You'll see green okra at many farmers' markets and you may even see a purple or red variety. Okra's vegetal flavor and delicate crunch is something like a cross between green beans and zucchini. For many, its most memorable characteristic is its unique texture. It has a rich, moist quality, but if cooked improperly, it can turn slimy. When cooking fresh whole pods using a dry-heat method such as searing, or when deep-frying, you needn't worry about excessive mucilage. For other cooking methods, salting the okra first helps reduce any sliminess. When shopping for okra, look for firm, unblemished pods no longer than 3 inches in length. Larger pods will often be tough, and no cooking method will prevent them from becoming slimy. Store fresh okra in a paper bag in the refrigerator for just a day or two.

Madras Okra Curry

Madras Okra Curry
Serves 4 to 6

Why This Recipe Works In Indian cuisine, okra has a long and varied history. Looking for an okra dish with main-course potential, we explored Indian treatments of the vegetable and found ourselves taken with a Madras-style okra curry with a plentiful, rich sauce, and okra pods that retained some of their fresh bite. For our version, we made a pantry-friendly sauce with onion, ginger, garlic, and coconut milk. Searing the okra whole—and not letting it stew in the sauce—kept it crisp-tender with an appealing texture, rather than letting it get slimy and mushy. Fresh cilantro sprigs and bright lime wedges balanced out our rich curry. We prefer the spicier flavor of Madras curry powder here, but you can substitute regular curry powder. Do not substitute frozen okra as it doesn't brown like fresh okra. Serve with Everyday White Rice (page 107).

- 6 tablespoons vegetable oil, divided
- 1½ pounds okra, stemmed
- 1 small onion, chopped fine
- 3 garlic cloves, minced
- 1 tablespoon grated fresh ginger
- 1 tablespoon Madras curry powder
- 2½ cups chicken or vegetable broth
- 1 cup canned coconut milk
- 2 teaspoons honey
- 1 teaspoon cornstarch
- ¼ teaspoon table salt
- 10 sprigs fresh cilantro, chopped
  Lime wedges

1. Heat 2 tablespoons oil in 12-inch skillet over medium-high heat until just smoking. Add half of okra to skillet and cook, stirring occasionally, until crisp-tender and well browned on most sides, 5 to 7 minutes; transfer to bowl. Repeat with 2 tablespoons oil and remaining okra; transfer to bowl. Let skillet cool slightly.

2. Heat remaining 2 tablespoons oil in now-empty skillet over medium heat until shimmering. Add onion and cook until softened, about 5 minutes. Stir in garlic, ginger, and curry powder and cook until fragrant, about 1 minute. Stir in broth, scraping up any browned bits, and bring to simmer. Cook, stirring occasionally, until reduced to 1¼ cups, 15 to 20 minutes.

3. Whisk coconut milk, honey, and cornstarch together in bowl to dissolve cornstarch, then whisk mixture into skillet. Bring to simmer and cook until slightly thickened, about 30 seconds. Stir in okra and any accumulated juices and salt and return to brief simmer to warm through. Season with salt and pepper to taste. Sprinkle with cilantro and serve with lime wedges.

Eggs Pipérade

Serves 6 to 8

Why This Recipe Works Peppers both sweet and hot overflow summer farmers' markets, and there are never enough ways to use them. One of the simplest and best is the Basque pepper and tomato sauté known as *pipérade*, which is often paired with scrambled eggs for an easy dinner. Pipérade delivers richness, acidity, and tempered heat from a combination of fresh sweet peppers, tomatoes, and fragrant spices like paprika. Since we had already perfected our scrambled egg technique, we focused our attention on achieving a great pipérade. We liked a combination of red bell peppers and Italian Cubanelle peppers for their sweetness and delicate fresh flavor. By using canned peeled tomatoes, we avoided chewy bits of tomato skin; draining the tomatoes of most of their juice kept the dish from being watery. Onion, garlic, bay leaf, and thyme offered aromatic complexity; a bit of sherry vinegar brought the flavors into focus. While in many pipérade recipes the eggs are scrambled with the vegetable mixture, we found that the liquid from the produce caused the eggs to cook up stringy and wet rather than fluffy and creamy. We opted to cook the eggs separately and then plate the two elements alongside one another to preserve the clean yellow color of the eggs. We prefer to make this dish with Cubanelle peppers, which are chartreuse in color and look similar to banana peppers; if you can't find them, you can substitute green bell peppers. You will need a 12-inch nonstick skillet with a tight-fitting lid for this recipe.

5 tablespoons extra-virgin olive oil, divided
1 large onion, chopped
1 bay leaf
2 teaspoons table salt, divided
4 garlic cloves, minced
2 teaspoons paprika
1 teaspoon minced fresh thyme or ¼ teaspoon dried
¾ teaspoon red pepper flakes
3 red bell peppers, stemmed, seeded, and cut into ½-inch-wide strips
3 Cubanelle peppers, stemmed, seeded, and cut into ½-inch-wide strips
1 (14-ounce) can whole peeled tomatoes, drained with ¼ cup juice reserved, chopped
3 tablespoons minced fresh parsley, divided
2 teaspoons sherry vinegar
12 large eggs
2 tablespoons water
¼ teaspoon pepper

1. Heat 3 tablespoons oil in 12-inch nonstick skillet over medium heat until shimmering. Add onion, bay leaf, and ½ teaspoon salt and cook until onion is softened and lightly browned, 5 to 7 minutes. Stir in garlic, paprika, thyme, and pepper flakes and cook until fragrant, about 1 minute. Add bell peppers, Cubanelle peppers, and 1 teaspoon salt, cover, and cook, stirring occasionally, until peppers begin to soften, about 10 minutes.

2. Reduce heat to medium-low. Uncover, add tomatoes and reserved juice, and cook, stirring occasionally, until mixture appears dry and peppers are tender but not mushy, 10 to 12 minutes. Off heat, discard bay leaf. Stir in 2 tablespoons parsley and vinegar and season with salt and pepper to taste. Transfer to bowl and cover to keep warm.

3. Beat eggs, water, pepper, and remaining ½ teaspoon salt with fork in bowl until thoroughly combined and mixture is pure yellow; do not overbeat.

4. Wipe skillet clean with paper towels. Heat remaining 2 tablespoons oil in now-empty skillet over medium heat until shimmering. Add egg mixture and, using rubber spatula, constantly and firmly scrape along bottom and sides of skillet until eggs begin to clump and spatula leaves trail on bottom of skillet, 1½ to 2 minutes.

5. Reduce heat to low and gently but constantly fold eggs until clumped and slightly wet, 30 to 60 seconds. Off heat, sprinkle with remaining 1 tablespoon parsley and serve immediately with pepper mixture.

Pepper and Onion Frittata with Arugula Salad

Serves 4 `FAST`

Why This Recipe Works The frittata is sometimes called the lazy man's omelet. After all, it contains the same ingredients but doesn't require folding the eggs around the filling, a skill that can take practice to master. We've got nothing against cooking eggs for dinner, and an easy frittata packed with seasonal produce and served with a fresh green salad sounded like a wonderful meal to throw into the summertime dinner rotation. We whisked a dozen eggs with some half-and-half, which tenderized the eggs and added a bit of richness. For the vegetables, we chose sweet, colorful bell peppers (red were our favorite here) and cooked them in a skillet with some aromatic onion until browned. We then poured in the egg mixture and let the eggs cook, scraping the pan to encourage curds as we would with scrambled eggs. When the eggs had begun to firm up but were still quite wet, we transferred the skillet to the oven to bake until the eggs were perfectly set up and browned.

To make this a meal, we also put together a simple salad of arugula, briny olives, and creamy goat cheese to serve alongside. Leftover fritatta also tastes great cold the next day.

12 large eggs
 3 tablespoons half-and-half
 ½ teaspoon table salt
 ¼ teaspoon pepper
3½ tablespoons extra-virgin olive oil, divided
 2 red bell peppers, stemmed, seeded, and sliced thin
 1 small onion, sliced thin
 2 ounces (2 cups) baby arugula
 ¼ cup pitted kalamata olives, halved
 2 teaspoons lemon juice
 2 ounces goat cheese, crumbled (½ cup)

1. Adjust oven rack to upper-middle position and heat oven to 375 degrees. Whisk eggs, half-and-half, salt, and pepper in large bowl until well combined.

2. Heat 1½ tablespoons oil in 12-inch ovensafe nonstick skillet over medium-high heat until shimmering. Add bell peppers and onion and cook until spotty brown, about 8 minutes. Reduce heat to medium-low and stir in egg mixture. Cook, using spatula to scrape bottom of skillet, until large curds form but eggs are still very wet, about 2 minutes. Smooth egg mixture into even layer. Transfer skillet to oven and bake until surface is golden brown, 8 to 10 minutes. Slide frittata onto serving platter.

3. Toss arugula, olives, lemon juice, and remaining 2 tablespoons oil together in bowl. Season with salt and pepper to taste. Pile salad alongside frittata, sprinkle with goat cheese, and serve warm or at room temperature.

Pasta with Pesto, Potatoes, and Green Beans

Serves 6

Why This Recipe Works The idea of combining potatoes and pasta—two starches—might seem unusual, but this dish from Liguria, Italy, is a classic way to serve pesto. We jumped at the chance to use just-dug potatoes in a satisfying, herbaceous pasta along with green beans and basil pesto. In addition to heartiness, the potatoes offer the key to the sauce's creaminess, due to the starch they release when vigorously mixed with the pasta. We found that waxy red potatoes made a creamy, but not grainy, sauce, as just enough of their starch sloughed off during stirring. Some recipes call for cooking the potatoes, green beans,

and pasta simultaneously in the same pot, but this often results in one or more elements being overcooked. Cooking them separately made the dish more foolproof. The generous amount of basil in our bright pesto lent even more color and fresh summer flavor. Since trofie, the traditional pasta shape for this dish, is hard to find, we typically reach for gemelli. Penne or rigatoni can also be used.

 ¼ cup pine nuts
 3 garlic cloves, unpeeled
 1 pound red potatoes, peeled and cut into ½-inch pieces
 ¾ teaspoon table salt, divided, plus salt for cooking potatoes and pasta
12 ounces green beans, trimmed and cut into 1½-inch lengths
 2 cups fresh basil leaves
 1 ounce Parmesan cheese, grated (½ cup)
 7 tablespoons extra-virgin olive oil
 1 pound gemelli or trofie
 2 tablespoons unsalted butter, cut into ½-inch pieces and chilled
 1 tablespoon lemon juice
 ½ teaspoon pepper

1. Toast pine nuts and garlic in 10-inch skillet over medium heat, stirring frequently, until pine nuts are golden and fragrant and garlic darkens slightly, 3 to 5 minutes. Transfer to bowl and let cool. Peel garlic and chop coarse; return to bowl.

2. Bring 3 quarts water to boil in large pot. Add potatoes and 1 tablespoon salt and cook until potatoes are tender but still hold their shape, 9 to 12 minutes. Using slotted spoon, transfer potatoes to rimmed baking sheet. (Do not discard water.)

3. Meanwhile, bring ½ cup water and ¼ teaspoon salt to boil in now-empty skillet over medium heat. Add green beans, cover, and cook until tender, 5 to 8 minutes. Drain green beans and transfer to sheet with potatoes.

4. Process basil, Parmesan, oil, pine nuts and garlic, and remaining ½ teaspoon salt in food processor until smooth, about 1 minute.

5. Bring potato cooking water back to boil, add pasta, and cook, stirring often, until al dente. Set colander in large bowl. Drain pasta in colander and return pasta to pot, reserving cooking water in bowl. Add butter, lemon juice, pepper, potatoes and green beans, pesto, and 1¼ cups reserved cooking water to pot and stir vigorously with rubber spatula until sauce takes on creamy appearance. Adjust consistency with remaining reserved cooking water as needed and season with salt and pepper to taste. Serve immediately.

Roasted Chicken with Radishes, Spinach, and Bacon

Serves 4

Why This Recipe Works An unusual combination of spicy, crunchy, bright red radishes and earthy, soft spinach turn a standard dinner of roasted chicken into something special and rustically summery. We first browned the chicken pieces in rendered bacon fat on the stovetop for a luxuriously rich flavor, and then transferred the skillet to the oven to finish cooking. Cooking the chicken in the bacon fat ensured both crisp, crackly skin and a subtle smoky flavor. After it came out of the oven, we removed the chicken from the skillet and then quickly cooked the radishes and spinach in the remaining fat for savory depth and seamlessly cohesive flavors throughout the dish. To ensure crispy chicken skin, resist the urge to move the chicken while browning it in step 2.

- 2 slices bacon, chopped fine
- 3 pounds bone-in chicken pieces (split breasts cut in half, drumsticks, and/or thighs), trimmed
- 2 teaspoons table salt, divided
- ¾ teaspoon pepper
- 10 ounces radishes, trimmed and quartered
- 2 garlic cloves, minced
- 10 ounces (10 cups) baby spinach
- 2 teaspoons lemon juice, plus lemon wedges for serving

1. Adjust oven rack to middle position and heat oven to 450 degrees. Cook bacon in 12-inch oven-safe skillet over medium-high heat until crispy, about 5 minutes. Using slotted spoon, transfer bacon to paper towel–lined plate; set aside for serving.

2. Pat chicken dry with paper towels and sprinkle with 1½ teaspoons salt and pepper. Heat fat left in skillet over medium-high heat until just smoking. Brown chicken skin side down, about 5 minutes. Flip chicken, transfer skillet to oven, and roast until breasts register 160 degrees and drumsticks/thighs register 175 degrees, about 15 minutes.

3. Remove skillet from oven. Being careful of hot skillet handle, transfer chicken skin side up to serving platter and let rest while preparing vegetables.

4. Pour off all but 1 tablespoon fat from skillet. Add radishes and remaining ½ teaspoon salt and cook over medium-high heat until tender, about 2 minutes. Stir in garlic and cook until fragrant, about 30 seconds. Stir in spinach, 1 handful at a time, and cook until wilted, about 2 minutes. Off heat, stir in lemon juice and reserved bacon. Serve chicken with vegetables and lemon wedges.

Pasta with Pesto, Potatoes, and Green Beans

Roasted Chicken with Radishes, Spinach, and Bacon

Pan-Roasted Cod with Amarillo Sauce

Serves 4

Why This Recipe Works We often associate tomatillos with bright green sauces. Here, however, we combined the tangy, almost citrusy tasting fruit with dried chiles and masa harina to make a rust-orange amarillo sauce—a lively mole-style sauce from Oaxaca—and used it to dress up mild white fish. Although typically aji amarillo chiles are used, most modern recipes use guajillos, which gave the mole a pleasant, mild heat. We complemented that chile flavor with some warm spices. Our aromatic base benefited from the addition of clam juice, which provided a subtle seafood backbone. We cooked the tomatillos only briefly to preserve their bright, tart flavor, before pureeing the sauce in the blender. We cooked the cod fillets simply, sprinkling them with just a bit of sugar to accelerate browning. This shortened the cooking time and ensured that the fish didn't dry out. Black sea bass, haddock, hake, and pollack are good substitutes for the cod. Because most fish fillets differ in thickness, some pieces may finish cooking before others—be sure to immediately remove any fillet that reaches 135 degrees. You will need a 12-inch ovensafe nonstick skillet for this recipe. Serve with corn tortillas, if desired.

Pan-Roasted Cod with Amarillo Sauce

- 3 guajillo chiles, stemmed, seeded, and torn into ½-inch pieces (6 tablespoons)
- 2 tablespoons vegetable oil, divided
- 1 onion, chopped
- 4 garlic cloves, peeled
- ½ teaspoon dried oregano
- ¼ teaspoon whole cumin seeds
- ⅛ teaspoon ground cloves
- ⅛ teaspoon ground allspice
- 3 tablespoons masa harina
- 1 (8-ounce) bottle clam juice
- 8 ounces tomatillos, husks and stems removed, rinsed well and dried, and cut into ½-inch pieces
- 6 sprigs cilantro
- 1¼ teaspoons table salt, divided
- ½ teaspoon pepper, divided
- 4 (6- to 8-ounce) skinless cod fillets, 1 inch thick
- ½ teaspoon sugar

1. Toast guajillos in medium saucepan over medium heat, stirring frequently, until fragrant, 2 to 6 minutes; transfer to bowl. Heat 1 tablespoon oil in now-empty saucepan over medium heat until shimmering. Add onion and cook until softened, about 5 minutes. Stir in garlic, oregano, cumin seeds, cloves, and allspice and cook until fragrant, about 30 seconds. Stir in masa harina and cook for 1 minute. Slowly whisk in clam juice, scraping up any browned bits and smoothing out any lumps.

2. Stir in guajillos, tomatillos, cilantro sprigs, ½ teaspoon salt, and ¼ teaspoon pepper. Bring to simmer and cook until tomatillos begin to soften, about 3 minutes. Carefully transfer mixture to blender and process until smooth, 1 to 2 minutes. Return to clean pot and cover to keep warm.

3. Adjust oven rack to middle position and heat oven to 425 degrees. Pat cod dry with paper towels, sprinkle with remaining ¾ teaspoon salt and remaining ¼ teaspoon pepper, then sprinkle sugar lightly over 1 side of each fillet.

4. Heat remaining 1 tablespoon oil in 12-inch ovensafe nonstick skillet over high heat until just smoking. Lay fillets sugared side down in skillet and press lightly to ensure even contact with skillet. Cook until browned, 1 to 1½ minutes.

5. Turn fillets over using 2 spatulas and transfer skillet to oven. Roast cod until fish flakes apart when gently prodded with paring knife and registers 135 degrees, 7 to 10 minutes. Serve with sauce.

Tomatillo and Pinto Bean Nachos
Serves 4 to 6

Why This Recipe Works Nachos for dinner...why not? While the beloved shareable appetizer can be drab when laden with meat and cheese, we set our sights on a lighter, fresher version that would satisfy as a summer meal. We started by preparing a bright, boldly seasoned sauce featuring juicy, mouth-puckering tomatillos. We chopped the tomatillos and sautéed them with corn, aromatics, and spices. To avoid ending up with soggy chips, we cooked the tomatillo mixture until all the moisture had evaporated, and we sprinkled pepper Jack cheese on the chips first to act as a protective layer. Rather than heavy refried beans, we chose canned pinto beans, and sprinkled them between each layer of filling. Fresh jalapeños added more flavor and texture. When everything was layered, we transferred the nachos to the oven to melt the cheese. Once the nachos came out, we added sliced radishes for fresh, cooling crunch. Our homemade Fresh Tomato Salsa (page 234) and Guacamole (page 235) are key for making this recipe stand out, but if you are short on time you can use store-bought. If using fresh corn, you will need one to two ears.

- 1 tablespoon vegetable oil
- 1 onion, chopped fine
- 3 garlic cloves, minced
- 2 teaspoons minced fresh oregano or ½ teaspoon dried
- 1 teaspoon ground coriander
- 1 teaspoon table salt
- 12 ounces tomatillos, husks and stems removed, rinsed well and dried, cut into ½-inch pieces
- 1 cup fresh or frozen corn, thawed
- 8 ounces tortilla chips
- 12 ounces pepper Jack cheese, shredded (3 cups)
- 1 (15-ounce) can pinto beans, rinsed
- 2 jalapeño chiles, stemmed and sliced thin
- 3 radishes, trimmed and sliced thin
- 1½ cups Guacamole (page 235)
- 1 cup Fresh Tomato Salsa (page 234)
- ½ cup sour cream
  Lime wedges

1. Adjust oven rack to middle position and heat oven to 400 degrees. Heat oil in 12-inch nonstick skillet over medium heat until shimmering. Add onion and cook until softened, about 5 minutes. Stir in garlic, oregano, coriander, and salt and cook until fragrant, about 30 seconds. Add tomatillos and corn, reduce heat to medium-low, and cook until tomatillos have released all their moisture and mixture is nearly dry, about 10 minutes. Let cool slightly.

2. Spread half of tortilla chips evenly into 13 by 9-inch baking dish. Sprinkle 1½ cups pepper Jack evenly over chips, then top evenly with half of tomatillo mixture, followed by half of beans and, finally, half of jalapeños. Repeat layering with remaining chips, pepper Jack, tomatillo mixture, beans, and jalapeños. Bake until cheese is melted and just beginning to brown, 7 to 10 minutes.

3. Let nachos cool for 2 minutes, then sprinkle with radishes. Drop scoops of guacamole, salsa, and sour cream around edges of nachos. Serve immediately, passing lime wedges separately.

Fresh Tomato Soup with Basil
Serves 4 to 6

Why This Recipe Works We thought we knew tomato soup: velvety smooth, creamy, comforting, and perfect for a cold winter day. But there's another kind of tomato soup—made without cream, bursting with fresh tomato essence—whose flavors are more appealing come summertime. Flavored with onions, garlic, and basil, it's perfect for using a surplus of ripe tomatoes. We concentrated the tomato flavor and evaporated excess moisture by roasting the tomatoes, then pureed them in a blender. We salted our reserved chopped tomatoes to soften them and added them at the end of cooking, boosting the tomato flavor. The success of this recipe depends on using ripe, in-season tomatoes.

- 6 pounds ripe tomatoes, cored (5 pounds quartered, 1 pound cut into ½-inch pieces)
- 2 onions, chopped
- 9 garlic cloves, peeled (8 whole, 1 minced)
- 3 tablespoons extra-virgin olive oil
- ¾ teaspoon table salt, divided
- ¼ teaspoon sugar
- 1 cup chopped fresh basil

1. Adjust oven rack to upper-middle position and heat oven to 450 degrees. Combine quartered tomatoes, onions, whole garlic cloves, oil, ½ teaspoon salt, and sugar in large roasting pan. Roast until tomatoes are brown in spots, about 1½ hours, stirring halfway through roasting. Let tomato mixture cool slightly.

2. Meanwhile, combine basil, diced tomatoes, minced garlic, and remaining ¼ teaspoon salt in bowl and let sit for 30 minutes. Working in batches, process roasted tomato mixture in food processor until smooth; transfer to large saucepan. Stir in diced tomato mixture and bring to simmer over medium heat. Cook until diced tomatoes are slightly softened, about 5 minutes. Season with salt and sugar to taste. Serve.

Pan-Seared Shrimp with Tomatoes and Avocado

Serves 4 FAST

Why This Recipe Works This fast and flavorful stovetop shrimp dish is enhanced with a spicy fresh tomato sauce. Shrimp need only about 2 minutes to cook through, which doesn't allow a lot of time to develop flavor. We made our shrimp tasty by using a very hot skillet to get some browning. We sprinkled the shrimp with a little sugar before cooking; the sugar caramelized and helped to develop a nice sear on the exterior of the shrimp. We also found it important to cook the shrimp in a single layer in the skillet (which meant two batches for this recipe); if the shrimp are crowded they will steam rather than brown. Letting the shrimp finish cooking gently in the tomato sauce off the heat kept them tender. If your shrimp are larger or smaller, be sure to alter the cooking time in step 2 accordingly. This dish is fairly spicy; to make it milder, use less chipotle chile. Serve with lime wedges.

 3 tomatoes, cored, seeded, and cut into ½-inch pieces
 6 scallions, white and green parts separated and sliced thin
 ¼ cup minced fresh cilantro
 3 garlic cloves, minced
 1 tablespoon lime juice
 1 teaspoon minced canned chipotle chile in adobo sauce
 ½ teaspoon table salt
 2 tablespoons vegetable oil, divided
 1½ pounds extra-large shrimp (21 to 25 per pound), peeled, deveined, and tails removed
 ¼ teaspoon pepper
 ⅛ teaspoon sugar
 1 avocado, halved, pitted, and cut into ½-inch pieces

1. Combine tomatoes, scallion whites, cilantro, garlic, lime juice, chipotle, and ¼ teaspoon salt in bowl.

2. Heat 1 tablespoon oil in 12-inch nonstick skillet over high heat until just smoking. Pat shrimp dry with paper towels and sprinkle with pepper, sugar, and remaining ¼ teaspoon salt. Add half of shrimp to skillet in single layer and cook, without stirring, until spotty brown and edges turn pink, about 1 minute. Remove skillet from heat, flip shrimp, and let sit until opaque in very center, about 30 seconds; transfer to bowl. Repeat with remaining 1 tablespoon oil and remaining shrimp; transfer to bowl.

3. Return now-empty skillet to high heat, add tomato mixture, and cook until tomatoes soften slightly, about 1 minute. Off heat, stir in shrimp, cover, and let sit until shrimp are cooked through, 1 to 2 minutes. Season with salt and pepper to taste, transfer to serving platter, and sprinkle with scallion greens and avocado. Serve.

Fresh Tomato Galette

Serves 4 to 6 MAKE AHEAD

Why This Recipe Works A rustic tomato tart is a fantastic way to showcase the sweetness and flavor of ripe, in-season tomatoes. But baking with tomatoes can be tricky due to their unpredictable juice. To bring out the best in the tomatoes' flavor, capture their appealing juiciness, and avoid a soggy tart, we salted the slices and let them sit in a colander to draw out excess moisture before building the tart. Shaking the colander well after a 30-minute rest helped ensure that no added liquid entered the crust. For added protection against sogginess, we lined the inside of the crust with a layer of mustard and shredded Gruyère cheese, which kept the crust crisp. Some chopped fresh basil sprinkled over the top enhanced this tart's summer appeal. Sharp cheddar cheese can be used in place of the Gruyère, if desired.

 1½ cups (7½ ounces) all-purpose flour
 2 teaspoons table salt, divided
 10 tablespoons unsalted butter, cut into ½-inch pieces and chilled
 6–7 tablespoons ice water
 1½ pounds mixed tomatoes, cored and sliced ¼ inch thick
 1 shallot, sliced thin
 2 tablespoons extra-virgin olive oil
 1 teaspoon minced fresh thyme
 1 garlic clove, minced
 ¼ teaspoon pepper
 2 teaspoons Dijon mustard
 3 ounces Gruyère cheese, shredded (¾ cup)
 2 tablespoons grated Parmesan cheese
 1 large egg, lightly beaten
 1 tablespoon chopped fresh basil

1. Process flour and ½ teaspoon salt in food processor until combined, about 3 seconds. Scatter butter over top and pulse until mixture resembles coarse crumbs, about 10 pulses.

Fresh Tomato Galette

5. Shake colander well to rid tomatoes of excess juice. Combine tomatoes, shallot, oil, thyme, garlic, pepper, and remaining ½ teaspoon salt in now-empty bowl. Spread mustard over dough, leaving 1½-inch border. Sprinkle Gruyère in even layer over mustard. Shingle tomatoes and shallot on top of Gruyère in concentric circles, keeping within 1½-inch border. Sprinkle Parmesan over tomato mixture.

6. Carefully grasp 1 edge of dough and fold up about 1 inch over filling. Repeat around circumference of tart, overlapping dough every 2 inches, gently pinching pleated dough to secure. Brush folded dough with egg (you won't need it all).

7. Bake until crust is golden brown and tomatoes are bubbling, 45 to 50 minutes. Transfer sheet to wire rack and let galette cool for 10 minutes. Using metal spatula, loosen galette from parchment and carefully slide onto wire rack; let cool until just warm, about 20 minutes. Sprinkle with basil. Cut into wedges and serve warm or at room temperature.

Penne with Garden Vegetable Sauce

Serves 4 to 6   MAKE AHEAD

Why This Recipe Works A fresh summer vegetable pasta sauce sounds easy, but it's actually more difficult than you'd think. The trick was figuring out how to get distinct pieces of crisp-tender vegetables with a saucy, flavorful base. We gathered a variety of veggies—zucchini, cherry tomatoes, carrots, and bell peppers—and started sautéing. However, the flavors became too homogeneous and the vegetables cooked at different rates; some were mushy, while others were too crisp. We had better luck when we cooked the vegetables in two batches. First, we sautéed the tomatoes, onion, carrots, and bell peppers until the tomatoes started to break down and created a pasta-clinging sauciness that enveloped the just-tender carrots and peppers. Porcini mushrooms, tomato paste, garlic, oregano, and just a little bit of red pepper flakes gave depth to the sauce without overwhelming the delicate vegetable flavors. We added the zucchini toward the very end to keep them from overcooking and turning mushy. A hefty portion of chopped basil, added just before serving, ensured that our dinner tasted—and looked— like it was fresh from the garden.

Transfer to large bowl. Sprinkle 6 tablespoons ice water over flour mixture. Using rubber spatula, stir and press dough until it sticks together, adding up to 1 tablespoon more ice water if dough doesn't come together.

2. Turn out dough onto lightly floured counter, form into 4-inch disk, wrap tightly in plastic wrap, and refrigerate for 1 hour. (Wrapped dough can be refrigerated for up to 2 days or frozen for up to 1 month.)

3. Toss tomatoes and 1 teaspoon salt together in second large bowl. Transfer tomatoes to colander and set colander in sink. Let tomatoes drain for 30 minutes.

4. Adjust oven rack to lower-middle position and heat oven to 375 degrees. Line rimmed baking sheet with parchment paper. Let chilled dough sit on counter to soften slightly, about 10 minutes, before rolling. Roll dough into 12-inch circle on lightly floured counter, then transfer to prepared sheet (dough may run up lip of sheet slightly; this is OK).

¼ cup extra-virgin olive oil
1 pound cherry tomatoes, halved
2 yellow bell peppers, stemmed, seeded, and chopped
1 onion, chopped
2 carrots, peeled and shredded
1½ teaspoons table salt, plus salt for cooking pasta
½ teaspoon pepper
½ ounce dried porcini mushrooms, rinsed and minced
3 tablespoons tomato paste
4 garlic cloves, minced
1 tablespoon minced fresh oregano or 1 teaspoon dried
⅛ teaspoon red pepper flakes
½ cup vegetable broth
2 zucchini, quartered lengthwise and sliced ¼ inch thick
1 pound penne
¼ cup chopped fresh basil
Grated Parmesan cheese

1. Heat oil in Dutch oven over medium heat until shimmering. Add tomatoes, bell peppers, onion, carrots, 1½ teaspoons salt, and pepper and cook, stirring occasionally, until vegetables are softened and tomatoes are broken down, 8 to 10 minutes.

2. Stir in mushrooms, tomato paste, garlic, oregano, and pepper flakes and cook until fragrant, about 1 minute. Stir in broth and bring to simmer. Stir in zucchini and cook until zucchini is just tender, about 4 minutes. (Sauce can be refrigerated for up to 2 days. Bring to room temperature before continuing with recipe.)

3. Meanwhile, bring 4 quarts water to boil in large pot. Add pasta and 1 tablespoon salt and cook, stirring often, until al dente. Reserve ½ cup cooking water, then drain pasta and return it to pot. Add sauce and toss to combine. Stir in basil and season with salt and pepper to taste. Add reserved cooking water as needed to adjust consistency. Serve with Parmesan.

RINSING DRIED PORCINI

To remove dirt or grit from dried porcini, place porcini in fine-mesh strainer and run under water, using your fingers as needed to rub grit out of crevices.

One-Pan Pork Tenderloin and Panzanella Salad

Serves 4 to 6

Why This Recipe Works Panzanella is a hearty salad of summer vegetables and toasted bread, which soaks up the dressing, becoming just a little chewy. We built a deceptively easy one-pan meal around the salad by adding roast pork tenderloin and a mix of fresh and roasted vegetables for complexity. First, we placed two pork tenderloins on a rimmed baking sheet and brushed them with a mixture of balsamic vinegar, brown sugar, and whole-grain mustard that complemented the sweet nuances of the pork and gave it some color. A bit of cornstarch ensured that the glaze stuck. Then, we surrounded the tenderloins with 1-inch pieces of summer squash, red onion, bell pepper, and baguette and roasted it all until the pork was rosy in the center, the vegetables were tender, and the bread was toasted and crunchy. While the tenderloins rested, we tossed the bread and vegetables with fresh cucumber, cherry tomatoes, and basil. To dress our salad, we whisked up a mustard-balsamic vinaigrette, adding salty capers along with a splash of their brine for a kick. Sourdough bread can be used in place of the baguette.

3 tablespoons balsamic vinegar, divided
2 tablespoons whole-grain mustard, divided
1 tablespoon packed brown sugar
1 teaspoon cornstarch
2 (12 to 16-ounce) pork tenderloins, trimmed
1½ teaspoons plus ⅛ teaspoon table salt, divided
1⅛ teaspoons pepper, divided
1 (12-inch) baguette, cut into 1-inch pieces
1 red onion, cut into 1-inch pieces
1 red bell pepper, stemmed, seeded, and cut into ½-inch-wide strips
1 yellow summer squash, quartered lengthwise and cut into 1-inch pieces
½ cup extra-virgin olive oil, divided
1 tablespoon capers, rinsed, plus 1 tablespoon brine
1 garlic clove, minced
½ seedless English cucumber, quartered lengthwise and cut into ½-inch pieces
6 ounces cherry tomatoes, halved
½ cup chopped fresh basil

1. Adjust oven rack to middle position and heat oven to 450 degrees. Whisk 1 tablespoon vinegar, 1 tablespoon mustard, sugar, and cornstarch in bowl until no lumps of cornstarch remain.

2. Pat tenderloins dry with paper towels and sprinkle with 1 teaspoon salt and ½ teaspoon pepper. Place tenderloins in center of rimmed baking sheet (it's OK if they are touching) and brush tops and sides with all of vinegar mixture.

3. Toss baguette, onion, bell pepper, squash, ¼ cup oil, ½ teaspoon salt, and ½ teaspoon pepper in large bowl until baguette and vegetables are well coated with oil. Distribute vegetable mixture around tenderloins on sheet. Roast until pork registers 140 degrees, about 20 minutes, stirring vegetable mixture halfway through roasting.

4. Meanwhile, whisk capers and brine, garlic, remaining 2 tablespoons vinegar, remaining 1 tablespoon mustard, remaining ⅛ teaspoon salt, remaining ⅛ teaspoon pepper, and remaining ¼ cup oil together in now-empty bowl.

5. Transfer tenderloins to carving board, tent with aluminum foil, and let rest for 10 minutes. While tenderloins rest, add cucumber, tomatoes, 6 tablespoons basil, and vegetable mixture to bowl with caper dressing and toss to combine.

6. Transfer salad to serving platter. Slice tenderloins ½ inch thick and arrange over salad. Sprinkle with remaining 2 tablespoons basil. Serve.

One-Pan Pork Tenderloin and Panzanella Salad

Red Curry Noodles with Shrimp, Summer Squash, and Bell Peppers

Serves 4

Why This Recipe Works This vibrant shrimp-and-noodle dish is packed with bold, contrasting flavors typical of Thai curries, as well as some of our favorite summer produce. The rice noodles were easy to prepare: The key was to soak them in boiling water until pliable but not fully tender, since they would finish cooking later in the curry sauce. We browned the peppers and then the squash in a skillet before setting them aside together in a bowl. For an easy but complex-tasting sauce, we bloomed red curry paste (a blend of red chiles, garlic, lemon grass, galangal, makrut lime, and coriander) in oil to release its flavor. After seasoning it with fish sauce and sugar, we added equal parts coconut milk and chicken broth, which gave us a deeply flavored sauce that wasn't too rich. We let the shrimp cook in the sauce and then removed them before adding the rice noodles and simmering them until tender. Fresh lime juice and cilantro balanced the sauce's richness and a sprinkle of peanuts added crunch. You can substitute small, firm zucchini for the yellow summer squash and red, orange, or yellow bell peppers for the green bell peppers.

Red Curry Noodles with Shrimp, Summer Squash, and Bell Peppers

12 ounces (¼-inch-wide) rice noodles
1 tablespoon vegetable oil, divided
2 green bell peppers, stemmed, seeded, and cut into
   1-inch pieces
2 yellow summer squash, quartered lengthwise and
   sliced crosswise ¼ inch thick
2 tablespoons red curry paste
2 tablespoons fish sauce
1 tablespoon packed brown sugar
1 cup canned coconut milk
1 cup chicken or vegetable broth
1 pound large shrimp (26 to 30 per pound),
   peeled and deveined
2 tablespoons lime juice, plus lime wedges for serving
¼ cup minced fresh cilantro
¼ cup dry-roasted peanuts, chopped

1. Bring 3 quarts water to boil in large saucepan. Place noodles in large bowl. Pour boiling water over noodles. Stir, then let soak until noodles are soft and pliable but not fully tender, 8 to 10 minutes, stirring once halfway through soaking. Drain noodles and rinse under cold running water until water runs clear. Drain well and set aside.

2. Heat ½ teaspoon oil in 12-inch nonstick skillet over high heat until just smoking. Add bell peppers and cook, stirring occasionally, until spotty brown, 2 to 3 minutes; transfer to large serving bowl. Add ½ teaspoon oil to now-empty skillet, and heat until just smoking. Add squash and cook, stirring occasionally, until spotty brown, 3 to 4 minutes; transfer to bowl with peppers.

3. Add remaining 2 teaspoons oil to now-empty skillet and reduce heat to medium. Add curry paste and cook, stirring constantly, until fragrant, about 30 seconds. Stir in fish sauce and sugar and cook for 30 seconds. Stir in coconut milk and broth and bring to simmer. Reduce heat to medium-low and gently simmer until sauce is thickened and reduced by about a quarter, 8 to 10 minutes.

4. When sauce has reduced, stir shrimp into sauce and cook, stirring occasionally, until shrimp are opaque, 2 to 3 minutes. Using slotted spoon, transfer shrimp to bowl with peppers and squash.

5. Return sauce to simmer over high heat. Add noodles and cook, stirring often, until sauce has thickened and noodles are well coated and tender, 2 to 3 minutes. Off heat, stir in lime juice. Transfer noodle mixture to bowl with shrimp and vegetables and toss to combine. Sprinkle with cilantro and peanuts. Serve with lime wedges.

Skillet Summer Vegetable Lasagna

Serves 4 FAST

Why This Recipe Works This deconstructed take on lasagna offers a comfort-food meal with a fraction of lasagna's typical fuss and incorporates plenty of seasonal produce. We started by layering sautéed onion and garlic, broken-up lasagna noodles, and diced tomatoes and their juice in the pan. The tomatoes' juice—mixed with a little water—let the noodles cook through and soften. Fresh flavor and bright color came in the form of zucchini and yellow summer squash. Adding the vegetables to the skillet halfway through cooking ensured that both the pasta and the vegetables were perfectly cooked. We avoided weighing down our lasagna with a large amount of melted cheese; instead, we swirled in some milky ricotta for creaminess and then dolloped on more just before serving. A handful of chopped basil added herbal depth. You will need a 12-inch skillet with a tight-fitting lid for this recipe.

2 tablespoons extra-virgin olive oil
1 onion, chopped fine
4 garlic cloves, minced
1 (28-ounce) can diced tomatoes, drained with
   juice reserved
1 teaspoon table salt
10 curly-edged lasagna noodles, broken into
   2-inch lengths
1 small zucchini, cut into ½-inch pieces
1 small yellow summer squash, cut into ½-inch pieces
¼ cup shredded fresh basil
8 ounces (1 cup) whole-milk ricotta cheese, divided

1. Heat oil in 12-inch skillet over medium-high heat until shimmering. Add onion and cook until softened, about 5 minutes. Add garlic and cook until fragrant, about 30 seconds.

2. Add water as needed to reserved tomato juice to equal 2 cups. Add tomato liquid and salt to skillet. Scatter noodles over onion-garlic mixture, layer tomatoes over noodles, and bring to simmer. Reduce heat to medium and cook, covered, stirring occasionally, for 10 minutes. Stir in zucchini and squash. Cook until noodles and squash are tender, about 8 minutes.

3. Add basil and ½ cup ricotta to skillet and stir until sauce is creamy. Season with salt and pepper to taste. Dollop remaining ½ cup ricotta over noodles and serve.

Summer Vegetable Gratin

Serves 4 `MAKE AHEAD`

Why This Recipe Works Casseroles aren't just for winter. A crispy, crumb-topped gratin is a wonderful way to use up an abundance of summer produce and makes for a meal by itself. But every version we tried ended up a watery, soggy mess thanks to the liquid the vegetables released. To remedy this, we salted the vegetables and let them drain before assembling the casserole. We baked the dish uncovered so that the remaining excess moisture would evaporate in the oven. Layering the tomatoes on top exposed them to more heat so that they ended up roasted and caramelized. To flavor the vegetables, we tossed them with an aromatic garlic-thyme oil and drizzled more oil over the top. Fresh bread crumbs tossed with Parmesan and shallots made an elegant topping. The success of this recipe depends on high-quality vegetables. Buy zucchini and summer squash of roughly the same diameter. We like the combination, but you can also use just zucchini or summer squash.

- 1 pound zucchini, sliced ¼ inch thick
- 1 pound yellow summer squash, sliced ¼ inch thick
- 1 teaspoon table salt, divided, plus salt for salting vegetables
- 1½ pounds ripe tomatoes, cored and sliced ¼ inch thick
- 6 tablespoons extra-virgin olive oil, divided
- 2 onions, halved and sliced thin
- 1 tablespoon minced fresh thyme
- 2 garlic cloves, minced
- ½ teaspoon pepper
- 1 slice hearty white sandwich bread, torn into quarters
- 2 ounces Parmesan cheese, grated (1 cup)
- 2 shallots, minced
- ¼ cup chopped fresh basil

1. Toss zucchini and summer squash with 1 teaspoon salt and let drain in colander until vegetables release at least 3 tablespoons liquid, about 45 minutes. Pat zucchini and summer squash dry firmly with paper towels, removing as much liquid as possible.

2. Spread tomatoes out over paper towel–lined baking sheet, sprinkle with ½ teaspoon salt, and let sit for 30 minutes. Thoroughly pat tomatoes dry with more paper towels.

3. Heat 1 tablespoon oil in 12-inch nonstick skillet over medium heat until shimmering. Add onions and remaining ½ teaspoon salt and cook, stirring occasionally, until softened and dark golden brown, 20 to 25 minutes; set aside.

4. Combine 3 tablespoons oil, thyme, garlic, and pepper in bowl; set aside. Process bread in food processor until finely ground, about 10 seconds, then combine with 1 tablespoon oil, Parmesan, and shallots in separate bowl; set aside.

Skillet Summer Vegetable Lasagna

Summer Vegetable Gratin

5. Adjust oven rack to upper-middle position and heat oven to 400 degrees. Grease 3-quart gratin dish (or 13 by 9-inch baking dish) with remaining 1 tablespoon oil. Toss zucchini and summer squash with half of garlic-oil mixture and arrange in greased baking dish. Sprinkle evenly with caramelized onions, then top with tomato slices, overlapping them slightly. Spoon remaining garlic-oil mixture evenly over tomatoes. (Gratin and bread-crumb mixture can be refrigerated separately for up to 24 hours.)

6. Bake until vegetables are tender and tomatoes are starting to brown on edges, 40 to 45 minutes. Remove baking dish from oven and increase heat to 450 degrees. Sprinkle bread-crumb mixture evenly over top and continue to bake gratin until bubbling and cheese is lightly browned, 5 to 10 minutes. Let cool for 10 minutes, then sprinkle with basil and serve warm or at room temperature.

ASSEMBLING A SUMMER VEGETABLE GRATIN

1. Arrange zucchini and summer squash in greased gratin dish.

2. Sprinkle caramelized onions evenly over top.

3. Lay tomato slices over onions, overlapping them slightly, and spoon remaining garlic-oil mixture evenly over top.

4. Bake until vegetables are tender and tomatoes are starting to brown on edges, then sprinkle bread-crumb mixture evenly over top. Bake until cheese is lightly browned, 5 to 10 minutes.

Pan-Seared Skirt Steak with Zucchini and Scallion Sauce

Serves 4 FAST

Why This Recipe Works Scallions are one of the onion family's best-known players, but these long-stalked alliums are often relegated to garnish status or thrown into dishes as an afterthought. Seeing the beautiful scallion bunches cropping up at the summer farm stands, we decided to give them a more prominent position in a steak dinner tied together by a vibrant scallion sauce. We chose thin, quick-cooking skirt steak, which we seared in a nonstick skillet until well browned but still tender and juicy. To make use of another farm-fresh vegetable, we sautéed zucchini until browned and softened. For our vibrant sauce, we processed scallion greens with parsley, olive oil, some water, red wine vinegar, and Dijon mustard, seasoning it with a bit of salt and pepper. Stirring the minced scallion whites in with the zucchini and then stirring in some of the sauce gave the side dish maximum scallion flavor. We served the zucchini with thinly sliced strips of the skirt steak, drizzling the remaining scallion sauce over the top.

- 1 cup fresh parsley leaves
- 8 scallions, white parts minced, green parts cut into 1-inch pieces
- ½ cup plus 3 tablespoons extra-virgin olive oil, divided
- ¼ cup water
- 4 teaspoons red wine vinegar
- 1 tablespoon Dijon mustard
- 1¼ teaspoons table salt, divided
- ¾ teaspoon pepper, divided
- 1 (1½-pound) skirt steak, trimmed and cut into 4 equal pieces
- 2 zucchini, cut into ½-inch pieces

1. Process parsley, scallion greens, ½ cup oil, water, vinegar, mustard, ½ teaspoon salt, and ½ teaspoon pepper in blender until smooth, about 1 minute. Set aside.

2. Pat steak dry with paper towels and sprinkle with remaining ¾ teaspoon salt and remaining ¼ teaspoon pepper. Heat 2 tablespoons oil in 12-inch nonstick skillet over medium-high heat until just smoking. Cook steak until well browned and meat registers 125 degrees (for medium-rare), about 2 minutes per side. Transfer steak to carving board and tent with foil.

3. Add remaining 1 tablespoon oil and zucchini to now-empty skillet and cook over medium-high heat, without stirring, until zucchini is well browned, about 2 minutes. Stir and continue to cook until softened, about 3 minutes. Off heat, add scallion whites and 2 tablespoons scallion sauce and stir to coat zucchini. Season with salt and pepper to taste. Slice steak thin against grain. Serve with zucchini and remaining scallion sauce.

Cod Baked in Foil with Zucchini and Tomatoes

Serves 4

Why This Recipe Works In addition to being easy and minimizing cleanup, baking fish and vegetables in a foil packet is a surprisingly flavorful cooking method. With no water to dilute flavor, everything steams in its own juices, yielding flaky fish and tender but firm vegetables flavored with their aromatic essences. We used mild white cod here, as more assertive salmon or tuna would overpower the vegetables. Placing the packets on the lower-middle rack of the oven close to the heat source concentrated the exuded liquid and deepened its flavor. Since the vegetables needed to cook at the same rate as the fish, dense vegetables were out of the running, as were absorbent vegetables such as eggplant, which cooked into mush. Light, clean-tasting zucchini, sliced into thin rounds, was a winner and a chopped tomato and olive oil "salsa" added sweetness, richness, and moisture that would encourage steaming. A splash of white wine gave the resulting broth added complexity. Black sea bass, haddock, hake, and pollack are good substitutes for the cod. If using a substitute, start checking for doneness at 12 minutes.

1 pound zucchini, sliced ¼ inch thick
1 teaspoon table salt, divided, plus salt for salting vegetables
2 plum tomatoes, cored, seeded, and chopped
2 tablespoons extra-virgin olive oil
2 garlic cloves, minced
1 teaspoon minced fresh oregano
⅛ teaspoon red pepper flakes
⅛ teaspoon plus ¼ teaspoon pepper, divided
¼ cup dry white wine
4 (6- to 8-ounce) skinless cod fillets, 1 inch thick
¼ cup chopped fresh basil
Lemon wedges

Cod Baked in Foil with Zucchini and Tomatoes

1. Toss zucchini with ½ teaspoon salt in bowl, transfer to colander, and let sit for 30 minutes. Pat zucchini dry thoroughly with paper towels, pressing firmly on each slice to remove as much liquid as possible. Meanwhile, combine tomatoes, oil, garlic, oregano, pepper flakes, ⅛ teaspoon pepper, and ¼ teaspoon salt in bowl.

2. Adjust oven rack to lower-middle position and heat oven to 450 degrees. Cut eight 12-inch sheets of aluminum foil; arrange four flat on counter. Shingle zucchini in center of foil sheets and sprinkle with wine. Pat cod dry with paper towels, sprinkle with remaining ¾ teaspoon salt and remaining ¼ teaspoon pepper, and place on top of zucchini. Spread tomato mixture over fish.

3. Place second square of foil on top of cod. Press edges of foil together and fold over several times until packet is well sealed and measures about 7 inches. Place packets on rimmed baking sheet, overlapping as needed.

4. Bake packets until cod registers 135 degrees, about 15 minutes. (To check temperature, poke thermometer through foil of 1 packet and into fish.) Carefully open foil, allowing steam to escape away from you. Using thin metal spatula, gently slide cod and vegetables, and any accumulated juices, onto plate. Sprinkle with basil and serve with lemon wedges.

Vegetable and Orzo Tian
Serves 4

Why This Recipe Works This striking casserole layers creamy orzo under a colorful topping of zucchini, summer squash, and tomatoes. While impressive, it's relatively hands-off, utilizing just one pan. To accomplish that, we had to get the pasta and vegetables to finish cooking simultaneously without sacrificing taste or texture. We achieved perfectly cooked pasta by tightly shingling the vegetables on the orzo's surface, trapping the moisture within the casserole. Shallots and garlic mixed into the orzo provided aromatic depth and sweetness. Parmesan added creaminess, and oregano and red pepper flakes lent floral, spicy notes. The pasta and vegetables were close to perfection after 20 minutes in a hot oven. We sprinkled more Parmesan on top and broiled the casserole briefly for an appealing presentation; chopped basil made for a fresh, bright finish. Look for vegetables with similar-size circumferences so that they are easy to shingle into the dish.

- 3 ounces Parmesan cheese, grated (1½ cups), divided
- 1 cup orzo
- 2 shallots, minced
- 3 tablespoons minced fresh oregano or 1 teaspoon dried
- 3 garlic cloves, minced
- ¼ teaspoon table salt
- ⅛ teaspoon red pepper flakes
- 1 zucchini, sliced ¼ inch thick
- 1 yellow summer squash, sliced ¼ inch thick
- 1 pound plum tomatoes, cored and sliced ¼ inch thick
- 1¾ cups vegetable broth
- 1 tablespoon extra-virgin olive oil
- 2 tablespoons chopped fresh basil

1. Adjust oven rack to middle position and heat oven to 425 degrees. Combine ½ cup Parmesan, orzo, shallots, oregano, garlic, salt, and pepper flakes in bowl. Spread mixture evenly into broiler-safe 3-quart gratin dish (or 13 by 9-inch baking dish). Alternately shingle zucchini, squash, and tomatoes in tidy rows on top of orzo.

2. Carefully pour broth over top of vegetables. Bake until orzo is just tender and most of broth is absorbed, about 20 minutes.

3. Remove dish from oven, adjust oven rack 9 inches from broiler element, and heat broiler. Drizzle vegetables with oil, season with salt and pepper, and sprinkle with remaining 1 cup Parmesan. Broil until nicely browned and bubbling around edges, about 5 minutes.

4. Remove dish from oven and let rest for 10 minutes. Sprinkle with basil and serve warm or at room temperature.

Zucchini Noodles with Roasted Tomatoes and Cream Sauce

Zucchini Noodles with Roasted Tomatoes and Cream Sauce
Serves 4

Why This Recipe Works If you haven't yet been convinced to spiralize vegetable noodles, this recipe will change your mind. Zucchini noodles are coated with a rich, creamy sauce and topped with an abundance of sweet, garlicky roasted tomatoes. Roasting the zucchini noodles rid them of excess moisture and ensured that the sauce wouldn't get washed out. Tossing the cherry tomatoes with tomato paste before roasting helped them to develop a caramelized depth of flavor, and five cloves of garlic gave them a supersavory boost. If possible, use smaller zucchini or summer squash, which have thinner skins and fewer seeds. Store-bought zucchini "noodles" can be used here if you don't have a spiralizer. You'll need 2½ pounds of noodles. Serve with crusty bread, if desired.

- 3 pounds zucchini or yellow summer squash, trimmed
- 1 pound cherry tomatoes
- 1 shallot, sliced thin
- 5 garlic cloves, minced

3 tablespoons extra-virgin olive oil, divided
1 tablespoon tomato paste
1 teaspoon dried oregano
¼ teaspoon red pepper flakes
1½ teaspoons table salt, divided
¾ teaspoon pepper, divided
1 cup heavy cream
2 tablespoons unsalted butter
1½ ounces Parmesan cheese, grated (¾ cup)
¼ cup fresh basil leaves, torn into ½-inch pieces

1. Adjust oven racks to upper-middle and lower-middle positions and heat oven to 375 degrees. Line 2 rimmed baking sheets with aluminum foil; set aside. Using spiralizer, cut zucchini into ⅛-inch-thick noodles, cutting noodles into 12-inch lengths with kitchen shears as you spiralize (about every 4 to 5 revolutions).

2. Toss tomatoes, shallot, garlic, 2 tablespoons oil, tomato paste, oregano, pepper flakes, ½ teaspoon salt, and ¼ teaspoon pepper together in bowl. Spread tomato mixture on 1 prepared sheet and place on lower rack. Roast, without stirring, until tomatoes are softened and skins begin to shrivel, about 25 minutes.

3. Meanwhile, toss zucchini with remaining 1 tablespoon oil, ½ teaspoon salt, and ¼ teaspoon pepper; spread on second prepared sheet and roast on upper rack until tender, 20 to 25 minutes. Transfer roasted zucchini to colander and shake to remove any excess liquid.

4. Bring cream and butter to simmer in large saucepan over medium heat. Reduce heat to low and simmer gently until mixture measures ⅔ cup, 12 to 15 minutes. Stir in Parmesan, remaining ½ teaspoon salt, and remaining ¼ teaspoon pepper and cook over low heat, stirring often, until Parmesan is melted.

5. Add zucchini to cream sauce and gently toss to combine. Transfer to serving platter and top with roasted tomatoes. Season with salt and pepper to taste, and sprinkle with basil. Serve noodles immediately.

Soupe au Pistou
Serves 6

Why This Recipe Works *Soupe au pistou* is a Provençal soup chock-full of vegetables, creamy white beans, and fragrant herbs—a celebration of the produce that returns to the markets in early summer. Virtually any vegetable can go in the pot, but we liked the flavors and varying shades of green provided by leeks, green beans, and zucchini. Traditional recipes use water for the base, but supplementing the water with vegetable broth promised a more rounded, flavorful base. Canned white beans

were convenient, and adding the bean liquid to the pot gave the soup body and a flavor that evoked long-simmered versions. This soup is always served with a dollop of pistou, France's answer to pesto. We simply whirled basil, Parmesan, olive oil, and garlic in a food processor. If you cannot find haricots verts (thin green beans), substitute regular green beans and cook them for an extra minute or two. You can substitute small shells or ditalini for the orecchiette (the cooking times may vary slightly). Serve with crusty bread.

Pistou
¾ cup fresh basil leaves
1 ounce Parmesan cheese, grated (½ cup)
⅓ cup extra-virgin olive oil
1 garlic clove, minced

Soup
1 tablespoon extra-virgin olive oil
1 leek, white and light green parts only, halved lengthwise, sliced ½ inch thick, and washed thoroughly
1 celery rib, cut into ½-inch pieces
1 carrot, peeled and sliced ¼ inch thick
½ teaspoon table salt
2 garlic cloves, minced
3 cups vegetable or chicken broth
3 cups water
½ cup orecchiette or other short pasta
8 ounces haricots verts or green beans, trimmed and cut into ½-inch lengths
1 (15-ounce) can cannellini or navy beans
1 small zucchini, halved lengthwise, seeded, and cut into ¼-inch pieces
1 large tomato, cored, seeded, and cut into ¼-inch pieces

1. For the pistou Process all ingredients in food processor until smooth, scraping down sides of bowl as needed, about 15 seconds. (Pistou can be refrigerated for up to 4 hours.)

2. For the soup Heat oil in Dutch oven over medium heat until shimmering. Add leek, celery, carrot, and salt and cook until vegetables are softened, 8 to 10 minutes. Stir in garlic and cook until fragrant, about 30 seconds. Stir in broth and water and bring to simmer.

3. Stir in pasta and simmer until slightly softened, about 5 minutes. Stir in haricots verts and simmer until bright green but still crunchy, 3 to 5 minutes. Stir in cannellini beans and their liquid, zucchini, and tomato and simmer until pasta and vegetables are tender, about 3 minutes. Season with salt and pepper to taste. Serve, topping individual portions with generous tablespoon of pistou.

CHAPTER 5

Keep Cool with Countertop Cooking

■ FAST (30 minutes or less total time)   ■ MAKE AHEAD
Photos (from left to right): Slow-Cooker Classic Barbecued Spareribs;
Pressure-Cooker Braised Striped Bass with Zucchini and Tomatoes

Slow-Cooker Lemony Chicken and Rice with Spinach and Feta

Slow-Cooker Jerk Chicken

Slow-Cooker Thai Chicken with Asparagus and Mushrooms

Serves 4
Cooking Time: 2 to 3 hours on low

Why This Recipe Works Ordering takeout is tempting on a hot summer's night. By using the slow cooker and a few shortcut ingredients, we created a boldly flavored Thai chicken dinner that was better than takeout and nearly as easy to get on the table. We swapped Thai red curry paste for an overwhelming list of traditional seasonings and enriched it with coconut milk to add more flavor to our sauce. Stirring in a portion of the coconut milk just before serving helped to deepen the coconut flavor. Bone-in chicken breasts stayed moist and tender as the sauce simmered and the rich flavors melded. We liked fresh asparagus and delicate shiitakes in this dish, but they turned to mush in the slow cooker. Luckily, just 5 minutes in the microwave turned them tender, so we added them at the end. We brightened the sauce with lime juice, fish sauce, and fresh cilantro and a little instant tapioca helped to thicken the sauce to a consistency that went perfectly with rice. Check the chicken's temperature after 2 hours of cooking and continue to monitor until it registers 160 degrees. You will need a 4- to 7-quart oval slow cooker for this recipe. This recipe will only work in a traditional slow cooker.

1   cup canned coconut milk, divided
2   tablespoons Thai red curry paste
1   tablespoon instant tapioca
1½ teaspoons table salt, divided
1¼ teaspoons pepper, divided
4   (12-ounce) bone-in split chicken breasts, skin removed, trimmed
1   pound asparagus, trimmed and cut into 1-inch lengths
1   pound shiitake mushrooms, stemmed and sliced ½ inch thick
1   tablespoon vegetable oil
2   tablespoons lime juice, plus extra for seasoning
1   tablespoon fish sauce, plus extra for seasoning
¼   cup minced fresh cilantro

1. Whisk ½ cup coconut milk, curry paste, tapioca, ½ teaspoon salt, and ½ teaspoon pepper together in slow cooker. Sprinkle chicken with remaining 1 teaspoon salt and remaining ¾ teaspoon pepper and arrange, skinned side up, in even layer in slow cooker. Cover and cook until chicken registers 160 degrees, 2 to 3 hours on low.

2. Microwave asparagus, mushrooms, and oil in bowl, stirring occasionally, until vegetables are tender, about 5 minutes.

3. Transfer chicken to serving platter and tent loosely with aluminum foil. Stir vegetables, remaining ½ cup coconut milk, lime juice, and fish sauce into cooking liquid and let sit until heated through, about 5 minutes. Stir in cilantro and season with extra lime juice and fish sauce to taste. Spoon sauce over chicken and serve.

Slow-Cooker Lemony Chicken and Rice with Spinach and Feta

Serves 4
Cooking Time: 4 to 5 hours on low

Why This Recipe Works For a chicken and rice dinner big on flavor but light on prep, we relied on the slow cooker and Mediterranean flavors. We included feta for its briny tang, lemon for brightness, and baby spinach for freshness and color. To start, we microwaved aromatics to develop their flavor before adding them to the slow cooker. We then added meaty chicken thighs and cooked them until tender. Once cooked, we removed the thighs and stirred in instant rice, then nestled the chicken on top and continued until the rice was cooked. Be sure to use instant rice (sometimes labeled minute rice); traditional rice takes much longer to cook and won't work here. You will need a 4- to 7-quart slow cooker for this recipe. This recipe will only work in a traditional slow cooker.

- 1 onion, chopped fine
- 2 tablespoons extra-virgin olive oil
- 3 garlic cloves, minced
- 2 teaspoons minced fresh oregano or ½ teaspoon dried
- 1 teaspoon table salt, divided
- ½ cup chicken broth
- 8 (5- to 7-ounce) bone-in chicken thighs, skin removed, trimmed
- ½ teaspoon pepper
- 1½ cups instant white rice
- 4 ounces (4 cups) baby spinach
- 1 teaspoon grated lemon zest plus 2 tablespoons juice
- 2 ounces feta cheese, crumbled (½ cup)
- 2 tablespoons minced fresh parsley

1. Microwave onion, oil, garlic, oregano, and ½ teaspoon salt in bowl, stirring occasionally, until onion is softened, about 5 minutes; transfer to slow cooker. Stir in broth. Sprinkle chicken with remaining ½ teaspoon salt and pepper and nestle into slow cooker. Cover and cook until chicken is tender, 4 to 5 hours on low.

2. Transfer chicken to plate. Stir rice into slow cooker. Arrange chicken on top of rice, adding any accumulated juices. Cover and cook on high until rice is tender, 20 to 30 minutes.

3. Transfer chicken to serving platter and tent loosely with aluminum foil. Gently stir spinach into slow cooker, 1 handful at a time, and let sit until wilted, about 5 minutes. Stir in lemon zest and juice, and season with salt and pepper to taste. Transfer rice to dish with chicken and sprinkle with feta and parsley. Serve.

Slow-Cooker Jerk Chicken

Serves 4 to 6
Cooking Time: 4 to 5 hours on low

Why This Recipe Works Jerk chicken hails from Jamaica and its island appeal makes it a great recipe for summer. We used the slow cooker to create an authentic-tasting jerk chicken—with fiery chiles, warm spices, and fragrant herbs—without firing up the grill. First, we made a smooth paste of the traditional mix of aromatics—scallions, garlic, habanero chiles (also called Scotch bonnets), and ginger—along with molasses, thyme, allspice, salt, and oil to bind everything together. We coated the chicken with some of this paste before cooking and saved the rest for basting later on. Following a slow braise in the slow cooker, we finished the tender chicken under the broiler, basting it with more of the paste until it was lightly charred and crisp. If you can't find habaneros, substitute 2 to 4 jalapeño chiles. For even more heat, include the chile seeds. You will need a 4- to 7-quart slow cooker for this recipe. This recipe will only work in a traditional slow cooker.

- 8 scallions, chopped
- ¼ cup vegetable oil
- 2 habanero chiles, stemmed and seeded
- 1 (1-inch) piece ginger, peeled and sliced into ¼-inch-thick rounds
- 2 tablespoons molasses
- 3 garlic cloves, peeled
- 1 tablespoon dried thyme
- 2 teaspoons ground allspice
- 1 teaspoon table salt
- 4 pounds bone-in chicken pieces (thighs and/or drumsticks), trimmed
  Lime wedges

1. Process scallions, oil, habaneros, ginger, molasses, garlic, thyme, allspice, and salt in food processor until smooth, about 30 seconds.

2. Lightly coat slow cooker with vegetable oil spray. Transfer ½ cup scallion mixture to prepared slow cooker; reserve remaining mixture. Add chicken to slow cooker and turn to coat evenly with scallion mixture. Cover and cook until chicken is tender, 4 to 5 hours on low.

3. Adjust oven rack 6 inches from broiler element and heat broiler. Set wire rack in aluminum foil-lined rimmed baking sheet and coat with vegetable oil spray. Transfer chicken to prepared rack; discard cooking liquid. Broil chicken until browned, about 10 minutes, flipping chicken halfway through broiling.

4. Brush chicken with half of reserved scallion mixture and continue to broil until lightly charred, about 5 minutes, flipping and brushing chicken with remaining scallion mixture halfway through broiling. Serve with lime wedges.

PREPARING CHILES SAFELY

Wear gloves when working with very hot peppers like habaneros to avoid direct contact with oils that supply heat. Wash your hands, knife, and cutting board well after prepping chiles.

Slow-Cooker Sweet and Tangy Pulled Chicken

Slow-Cooker Sweet and Tangy Pulled Chicken

Serves 4
Cooking Time: 2 to 3 hours on low

Why This Recipe Works Pulled chicken is a barbecue mainstay, but making it at home can be a labor of love. A simple spice mixture and a quick homemade barbecue sauce made it easy to turn slow-cooked bone-in chicken into tangy, silky, shredded chicken—perfect for piling onto buns for an easy dinner. Quickly microwaving the aromatics together with chili powder, paprika, and cayenne softened the onions and infused them with layers of barbecue flavor while at the same time blooming the spices. Simply seasoning the chicken with salt and pepper before nestling the breasts into our quick sauce mixture was enough to infuse the chicken with its rich essence. Adding 2 tablespoons of vinegar at the end of cooking, along with a small amount of mustard, ensured that the sauce was the perfect consistency and retained its bright flavors. Check the chicken's temperature after 2 hours of cooking and continue to monitor until it registers 160 degrees. Serve with pickle chips and Sweet and Tangy Coleslaw. You will need a 4- to 7-quart slow cooker for this recipe. This recipe will only work in a traditional slow cooker.

- 1 onion, chopped fine
- ¼ cup tomato paste
- 1 tablespoon chili powder
- 1 tablespoon vegetable oil
- 1 teaspoon paprika
- ½ teaspoon table salt
- ¼ teaspoon pepper
- ⅛ teaspoon cayenne pepper
- ¼ cup ketchup
- 2 tablespoons molasses
- 2 (12-ounce) bone-in split chicken breasts, skin removed, trimmed
- 2 tablespoons cider vinegar
- 2 teaspoons Dijon mustard
- 4 hamburger buns

1. Lightly coat slow cooker with vegetable oil spray. Microwave onion, tomato paste, chili powder, oil, paprika, salt, pepper, and cayenne in bowl, stirring occasionally, until onion is softened, about 5 minutes; transfer to prepared slow cooker. Stir in ketchup and molasses. Add chicken to slow cooker and coat evenly with sauce mixture. Cover and cook until chicken registers 160 degrees, 2 to 3 hours on low.

2. Transfer chicken to cutting board, let cool slightly, then shred into bite-size pieces using 2 forks; discard bones. Stir vinegar and mustard into sauce. Adjust consistency with hot water as needed. Stir in chicken and season with salt and pepper to taste. Serve on hamburger buns.

Sweet and Tangy Coleslaw
Serves 4

If you don't have a salad spinner, use a colander to drain the cabbage, pressing out the excess moisture with a rubber spatula. This recipe can be easily doubled.

- ¼ cup cider vinegar, plus extra for seasoning
- 2 tablespoons vegetable oil
- ¼ teaspoon celery seeds
- ¼ teaspoon pepper
- ½ head green or red cabbage, cored and shredded (6 cups)
- ¼ cup sugar, plus extra for seasoning
- 1 teaspoon table salt
- 1 large carrot, peeled and shredded
- 2 tablespoons chopped fresh parsley

1. Whisk vinegar, oil, celery seeds, and pepper together in medium bowl. Place bowl in freezer and chill until dressing is cold, at least 15 minutes or up to 30 minutes.

2. Meanwhile, in large bowl, toss cabbage with sugar and salt. Cover and microwave until cabbage is just beginning to wilt, about 1 minute. Stir briefly, cover, and continue to microwave until cabbage is partially wilted and has reduced in volume by one-third, 30 to 60 seconds.

3. Transfer cabbage mixture to salad spinner and spin until excess water is removed, 10 to 20 seconds. Remove bowl from freezer, add cabbage mixture, carrot, and parsley to cold dressing, and toss to coat. Season with salt, pepper, vinegar, and sugar to taste. Refrigerate until chilled, about 15 minutes. Toss coleslaw again before serving.

Slow-Cooker Tomatillo Chicken Chili

Serves 6 to 8
Cooking Time: 4 to 5 hours on low

Why This Recipe Works White chicken chili is a fresher, lighter cousin of thick red chili, making it an appealing option in the summer months. The fresh chiles, herbs, and spices take center stage. To achieve a great chicken chili in the slow cooker, we needed to build flavor every step of the way. We started by choosing convenient boneless, skinless chicken thighs. They could be added to the slow cooker whole, then easily broken into pieces once fully cooked, and they stayed juicy. For the base of our chili, we used canned hominy, pureeing some of the hominy with chicken broth to give the chili an appealing texture and a hearty corn flavor. Microwaving onion and garlic along with a combination of cumin and coriander also added a richer, deeper flavor. Finally, adding store-bought tomatillo salsa—a zesty combination of green tomatoes, chiles, and cilantro—was a quick and easy way to give our chili a boost of fresh flavor. Jarred tomatillo salsa is also called "salsa verde." Serve with your favorite chili garnishes. You will need a 5- to 7-quart slow cooker for this recipe. This recipe will only work in a traditional slow cooker.

- 2 (15-ounce) cans hominy, rinsed, divided
- 4 cups chicken broth, divided
- 2 cups chopped onions
- 2 tablespoons minced garlic
- 2 tablespoons extra-virgin olive oil, divided
- 4 teaspoons ground cumin
- 2 teaspoons ground coriander
- 4 pounds boneless, skinless chicken thighs, trimmed
- 3 poblano chiles, stemmed, seeded, and minced
- 1 cup jarred tomatillo salsa
- ¼ cup minced fresh cilantro

1. Process half of hominy and 2 cups broth in blender until smooth, about 1 minute; transfer to slow cooker.

2. Microwave onions, garlic, 1 tablespoon oil, cumin, and coriander in bowl, stirring occasionally, until onions are softened, about 5 minutes; transfer to slow cooker. Stir in remaining hominy and remaining 2 cups broth. Season chicken with salt and pepper and nestle into slow cooker. Cover and cook until chicken is tender, 4 to 5 hours on low.

3. Using large spoon, skim excess fat from surface of stew. Break chicken into about 1-inch pieces with tongs.

4. Microwave poblanos and remaining 1 tablespoon oil in bowl, stirring occasionally, until tender, about 8 minutes. Stir poblanos and salsa into chili and let sit until heated through, about 2 minutes. Stir in cilantro and season with salt and pepper to taste. Serve.

Slow-Cooker Shredded Beef Tacos with Cabbage-Carrot Slaw

Serves 4 to 6
Cooking Time: 7 to 8 hours on low or 4 to 5 hours on high

Why This Recipe Works This easy-to-prepare slow-cooker beef taco filling makes for a great weeknight meal in the summer. We turned to chuck roast, with its big beefy flavor, as the basis for the filling because it becomes meltingly tender and shreddable in the slow cooker—plus it's inexpensive and easy to find. Cutting the roast into 1½-inch pieces helped it cook faster and, as a result, become even more tender than when left whole. To make our red sauce we built a flavorful mixture of dried ancho chiles, chipotle chiles, tomato paste, and a hint of cinnamon. The different types of chiles created layers of heat without turning the sauce overly spicy. We bloomed the aromatics, including the dried chiles, with oil in the microwave to bring out their full flavor and added them to the slow cooker with a little honey to balance the heat, and water to distribute the spices evenly. Once the beef was pull-apart tender, we simply pureed the braising liquid into a rich, smooth sauce and tossed it with the shredded beef. To complement the warm spices of the beef, we topped our tacos with a cool and tangy cabbage slaw, which we kept simple with just a splash of lime juice. You will need a 4- to 7-quart slow cooker for this recipe. This recipe will only work in a traditional slow cooker.

½ onion, chopped fine
1 ounce (2 to 3) dried ancho chiles, stemmed, seeded, and torn into 1-inch pieces (½ cup)
3 garlic cloves, minced
1 tablespoon tomato paste
1 tablespoon vegetable oil
1 teaspoon minced canned chipotle chile in adobo sauce
½ teaspoon ground cinnamon
¾ cup water

1 tablespoon honey
2 pounds boneless beef chuck-eye roast, pulled apart at seams, trimmed, and cut into 1½-inch pieces
1 teaspoon table salt, divided
½ teaspoon pepper
½ head napa cabbage, cored and sliced thin (6 cups)
1 carrot, peeled and shredded
1 jalapeño chile, stemmed, seeded, and sliced thin
¼ cup lime juice (2 limes), plus lime wedges for serving
¼ cup chopped fresh cilantro
12–18 (6-inch) corn tortillas, warmed
Crumbled queso fresco

1. Microwave onion, anchos, garlic, tomato paste, oil, chipotle, and cinnamon in bowl, stirring occasionally, until onion is softened, about 5 minutes; transfer to slow cooker. Stir in water and honey. Sprinkle beef with ½ teaspoon salt and pepper and stir into slow cooker. Cover and cook until beef is tender, 7 to 8 hours on low or 4 to 5 hours on high.

2. Combine cabbage, carrot, jalapeño, lime juice, cilantro, and remaining ½ teaspoon salt in large bowl. Cover and refrigerate until ready to serve.

3. Using slotted spoon, transfer beef to another large bowl. Using potato masher, smash beef until coarsely shredded; cover to keep warm.

4. Process cooking liquid in blender until smooth, about 1 minute. Adjust sauce consistency with extra hot water as needed. Season with salt and pepper to taste. Toss beef with 1 cup sauce. Toss slaw to recombine. Serve beef with tortillas, slaw, and queso fresco, passing lime wedges and remaining sauce separately.

NOTES FROM THE TEST KITCHEN

OUR FAVORITE SLOW COOKER
We highly recommend the **KitchenAid 6-Quart Slow-Cooker with Solid Glass Lid.** Its control panel is simple to set and monitor. Its thick stoneware crock, insulated housing, and built-in thermal sensor are all well-designed—and at a moderate price.

Slow-Cooker Korean Lettuce Wraps

Serves 4 to 6
Cooking Time: 8 to 9 hours on low or 5 to 6 hours on high

Why This Recipe Works Tender short ribs covered in a sweet-spicy glaze are classic Korean BBQ fare and they make an easy summer dinner option when prepared in a slow cooker. For a signature Korean glaze, we created a base of fruity hoisin sauce, gochujang (a Korean chile-soybean paste), fresh ginger, garlic, and a little toasted sesame oil. Instead of adding extra liquid (broth or water) to our base as we do for most braises, we allowed the meat's natural juices to meld with the glaze base to build a flavor-rich sauce. A tablespoon of instant tapioca helped to ensure the glaze was properly thickened. Rice vinegar and more hoisin after cooking brightened the flavor of the dish, while scallions provided welcome notes of freshness. We prefer to eat these tender short rib pieces wrapped in a lettuce leaf and eaten like a taco, but they are equally delicious served over Everyday White Rice (page 107). If you can't find gochujang, substitute an equal amount of sriracha. You will need a 4- to 7-quart slow cooker for this recipe. This recipe will only work in a traditional slow cooker.

- ½ cup plus 1 tablespoon hoisin sauce, divided
- 2 tablespoons gochujang
- 4 teaspoons grated fresh ginger
- 4 garlic cloves, minced
- 1 tablespoon instant tapioca
- 3 pounds boneless English-style short ribs, trimmed
- ¾ teaspoon pepper
- 1 tablespoon rice vinegar
- 2 teaspoons toasted sesame oil
- 2 scallions, sliced thin
- 2 heads Bibb lettuce (8 ounces each), leaves separated

1. Combine ½ cup hoisin, gochujang, ginger, garlic, and tapioca in slow cooker. Sprinkle short ribs with pepper and nestle into slow cooker. Cover and cook until beef is tender and fork slips easily in and out of meat, 8 to 9 hours on low or 5 to 6 hours on high.

2. Transfer short ribs to cutting board, let cool slightly, then pull apart into large pieces using 2 forks; tent with aluminum foil to keep warm.

3. Transfer cooking liquid to fat separator and let sit for 5 minutes. Whisk defatted liquid, vinegar, oil, and remaining 1 tablespoon hoisin together in large bowl. Add beef and scallions and toss to combine. Season with salt and pepper to taste. Serve beef with lettuce leaves.

Slow-Cooker Shredded Beef Tacos with Cabbage-Carrot Slaw

Slow-Cooker Korean Lettuce Wraps

Slow-Cooker Street Fair Sausages with Peppers and Onions

Serves 4
Cooking Time: 2 to 3 hours on low

Why This Recipe Works No need to stand at the grill when you can make a fun and easy meal of tender, perfectly cooked Italian sausages and superflavorful peppers and onions in your slow cooker. First, we jump-started the vegetables in the microwave to ensure that they'd cook through, then we added them to the slow cooker and nestled in raw Italian sausages. To season the vegetables as they cooked, we used a potent mixture of chicken broth, tomato paste, and garlic. As they simmered, the peppers and onions absorbed the flavors of the sausage and braising liquid. Once the sausages were cooked through, all we needed to do was strain the peppers and onions and pile them high on sub rolls with the juicy sausages. You will need a 4- to 7-quart oval slow cooker for this recipe. This recipe will only work in a traditional slow cooker.

- 2 red or green bell peppers, stemmed, seeded, and cut into ¾-inch-wide strips
- 2 onions, sliced into ½-inch-thick rounds
- 2 tablespoons tomato paste
- 1 tablespoon vegetable oil
- 1 garlic clove, minced
- ½ cup chicken broth
- 1½ pounds hot or sweet Italian sausage
- 4 (6-inch) Italian sub rolls, split lengthwise

1. Microwave peppers, onions, tomato paste, oil, and garlic in bowl, stirring occasionally, until vegetables are softened, about 8 minutes; transfer to slow cooker. Stir in broth. Nestle sausage into slow cooker, cover, and cook until sausage is tender, 2 to 3 hours on low.

2. Transfer sausage to cutting board. Strain pepper-onion mixture, discarding cooking liquid, and transfer to bowl. Season with salt and pepper to taste. Cut sausage into 2-inch pieces. Serve sausage on rolls with pepper-onion mixture.

Slow-Cooker Pork Carnitas

Slow-Cooker Pork Carnitas

Serves 6 to 8
Cooking Time: 8 to 9 hours on low or 5 to 6 hours on high

Why This Recipe Works To achieve a slow-cooker version of this classic Mexican pulled pork dish, we cut pork shoulder into chunks and combined the meat with onion, orange zest and juice, lime zest and juice, garlic, ground cumin, oregano, and hefty amounts of salt and pepper. As the meat cooked, it released just the right amount of liquid to help it braise and become tender. To get the characteristic crispiness of the dish, we turned to the stovetop and a nonstick skillet. We mashed the pork pieces, added them to the hot skillet along with some of the intensely flavorful juices, and cooked the mixture until the pork began to turn crispy. Pork butt roast is often labeled Boston butt in the supermarket. Do not overtrim the pork; this extra fat is essential for keeping the pork moist and helping it brown when sautéed in step 3. Serve with sour cream, chopped onion, chopped cilantro, thinly sliced radishes, and/or lime wedges. You will need a 4- to 7-quart slow cooker for this recipe. This recipe will only work in a traditional slow cooker.

4 pounds boneless pork butt roast, pulled apart at seams, trimmed, and cut into 1½-inch pieces
1 small onion, peeled and halved
3 (2-inch) strips orange zest plus ½ cup juice
3 (2-inch) strips lime zest plus 2 tablespoons juice
5 garlic cloves, minced
1 tablespoon ground cumin
1 tablespoon dried oregano
2 teaspoons table salt
1½ teaspoons pepper
2 bay leaves
2 tablespoons vegetable oil
18–24 (6-inch) corn tortillas, warmed

1. Combine pork, onion, orange zest and juice, lime zest and juice, garlic, cumin, oregano, salt, pepper, and bay leaves in slow cooker. Cover and cook until pork is tender, 8 to 9 hours on low or 5 to 6 hours on high.

2. Using slotted spoon, transfer pork to large bowl. Using potato masher, smash pork until coarsely shredded. Strain cooking liquid into separate bowl; discard solids.

3. Heat oil in 12-inch nonstick skillet over medium-high heat until shimmering. Add pork to skillet. Whisk cooking liquid to recombine, then add 1 cup to skillet with pork. Cook, stirring occasionally, until liquid has evaporated and pork is evenly browned and crisp in spots, 10 to 15 minutes. Season with salt and pepper to taste. Transfer pork to serving platter and moisten with remaining cooking liquid as needed. Serve with tortillas.

Slow-Cooker Classic Barbecued Spareribs

Serves 4 to 6
Cooking Time: 7 to 8 hours on low or 4 to 5 hours on high

Why This Recipe Works We wanted fall-off-the-bone-tender barbecued pork spareribs with grilled flavor that we could make in our slow cooker and not actually have to grill. We started by covering the ribs with a dry spice rub for deep flavor. To fit two racks of spareribs into the slow cooker, we cut them in half and stood the racks upright around the slow cooker's perimeter, overlapping them slightly. We found that leaving the membrane coating the underside of the ribs attached helped hold the racks together as they cooked. Once the ribs were fully tender, we transferred them to a wire rack set in a baking sheet, brushed them with a simple pantry barbecue sauce, and broiled them to develop a lightly charred exterior. Avoid buying ribs labeled

"spareribs"; their large size and irregular shape make them unwieldy in a slow cooker. St. Louis–style spareribs are smaller and more uniform in size. You can substitute an equal amount of baby back ribs; reduce the cooking time to 4 to 5 hours on low or 3 to 4 hours on high. You will need a 5- to 7-quart slow cooker for this recipe. This recipe will only work in a traditional slow cooker.

3 tablespoons paprika
2 tablespoons packed brown sugar
2 teaspoons onion powder
2 teaspoons garlic powder
¼ teaspoon cayenne pepper
1 tablespoon pepper
½ teaspoon table salt
2 (2½- to 3-pound) racks St. Louis–style spareribs, trimmed and halved
½ cup ketchup
6 tablespoons molasses
2 tablespoons Dijon mustard
1 tablespoon cider vinegar
½ teaspoon liquid smoke

1. Combine paprika, sugar, onion powder, garlic powder, cayenne, pepper, and salt in bowl. Pat ribs dry with paper towels; rub with spice mixture.

2. Arrange ribs upright in slow cooker, with thick ends pointing down and meaty sides against wall (ribs will overlap). Cover and cook until ribs are just tender, 7 to 8 hours on low or 4 to 5 hours on high.

3. Adjust oven rack 4 inches from broiler element and heat broiler. Set wire rack in aluminum foil–lined rimmed baking sheet; coat with vegetable oil spray. Transfer ribs meaty side up to prepared rack; let sit until surface is dry, about 10 minutes.

4. Whisk ketchup, molasses, mustard, vinegar, and liquid smoke together in bowl. Brush ribs with half of sauce; broil until sauce is bubbling and beginning to char, about 5 minutes. Brush ribs with remaining sauce, tent loosely with foil, and let rest for 10 minutes. Cut ribs in between bones to separate. Serve.

ARRANGING RIBS IN THE SLOW COOKER

To ensure that the ribs cook evenly, stand the racks up along the perimeter of the slow cooker with the wide end down and the meatier side of the ribs facing the slow-cooker insert wall.

Slow-Cooker Salmon with
Mediterranean White Rice Salad

Slow-Cooker Sicilian
Fish Stew

Slow-Cooker Salmon with Mediterranean White Rice Salad

Serves 4
Cooking Time: 1 to 2 hours on low

Why This Recipe Works Salmon is a go-to choice for summer dinners and we wanted to develop an easy slow-cooker meal of beautifully moist fish and perfectly cooked rice. By using convenient instant rice, we found that we were able to cook both the rice and the salmon in the same amount of time. We kept the salmon simple, but wanted to give our rice some bold flavors. We decided on a Greek profile, using red wine vinegar, honey, garlic, and oregano in a vinaigrette. Once the rice was cooked, we stirred cherry tomatoes, whole parsley leaves, feta, and the vinaigrette into it. Look for salmon fillets of similar thickness to ensure that they cook at the same rate. Leave the skin on the salmon to keep the bottom of the fillets from overcooking and to make it easier to skin the fillets once done. Be sure to use instant rice (sometimes labeled minute rice); traditional rice takes much longer to cook and won't work here. For an accurate measurement of boiling water, bring a full kettle of water to a boil and then measure out the desired amount. Check the salmon's temperature after 1 hour of cooking and continue to monitor until it registers 135 degrees. You will need a 4- to 7-quart oval slow cooker for this recipe. This recipe will only work in a traditional slow cooker.

1⅔ cups boiling water
1½ cups instant white rice
⅓ cup extra-virgin olive oil, divided
1 teaspoon table salt, divided
¾ teaspoon pepper, divided
4 (6- to 8-ounce) skin-on salmon fillets,
    1 to 1½ inches thick
¼ cup red wine vinegar
1 tablespoon honey
2 teaspoons minced fresh oregano
2 garlic cloves, minced
8 ounces cherry tomatoes, quartered
½ cup fresh parsley leaves
2 ounces feta cheese, crumbled (½ cup)
    Lemon wedges

1. Lightly coat slow cooker with vegetable oil spray. Combine boiling water, rice, 1 tablespoon oil, ½ teaspoon salt, and ½ teaspoon pepper in prepared slow cooker. Gently press 16 by 12-inch sheet of parchment paper onto surface of water, folding down edges as needed.

2. Sprinkle salmon with remaining ½ teaspoon salt and remaining ¼ teaspoon pepper and arrange, skin side down, in even layer on top of parchment. Cover and cook until salmon is opaque throughout when checked with tip of paring knife and registers 135 degrees (for medium), 1 to 2 hours on low.

3. Using 2 metal spatulas, transfer salmon to serving platter; discard parchment and remove any white albumin from salmon. Whisk vinegar, honey, oregano, garlic, and remaining oil together in bowl. Fluff rice with fork, then gently fold in tomatoes, parsley, feta, and ½ cup vinaigrette. Season with salt and pepper to taste. Drizzle remaining vinaigrette over salmon and serve with salad and lemon wedges.

CREATING A PARCHMENT SHIELD

Press 16 by 12-inch sheet of parchment paper firmly onto rice or vegetables, folding down edges as needed.

Slow-Cooker Sicilian Fish Stew
Serves 6 to 8
Cooking Time: 4 to 6 hours on low or 3 to 5 hours on high

Why This Recipe Works In Sicily, fish is combined with tomatoes and local ingredients to create a simple stew that intermingles salty, sweet, and sour flavors. For our slow cooker riff on this stew, we created a balanced tomatoey broth base from the trio of onions, celery, and garlic, which we bloomed in the microwave along with tomato paste and thyme. Clam juice gave us the brininess of the sea, and a little white wine gave us much needed acidity. Golden raisins and capers imparted nice punches of sweet and salty flavor. This stew is typically made with firm white-fleshed fillets, such as snapper. However, we preferred the stronger flavor and meaty texture of swordfish. Cooking the swordfish for only the last half-hour ensured tender, flaky fish that remained moist. To top our stew with a hit of texture and flavor, we went with a slight twist on gremolata, a classic Italian herb condiment, swapping in mint and orange for the usual lemon and parsley to give us nuanced freshness. Halibut is a good substitute for swordfish. Serve with crusty bread or Garlic Toasts (page 169) to dip into the broth. You will need a 4- to 7-quart slow cooker for this recipe. This recipe will only work in a traditional slow cooker.

- 2 onions, chopped fine
- 1 celery rib, chopped fine
- 2 tablespoons extra-virgin olive oil
- 2 tablespoons tomato paste
- 4 garlic cloves, minced, divided
- 1 teaspoon minced fresh thyme or ¼ teaspoon dried
- 1 teaspoon table salt, divided
- ½ teaspoon pepper, divided
  Pinch red pepper flakes
- 2 (8-ounce) bottles clam juice
- 1 (14.5-ounce) can diced tomatoes, drained
- ¼ cup dry white wine
- ¼ cup golden raisins
- 2 tablespoons capers, rinsed
- 1½ pounds skinless swordfish steaks, 1 to 1½ inches thick, cut into 1-inch pieces
- ¼ cup pine nuts, toasted and chopped
- ¼ cup minced fresh mint
- 1 teaspoon grated orange zest

1. Microwave onions, celery, oil, tomato paste, three-quarters of garlic, thyme, ½ teaspoon salt, ¼ teaspoon pepper, and pepper flakes in bowl, stirring occasionally, until vegetables are softened, about 5 minutes; transfer to slow cooker. Stir in clam juice, tomatoes, wine, raisins, and capers, cover, and cook until flavors meld, 4 to 6 hours on low or 3 to 5 hours on high.

2. Sprinkle swordfish with remaining ½ teaspoon salt and remaining ¼ teaspoon pepper and stir into stew. Cover and cook on high until swordfish flakes apart when gently prodded with paring knife, about 30 minutes.

3. Combine pine nuts, mint, orange zest, and remaining garlic in bowl. Season stew with salt and pepper to taste. Serve, topping individual portions with pine nut mixture.

INGREDIENT SPOTLIGHT

CAPERS
Capers are one of the test kitchen's favorite stealthy ingredients. These small buds are both salty and lightly acidic; we love their briny, vegetal flavor and subtle crunch. For everyday cooking, we like the convenience of brined capers and we prefer a small size known as nonpareil. Once opened, a jar of capers can last in the refrigerator for months. Our favorite brand is **Reese Non Pareil Capers**.

Slow-Cooker Poached Swordfish with Warm Tomato and Olive Relish

Serves 4
Cooking Time: 1 to 2 hours on low

Why This Recipe Works Hearty swordfish steaks are a great option for gentle poaching in the slow cooker because the low heat renders the fish exceptionally tender. To keep the bottom of the fish from overcooking, we propped the steaks up on lemon slices. A summery Mediterranean-style tomato and olive relish dressed up our swordfish and added big flavor. Look for swordfish steaks of similar thickness to ensure that they cook at the same rate. Halibut is a good substitute for swordfish. Check the swordfish's temperature after 1 hour of cooking and continue to monitor until it registers 140 degrees. You will need a 4- to 7-quart oval slow cooker for this recipe. This recipe will only work in a traditional slow cooker.

- 1 lemon, sliced ¼ inch thick
- 2 tablespoons minced fresh parsley, stems reserved
- ¼ cup dry white wine
- 4 (6- to 8-ounce) skinless swordfish steaks, 1 to 1½ inches thick
- ½ teaspoon table salt
- ¼ teaspoon pepper
- 1 pound cherry tomatoes, halved
- ½ cup pitted salt-cured black olives, rinsed and halved
- 3 garlic cloves, minced
- ¼ cup extra-virgin olive oil

1. Fold sheet of aluminum foil into 12 by 7-inch sling and press widthwise into slow cooker. Arrange lemon slices in single layer in bottom of prepared slow cooker. Scatter parsley stems over lemon slices. Add wine to slow cooker, then add water until liquid level is even with lemon slices (about ¼ cup). Sprinkle swordfish with salt and pepper and arrange in even layer on top of parsley stems. Cover and cook until swordfish flakes apart when gently prodded with paring knife and registers 140 degrees, 1 to 2 hours on low.

2. Microwave tomatoes, olives, and garlic in bowl until tomatoes begin to break down, about 4 minutes. Stir in oil and minced parsley and season with salt and pepper to taste. Using sling, transfer swordfish to baking sheet. Gently lift and tilt steaks with spatula to remove parsley stems and lemon slices; transfer to serving platter. Discard poaching liquid and remove any white albumin from swordfish. Serve with relish.

MAKING A FOIL SLING

Fold sheet of aluminum foil into 12 by 7-inch rectangle and press it widthwise into slow cooker. Before serving, use edges of sling as handles to lift fish or other delicate items out of slow cooker fully intact.

Slow-Cooker Shrimp with Spiced Quinoa and Corn Salad

Serves 4
Cooking Time: 3 to 4 hours on low or 2 to 3 hours on high

Why This Recipe Works We wanted to make a main course seafood and quinoa salad that was easy to prepare and that was tailored to the slow cooker. To keep the grains separate and fluffy during cooking, we quickly toasted them in the microwave before adding them to the slow cooker. The heat of the slow cooker further toasted the grains, giving a nicely caramelized flavor to the salad. We then added in some shrimp and corn to round out our Southwestern-themed salad. A sprinkling of cotija cheese was a delicious finishing touch. A salsa made with ripe tomatoes, cilantro, and some lime juice perfectly complemented our salad with fresh summery flavor. We like the convenience of prewashed quinoa; rinsing removes the quinoa's bitter protective coating (called saponin). If you buy unwashed quinoa, rinse it and then spread it out on a clean dish towel to dry for 15 minutes. You will need a 4- to 7-quart oval slow cooker for this recipe. This recipe will only work in a traditional slow cooker.

- 1 cup prewashed white quinoa, rinsed
- 2 scallions, white parts minced, green parts cut into ½-inch pieces
- 2 jalapeño chiles, stemmed, seeded, and minced
- 5 teaspoons extra-virgin olive oil, divided
- 1 teaspoon chili powder
- 1⅓ cups water
- ¾ teaspoon table salt, divided
- 1 pound medium-large shrimp (31 to 40 per pound), peeled, deveined, and tails removed
- ½ teaspoon pepper, divided
- ¾ cup fresh or frozen thawed corn

Slow-Cooker Shrimp with Spiced Quinoa and Corn Salad

3 tomatoes, cored and chopped
⅓ cup minced fresh cilantro
1 tablespoon lime juice
2 ounces cotija cheese, crumbled (½ cup)

1. Lightly coat slow cooker with vegetable oil spray. Microwave quinoa, scallion whites, jalapeños, 2 teaspoons oil, and chili powder in bowl, stirring occasionally, until vegetables are softened, about 2 minutes; transfer to prepared slow cooker. Stir in water and ½ teaspoon salt. Cover and cook until water is absorbed and quinoa is tender, 3 to 4 hours on low or 2 to 3 hours on high.

2. Sprinkle shrimp with ¼ teaspoon pepper. Fluff quinoa with fork, then nestle shrimp into quinoa and sprinkle with corn. Cover and cook on high until shrimp are opaque throughout, 30 to 40 minutes.

3. Combine tomatoes, cilantro, lime juice, scallion greens, remaining 1 tablespoon oil, remaining ¼ teaspoon salt, and remaining ¼ teaspoon pepper in bowl. Sprinkle quinoa and shrimp with cotija and serve, passing salsa separately.

Slow-Cooker Garden Minestrone
Serves 6 to 8
Cooking Time: 8 to 10 hours on high

Why This Recipe Works Creating anything garden-fresh in a slow cooker is a tall order, but our lively minestrone marries a flavorful tomato broth, fresh vegetables, beans, and pasta. After microwaving the aromatics we added broth and tomato sauce along with carrots and dried beans—both of which could sustain a long stay in a slow cooker. Zucchini and chard were added at the end of cooking, and precooked pasta was stirred in last. Serve with crusty bread or Garlic Toasts (page 169) to dip into the broth. You will need a 4- to 7-quart slow cooker for this recipe. This recipe will only work in a traditional slow cooker.

1 onion, chopped fine
4 garlic cloves, minced
1 tablespoon plus 1 teaspoon extra-virgin olive oil, divided, plus extra for serving
1½ teaspoons minced fresh oregano or ½ teaspoon dried
⅛ teaspoon red pepper flakes
8 cups chicken or vegetable broth
1 (15-ounce) can tomato sauce
1 cup dried great Northern or cannellini beans, picked over and rinsed
2 carrots, peeled and cut into ½-inch pieces
½ cup small pasta, such as ditalini, tubettini, or elbow macaroni
 Table salt, for cooking pasta
1 zucchini, quartered lengthwise and sliced ¼ inch thick
8 ounces Swiss chard, stemmed and sliced ½ inch thick
½ cup chopped fresh basil
 Grated Parmesan cheese

1. Microwave onion, garlic, 1 tablespoon oil, oregano, and pepper flakes in bowl, stirring occasionally, until onion is softened, about 5 minutes; transfer to slow cooker. Stir in broth, tomato sauce, beans, and carrots. Cover and cook until beans are tender, 8 to 10 hours on high.

2. Meanwhile, bring 2 quarts water to boil in large saucepan. Add pasta and 1½ teaspoons salt and cook, stirring often, until al dente. Drain pasta, rinse with cold water, then toss with remaining 1 teaspoon oil in bowl; set aside.

3. Stir zucchini and chard into soup, cover, and cook on high until tender, 20 to 30 minutes. Stir in pasta and let sit until heated through, about 5 minutes. Stir in basil and season with salt and pepper to taste. Serve, passing Parmesan and extra oil separately.

Slow-Cooker Black Bean Chili

Serves 6 to 8
Cooking Time: 8 to 10 hours on high

Why This Recipe Works Our rich and hearty vegetarian bean chili is so satisfying and flavorful, no one will miss the meat. Vegetarian versions of black bean chili can be tricky since there are no ham products, like meaty, smoky ham hocks, to build flavor over the long cooking time. To achieve the full flavors we expected from black bean chili, we started by browning a generous amount of aromatics and spices. This additional step was promising, but the chili still seemed pretty lean. Though a bit odd for a chili, a surprise ingredient, mustard seeds, added an appealing pungency and the level of complexity we were looking for. To bulk up the chili, we added red bell peppers, white mushrooms, and canned tomatoes. We added the tomatoes at the end because otherwise their acidity prevented the beans from cooking through fully. Minced cilantro and a spritz of fresh lime provide welcome brightness and are a must. Serve with your favorite chili garnishes. You will need a 4- to 7-quart slow cooker for this recipe. This recipe will only work in a traditional slow cooker.

2 tablespoons vegetable oil

2 onions, chopped fine

2 red bell peppers, stemmed, seeded, and chopped fine

2 jalapeño chiles, stemmed, seeded, and minced

9 garlic cloves, minced

3 tablespoons chili powder

4 teaspoons mustard seeds

1 tablespoon minced canned chipotle chile in adobo sauce

1 tablespoon ground cumin

1 tablespoon dried oregano

2½ cups vegetable or chicken broth, divided, plus extra as needed

2½ cups water

1 pound (2½ cups) dried black beans, picked over and rinsed

10 ounces white mushrooms, trimmed and halved if small or quartered if large

2 bay leaves

1 (28-ounce) can whole peeled tomatoes, drained and cut into ½-inch pieces

2 tablespoons minced fresh cilantro
Lime wedges

Slow-Cooker Black Bean Chili

1. Heat oil in 12-inch skillet over medium heat until shimmering. Add onions and bell peppers and cook until vegetables are softened and lightly browned, 8 to 10 minutes. Stir in jalapeños, garlic, chili powder, mustard seeds, chipotle, cumin, and oregano and cook until fragrant, about 1 minute. Stir in 1 cup broth, scraping up any browned bits; transfer to slow cooker.

2. Stir remaining 1½ cups broth, water, beans, mushrooms, and bay leaves into slow cooker. Cover and cook until beans are tender, 8 to 10 hours on high.

3. Discard bay leaves. Transfer 1 cup cooked beans to bowl and mash with potato masher until mostly smooth. Stir mashed beans and tomatoes into chili and let sit until heated through, about 5 minutes. Adjust consistency with extra hot broth as needed. Stir in cilantro and season with salt and pepper to taste. Serve with lime wedges.

Slow-Cooker Southern Braised Collard Greens with Pork

Serves 4 to 6 `MAKE AHEAD`
Cooking Time: 9 to 10 hours on low or 6 to 7 hours on high

Why This Recipe Works Slow cooking fresh hearty greens in liquid tempers their assertive bitterness, and using the slow cooker is a very convenient way to make them as a side for a barbecue. Upon testing, we found 4 cups of liquid to be ideal for 2 pounds of greens. This may not sound like a lot, but given the lack of significant evaporation and the slow cooker's moist environment, that amount went a long way to ensure properly cooked collards without the need for them to be fully submerged. A combination of chicken broth (rather than water) and aromatics (onion and garlic) helped the greens develop great flavor, while a ham hock imparted characteristic smokiness. To round things out, pepper flakes were added for some subtle heat. We brightened up the liquid at the end of cooking with cider vinegar, and the leftover cooking liquid can be sopped up with cornbread or biscuits, or used to cook a second batch of collard greens, as is traditionally done in the South. You will need a 5- to 7-quart slow cooker for this recipe. This recipe will only work in a traditional slow cooker.

- 1 onion, chopped fine
- 6 garlic cloves, minced
- 1 tablespoon vegetable oil
- ½ teaspoon table salt
- ½ teaspoon red pepper flakes
- 2 pounds collard greens, stemmed and cut into 1-inch pieces
- 4 cups chicken broth
- 1 (12-ounce) smoked ham hock, rinsed
- 2 tablespoons cider vinegar, plus extra for seasoning
  Hot sauce

1. Lightly coat slow cooker with vegetable oil spray. Microwave onion, garlic, oil, salt, and pepper flakes in bowl, stirring occasionally, until onion is softened, about 5 minutes; transfer to prepared slow cooker. Stir in collard greens and broth. Nestle ham hock into slow cooker. Cover and cook until collard greens are tender, 9 to 10 hours on low or 6 to 7 hours on high.

2. Transfer ham hock to cutting board, let cool slightly, then shred into bite-size pieces using 2 forks; discard fat, skin, and bones. Stir ham and vinegar into collard greens. Season with salt, pepper, and extra vinegar to taste. Serve with hot sauce. (Collard greens can be held on warm or low setting for up to 2 hours.)

Farmers' Market Find   Hearty Greens

Several varieties of what we call hearty greens are available during the summer months and are ideal for braising. When harvested young, the "baby" versions of these greens are tender and perfect for eating raw in salads. When shopping, make sure the leaves of the greens are not yellowing, browning, or wilting. If you have a choice, purchase bunches of greens with thinner rather than thicker stems; the leaves will be more tender. To store any hearty green, wrap it in paper towels inside an open plastic produce bag in the refrigerator for several days.

Collard Greens Collard greens have large flat, stiff leaves with firm veins in them. They have a mild flavor and taste a bit like cabbage, which they technically are.

Kale Curly kale (also called green kale) has broad, dark green, frilly leaves. It has an earthy, grassy flavor that takes on nutty notes when cooked. It has double the amount of Vitamin A typically found in other leafy greens. Lacinato kale (also called Tuscan kale, dinosaur kale, or black kale) has long, slender, very dark green leaves. It has a sweet, mineral-y flavor and a tender texture when eaten raw, and it becomes robust and rich when braised.

Mustard Greens "Mustard greens" actually encompasses several varieties. Most commonly you'll see narrow, bright green, frilly leaves with a leafier, less leathery texture than other hearty greens. Mustard greens can also have a purplish tinge, and the leaves can also be flat. They're peppery and pleasantly sharp-hot in flavor.

Swiss Chard Swiss chard is like two vegetables in one: the dark green leaves, which can be treated like spinach or any similar hearty green, and the thick white or colored stems, which have a sturdier texture more akin to celery. Fordhook Giant is the classic white-stemmed, white-veined variety with dark green leaves. It is sometimes called "green chard" or "white chard." Ruby Red, or Rhubarb, chard is the next most common variety, with deep red stems and red veins running through the green leaves. "Rainbow chard" is a type called Bright Lights, featuring pink, yellow, orange, and crimson stems.

Slow-Cooker Summer Barley Salad

Serves 4 to 6
Cooking Time: 3 to 4 hours on low or 2 to 3 hours on high

Why This Recipe Works To showcase the appealingly nutty taste of barley, we kept the flavors simple—just lemon and coriander—and constructed a summery salad that paired the barley with piles of fresh veggies and a yogurt-herb dressing. Using the right liquid-to-barley ratio for the slow cooker was essential for getting perfectly cooked grains. To maintain a bit of the grains' toothsome structure and ensure even cooking, we briefly toasted the barley in the microwave before adding it to the slow cooker. To make this grain salad a perfect addition to the summer dinner table, we included in-season summer squash and some bright cherry tomatoes. A tangy yogurt dressing loaded with minced fresh chives and some lemon zest rounded out the salad's flavor profile. Do not substitute hulled, hull-less, quick-cooking, or presteamed barley (read the ingredient list on the package to determine this) in this recipe. You will need a 4- to 7-quart slow cooker for this recipe. This recipe will only work in a traditional slow cooker.

- 1 cup pearled barley, rinsed
- 3 tablespoons extra-virgin olive oil, divided
- 1 teaspoon ground coriander
- 1 tablespoon grated lemon zest plus 1 tablespoon juice, divided
- ¾ teaspoon table salt, divided
- 1 pound yellow summer squash or zucchini
- 10 ounces cherry tomatoes, halved
- ½ cup fresh parsley leaves
- ⅓ cup plain yogurt
- 2 tablespoons minced fresh chives
- 1 garlic clove, minced
- ¼ teaspoon pepper

1. Lightly coat slow cooker with vegetable oil spray. Microwave barley, 1 tablespoon oil, and coriander in bowl, stirring occasionally, until barley is lightly toasted and fragrant, about 3 minutes; transfer to prepared slow cooker. Stir in 2¼ cups water, 2 teaspoons lemon zest, and ½ teaspoon salt. Cover and cook until barley is tender, 3 to 4 hours on low or 2 to 3 hours on high.

2. Drain barley, if needed, and transfer to large serving bowl; let cool slightly. Using vegetable peeler or mandoline, shave squash lengthwise into very thin ribbons. Add squash ribbons, tomatoes, and parsley to bowl with barley and gently toss to combine.

3. Whisk yogurt, chives, garlic, lemon juice, remaining ¼ teaspoon salt, pepper, remaining 2 tablespoons oil, and remaining 1 teaspoon lemon zest together in separate bowl. Add dressing to salad and toss to coat. Season with salt and pepper to taste. Serve.

Slow-Cooker Lentil Salad with Radishes, Cilantro, and Pepitas

Serves 4
Cooking Time: 3 to 4 hours on low or 2 to 3 hours on high

Why This Recipe Works Lentil salad is a hearty vegetarian warm-weather main course option. Ours includes crisp radishes and red bell pepper, fresh cilantro, and roasted pepitas. We discovered that cooking the lentils with plenty of liquid was necessary to ensure even cooking. Adding a little salt and vinegar to the cooking liquid (we preferred water for a pure lentil flavor) gave us lentils that were firm yet creamy. We added aromatics to the water for a flavorful backbone. Once the lentils were cooked and drained, we added our fresh ingredients. In addition to the radishes, a jalapeño and a minced shallot lent some bite and complexity. *Queso fresco* added the finishing touch. We prefer *lentilles du Puy* (French green lentils) for this recipe, but it will work with any type of lentil except red or yellow. You will need a 4- to 7-quart slow cooker for this recipe. This recipe will only work in a traditional slow cooker.

- 1 cup dried lentilles du Puy (French green lentils), picked over and rinsed
- 3 tablespoons lime juice, divided
- 3 garlic cloves, minced
- 1 tablespoon ground cumin
- 1½ teaspoons dried oregano
- 1 teaspoon table salt, divided
- 6 radishes, trimmed, halved, and sliced thin
- 1 red bell pepper, stemmed, seeded, and cut into ½-inch pieces
- ¼ cup fresh cilantro leaves
- ¼ cup extra-virgin olive oil
- 1 jalapeño chile, stemmed, seeded, and minced
- 1 shallot, minced
- 2 tablespoons roasted pepitas
- 2 ounces queso fresco, crumbled (½ cup)

1. Combine 4 cups water, lentils, 1 tablespoon lime juice, garlic, cumin, oregano, and ¾ teaspoon salt in slow cooker. Cover and cook until lentils are tender, 3 to 4 hours on low or 2 to 3 hours on high.

2. Drain lentils and transfer to large serving bowl; let cool slightly. Add radishes, bell pepper, cilantro, oil, jalapeño, shallot, remaining ¼ teaspoon salt, and remaining 2 tablespoons lime juice; gently toss to combine. Season with salt and pepper to taste. Sprinkle with pepitas and queso fresco. Serve.

Slow-Cooker Refried Beans
Serves 6   MAKE AHEAD
Cooking Time: 8 to 9 hours on high

Why This Recipe Works Homemade refried beans, rich with pork flavor, subtle heat, and warm spices, are welcome at any barbecue. They are worlds apart from the canned stuff, but making them takes time; so we put our slow cooker to work. We started with dried pintos and added them right to the slow cooker—no advance soaking or simmering needed. Chicken broth provided the cooking liquid, and garlic, onion, and cumin offered aromatic and warm spice notes while a poblano chile upped the heat. To deepen the flavor of the aromatics and cumin, we microwaved them with smoky bacon. Once the beans were tender, we discarded the bacon and mashed the beans. Cilantro and lime juice added bright south-of-the-border flavor. You will need a 4- to 7-quart slow cooker for this recipe. This recipe will only work in a traditional slow cooker.

- 1 onion, chopped fine
- 1 poblano chile, stemmed, seeded, and minced
- 2 slices bacon
- 3 garlic cloves, minced
- 1 tablespoon ground cumin
- 1 pound (2½ cups) dried pinto beans, picked over and rinsed
- 6 cups chicken broth, plus extra as needed
- 3 tablespoons minced fresh cilantro
- 1 tablespoon lime juice, plus extra as needed
- ½ teaspoon table salt

1. Microwave onion, poblano, bacon, garlic, and cumin in bowl, stirring occasionally, until vegetables are softened, about 5 minutes; transfer to slow cooker. Stir in beans and broth, cover, and cook until beans are tender, 8 to 9 hours on high.

2. Discard bacon. Drain beans, reserving 1 cup cooking liquid. Return beans and reserved cooking liquid to now-empty slow cooker and mash with potato masher until smooth. Stir in cilantro, lime juice, and salt. Season with salt, pepper, and extra lime juice to taste. Serve. (Beans can be held on warm or low setting for up to 2 hours; adjust consistency with extra hot broth as needed before serving.)

Slow-Cooker Summer Barley Salad

Slow-Cooker Lentil Salad with Radishes, Cilantro, and Pepitas

Pressure-Cooker
Spanish-Style
Chicken and
Couscous

Pressure-Cooker Teriyaki
Chicken Thighs with
Carrots and Snow Peas

Pressure-Cooker Spanish-Style Chicken and Couscous

Serves 4

Why This Recipe Works Bursting with the aromatic flavors of saffron, chorizo, and garlic, our Spanish-inspired chicken dish is a winning weeknight dinner on a summer night. Instead of rice, we used couscous here, which fit well with the Spanish flavor profile and couldn't have been simpler to prepare with the chicken: It didn't require cooking at all, just soaking, which meant we could add it to the pot after pressure cooking and allow it to simply absorb the ultraflavorful cooking liquid. Saffron gave the dish an authentic Spanish feel, and peas and fresh parsley added summery bursts of color and freshness. This recipe will only work in an electric pressure cooker.

4 (12-ounce) bone-in split chicken breasts, trimmed
1¼ teaspoons table salt, divided
¾ teaspoon pepper
1 tablespoon extra-virgin olive oil
1 red bell pepper, stemmed, seeded, and chopped fine
4 ounces Spanish-style chorizo sausage, cut into ¼-inch pieces
4 garlic cloves, minced
⅛ teaspoon saffron threads, crumbled
½ cup chicken broth
1½ cups couscous
1 cup frozen peas, thawed
2 teaspoons lemon juice
3 tablespoons minced fresh parsley

1. Pat chicken dry with paper towels and sprinkle with 1 teaspoon salt and pepper. Using highest sauté or browning function, heat oil in pressure cooker for 5 minutes (or until just smoking.) Place half of chicken, skin side down, in pressure cooker and cook until browned, 5 to 7 minutes; transfer to plate. Repeat with remaining chicken; transfer to plate.

2. Add bell pepper, chorizo, and remaining ¼ teaspoon salt to fat left in pressure cooker and cook until bell pepper is softened, 3 to 5 minutes. Stir in garlic and saffron and cook until fragrant, about 30 seconds. Stir in broth, scraping up any browned bits. Nestle chicken, skin side up, into pressure cooker, adding any accumulated juices.

3. Lock lid in place and close pressure release valve. Select high pressure cook function and cook for 17 minutes. (If using Instant Pot, decrease cooking time to 9 minutes.) Turn off pressure cooker and quick-release pressure. Carefully remove lid, allowing steam to escape away from you.

4. Transfer chicken to serving platter and discard skin, if desired. Tent with aluminum foil and let rest while preparing couscous.

5. Stir couscous, peas, and lemon juice into pressure cooker, cover, and let sit until couscous is tender, about 5 minutes. Add parsley and fluff couscous gently with fork to combine. Season with salt and pepper to taste. Serve with chicken.

Pressure-Cooker Teriyaki Chicken Thighs with Carrots and Snow Peas
Serves 4

Why This Recipe Works Carrots and peas often go hand-in-hand, and when they're summertime fresh we love to showcase this pairing in a main dish. Another classic pairing? Chicken and teriyaki—a sauce we knew would perfectly complement our vegetable duo. For a fuss-free method that delivered a truly great chicken teriyaki, we started with bone-in, skin-on chicken thighs. We seared the chicken to get some browning and get rid of excess fat. Salty soy sauce, enhanced with sugar, ginger, and garlic, not only contributed to the classic teriyaki profile, but also seasoned the chicken as it cooked. We used the chicken's resting time to thicken the sauce using the sauté function; a mixture of cornstarch and mirin gave the sauce a satiny texture and a bit of acidity and sweetness. Since we were already simmering the sauce, we quickly cooked the carrots and snow peas in the sauce as well for maximum flavor throughout the finished dish. Mirin, a sweet Japanese rice wine, can be found in the international section of most major supermarkets and in most Asian markets. If you cannot find it, use 2 tablespoons white wine and an extra teaspoon of sugar. Serve with Everyday White Rice (page 107). This recipe will only work in an electric pressure cooker.

8 (5- to 7-ounce) bone-in chicken thighs, trimmed
¾ teaspoon pepper
1 tablespoon vegetable oil
½ cup soy sauce
½ cup sugar
½ teaspoon grated fresh ginger
1 garlic clove, minced
3 tablespoons mirin
2 tablespoons cornstarch
3 carrots, peeled and sliced thin on bias
8 ounces snow peas, strings removed
2 scallions, sliced thin on bias

1. Pat chicken dry with paper towels and sprinkle with pepper. Using highest sauté or browning function, heat oil in pressure cooker for 5 minutes (or until just smoking). Place half of chicken, skin side down, in pressure cooker and cook until browned, 5 to 7 minutes; transfer to plate. Repeat with remaining chicken; transfer to plate. Turn off pressure cooker and discard any fat left in pot.

2. Whisk soy sauce, sugar, ginger, and garlic together in now-empty pressure cooker, scraping up any browned bits. Nestle chicken, skin side up, into pressure cooker, adding any accumulated juices.

3. Lock lid in place and close pressure release valve. Select high pressure cook function and cook for 9 minutes. Turn off pressure cooker and quick-release pressure. Carefully remove lid, allowing steam to escape away from you.

4. Transfer chicken to serving platter and discard skin, if desired. Tent with aluminum foil and let rest while cooking vegetables.

5. Whisk mirin and cornstarch in bowl until no lumps remain, then whisk mixture into sauce. Stir in carrots and cook using highest sauté or browning function until crisp-tender, about 5 minutes. Turn off pressure cooker. Stir in snow peas and let sit until heated through and crisp-tender, about 30 seconds. Transfer vegetable-sauce mixture to serving platter with chicken. Sprinkle with scallions and serve.

PREPARING FRESH GINGER
Although we love the floral pungency of fresh ginger, it has a distractingly fibrous texture when minced or coarsely grated. To prevent this, we use a rasp-style grater to grate the ginger to a fine pulp.

1. To quickly peel knob of ginger, hold it firmly against cutting board and use edge of teaspoon to scrape away thin, brown skin.

2. To grate ginger, peel just small section of large piece of ginger, then grate peeled portion using rasp-style grater, using unpeeled ginger as handle to keep your fingers safely away from grater.

Pressure-Cooker Chicken in a Pot with Lemon-Herb Sauce

Pressure-Cooker Braised Pork with Broccoli Rabe and Sage

Pressure-Cooker Chicken in a Pot with Lemon-Herb Sauce

Serves 4

Why This Recipe Works It might sound odd to cook a whole chicken in the summertime when you want to avoid heat—and your oven. But with a pressure cooker, you can do both, as well as make an easy, herb-filled sauce to elevate chicken from basic to bursting with flavor. We started with a 4-pound chicken, which fit nicely into the narrow pot of a pressure cooker. Since we wanted to focus on achieving succulent meat and not on getting crisp skin, we didn't bother with the time-consuming step of browning the chicken; sautéing some onion and garlic in the pot gave the chicken and the jus layers of deep flavor. Pressure cooking produced a chicken with perfectly cooked light and dark meat. A couple of tablespoons of flour, added at the start, ensured that our jus was transformed into a velvety smooth sauce after cooking. Butter, lemon juice, and garden-fresh herbs gave our sauce a final boost of rich, bright flavor. This recipe will only work in an electric pressure cooker.

1 tablespoon vegetable oil
1 onion, chopped fine
2 tablespoons all-purpose flour
3 garlic cloves, minced
2 teaspoons minced fresh rosemary
½ cup dry white wine
1 cup chicken broth
1 (4-pound) whole chicken, giblets discarded
1 teaspoon table salt
½ teaspoon pepper
2 tablespoons unsalted butter, cut into
  2 pieces and chilled
2 tablespoons lemon juice
¼ cup minced fresh chives, parsley, or tarragon

1. Using highest sauté or browning function, heat oil in pressure cooker until shimmering. Add onion and cook until softened, 3 to 5 minutes. Stir in flour, garlic, and rosemary and cook until fragrant, about 1 minute. Slowly whisk in wine, scraping up any browned bits and smoothing out any lumps, then stir in broth. Sprinkle chicken with salt and pepper and place breast side up into pressure cooker.

2. Lock lid in place and close pressure release valve. Select high pressure cook function and cook for 30 minutes. Turn off pressure cooker and quick-release pressure. Carefully remove lid, allowing steam to escape away from you.

3. Transfer chicken to carving board, tent with aluminum foil, and let rest for 5 to 10 minutes. Let cooking liquid settle, then skim excess fat from surface using large spoon. Whisk in butter, lemon juice, and chives. Carve chicken, discarding chicken skin if desired. Serve with sauce.

Pressure-Cooker Braised Pork with Broccoli Rabe and Sage

Serves 4

Why This Recipe Works Using a pressure cooker is a great way to cook pork without turning on the oven, in summer or at any other time of year. This simple braised pork meal is far greater than the sum of its parts: Tender, meaty pork and deliciously bitter broccoli rabe are joined in a silky, aromatic sauce. We started by browning pieces of juicy, richly flavored pork butt, then combined garlic, white wine, and aromatic sage with the fond in the pot (with just a touch of flour to add body) to build the braising liquid. After releasing the pressure, we removed the tender pork. As it rested, we cooked the broccoli rabe in the remaining sauce for just 3 minutes using the sauté function. A half teaspoon of freshly grated orange zest added a burst of brightness. Pork butt roast is often labeled Boston butt in the supermarket. This recipe will only work in an electric pressure cooker.

1½ pounds boneless pork butt roast, trimmed and cut into 2-inch pieces
½ teaspoon table salt
½ teaspoon pepper
1 tablespoon extra-virgin olive oil
2 tablespoons minced fresh sage, divided
5 garlic cloves, peeled and smashed
1 tablespoon all-purpose flour
¼ cup chicken broth
¼ cup dry white wine
1 pound broccoli rabe, trimmed and cut into 1-inch pieces
½ teaspoon grated orange zest

1. Pat pork dry with paper towels and sprinkle with salt and pepper. Using highest sauté or browning function, heat oil in pressure cooker for 5 minutes (or until just smoking). Brown pork on all sides, 6 to 8 minutes; transfer to plate.

2. Add 1 tablespoon sage, garlic, and flour to fat left in pot and cook, using highest sauté or browning function, until fragrant, about 1 minute. Stir in broth and wine, scraping up any browned bits. Return pork to pot along with any accumulated juices. Lock lid in place and close pressure release valve. Select high pressure cook function and cook for 30 minutes.

3. Turn off pressure cooker and let pressure release naturally for 15 minutes. Quick-release any remaining pressure, then carefully remove lid, allowing steam to escape away from you. Transfer pork to serving platter, tent with aluminum foil, and let rest while preparing broccoli rabe.

4. Whisk sauce until smooth and bring to simmer using highest sauté or browning function. Stir in broccoli rabe and cook, partially covered, until tender and bright green, about 3 minutes. Stir in orange zest and remaining 1 tablespoon sage. Serve pork with broccoli rabe mixture.

TRIMMING BROCCOLI RABE

1. Trim off and discard very thick stalk ends, about 2 inches from bottom of stalks.

2. Cut remaining stems and florets into pieces according to recipe directions.

NOTES FROM THE TEST KITCHEN

OUR FAVORITE PRESSURE COOKER
We recommend the **Zavor LUX LCD 8-Quart Multicooker**. This model has a clear LCD interface that is easy to use and always tells you exactly what it is doing. A sensor alerts you when the lid isn't properly sealed.

Pressure-Cooker North Carolina–Style Pulled Pork
Serves 8

Why This Recipe Works Pulled pork consists of succulent, smoky meat napped in a tangy vinegar-y sauce; it's a barbecue staple. Traditional recipes can require a full day of closely monitoring a grill but we streamlined this labor-intensive dish without losing out on any of the flavor. We started with a traditional pork butt roast and let the moist heat of the pressure cooker effortlessly tenderize this tough cut. The only thing the multicooker couldn't do was give the meat smoky flavor, but this was an easy fix: We added liquid smoke to the braising liquid—no grill required. We infused the pork with classic barbecue flavors by rubbing it with a sweet and spicy dry rub made with brown sugar, paprika, chili powder, and cumin. We also used our simple sauce as our braising liquid, which helped to deepen the flavor of the sauce. Once the pork was cooked, we removed it from the pot to shred it and reduced the sauce to a thick consistency. Don't shred the meat too fine in step 3; it will break up more as the meat is combined with the sauce. Pork butt roast is often labeled Boston butt in the supermarket. This recipe will only work in an electric pressure cooker.

- 3 tablespoons packed brown sugar, plus extra as needed
- 2 tablespoons paprika
- 2 tablespoons chili powder
- 2 teaspoons ground cumin
- 1 teaspoon table salt
- ½ teaspoon pepper
- 1 (4-pound) boneless pork butt roast, trimmed and quartered
- ¾ cup plus 1 tablespoon cider vinegar, divided, plus extra for seasoning
- ½ cup water
- ½ cup ketchup
- ½ teaspoon liquid smoke
- 8 hamburger buns

1. Combine sugar, paprika, chili powder, cumin, salt, and pepper in bowl, then rub mixture evenly over pork. Combine ¾ cup vinegar, water, ketchup, and liquid smoke in pressure cooker, then nestle pork into pot.

2. Lock lid in place and close pressure release valve. Select high pressure cook function and cook for 45 minutes. Turn off pressure cooker and let pressure release naturally for 15 minutes. Quick-release any remaining pressure, then carefully remove lid, allowing steam to escape away from you.

3. Transfer pork to large bowl, let cool slightly, then shred into bite-size pieces, discarding any excess fat.

4. Let braising liquid settle, then skim excess fat from surface using large spoon. Using highest sauté or browning function, cook liquid until reduced to about 2 cups, 15 to 20 minutes. Stir in remaining 1 tablespoon vinegar and season with salt, pepper, extra sugar, and extra vinegar to taste. Stir 1 cup sauce into shredded pork, then add extra sauce to taste. Serve shredded pork on buns, passing remaining sauce separately.

Pressure-Cooker Lamb Meatballs with Couscous, Pickled Onions, and Tahini
Serves 4

Why This Recipe Works We took advantage of the convenience of deeply flavored jarred roasted red peppers and chose a Mediterranean backdrop for a dish starring lamb meatballs, knowing that lamb's robust, almost grassy notes would make a perfect companion to this combination of flavors. Tahini, a potent paste made from toasted sesame seeds, is a regular in Mediterranean dishes, so to play off our chosen flavor profile, we created a savory tahini sauce and made it do double duty by mixing it with bread crumbs as a riff on a panade (typically made from bread pieces soaked and mashed in milk or yogurt and then mixed into meatballs to keep them moist). We also spooned some of the sauce over the finished meatballs, which we nestled on a bed of warmly spiced couscous mixed with our roasted red peppers and some pickled onions. The meatballs cooked in just 1 minute under pressure, and as they rested separately, we simply stirred the couscous into the remaining liquid and allowed it to cook in the residual heat and absorb the bold and delicious flavors. This recipe will only work in an electric pressure cooker.

- ½ cup Tahini Sauce (page 164), divided
- 3 tablespoons panko bread crumbs
- 1 pound ground lamb
- ¼ cup chopped fresh mint, divided
- 1 teaspoon ground cinnamon, divided
- 1 teaspoon ground cumin, divided
- ½ teaspoon table salt, divided
- 1 tablespoon extra-virgin olive oil
- 1 onion, chopped fine
- ⅛ teaspoon cayenne pepper
- 1 cup chicken broth

1 cup couscous
½ cup jarred roasted red peppers, rinsed, patted dry, and chopped
1 teaspoon grated lemon zest plus 1 tablespoon juice
⅓ cup Quick Pickled Red Onions (page 100)

1. Using fork, mash ¼ cup tahini sauce and panko together in bowl to form paste. Add ground lamb, 2 tablespoons mint, ½ teaspoon cinnamon, ½ teaspoon cumin, and ¼ teaspoon salt and knead with hands until thoroughly combined. Pinch off and roll mixture into twelve 1½-inch meatballs.

2. Using highest sauté or browning function, heat oil in pressure cooker until shimmering. Add onion and remaining ¼ teaspoon salt and cook until onion is softened, about 5 minutes. Stir in remaining ½ teaspoon cinnamon, remaining ½ teaspoon cumin, and cayenne and cook until fragrant, about 30 seconds. Stir in broth, scraping up any browned bits. Add meatballs to pot. Lock lid in place and close pressure release valve. Select high pressure cook function and cook for 1 minute.

3. Turn off pressure cooker and quick-release pressure. Carefully remove lid, allowing steam to escape away from you. Using slotted spoon, transfer meatballs to plate, tent with aluminum foil, and let rest while finishing couscous.

4. Using highest sauté or browning function, bring liquid in pot to simmer. Stir in couscous, red peppers, and lemon zest and juice. Turn off pressure cooker, cover, and let sit for 10 minutes. Fluff couscous gently with fork and transfer to serving platter. Arrange meatballs on top and drizzle with remaining ¼ cup tahini sauce. Sprinkle with pickled onions and remaining 2 tablespoons mint. Serve.

Tahini Sauce
Makes about 1 cup
Our favorite brand of tahini is Ziyad.

½ cup tahini
½ cup water
¼ cup lemon juice (2 lemons)
2 garlic cloves, minced

Whisk tahini, water, lemon juice, and garlic in bowl until smooth (mixture will appear broken at first). Season with salt and pepper to taste. Let sit at room temperature for at least 30 minutes to allow flavors to meld. (Sauce can be refrigerated for up to 4 days; bring to room temperature before serving.)

Pressure-Cooker North Carolina–Style Pulled Pork

Pressure-Cooker Lamb Meatballs with Couscous, Pickled Onions, and Tahini

In the height of summer, zucchini and yellow summer squash are beyond plentiful. The little green and yellow squashes (and some not so little) are piled high at seemingly every farmstand, farmers' market, and supermarket. These squashes are very easy to grow, thriving in many different climates and soil conditions. Despite their name, these squashes are actually more closely related to cucumbers and watermelon than to winter squash. Choose zucchini and other summer squashes that are firm and without soft spots. The skins should be free of blemishes and have a vibrant green or yellow color. Zucchini and yellow squash are fairly perishable; store them in the refrigerator in a partially sealed zipper-lock bag for up to five days.

Summer Squash Summer squash encompasses several varieties of yellow squash, as well as zucchini, all of which share similar characteristics and flavor. Yellow squash has a fat bottom and a tapered neck, unlike zucchini, which is more uniform along its length. Yellow squashes can either be straight or have a curved neck (these are called crooknecks). There is also a yellow variety of zucchini, with a golden skin.

Pattypan Squash Pattypan squash is small, squat, and round and shares many of the same qualities as its ubiquitous relatives: It's crisp and bright when raw and silky and buttery when cooked. It is most tender when young and becomes especially sweet and flavorful when roasted (page 305).

Squash Blossoms Most commonly from the zucchini plant, squash blossoms are easily treated like a full-fledged vegetable. These ephemeral treats have been described as having a flavor like "squash perfume." Zucchini blossoms are available at farmers' markets starting in June and remain through the summer. They are often stuffed with cheese and flash-fried but they also make a wonderful topping for a white pizza or a filling ingredient for frittatas. In Mexico, they are used in quesadillas. Or simply eat them raw, tossed into a green salad.

Pressure-Cooker Braised Striped Bass with Zucchini and Tomatoes

Serves 4

Why This Recipe Works We thought the winning combination of zucchini and tomatoes would make the perfect companion to meaty fish for a satisfying light meal. For this dish, we chose canned whole tomatoes to pair with our zucchini instead of fresh since we knew they'd hold up better during cooking, and we could also make use of the tomatoes' concentrated juice in our stewing liquid. For the fish, we chose flaky-yet-meaty striped bass, which held its pleasant texture during cooking in the pressure cooker. Olives added briny depth to the finished dish, and shredded mint brought brightness and fresh herbal notes. Halibut and swordfish are good substitutes for the striped bass here. To prevent the striped bass from overcooking, be sure to turn off the pressure cooker as soon as it reaches pressure. The striped bass should register about 130 degrees after cooking; if it doesn't, partially cover the pot with the lid and continue to cook using the highest sauté or browning function until the desired temperature is achieved. This recipe will only work in an electric pressure cooker.

  2 tablespoons extra-virgin olive oil, divided, plus extra for drizzling
  3 zucchini (8 ounces each), halved lengthwise and sliced ¼ inch thick
  1 onion, chopped
  ¾ teaspoon table salt, divided
  3 garlic cloves, minced
  1 teaspoon minced fresh oregano or ¼ teaspoon dried
  ¼ teaspoon red pepper flakes
  1 (28-ounce) can whole peeled tomatoes, drained with juice reserved, halved
1½ pounds skinless striped bass, 1½ inches thick, cut into 2-inch pieces
  ¼ teaspoon pepper
  2 tablespoons chopped pitted kalamata olives
  2 tablespoons shredded fresh mint

1. Using highest sauté or browning function, heat 1 tablespoon oil in pressure cooker for 5 minutes (or until just smoking). Add zucchini and cook until tender, about 5 minutes; transfer to bowl and set aside.

2. Add remaining 1 tablespoon oil, onion, and ¼ teaspoon salt to now-empty pot and cook, using highest sauté or browning function, until onion is softened, about 5 minutes. Stir in garlic, oregano, and pepper flakes and cook until fragrant, about 30 seconds. Stir in tomatoes and reserved juice.

3. Sprinkle bass with remaining ½ teaspoon salt and pepper. Nestle bass into tomato mixture and spoon some of cooking liquid on top of pieces. Lock lid in place and close pressure release valve. Select high pressure cook function and cook for 1 minute. Turn off pressure cooker and quick-release pressure. (If using Instant Pot, immediately turn off pot once pressure has been reached and quick-release pressure.) Carefully remove lid, allowing steam to escape away from you.

4. Transfer bass to plate, tent with aluminum foil, and let rest while finishing vegetables. Stir zucchini into pot and let sit until heated through, about 5 minutes. Stir in olives and season with salt and pepper to taste. Serve bass with vegetables, sprinkling individual portions with mint and drizzling with extra oil.

Pressure-Cooker Poached Salmon with Cucumber and Tomato Salad

Serves 4   FAST

Why This Recipe Works Salmon is a crowd-pleasing fish choice and we found that the pressure cooker makes the process of cooking it foolproof: The consistent moisture level and temperature, as well as the precise timing, safeguards against overcooking, producing evenly cooked salmon each and every time. Cooking the salmon on a foil sling made it easy to transfer in and out of the pressure cooker, and propping the fish up on lemon slices insulated it from the direct heat while imparting the fish with bright citrus flavor. This method produced great salmon in under an hour and guaranteed that it was cooked perfectly. To build a rounded summery dinner around our perfectly cooked fish, we made a fresh and light salad with fresh cucumber, tomatoes, and herbs, and added in some kalamata olives for a briny touch. This recipe will only work in an electric pressure cooker.

1 lemon, sliced ¼ inch thick, plus 1 teaspoon grated lemon zest and 2 tablespoons juice
¼ cup fresh parsley leaves, stems reserved
1 tablespoon chopped fresh dill, stems reserved
1 (1½-pound) skinless center-cut salmon fillet, 1 to 1½ inches thick, sliced crosswise into 4 equal pieces
½ teaspoon table salt
¼ teaspoon pepper
3 tablespoons extra-virgin olive oil
1 shallot, minced
2 tablespoons capers, rinsed and minced

Pressure-Cooker Poached Salmon with Cucumber and Tomato Salad

1 English cucumber, halved lengthwise and sliced thin
8 ounces cherry tomatoes, halved
¾ cup pitted kalamata olives, halved

1. Fold sheet of aluminum foil into 12 by 7-inch sling. Press sling into pressure cooker, allowing narrow edges to rest along sides of insert. Arrange lemon slices in single layer on prepared sling, then scatter parsley and dill stems over top. Add water until liquid level is even with lemon slices (about ½ cup). Sprinkle flesh side of salmon with salt and pepper and arrange skinned side down in even layer on top of herb stems.

2. Lock lid in place and close pressure release valve. Select high pressure cook function and cook for 5 minutes. (If using Instant Pot, reduce cooking time to 3 minutes.) Turn off pressure cooker and quick-release pressure. Carefully remove lid, allowing steam to escape away from you.

3. Meanwhile, whisk oil, shallot, capers, lemon zest and juice, and chopped dill together in large bowl. Add cucumber, tomatoes, olives, and parsley leaves and gently toss to combine. Season with salt and pepper to taste.

4. Using sling, transfer salmon to baking sheet; discard poaching liquid. Gently lift and tilt fillets with spatula to remove herb stems and lemon slices and remove any white albumin. Transfer salmon to individual plates and serve with salad.

Pressure-Cooker
Shrimp with Tomatoes
and Warm Spices

Pressure-Cooker Mussels with
White Wine and Garlic

Pressure-Cooker Shrimp with Tomatoes and Warm Spices

Serves 4

Why This Recipe Works Succulent shrimp poached in roasty tomatoes and bell pepper perfumed by the warm spice blend *ras el hanout* is our idea of elevated comfort food, and countertop cooking makes this meal a breeze to prepare. Cooked under pressure, the vegetables in this dish softened and their flavor intensified. The shrimp gently cooked in the residual heat of the cooked tomato mixture. Olives provided pops of briny saltiness, and scallions and a drizzle of extra-virgin olive oil provided a fresh, rich finish. Do not substitute larger shrimp here; they will not cook through in time. Serve over Everyday White Rice (page 107) or Couscous (page 172). You can find ras el hanout in the spice aisle of most well-stocked supermarkets. This recipe will only work in an electric pressure cooker.

1 pound large shrimp (26 to 30 per pound), peeled and deveined
2 tablespoons extra-virgin olive oil, divided, plus extra for drizzling
5 garlic cloves, minced, divided
1 teaspoon grated lemon zest
½ teaspoon table salt, divided
⅛ teaspoon pepper
1 red or green bell pepper, stemmed, seeded, and chopped
1 small onion, chopped
1 tablespoon ras el hanout
½ teaspoon ground ginger
1 (28-ounce) can whole peeled tomatoes, drained with juice reserved, chopped
¼ cup pitted brine-cured green or black olives, chopped
2 tablespoons coarsely chopped fresh parsley
2 scallions, sliced thin on bias

1. Toss shrimp with 1 tablespoon oil, 1 teaspoon garlic, lemon zest, ¼ teaspoon salt, and pepper; refrigerate until ready to use.

2. Using highest sauté or browning function, heat remaining 1 tablespoon oil in pressure cooker until shimmering. Add pepper, onion, and remaining ¼ teaspoon salt and cook until vegetables are softened, about 5 minutes. Stir in remaining garlic, ras el hanout, and ginger and cook until fragrant, about 30 seconds. Stir in tomatoes and reserved juice.

3. Lock lid in place and close pressure release valve. Select high pressure cook function and cook for 15 minutes. Turn off pressure cooker and quick-release pressure. Carefully remove lid, allowing steam to escape away from you.

4. Stir shrimp into tomato mixture, cover, and let sit until opaque throughout, 5 to 7 minutes. Stir in olives and parsley and season with salt and pepper to taste. Sprinkle individual portions with scallions and drizzle with extra oil before serving.

Pressure-Cooker Mussels with White Wine and Garlic

Serves 4 to 6 FAST

Why This Recipe Works Paired with some crusty bread and a simple salad, mussels are a summertime favorite for a light seafood meal. But getting them perfectly cooked can be tricky, with most stovetop recipes inevitably turning out some overcooked and some undercooked mussels. We made cooking mussels absolutely foolproof by using our pressure cooker, which evenly surrounded the mussels with steam and resulted in a pot full of tender, plump mussels every time. We needed to cook the mussels for just 1 minute. To infuse the mussels with lots of flavor, we sautéed garlic, thyme, and red pepper flakes in butter, and used wine as the cooking liquid. We finished the mussels with some minced fresh parsley. You can substitute 3 pounds of littleneck clams for the mussels; increase the cooking time to 2 minutes. Discard any raw mussels with an unpleasant odor or with a cracked or broken shell or a shell that won't close. Serve with Garlic Toasts or crusty bread. This recipe will only work in an electric pressure cooker.

- 4 tablespoons unsalted butter
- 4 garlic cloves, sliced thin
- 4 sprigs fresh thyme
- ¼ teaspoon table salt
  Pinch red pepper flakes
- 2 bay leaves
- 3 pounds mussels, scrubbed and debearded
- ½ cup dry white wine
- 2 tablespoons minced fresh parsley

1. Using highest sauté or browning function, melt butter in pressure cooker. Add garlic, thyme sprigs, salt, pepper flakes, and bay leaves and cook until fragrant, about 30 seconds. Stir in mussels and wine.

2. Lock lid in place and close pressure release valve. Select high pressure cook function and cook for 1 minute. Turn off pressure cooker and quick-release pressure. Carefully remove lid, allowing steam to escape away from you.

3. Discard thyme sprigs, bay leaves, and any mussels that have not opened. Stir in parsley and transfer to large serving bowl. Serve.

DEBEARDING MUSSELS
When you buy mussels, you might notice that some of the mussels have a weedy piece (known as a beard) protruding from their shells. Though the beard is harmless, it does look unattractive in dishes, so you should remove it. Because it's fairly small, it can be difficult to tug out of place. To remove it easily, use this technique:

Trap beard between side of a small knife and your thumb and pull to remove it. Make sure to throw away mussels with cracked shells. If any mussels are open, tap them. If they do not close up again, toss them out.

Garlic Toasts
Makes 8 slices
Be sure to use a high-quality crusty bread, such as a baguette; do not use sliced sandwich bread.

- 8 (1-inch-thick) slices rustic bread
- 1 large garlic clove, peeled
- 3 tablespoons extra-virgin olive oil

Adjust oven rack 6 inches from broiler element and heat broiler. Spread bread evenly in rimmed baking sheet and broil, flipping as needed, until well toasted on both sides, about 4 minutes. Briefly rub 1 side of each toast with garlic, drizzle with oil, and season with salt and pepper to taste. Serve.

Pressure-Cooker Beet and Watercress Salad with Orange and Dill

Pressure-Cooker Rustic Garlic Toasts with Stewed Tomatoes, Shaved Fennel, and Burrata

Pressure-Cooker Beet and Watercress Salad with Orange and Dill
Serves 4 FAST

Why This Recipe Works Beets are a beloved late summer vegetable, but cooking them can be messy and time-consuming. We used the pressure cooker to make beets simpler to prepare so they could star in a satisfying beet salad. The salad had a medley of contrasting flavors and textures and enough heft to make a light weeknight dinner. After cooking the beets under pressure with caraway seeds and water (no peeling required), we stirred the intensely flavored cooking liquid into some creamy Greek yogurt, turning it a spectacular pink, perfect as a base to some lightly dressed, peppery watercress. Some orange zest brightened up the beets, and we arranged them on top of the greens. A sprinkling of dill brought out the anise notes of the caraway seeds, and hazelnuts and coarse sea salt added rich crunchiness. To make this a heartier meal, add Easy-Peel Hard-Cooked Eggs (page 54) and serve with crusty bread. This recipe will only work in an electric pressure cooker.

2 pounds beets, scrubbed, trimmed, and cut into ¾-inch pieces
½ cup water
1 teaspoon caraway seeds
½ teaspoon table salt
1 cup plain Greek yogurt
1 small garlic clove, minced to paste
5 ounces (5 cups) watercress, torn into bite-size pieces
1 tablespoon extra-virgin olive oil, divided, plus extra for drizzling
1 tablespoon white wine vinegar, divided
1 teaspoon grated orange zest plus 2 tablespoons juice
¼ cup hazelnuts, toasted, skinned, and chopped
¼ cup coarsely chopped fresh dill
Coarse sea salt

1. Combine beets, water, caraway seeds, and table salt in pressure cooker. Lock lid in place and close pressure release valve. Select high pressure cook function and cook for 8 minutes. Turn off pressure cooker and quick-release pressure. Carefully remove lid, allowing steam to escape away from you.

2. Using slotted spoon, transfer beets to plate; set aside to cool slightly. Combine yogurt, garlic, and 3 tablespoons beet cooking liquid in bowl; discard remaining cooking liquid. In separate large bowl, toss watercress with 2 teaspoons oil and 1 teaspoon vinegar. Season with salt and pepper to taste.

3. Spread yogurt mixture over surface of serving platter. Arrange watercress on top of yogurt mixture, leaving 1-inch border of yogurt mixture. Add beets to now-empty large bowl and toss with orange zest and juice, remaining 2 teaspoons vinegar, and remaining 1 teaspoon oil. Season with salt and pepper to taste. Arrange beets on top of watercress mixture. Drizzle with extra oil and sprinkle with dill, hazelnuts, and sea salt to taste. Serve.

Pressure-Cooker Green Beans with Tomatoes and Basil

Serves 4

Why This Recipe Works Unlike crisp-tender green beans that have been steamed or sautéed, braised green beans boast a uniquely soft texture without being mushy. Unfortunately, achieving this can require 2 hours of simmering. To get ultra-tender braised green beans in a fraction of the time, we used the quick cooking, even heat of a pressure cooker. For a more substantial meal, we added chunks of Yukon Gold potatoes, which turned tender in the same amount of time as the beans. Canned tomatoes supplied sweetness, while their juice along with a little water provided just enough braising liquid for the beans. Shaved Parmesan, a final drizzle of fruity extra-virgin olive oil, and toasted pine nuts added richness and textural contrast. To make this a heartier meal, add Easy-Peel Hard-Cooked Eggs (page 54) and serve with crusty bread. This recipe will only work in an electric pressure cooker.

- 2 tablespoons extra-virgin olive oil, plus extra for drizzling
- 1 onion, chopped fine
- 2 tablespoons minced fresh oregano or 2 teaspoons dried
- 2 tablespoons tomato paste
- 4 garlic cloves, minced
- 1 (14.5-ounce) can whole peeled tomatoes, drained with juice reserved, chopped
- ½ cup water
- 1½ pounds green beans, trimmed and cut into 2-inch lengths
- 1 pound Yukon Gold potatoes, peeled and cut into 1-inch pieces
- 1 teaspoon table salt
- ¼ teaspoon pepper
- 3 tablespoons chopped fresh basil or parsley
- 2 tablespoons toasted pine nuts
  Shaved Parmesan cheese

1. Using highest sauté function, heat oil in pressure cooker until shimmering. Add onion and cook until softened, about 5 minutes. Stir in oregano, tomato paste, and garlic and cook until fragrant, about 30 seconds. Stir in tomatoes and their juice, water, salt, and pepper, then stir in green beans and potatoes. Lock lid in place and close pressure release valve. Select high pressure cook function and cook for 5 minutes.

2. Turn off pressure cooker and quick-release pressure. Carefully remove lid, allowing steam to escape away from you. Season with salt and pepper to taste. Sprinkle individual portions with basil, pine nuts, and Parmesan and drizzle with extra oil. Serve.

Pressure-Cooker Rustic Garlic Toasts with Stewed Tomatoes, Shaved Fennel, and Burrata

Serves 4

Why This Recipe Works Burrata is a decadent version of mozzarella in which the supple cheese is bound around a filling of cream and soft curds. It is commonly served with tomatoes, whose natural acidity tempers the richness of the cheese. Here, we also like to add fresh fennel, and some toasty bread for a light vegetarian meal. Cooking whole peeled tomatoes in the pressure cooker turned them tender, and their freshness almost intensified under pressure. We spooned them over Garlic Toasts (page 169), and added a salad of arugula and shaved fennel. We drizzled the burrata with a sweet-sour balsamic glaze. To crush fennel seeds, place them on a cutting board and rock the bottom edge of a skillet over them until they crack. To make a balsamic glaze, simmer ¼ cup balsamic vinegar and 2 tablespoons brown sugar in a small saucepan set over medium heat until slightly thickened, about 3 minutes. This recipe will only work in an electric pressure cooker.

- 2 tablespoons extra-virgin olive oil, divided, plus extra for drizzling
- 5 garlic cloves, sliced thin
- 1½ teaspoons fennel seeds, lightly cracked
- 1 (28-ounce) can whole peeled tomatoes, drained with juice reserved, halved
- ⅛ teaspoon table salt
- 8 ounces burrata cheese, room temperature
- 1 fennel bulb, 1 tablespoon fronds chopped, stalks discarded, bulb halved, cored, and sliced thin
- 4 ounces (4 cups) baby arugula
- 1 recipe Garlic Toasts (page 169)
  Balsamic glaze

1. Using highest sauté function, cook 1 tablespoon oil, garlic, and fennel seeds in pressure cooker until fragrant and garlic is light-golden brown, about 3 minutes. Stir in tomatoes and reserved juice and salt. Lock lid in place and close pressure release valve. Select high pressure cook function and cook for 2 minutes.

2. Turn off pressure cooker and quick-release pressure. Carefully remove lid, allowing steam to escape away from you. Continue to cook tomatoes using highest sauté function until sauce is slightly thickened, about 5 minutes.

3. Place burrata on plate and cut into 1-inch pieces, collecting creamy liquid. Toss fennel and arugula with remaining 1 tablespoon oil in large bowl. Season with salt and pepper to taste. Arrange toasts on individual serving plates and top with tomatoes, fennel-arugula salad, and burrata and any accumulated liquid. Drizzle with glaze and extra oil. Serve.

Pressure-Cooker Ratatouille
Serves 4

Why This Recipe Works Classic ratatouille, a summery Provençal vegetable dish, is chock-full of our favorite seasonal produce. The downside is that most of these vegetables have high water contents, making it too easy to end up with soggy ratatouille. We wanted a streamlined recipe with great flavor and texture that we could prep and walk away from using our pressure cooker. Sautéing the peppers released some of their moisture and concentrated their flavor. Garlic, pepper flakes, and herbes de Provence added spice and characteristic backbone. The best part? We found that pretreating the eggplant wasn't necessary—cutting it small helped shorten the cook time as well as ensuring it would break down and help create a thicker sauce. Canned whole tomatoes and zucchini rounded out the vegetable medley. A splash of vinegar helped wake up the flavors of the sweet vegetables, and bright pesto gave it a fresh, rich finish, with plenty of flavor. Serve with Couscous, Everyday White Rice (page 107), grains, or crusty bread. This recipe will only work in an electric pressure cooker.

- 2 tablespoons extra-virgin olive oil
- 2 red or yellow bell peppers, stemmed, seeded, and cut into 1-inch pieces
- 1 onion, chopped fine
- 1 teaspoon table salt
- 4 garlic cloves, minced
- 1 teaspoon herbes de Provence
- ¼ teaspoon red pepper flakes

- 1 (28-ounce) can whole peeled tomatoes, drained with juice reserved, chopped
- 1 pound eggplant, cut into ½-inch pieces
- 1 pound zucchini, quartered lengthwise and sliced 1 inch thick
- 1 tablespoon sherry vinegar
- ¼ cup basil pesto, plus extra for serving

1. Using highest sauté or browning function, heat oil in pressure cooker until shimmering. Add peppers, onion, and salt and cook until softened, about 5 minutes. Stir in garlic, herbes de Provence, and pepper flakes and cook until fragrant, about 30 seconds. Stir in tomatoes and their juice, eggplant, and zucchini. Lock lid in place and close pressure release valve. Select high pressure cook function and cook for 1 minute.

2. Turn off pressure cooker and quick-release pressure. Carefully remove lid, allowing steam to escape away from you. Using highest sauté or browning function, continue to cook vegetable mixture until zucchini is tender and sauce has thickened slightly, 3 to 5 minutes. Stir in vinegar and season with salt and pepper to taste. Dollop individual portions with pesto and serve, passing extra pesto separately.

Couscous
Serves 4 to 6
Be sure to use regular (or fine-grain) couscous; large-grain couscous, often labeled "Israeli-style," takes much longer to cook and won't work in this recipe. Use a large fork to fluff the couscous grains; a spoon or spatula can mash its light texture.

- 2 tablespoons unsalted butter
- 2 cups couscous
- 1 cup water
- 1 cup chicken broth
- 1 teaspoon table salt

1. Melt butter in medium saucepan over medium-high heat. Add couscous and cook, stirring frequently, until grains are just beginning to brown, about 5 minutes.

2. Add water, broth, and salt; stir briefly to combine, cover, and remove saucepan from heat. Let sit until grains are tender, about 7 minutes. Uncover and fluff grains with fork. Season with pepper to taste and serve.

Pressure-Cooker
Boston Baked Beans

Serves 6

Why This Recipe Works Boston baked beans—tender navy beans in a sweet-savory sauce—are a cookout favorite. Using a pressure cooker to make them freed up our time: The even, steady heat and closed environment (meaning limited evaporation) made this dish hands-off. Brining the beans seasoned them and helped them hold their shape while cooking. After brining, we merely combined the beans and other ingredients in the pressure cooker and locked on the lid. You'll get fewer blowouts if you soak the beans overnight, but if you're pressed for time you can quick-salt-soak your beans: In step 1, combine the salt, water, and beans in the pressure cooker and bring everything to a boil using the highest sauté or browning function. Turn off the pressure cooker, cover, and let the beans sit for 1 hour. Drain and rinse the beans and proceed with the recipe as directed. This recipe will only work in an electric pressure cooker.

1½ tablespoons table salt, for brining
1 pound (2½ cups) dried navy beans, picked over and rinsed
6 ounces salt pork, rind removed, rinsed, and cut into 3 pieces
1 onion, halved
½ cup molasses
2 tablespoons packed dark brown sugar
2 tablespoons vegetable oil
1 tablespoon soy sauce
2 teaspoons dry mustard
1 teaspoon table salt
½ teaspoon pepper
½ teaspoon baking soda
1 bay leaf

1. Dissolve 1½ tablespoons salt in 8 cups cold water in large container. Add beans and let soak at room temperature for at least 8 hours or up to 24 hours. Drain and rinse well.

2. Combine soaked beans, 2½ cups water, salt pork, onion, molasses, sugar, oil, soy sauce, mustard, 1 teaspoon salt, pepper, baking soda, and bay leaf in pressure cooker.

3. Lock lid in place and close pressure release valve. Select high pressure cook function and cook for 50 minutes. Turn off pressure cooker and let pressure release naturally for 15 minutes. Quick-release any remaining pressure, then carefully remove lid, allowing steam to escape away from you.

4. Discard bay leaf and onion. If necessary, continue to cook beans using highest sauté or browning function until sauce has thickened and clings to beans. Serve.

Pressure-Cooker Ratatouille

**Pressure-Cooker
Boston Baked Beans**

Dinner Off the Grill

For grilled burgers and tacos, see Burgers, Sandwiches, and Tacos (pages 70–103). For more grilled salads, see Dinner-Size Salads (pages 38–69)

■ FAST (30 minutes or less total time) ■ MAKE AHEAD

Photos (clockwise from top left): Paprika-and-Lime-Rubbed Chicken with Grilled Vegetable Succotash; Grilled Paella; Grilled Porterhouse or T-Bone Steaks; Grilled Caesar Salad

Using a Charcoal Grill

Grilling food turns it into something special and there's no better time to grill than in the summer. Each recipe in this chapter contains specific instructions for cooking on either a charcoal or a gas grill. Follow the fire setup instructions carefully to ensure recipe success.

USE A CHIMNEY STARTER

We strongly recommend using a chimney starter for charcoal fires. (Lighter fluid imparts an off-flavor to grilled foods.) This simple device gets all of the charcoal ready at once. Fill the bottom of the chimney starter with crumpled newspaper, set it on the charcoal grate, and fill the top with charcoal as directed. A large starter holds about 6 quarts of charcoal.

GET THE COALS HOT

Allow the charcoal to burn until the briquettes on top are partially covered with a thin layer of gray ash. The ash is a sign that the coals are fully lit and hot and are ready to be turned out into the grill. Don't pour out the coals prematurely; you will be left with unlit coals at the bottom of the pile that may never ignite, as well as a cooler fire.

ARRANGE THE COALS CAREFULLY

Once the coals are covered with gray ash, empty them evenly onto the charcoal grate or as instructed in the recipe. A single-level fire is a common fire setup that delivers a uniform level of heat across the entire cooking surface.

USING A DISPOSABLE PAN

Some fire setups call for using a disposable aluminum pan. Piling coals on either side of the pan creates a cool area over the pan for foods such as bone-in chicken. Alternatively, corralling the coals in the pan concentrates the heat to create an intense fire ideal for quicker-cooking foods such as burgers and scallops.

MODIFIED TWO-LEVEL (HALF-GRILL) CHARCOAL FIRE

A half-grill fire has two cooking zones for foods that require longer cooking: You can brown the food on the hotter side and finish it on the cooler side's indirect heat. To set up this fire, distribute ash-covered coals over half of the grill, piling them in an even layer. Leave the other half free of coals.

CLEAN AND OIL THE COOKING GRATE

Properly heating and cleaning your grill are important steps to successful grilling. To ensure that food will release with ease, heat the grate before scraping it clean with a grill brush. For further insurance against sticking, dip a wad of paper towels into vegetable oil and run it over the cleaned grate several times.

Grilled Chicken Kebabs with Garlic and Herb Marinade

Serves 4 `MAKE AHEAD`

Why This Recipe Works Chicken kebabs are a great way to take boneless, skinless chicken breasts up a notch, but the lean meat requires some help to keep from becoming dried out over a hot grill. To counter this, we started with a simple olive oil marinade. Brining meat helps it retain moisture, but we worried that a true brine would make the small pieces of chicken too salty. Instead, we simply added a teaspoon of salt to the marinade, along with a mix of herbs and garlic—you can tweak the herbs based on what you like best, or try one of our spiced-up variations. Because there is no acid in the marinade and thus no danger of breaking down the texture of the meat, the chicken can be soaked for up to 24 hours before cooking. You will need four 12-inch metal skewers for this recipe.

½ cup extra-virgin olive oil
¼ cup chopped fresh chives or minced fresh basil, parsley, tarragon, oregano, cilantro, or mint; or 2 tablespoons minced fresh thyme or rosemary
6 garlic cloves, minced
1 teaspoon table salt
½ teaspoon pepper
1½ pounds boneless, skinless chicken breasts, trimmed and cut into 1-inch pieces
2 red bell peppers, stemmed, seeded, and cut into 1-inch pieces
1 large red onion, cut into 1-inch pieces, 3 layers thick

1. Whisk oil, herbs, garlic, salt, and pepper together in small bowl. Combine marinade and chicken in 1-gallon zipper-lock bag; seal bag and refrigerate, turning once or twice, for at least 3 hours or up to 24 hours.

2. Remove chicken from marinade. Thread each of four 12-inch metal skewers with 2 pieces bell pepper, 1 section onion, 2 pieces chicken, and 1 section onion. Repeat twice more, ending with 2 additional pieces bell pepper.

3A. For a charcoal grill Open bottom vent completely. Light large chimney starter filled with charcoal briquettes (6 quarts). When top coals are partially covered with ash, pour evenly over grill. Set cooking grate in place, cover, and open lid vent completely. Heat grill until hot, about 5 minutes.

3B. For a gas grill Turn all burners to high, cover, and heat grill until hot, about 15 minutes. Leave all burners on high.

4. Clean and oil cooking grate. Place kebabs on grill. Cook (covered if using gas), turning as needed, until vegetables and chicken are charred around edges and chicken is cooked through, about 12 minutes. Transfer kebabs to serving platter and serve.

Grilled Chicken Kebabs with Garlic and Herb Marinade

VARIATIONS
Grilled Chicken Kebabs with Middle Eastern Marinade

Substitute ¼ cup minced fresh mint or parsley (alone or in combination) for herbs and add ½ teaspoon ground cinnamon, ½ teaspoon ground allspice, and ¼ teaspoon cayenne pepper to marinade.

Grilled Chicken Kebabs with Mediterranean Marinade

Substitute following mixture for herb marinade: Combine ½ cup plain whole-milk yogurt, ¼ cup extra-virgin olive oil, 3 minced garlic cloves, 2 teaspoons dried thyme, 2 teaspoons dried oregano, 1 teaspoon table salt, 1 teaspoon pepper, and ¼ teaspoon cayenne pepper. In step 2, marinate chicken for 3 to 6 hours. Whisk ¼ cup extra-virgin olive oil, 1 minced garlic clove, 2 tablespoons chopped fresh basil, and 3 tablespoons lemon juice together in bowl; set aside. Skewer chicken and grill as directed. Brush cooked kebabs with lemon dressing before serving.

Chicken Souvlaki
Serves 4 to 6

Why This Recipe Works *Souvlaki* is a Greek grilled specialty consisting of chunks of marinated meat threaded onto skewers, sometimes with vegetables such as green pepper and onion. Chicken souvlaki is almost always made with boneless, skinless breasts, which have a marked tendency to dry out when grilled. To help prevent this, we swapped traditional overnight marinating for a quick brine while the grill heated. We then tossed the chicken with a flavorful mixture of lemon, olive oil, herbs, and honey right before grilling. To prevent the end pieces from overcooking, we protected them by threading pepper and onion pieces on the ends of the skewers. Once the chicken was cooked, we tossed it with the reserved marinade to ensure that it was brightly flavored. We like the chicken in a wrap, but you may skip the pita and serve the chicken, vegetables, and tzatziki with rice. If using kosher chicken, do not brine in step 1. You will need four 12-inch metal skewers for this recipe.

Chicken Souvlaki

- 2 tablespoons table salt, for brining
- 1½ pounds boneless, skinless chicken breasts, trimmed and cut into 1-inch pieces
- ⅓ cup extra-virgin olive oil
- 2 tablespoons minced fresh parsley
- 1 teaspoon finely grated lemon zest plus ¼ cup juice (2 lemons)
- 1 teaspoon honey
- 1 teaspoon dried oregano
- ½ teaspoon pepper
- 1 green bell pepper, quartered, stemmed, seeded, and each quarter cut into 4 pieces
- 1 small red onion, halved through root end, each half cut into 4 chunks
- 4–6 (8-inch) pita breads
- 1 cup Tzatziki (page 20)

1. Dissolve 2 tablespoons salt in 1 quart cold water in large container. Submerge chicken in brine, cover, and refrigerate for 30 minutes. Combine oil, parsley, lemon zest and juice, honey, oregano, and pepper in medium bowl. Reserve ¼ cup oil mixture in large bowl.

2. Remove chicken from brine and pat dry with paper towels. Toss chicken with remaining oil mixture. Thread 4 pieces of bell pepper, concave side up, onto one 12-inch metal skewer. Thread one-quarter of chicken onto skewer. Thread 2 pieces of onion onto skewer and place skewer on plate. Repeat skewering remaining chicken and vegetables on 3 more skewers. Lightly moisten 2 pita breads with water. Sandwich unmoistened pitas between moistened pitas and wrap stack tightly in lightly greased heavy-duty aluminum foil.

3A. For a charcoal grill Open bottom vent completely. Light large chimney starter mounded with charcoal briquettes (7 quarts). When top coals are partially covered with ash, pour evenly over half of grill. Set cooking grate in place, cover, and open lid vent completely. Heat grill until hot, about 5 minutes.

3B. For a gas grill Turn all burners to high, cover, and heat grill until hot, about 15 minutes. Leave primary burner on high and turn off other burner(s).

4. Clean and oil cooking grate. Place skewers on hotter side of grill and cook, turning occasionally, until chicken and vegetables are well browned and chicken registers 160 degrees, 15 to 20 minutes. Using tongs, slide chicken and vegetables off skewers into bowl of reserved oil mixture. Toss gently, breaking up onion pieces. Cover loosely with foil and let sit while heating pitas.

5. Place packet of pitas on cooler side of grill and flip occasionally until heated through, about 5 minutes. Lay each warm pita on 12-inch square of foil. Spread each pita with 2 tablespoons tzatziki. Distribute chicken and vegetables evenly among pitas, placing in middle of each pita. Roll into cylindrical shape and serve.

Grilled Lemon-Parsley Chicken Breasts

Serves 4

Why This Recipe Works Chicken breasts that come off the grill juicy and flavorful are a crowd-pleasing main dish perfect for pairing with colorful vegetables or a refreshing salad for a simple summertime meal. We first marinated the chicken breasts in a simple combination of olive oil, lemon juice, garlic, parsley, salt, pepper, and a bit of sugar, which helped keep them from drying out while cooking. We kept the marinade's acidity low by reducing the lemon juice to avoid mushy chicken but added the bright lemon flavor back in by drizzling the cooked chicken with a complementary vinaigrette before serving. Cooked over a hot, single-level fire, the outer layers of the chicken breasts burned before the inside was cooked through, so we ended up using a two-level fire. We cooked the chicken, covered, over the cooler side of the grill until it was almost done and then finished it with a quick sear for perfectly cooked breasts. The flavors of the citrus-herb marinade are easy to switch up—we provide two other flavor options. The chicken should be marinated for no less than 30 minutes and no more than 1 hour. Serve with a simply prepared vegetable or use in sandwiches or salad.

- 6 tablespoons extra-virgin olive oil, divided
- 2 tablespoons lemon juice, divided
- 1 tablespoon minced fresh parsley
- 1¼ teaspoons sugar, divided
- 1 teaspoon Dijon mustard
- ¾ teaspoon table salt, divided
- ¾ teaspoon pepper, divided
- 2 tablespoons water
- 3 garlic cloves, minced
- 4 (6- to 8-ounce) boneless, skinless chicken breasts, trimmed

1. Whisk 3 tablespoons oil, 1 tablespoon lemon juice, parsley, ¼ teaspoon sugar, mustard, ¼ teaspoon salt, and ¼ teaspoon pepper together in bowl and set aside for serving.

2. Whisk water, garlic, remaining 3 tablespoons oil, remaining 1 tablespoon lemon juice, remaining 1 teaspoon sugar, remaining ½ teaspoon salt, and remaining ½ teaspoon pepper together in bowl. Place marinade and chicken in 1-gallon zipper-lock bag and toss to coat; press out as much air as possible and seal bag. Refrigerate for at least 30 minutes or up to 1 hour, flipping bag every 15 minutes.

3A. For a charcoal grill Open bottom vent completely. Light large chimney starter filled with charcoal briquettes (6 quarts). When top coals are partially covered with ash, pour evenly over half of grill. Set cooking grate in place, cover, and open lid vent completely. Heat grill until hot, about 5 minutes.

3B. For a gas grill Turn all burners to high, cover, and heat grill until hot, about 15 minutes. Leave primary burner on high and turn off other burner(s).

4. Clean and oil cooking grate. Remove chicken from bag, allowing excess marinade to drip off. Place chicken on cooler side of grill, smooth side down, with thicker sides facing coals and flames. Cover and cook until bottom of chicken just begins to develop light grill marks and is no longer translucent, 6 to 9 minutes.

5. Flip chicken and rotate so that thinner sides face coals and flames. Cover and continue to cook until chicken is opaque and firm to touch and registers 140 degrees, 6 to 9 minutes.

6. Move chicken to hotter side of grill and cook until dark grill marks appear on both sides and chicken registers 160 degrees, 2 to 6 minutes.

7. Transfer chicken to carving board, tent with aluminum foil, and let rest for 5 to 10 minutes. Slice each breast on bias into ¼-inch-thick slices and transfer to individual plates. Drizzle with reserved vinaigrette and serve.

VARIATIONS

Grilled Chipotle-Lime Chicken Breasts
Substitute lime juice for lemon juice and use extra teaspoon lime juice in reserved vinaigrette in step 1. Substitute 1 teaspoon minced chipotle chile in adobo sauce for mustard and cilantro for parsley.

Grilled Orange-Tarragon Chicken Breasts
Substitute orange juice for lemon juice and tarragon for parsley. Add ¼ teaspoon grated orange zest to reserved vinaigrette in step 1.

CREATING A SINGLE-LEVEL OR OTHER GAS FIRE

To create a single-level fire on a gas grill, turn all the burners to the heat setting specified in the recipe after preheating the grill. To create other fires, adjust the primary burner as directed in the recipe and turn off or adjust the other burner(s).

Grilled Bone-In Chicken
Serves 4 to 6

Why This Recipe Works Smoky bone-in chicken with subtle charred flavor is a must-have in your summer dinner rotation. But flare-ups can turn chicken into a charred mess if you're not paying attention. We wanted to avoid this pitfall by starting the chicken over a relatively cool area of the grill. This allowed the fat in the chicken skin to render slowly, thereby avoiding flare-ups and encouraging ultracrisp skin. Finishing it over the hotter side of the grill yielded beautifully well-browned chicken. In addition to the quality of the finished product, we loved this approach because it was effectively hands-off: We didn't have to constantly move and monitor the chicken pieces. This recipe works with breasts, legs, thighs, or a combination of parts. For extra flavor, rub the chicken with Cajun or Tex-Mex Spice Rubs before cooking, or brush with barbecue sauce during the final few minutes of grilling.

- 4 pounds bone-in chicken pieces (split breasts cut in half crosswise, drumsticks, and/or thighs), trimmed
- 1 teaspoon table salt
- ½ teaspoon pepper
- 1 (13 by 9-inch) disposable aluminum roasting pan (if using charcoal)

1. Pat chicken dry with paper towels and sprinkle with salt and pepper.

2A. For a charcoal grill Open bottom vent completely and place disposable pan in center of grill. Light large chimney starter filled with charcoal briquettes (6 quarts). When top coals are partially covered with ash, pour into 2 even piles on either side of disposable pan. Set cooking grate in place, cover, and open lid vent completely. Heat grill until hot, about 5 minutes.

2B. For a gas grill Turn all burners to high, cover, and heat grill until hot, about 15 minutes. Turn all burners to medium-low.

3. Clean and oil cooking grate. Place chicken, skin side down, on grill (over disposable pan if using charcoal). Cover and cook until skin is crisp and golden, about 20 minutes.

4. Slide chicken to hotter sides of grill if using charcoal, or turn all burners to medium-high if using gas. Cook (covered if using gas), turning as needed, until well browned on both sides and breasts register 160 degrees and drumsticks/thighs register 175 degrees, 5 to 15 minutes.

5. Transfer chicken to serving platter, tent with aluminum foil, and let rest for 5 to 10 minutes before serving.

VARIATIONS
Grilled Bone-In Chicken with Cajun Spice Rub
Makes about 1 cup

- ½ cup paprika
- 2 tablespoons kosher salt
- 2 tablespoons garlic powder
- 1 tablespoon dried thyme
- 2 teaspoons ground celery seeds
- 2 teaspoons pepper
- 2 teaspoons cayenne pepper

Combine all ingredients in bowl. Substitute ⅓ cup spice rub for salt and pepper. Remaining spice rub can be stored in airtight container for up to 3 months.

Grilled Bone-In Chicken with Tex-Mex Spice Rub
Makes about 1 cup

- ¼ cup ground cumin
- 2 tablespoons chili powder
- 2 tablespoons ground coriander
- 2 tablespoons dried oregano
- 2 tablespoons garlic powder
- 4 teaspoons kosher salt
- 2 teaspoons unsweetened cocoa powder
- 1 teaspoon cayenne pepper

Combine all ingredients in bowl. Substitute ⅓ cup spice rub for salt and pepper. Remaining spice rub can be stored in airtight container for up to 3 months.

Teriyaki Chicken with Grilled Bok Choy and Pineapple
Serves 4

Why This Recipe Works Teriyaki-sauced grilled chicken and grilled fresh produce make an ideal summer meal. A quick homemade teriyaki sauce beats out the bottled stuff. We brushed our sauce on bone-in chicken thighs toward the end of grilling so it would not burn. For the vegetable component, we chose baby bok choy, which takes on complexity when grilled and balanced the savory chicken. The caramelized sweetness of grilled pineapple rounded out our plate. You can buy and use fresh peeled and cored pineapple in this recipe if you prefer; canned pineapple rings will also work in a pinch.

⅓ cup soy sauce

¼ cup sugar

2 tablespoons mirin

1 tablespoon grated fresh ginger

1 teaspoon cornstarch

4 heads baby bok choy (4 ounces each), halved lengthwise

1 tablespoon vegetable oil

1½ teaspoons table salt, divided

¾ teaspoon pepper, divided

1 pineapple (about 4 pounds), peeled, cored, and sliced lengthwise into 1-inch-thick planks

8 (5- to 7-ounce) bone-in chicken thighs

2 scallions, sliced thin on bias

1. Whisk soy sauce, sugar, mirin, ginger, and cornstarch together in small saucepan. Bring to boil over medium-high heat and cook until thickened, about 2 minutes.

2. Place bok choy in bowl, cover, and microwave until beginning to soften, 3 to 5 minutes. Drain any liquid from bowl and toss bok choy with oil, ½ teaspoon salt, and ¼ teaspoon pepper.

3. Brush pineapple planks with 2 tablespoons teriyaki sauce. Trim chicken, pat dry with paper towels, and sprinkle with remaining 1 teaspoon salt and remaining ½ teaspoon pepper.

4A. For a charcoal grill Open bottom vent completely. Light large chimney starter full of charcoal briquettes (6 quarts). When top coals are partially covered with ash, pour two-thirds evenly over half of grill, then pour remaining coals over other half of grill. Set cooking grate in place, cover, and open lid vent completely. Heat grill until hot, about 5 minutes.

4B. For a gas grill Turn all burners to high, cover, and heat grill until hot, about 15 minutes. Leave primary burner on high and turn other burner(s) to low.

5. Clean and oil cooking grate. Place chicken, skin side down, on cooler side of grill. Cover and cook until chicken registers 175 degrees, 20 to 25 minutes. Halfway through cooking rearrange so all pieces get equal exposure to heat source.

6. While chicken cooks on cooler side, place pineapple and bok choy (in batches, if necessary), on hotter side of grill and cook, covered, until lightly charred and tender, 2 to 5 minutes, flipping halfway through cooking; transfer to serving platter as they finish cooking and tent with aluminum foil.

7. Transfer chicken pieces, skin side up, to hotter side of grill. Brush chicken all over with ¼ cup teriyaki sauce and continue to grill, uncovered and flipping often, until sauce begins to caramelize, about 5 minutes; transfer to serving platter, and let rest for 5 to 10 minutes. Brush remaining sauce over chicken and pineapple, sprinkle with scallions, and serve with bok choy.

Grilled Bone-In Chicken

Teriyaki Chicken with Grilled Bok Choy and Pineapple

Classic Barbecued Chicken
Serves 4 to 6

Why This Recipe Works Classic barbecued chicken is one of America's favorite summer foods. But despite its popularity, barbecued chicken recipes cause backyard grillers plenty of headaches. We set out to develop a recipe for barbecued chicken with perfect, evenly cooked meat, golden-brown skin, and intense, multidimensional barbecue flavor. Most recipes call for searing chicken quickly over high heat, but we found that starting barbecued chicken over low heat slowly rendered the fat without the danger of flare-ups and gave us evenly cooked meat all the way through. Our homemade sauce has the perfect balance of sweetness and smokiness from brewed coffee, vinegar, and molasses. We created a complex layer of barbecue flavor by applying the sauce in coats and turning the chicken as it cooked over moderate heat. The sauce turned out thick and caramelized, and it perfectly glazed the chicken. Using homemade barbecue sauce makes a big difference, but you can substitute 3 cups of store-bought sauce. Don't try to grill more than 10 pieces of chicken at a time; you won't be able to line them up as directed in step 6. You can use a mix of chicken breasts, thighs, and drumsticks, making sure they add up to 10 pieces.

Barbecue Sauce
- 1 tablespoon vegetable oil
- 1 onion, chopped fine
- Pinch table salt
- 4 cups chicken broth
- 1¼ cups cider vinegar
- 1 cup brewed coffee
- ¾ cup molasses
- ½ cup tomato paste
- ½ cup ketchup
- 2 tablespoons brown mustard
- 1 tablespoon hot sauce
- ½ teaspoon garlic powder
- ¼ teaspoon liquid smoke

Chicken
- ½ teaspoon table salt
- 1 teaspoon pepper
- ¼ teaspoon cayenne pepper
- 3 pounds bone-in chicken pieces (split breasts cut in half crosswise, drumsticks, and/or thighs), trimmed
- 1 (13 by 9-inch) disposable aluminum roasting pan (if using charcoal)

Classic Barbecued Chicken

1. For the barbecue sauce Heat oil in large saucepan over medium heat until shimmering. Add onion and salt and cook until softened, 5 to 7 minutes. Whisk in broth, vinegar, coffee, molasses, tomato paste, ketchup, mustard, hot sauce, and garlic powder.

2. Bring sauce to simmer and cook, stirring occasionally, until thickened and measures 4 cups, about 1 hour. Off heat, stir in liquid smoke. Let sauce cool completely. Season with salt and pepper to taste. Reserve 2 cups barbecue sauce for cooking; set aside remaining sauce for serving.

3. For the chicken Combine salt, pepper, and cayenne in bowl. Pat chicken dry with paper towels and rub with spices.

4A. For a charcoal grill Open bottom vent completely and place disposable pan on 1 side of grill. Light large chimney starter filled with charcoal briquettes (6 quarts). When top coals are partially covered with ash, pour evenly over other side of grill. Set cooking grate in place, cover, and open lid vent completely. Heat grill until hot, about 5 minutes.

4B. For a gas grill Turn all burners to high, cover, and heat grill until hot, about 15 minutes. Leave primary burner on high and turn off other burner(s). (Adjust primary burner as needed to maintain grill temperature around 350 degrees.)

5. Clean and oil cooking grate. Place chicken, skin side down, on cooler side of grill. Cover and cook until chicken begins to brown, 30 to 35 minutes.

6. Slide chicken into single line between hotter and cooler sides of grill. Cook uncovered, flipping chicken and brushing every 5 minutes with some of sauce reserved for cooking, until sticky, about 20 minutes.

7. Slide chicken to hotter side of grill and cook, uncovered, flipping and brushing with remaining sauce for cooking, until well glazed, breasts register 160 degrees, and drumsticks/thighs register 175 degrees, about 5 minutes. Transfer chicken to serving platter, tent with aluminum foil, and let rest for 5 to 10 minutes. Serve with remaining sauce.

Paprika-and-Lime-Rubbed Chicken with Grilled Vegetable Succotash
Serves 4

Why This Recipe Works All of the elements of this brightly flavored meal of zesty chicken and fresh summer succotash come together quickly on the grill. We made a spice rub of smoked paprika, lime zest, sugar, cumin, salt, and pepper and used it to coat the chicken parts. Cooking the chicken on the cooler side of the grill helped us avoid flare-ups while still giving it great grilled flavor and char. To bring in even more grilled flavor, we grilled the vegetables for our succotash, too, placing corn cobs, onion rounds, and skewered cherry tomatoes on the hotter side of the grill while the chicken cooked on the cooler side. We chopped the grilled onions and cut the corn from the cobs after cooking and tossed the vegetables with a simple dressing, including more lime zest and paprika to reinforce the flavors of the spice-rubbed chicken, plus some cilantro for fresh herbal notes. To round out our grilled succotash, we added canned butter beans, which were superquick to prepare and added a creamy consistency and pleasant mild flavor. You will need four 12-inch metal skewers for this recipe.

12 ounces cherry tomatoes
3 ears corn, husks and silk removed
1 red onion, sliced crosswise into ½-inch-thick rounds
¼ cup extra-virgin olive oil, divided
1 teaspoon table salt, divided
¾ teaspoon pepper, divided
1 tablespoon plus ½ teaspoon smoked hot paprika, divided

4 teaspoons grated lime zest, divided, plus 2 tablespoons juice (2 limes), and lime wedges for serving
1½ teaspoons packed dark brown sugar
1 teaspoon ground cumin
3 pounds bone-in chicken pieces (split breasts cut in half crosswise, drumsticks, and/or thighs), trimmed
3 tablespoons minced fresh cilantro, divided
2 garlic cloves, minced
1 (15-ounce) can butter beans, rinsed

1. Thread tomatoes onto four 12-inch metal skewers. Brush corn, onion, and tomato skewers with 2 tablespoons oil and sprinkle with ½ teaspoon salt and ¼ teaspoon pepper.

2. Combine 1 tablespoon paprika, 1 tablespoon lime zest, sugar, cumin, remaining ½ teaspoon salt, and remaining ½ teaspoon pepper together in large bowl. Pat chicken dry with paper towels, transfer to bowl with spice mixture, and stir to coat evenly.

3A. For a charcoal grill Open bottom vent completely. Light large chimney starter full of charcoal briquettes (6 quarts). When top coals are partially covered with ash, pour two-thirds evenly over half of grill, then pour remaining coals over other half of grill. Set cooking grate in place, cover, and open lid vent completely. Heat grill until hot, about 5 minutes.

3B. For a gas grill Turn all burners to high, cover, and heat grill until hot, about 15 minutes. Leave primary burner on high and turn other burner(s) to low.

4. Clean and oil cooking grate. Place chicken, skin side down, on cooler side of grill. Cover and cook until skin is well browned and slightly charred and breasts register 160 degrees and drumsticks/thighs register 175 degrees, 20 to 30 minutes, flipping as needed and rearranging so all pieces get equal exposure to heat source. Transfer chicken pieces to serving platter as they finish cooking, tent with aluminum foil, and let rest.

5. While chicken cooks on cooler side, place corn, onion rounds, and tomato skewers on hotter side of grill. Cook tomatoes, covered, turning as needed, until skins begin to blister, about 2 minutes; transfer to serving platter. Continue to cook corn and onion, covered, turning occasionally, until lightly charred on all sides, 8 to 10 minutes; transfer corn and onion to cutting board as they finish cooking and cover with foil.

6. Chop grilled onions and cut corn kernels from cobs. Whisk remaining 1 teaspoon lime zest, lime juice, 2 tablespoons cilantro, garlic, remaining ½ teaspoon paprika, and remaining 2 tablespoons oil together in large bowl. Add beans, tomatoes, chopped onion, and corn to bowl and toss to combine. Season with salt and pepper to taste. Sprinkle remaining 1 tablespoon cilantro over chicken. Serve with succotash and lime wedges.

Indian-Spiced Chicken with Radicchio and Grilled Naan

Grilled Butterflied Lemon Chicken

Indian-Spiced Chicken with Radicchio and Grilled Naan

Serves 4

Why This Recipe Works We love Indian takeout, especially delectable tandoori chicken, but in the summer we also like to take advantage of the weather and make our own dinner on the grill. We skipped the takeout and instead made an Indian-style chicken dinner at home with a grilled vegetable side and a cooling yogurt sauce. Garam masala was convenient to employ and made for deeply flavorful chicken. We coated the chicken parts in a mixture of the garam masala and some salt before grilling. To round out the meal, we grilled some beautiful red radicchio, which made a surprisingly great pairing for the Indian-spiced chicken; its crispy edges and bitter notes were an excellent complement to the richness of the chicken. To further balance out the flavors of the meal, we made a simple, bright sauce of plain yogurt, fresh lime juice, and chopped fresh cilantro for some color and kick. Finally, we completed our Indian meal with quickly grilled store-bought naan.

- ¾ cup plain whole-milk yogurt
- 2 tablespoons fresh lime juice
- 2 tablespoons finely chopped fresh cilantro, divided
- 1¼ teaspoons table salt, divided
- 1 tablespoon garam masala
- 3 pounds bone-in chicken pieces (split breasts cut in half crosswise, drumsticks, and/or thighs), trimmed
- 1 head radicchio (10 ounces), cut into quarters, leaving core intact
- 1 tablespoon extra-virgin olive oil
- ⅛ teaspoon pepper
- 2 naan breads, halved

1. Stir yogurt, lime juice, 1 tablespoon cilantro, and ½ teaspoon salt in small bowl until smooth; set aside sauce for serving. Mix garam masala and ½ teaspoon salt together in large bowl.

2. Pat chicken dry with paper towels, transfer to bowl with spice mixture, and stir to coat evenly. Brush radicchio with oil and sprinkle with remaining ¼ teaspoon salt and pepper

3A. For a charcoal grill Open bottom vent completely. Light large chimney starter full of charcoal briquettes (6 quarts). When top coals are partially covered with ash, pour two-thirds evenly over half of grill, then pour remaining coals over other half of grill. Set cooking grate in place, cover, and open lid vent completely. Heat grill until hot, about 5 minutes.

3B. For a gas grill Turn all burners to high, cover, and heat grill until hot, about 15 minutes. Leave primary burner on high and turn other burner(s) to low.

4. Clean and oil cooking grate. Place chicken, skin side down, on cooler side of grill. Cover and cook until skin is well browned and slightly charred and breasts register 160 degrees and drumsticks/thighs register 175 degrees, 20 to 30 minutes, flipping as needed and rearranging so all pieces get equal exposure to heat source. Transfer chicken pieces to serving platter as they finish cooking. Tent with aluminum foil and let rest.

5. While chicken cooks on cooler side, place radicchio on hotter side of grill. Cook, flipping as needed, until softened and lightly charred, 3 to 5 minutes. Transfer radicchio to serving platter and tent with foil. While chicken rests, grill naan on hotter side of grill, uncovered, until warmed through, 1 minute per side. Sprinkle chicken with remaining 1 tablespoon cilantro and serve with reserved sauce and naan.

Grilled Butterflied Lemon Chicken
Serves 8 `MAKE AHEAD`

Why This Recipe Works Lemony chicken is always a winning idea, and butterflying is a great way to prepare whole chickens for grilling to achieve succulent meat and irresistibly crisped skin. For perfectly grilled butterflied lemon chicken, we banked all the coals on one side of the grill, placed the chicken opposite the coals, and set the lid on the grill. The relatively gentle heat rendered the fat slowly and resulted in a moister bird. Placing the chicken skin side down reduced the cooking time and maximized the amount of fat rendered. A final sear directly over the dying coals at the end of cooking crisped and browned the skin nicely. To finish the chicken with intense lemon flavor, we caramelized lemon halves over the grill and made a sauce from their juice.

- 2 (4-pound) whole chickens, giblets discarded
- 5 lemons, divided
- 2½ teaspoons table salt, divided
- 1¾ teaspoons pepper, divided
- 1 (13 by 9-inch) disposable aluminum roasting pan (if using charcoal)
- 1 garlic clove, minced
- 2 tablespoons minced fresh parsley
- 2 teaspoons Dijon mustard
- 1 teaspoon sugar
- ⅔ cup extra-virgin olive oil

1. Set wire rack in rimmed baking sheet. Working with 1 chicken at a time, place chicken breast side down on cutting board. Using kitchen shears, cut through bones on either side of backbone; discard backbone. Trim chicken of excess fat and skin. Flip chicken over and press on breastbone to flatten. Cover chicken with plastic wrap and pound breasts with meat pounder to even thickness.

2. Grate 2 teaspoons zest from 1 lemon (halve and reserve lemon) and mix with 1½ teaspoons salt and 1 teaspoon pepper in bowl. Pat chickens dry with paper towels and, using your fingers or handle of wooden spoon, gently loosen skin covering breasts and thighs. Rub zest mixture under skin, then sprinkle exterior of chickens with ½ teaspoon salt and ¼ teaspoon pepper. Tuck wingtips behind breasts and transfer chickens to prepared rack. Refrigerate, uncovered, for at least 1 hour or up to 24 hours.

3A. For a charcoal grill Open bottom vent completely and place disposable pan on 1 side of grill with long side of pan facing center of grill. Light large chimney starter filled with charcoal briquettes (6 quarts). When top coals are partially covered with ash, pour evenly over other half of grill (opposite disposable pan). Scatter 20 unlit coals on top of lit coals. Set cooking grate in place, cover, and open lid vent completely. Heat grill until hot, about 5 minutes.

BUTTERFLYING A CHICKEN

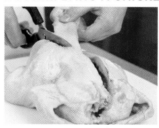

1. Cut through bones on either side of backbone, remove backbone, and trim any excess fat and skin around neck.

2. Flip chicken over and use heel of your hand to flatten breastbone.

3. Cover chicken with plastic wrap and pound breast to be same thickness as legs and thighs.

3B. For a gas grill Turn all burners to high, cover, and heat grill until hot, about 15 minutes. Leave primary burner on high and turn other burner(s) to low. (Adjust primary burner as needed to maintain grill temperature of 350 to 375 degrees.)

4. Clean and oil cooking grate. Halve remaining 4 lemons and place, along with reserved lemon halves, cut side down on hotter side of grill. Place chickens skin side down on cooler side of grill, with legs pointing toward fire; cover, placing lid vent over chickens on charcoal grill.

5. Grill lemons until deep brown and caramelized, 5 to 8 minutes; transfer to bowl. Continue to grill chickens, covered, until breasts register 160 degrees and thighs register 175 degrees, 40 to 50 minutes. Slide chickens to hotter side of grill and cook, uncovered, until skin is well browned, 2 to 4 minutes. Transfer chickens to carving board skin side up, tent with aluminum foil, and let rest for 15 minutes.

6. Meanwhile, squeeze ⅓ cup juice from grilled lemons into bowl. (Cut any unsqueezed lemons into wedges for serving.) Using flat side of knife, mash garlic and remaining ½ teaspoon salt into paste and add to bowl with lemon juice. Whisk in parsley, mustard, sugar, and remaining ½ teaspoon pepper. Slowly whisk in oil until emulsified.

7. Carve chickens, transfer to serving platter, and pour ⅓ cup vinaigrette over chicken. Serve, passing remaining vinaigrette and grilled lemon wedges separately.

Grill-Roasted Beer Can Chicken
Serves 3 to 4

Why This Recipe Works Beer can chicken is the real deal: The bird is rubbed with spices, an open, partially filled beer can is inserted into its cavity, and the bird is grill-roasted upright. The beer turns to steam as the chicken roasts, which makes the meat remarkably juicy and rich-textured. And the dry heat crisps the skin and renders the fat away. It's a near-perfect way to cook a chicken. Banking the coals on either side of the grill allowed for a cooler spot in the middle where the chicken could cook through evenly and gently. A chimney starter two-thirds full provided just enough coals to maintain the grill at the proper temperature for the entire cooking time. A few wood chips contributed a pleasing smoky flavor that didn't overwhelm the chicken. A simple but flavorful spice blend provided a rub that was rich and a little spicy, the perfect complement to the smokiness. If you'd like to use wood chunks instead of wood chips when using a charcoal grill, substitute two medium wood chunks, soaked in water for 1 hour, for the wood chip packet. If you prefer, use lemonade instead of beer; fill an empty 12-ounce soda or beer can with 10 ounces (1¼ cups) of lemonade and proceed as directed.

Spice Rub
- 1 tablespoon packed brown sugar
- 1 tablespoon paprika
- 1 teaspoon table salt
- 1½ teaspoons pepper
- ½ teaspoon cayenne

Chicken
- 1 (12-ounce) can beer
- 2 bay leaves
- 1 (3½- to 4-pound) whole chicken, giblets discarded
- 2 cups wood chips, soaked in water for 15 minutes and drained
- 1 (13 by 9-inch) disposable aluminum roasting pan (if using charcoal)

1. For the spice rub Combine all ingredients in small bowl.

2. For the chicken Open beer can and pour out (or drink) about ¼ cup. With church key can opener, punch 2 more large holes in top of can (for total of 3 holes). Crumble bay leaves into beer.

3. Pat chicken dry with paper towels. Rub chicken evenly, inside and out, with spice rub, gently loosening skin over breast and rubbing spice rub directly onto meat. Using skewer, poke skin all over. Slide chicken over beer can so that drumsticks reach down to bottom of can and chicken stands upright; set aside at room temperature.

4. Using large piece of heavy-duty aluminum foil, wrap chips in 8 by 4½-inch foil packet. (Make sure chips do not poke holes in sides or bottom of packet.) Cut 2 evenly spaced 2-inch slits in top of packet.

5A. For a charcoal grill Open bottom vent halfway and place disposable pan in center of grill. Light large chimney starter two-thirds filled with charcoal briquettes (4 quarts). When top coals are partially covered with ash, pour into 2 even piles on either side of disposable pan. Place wood chip packet on 1 pile of coals. Set cooking grate in place, cover, and open lid vent halfway. Heat grill until hot and wood chips are smoking, about 5 minutes.

SETTING UP BEER CAN CHICKEN

With legs pointing down, slide chicken over open beer can. Two legs and beer can form tripod that steadies chicken on grill.

5B. For a gas grill Remove cooking grate and place wood chip packet directly on primary burner. Set cooking grate in place, turn all burners to high, cover, and heat grill until hot and wood chips are smoking, about 15 minutes. Turn all burners to medium. (Adjust burners as needed to maintain grill temperature of 325 degrees.)

6. Clean and oil cooking grate. Place chicken (with can) in center of grill (over roasting pan if using charcoal), using drumsticks to help steady bird. Cover (position lid vent over chicken if using charcoal) and cook until breast registers 160 degrees and thighs register 175 degrees, 1 to 1½ hours.

7. Using large wad of paper towels, carefully transfer chicken (with can) to tray, making sure to keep can upright. Tent with foil and let rest for 15 minutes. Carefully lift chicken off can and onto carving board. Discard remaining beer and can. Carve chicken and serve.

Grilled Boneless Steaks
Serves 4

Why This Recipe Works A simple grilled steak can be the focal point for countless summer dinners paired with any number of side dishes or salads, so a foolproof recipe is an essential part of any home griller's arsenal. Turning out perfectly grilled steaks with flavorful, charred exteriors and rosy, medium-rare interiors required a few tricks. The first trick was to buy decent steaks—we preferred strip steaks, rib-eye steaks, filets mignons, sirloin steaks, or flank steaks. Second, to bring out its flavor, we seasoned the meat with salt and let it sit before cooking. Third, we brushed the steaks with oil in order to get a good sear; the oil was especially helpful for thin or lean steaks such as flank and filet mignon. Then, to ensure that these steaks came off the grill with charred exteriors and perfectly tender interiors, we built a fire with two heat zones; we started the steaks over the hotter side and moved them to the cooler side to finish cooking through. We found that letting the steaks rest before serving is key—if sliced into right off the grill, the meat will exude its flavorful juices and be dry. Try to buy steaks of even thickness so they cook at the same rate. If cooking filet mignon, look for steaks that are a bit thicker, about 2 inches. We prefer these steaks cooked to medium-rare but if you prefer them more or less done, see our guidelines on page 188.

2–2½ pounds boneless beef steaks,
      1 to 2 inches thick, trimmed
1 teaspoon kosher salt
   Vegetable oil
½ teaspoon pepper

Grilled Boneless Steaks

1. Sprinkle steaks evenly with salt and let sit at room temperature for 1 hour. Pat steaks dry with paper towels, brush lightly with oil, and sprinkle with pepper.

2A. For a charcoal grill Open bottom vent completely. Light large chimney starter filled with charcoal briquettes (6 quarts). When top coals are partially covered with ash, pour two-thirds evenly over half of grill, then pour remaining coals over other half of grill. Set cooking grate in place, cover, and open lid vent completely. Heat grill until hot, about 5 minutes.

2B. For a gas grill Turn all burners to high, cover, and heat grill until hot, about 15 minutes. Leave primary burner on high and turn other burner(s) to medium.

3. Clean and oil cooking grate. Place steaks on hotter side of grill. Cook (covered if using gas), turning steaks as needed, until nicely charred on both sides, 4 to 6 minutes. Slide steaks to cooler side of grill and continue to cook until meat registers 120 to 125 degrees (for medium-rare), 4 to 8 minutes.

4. Transfer steaks to serving platter, tent with aluminum foil, and let rest for 5 to 10 minutes before serving.

DONENESS TEMPERATURES FOR MEAT, POULTRY, AND FISH

Do not guess at doneness; use a thermometer. We list below the final cooking temperatures of meat, poultry, and fish. Note that the temperature of beef and pork (but not poultry or fish) will continue to rise after cooking (this is known as carryover cooking). For this reason, we list both the cooking and serving temperatures.

INGREDIENT	DONENESS TEMPERATURE
Beef and Lamb	
Chops, Steaks, and Roasts	
Rare	115 to 120 degrees (120 to 125 degrees after resting)
Medium-Rare	120 to 125 degrees (125 to 130 degrees after resting)
Medium	130 to 135 degrees (135 to 140 degrees after resting)
Medium-Well	140 to 145 degrees (145 to 150 degrees after resting)
Well-Done	150 to 155 degrees (155 to 160 degrees after resting)
Pork	
Chops and Tenderloin	
Medium-Well	145 degrees (150 degrees after resting)
Well-Done	160 degrees
Loin Roasts	
Medium-Well	140 degrees (145 degrees after resting)
Well-Done	160 degrees
Poultry	
Breasts	160 degrees
Thighs and drumsticks	175 degrees
Fish	
Rare	110 degrees (for tuna only)
Medium-Rare	125 degrees (for tuna or salmon)
Medium	135 to 140 degrees (for white-fleshed fish)

Grilled Porterhouse or T-Bone Steaks

Serves 4 to 6

Why This Recipe Works Porterhouse and T-bone steaks are really two steaks in one—a tender New York strip steak on one side of the bone and a buttery, quicker-cooking tenderloin on the other. For our on-the-grill version, we knew that the challenge would be cooking both parts to the perfect doneness at the same time. As we do with boneless steaks, we made a two-level fire for our porterhouse steaks. We first seared the steaks over the hotter side and then slid them to the cooler side to cook through. We positioned the steaks so the tenderloin always faced the cooler side of the grill—this prevented it from overcooking. And when moving the steaks to the cooler side, we made sure the big bone along the bottom of each steak faced the hotter side of the grill, to protect the narrow top of the steak from drying out. Salting the meat and letting it sit for 1 hour before grilling boosted its flavor from crust to bone. Be sure to buy steaks that are at least 1 inch thick. We prefer these steaks cooked to medium-rare but if you prefer them more or less done, see our guidelines at left.

2 (1¾-pound) porterhouse or T-bone steaks, 1 to 1½ inches thick, trimmed
1 teaspoon table salt
1 teaspoon pepper

1. Sprinkle each steak evenly with ½ teaspoon salt and let sit at room temperature for 1 hour. Pat steaks dry with paper towels and sprinkle with pepper.

2A. For a charcoal grill Open bottom vent completely. Light large chimney starter three-quarters filled with charcoal briquettes (4½ quarts). When top coals are partially covered with ash, pour evenly over half of grill. Set cooking grate in place, cover, and open lid vent completely. Heat grill until hot, about 5 minutes.

2B. For a gas grill Turn all burners to high, cover, and heat grill until hot, about 15 minutes. Leave primary burner on high and turn other burner(s) to low.

3. Clean and oil cooking grate. Place steaks on hotter side of grill with tenderloin sides facing cooler side of grill. Cook (covered if using gas) until dark crust forms, 6 to 8 minutes. Flip and turn steaks so that tenderloin sides are still facing cooler side of grill. Cook until dark brown crust forms on second side, 6 to 8 minutes.

4. Slide steaks to cooler side of grill and turn so that bone sides are facing hotter side of grill. Cover grill and cook, turning steaks as needed, until meat registers 120 to 125 degrees (for medium-rare), 2 to 4 minutes.

5. Transfer steaks to carving board, tent with aluminum foil, and let rest for 5 to 10 minutes. Cut strip and tenderloin pieces off bones, then slice each piece ¼ inch thick. Serve.

Grilled Beef Kebabs with Lemon-Rosemary Marinade

Serves 4 to 6

Why This Recipe Works You can't argue with the appeal of a summer dinner consisting of chunks of beef with a perfect char and juicy interior, all thoroughly seasoned and paired with browned, tender grilled vegetables. For the meat, we avoided precut chunks from the supermarket and instead made our own. We chose well-marbled steak tips for their beefy flavor and tender texture and cut the meat into generous 2-inch cubes. For the marinade, we combined salt for moisture, oil for flavor, and sugar for browning. For depth of flavor, we added tomato paste, seasonings and herbs, and beef broth. Just an hour of marinating gave the meat all the seasoning it needed. We chose three grill favorites for the vegetables: bell pepper, red onion, and zucchini. Grilling the beef and vegetables on separate skewers over our tweaked version of a two-level fire allowed the vegetables to cook at a lower temperature while the beef seared over the hotter center area so both parts came out perfectly cooked within a few minutes of each other. The flavors of the marinade are easy to change up for a wealth of variations; try our spicy red curry or savory North African–inspired mixes. Sirloin steak tips are often sold as flap meat. They can be packaged as whole steaks, cubes, or strips. We prefer to buy whole steaks so we can cut our own steak tips. If you have long, thin pieces of meat, roll or fold them into approximate 2-inch cubes. You will need four 12-inch metal skewers for this recipe. We prefer this steak cooked to medium-rare but if you prefer it more or less done, see our guidelines on page 188.

Marinade
- 1 onion, chopped
- ⅓ cup beef broth
- ⅓ cup vegetable oil
- 3 tablespoons tomato paste
- 6 garlic cloves, chopped
- 2 tablespoons chopped fresh rosemary
- 2 teaspoons grated lemon zest
- 2 teaspoons table salt
- 1½ teaspoons sugar
- ¾ teaspoon pepper

Grilled Beef Kebabs with North African Marinade

Beef and Vegetables
- 2 pounds sirloin steak tips, trimmed and cut into 2-inch pieces
- 1 large zucchini, halved lengthwise and sliced 1 inch thick
- 1 large red bell pepper, stemmed, seeded, and cut into 1½-inch pieces
- 1 large red onion, cut into 1-inch pieces, 3 layers thick

1. For the marinade Process all ingredients in blender until smooth, about 45 seconds. Measure out ¾ cup marinade and set aside for vegetables.

2. For the beef and vegetables Combine remaining marinade and beef in 1-gallon zipper-lock bag and toss to coat; press out as much air as possible and seal bag. Refrigerate for 1 to 2 hours, flipping bag every 30 minutes. Gently combine zucchini, bell pepper, and onion with reserved marinade in bowl. Cover and let sit at room temperature for 30 minutes.

3. Remove beef from bag, pat dry with paper towels, and thread tightly onto two 12-inch metal skewers. Thread vegetables onto two 12-inch metal skewers, in alternating pattern of zucchini, bell pepper, and onion.

4A. For a charcoal grill Open bottom vent completely. Light large chimney starter mounded with charcoal briquettes (7 quarts). When top coals are partially covered with ash, pour evenly over center of grill, leaving 2-inch gap between grill wall and charcoal. Set cooking grate in place, cover, and open lid vent completely. Heat grill until hot, about 5 minutes.

4B. For a gas grill Turn all burners to high, cover, and heat grill until hot, about 15 minutes. Leave primary burner on high and turn other burner(s) to medium-low.

5. Clean and oil cooking grate. Place beef skewers on grill (directly over coals if using charcoal or over hotter side if using gas). Place vegetable skewers on cooler part(s) of grill (near edge of coals if using charcoal). Cook (covered if using gas), turning skewers every 3 to 4 minutes, until beef is well browned and registers 120 to 125 degrees (for medium-rare), 12 to 16 minutes.

6. Transfer beef skewers to serving platter and tent with aluminum foil. Continue cooking vegetable skewers until tender and lightly charred, about 5 minutes. Serve.

VARIATIONS

Grilled Beef Kebabs with North African Marinade

Substitute 20 cilantro sprigs, 2 teaspoons paprika, 1½ teaspoons ground cumin, and ½ teaspoon cayenne pepper for rosemary and lemon zest.

Grilled Beef Kebabs with Red Curry Marinade

Substitute ½ cup packed fresh basil leaves, 3 tablespoons red curry paste, 2 teaspoons grated lime zest, and 2 teaspoons grated fresh ginger for lemon zest and rosemary in marinade.

Grilled Flank Steak with Vegetables and Salsa Verde

Serves 4

Why This Recipe Works Rich and beefy flank steak is thin, flat, and quick-cooking, making it ideal for grilling. We paired our flank steak with a pungent, easy-to-make Italian salsa verde chock-full of straight-from-the-garden flavor. The sauce elevated the simple char-grilled steak and added a welcome freshness. For the vegetables, we chose a combination of fresh zucchini and earthy eggplant, which perfectly complemented the Italian flavors of the sauce. These hearty summer vegetables were also a perfect match for the high heat of the grill. Slicing flank steak against the grain before serving (that is, perpendicular to the orientation of the muscle fibers) makes this relatively tough cut much more tender. We prefer our steaks cooked to medium-rare but if you prefer them more or less done, see our guidelines on page 188.

<table>
<tr><td>2</td><td>zucchini, sliced lengthwise into ¾-inch-thick planks</td></tr>
<tr><td>1</td><td>pound eggplant, sliced lengthwise into ¾-inch-thick planks</td></tr>
<tr><td>5</td><td>tablespoons extra-virgin olive oil, divided</td></tr>
<tr><td>1⅛</td><td>teaspoons table salt, divided</td></tr>
<tr><td>1</td><td>teaspoon pepper, divided</td></tr>
<tr><td>1</td><td>(1½-pound) flank steak, trimmed</td></tr>
<tr><td>1½</td><td>cups fresh parsley leaves</td></tr>
<tr><td>½</td><td>cup fresh mint leaves</td></tr>
<tr><td>1½</td><td>tablespoons white wine vinegar</td></tr>
<tr><td>1</td><td>tablespoon capers, rinsed</td></tr>
<tr><td>1</td><td>tablespoon water</td></tr>
<tr><td>2</td><td>anchovy fillets, rinsed and patted dry</td></tr>
<tr><td>1</td><td>garlic clove, minced</td></tr>
</table>

1. Brush zucchini and eggplant with 1 tablespoon oil and sprinkle with ½ teaspoon salt and ¼ teaspoon pepper.

2. Pat steak dry with paper towels, and sprinkle with ½ teaspoon salt and remaining ¾ teaspoon pepper.

3A. For a charcoal grill Open bottom vent completely. Light large chimney starter filled with charcoal briquettes (6 quarts). When top coals are partially covered with ash, pour evenly over grill. Set cooking grate in place, cover, and open lid vent completely. Heat grill until hot, about 5 minutes.

3B. For a gas grill Turn all burners to high, cover, and heat grill until hot, about 15 minutes. Leave all burners on high.

4. Clean and oil cooking grate. Place steak and vegetables on grill. Cover and cook, flipping steak and turning vegetables as needed, until steak is well browned and registers 120 to 125 degrees (for medium-rare) and vegetables are slightly charred and tender, 7 to 12 minutes. Transfer steak and vegetables to carving board as they finish cooking, tent with aluminum foil, and let rest.

5. While steak rests, pulse parsley, mint, vinegar, capers, water, anchovies, garlic, remaining ¼ cup oil, and remaining ⅛ teaspoon salt in food processor until finely chopped, about 15 pulses, scraping down sides of bowl as needed. Transfer to bowl.

6. Cut zucchini and eggplant into 2-inch pieces. Arrange vegetables on serving platter and season with salt and pepper to taste. Slice steak thin against grain and arrange on serving platter with vegetables. Drizzle steak with ¼ cup salsa verde. Serve, passing remaining salsa verde separately.

Grilled Mojo-Marinated Skirt Steak

Serves 4 to 6

Why This Recipe Works A mojo marinade is a complexly flavored, citrusy, garlicky concoction from Cuba that's great for jazzing up grilled meat. For a mojo-marinated steak recipe, we chose the outside skirt steak, which has ample surface area for soaking up the flavors of the marinade. Soy sauce in the marinade seasoned the meat, and its glutamates enhanced the meat's beefiness. We rubbed a thin coating of baking soda over the steaks before grilling them over high heat to guarantee great browning. To emphasize the mojo flavor, we boiled the marinade to make it food-safe and turned it into a sauce that we drizzled over the steaks. Skirt steaks come from two different muscles and are sometimes labeled as inside skirt steak or outside skirt steak. The more desirable outside skirt steak measures 3 to 4 inches wide and ½ to 1 inch thick. Avoid the inside skirt steak, which typically measures 5 to 7 inches wide and ¼ to ½ inch thick, as it is very chewy. Skirt steak is most tender when cooked to medium (130 to 135 degrees).

- 6 garlic cloves, minced
- 2 tablespoons soy sauce
- 1 teaspoon grated lime zest plus ¼ cup juice (2 limes), divided
- 1 teaspoon ground cumin
- 1 teaspoon dried oregano
- ½ teaspoon table salt
- ½ teaspoon grated orange zest plus ½ cup juice
- ¼ teaspoon red pepper flakes
- 2 pounds skirt steak, trimmed and cut with grain into 6- to 8-inch-long steaks
- 2 tablespoons extra-virgin olive oil, divided
- 1 teaspoon baking soda

1. Combine garlic, soy sauce, 2 tablespoons lime juice, cumin, oregano, salt, orange juice, and pepper flakes in 13 by 9-inch baking dish. Place steaks in dish. Flip steaks to coat both sides with marinade. Cover and refrigerate for 1 hour, flipping steaks halfway through refrigerating.

2. Remove steaks from marinade and transfer marinade to small saucepan. Pat steaks dry with paper towels. Combine 1 tablespoon oil and baking soda in small bowl. Rub oil mixture evenly onto both sides of each steak.

3. Bring marinade to boil over high heat and boil for 30 seconds. Transfer to bowl and stir in lime zest, orange zest, remaining 2 tablespoons lime juice, and remaining 1 tablespoon oil. Set aside sauce.

Grilled Flank Steak with Vegetables and Salsa Verde

Grilled Mojo-Marinated Skirt Steak

4A. For a charcoal grill About 25 minutes before grilling, open bottom vent completely. Light large chimney starter filled with charcoal briquettes (6 quarts). When top coals are partially covered with ash, pour evenly over half of grill. Set cooking grate in place, cover, and open lid vent completely. Heat grill until hot, about 5 minutes.

4B. For a gas grill Turn all burners to high, cover, and heat grill until hot, about 15 minutes. Turn off 1 burner (if using grill with more than 2 burners, turn off burner farthest from primary burner) and leave other burner(s) on high.

5. Clean and oil cooking grate. Cook steaks on hotter side of grill until well browned and meat registers 130 to 135 (for medium), 2 to 4 minutes per side. (Move steaks to cooler side of grill before taking temperature to prevent them from overcooking.) Transfer steaks to cutting board, tent with aluminum foil, and let rest for 10 minutes. Cut steaks on bias against grain into ½-inch-thick slices. Arrange slices on serving platter, drizzle with 2 tablespoons sauce, and serve, passing extra sauce separately.

Grill-Smoked Herb-Rubbed Flat-Iron Steaks

Serves 4 to 6

Why This Recipe Works Smoking steaks can lend them complexity, but most recipes overwhelm the meat's delicate flavor with too much smoke. We found that the key was using a small amount of wood chips and cooking the steaks quickly over direct heat so that they were just kissed with smoke. Since wood chips pack differently, we weighed the chips for more control over the smoke quantity. Salting the steaks for an hour before cooking ensured that the seasoning penetrated below the meat's surface, and coating them with an herb-spice rub lent an extra layer of fresh summer flavor that complemented the smoke. We also grilled lemons to serve with the steaks for a hit of brightness. You can substitute blade steaks for the flat-iron steaks, if desired. We like both cuts cooked to medium (130 to 135 degrees). We like hickory chips in this recipe, but other kinds of wood chips will work. Gas grills are not as efficient at smoking meat as charcoal grills, so we recommend using 1½ cups of wood chips if using a gas grill. Wood chunks are not recommended for this recipe.

- 2 teaspoons dried thyme
- 1 teaspoon dried rosemary
- ¾ teaspoon fennel seeds
- ½ teaspoon black peppercorns
- ¼ teaspoon red pepper flakes
- 4 (6- to 8-ounce) flat-iron steaks, ¾ to 1 inch thick, trimmed
- 1 tablespoon kosher salt
- 1–1½ cups wood chips
  - Vegetable oil spray
- 2 lemons, quartered lengthwise

1. Grind thyme, rosemary, fennel seeds, peppercorns, and pepper flakes in spice grinder or with mortar and pestle until coarsely ground. Transfer to small bowl. Pat steaks dry with paper towels. Rub steaks evenly on both sides with salt and place on wire rack set in rimmed baking sheet. Let stand at room temperature for 1 hour. (After 30 minutes, prepare grill.)

2. Just before grilling, soak wood chips in water for 15 minutes, then drain. Using large piece of heavy-duty aluminum foil, wrap wood chips (1 cup if using charcoal; 1½ cups if using gas) in 8 by 4½-inch foil packet. (Make sure chips do not poke holes in sides or bottom of packet.) Cut 2 evenly spaced 2-inch slits in top of packet.

3A. For a charcoal grill Open bottom vent completely. Light large chimney starter filled with charcoal briquettes (6 quarts). When top coals are partially covered with ash, pour evenly over half of grill. Place wood chip packet on coals. Set cooking grate in place, cover, and open lid vent completely. Heat grill until hot and wood chips are smoking, about 5 minutes.

3B. For a gas grill Remove cooking grate and place wood chip packet directly on primary burner. Set grate in place, turn all burners to high, cover, and heat grill until hot and wood chips are smoking, about 15 minutes. Leave primary burner on high and turn other burner(s) to medium.

MAKING A FOIL PACKET FOR WOOD CHIPS

1. Soak wood chips in water for 15 minutes; spread drained chips in center of 15 by 12-inch piece of heavy-duty aluminum foil. Fold to seal edges, then cut 2 evenly spaced 2-inch slits in top of packet to allow smoke to escape.

2. Place aluminum foil packet of chips on lit coals of charcoal grill or over primary burner on gas grill.

4. Clean and oil cooking grate. Sprinkle half of herb rub evenly over 1 side of steaks and press to adhere. Lightly spray herb-rubbed side of steaks with oil spray, about 3 seconds. Flip steaks and repeat process of sprinkling and pressing steaks with remaining herb rub and coating with oil spray on second side.

5. Place lemons and steaks on hotter side of grill, cover (position lid vent over steaks if using charcoal), and cook until lemons and steaks are well browned on both sides and meat registers 130 to 135 degrees (for medium), 4 to 6 minutes per side. (If steaks are fully charred before reaching desired temperature, move to cooler side of grill, cover, and continue to cook.) Transfer lemons and steaks to clean wire rack set in rimmed baking sheet, tent with foil, and let rest for 10 minutes. Slice steaks thin against grain and serve, passing lemons separately.

Smoked Roast Beef
Serves 6 to 8

Why This Recipe Works We turned an inexpensive eye round into a tender roast on the grill. To tenderize the meat, we used a ketchup-salt-herb rub. Then we slow-cooked the roast over indirect heat with a foil shield around the meat. Its shape helped it to cook evenly. If using charcoal, you will need to light two fires: the first to slow-smoke the meat, and the second to sear it after a rest. If using a gas grill, simply turn it off between uses. To use wood chunks instead of wood chips when using a charcoal grill, substitute one medium wood chunk, soaked in water for 1 hour, for the wood chip packet. For medium roast beef, cook it to 130 to 135 degrees. You don't need to rest the meat again after step 5; it may be served immediately.

    2   tablespoons ketchup
    2   teaspoons table salt
    2   teaspoons pepper
    ½   teaspoon dried thyme
    ½   teaspoon dried oregano
    ½   teaspoon dried rosemary
    1   (4-pound) boneless eye-round roast, trimmed
    1   cup wood chips
    2   teaspoons vegetable oil

1. Combine ketchup, salt, pepper, thyme, oregano, and rosemary in bowl. Rub ketchup mixture all over roast, then wrap roast in plastic wrap and refrigerate for at least 6 hours or up to 24 hours. Just before grilling, soak wood chips in water for 15 minutes, then drain. Using large piece of heavy-duty aluminum foil, wrap chips in 8 by 4½-inch foil packet. (Make sure chips do not poke holes in sides or bottom of packet.) Cut 2 evenly spaced 2-inch slits in top of packet.

Grill-Smoked Herb-Rubbed Flat-Iron Steaks

Smoked Roast Beef

2A. For a charcoal grill Open bottom vent halfway. Light large chimney starter half filled with charcoal briquettes (3 quarts). When top coals are partially covered with ash, pour into steeply banked pile against side of grill. Place wood chip packet on coals. Set cooking grate in place, cover, and open lid vent halfway. Heat grill until hot and wood chips are smoking, about 5 minutes.

2B. For a gas grill Remove cooking grate and place wood chip packet directly on primary burner. Set cooking grate in place, turn all burners to high, cover, and heat grill until hot and wood chips are smoking, about 15 minutes. Turn primary burner to medium-high and turn off other burner(s). (Adjust primary burner as needed to maintain grill temperature of 325 degrees.)

3. Set wire rack in rimmed baking sheet. Unwrap roast. Make two ½-inch folds on long side of 18-inch length of foil to form reinforced edge. Place foil in center of cooking grate, with reinforced edge over hotter side of grill. Place roast on cooler side of grill so that it covers one-third of foil. Lift and bend edges of foil to shield roast, tucking in edges. Cook, covered, until meat registers 120 to 125 degrees (for medium-rare), 1½ to 1¾ hours. Remove roast from grill, transfer to prepared wire rack, and tent with foil. Let roast rest for 30 minutes or up to 1 hour.

4A. For a charcoal grill Open bottom vent completely. Light large chimney starter filled with charcoal briquettes (6 quarts). When top coals are partially covered with ash, pour into pile over spent coals. Set cooking grate in place, cover, and open lid vent completely. Heat grill until hot, about 5 minutes.

4B. For a gas grill Turn all burners to high, cover, and heat grill until hot, about 5 minutes. Leave all burners on high.

5. Clean and oil cooking grate. Brush roast all over with oil. Grill (directly over coals if using charcoal; covered if using gas), turning frequently, until charred on all sides, 8 to 12 minutes. Transfer meat to carving board, slice thin, and serve.

Barbecued Burnt Ends
Serve 8 to 10

Why This Recipe Works Real burnt ends are all about moist meat and charred bark, but most pit masters use fatty point-cut brisket. To make the leaner flat-cut brisket work, we cut it into strips and brined it for maximum moisture and flavor. Three hours of smoke on the grill—with a water pan for more moisture—followed by a few hours in a low oven ensured tender brisket with plenty of char. We cut the meat into cubes before tossing it with our homemade sauce. Look for a brisket with a significant fat cap. This recipe takes about 8 hours to prepare. The meat can be brined ahead of time, transferred to a zipper-lock bag, and refrigerated for up to a day. If you don't

Barbecued Burnt Ends

have ½ cup of juices from the rested brisket, supplement with beef broth. If you'd like to use wood chunks instead of wood chips when using a charcoal grill, substitute three medium wood chunks, soaked in water for 1 hour, for the wood chip packets.

Brisket and Rub

- 2 cups kosher salt, for brining
- ½ cup granulated sugar, for brining
- 1 (5- to 6-pound) beef brisket, flat cut, untrimmed
- ¼ cup packed brown sugar
- 2 tablespoons pepper
- 1 tablespoon kosher salt
- 4 cups wood chips
- 1 (13 by 9-inch) disposable aluminum roasting pan (if using charcoal) or 2 (8½ by 6-inch) disposable aluminum pans (if using gas)

Barbecue Sauce

- ¾ cup ketchup
- ¼ cup packed brown sugar
- 2 tablespoons cider vinegar
- 2 tablespoons Worcestershire sauce
- 2 teaspoons granulated garlic
- ¼ teaspoon cayenne pepper

1. For the brisket and rub Dissolve 2 cups salt and ½ cup granulated sugar in 4 quarts cold water in large container. Slice brisket with grain into 1½-inch-thick strips. Add brisket strips to brine, cover, and refrigerate for 2 hours. Remove brisket from brine and pat dry with paper towels.

2. Combine brown sugar, pepper, and 1 tablespoon salt in bowl. Season brisket all over with rub. Just before grilling, soak wood chips in water for 15 minutes, then drain. Using 2 large pieces of heavy-duty aluminum foil, wrap wood chips in two 8 by 4½-inch foil packets. (Make sure chips do not poke holes in sides or bottom of packets.) Cut 2 evenly spaced 2-inch slits in top of packets.

3A. For a charcoal grill Open bottom vent halfway and place disposable pan filled with 2 quarts water on one side of grill, with long side of pan facing center of grill. Arrange 3 quarts unlit charcoal briquettes on opposite side of grill and place 1 wood chip packet on coals. Light large chimney starter half filled with charcoal briquettes (3 quarts). When top coals are partially covered with ash, pour evenly over unlit coals and wood chip packet. Place remaining wood chip packet on lit coals. Set cooking grate in place, cover, and open lid vent halfway. Heat grill until hot and wood chips are smoking, about 5 minutes.

3B. For a gas grill Add ½ cup ice cubes to 1 wood chip packet. Remove cooking grate and place both wood chip packets directly on primary burner; place disposable pans each filled with 2 cups water directly on secondary burner(s). Set grate in place, turn all burners to high, cover, and heat grill until hot and wood chips are smoking, about 15 minutes. Leave primary burner on high and turn off other burner(s). (Adjust primary burner as needed to maintain grill temperature of 275 to 300 degrees.)

4. Clean and oil cooking grate. Arrange brisket on cooler side of grill as far from heat source as possible. Cover (positioning lid vent over brisket for charcoal) and cook without opening for 3 hours.

5. Adjust oven rack to middle position and heat oven to 275 degrees. Remove brisket from grill and transfer to rimmed baking sheet. Cover sheet tightly with foil. Roast until fork slips easily in and out of meat and meat registers 210 degrees, about 2 hours. Remove from oven, leave covered, and let rest for 1 hour. Remove foil, transfer brisket to carving board, and pour accumulated juices into fat separator.

6. For the barbecue sauce Combine ketchup, sugar, vinegar, Worcestershire, granulated garlic, cayenne, and ½ cup defatted brisket juices in medium saucepan. Bring to simmer over medium heat and cook until slightly thickened, about 5 minutes.

7. Cut brisket strips crosswise into 1- to 2-inch pieces. Combine brisket pieces and barbecue sauce in large bowl and toss to combine. Serve.

CUTTING BRISKET INTO STRIPS

Slice flat-cut brisket into 1½-inch strips to create more surface area to facilitate brining, browning, and smoke absorption during cooking.

Texas Barbecue Brisket
Serves 12 to 15 `MAKE AHEAD`

Why This Recipe Works Authentic Texas-style smoked brisket—with a tender, juicy interior encased in a dark, peppery bark—is an irresistible dish worth firing up the grill for. We started with a 10- to 12-pound whole brisket (both the point and flat cuts). Seasoning the brisket overnight with salt and pepper enhanced the flavor of the meat without masking any of its beefiness. To avoid drying out the meat as it cooked, we used a grill setup called a charcoal snake. This C-shaped array of smoldering briquettes provided low, slow, indirect heat to the center of the grill for upwards of 6 hours, so we needed to refuel only once during the exceptionally long cooking time. Cooking the brisket fat side down gave it a protective barrier against the direct heat of the fire. And wrapping the brisket in aluminum foil toward the end of its cooking time and letting it rest in a cooler for 2 hours before serving helped keep it ultramoist and juicy. The brisket must be seasoned at least 12 hours before cooking. We call for a whole beef brisket here, with both the flat and point cuts intact; you may need to special-order this cut.

1 (10- to 12-pound) whole beef brisket, untrimmed
¼ cup kosher salt
¼ cup pepper
5 (3-inch) wood chunks
1 (13 by 9-inch) disposable aluminum roasting pan

1. With brisket positioned point side up, use sharp knife to trim fat cap to ½- to ¼-inch thickness. Remove excess fat from deep pocket where flat and point are attached. Trim and discard short edge of flat if less than 1 inch thick. Flip brisket and remove any large deposits of fat from underside.

2. Combine salt and pepper in bowl. Place brisket on rimmed baking sheet and sprinkle all over with salt mixture. Cover loosely with plastic wrap and refrigerate for 12 to 24 hours.

3. Open bottom vent completely. Set up charcoal snake: Arrange 58 briquettes, 2 briquettes wide, around perimeter of grill, overlapping slightly so briquettes are touching, leaving 8-inch gap between ends of snake. Place second layer of 58 briquettes, also 2 briquettes wide, on top of first. (Completed snake should be 2 briquettes wide by 2 briquettes high.)

4. Starting 4 inches from 1 end of snake, evenly space wood chunks on top of snake. Place disposable pan in center of grill. Fill disposable pan with 6 cups water. Light chimney starter filled with 10 briquettes (pile briquettes on 1 side of chimney). When coals are partially covered with ash, pour over 1 end of snake. (Make sure lit coals touch only 1 end of snake.)

5. Set cooking grate in place. Clean and oil cooking grate. Place brisket, fat side down, directly over water pan, with point end facing gap in snake. Insert temperature probe into side of upper third of point. Cover grill, open lid vent completely, and position lid vent over gap in snake. Cook, undisturbed and without lifting lid, until meat registers 170 degrees, 4 to 5 hours.

6. Place 2 large sheets of aluminum foil on rimmed baking sheet. Remove temperature probe from brisket. Using oven mitts, lift brisket and transfer to center of foil, fat side down. Wrap brisket tightly with first layer of foil, minimizing air pockets between foil and brisket. Rotate brisket 90 degrees and wrap with second layer of foil. (Use additional foil, if necessary, to completely wrap brisket.) Make small mark on foil with marker to keep track of fat/point side. Foil wrap should be airtight.

7. Remove cooking grate. Starting at still-unlit end of snake, pour 3 quarts unlit briquettes about halfway around perimeter of grill over gap and spent coals. Replace cooking grate. Return foil-wrapped brisket to grill over water pan, fat side down, with point end facing where gap in snake used to be. Reinsert temperature probe into point. Cover grill and continue to cook until meat registers 205 degrees, 1 to 2 hours.

8. Remove temperature probe. Transfer foil-wrapped brisket to cooler, point side up. Close cooler and let rest for at least 2 hours or up to 3 hours. Transfer brisket to carving board, unwrap, and position fat side up. Slice flat against grain ¼ inch thick, stopping once you reach base of point. Rotate point 90 degrees and slice point against grain (perpendicular to first cut) ⅜ inch thick. Serve.

BUILDING A CHARCOAL SNAKE

Count out 2 piles of 58 briquettes. Arrange 1 pile, in C shape 2 briquettes wide, around perimeter of cooking grate. Arrange second pile on top of first layer. Evenly space wood chunks on top of second layer.

Grilled Pork Cutlets and Zucchini with Feta and Mint Compound Butter
Serves 4 `FAST`

Why This Recipe Works Compound butters, which are merely softened butter with flavorings whisked in, needn't be reserved for meals cooked indoors. They are easy to prepare and can offer a welcome boost of flavor to a wide range of grilled dishes. We made an herbaceous compound butter loaded with chopped fresh mint, floral orange zest (which provided a subtle sweetness) and crumbles of briny feta cheese. We topped lean grilled pork cutlets and spears of grilled zucchini with our butter, which melted on the warm pork and zucchini and turned into a sauce. Packaged pork loin cutlets are convenient, but we often find them to be inconsistent in size and thickness. Instead, we made our own cutlets by cutting pork tenderloin into pieces and pounding them into ¼-inch-thick cutlets to ensure even cooking.

> 2 (12- to 16-ounce) pork tenderloins, trimmed, each cut into 4 equal pieces and pounded ¼-inch thick
> 1 teaspoon table salt, divided
> ½ teaspoon plus ⅛ teaspoon pepper, divided
> 4 tablespoons unsalted butter, softened
> 1 ounce feta cheese, crumbled (¼ cup)
> 1 tablespoon chopped fresh mint
> ½ teaspoon grated orange zest
> 4 small zucchini (6 ounces each), halved lengthwise
> 1 tablespoon vegetable oil

1. Pat pork dry with paper towels and sprinkle with ½ teaspoon salt and ¼ teaspoon pepper. Let sit for 10 minutes.

2. Meanwhile, combine butter, feta, mint, orange zest, ¼ teaspoon salt, and ¼ teaspoon pepper in bowl; set aside. Brush zucchini with oil and sprinkle with remaining ¼ teaspoon salt and remaining ⅛ teaspoon pepper.

3A. For a charcoal grill Open bottom vent completely. Light large chimney starter filled with charcoal briquettes (6 quarts). When top coals are partially covered with ash, pour evenly over grill. Set cooking grate in place, cover, and open lid vent completely. Heat grill until hot, about 5 minutes.

3B. For a gas grill Turn all burners to high, cover, and heat grill until hot, about 15 minutes. Leave all burners on high.

4. Clean and oil cooking grate. Grill pork, uncovered, until lightly charred and cooked through, about 2 minutes per side. Transfer to serving platter, tent with aluminum foil, and let rest while cooking zucchini. Grill zucchini, uncovered, until tender, about 3 minutes per side. Top pork and zucchini with compound butter. Serve.

Grilled Pork Chops with Plums
Serves 4

Why This Recipe Works For a fresher take on pork with prunes, we paired quick-grilling pork chops with fresh plums—one of late summer's finest fruits. We first rubbed the halved and pitted plums with some sugar to promote caramelization and browning on the grill. Then we sprinkled the pork chops with a savory-sweet spice mixture of coriander, ginger, salt, and pepper, and a bit of sugar to play off the sweetness of the plums. The pork chops cooked quickly, needing only 2 to 3 minutes on each side to become nicely browned. After grilling the chops, we popped the plums halves onto the grill and quickly cooked them until slightly brown and caramelized. They emerged juicy with concentrated sweetness, making the perfect accompaniment to our tender pork chops.

- 2   tablespoons extra-virgin olive oil
- 1   tablespoon lemon juice
- 4   plums, halved and pitted
- 2   tablespoons packed brown sugar, divided
- 1½ teaspoons ground coriander
- ½   teaspoon table salt
- ½   teaspoon ground ginger
- ¼   teaspoon pepper
- 4   (6-ounce) bone-in pork rib or center-cut chops, ½ inch thick, trimmed
- 3   ounces (3 cups) baby arugula

1. Whisk oil and lemon juice together in medium bowl; set aside dressing. Rub cut sides of plums with 1 tablespoon sugar. Combine coriander, salt, ginger, pepper, and remaining 1 tablespoon sugar in small bowl. Pat pork dry with paper towels and sprinkle all over with spice mixture.

2A. For a charcoal grill Open bottom vent completely. Light large chimney starter filled with charcoal briquettes (6 quarts). When top coals are partially covered with ash, pour evenly over grill. Set cooking grate in place, cover, and open lid vent completely. Heat grill until hot, about 5 minutes.

2B. For a gas grill Turn all burners to high, cover, and heat grill until hot, about 15 minutes. Leave all burners on high.

3. Clean and oil cooking grate. Grill pork until browned and meat registers 140 degrees, 2 to 3 minutes per side. Transfer to serving platter, tent with foil, and let rest for 10 minutes. Meanwhile, grill plums until caramelized and tender, about 3 minutes per side.

4. Add plums and arugula to bowl with dressing and toss to combine. Transfer to serving platter with pork and serve.

Grilled Pork Cutlets and Zucchini with Feta and Mint Compound Butter

Grilled Pork Chops with Plums

Grilled Pork Tenderloin and Summer Squash with Chimichurri

Grill-Roasted Bone-In Pork Rib Roast

Grilled Pork Tenderloin and Summer Squash with Chimichurri

Serves 4 FAST

Why This Recipe Works Chimichurri is a supremely fresh-tasting sauce made from chopped herbs, minced garlic, olive oil, and some vinegar—it's perfect for turning simple grilled meat and vegetables into something more special. To put a summery spin on pork tenderloin, we made a verdant chimichurri using garden-fresh parsley and cilantro and grilled the pork to add smoky flavor. After cooking the pork, we put some yellow summer squash, cut into long planks, on the grill and cooked them until nicely charred. Turning the grilled pork and vegetables into a lively dinner was as simple as topping both the meat and the squash with our bright chimichurri. You can use fresh mint in place of the cilantro in the chimichurri sauce.

- 6 tablespoons extra-virgin olive oil, divided
- ¼ cup minced fresh parsley
- ¼ cup minced fresh cilantro
- 3 tablespoons red wine vinegar
- 1 garlic clove, minced
- 1 teaspoon table salt, divided
- ¾ teaspoon plus ⅛ teaspoon pepper, divided
- ½ teaspoon dried oregano
- 2 (1-pound) pork tenderloins, trimmed and pounded ½ inch thick
- 1 tablespoon packed brown sugar
- 4 yellow summer squash, cut lengthwise into ½-inch-thick planks

1. Combine ¼ cup oil, parsley, cilantro, vinegar, garlic, ¼ teaspoon salt, ¼ teaspoon pepper, and oregano in bowl; set aside for serving. Sprinkle pork with sugar, ½ teaspoon salt, and ½ teaspoon pepper. Brush squash with remaining 2 tablespoons oil and sprinkle with remaining ¼ teaspoon salt and remaining ⅛ teaspoon pepper.

2A. For a charcoal grill Open bottom vent completely. Light large chimney starter filled with charcoal briquettes (6 quarts). When top coals are partially covered with ash, pour evenly over grill. Set cooking grate in place, cover, and open lid vent completely. Heat grill until hot, about 5 minutes.

2B. For a gas grill Turn all burners to high, cover, and heat grill until hot, about 15 minutes. Leave all burners on high.

3. Clean and oil cooking grate. Grill pork until lightly browned and registers 140 degrees, about 2 minutes per side. Transfer pork to carving board, tent with foil, and let rest while grilling squash.

4. Grill squash until charred and tender, 3 to 5 minutes per side; transfer to serving platter. Slice pork on bias ½ inch thick and transfer to platter with squash. Top with chimichurri and serve.

REMOVING PORK SILVERSKIN

Silverskin is a swath of connective tissue located between the meat and the fat that covers its surface. To remove silverskin, simply slip a knife under it, tilt the blade slightly upward, and use a gentle back-and-forth motion.

Grill-Roasted Bone-In Pork Rib Roast

Serves 6 to 8   MAKE AHEAD

Why This Recipe Works The biggest challenge when grilling a bulky cut of meat like a pork rib roast is getting the interior cooked to the proper temperature without charring the exterior. We wanted a tender, juicy grilled roast with a thick mahogany crust and plenty of deep, rich flavor. After testing three possible cuts from the loin, we determined that we liked the center-cut rib roast for its flavor and simplicity. Because the meat is a single muscle attached along one side to the bones, there is no need to tie the roast for a tidy presentation. We figured that with such a large roast, using a two-level fire would be essential. But we were surprised to discover that we could cook the roast on the cooler side for the duration. After an hour a mahogany crust developed—no high-temperature sear needed. We found it important to position the roast away—but not too far

away—from the coals or flames with the bones facing away from the fire. Letting the roast rest for a full 30 minutes after it finished on the grill allowed the meat to reabsorb some of the juices lost during cooking. For easier carving, ask the butcher to remove the tip of the chine bone and to cut the remainder of the chine bone between each rib. If you'd like to use wood chunks instead of wood chips when using a charcoal grill, substitute one medium wood chunk, soaked in water for 1 hour, for the wood chip packet.

1 (4- to 5-pound) center-cut bone-in pork rib roast, chine bone removed, fat trimmed to ¼ inch
4 teaspoons kosher salt
1 cup wood chips
1½ teaspoons pepper

1. Pat roast dry with paper towels. Lightly score fat cap in 1-inch crosshatch pattern, being careful not to cut into meat. Sprinkle roast with salt. Wrap roast in plastic wrap and refrigerate for at least 6 hours or up to 24 hours.

2. Just before grilling, soak wood chips in water for 15 minutes, then drain. Using large piece of heavy-duty aluminum foil, wrap chips in 8 by 4½-inch foil packet. (Make sure chips do not poke holes in sides or bottom of packet.) Cut 2 evenly spaced 2-inch slits in top of packet.

3A. For a charcoal grill Open bottom vent halfway. Light large chimney starter filled with charcoal briquettes (6 quarts). When top coals are partially covered with ash, pour into steeply banked pile against side of grill. Place wood chip packet on coals. Set cooking grate in place, cover, and open lid vent halfway. Heat grill until hot and wood chips are smoking, about 5 minutes.

3B. For a gas grill Remove cooking grate and place wood chip packet directly on primary burner. Set cooking grate in place, turn all burners to high, cover, and heat grill until hot and wood chips are smoking, about 15 minutes. Turn primary burner to medium-high and turn off other burner(s). (Adjust primary burner as needed during cooking to maintain grill temperature of 325 degrees.)

4. Clean and oil cooking grate. Unwrap roast and season with pepper. Place roast on grate with meat near, but not over, coals and flames and bones facing away from coals and flames. Cover (position lid vent over meat if using charcoal) and cook until meat registers 140 degrees, 1¼ to 1½ hours.

5. Transfer roast to carving board, tent with aluminum foil, and let rest for 30 minutes. Carve into thick slices by cutting between ribs. Serve.

VARIATION
Grill-Roasted Bone-In Pork Rib Roast with Orange Salsa with Cuban Flavors
Makes about 2½ cups
To make this salsa spicier, reserve and add the chile seeds.

- ½ teaspoon grated orange zest, plus 5 oranges peeled and segmented, each segment quartered crosswise
- ½ cup finely chopped red onion
- 1 jalapeño chile, stemmed, seeded, and minced
- 2 tablespoons lime juice
- 2 tablespoons minced fresh parsley
- 1 tablespoon extra-virgin olive oil
- 2 teaspoons packed brown sugar
- 1½ teaspoons distilled white vinegar
- 1½ teaspoons minced fresh oregano
- 1 garlic clove, minced
- ½ teaspoon ground cumin
- ½ teaspoon table salt
- ½ teaspoon pepper

Combine all ingredients in bowl. Serve with pork roast.

Barbecued Pulled Pork
Serves 8 `MAKE AHEAD`

Why This Recipe Works Barbecued pulled pork is essential summer cookout fare, but most recipes demand the attention of the cook for 8 hours or more. We wanted to find a way to make moist, fork-tender pulled pork without the marathon cooking time and constant attention to the grill. For the seasoning, we found that keeping it simple produced great results. A blend of spices—paprika, chili powder, and cumin, along with some salt, sugar, and two peppers—provided plenty of complexity and bold flavor. Simply massaging the rub into the meat was straightforward and effective. Placing the roast in a disposable roasting pan on the grill helped protect it from the heat so there was no risk of scorching, while wood chips provided plenty of smoky flavor. We then finished the pork in the oven at a relatively low temperature. This method produced almost the same results as the traditional barbecue, but in considerably less time and with much less effort. Resting the pork for an hour inside a paper grocery sack allowed time for the flavorful juices to be reabsorbed. Pork butt roast is often labeled Boston butt

in the supermarket. Preparing pulled pork requires little effort but lots of time. Plan on 10 hours from start to finish. If you'd like to use wood chunks instead of wood chips when using a charcoal grill, substitute four medium wood chunks, soaked in water for 1 hour, for the wood chip packets. To complement the pulled pork, you can choose between Eastern North Carolina Barbecue Sauce, Western South Carolina Barbecue Sauce, and Mid-South Carolina Mustard Sauce. Serve on plain white bread or warmed rolls with dill pickle chips and coleslaw.

Dry Rub
- ¼ cup paprika
- 2 tablespoons chili powder
- 2 tablespoons packed dark brown sugar
- 2 tablespoons table salt
- 1 tablespoon pepper
- 1 tablespoon ground cumin
- 1 teaspoon cayenne pepper

Pork
- 1 (6- to 8-pound) bone-in pork butt roast, trimmed
- 4 cups wood chips
- 1 (13 by 9-inch) disposable aluminum roasting pan
- 1 brown paper grocery bag
- 2 cups barbecue sauce (recipes follow)

1. For the dry rub Combine all ingredients in bowl.

2. For the pork Pat pork dry with paper towels, then massage dry rub into meat. Wrap roast in plastic wrap and refrigerate for at least 3 hours or up to 3 days.

3. At least 1 hour prior to cooking, remove roast from refrigerator, unwrap, and let sit at room temperature. Just before grilling, soak wood chips in water for 15 minutes, then drain. Using 2 large pieces of heavy-duty aluminum foil, wrap chips in two 8 by 4½-inch foil packets. (Make sure chips do not poke holes in sides or bottom of packets.) Cut 2 evenly spaced 2-inch slits in top of each packet.

4A. For a charcoal grill Open bottom vent halfway. Light large chimney starter three-quarters filled with charcoal briquettes (4½ quarts). When top coals are partially covered with ash, pour evenly over half of grill. Place wood chip packets on coals. Set cooking grate in place, cover, and open lid vent halfway. Heat grill until hot and wood chips are smoking, about 5 minutes.

4B. For a gas grill Remove cooking grate and place wood chip packets directly on primary burner. Set cooking grate in place, turn all burners to high, cover, and heat grill until hot and wood chips are smoking, about 15 minutes. Turn primary burner to medium-high and turn off other burner(s). (Adjust primary burner as needed to maintain grill temperature of 325 degrees.)

5. Set roast in disposable pan, place on cooler side of grill, cover, and cook for 3 hours. During final 20 minutes of cooking, adjust oven rack to lower-middle position and heat oven to 325 degrees.

6. Wrap disposable pan with heavy-duty foil and cook in oven until meat is fork-tender, about 2 hours.

7. Carefully slide foil-wrapped pan with roast into brown paper bag. Crimp end shut and let rest for 1 hour.

8. Transfer roast to carving board and unwrap. Separate roast into muscle sections, removing fat, if desired, and tearing meat into shreds with your fingers. Place shredded meat in large bowl and toss with 1 cup barbecue sauce. Serve, passing remaining sauce separately.

Eastern North Carolina Barbecue Sauce
Makes about 2 cups

- 1 cup distilled white vinegar
- 1 cup cider vinegar
- 1 tablespoon sugar
- 1 tablespoon red pepper flakes
- 1 tablespoon hot sauce

Mix all ingredients together in bowl and season with salt and pepper to taste. (Sauce can be refrigerated for up to 4 days.)

Western South Carolina Barbecue Sauce
Makes about 2 cups

- 1 tablespoon vegetable oil
- ½ cup finely chopped onion
- 2 garlic cloves, minced
- ½ cup cider vinegar
- ½ cup Worcestershire sauce
- 1 tablespoon dry mustard
- 1 tablespoon packed dark brown sugar
- 1 tablespoon paprika
- 1 teaspoon table salt
- 1 teaspoon cayenne pepper
- 1 cup ketchup

Heat oil in small saucepan over medium heat. Add onion and cook, stirring occasionally, until softened, 5 to 7 minutes. Stir in garlic and cook until fragrant, about 30 seconds.

Barbecued Pulled Pork

Stir in vinegar, Worcestershire, mustard, sugar, paprika, salt, and cayenne, bring to simmer, and stir in ketchup. Cook over low heat until thickened, about 15 minutes. (Sauce can be refrigerated for up to 4 days.)

Mid-South Carolina Mustard Sauce
Makes about 2½ cups

- 1 cup cider vinegar
- 1 cup vegetable oil
- 6 tablespoons Dijon mustard
- 2 tablespoons maple syrup or honey
- 4 teaspoons Worcestershire sauce
- 1 teaspoon hot sauce

Mix all ingredients together in bowl and season with salt and pepper to taste. Use 2 cups sauce in recipe. (Remaining sauce can be refrigerated for up to 4 days.)

Barbecued Baby Back Ribs
Serves 4

Why This Recipe Works There's nothing as satisfying as a plate of eat-with-your-hands, juicy, tender baby back ribs. We wanted ribs that were fully seasoned with an intense smokiness. In other words, we wanted ribs that would be well worth the time and effort. Meaty ribs—racks as close to 2 pounds as possible—provided substantial, satisfying portions. Leaving the skin-like membrane on the ribs during cooking helped retain flavor and moistness and helped form a crispy crust. A brief stint in a standard salt-and-sugar brine ensured moist, well-seasoned ribs, while a simple spice rub of chili powder, cayenne, cumin, and brown sugar provided a good balance of sweet and spicy flavors and formed a nice, crisp crust. We barbecued the ribs for a couple of hours on the cooler side of the grill with wood chips and then moved them to a baking sheet and covered them with foil to gently finish cooking in the oven, which made for moist, tender baby back ribs with an intense smoky flavor. If you'd like to use wood chunks instead of wood chips when using a charcoal grill, substitute two medium wood chunks, soaked in water for 1 hour, for the wood chip packet. You do not have to remove the membrane on the ribs in this recipe.

Barbecued Baby Back Ribs

½ cup sugar, for brining
½ cup table salt, for brining
2 (1½- to 2-pound) racks baby back ribs, trimmed
3½ teaspoons paprika
1¾ teaspoons ground cumin
1½ teaspoons chili powder
1½ teaspoons packed dark brown sugar
1 teaspoon white pepper
¾ teaspoon dried oregano
¾ teaspoon table salt
¾ teaspoon pepper
½ teaspoon cayenne pepper
2 cups wood chips

1. Dissolve ½ cup sugar and ½ cup salt in 4 quarts cold water in large container. Submerge racks in brine, cover, and refrigerate for 1 hour. Remove pork from brine and pat dry with paper towels.

2. Combine paprika, cumin, chili powder, brown sugar, white pepper, oregano, ¾ teaspoon salt, pepper, and cayenne in small bowl. Rub each rack with 1 tablespoon spice rub. Let ribs sit at room temperature for 1 hour.

3. Just before grilling, soak wood chips in water for 15 minutes, then drain. Using large piece of heavy-duty aluminum foil, wrap chips in 8 by 4½-inch foil packet. (Make sure chips do not poke holes in sides or bottom of packet.) Cut 2 evenly spaced 2-inch slits in top of packet.

4A. For a charcoal grill Open bottom vent halfway. Light large chimney starter three-quarters filled with charcoal briquettes (4½ quarts). When top coals are partially covered with ash, pour evenly over half of grill. Place wood chip packet on coals. Set cooking grate in place, cover, and open lid vent halfway. Heat grill until hot and wood chips are smoking, about 5 minutes.

4B. For a gas grill Remove cooking grate and place wood chip packet directly on primary burner. Set cooking grate in place, turn all burners to high, cover, and heat grill until hot and wood chips are smoking, about 15 minutes. Turn primary burner to medium-high and turn off other burner(s). (Adjust primary burner as needed to maintain grill temperature of 300 to 325 degrees.)

5. Clean and oil cooking grate. Place ribs meaty side down on cooler side of grill. Cover (position lid vent over meat if using charcoal) and cook until ribs are deep red and smoky, about 2 hours, flipping and rotating racks halfway through grilling. During final 20 minutes of grilling, adjust oven rack to lower-middle position and heat oven to 325 degrees.

6. Transfer ribs to wire rack set in rimmed baking sheet. Cover tightly with foil and cook in oven until tender, 1 to 2 hours.

7. Remove ribs from oven, loosen foil to release steam, and let rest for 30 minutes. Slice ribs between bones and serve.

Kansas City Sticky Ribs
Serves 4 to 6 `MAKE AHEAD`

Why This Recipe Works For barbecue fans who like to get their hands dirty, Kansas City sticky ribs are just the ticket. To bring the smoky flavor, tender meat, and signature sticky barbecue sauce home without hours by the grill, we focused on keeping the ribs moist while speeding up their cooking time. After treating a rack of St. Louis–style spareribs with a spicy rub, we readied our grill. Wood chips gave the ribs great smoky flavor, and we kept the meat moist by capturing the escaping steam with a sheet of aluminum foil placed directly on top of the ribs. Even on the cooler side of the grill, the ribs still developed a nice crusty exterior. After spreading on a thick coating of our homemade barbecue sauce, we wrapped the ribs tightly in foil to prevent the sauce from charring, added more hot coals and wood chips, and let the ribs cook for a final hour. More sauce brushed on before serving added a final layer of flavor. We like St. Louis–style racks, but if you can't find them, baby back ribs will work fine. If you'd like to use wood chunks instead of wood chips when using a charcoal grill, substitute two medium wood chunks, soaked in water for 1 hour, for the wood chip packets.

Ribs
- 3 tablespoons paprika
- 2 tablespoons brown sugar
- 1 tablespoon table salt
- 1 tablespoon pepper
- ¼ teaspoon cayenne pepper
- 2 (2½- to 3-pound) full racks pork spareribs, trimmed of any large pieces of fat and membrane removed
- 2 cups wood chips
- 1 (13 by 9-inch) disposable aluminum roasting pan (if using charcoal)

Kansas City Barbecue Sauce
- 1 tablespoon vegetable oil
- 1 onion, chopped fine
  Pinch table salt
- 4 cups chicken broth
- 1 cup root beer
- 1 cup cider vinegar
- 1 cup dark corn syrup
- ½ cup molasses
- ½ cup tomato paste
- ½ cup ketchup
- 2 tablespoons brown mustard
- 1 tablespoon hot sauce
- ½ teaspoon garlic powder
- ¼ teaspoon liquid smoke

1. For the ribs Combine paprika, sugar, salt, pepper, and cayenne in bowl. Pat ribs dry with paper towels and rub evenly with spice mixture. Wrap ribs in plastic wrap and let sit at room temperature for at least 1 hour or refrigerate for up to 24 hours. (If refrigerated, let sit at room temperature for 1 hour before grilling.) Just before grilling, soak wood chips in water for 15 minutes, then drain. Using 2 large pieces of heavy-duty aluminum foil, wrap chips in two 8 by 4½-inch foil packets. (Make sure chips do not poke holes in sides or bottom of packet.) Cut 2 evenly spaced 2-inch slits in top of packets.

2. For the Kansas City barbecue sauce Meanwhile, heat oil in large saucepan over medium heat until shimmering. Add onion and salt and cook until softened, 5 to 7 minutes. Whisk in broth, root beer, vinegar, corn syrup, molasses, tomato paste, ketchup, mustard, hot sauce, and garlic powder. Bring sauce to simmer and cook, stirring occasionally, until reduced to 4 cups, about 1 hour. Off heat, stir in liquid smoke. Let sauce cool to room temperature. Season with salt and pepper to taste. Measure out 1 cup barbecue sauce for cooking; set aside remaining sauce for serving. (Sauce can be refrigerated for up to 4 days.)

3A. For a charcoal grill Open bottom vent halfway and place disposable pan on 1 side of grill. Light large chimney starter three-quarters filled with charcoal briquettes (4½ quarts). When top coals are partially covered with ash, pour into steeply banked pile against side of grill (opposite disposable pan). Place 1 wood chip packet on coals. Set cooking grate in place, cover, and open lid vent halfway. Heat grill until hot and wood chips are smoking, about 5 minutes.

3B. For a gas grill Remove cooking grate and place wood chip packets directly on primary burner. Set cooking grate in place, turn all burners to high, cover, and heat grill until hot and wood chips are smoking, about 15 minutes. Turn primary burner to medium-high and turn off other burner(s). (Adjust primary burner as needed to maintain grill temperature around 325 degrees.)

REMOVING THE MEMBRANE FROM SPARERIBS

1. Slip tip of paring knife under edge of membrane on each rack to loosen it.

2. Gripping loosened edge with paper towel, slowly pull off membrane. It should come off in single piece.

4. Clean and oil cooking grate. Unwrap ribs and place, meat side down, on cooler side of grill; ribs may overlap slightly. Place sheet of foil directly on top of ribs. Cover (position lid vent over meat if using charcoal) and cook until ribs are deep red and smoky, about 2 hours, flipping and rotating racks halfway through cooking. During final 20 minutes of grilling, if using charcoal, light another large chimney starter three-quarters filled with charcoal (4½ quarts). When top coals are partially covered with ash, pour hot coals on top of spent coals and top with remaining wood chip packet. Flip and rotate ribs and cook, covered, for 1 hour.

5. Remove ribs from grill, brush evenly with 1 cup sauce, and wrap tightly with foil. Lay foil-wrapped ribs on grill and cook until tender, about 1 hour.

6. Transfer ribs (still in foil) to cutting board and let rest for 30 minutes. Unwrap ribs and brush with additional sauce. Slice ribs between bones and serve with remaining sauce.

Sweet and Tangy Grilled Country-Style Pork Ribs

Serves 4 to 6   `MAKE AHEAD`

Why This Recipe Works Country-style ribs are less like baby back ribs or spareribs and more like well-marbled pork chops. They contain both lean loin meat and a section of dark shoulder meat. The trick to cooking these on the grill was getting both parts to cook evenly. We started with a simple dry rub of chili powder, cayenne, salt, and brown sugar, which would encourage browning while adding a complex sweetness. Though cooking the ribs to 175 degrees delivered perfect dark meat, the light meat was woefully dry. On the flip side, pulling the ribs off the grill when they hit 135 to 140 degrees produced juicy light meat but chewy, underdone dark meat. A compromise was in order: 150 degrees. The fat in the ribs moistened the light meat enough that the slight overcooking wasn't noticeable, while the dark meat still had a little tug to it but was nevertheless tender. We started the ribs over the hotter side of the grill for excellent browning, then finished them on the cooler side, where it was easy to baste the ribs with barbecue sauce and allow it to slowly caramelize without burning. When purchasing bone-in country-style ribs, look for those that are approximately 1 inch thick and that contain a large proportion of dark meat. Be sure to carefully trim the pork to reduce the number of flare-ups when the pork is grilled. This recipe requires refrigerating the spice-rubbed ribs for at least 1 hour or up to 24 hours before grilling.

Pork

- 4 teaspoons packed brown sugar
- 1 tablespoon kosher salt
- 1 tablespoon chili powder
- ⅛ teaspoon cayenne pepper
- 4 pounds bone-in country-style pork ribs, trimmed

Sweet and Tangy Sauce

- 1 cup ketchup
- 5 tablespoons molasses
- 3 tablespoons cider vinegar
- 2 tablespoons Worcestershire sauce
- 2 tablespoons Dijon mustard
- ¼ teaspoon pepper
- 2 tablespoons vegetable oil
- ⅓ cup grated onion
- 1 garlic clove, minced
- 1 teaspoon chili powder
- ¼ teaspoon cayenne pepper

1. For the pork Combine sugar, salt, chili powder and cayenne in bowl. Pat ribs dry. Rub mixture all over ribs. Wrap ribs in plastic and refrigerate for at least 1 hour or up to 24 hours.

2. For the sweet and tangy sauce Whisk ketchup, molasses, vinegar, Worcestershire, mustard, and pepper together in bowl. Heat oil in medium saucepan over medium heat until shimmering. Add onion and garlic; cook until onion is softened, 2 to 4 minutes. Add chili powder and cayenne and cook until fragrant, about 30 seconds. Whisk in ketchup mixture and bring to boil. Reduce heat to medium-low and simmer for 5 minutes. Transfer ½ cup of sauce to small bowl for basting and set aside remaining sauce for serving. (Sauce can be refrigerated for up to 1 week.)

3A. For a charcoal grill Open bottom vent halfway. Light large chimney starter filled with charcoal briquettes (6 quarts). When top coals are partially covered with ash, pour evenly over half of grill. Set cooking grate in place, cover, and open lid vent halfway. Heat grill until hot, about 5 minutes.

3B. For a gas grill Turn all burners to high, cover, and heat grill until hot, about 15 minutes. Leave primary burner on high and turn off other burner(s). (Adjust primary burner as needed to maintain grill temperature around 350 degrees.)

4. Clean and oil cooking grate. Unwrap ribs. Place ribs on hotter side of grill and cook until well browned on both sides, 4 to 7 minutes. Move ribs to cooler side of grill and brush top side with ¼ cup sauce for basting. Cover and cook for 6 minutes. Flip ribs and brush with remaining ¼ cup sauce for basting. Cover and continue to cook until pork registers 150 degrees, 5 to 10 minutes. Transfer ribs to serving platter, tent with foil and let rest for 10 minutes. Serve, passing reserved sauce separately.

Grilled Sausages with Bell Peppers and Onions

Serves 6

Why This Recipe Works The combination of sausages with plenty of charred flavor and perfectly grilled peppers and onions makes a humble but delicious summertime meal. To properly cook both the sausages and the vegetables, we discovered that we needed to stagger the cooking process. We cooked the sausages gently on the cooler side of the grill until they were nearly done and then moved them to the hotter side to develop nice grill marks and a slight char. For the vegetables, we relied on the microwave to jump-start their cooking. We then transferred them to a disposable aluminum pan set on the hotter side of the grill, which acted as our makeshift ballpark flat-top grill. We seasoned the vegetables with vinegar, salt, and pepper, and they reached perfect tenderness just as the sausages finished cooking. Just before serving, we transferred the sausages to the disposable pan, covered it with aluminum foil, and let everything rest for a few minutes before serving. You can substitute hot Italian sausages for sweet, if desired. Minimal flare-ups are to be expected when grilling the sausages on the hotter side of the grill; they give the sausages color and flavor.

- 3 red bell peppers, stemmed, seeded, and cut into ¼-inch-wide strips
- 2 onions, halved and sliced ¼ inch thick
- 3 tablespoons distilled white vinegar
- 2 tablespoons sugar
- 1 tablespoon vegetable oil
- ½ teaspoon table salt
- ½ teaspoon pepper
- 1 (13 by 9-inch) disposable aluminum roasting pan
- 2 pounds sweet Italian sausage
- 12 (6-inch) Italian sub rolls

1. Toss bell peppers, onions, vinegar, sugar, oil, salt, and pepper together in bowl. Microwave, covered, until vegetables are just tender, about 6 minutes. Pour vegetable mixture and any accumulated juices into disposable pan.

2A. For a charcoal grill Open bottom vent completely. Light large chimney starter filled with charcoal briquettes (6 quarts). When top coals are partially covered with ash, pour evenly over half of grill. Set cooking grate in place, cover, and open lid vent completely. Heat grill until hot, about 5 minutes.

2B. For a gas grill Turn all burners to high, cover, and heat grill until hot, about 15 minutes. Leave primary burner on high and turn off other burner(s). (Adjust primary burner as needed to maintain grill temperature between 375 and 400 degrees.)

Sweet and Tangy Grilled Country-Style Pork Ribs

Grilled Sausages with Bell Peppers and Onions

Vietnamese Grilled Pork Patties with Rice Noodles and Salad (Bun Cha)

Grilled Lamb Shoulder Chops with Zucchini and Corn Salad

3. Clean and oil cooking grate. Place disposable pan on hotter side of grill (over primary burner if using gas). Cover and cook for 20 minutes.

4. Place sausages on cooler side of grill and stir vegetable mixture; cover and cook for 8 minutes. Flip sausages and stir vegetable mixture again; cover and cook until sausages register 150 degrees and vegetables are softened and beginning to brown, about 8 minutes.

5. Transfer sausages to disposable pan with vegetables; slide disposable pan to cooler side of grill, then transfer sausages from disposable pan to hotter side of grill. Cook sausages, uncovered, turning often, until well browned and registering 160 degrees, 2 to 3 minutes (there may be flare-ups).

6. Return sausages to disposable pan with vegetables. Remove disposable pan from grill, tent with aluminum foil, and let rest for 5 minutes. Divide sausages and vegetables among rolls. Serve.

Vietnamese Grilled Pork Patties with Rice Noodles and Salad (Bun Cha)
Serves 4 to 6

Why This Recipe Works Vietnamese *bun cha*—a vibrant mix of grilled pork, crisp salad, and delicate rice vermicelli, all united by a light yet potent sauce—is an ideal meal for a hot summer night. We started by boiling dried rice vermicelli, then we rinsed the noodles and spread them on a platter to dry. We mixed up a bold and zesty sauce known as *nuoc cham* using lime juice, sugar, and fish sauce. To ensure that every drop of the sauce was flavored with garlic and chile, we used a portion of the sugar to help grind the ingredients into a fine paste. For juicy pork patties, we mixed baking soda into ground pork, which raised the meat's pH and helped it to retain moisture and brown during the brief grilling time. We also seasoned the pork with shallot, fish sauce, sugar, and pepper. Briefly soaking the grilled patties in the sauce further flavored the patties and imbued the sauce with grill flavor. Look for dried rice vermicelli in the Asian section of your supermarket. We prefer the more delicate springiness of vermicelli made from 100 percent rice flour to those that include a secondary starch such as cornstarch. If you can find only the latter, just cook them longer—up to 12 minutes. For a less spicy sauce, use only half the Thai chile. For the cilantro, use the leaves and the thin, delicate stems, not the thicker ones close to the root. To serve, place platters of noodles, salad, sauce, and pork patties on the table and allow diners to combine components to their taste. The sauce is potent, so use it sparingly.

Noodles and Salad

- 8 ounces rice vermicelli
- 1 head Boston lettuce (8 ounces), torn into bite-size pieces
- 1 English cucumber, peeled, quartered lengthwise, seeded, and sliced thin on bias
- 1 cup fresh cilantro leaves and stems
- 1 cup fresh mint leaves, torn if large

Sauce

- 1 small Thai chile, stemmed and minced
- 3 tablespoons sugar, divided
- 1 garlic clove, minced
- ⅔ cup hot water
- 5 tablespoons fish sauce
- ¼ cup lime juice (2 limes)

Pork Patties

- 1 large shallot, minced
- 1 tablespoon fish sauce
- 1½ teaspoons sugar
- ½ teaspoon baking soda
- ½ teaspoon pepper
- 1 pound ground pork

1. For the noodles and salad Bring 4 quarts water to boil in large pot. Stir in noodles and cook until tender but not mushy, 4 to 12 minutes. Drain noodles and rinse under cold running water until cool. Drain noodles very well, spread on large plate, and let stand at room temperature to dry. Arrange lettuce, cucumber, cilantro, and mint separately on large platter and refrigerate until needed.

2. For the sauce Using mortar and pestle (or on cutting board using flat side of chef's knife), mash Thai chile, 1 tablespoon sugar, and garlic to fine paste. Transfer to medium bowl and add hot water and remaining 2 tablespoons sugar. Stir until sugar is dissolved. Stir in fish sauce and lime juice. Set aside.

3. For the pork patties Combine shallot, fish sauce, sugar, baking soda, and pepper in medium bowl. Add pork and mix until well combined. Shape pork mixture into 12 patties, each about 2½ inches wide and ½ inch thick.

4A. For a charcoal grill Open bottom vent completely. Light large chimney starter filled with charcoal briquettes (6 quarts). When top coals are partially covered with ash, pour evenly over half of grill. Set cooking grate in place, cover, and open lid vent completely. Heat grill until hot, about 5 minutes.

4B. For a gas grill Turn all burners to high, cover, and heat grill until hot, about 15 minutes. Leave all burners on high.

5. Clean and oil cooking grate. Cook patties (directly over coals if using charcoal; covered if using gas) until well charred, 3 to 4 minutes per side. Transfer grilled patties to bowl with sauce and gently toss to coat. Let sit for 5 minutes.

6. Transfer patties to serving platter, reserving sauce. Serve noodles, salad, sauce, and pork patties separately.

Grilled Lamb Shoulder Chops with Zucchini and Corn Salad

Serves 4

Why This Recipe Works Grill-charred corn and zucchini brushed with a simple marinade gave this summery salad tons of flavor. We grilled the corn and the zucchini side by side after coating the vegetables in a pungent mixture of olive oil, garlic, red pepper flakes, and salt and pepper. For a protein to grill and serve with our char-flavored salad, we chose inexpensive lamb shoulder chops—they are a great match with the grill because their distinctive gutsy flavor holds up well to the smoke. They're also a fun way to mix things up when you're used to grilling beef steaks, pork chops, or other more common cuts of meat. To imbue our lamb with flavor, we marinated the chops in a mixture of olive oil, garlic, salt, and pepper. We like our lamb shoulder chops cooked to medium as this cut can be tough if cooked any less than that.

- ½ cup extra-virgin olive oil, divided
- 3 garlic cloves, minced, divided
- 1 teaspoon table salt, divided
- ¾ teaspoon pepper, divided
- 4 (8- to 12-ounce) lamb shoulder chops (blade or round bone), ¾ to 1 inch thick, trimmed
- ⅛ teaspoon red pepper flakes
- 2 ears corn, husks and silk removed
- 1½ pounds zucchini, sliced lengthwise into ½-inch-thick planks
- 2 tablespoons chopped fresh basil
- 4 teaspoons lemon juice
- 2 ounces feta cheese, crumbled (½ cup)

1. Whisk 3 tablespoons oil, one-third of garlic, ½ teaspoon salt, and ½ teaspoon pepper together in baking dish. Add lamb chops to marinade and turn to coat.

2. Whisk pepper flakes, remaining 5 tablespoons oil, remaining garlic, remaining ½ teaspoon salt, and remaining ¼ teaspoon pepper together in large bowl. Brush corn with 1 tablespoon oil mixture. Add zucchini to remaining oil mixture in bowl and toss to coat.

3A. For a charcoal grill Open bottom vent completely. Light large chimney starter three-quarters filled with charcoal briquettes (4½ quarts). When top coals are partially covered with ash, pour evenly over grill. Set cooking grate in place, cover, and open lid vent completely. Heat grill until hot, about 5 minutes.

3B. For a gas grill Turn all burners to high, cover, and heat grill until hot, about 15 minutes. Turn all burners to medium-high.

4. Clean and oil cooking grate. Place corn and zucchini on grill; do not wash bowl, reserving any oil mixture remaining. Grill, uncovered, turning corn every 2 to 3 minutes until kernels are lightly charred all over, 10 to 15 minutes total, and zucchini is well browned and tender (not mushy), 5 to 7 minutes per side; transfer to plate. Turn all burners to high if using gas.

5. Place chops on grill and cook, covered, until browned and meat registers 130 to 135 degrees (for medium), 4 to 6 minutes per side. Transfer chops to serving platter, tent with aluminum foil, and let rest.

6. While lamb rests, cut kernels from cobs. Cut zucchini on bias into ½-inch-thick slices. Add vegetables to bowl with reserved oil mixture. Add basil and lemon juice to vegetables and toss to combine. Season with salt and pepper to taste. Transfer salad to serving platter and sprinkle feta over top. Serve with lamb chops.

Grilled Lamb Kofte
Serves 4 to 6 `MAKE AHEAD`

Why This Recipe Works In the Middle East, kebabs called *kofte* feature ground meat, not chunks, mixed with lots of spices and fresh herbs. Our challenge was to get their sausage-like texture just right. Because the patties are small, the meat easily overcooks and becomes dry. Plus, since kofte is kneaded by hand in order to get the meat proteins to cross-link and take on a resilient texture, it's easy to make it too springy—or not springy enough. We skipped the traditional bread panade in favor of a little gelatin to keep our kofte moist after grilling. Pine nuts added richness and texture. For the spices, we used a variation on the common Middle Eastern spice blend called *baharat*, which contains black pepper, cumin, coriander, and chile pepper. For a cooling sauce to balance the spices of the kofte we made a yogurt-garlic-tahini-lemon mixture. Use the large holes of a box grater to grate the onion for this recipe. You will need eight 12-inch metal skewers for the kofte.

Yogurt-Garlic Sauce
- 1 cup plain whole-milk yogurt
- 2 tablespoons lemon juice
- 2 tablespoons tahini
- 1 garlic clove, minced
- ½ teaspoon table salt

Kofte
- ½ cup pine nuts
- 4 garlic cloves, peeled
- 1½ teaspoons hot smoked paprika
- 1 teaspoon table salt
- 1 teaspoon ground cumin
- ½ teaspoon pepper
- ¼ teaspoon ground coriander
- ¼ teaspoon ground cloves
- ⅛ teaspoon ground nutmeg
- ⅛ teaspoon ground cinnamon
- 1½ pounds ground lamb
- ½ cup grated onion, drained
- ⅓ cup minced fresh parsley
- ⅓ cup minced fresh mint
- 1½ teaspoons unflavored gelatin
- 1 (13 by 9-inch) disposable aluminum roasting pan (if using charcoal)

1. For the sauce Whisk all ingredients together in bowl.

2. For the kofte Process pine nuts, garlic, paprika, salt, cumin, pepper, coriander, cloves, nutmeg, and cinnamon into paste in food processor, 30 to 45 seconds; transfer to large bowl. Add lamb, onion, parsley, mint, and gelatin to bowl and knead with your hands until thoroughly combined and mixture feels slightly sticky, about 2 minutes.

3. Divide mixture into 8 equal portions. Shape each portion into 5-inch-long cylinder about 1 inch in diameter. Using eight 12-inch metal skewers, thread 1 cylinder onto each skewer, pressing gently to adhere. Transfer skewers to lightly greased baking sheet, cover with plastic wrap, and refrigerate for 1 hour or up to 24 hours.

4A. For a charcoal grill Using skewer, poke 12 holes in bottom of disposable pan. Open bottom vent completely and place disposable pan in center of grill. Light large chimney starter two-thirds filled with charcoal briquettes (4 quarts). When top coals are partially covered with ash, pour into disposable pan. Set cooking grate in place, cover, and open lid vent completely. Heat grill until hot, about 5 minutes.

4B. For a gas grill Turn all burners to high, cover, and heat grill until hot, about 15 minutes. Leave all burners on high.

5. Clean and oil cooking grate. Place skewers on grill (directly over coals if using charcoal) at 45-degree angle to grate bars. Cook (covered if using gas) until browned and meat easily releases from grill, 4 to 7 minutes. Flip skewers and continue to cook until browned on second side and meat registers 160 degrees, about 6 minutes. Transfer skewers to serving platter and serve, passing yogurt-garlic sauce separately.

Swordfish Kebabs with Zucchini Ribbon Salad

Serves 4

Why This Recipe Works Swordfish is a favorite fish for grilling. It has a robust taste all its own and needs costarring ingredients with just as much oomph. For our skewers, we paired swordfish with a lively salad of attractive shaved zucchini ribbons, tender baby kale, salty ricotta salata, and bright fresh mint. We used Italian seasoning as a deeply flavorful and convenient rub on the swordfish and grilled the fish to perfection before serving the kebabs with our fresh, summery salad. Crumbled feta cheese can be substituted for the ricotta salata. You will need four 12-inch metal skewers for this recipe.

    7   tablespoons extra-virgin olive oil, divided
    ¼   cup lemon juice (2 lemons), divided
    1   tablespoon dried Italian seasoning
    1½ teaspoons table salt, divided
    1½ teaspoons pepper, divided
    2   pounds skinless swordfish steaks,
        1 inch thick, cut into 1-inch pieces
    3   zucchini (8 ounces each), shaved into
        ribbons with vegetable peeler,
        seeds discarded
    3   ounces (3 cups) baby kale
    3   ounces ricotta salata, shaved
    2   tablespoons chopped fresh mint

1. Whisk ¼ cup oil, 2 tablespoons lemon juice, Italian seasoning, ½ teaspoon salt, and ½ teaspoon pepper together in large bowl. Add swordfish and toss to coat. Thread swordfish evenly onto four 12-inch metal skewers.

2. Whisk remaining 3 tablespoons oil, remaining 2 tablespoons lemon juice, remaining 1 teaspoon salt, and remaining 1 teaspoon pepper together in second large bowl; set dressing aside.

Grilled Lamb Kofte

Swordfish Kebabs with
Zucchini Ribbon Salad

3A. For a charcoal grill Open bottom vent completely. Light large chimney starter filled with charcoal briquettes (6 quarts). When top coals are partially covered with ash, pour evenly over grill. Set cooking grate in place, cover, and open lid vent completely. Heat grill until hot, about 5 minutes.

3B. For a gas grill Turn all burners to high, cover, and heat grill until hot, about 15 minutes. Leave all burners on high.

4. Clean and oil cooking grate. Grill skewers, turning often, until swordfish registers 140 degrees, 9 to 12 minutes. Transfer to serving platter. Add zucchini, kale, ricotta salata, and mint to bowl with dressing and toss to coat. Serve with swordfish.

Grilled Salmon Steaks with Lemon-Caper Sauce

Serves 4

Why This Recipe Works Hearty salmon steaks are a common choice for summer grilling, but in spite of their thick cut they often end up with a burnt exterior and a dry, flavorless interior. Plus, no matter how much seasoning goes on the outside, it never seems to permeate the whole steak. To make the process fool-proof, we first turned the oblong steaks into sturdy medallions. By carefully removing a bit of skin from one tail of the steak, tightly wrapping the skin of the other tail around the skinned portion, and then tying the whole thing with kitchen twine, we made neat steaks that cooked evenly and could be easily moved around the grill. We used a two-level cooking approach, beginning with an initial sear over the hotter part of the grill. While the steaks seared, we made a simple, bright lemon and caper sauce directly in a disposable aluminum pan over the cooler side of the grill. When the steaks were browned, we transferred them to the pan, coated them with the sauce, and finished cooking them over the lower heat directly in the sauce, which ensured that they stayed moist and tender. Before eating, lift out the small circular bone from the center of each steak. Arctic char and wild salmon are good substitutes for the salmon. If using, make sure to cook them to 120 degrees.

Lemon-Caper Sauce

- 3 tablespoons unsalted butter, cut into 3 pieces
- 1 teaspoon grated lemon zest plus 6 tablespoons juice (2 lemons)
- 1 shallot, minced
- 1 tablespoon capers, rinsed
- ⅛ teaspoon table salt
- 1 (13 by 9-inch) disposable aluminum roasting pan

Grilled Salmon Steaks with Lime-Cilantro Sauce

Salmon

- 4 (10-ounce) skin-on salmon steaks, 1 to 1½ inches thick
- 1 teaspoon table salt
- ½ teaspoon pepper
- 2 tablespoons vegetable oil
- 2 tablespoons minced fresh parsley

1. For the sauce Combine butter, lemon zest and juice, shallot, capers, and salt in disposable pan.

2. For the salmon Pat salmon dry with paper towels. Working with 1 steak at a time, carefully trim 1½ inches of skin from 1 tail. Tightly wrap other tail around skinned portion and tie steak with kitchen twine. Sprinkle salmon with salt and pepper and brush both sides with oil.

3A. For a charcoal grill Open bottom vent completely. Light large chimney starter filled with charcoal briquettes (6 quarts). When top coals are partially covered with ash, pour evenly over half of grill. Set cooking grate in place, cover, and open lid vent completely. Heat grill until hot, about 5 minutes.

3B. For a gas grill Turn all burners to high, cover, and heat grill until hot, about 15 minutes. Leave primary burner on high and turn off other burner(s).

4. Clean cooking grate, then repeatedly brush grate with well-oiled paper towels until black and glossy, 5 to 10 times. Place salmon on hotter side of grill. Cook, turning once, until browned on both sides, 4 to 6 minutes. Meanwhile, set disposable pan with butter mixture on cooler side of grill and cook until butter has melted, about 2 minutes.

5. Transfer salmon to disposable pan and gently turn to coat with butter mixture. Cook (covered if using gas) until center of salmon is still translucent when checked with tip of paring knife and registers 125 degrees (for medium-rare), 6 to 14 minutes, flipping salmon and rotating pan halfway through grilling. Remove twine and transfer salmon to serving platter. Off heat, whisk parsley into sauce. Drizzle sauce over steaks. Serve.

VARIATIONS

Grilled Salmon Steaks with Orange-Ginger Sauce
Replace lemon zest and juice with orange zest and orange juice. Omit shallot and capers; add 1 tablespoon grated fresh ginger and 1 tablespoon soy sauce to mixture in step 1. Substitute 1 thinly sliced scallion for parsley in step 3.

Grilled Salmon Steaks with Lime-Cilantro Sauce
Replace lemon zest and juice with lime zest and lime juice. Omit shallot and capers; add 2 minced garlic cloves and ½ teaspoon ground cumin to mixture in step 1. Substitute cilantro for parsley in step 3.

PREPPING SALMON MEDALLIONS

1. Remove 1½ inches of skin from 1 tail of each steak.

2. Tuck skinned portion into center of steak, wrap other tail around it, and tie with kitchen twine.

Grill-Smoked Salmon
Serves 6

Why This Recipe Works We wanted to capture the intense, smoky flavor of smoked fish, but we also wanted to skip the specialized equipment and make this dish less of a project recipe. To prepare the salmon for smoking, we quick-cured the fish with a mixture of salt and sugar, which firmed it up and seasoned it inside and out. We then cooked the fish indirectly over a gentle fire with ample smoke. We also cut our large fillet into individual portions to make serving simple. This small step delivered big results: First, it ensured more thorough smoke exposure (without increasing the time) by creating more surface area. Second, the smaller pieces of delicate salmon were far easier to get off the grill intact than one large fillet. To ensure uniform pieces of fish that cooked at the same rate, we found it best to buy a whole center-cut fillet and cut it into six pieces ourselves. Arctic char and wild salmon are good substitutes for the salmon. If using, make sure to cook them to 120 degrees. If you'd like to use wood chunks instead of wood chips when using a charcoal grill, substitute two medium wood chunks, soaked in water for 1 hour, for the wood chip packet.

1 (2½-pound) skin-on salmon fillet,
   1 to 1½ inches thick
2 tablespoons sugar
1 tablespoon kosher salt
2 cups wood chips, 1 cup soaked in
   water for 15 minutes and drained

1. Cut salmon crosswise into 6 fillets. Combine sugar and salt in bowl. Set salmon, skin side down, on wire rack set in rimmed baking sheet and sprinkle flesh side evenly with sugar mixture. Refrigerate, uncovered, for 1 hour. Meanwhile, using large piece of heavy-duty aluminum foil, wrap both soaked wood chips and remaining 1 cup unsoaked chips in 8 by 4½-inch foil packet. (Make sure chips do not poke holes in sides or bottom of packet.) Cut 2 evenly spaced 2-inch slits in top of packet.

2. Brush any excess salt and sugar from salmon using paper towels and blot salmon dry. Return fish to wire rack and refrigerate, uncovered, until ready to cook. Fold piece of heavy-duty foil into 18 by 6-inch rectangle.

3A. For a charcoal grill Open bottom vent halfway. Light large chimney starter one-third filled with charcoal briquettes (2 quarts). When top coals are partially covered with ash, pour into steeply banked pile against side of grill. Place wood chip packet on coals. Set cooking grate in place, cover, and open lid vent halfway. Heat grill until hot and wood chips are smoking, about 5 minutes.

3B. For a gas grill Remove cooking grate and place wood chip packet directly on primary burner. Set cooking grate in place and turn primary burner to high (leave other burner[s] off). Cover and heat grill until hot and wood chips begin to smoke, 15 to 25 minutes. Turn primary burner to medium. (Adjust primary burner as needed to maintain grill temperature between 275 to 300 degrees.)

4. Clean and oil cooking grate. Place foil rectangle on cooler side of grill and place salmon fillets on foil, spaced at least ½ inch apart. Cover (position lid vent over fish if using charcoal) and cook until center of salmon is still translucent when checked with tip of paring knife and registers 125 degrees (for medium-rare), 30 to 40 minutes. Transfer to serving platter. Serve warm or at room temperature.

Grilled Blackened Red Snapper
Serves 4

Why This Recipe Works Blackened fish is usually prepared in a cast-iron skillet, but that can lead to one smoky kitchen. We were done with the smoke but we wanted our fillets to have a dark brown, crusty, sweet-smoky, toasted-spice exterior, providing a rich contrast to the moist, mild-flavored fish inside. We thought we'd solve our problems by throwing the fish on the grill. Unfortunately, this move created a host of other issues, including that the fish stuck to the grate, the outside of the fish was way overdone by the time the flesh had cooked through, and the skin-on fillets curled midway through cooking. The curling problem was easy to fix: We simply needed to score the skin. To prevent sticking, we made sure the grill was hot when we put the fish on and oiled the grate multiple times to ensure a clean surface. Finally, to give the fish its flavorful blackened-but-not-burned coating, we bloomed our spice mixture in melted butter, allowed it to cool, and then applied the coating to the fish. Once on the grill, the spice crust acquired the proper depth and richness while the fish cooked through.

Pineapple and Cucumber Salsa with Mint
- ½ large pineapple, peeled, cored, and cut into ¼-inch pieces
- ½ cucumber, peeled, halved lengthwise, seeded, and cut into ¼-inch pieces
- 1 small shallot, minced
- 1 serrano chile, stemmed, seeded, and minced
- 2 tablespoons chopped fresh mint
- 1 tablespoon lime juice, plus extra as needed
- ½ teaspoon grated fresh ginger
- ½ teaspoon table salt

Fish
- 2 tablespoons paprika
- 2 teaspoons onion powder
- 2 teaspoons garlic powder
- ¾ teaspoon ground coriander
- ½ teaspoon table salt
- ¼ teaspoon pepper
- ¼ teaspoon cayenne pepper
- ¼ teaspoon white pepper
- 3 tablespoons unsalted butter
- 4 (6- to 8-ounce) skin-on red snapper fillets, ¾ inch thick

1. For the salsa Combine pineapple, cucumber, shallot, chile, mint, lime juice, ginger, and salt in bowl and let sit at room temperature for 15 to 30 minutes. Set aside for serving.

2. For the fish Combine paprika, onion powder, garlic powder, coriander, salt, pepper, cayenne, and white pepper in bowl. Melt butter in 10-inch skillet over medium heat. Stir in spice mixture and cook, stirring often, until fragrant and spices turn dark rust color, 2 to 3 minutes. Transfer mixture to pie plate and let cool to room temperature. Use fork to break up any large clumps.

3. Pat snapper dry with paper towels. Using sharp knife, make shallow diagonal slashes every inch along skin side of fish, being careful not to cut into flesh. Using your fingers, rub spice mixture evenly over top, bottom, and sides of fish (you should use all of spice mixture).

4A. For a charcoal grill Open bottom vent completely. Light large chimney starter two-thirds filled with charcoal briquettes (4 quarts). When top coals are partially covered with ash, pour evenly over half of grill. Set cooking grate in place, cover, and open lid vent completely. Heat grill until hot, about 5 minutes.

4B. For a gas grill Turn all burners to high, cover, and heat grill until hot, about 15 minutes. Leave all burners on high.

5. Clean cooking grate, then repeatedly brush grate with well-oiled paper towels until black and glossy, 5 to 10 times.

6. Place snapper skin side down on grill (on hotter side if using charcoal) with fillets perpendicular to grate. Cook until skin is very dark brown and crisp, 3 to 5 minutes. Carefully flip snapper and continue to cook until dark brown and beginning to flake when prodded with paring knife and registers 140 degrees, about 5 minutes. Serve with salsa.

Grilled Whole Red Snapper
Serves 4

Why This Recipe Works Grilling a whole fish is super appealing in the summer and makes for an impressive dinner centerpiece. But it also has its challenges: the skin can stick fast to the grill and the meat can cook unevenly. We wanted a foolproof way to conquer these challenges. Using semifirm, midsize, mild-flavored fish was the first step to success. Making shallow diagonal slashes on the skin helped ensure even cooking and enabled us to gauge the doneness more easily. To prevent the skin from sticking, we greased the cooking grate and coated the fish with a film of oil. We used two thin metal spatulas to flip the delicate fish once the first side was done. They also made it easier to remove the cooked fish from the grill. The cooked fish needed only a few cuts for us to use one of our spatulas to lift away the meat from the bones on each side in a single piece. A fresh relish or vinaigrette is the perfect complement to the simple grilled fish. If your fish are a little larger (between 1½ and 2 pounds), simply grill them a minute or two longer on each side. Fish weighing more than 2 pounds will be hard to maneuver on the grill and should be avoided. Serve with lemon wedges and Chermoula (page 294), if desired.

- 2 whole red snapper or striped bass (about 1½ pounds each), scaled, gutted, and fins snipped off with scissors
- 3 tablespoons extra-virgin olive oil
- 1½ teaspoons table salt
- ¾ teaspoon pepper
  Lemon wedges

1A. For a charcoal grill Open bottom vent completely. Light large chimney starter filled with charcoal briquettes (6 quarts). When top coals are partially covered with ash, pour evenly over grill. Set cooking grate in place, cover, and open lid vent completely. Heat grill until hot, about 5 minutes.

1B. For a gas grill Turn all burners to high, cover, and heat grill until hot, about 15 minutes. Leave all burners on high.

2. Rinse each snapper under cold running water and pat dry with paper towels inside and out. Using sharp knife, make 3 or 4 shallow slashes, about 2 inches apart, on both sides of fish. Rub fish with oil and sprinkle with salt and pepper on inside and outside.

3. Clean cooking grate, then repeatedly brush grate with well-oiled paper towels until black and glossy, 5 to 10 times. Lay snapper on grill, perpendicular to grate bars. Cook (covered if using gas) until side of snapper facing heat source is browned and crisp, 6 to 7 minutes. Using thin metal spatula, lift bottom of thick backbone edge of fish from cooking grate just enough to slide second thin metal spatula under fish. Remove first spatula,

Grilled Whole Red Snapper

then use it to support raw side of fish as you use second spatula to flip fish over. Cook (covered if using gas) until flesh is no longer translucent at center, skin on both sides of each snapper is blistered and crisp, and snapper registers 140 degrees, 6 to 8 minutes. Carefully transfer snapper to serving platter and let rest for 5 minutes.

SERVING WHOLE FISH

1. Make vertical cut just behind head from top to belly, then cut along back of fish from head to tail.

2. Starting at head and working toward tail, use metal spatula to lift meat away from bones. Repeat on second side.

Grilled Scallops

Grilled Jalapeño and Lime Shrimp Skewers

4. Fillet each snapper by making vertical cut just behind head from top of snapper to belly. Make another cut along top of snapper from head to tail. Use spatula to lift meat from bones, starting at head end and running spatula over bones to lift out fillet. Repeat on other side of snapper. Discard head and skeleton and serve with lemon wedges.

Grilled Scallops
Serves 4

Why This Recipe Works In theory, scallops are tailor-made for the grill. The superhot fire should deeply brown their exteriors while leaving their centers plump and moist. Unfortunately, in reality, by the time the scallops develop a good sear, they're usually overcooked and rubbery. And then there's the problem of trying to flip them when they inevitably stick to the cooking grate. To avoid overcooking the scallops yet still develop a brown crust, we needed a quick blast of heat, so we built the hottest fire possible by corralling the coals in a disposable aluminum pan set in the bottom of the grill. To make flipping easier, we lightly coated the scallops with a slurry of vegetable oil, flour, cornstarch, and sugar and threaded them onto doubled metal skewers. The slurry kept the scallops from sticking to the cooking grate, the sugar promoted browning, and the two skewers prevented the scallops from spinning when flipped. Thoroughly oiling the grate also helped get our scallops off the grill in one piece. We created two boldly flavored vinaigrettes to complement the juicy, smoky scallops; one with chili sauce and lime and one with fresh basil and chives. We recommend buying "dry" scallops, which don't have chemical additives and taste better than "wet." Dry scallops will look ivory or pinkish; wet scallops are bright white. To double-skewer the scallops, thread four to six scallops onto one skewer and then place a second skewer through the scallops parallel to and about ¼ inch from the first. You will need eight to twelve 12-inch metal skewers for this recipe. If you use a charcoal grill, make sure the roasting pan you use is at least 2¾ inches deep.

1½ pounds large sea scallops, tendons removed
1 (13 by 9-inch) disposable aluminum roasting pan (if using charcoal)
2 tablespoons vegetable oil
1 tablespoon all-purpose flour
1 teaspoon cornstarch
1 teaspoon sugar
½ teaspoon kosher salt
½ teaspoon pepper
  Lemon wedges
1 recipe vinaigrette (optional) (recipes follow)

1. Place scallops on rimmed baking sheet lined with clean dish towel. Place second clean dish towel on top of scallops and press gently on towel to blot liquid. Let scallops sit at room temperature, covered with towel, for 10 minutes. Thread scallops onto doubled 12-inch metal skewers so that flat sides will directly touch cooking grate, 4 to 6 scallops per pair of skewers. Return skewered scallops to towel-lined sheet; refrigerate, covered with second towel, while preparing grill.

2A. For a charcoal grill Light large chimney starter mounded with charcoal briquettes (7 quarts). Poke twelve ½-inch holes in bottom of disposable pan and place in center of grill. When top coals are partially covered with ash, pour into disposable pan.

2B. For a gas grill Turn all burners to high, cover, and heat grill until very hot, about 15 minutes. Leave all burners on high.

3. Clean cooking grate, then repeatedly brush grate with well-oiled paper towels until grate is black and glossy, 5 to 10 times.

4. Whisk oil, flour, cornstarch, and sugar together in small bowl. Brush both sides of skewered scallops with oil mixture and sprinkle with salt and pepper. Place skewered scallops on grill (directly over coals if using charcoal). Cook scallops (covered if using gas), without moving them, until lightly browned, 2½ to 4 minutes. Carefully flip skewers and continue to cook until second side is browned, sides of scallops are firm, and centers are opaque, 2 to 4 minutes. Serve immediately with lemon wedges and vinaigrette, if using.

Chile-Lime Vinaigrette
Makes about 1 cup

2 tablespoons honey
1 tablespoon sriracha
2 teaspoons fish sauce
1 teaspoon finely grated lime zest plus
  3 tablespoons juice (2 limes)
½ cup vegetable oil

Whisk honey, sriracha, fish sauce, and lime zest and juice until combined. Whisking constantly, slowly drizzle in oil until emulsified.

Basil Vinaigrette
Makes about 1 cup
If you don't have champagne vinegar, white wine vinegar will also work here.

1 cup fresh basil leaves
3 tablespoons minced fresh chives
2 tablespoons champagne vinegar
2 garlic cloves, minced
2 teaspoons sugar
1 teaspoon table salt
½ teaspoon pepper
⅔ cup vegetable oil

Pulse basil, chives, vinegar, garlic, sugar, salt, and pepper in blender until roughly chopped. With blender running, slowly drizzle in oil until emulsified, scraping down sides of blender jar as needed.

Grilled Jalapeño and Lime Shrimp Skewers

Serves 4

Why This Recipe Works We wanted tender grilled shrimp with a smoky, charred crust and chile flavor that was more than just superficial. To achieve this, we sprinkled one side of the shrimp with sugar to promote browning and cooked the shrimp sugar side down over the hot side of the grill for a few minutes. We then flipped the skewers to gently finish cooking on the cool side of the grill. Creating a flavorful marinade that doubled as a sauce gave our shrimp skewers a spicy, assertive kick. And butterflying the shrimp before marinating and grilling them opened up more shrimp flesh for the marinade and finishing sauce to flavor. We prefer flat metal skewers that are at least 14 inches long for this recipe.

Marinade
1–2 jalapeño chiles, stemmed, seeded, and chopped
3 tablespoons extra-virgin olive oil
6 garlic cloves, minced
1 teaspoon grated lime zest plus 5 tablespoons juice (3 limes)
½ teaspoon table salt
½ teaspoon ground cumin
¼ teaspoon cayenne pepper

Shrimp
1½ pounds extra-large shrimp (21 to 25 per pound), peeled and deveined
½ teaspoon sugar
1 tablespoon minced fresh cilantro

1. For the marinade Process all ingredients in food processor until smooth, about 15 seconds. Reserve 2 tablespoons marinade; transfer remaining marinade to medium bowl.

2. For the shrimp Pat shrimp dry with paper towels. To butterfly shrimp, use paring knife to make shallow cut down outside curve of shrimp. Add shrimp to bowl with marinade and toss to coat. Cover and refrigerate for 30 minutes to 1 hour.

3A. For a charcoal grill Open bottom vent completely. Light large chimney starter filled with charcoal briquettes (6 quarts). When top coals are partially covered with ash, pour evenly over half of grill. Set cooking grate in place, cover, and open lid vent completely. Heat grill until hot, about 5 minutes.

3B. For a gas grill Turn all burners to high, cover, and heat grill until hot, about 15 minutes.

4. Clean and oil cooking grate. Thread marinated shrimp on skewers. (Alternate direction of each shrimp as you pack them tightly on skewer to allow about a dozen shrimp to fit snugly on each skewer.) Sprinkle 1 side of skewered shrimp with sugar. Grill shrimp, sugared side down, over hot side of grill (covered if using gas), until lightly charred, 3 to 4 minutes. Flip skewers and move to cool side of grill (if using charcoal) or turn all burners off (if using gas), and cook, covered, until other side of shrimp is no longer translucent, 1 to 2 minutes. Using tongs, slide shrimp into clean medium bowl and toss with reserved marinade. Sprinkle with cilantro and serve.

VARIATION

Grilled Red Chile and Ginger Shrimp Skewers
Replace marinade with 1 to 3 seeded and chopped small red chiles (or jalapeños), 1 minced scallion, 3 tablespoons rice vinegar, 2 tablespoons soy sauce, 1 tablespoon toasted sesame oil, 1 tablespoon grated fresh ginger, 2 teaspoons sugar, and 1 minced garlic clove. Prepare and grill shrimp as directed. Replace cilantro with 1 thinly sliced scallion and serve with lime wedges.

HOW TO SKEWER SHRIMP

1. Make shallow cut down outside curve of shrimp to open up flesh.

2. Alternate direction of each shrimp as you pack them tightly on skewer.

New England Clambake
Serves 4

Why This Recipe Works Clambakes are a rite of summer all along the East Coast. Shellfish and vegetables are layered with seaweed and piled on top of white-hot rocks in a wide sandpit. The food then steams beneath a wet tarp until it's done. This feast usually takes more than a day to prepare and cook. We wanted to make it faster and more approachable by translating it to the grill. The biggest challenge was that our grill was only big enough to handle half the ingredients at a time. Since charcoal dies down as it burns, we had to decide which items would need the hotter temperature of the first round of grilling but could also sit the longest before serving. We chose to lead off with the corn, sausage, and potatoes and follow by the lobsters and clams. We also gave the potatoes a jump-start in the microwave and skewered them to make them more manageable. This grilled clambake captured all the smoky flavor of the traditional version—with no shovel required. Look for potatoes that are 1 to 2 inches in diameter; if your potatoes are larger, quarter them and increase the microwaving time as needed in step 2. Because the skewers go into the microwave, use wooden, not metal, skewers.

½ cup table salt, for brining
4 ears corn, husks and silk removed
½ teaspoon plus ⅛ teaspoon pepper, divided
1 pound small red potatoes, unpeeled, halved
2 (12-inch) wooden skewers
4 tablespoons unsalted butter, melted, divided, plus extra for serving
¾ teaspoon table salt, divided
2 (1¼- to 1½-pound) live lobsters
1 pound kielbasa
2 pounds littleneck clams, scrubbed
   Lemon wedges

1. Dissolve ½ cup salt in 4 quarts cold water in large pot. Add corn and soak for at least 30 minutes or up to 8 hours. Before grilling, remove corn from water, pat dry with paper towels, and sprinkle with ¼ teaspoon pepper.

2. Skewer potatoes, then lay them in single layer on large plate. Brush with 1 tablespoon melted butter and sprinkle with ¼ teaspoon salt and ⅛ teaspoon pepper. Microwave until potatoes begin to soften, about 6 minutes, flipping them halfway through microwaving. Brush with 1 tablespoon melted butter.

3. Split lobsters in half lengthwise, removing internal organs. Using back of chef's knife, whack 1 side of each claw to crack shell. Brush tail meat with 1 tablespoon melted butter, and sprinkle with remaining ½ teaspoon salt and remaining ¼ teaspoon pepper.

New England Clambake

4A. For a charcoal grill Open bottom vent completely. Light large chimney starter filled with charcoal briquettes (6 quarts). When top coals are partially covered with ash, pour evenly over grill. Set cooking grate in place, cover, and open lid vent completely. Heat grill until hot, about 5 minutes.

4B. For a gas grill Turn all burners to high, cover, and heat grill until hot, about 15 minutes. Adjust burners as needed to maintain grill temperature at 325 degrees.

5. Clean and oil cooking grate. Place kielbasa, corn, and skewered potatoes on grill. Cook until kielbasa is seared and hot throughout, corn is lightly charred, and potatoes are brown and tender, 10 to 16 minutes, turning as needed. Transfer vegetables and sausage as they finish cooking to serving platter, and tent with aluminum foil.

6. Lay lobsters, flesh side down, and clams on grill. Cook until clams have opened and lobsters are cooked through, 8 to 14 minutes, flipping lobsters and brushing lobster tail meat with remaining 1 tablespoon butter halfway through grilling. As lobsters and clams finish cooking, transfer them to serving platter with vegetables and sausage, preserving any juices that have accumulated inside their shells.

7. Slice kielbasa into 1-inch pieces and remove skewers from potatoes. Serve with lemon wedges and extra melted butter. Use lobster picks to reach meat inside claws and knuckles.

Grilled Paella
Serves 8

Why This Recipe Works This flavor-packed Spanish rice dish is a perfect one-pot showpiece for entertaining. Many modern recipes are cooked on the stove, but paella was originally made on the grill, so we started there. A large roasting pan was easy to maneuver, and its surface area maximized the amount of rice in contact with the pan, which formed the caramelized crust known as *socarrat*. Building a large grill fire and fueling it with fresh coals (which ignited during cooking) ensured that the heat would last throughout cooking. We streamlined the recipe by using roasted red peppers and tomato paste instead of fresh peppers and tomatoes. Staggering the addition of the proteins ensured that each element was perfectly cooked. Grilling the chicken thighs infused them with smoky flavor and gave them a head start on cooking, and arranging them around the cooler perimeter of the pan helped them stay moist. Nestling the clams and shrimp into the center of the pan allowed them to release their flavorful juices into the rice without overcooking. If littleneck clams are not available, increase the shrimp to 1½ pounds and season the shrimp in step 1 with ½ teaspoon salt. You will need a heavy-duty roasting pan that measures at least 11 by 14 inches for this recipe. If the exterior of your roasting pan is dark, the cooking times will be on the lower side of the ranges given. You can also cook this recipe in a paella pan that is 15 to 17 inches in diameter.

1½ pounds boneless, skinless chicken thighs, trimmed and halved crosswise
1¼ teaspoons table salt, divided
1 teaspoon pepper
12 ounces jumbo shrimp (16 to 20 per pound), peeled and deveined
5 tablespoons extra-virgin olive oil, divided
6 garlic cloves, minced, divided
1¾ teaspoons hot smoked paprika, divided
3 tablespoons tomato paste
4 cups chicken broth
1 (8-ounce) bottle clam juice
⅔ cup dry sherry
  Pinch saffron threads, crumbled (optional)
1 onion, chopped fine
½ cup jarred roasted red peppers, rinsed, patted dry, and chopped fine
3 cups Arborio rice
1 pound littleneck clams, scrubbed
8 ounces Spanish-style chorizo sausage, cut into ½-inch pieces
1 cup frozen peas, thawed
  Lemon wedges

1. Pat chicken dry with paper towels and sprinkle both sides with ½ teaspoon salt and 1 teaspoon pepper. Toss shrimp with 1½ teaspoons oil, ½ teaspoon garlic, ¼ teaspoon paprika, and ¼ teaspoon salt in bowl until evenly coated. Set aside.

2. Heat 1½ teaspoons oil in medium saucepan over medium heat until shimmering. Add remaining garlic and cook, stirring constantly, until garlic sticks to bottom of saucepan and begins to brown, about 1 minute. Add tomato paste and remaining 1½ teaspoons paprika and continue to cook, stirring constantly, until dark brown bits form on bottom of saucepan, about 1 minute. Stir in broth, clam juice, sherry, and saffron, if using. Increase heat to high and bring to boil. Remove saucepan from heat and set aside.

3A. For a charcoal grill Open bottom vent completely. Light large chimney starter mounded with charcoal briquettes (7 quarts). When top coals are partially covered with ash, pour evenly over grill. Using tongs, arrange 20 unlit briquettes evenly over coals. Set cooking grate in place, cover, and open lid vent completely. Heat grill until hot, about 5 minutes.

3B. For a gas grill Turn all burners to high, cover, and heat grill until hot, about 15 minutes. Leave all burners on high.

4. Clean and oil cooking grate. Place chicken on grill and cook until both sides are lightly browned, 5 to 7 minutes; transfer chicken to plate and clean cooking grate.

5. Place roasting pan on grill (turning burners to medium-high if using gas) and add remaining ¼ cup oil. When oil begins to shimmer, add onion, red peppers, and remaining ½ teaspoon salt. Cook, stirring frequently, until onion begins to brown, 4 to 7 minutes. Stir in rice (turning burners to medium if using gas) until grains are well coated with oil.

6. Arrange chicken around perimeter of pan. Pour chicken broth mixture and any accumulated chicken juices over rice. Smooth rice into even layer, making sure nothing sticks to sides of pan and no rice rests atop chicken. When liquid reaches gentle simmer, place shrimp in center of pan in single layer. Arrange clams in center of pan, evenly dispersing with shrimp and pushing hinge side of clams into rice slightly so they stand up. Distribute chorizo evenly over surface of rice. Cook, moving and rotating pan to maintain gentle simmer across entire surface of pan, until rice is almost cooked through, 12 to 18 minutes. (If using gas, adjust burners as needed to maintain simmer.)

7. Sprinkle peas evenly over paella, cover grill, and cook until liquid is fully absorbed and rice on bottom of pan sizzles, 5 to 8 minutes. Continue to cook, uncovered, checking frequently, until uniform golden-brown crust forms on bottom of pan, 8 to 15 minutes. (Rotate and slide pan around grill as necessary to ensure even crust formation.) Remove from grill, cover with aluminum foil, and let sit for 10 minutes. Serve with lemon wedges.

Grilled Vegetable Kebabs with Grilled Lemon Dressing

Serves 4

Why This Recipe Works Typical kebabs are made with meat, but we also love them with delicious vegetables with a crisp, charred exterior and a juicy, tender interior. To start our vegetables with great flavor, we tossed them with half of our dressing base before skewering and grilling them. We also grilled lemon quarters to tone down their acidity and give the juice a deeper, more complex flavor when added to the dressing. Bell peppers and zucchini are classic grilling vegetables for good reason: Bell peppers sweeten over the flame, while zucchini hold their shape and meaty texture. Portobello mushroom caps were the perfect addition to the kebabs. You will need eight 12-inch metal skewers for this recipe.

¼ cup extra-virgin olive oil
1 teaspoon Dijon mustard
1 teaspoon minced fresh rosemary
1 garlic clove, minced
½ teaspoon table salt
¼ teaspoon pepper
6 portobello mushroom caps (5 inches in diameter), quartered
2 zucchini, halved lengthwise and sliced ¾ inch thick
2 red bell peppers, stemmed, seeded, and cut into 1½-inch pieces
2 lemons, quartered

1. Whisk oil, mustard, rosemary, garlic, salt, and pepper together in large bowl. Measure half of mixture into separate bowl and set aside for serving. Toss mushrooms, zucchini, and bell peppers with remaining oil mixture, then thread in alternating order onto eight 12-inch metal skewers.

2A. For a charcoal grill Open bottom vent completely. Light large chimney starter half filled with charcoal briquettes (3 quarts). When top coals are partially covered with ash, pour evenly over grill. Set cooking grate in place, cover, and open lid vent completely. Heat grill until hot, about 5 minutes.

2B. For a gas grill Turn all burners to high, cover, and heat grill until hot, about 15 minutes. Turn all burners to medium.

3. Clean and oil cooking grate. Place kebabs and lemons on grill. Cook (covered if using gas), turning as needed, until vegetables are tender and well browned and lemons are juicy and slightly charred, 16 to 18 minutes. Transfer kebabs and 6 lemon quarters to platter, removing skewers.

4. Juice remaining 2 lemon quarters and whisk into reserved oil mixture. Drizzle vegetables with dressing and serve.

Grilled Vegetable and Halloumi Salad

Serves 4 to 6

Why This Recipe Works This warm, hearty salad is the ultimate combination of perfectly charred vegetables and chunks of briny halloumi cheese. Halloumi has a solid consistency and high melting point, making it perfect for grilling. After just 10 minutes on the grill, the radicchio, eggplant, zucchini, and cheese were perfectly browned, tender, and redolent with smoky flavor. We chopped all the vegetables before tossing everything with a honey and thyme vinaigrette.

- 3 tablespoons honey
- 1 tablespoon minced fresh thyme
- ½ teaspoon grated lemon zest plus 3 tablespoons juice
- 1 garlic clove, minced
- ¾ teaspoon table salt, divided
- ⅛ teaspoon plus ½ teaspoon pepper, divided
- 1 pound eggplant, sliced into ½-inch-thick rounds
- 1 head radicchio (10 ounces), quartered
- 1 zucchini, halved lengthwise
- 1 (8-ounce) block halloumi cheese, sliced into ½-inch-thick slabs
- ¼ cup extra-virgin olive oil, divided

1. Whisk honey, thyme, lemon zest and juice, garlic, ¼ teaspoon salt, and ⅛ teaspoon pepper together in large bowl; set aside. Brush eggplant, radicchio, zucchini, and halloumi with 2 tablespoons oil and season with remaining ½ teaspoon salt and remaining ½ teaspoon pepper.

2A. For a charcoal grill Open bottom vent completely. Light large chimney starter half filled with charcoal briquettes (3 quarts). When top coals are partially covered with ash, pour evenly over grill. Set cooking grate in place, cover, and open lid vent completely. Heat grill until hot, about 5 minutes.

2B. For a gas grill Turn all burners to high, cover, and heat grill until hot, about 15 minutes. Turn all burners to medium.

3. Clean and oil cooking grate. Place vegetables and cheese on grill. Cook (covered if using gas), flipping as needed, until radicchio is softened and lightly charred, 3 to 5 minutes, and remaining vegetables and cheese are softened and lightly charred, about 10 minutes. Transfer vegetables and cheese to cutting board as they finish cooking, let cool slightly, then cut into 1-inch pieces.

4. Whisking constantly, slowly drizzle remaining 2 tablespoons oil into honey mixture. Add vegetables and cheese and gently toss to coat. Season with salt and pepper to taste. Serve.

Grilled Vegetable Kebabs with Grilled Lemon Dressing

Grilled Vegetable and Halloumi Salad

Grilled Artichokes with Lemon Butter

Grilled Artichokes with Lemon Butter

Serves 4

Why This Recipe Works Artichokes are often steamed, but grilling them is a nice alternative preparation that brings a bit of smoky char and enhances their nutty flavor. We parboiled artichokes in a broth with lemon juice, red pepper flakes, and salt to ensure that they were completely tender and thoroughly seasoned. Tossing in extra-virgin olive oil before grilling helped develop flavorful char marks on the grill. A simple blend of lemon zest and juice, garlic, and butter came together easily in the microwave and was perfect for dipping or drizzling. If your artichokes are larger than 8 to 10 ounces, strip away another layer or two of the toughest outer leaves.

½ teaspoon table salt, plus salt for cooking artichokes
½ teaspoon red pepper flakes
2 lemons, divided
4 artichokes (8 to 10 ounces each)
6 tablespoons unsalted butter
1 garlic clove, minced to paste
¼ teaspoon pepper
2 tablespoons extra-virgin olive oil

1. Combine 3 quarts water, 3 tablespoons salt, and pepper flakes in Dutch oven. Cut 1 lemon in half; squeeze juice into pot, then add spent halves. Bring to boil over high heat.

2. Meanwhile, working with 1 artichoke at a time, trim end of stem and cut off top quarter of artichoke. Break off bottom 3 or 4 rows of tough outer leaves by pulling them downward. Using kitchen shears, trim off top portion of outer leaves. Using paring knife, trim stem and base, removing any dark green parts.

3. Add artichokes to pot with boiling water mixture, cover, and reduce heat to medium-low. Simmer until tip of paring knife inserted into base of artichoke meets no resistance, 25 to 28 minutes, stirring occasionally.

4. Meanwhile, grate 2 teaspoons zest from remaining lemon; combine with butter, garlic, pepper, and ½ teaspoon salt in bowl. Microwave at 50 percent power until butter is melted and bubbling and garlic is fragrant, about 2 minutes, stirring occasionally. Squeeze 1½ tablespoons juice from zested lemon and stir into butter. Season with salt and pepper to taste.

5. Set wire rack in rimmed baking sheet. Place artichokes stem side up on prepared rack and let drain for 10 minutes. Cut artichokes in half lengthwise. Remove fuzzy choke and any tiny inner purple-tinged leaves using small spoon, leaving small cavity in center of each half.

Farmers' Market Find   Artichokes

Artichokes are the immature flower buds of a perennial plant in the thistle family. They are commonly marketed in three sizes: small (2 to 4 ounces), medium (8 to 10 ounces), and large (12 ounces or more). We like medium artichokes best for braising, roasting, and grilling. They are easy to prepare, and one artichoke conveniently serves one person. Small artichokes are perfect for frying and marinating. Ninety percent of the work that goes into preparing most artichoke dishes is cleaning and trimming the artichokes, but it's well worth it to discover the delicious inner edible portions. When selecting artichokes, look for leaves that are tight, compact, and bright green. If you give an artichoke a squeeze, its leaves should squeak as they rub together (evidence that the artichoke still possesses much of its moisture). The leaves should snap off cleanly. Artichokes will keep in the refrigerator for up to five days if sprinkled lightly with water and stored in a zipper-lock bag.

6A. For a charcoal grill Open bottom vent completely. Light large chimney starter filled with charcoal briquettes (6 quarts). When top coals are partially covered with ash, pour evenly over grill. Set cooking grate in place, cover, and open lid vent completely. Heat grill until hot, about 5 minutes.

6B. For a gas grill Turn all burners to high, cover, and heat grill until hot, about 15 minutes. Leave all burners on high.

7. Clean and oil cooking grate. Brush artichokes with oil. Place artichokes on grill and cook (covered if using gas) until lightly charred, 2 to 4 minutes per side. Transfer artichokes to serving platter and tent with aluminum foil. Briefly rewarm lemon butter in microwave, if necessary, and serve with artichokes.

TRIMMING ARTICHOKES

1. Using sharp chef's knife, trim off end of stem and cut off top quarter of artichoke.

2. Break off bottom 3 or 4 rows of tough outer leaves by pulling them downward.

Grilled Asparagus

Serves 4 `FAST`

Why This Recipe Works The main challenge with grilling delicate asparagus is protecting it from overcooking while still developing a good char. For great grilled asparagus, we opted for thicker spears, which combined maximum browning potential with a meaty, crisp-tender texture. A medium-hot fire worked best—the spears were on and off the grill in less than 10 minutes. Brushing the spears with butter rather than oil before grilling gave us crispy, nutty asparagus. Look for asparagus spears between ½ and ¾ inch in diameter. You can use white or green asparagus in this recipe; if using white, peel just the outermost layer of the bottom halves of the spears.

1½ pounds thick asparagus
3 tablespoons unsalted butter, melted
½ teaspoon table salt
¼ teaspoon pepper

1. Trim bottom inch of asparagus spears and discard. Peel bottom halves of spears until white flesh is exposed. Brush asparagus with melted butter and sprinkle with salt and pepper.

2A. For a charcoal grill Open bottom vent completely. Light large chimney starter three-quarters filled with charcoal briquettes (4½ quarts). When top coals are partially covered with ash, pour evenly over grill. Set cooking grate in place, cover, and open lid vent completely. Heat grill until hot, about 5 minutes.

2B. For a gas grill Turn all burners to high, cover, and heat grill until hot, about 15 minutes. Turn all burners to medium-high.

3. Clean and oil cooking grate. Place asparagus in even layer on grill and cook until browned and tip of paring knife inserted at base of largest spear meets little resistance, 4 to 10 minutes, turning halfway through cooking. Transfer asparagus to serving platter and serve.

VARIATIONS
Grilled Asparagus with Cumin Butter
Add 2 minced small garlic cloves, 1 teaspoon grated lemon zest, ½ teaspoon ground cumin, and ½ teaspoon ground coriander to melted butter.

Grilled Asparagus with Garlic Butter
Add 3 minced small garlic cloves to melted butter.

Grilled Broccoli with Lemon and Parmesan

Serves 6 to 8

Why This Recipe Works For vivid green broccoli florets with flavorful char, there's no beating the grill. To avoid toughness, we peeled the stalks with a vegetable peeler and cut the head into spears small enough to cook quickly but large enough to grill easily. Since grilling alone would yield dry broccoli, we tossed the spears in olive oil and water and steamed them in sealed foil packets on the grill. As soon as the stalks and florets were evenly cooked, we placed them directly on the grill to give them perfect grill marks and plenty of flavor. A squeeze of grilled lemon and a sprinkling of Parmesan sealed the deal. To keep the packs from tearing, use heavy-duty aluminum foil. Use the large holes of a box grater to shred the Parmesan.

¼ cup extra-virgin olive oil, plus extra for drizzling
1 tablespoon water
¾ teaspoon table salt
½ teaspoon pepper
2 pounds broccoli
1 lemon, halved
¼ cup shredded Parmesan cheese

1. Cut two 26 by 12-inch sheets of heavy-duty aluminum foil. Whisk oil, water, salt, and pepper together in large bowl.

2. Trim stalks so each entire head of broccoli measures 6 to 7 inches long. Trim tough outer peel from stalks, then cut heads in half lengthwise into spears (stems should be ½ to ¾ inch thick and florets 3 to 4 inches wide). Add broccoli to oil mixture and toss well to coat.

3. Divide broccoli between sheets of foil, cut side down and alternating direction of florets and stalks. Bring short sides of foil together and crimp tightly. Crimp long ends to seal packs tightly.

4A. For a charcoal grill Open bottom vent completely. Light large chimney starter filled with charcoal briquettes (6 quarts). When top coals are partially covered with ash, pour evenly over half of grill. Set cooking grate in place, cover, and open lid vent completely. Heat grill until hot, about 5 minutes.

4B. For a gas grill Turn all burners to high, cover, and heat grill until hot, about 15 minutes. Turn all burners to medium-high. (Adjust burners as needed to maintain grill temperature around 400 degrees.)

5. Clean and oil cooking grate. Arrange packets evenly on grill (over coals if using charcoal), cover, and cook for 8 minutes, flipping packets halfway through cooking.

6. Transfer packets to rimmed baking sheet and, using scissors, carefully cut open, allowing steam to escape away from you. (Broccoli should be bright green and fork inserted into stalks should meet some resistance.)

7. Discard foil and place broccoli and lemon halves cut side down on grill (over coals if using charcoal). Grill (covered if using gas), turning broccoli about every 2 minutes, until stalks are fork-tender and well charred on all sides, 6 to 8 minutes. Transfer broccoli to now-empty sheet as it finishes cooking. Grill lemon halves until well charred on cut side, 6 to 8 minutes.

8. Transfer broccoli to cutting board and cut into 2-inch pieces. Transfer to serving platter and season with salt and pepper to taste. Squeeze lemon over broccoli to taste, sprinkle with Parmesan, and drizzle with extra oil. Serve.

Grilled Brined Carrots with Cilantro-Yogurt Sauce

Serves 4

Why This Recipe Works We love grilling whole carrots, but let's face it: They are tricky to season evenly. Dusting whole raw carrots with salt is like throwing a tennis ball at a wall—it just bounces right off. But 45 minutes in a salty bath changes the game, infusing the carrots evenly. Whereas we brine meat to increase tenderness and season, our goal here was primarily seasoning (though the carrots did soften slightly in the brine). We grilled them quickly over a hot fire to develop char and smoky flavor without sacrificing crunch. Drizzled with a piquant cilantro-yogurt sauce and sprinkled with peanuts and fresh herbs, these carrots might just become your new favorite side dish during grilling season. Look for carrots that are 3 to 5 inches long and ½ to 1 inch in diameter. Peeled carrots will absorb salt more rapidly, so we don't recommend peeling them for this recipe. If you can't find carrots with their tops attached or the greens aren't in good shape, use thin carrots and 2 cups cilantro.

1½ pounds young carrots with greens attached, carrots unpeeled, greens chopped (1¼ cups), divided
¼ cup table salt for brining
1¼ cups chopped fresh cilantro leaves and stems, divided
½ cup plain Greek yogurt
¼ cup dry-roasted peanuts, chopped, divided
1 jalapeño chile, stemmed, seeds reserved, and minced
1 ice cube
1 teaspoon grated fresh ginger
1 garlic clove, minced
¼ teaspoon ground coriander

1. Rinse and scrub carrots to remove any dirt. Dissolve salt in 1 quart water in large bowl. Submerge carrots in brine and let sit at room temperature for at least 45 minutes or up to 1 hour. (Carrots brined with this salt concentration will start to taste too salty if brined longer than 1 hour. Brined carrots can be removed from brine, patted dry, and refrigerated for up to 3 hours before cooking.) Transfer carrots to paper towel–lined plate and pat dry. Discard brine.

2. Meanwhile, process 1 cup cilantro, yogurt, 3 tablespoons peanuts, jalapeño, ice cube, ginger, garlic, coriander, and 1 cup carrot greens in blender on high speed until smooth and creamy, about 2 minutes, scraping down sides of blender jar halfway through processing. Taste for spiciness; if desired, add more spice by blending in reserved jalapeño seeds. Season with salt to taste. Transfer yogurt sauce to small bowl, cover, and refrigerate until ready to serve.

3A. For a charcoal grill Open bottom vent completely. Light large chimney starter filled with charcoal briquettes (6 quarts). When top coals are partially covered with ash, pour evenly over half of grill. Set cooking grate in place, cover, and open lid vent completely. Heat grill until hot, about 5 minutes.

3B. For a gas grill Turn all burners to high, cover, and heat grill until hot, about 15 minutes. Leave all burners on high.

4. Clean and oil cooking grate. Place carrots on grill (directly over coals if using charcoal) and cook, turning occasionally, until carrots are well charred on all sides and exteriors are just beginning to soften, 3 to 5 minutes for very small carrots or 5 to 7 minutes for larger ones. Transfer to serving platter.

5. Drizzle yogurt sauce over carrots, then sprinkle with remaining ¼ cup cilantro, remaining ¼ cup carrot greens, and remaining 1 tablespoon peanuts. Serve.

VARIATION

Grilled Brined Asparagus with Cilantro-Yogurt Sauce

Look for asparagus that is at least ½ inch thick at base.

Substitute 2 pounds thick asparagus, trimmed, for carrots and additional 1¼ cups chopped cilantro for carrot greens. Cook asparagus, turning occasionally, until spears are charred on all sides and just beginning to soften on exteriors, 2 to 4 minutes.

Husk-Grilled Corn
Serves 6

Why This Recipe Works Grilled corn on the cob is a classic. We started the corn with the husk on to prevent the kernels from drying out. But we found that if we left the husk on the whole time, the corn kernels didn't pick up the grill's signature smoky accent. By shucking the corn, rolling the ears in butter, and then returning the ears to the grill, we were able to perfectly cara-melize the kernels and maximize the grill flavor. One last roll in the butter and our corn was ready. Substitute a flavored butter for plain, if desired. Set up a cutting board and knife next to your grill to avoid traveling back and forth between kitchen and grill.

6 ears corn, husks and silk left intact
6 tablespoons unsalted butter, softened
½ teaspoon table salt
½ teaspoon pepper

1. Cut and remove silk protruding from top of each ear of corn. Combine butter, salt, and pepper in bowl. Fold one 14 by 12-inch piece heavy-duty aluminum foil in half to

Husk-Grilled Corn

create 7 by 12-inch rectangle; then crimp into boat shape long and wide enough to accommodate 1 ear of corn. Transfer butter mixture to prepared foil boat.

2A. For a charcoal grill Open bottom vent completely. Light large chimney starter mounded with charcoal briquettes (7 quarts). When top coals are partially covered with ash, pour evenly over half of grill. Set cooking grate in place, cover, and open lid vent completely. Heat grill until hot, about 5 minutes.

2B. For a gas grill Turn all burners to high, cover, and heat grill until hot, about 15 minutes. Leave all burners on high.

3. Clean and oil cooking grate. Place corn on grill (over coals, with stem ends facing cooler side of grill, for charcoal). Cover and cook, turning corn every 3 minutes, until husks have blackened all over, 12 to 15 minutes. (To check for doneness, carefully peel down small portion of husk. If corn is steaming and bright yellow, it is ready.) Transfer corn to cutting board. Using chef's knife, cut base from corn. Using dish towel to hold corn, peel away and discard husk and silk with tongs.

4. Roll each ear of corn in butter mixture to coat lightly and return to grill (over coals for charcoal). Cook, turning as needed to char corn lightly on each side, about 5 minutes total. Remove corn from grill and roll each ear again in butter mixture. Transfer corn to serving platter. Serve, passing any remaining butter mixture.

Mexican-Style Grilled Corn
Serves 6

Why This Recipe Works In Mexico, street vendors add kick to grilled corn by slathering it with a creamy, spicy, cheesy sauce. The corn takes on an irresistibly sweet, smoky, charred flavor, which is heightened by the lime juice and chili powder in the sauce. For our own rendition of this south-of-the border street fare, we ditched the husks, coated the ears with oil to prevent sticking, and grilled them directly on the grate over a hot fire so the corn could develop plenty of char. The traditional base for the sauce is crema, a thick, soured Mexican cream. But given its limited availability in supermarkets, we replaced the crema with a combination of mayonnaise (for richness) and sour cream (for tanginess). If you can't find *queso fresco*, you can use either cotija or Pecorino Romano.

- 1½ ounces queso fresco, crumbled (⅓ cup)
- ¼ cup mayonnaise
- 3 tablespoons sour cream
- 3 tablespoons minced fresh cilantro
- 4 teaspoons lime juice
- 1 garlic clove, minced
- ¾ teaspoon chili powder, divided
- ¼ teaspoon pepper
- ¼ teaspoon cayenne pepper
- 4 teaspoons vegetable oil
- ¼ teaspoon table salt
- 6 ears corn, husks and silk removed

1. Combine queso fresco, mayonnaise, sour cream, cilantro, lime juice, garlic, ¼ teaspoon chili powder, pepper, and cayenne in large bowl; set aside. In second large bowl, combine oil, salt, and remaining ½ teaspoon chili powder. Add corn to oil mixture and toss to coat.

2A. For a charcoal grill Open bottom vent completely. Light large chimney starter filled with charcoal briquettes (6 quarts). When top coals are partially covered with ash, pour evenly over half of grill. Set cooking grate in place, cover, and open lid vent completely. Heat grill until hot, about 5 minutes.

2B. For a gas grill Turn all burners to high, cover, and heat grill until hot, about 15 minutes. Leave all burners on high.

3. Clean and oil cooking grate. Place corn on grill (on hotter side if using charcoal) and cook (covered if using gas), turning as needed, until lightly charred on all sides, 7 to 12 minutes. Transfer corn to bowl with cheese mixture and toss to coat. Serve.

Grilled Eggplant with Chermoula

Grilled Eggplant with Chermoula
Serves 4 to 6

Why This Recipe Works On its own, grilled eggplant is great—it's meaty and deep in flavor. But it's even better when bathed in fragrant chermoula. The North African condiment's zestiness gives the rich vegetable welcome dimension. Unfortunately, grilled eggplant can easily turn out leathery or spongy. After a series of tests, we found that ¼-inch-thick rounds worked best; the interiors became tender by the time the exteriors were nicely grill-marked. Since it was necessary to brush the rounds with olive oil so they didn't stick to the grill, we infused that oil with minced garlic and red pepper flakes to add even more flavor. And we saved the browned and crisped minced garlic used to make the garlic oil to sprinkle on top with the chermoula. It is important to slice the eggplant thin so that the slices will cook through by the time the exterior is browned.

6 tablespoons extra-virgin olive oil
5 garlic cloves, minced
⅛ teaspoon red pepper flakes
2 pounds eggplant, sliced into ¼-inch-thick rounds
½ teaspoon table salt
¼ teaspoon pepper
1 cup Chermoula (page 294)

1. Combine oil, garlic, and pepper flakes in bowl. Microwave until garlic is golden brown and crisp, about 2 minutes. Strain garlic oil through fine-mesh strainer into small bowl. Reserve garlic oil and garlic separately.

2A. For a charcoal grill Open bottom vent completely. Light large chimney starter filled with charcoal briquettes (6 quarts). When top coals are partially covered with ash, pour evenly over grill. Set cooking grate in place, cover, and open lid vent completely. Heat grill until hot, about 5 minutes.

2B. For a gas grill Turn all burners to high, cover, and heat grill until hot, about 15 minutes. Turn all burners to medium-high.

3. Clean and oil cooking grate. Brush eggplant with garlic oil and sprinkle with salt and pepper. Place half of eggplant on grill and cook (covered if using gas) until browned and tender, about 4 minutes per side; transfer to serving platter. Repeat with remaining eggplant; transfer to serving platter. Drizzle chermoula over eggplant and sprinkle with garlic. Serve.

Grilled Caesar Salad
Serves 6

Why This Recipe Works The smoky char of the grill brings a whole new dimension to the crunchy, tangy, and savory flavors of Caesar salad. To develop good char and maintain crisp lettuce without ending up with scorched, wilted, even slimy leaves, we used sturdy, compact romaine hearts, which withstood the heat of the grill better than whole heads. Halving them lengthwise and grilling on just one side gave them plenty of surface area for charring without turning limp. A hot fire meant that the heat didn't have time to penetrate and wilt the crunchy inner leaves before the exterior developed grill marks. Our boldly seasoned Caesar dressing replaced the raw egg with mayonnaise, and brushing the dressing on the cut side of the uncooked lettuce allowed it to pick up a mildly smoky flavor on the grill along with the lettuce. For the croutons, we brushed baguette slices with olive oil, toasted them over the coals, and then rubbed them with a garlic clove. We combined the lettuce and croutons, drizzled on extra dressing, and dusted everything with Parmesan.

Dressing
- 1 tablespoon lemon juice
- 1 garlic clove, minced
- ½ cup mayonnaise
- ¼ cup grated Parmesan cheese
- 1 tablespoon white wine vinegar
- 1 tablespoon Worcestershire sauce
- 1 tablespoon Dijon mustard
- 2 anchovy fillets, rinsed
- ½ teaspoon table salt
- ½ teaspoon pepper
- ¼ cup extra-virgin olive oil

Salad
- 1 (12-inch) baguette, sliced ½ inch thick on bias
- 3 tablespoons extra-virgin olive oil
- 1 garlic clove, peeled
- 3 romaine lettuce hearts (18 ounces), halved lengthwise through cores
- ¼ cup grated Parmesan cheese

1. For the dressing Combine lemon juice and garlic in bowl and let sit for 10 minutes. Process lemon-garlic mixture, mayonnaise, Parmesan, vinegar, Worcestershire, mustard, anchovies, salt, and pepper in blender until smooth, about 30 seconds. With blender running, slowly add oil until incorporated. Measure out and reserve 6 tablespoons dressing for brushing romaine.

2A. For a charcoal grill Open bottom vent completely. Light large chimney starter filled with charcoal briquettes (6 quarts). When top coals are partially covered with ash, pour evenly over half of grill. Set cooking grate in place, cover, and open lid vent completely. Heat grill until hot, about 5 minutes.

2B. For a gas grill Turn all burners to high, cover, and heat grill until hot, about 15 minutes. Leave all burners on high.

3. For the salad Clean and oil cooking grate. Brush bread with oil and grill (over coals if using charcoal), uncovered, until browned, about 1 minute per side. Transfer to serving platter and rub with garlic clove. Brush cut sides of lettuce with half of reserved dressing. Place half of lettuce, cut side down, on grill (over coals if using charcoal). Grill, uncovered, until lightly charred, 1 to 2 minutes. Transfer to serving platter with bread. Repeat with remaining reserved dressing and lettuce. Drizzle lettuce with remaining dressing. Sprinkle with Parmesan. Serve.

Grill-Roasted Peppers

Grill-Roasted Peppers
Serves 4   MAKE AHEAD

Why This Recipe Works Roasting red peppers on the grill turns their flesh from juicy and crunchy to smoky and tender. We tossed stemmed and cored peppers in garlic-infused olive oil, allowing the oil to soak into the interiors' exposed flesh. To prevent flare-ups, we grilled the peppers in a foil-covered disposable pan, drained them, and placed them directly on the hot grate to char. After easily scraping the charred skins from the peppers, we tossed them in a vinaigrette made from the leftover oil and liquid released from the peppers. The finished peppers were tender, smoky, and infused with a heady garlic flavor that complemented the intensified sweetness that grilling had brought to the vegetables.

¼ cup extra-virgin olive oil
3 garlic cloves, peeled and smashed
½ teaspoon table salt
¼ teaspoon pepper
1 (13 by 9-inch) disposable aluminum roasting pan
6 red bell peppers
1 tablespoon sherry vinegar

1. Combine oil, garlic, salt, and pepper in disposable pan. Using paring knife, cut around stems of peppers and remove cores and seeds. Place peppers in pan and turn to coat with oil. Cover pan tightly with aluminum foil.

2A. For a charcoal grill Open bottom vent completely. Light large chimney starter filled with charcoal briquettes (6 quarts). When top coals are partially covered with ash, pour evenly over half of grill. Set cooking grate in place, cover, and open lid vent completely. Heat grill until hot, about 5 minutes.

2B. For a gas grill Turn all burners to high, cover, and heat grill until hot, about 15 minutes. Turn all burners to medium-high.

3. Clean and oil cooking grate. Place pan on grill (over hotter side for charcoal) and cook, covered, until peppers are just tender and skins begin to blister, 10 to 15 minutes, rotating and shaking pan halfway through cooking.

4. Remove pan from heat and carefully remove foil (reserve foil to use later). Using tongs, remove peppers from pan, allowing juices to drip back into pan, and place on grill (over hotter side if using charcoal). Grill peppers, covered, turning every few minutes until skins are blackened, 10 to 15 minutes.

5. Transfer juices and garlic in pan to medium bowl and whisk in vinegar. Remove peppers from grill, return to now-empty pan, and cover tightly with foil. Let peppers steam for 5 minutes. Using spoon, scrape blackened skin off each pepper. Quarter peppers lengthwise, add to vinaigrette in bowl, and toss to combine. Season with salt and pepper to taste, and serve. (Peppers can be refrigerated for up to 5 days.)

VARIATION
Grill-Roasted Peppers with Rosemary
Add 1 sprig rosemary to oil mixture in step 1 (discard after grilling). Substitute red wine vinegar for sherry vinegar.

Farmers' Market Find   Sweet Peppers

From sweet bell peppers to the hottest habanero, all peppers prefer a long, warm growing season. Most peppers are available year-round at the grocery store, though their traditional season is late summer into early fall. All sweet peppers start out green and eventually turn red, orange, yellow, purple, brown, or multicolored on the vine. Red peppers have been left on the plant the longest, and they are much sweeter than other peppers. Because they are the ripest, they also have the shortest shelf life. Select firm, crisp peppers that feel heavy for their size and are glossy-looking and vibrant in color; avoid any with shriveled, wrinkled, or soft spots. Store peppers in a perforated plastic bag in the crisper drawer. Green peppers will keep about a week, while yellow, orange, and red varieties should be eaten within four days.

Sweet peppers Bell peppers are the only pepper variety that do not produce capsaicin, the compound that gives chile peppers their heat. Hothouse bell peppers are the readily available supermarket standard. Bell peppers grown in a field instead of a hothouse are more elongated and irregularly shaped. Bell peppers get a lot of use in the test kitchen as we tend to gravitate toward their sweetness in our cooking.

Cubanelles Sweet, yet mildly pungent, Cubanelles are often called Italian frying peppers. They are long and skinny and thin-walled. They are usually sold when they are light yellowish-green but they will turn orange or bright red if allowed to ripen on the plant. You might see them mislabelled as banana peppers; the two look similar, though Cubanelles tend to be less tapered.

Pimentos The pimento is a sweet pepper, but it's not a bell pepper. Pimentos are a heart-shaped variety of red pepper that is slightly sweeter than a red bell pepper. They are occasionally available fresh but are usually bought jarred or canned in an acidic brine. We love them in the picnic classic Pimento Cheese Spread (page 238).

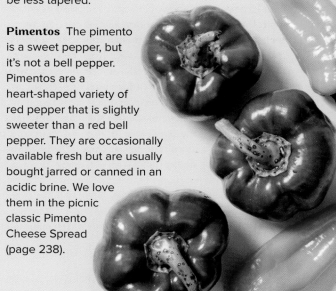

Grilled Potatoes with Garlic and Rosemary

Serves 4

Why This Recipe Works Grilled potatoes are a summertime classic. We wanted to put a new spin on this dish by adding earthy, aromatic rosemary and garlic. Unfortunately, we found it difficult to add sufficient flavor to plain grilled potatoes. Coating the potatoes with oil, garlic, and rosemary produced burnt, bitter garlic and charred rosemary. Could we find a better solution? It turned out that we needed to apply the garlic-oil mixture to the potatoes not just once but three times. Before cooking, we pierced the potatoes, skewered them, seasoned them with salt, brushed on the garlic-rosemary oil, and precooked them in the microwave. Then, before grilling, we brushed them again with the infused oil. After grilling, we tossed them with the oil yet again. Now we finally had it—tender potatoes infused with smoky grilled flavor and enlivened with the bold taste of garlic and rosemary. This recipe works best with small potatoes that are about 1½ inches in diameter. If using medium potatoes, 2 to 3 inches in diameter, quarter them. If the potatoes are larger than 3 inches in diameter, cut each potato into eighths. Because the skewers go into the microwave, use wooden, not metal, skewers.

- ¼ cup extra-virgin olive oil
- 9 garlic cloves, minced
- 1 teaspoon chopped fresh rosemary
- 1 teaspoon table salt, divided
- 2 pounds small red potatoes, unpeeled, halved
- 4 (12-inch) wooden skewers
- 2 tablespoons chopped fresh chives

1. Heat oil, garlic, rosemary, and ½ teaspoon salt in 8-inch skillet over medium heat until sizzling, about 3 minutes. Reduce heat to medium-low and continue to cook until garlic is light blond, about 3 minutes.

2. Strain mixture through fine-mesh strainer into small bowl; press on solids to extract as much liquid as possible. Measure 1 tablespoon solids and 1 tablespoon oil into large bowl and set aside. Discard remaining solids and reserve remaining oil.

3. Skewer potatoes and place in single layer on large plate. Poke each potato several times with skewer. Brush with 1 table-spoon strained oil and sprinkle with remaining ½ teaspoon salt. Microwave until potatoes offer slight resistance when pierced with paring knife, about 8 minutes, turning halfway through microwaving. Transfer potatoes to baking sheet coated with 1 tablespoon strained oil. Brush potatoes with remaining strained oil and season with salt and pepper.

4A. For a charcoal grill Open bottom vent completely. Light large chimney starter filled with charcoal briquettes (6 quarts). When top coals are partially covered with ash, pour two-thirds evenly over half of grill, then pour remaining coals over other half of grill. Set cooking grate in place, cover, and open lid vent completely. Heat grill until hot, about 5 minutes.

4B. For a gas grill Turn all burners to high, cover, and heat grill until hot, about 15 minutes. Turn all burners to medium-high.

5. Clean and oil cooking grate. Place potatoes on grill (on hotter side if using charcoal) and cook (covered if using gas) until grill marks appear, 3 to 5 minutes, flipping potatoes half-way through cooking. Move potatoes to cooler side of grill (if using charcoal) or turn all burners to medium-low (if using gas). Cover and continue to cook until paring knife slips in and out of potatoes easily, 5 to 8 minutes.

6. Remove potatoes from skewers and transfer to bowl with reserved garlic-oil mixture. Add chives, season with salt and pepper to taste, and toss until thoroughly coated. Serve.

Grilled Radicchio

Serves 4 to 6 `FAST`

Why This Recipe Works When grilled, the beautiful red-purple leaves of radicchio become lightly crisp and smoky-tasting. To keep the fragile radicchio from falling apart on the grill, we cut it through the core end into thick wedges. And for leaves that were smoky but not singed, we found it was necessary to coat the leaves liberally with olive oil; we infused that oil with extra flavor by microwaving it with garlic and rosemary before brushing it on the radicchio wedges. For optimal browning, we flipped each wedge of radicchio so that the two cut sides of the wedges could rest directly against the grill grate. This simple side is great with grilled steaks.

- 6 tablespoons extra-virgin olive oil
- 1 garlic clove, minced
- 1 teaspoon minced fresh rosemary or ¼ teaspoon dried
- 3 heads radicchio (10 ounces each), quartered
- 1 teaspoon table salt
- ½ teaspoon pepper

1. Microwave oil, garlic, and rosemary in bowl until bubbling, about 1 minute; let mixture steep for 1 minute. Brush radicchio with ¼ cup oil mixture and sprinkle with salt and pepper.

2A. For a charcoal grill Open bottom vent completely. Light large chimney starter half filled with charcoal briquettes (3 quarts). When top coals are partially covered with ash, pour evenly over grill. Set cooking grate in place, cover, and open lid vent completely. Heat grill until hot, about 5 minutes.

2B. For a gas grill Turn all burners to high, cover, and heat grill until hot, about 15 minutes. Turn all burners to medium.

3. Clean and oil cooking grate. Place radicchio on grill. Cook (covered if using gas), flipping as needed, until radicchio is softened and lightly charred, 3 to 5 minutes. Transfer to serving platter and drizzle with remaining oil mixture. Serve.

Brined Grilled Zucchini with Mint Salsa Verde

Serves 4

Why This Recipe Works Grilled zucchini often falls victim to both underseasoning and overcooking. Try to address the former by cutting the zucchini into thin planks that can be seasoned more thoroughly, and you end up exacerbating the latter, as thinner pieces overcook in a flash. To achieve well-seasoned, crisp-tender zucchini, we ditched the planks, halved the zucchini lengthwise, and mixed up a brine. Meat normally gets all the brining love, but a 45-minute soak in a saltwater solution produced incredibly well-seasoned zucchini. During brining, salt diffuses from an area of greater salt concentration (our 10-percent-salt brine) to an area of lesser concentration (our soon-to-be-delicious zucchini). We quickly grilled the brined zucchini to pick up great char and smoky flavor, without turning it to mush. We paired the zucchini with a punchy riff on salsa verde, packed with refreshing herbs, garlic and red pepper flakes for heat, and capers and vinegar for an acidic bite. Look for zucchini that are about 2 inches in diameter. Zucchini brined with this salt concentration will start to taste too salty if brined longer than 1 hour. Brined zucchini can be removed from brine, patted dry, and refrigerated for up to 3 hours before cooking. This is a perfect side dish for times when you're firing up the grill for other items on your dinner menu. Grilled zucchini are great when served warm or even at room temperature, so if you're going to be grilling other items as well, we recommend grilling the zucchini first.

Grilled Potatoes with Garlic and Rosemary

Brined Grilled Zucchini with Mint Salsa Verde

½ cup plus 2 tablespoons kosher salt, for brining
  2 pounds zucchini (3 large zucchini), halved lengthwise
  1 cup fresh mint, chopped fine
  1 cup fresh parsley, chopped fine
  ¼ cup extra-virgin olive oil
  3 tablespoons white wine vinegar
  2 tablespoons capers, rinsed and minced
  2 garlic cloves, minced
  1 teaspoon red pepper flakes

1. Dissolve salt in 1 quart water in large bowl. Add zucchini to brine and weigh down with plate to keep submerged. Let sit at room temperature for at least 45 minutes or up to 1 hour. Transfer zucchini to paper towel–lined plate and pat dry. Discard brine.

2A. For a charcoal grill Open bottom vent completely. Light large chimney starter filled with charcoal briquettes (6 quarts). When top coals are partially covered with ash, pour evenly over half of grill. Set cooking grate in place, cover, and open lid vent completely. Heat grill until hot, about 5 minutes.

2B. For a gas grill Turn all burners to high, cover, and heat grill until hot, about 15 minutes. Leave all burners on high.

3. Clean and oil cooking grate. Place zucchini, cut side down, on grill (directly over coals if using charcoal) and cook until zucchini are well charred on bottom and flesh just begins to soften, 3 to 4 minutes. Flip zucchini and continue to cook until skin side is charred, about 2 minutes longer. (Zucchini should be slightly soft at edges but still firm at centers.) Transfer to serving plate.

4. Stir together mint, parsley, oil, vinegar, capers, garlic, and pepper flakes in small bowl. Season with salt to taste. Spoon salsa verde over zucchini and serve.

Grilled Pizza
Serves 4 to 6   `MAKE AHEAD`

Why This Recipe Works The dough for our grilled pizza is easy to make in the food processor and proofs for at least 24 hours in the refrigerator, where it develops complex flavor. To ensure that it cooked up thin, we used a tiny amount of yeast to reduce air bubbles and a relatively high percentage of water, which made a relatively slack dough that stretched easily. Stretching the dough on a generously oiled baking sheet prevented it from sticking to our hands or the grill and also helped the exterior fry and crisp. To ensure that the toppings cooked quickly on the grill, we preheated the sauce and used

Grilled Pizza

a combination of fast-melting fresh mozzarella and finely grated Parmesan; we also sprinkled the Parmesan evenly over the dough to create a flavorful barrier against moisture before dolloping (rather than slathering) on the sauce and scattering chunks of cheese, all of which helped maintain the dough's crisp texture. To prevent a hot spot at the center that would burn the crust, we placed the coals only around the perimeter of the grill rather than spreading them in an even layer. The dough must sit for at least 24 hours before shaping. It's important to use ice water in the dough to prevent it from overheating in the food processor. We recommend pargrilling, topping, and grilling in quick succession and serving the pizzas one at a time, rather than all at once.

Dough
  3 cups (16½ ounces) King Arthur bread flour
  1 tablespoon sugar
  ¼ teaspoon instant or rapid-rise yeast
  1¼ cups plus 2 tablespoons ice water (11 ounces)
  1 tablespoon vegetable oil, plus extra for counter
  1½ teaspoons table salt

Sauce

- 1 (14-ounce) can whole peeled tomatoes, drained with juice reserved
- 2 tablespoons extra-virgin olive oil
- 2 teaspoons minced fresh oregano
- ½ teaspoon sugar, plus extra for seasoning
- ½ teaspoon table salt
- ¼ teaspoon red pepper flakes

Pizza

- ½ cup plus 1 tablespoon extra-virgin olive oil, divided, plus extra for drizzling
- 3 ounces Parmesan cheese, grated (1½ cups)
- 8 ounces fresh whole-milk mozzarella cheese, torn into bite-size pieces (2 cups)
- 3 tablespoons shredded fresh basil
  Coarse sea salt

1. For the dough Process flour, sugar, and yeast in food processor until combined, about 2 seconds. With processor running, slowly add ice water; process until dough is just combined and no dry flour remains, about 10 seconds. Let dough sit for 10 minutes.

2. Add oil and salt to dough and process until dough forms satiny, sticky ball that clears sides of bowl, 30 to 60 seconds. Transfer dough to lightly oiled counter and knead until smooth, about 1 minute. Divide dough into 3 equal pieces (about 9⅓ ounces each). Shape each piece into tight ball, transfer to well-oiled baking sheet (alternatively, place dough balls in individual well-oiled bowls), and coat top of each ball lightly with oil. Cover tightly with plastic wrap (taking care not to compress dough) and refrigerate for at least 24 hours or up to 3 days.

3. For the sauce Pulse tomatoes in food processor until finely chopped, 12 to 15 pulses. Transfer to medium bowl and stir in reserved juice, oil, oregano, sugar, salt, and pepper flakes. Season with extra sugar and salt to taste, cover, and refrigerate until ready to use.

4. One hour before cooking pizza, remove dough from refrigerator and let sit at room temperature.

5A. For a charcoal grill Open bottom vent halfway. Light large chimney starter three-quarters filled with charcoal briquettes (4½ quarts). When top coals are partially covered with ash, pour into ring around grill perimeter, leaving 8-inch clearing in center. Set cooking grate in place, cover, and open lid vent halfway. Heat grill until hot, about 5 minutes.

5B. For a gas grill Turn all burners to high, cover, and heat grill until hot, about 15 minutes. Leave all burners on high.

6. While grill is heating, transfer sauce to small saucepan and bring to simmer over medium heat. Cover and keep warm.

7. For the pizza Clean and oil cooking grate. Pour ¼ cup oil onto center of rimmed baking sheet. Transfer 1 dough round to sheet and coat both sides of dough with oil. Using your fingertips and palms, gently press and stretch dough toward edges of sheet to form rough 16 by 12-inch oval of even thickness. Using both your hands, lift dough and carefully transfer to grill. (When transferring dough from sheet to grill, it will droop slightly to form half-moon or snowshoe shape.) Cook (over clearing if using charcoal; covered if using gas) until grill marks form, 2 to 3 minutes. Using tongs and spatula, carefully peel dough from grate, then rotate dough 90 degrees and continue to cook (covered if using gas) until second set of grill marks appears, 2 to 3 minutes. Flip dough and cook (covered if using gas) until second side of dough is lightly charred in spots, 2 to 3 minutes. Using tongs or pizza peel, transfer crust to cutting board, inverting so side that was grilled first is facing down. Repeat with remaining 2 dough rounds, adding 1 tablespoon oil to sheet for each round and keeping grill cover closed when not in use to retain heat.

8. Drizzle top of 1 crust with 1 tablespoon oil. Sprinkle one-third of Parmesan evenly over surface. Arrange one-third of mozzarella pieces, evenly spaced, on surface of pizza. Dollop one-third of sauce in evenly spaced 1-tablespoon mounds over surface of pizza.

9. Using pizza peel or overturned rimmed baking sheet, transfer pizza to grill; cover and cook until bottom is well browned and mozzarella is melted, 3 to 5 minutes, checking bottom and turning pizza frequently to prevent burning. Transfer pizza to cutting board, sprinkle with 1 tablespoon basil, drizzle lightly with extra oil, and season with salt to taste. Cut into wedges and serve. Repeat with remaining 2 crusts.

INGREDIENT SPOTLIGHT

FRESH MOZZARELLA

Our winning cheese is **BelGioioso Fresh Mozzarella**. It has all the qualities we want in fresh mozzarella: balanced tang, moderate sodium, and high moisture. These attributes work together to create a cheese with a savory richness; a buttery, tender curd; and a clean, milky flavor. One note: Our winning cheese comes packaged in a vacuum-sealed ball. The company also produces a brine-packed fresh mozzarella and confirmed that this is made using a slightly different process. We sampled it before settling on our lineup, but tasters preferred the vacuum-packed version.

Picnic-Table Favorites

■ FAST (30 minutes or less total time)   ■ NO COOK   ■ MAKE AHEAD
Photos (clockwise from top right): Watermelon Salad with Basil and Feta; Pimento Cheese Spread; Classic Potato Salad; Spice-Rubbed Picnic Chicken; Capicola Picnic Sandwich with Artichoke Spread

Fresh Tomato Salsa

Serves 12 (Makes about 3 cups) `NO COOK`

Why This Recipe Works When you're assembling a casual summer meal to eat outdoors, mixing up a fresh tomato salsa is often a good idea. Beyond making an easy accompaniment for chips, the quintessential summer condiment adds a burst of bold summer flavor when dolloped on chicken, fish, steak, tacos, sandwiches, bruschetta, or even salad. Fresh salsa should be chunky and brightly flavored, but even at peak tomato season many versions are soggy and bland. We solved the problem of watery salsa by draining diced tomatoes (skin, seeds, and all) in a colander. For authentic flavors that would support but not overpower the tomatoes, we added red onions (preferred over other varieties), moderately spicy jalapeño chiles, and lime juice, seasoning to taste with both salt and sugar plus more lime juice to achieve balanced flavor.

Fresh Tomato Salsa

- 1½ pounds tomatoes, cored and cut into ½-inch pieces
- ½ cup finely chopped red onion
- ¼ cup chopped fresh cilantro
- 1 large jalapeño chile, stemmed, seeds reserved, and minced
- 1 small garlic clove, minced
- 2 teaspoons lime juice, plus extra for seasoning
  Sugar

Place tomatoes in colander and let drain for 30 minutes. As tomatoes drain, layer onion, cilantro, jalapeño, and garlic on top. Shake colander to drain excess juice, then transfer vegetables to serving bowl. Stir in lime juice. Add reserved jalapeño seeds to increase heat as desired. Season with salt, pepper, sugar, and extra lime juice to taste before serving.

One-Minute Tomato and Black Bean Salsa

Serves 12 (Makes about 3 cups)
`FAST` `NO COOK` `MAKE AHEAD`

Why This Recipe Works A simple salsa is the perfect quick snack for a summer day, and the variety of store-bought salsas seems endless. But many fail to deliver on flavor, so we set out to create a superior salsa that required little more time and effort than opening a jar. For the fastest route to bright flavor, we eschewed fresh tomatoes in favor of canned diced tomatoes. Jarred jalapeños were a tangy, piquant, and convenient flavor booster. With a few pantry-friendly ingredients—red onion, cilantro, lime juice, garlic, chili powder, and salt—we rounded out and enhanced the flavor of the tomatoes. For a thick, chunky consistency, we pulsed the ingredients in the food processor, and we strained the mixture to avoid a soupy salsa. Black beans, another convenient canned item, beefed up the flavor and texture of this hearty dip.

- ½ small red onion, cut into 1-inch pieces
- ½ cup fresh cilantro leaves
- ¼ cup jarred sliced jalapeños
- 2 tablespoons lime juice
- 2 garlic cloves, peeled and chopped
- ½ teaspoon chili powder
- ½ teaspoon table salt
- 1 (28-ounce) can diced tomatoes, drained
- 1 cup canned black beans, drained

Pulse onion, cilantro, jalapeños, lime juice, garlic, chili powder, and salt in food processor until coarsely chopped, about 5 pulses, scraping down sides of bowl as needed. Add tomatoes and pulse until combined, about 3 pulses. Drain salsa briefly in fine-mesh strainer, then transfer to bowl. Stir in black beans and season with salt and pepper to taste. (Salsa can be refrigerated for up to 2 days.)

Guacamole

Serves 8 (Makes about 2 cups)

`FAST` `NO COOK` `MAKE AHEAD`

Why This Recipe Works For a fast and easy dip that's perfect for a patio party or park picnic, you can't beat a bowl (or two) of guacamole. Store-bought containers of guacamole often lack any real flavor and are disconcertingly smooth, but our simple, sophisticated guac is all about bold flavor and great texture. First, we chopped the avocados into small pieces. Next, we minced onion, chile, and lime zest together to ensure that these strong flavors would be evenly distributed. We liked the textural contrast and fresh flavor that onion and tomato brought to our guacamole. Mashing everything together with a whisk and then gently folding in the tomato and cilantro made the guac cohesive but still chunky. Serve with tortilla chips.

- 2 tablespoons finely chopped onion
- 1 serrano chile, stemmed, seeded, and chopped fine
- ¼ teaspoon grated lime zest plus 1½ tablespoons juice
- 1 teaspoon kosher salt
- 3 ripe avocados, halved, pitted, and cut into ½-inch pieces
- 1 plum tomato, cored, seeded, and minced
- 2 tablespoons chopped fresh cilantro

Chop and mash onion, chile, and lime zest with salt until very finely minced and homogeneous. Transfer to medium serving bowl and stir in lime juice. Add avocados and, using sturdy whisk, mash and stir mixture until well combined with some ¼- to ½-inch pieces remaining. Fold in tomato and cilantro and season with salt to taste. Serve. (Guacamole can be refrigerated for up to 24 hours with plastic wrap pressed directly against its surface. To serve, bring to room temperature and season with lime juice and salt to taste.)

VARIATIONS

Habanero and Mango Guacamole
Substitute 1 stemmed, seeded, and minced habanero chile for serrano and ½ mango, peeled and cut into ¼-inch pieces, for tomato.

Feta and Arugula Guacamole
Substitute ½ cup chopped baby arugula for tomato. Add 1 cup crumbled feta cheese with cilantro.

Farmers' Market Find   Tomatoes

A ripe tomato is synonymous with summer, but beyond buying in season (or growing your own), what's the best way to ensure you get the juiciest, most flavorful fruit? Buy a locally grown one from a small farmer. The shorter the distance the tomato has to travel, the riper it can be when picked. Small-farm tomatoes are less likely to have been bred for sturdiness rather than flavor, or put under strain to produce high yields that can result in fruit lacking in sugars and flavor compounds. At farmers' markets, you will see plenty of oddly shaped tomatoes, which are completely fine. Even cracked skin, which you see often on heirloom varieties, is OK. Avoid tomatoes that are bruised, overly soft, or leaking juice. Choose tomatoes that smell fruity and feel heavy for their size. Store ripe tomatoes in the fridge.

Tomatoes are most abundant at the peak of summer, but depending on the variety, they may be at the market earlier or later in the season. How the tomato is grown can also impact the seasonality: field-ripened tomatoes are often only available in the height of summer, but hothouse tomatoes (grown in greenhouses) will sometimes appear before other varieties or stay available for longer.

HEIRLOOM VERSUS HYBRID

Heirloom This term gets bandied about, but any variety not associated with large-scale commercial production may be labeled as heirloom. Most have been grown for decades from naturally pollinated plants and seeds that haven't been hybridized for productivity. There are hundreds of varieties of heirloom tomatoes in every shade from deep purple to pale yellow or green, and their names are as unique as they are. Some you might see at the market include Brandywine, Cherokee Purple, Marvel Striped, Ivory Pear, and San Marzano (an heirloom variety of plum tomato).

Hybrid A hybrid tomato is a cross between different varieties, carefully bred for beneficial qualities such as disease resistance, even shape, and uniform size. When properly grown, hybrids can be just as sweet and juicy as heirlooms at half the price. Some kinds available at farmers' markets are Early Girl, Sun Gold, Roma, and Juliet.

Fresh Corn Salsa with Tomato

Creamy Herbed Spinach Dip

Roasted Tomatillo Salsa
Serves 8 (Makes about 2 cups) `MAKE AHEAD`

Why This Recipe Works A counterpart to bold tomato salsa, tangy *salsa verde* (green salsa) highlights the bright, citrusy notes of tomatillos, which are also abundant in the summer months. While some green salsas use raw tomatillos, most call for cooking them by either boiling or roasting. Cooking softens the fruit, which can be quite firm, and mellows its bracing acidity. We found that charring half of the tomatillos under the broiler and leaving the other half raw produced a salsa with clean, fresh flavor and subtle smoky nuances. We combined the tomatillos with traditional salsa seasonings (jalapeño, onion, garlic, cilantro, lime juice, and salt) in a food processor and pulsed them to a chunky consistency. Serve with tortilla chips or dollop on steaks, chicken, or fish.

- 1 pound tomatillos, husks and stems removed, rinsed well and dried, divided
- 1 teaspoon vegetable oil
- 1 small white onion, chopped
- 1 jalapeño chile, stemmed, halved, and seeded
- ½ cup fresh cilantro leaves
- 2 tablespoons lime juice
- 1 garlic clove, minced
- ¼ teaspoon table salt
- 2 teaspoons extra-virgin olive oil
  Sugar

1. Adjust oven rack 6 inches from broiler element and heat broiler. Line rimmed baking sheet with aluminum foil. Toss half of tomatillos with vegetable oil and transfer to prepared sheet. Broil until tomatillos are spotty brown and skins begin to burst, 7 to 10 minutes. Transfer tomatillos to food processor and let cool completely.

2. Halve remaining tomatillos and add to food processor with broiled tomatillos. Add onion, jalapeño, cilantro, lime juice, garlic, and salt. Pulse until slightly chunky, 16 to 18 pulses. Transfer salsa to serving bowl, cover, and let sit at room temperature for at least 30 minutes. Stir in olive oil and season with salt and sugar to taste before serving. (Salsa can be refrigerated for up to 2 days.)

Fresh Corn Salsa with Tomato
Serves 12 (Makes 3 cups)

Why This Recipe Works Corn's natural sweetness makes it an exemplary foil for salsa's signature spicy chiles and tart citrus juice. The key was how to handle the corn. Grilled corn was impractical and raw corn was too chewy. We found that if we added the kernels to boiling water and then let them sit off the heat for 10 minutes they acquired just the right texture, becoming juicy and crisp. A little baking soda added to the water softened their hulls so that the kernels burst with sweetness. For the other ingredients, fruits that were sweet but with a hint of acidity (like tomato, pineapple, and peach) worked well. An avocado variation made a nice change of pace. Herbs and chiles were essential additions, as was finely minced shallot. We whisked a tablespoon of vegetable oil and a tiny bit of honey into lime juice for a tangy dressing with enough body to cling to the vegetables. Do not substitute frozen corn for fresh. Serve with tortillas or dollop on steaks, chicken, or fish.

- 2 ears corn, kernels cut from cobs (about 2 cups)
- ¼ teaspoon baking soda
- ¼ teaspoon plus ⅛ teaspoon table salt, divided
- 2 tablespoons lime juice
- 1 tablespoon vegetable oil
- ½ teaspoon honey
- 1 tomato, cored, seeded, and cut into ¼-inch pieces
- 1 shallot, minced
- 1 jalapeño chile, stemmed, seeded, and minced
- ¼ cup chopped fresh cilantro

1. Bring 2 cups water to boil in small saucepan over high heat. Stir in corn, baking soda, and ¼ teaspoon salt, then let sit off heat for 10 minutes. Drain corn and let cool slightly, about 10 minutes.

2. Whisk lime juice, oil, honey, and remaining ⅛ teaspoon salt together in bowl. Add drained corn, tomato, shallot, jalapeño, and cilantro and toss to combine. Let sit for 10 minutes. Season with salt and pepper to taste. Serve.

VARIATIONS
Fresh Corn Salsa with Avocado and Toasted Cumin
Add ½ teaspoon toasted cumin seeds and ⅛ teaspoon cayenne pepper to lime juice mixture in step 2. Substitute 1 avocado, cut into ¼-inch pieces, and 3 thinly sliced scallions for tomato.

Fresh Corn Salsa with Jícama and Pineapple
Substitute ¾ cup ¼-inch pieces pineapple and ½ cup ¼-inch pieces jícama for tomato. Substitute 1 minced serrano chile for jalapeño.

Fresh Corn Salsa with Peaches and Radishes
Substitute 1 peeled and pitted peach, cut into ¼-inch pieces, and 4 thinly sliced radishes for tomato. Substitute 1 minced habanero chile for jalapeño, and basil for cilantro.

Creamy Herbed Spinach Dip
Serves 8 (Makes about 1½ cups)

`FAST` `NO COOK` `MAKE AHEAD`

Why This Recipe Works A quick, simple spinach dip works equally as well with chips for a casual snack as it does with crudité for an upscale picnic appetizer. But spinach dips made with sour cream and soup mixes are flat, overly salty, and stale-tasting, so we decided to ditch the mix and create a rich, thick, and creamy spinach dip brimming with big, bold flavors. We were surprised to discover that frozen spinach actually made a better-tasting dip with a vibrant, more intense flavor than one made with fresh spinach. Instead of thawing the spinach completely, we only partially thawed it, allowing the chunks of icy spinach to thoroughly cool the dip. We used a food processor to chop the spinach and then enriched it with sour cream, mayonnaise, and a mixture of fresh herbs and seasonings. The garlic must be minced before going into the food processor; otherwise, the dip will contain large chunks of garlic.

- 10 ounces frozen chopped spinach, thawed and squeezed dry
- ½ cup sour cream
- ½ cup mayonnaise
- 3 scallions, white parts only, sliced thin
- ½ cup fresh parsley leaves
- 1 tablespoon minced fresh dill
- 1 small garlic clove, minced
- ½ teaspoon table salt
- ¼ teaspoon pepper
- ¼ teaspoon hot sauce
- ½ red bell pepper, chopped fine

Process spinach, sour cream, mayonnaise, scallions, parsley, dill, garlic, salt, pepper, and hot sauce in food processor until smooth and creamy, about 30 seconds. Transfer mixture to serving bowl and stir in bell pepper; serve. (Dip can be refrigerated for up to 2 days.)

Seven-Layer Dip

Serves 8 to 10 `NO COOK` `MAKE AHEAD`

Why This Recipe Works The ubiquitous backyard barbecue and block party favorite packs a punch (both visual and flavorful) with its distinctive layers of Southwestern-inspired ingredients. But too often, the dip relies heavily on canned and processed ingredients and inevitably turns out messy and bland. We wanted to up the ante on this party classic. Rather than canned refried beans, we opted for a fresher layer made with canned black beans mashed with garlic, chili powder, and lime juice. To prevent the sour cream layer from becoming runny, we combined it with a generous amount of pepper Jack cheese. Homemade guacamole far surpassed store-bought. Tasters rejected store-bought salsa as well, so we made a quick, fresh pico de gallo with chopped tomatoes, jalapeños, cilantro, scallions, and lime juice. A layer of sliced scallions added bite and color. Our six layers were so packed with flavor, we decided to eliminate the usual canned black olives, finding their metallic flavor distracting. This recipe is usually served in a clear dish so you can see the layers. For a crowd, double the recipe and serve in a 13 by 9-inch glass baking dish. If you don't have time to make fresh guacamole as called for, simply mash three avocados with 3 tablespoons lime juice and ½ teaspoon table salt. Serve with tortilla chips.

- 4 large tomatoes, cored, seeded, and chopped fine
- 6 scallions (2 minced; 4, green parts only, sliced thin), divided
- 2 jalapeño chiles, stemmed, seeded, and minced
- 3 tablespoons minced fresh cilantro
- 2 tablespoons plus 2 teaspoons lime juice (2 limes), divided
- ¼ teaspoon table salt, divided
- 1 (15-ounce) can black beans, drained but not rinsed
- 2 garlic cloves, minced
- ¾ teaspoon chili powder
- 1 pound pepper Jack cheese, shredded (4 cups), divided
- 1½ cups sour cream
- 1 recipe Guacamole (page 235)

1. Combine tomatoes, minced scallions, jalapeños, cilantro, 2 tablespoons lime juice, and ⅛ teaspoon salt in bowl. Let sit until tomatoes begin to soften, about 30 minutes. Drain mixture, discard liquid, and return to bowl.

2. Meanwhile, pulse beans, garlic, chili powder, remaining 2 teaspoons lime juice, and remaining ⅛ teaspoon salt in food processor to coarse paste, about 15 pulses. Spread bean mixture evenly into 8-inch square baking dish or 1-quart glass bowl.

3. Pulse 2½ cups pepper Jack and sour cream in food processor until smooth, about 15 pulses. Spread sour cream mixture evenly over bean layer. Top evenly with remaining 1½ cups pepper Jack, followed by guacamole and, finally, drained tomato mixture. (Dip can be refrigerated for up to 24 hours; bring to room temperature before serving.) Sprinkle with sliced scallion greens before serving.

Pimento Cheese Spread

Serves 8 (Makes about 2½ cups)
`FAST` `NO COOK` `MAKE AHEAD`

Why This Recipe Works A popular Southern spread, this deconstructed cheese ball would be right at home served at a barbecue or picnic to slather on crackers, raw vegetables, sandwiches, or even burgers. Drained jarred pimentos give the cheesy spread its name and trademark color. You can buy it premade, but homemade spreads are infinitely better and take just about 10 minutes. Most recipes use a combination of extra-sharp cheddar cheese and a milder cheddar or Monterey Jack, but we found that batches made with all extra-sharp cheese tasted more complex and satisfying. To give our spread a well-rounded flavor and a little kick, we also added some Worcestershire sauce, minced garlic, and a dash or two of hot sauce. Finally, we mixed in just enough mayonnaise to bind everything together. Both white and orange extra-sharp cheddar work well here. Don't substitute store-bought preshredded cheese; it doesn't blend well and produces a dry spread. If you can't find jarred pimentos, an equal amount of roasted red peppers may be substituted. In order for this spread to be gluten-free, you must use gluten-free Worcestershire sauce.

- ½ cup jarred pimentos, drained and patted dry
- 6 tablespoons mayonnaise
- 2 garlic cloves, minced
- 1½ teaspoons Worcestershire sauce
- 1 teaspoon hot sauce, plus extra to taste
- 1 pound extra-sharp cheddar cheese, shredded (4 cups)

Process pimentos, mayonnaise, garlic, Worcestershire, and hot sauce in food processor until smooth, about 20 seconds. Add cheddar and pulse until uniformly blended, with fine bits of cheese throughout, about 20 pulses. Season with salt, pepper, and extra hot sauce to taste, and serve. (Spread can be refrigerated for up to 2 weeks; bring to room temperature before serving.)

Turkey Picnic Sandwich with Sun-Dried Tomato Spread

Serves 4 `MAKE AHEAD`

Why This Recipe Works Here's the perfect sandwich for a picnic in the park, a hike in the hills, or a day at the beach. Featuring layers of meat, cheese, and veggies pressed within a rectangular loaf of bread, it can be made a day in advance and survives jostling without falling apart. To design it, we needed the right bread and found that using a whole loaf produced a sturdier sandwich than slices of bread did (plus, a huge sandwich is fun!). But store-bought loaves proved either too soft, too tough, or simply too stale, so we opted for a (semi) homemade loaf using store-bought pizza dough, which baked up soft, pleasantly chewy, and fresh. To get some mileage out of our bread, we came up with three meat-cheese-vegetable combos, each paired with a supersavory spread that we whizzed in the food processor and that glued the sandwich together without turning it soggy. Pressing the sandwich fused the layers, making it sturdy enough for travel and easier to bite through. Letting the pizza dough sit at room temperature for 1 hour makes it easier to shape. If you don't have a Dutch oven, you can use a baking sheet or skillet loaded with hefty canned goods to press the sandwich.

Sandwich
- 1 pound store-bought pizza dough
- 1 teaspoon extra-virgin olive oil
- 4 ounces sliced Muenster cheese
- 8 ounces thinly sliced deli turkey
- ½ cup fresh parsley leaves
- 1¼ cups jarred roasted red peppers, drained and patted dry

Spread
- ¾ cup oil-packed sun-dried tomatoes, drained and patted dry
- ¼ cup sliced almonds, toasted
- ¼ cup capers, rinsed
- 1 teaspoon lemon juice
- 1 small garlic clove, minced
- ¼ teaspoon table salt
- ¼ teaspoon red pepper flakes
- 6 tablespoons extra-virgin olive oil

1. For the sandwich Line rimmed baking sheet with parchment paper and grease parchment. Place dough on prepared sheet. Cover loosely with greased plastic wrap and let sit at room temperature for 1 hour.

Seven-Layer Dip

Turkey Picnic Sandwich with Sun-Dried Tomato Spread

2. Adjust oven rack to upper-middle position and heat oven to 425 degrees. Keeping dough on sheet, use your hands to shape dough into rough 7-inch square (edges may be rounded; this is OK). Brush top of dough with oil. Bake until light golden brown, 13 to 15 minutes. Let cool completely on sheet, about 1 hour.

3. For the spread Meanwhile, process tomatoes, almonds, capers, lemon juice, garlic, salt, and pepper flakes in food processor until finely chopped, about 20 seconds, scraping down sides of bowl as needed. Transfer to bowl and stir in oil.

4. Slice bread in half horizontally. Spread tomato mixture on cut sides of bread, about ½ cup per piece (use all of it). Layer Muenster, turkey, parsley, and red peppers on bread bottom. Cap with bread top and wrap sandwich tightly in double layer of plastic.

5. Place Dutch oven on top of sandwich and let sit at room temperature for 1 hour. (Pressed sandwich can be refrigerated for up to 24 hours. Let come to room temperature before serving.) Unwrap sandwich, cut into quarters, and serve. (Sandwich can be kept unrefrigerated for up to 2 hours.)

VARIATIONS

Capicola Picnic Sandwich with Artichoke Spread
Substitute provolone for Muenster, hot capicola for turkey, and 1 thinly sliced small fennel bulb for roasted red peppers. For spread, substitute 1 (14-ounce) can artichoke hearts, drained and patted dry, for sun-dried tomatoes; ¼ cup chopped jarred hot cherry peppers for almonds; and 1 teaspoon chopped fresh thyme for capers.

Ham Picnic Sandwich with Olive Spread
Substitute mozzarella for Muenster, Black Forest ham for turkey, and 1 cup shredded carrots for red peppers. For spread, substitute pitted kalamata olives for sun-dried tomatoes and ½ cup fresh parsley leaves for almonds.

Spice-Rubbed Picnic Chicken
Serves 8 MAKE AHEAD

Why This Recipe Works We wanted a recipe for chicken that would be easy to pack (and eat) for a picnic; chicken that was moist, tender, and well seasoned even when served cold, with spicy and slightly sweet barbecue flavors. Cold barbecued chicken presents numerous challenges: The meat may be dry, the skin flabby, and the chicken covered with a sticky, messy sauce. We first threw out the idea of a sticky sauce,

substituting a robust dry rub (brown sugar, chili powder, paprika, and cayenne pepper) that reproduced barbecue flavor. We partly solved the flabby skin problem by diligently trimming the chicken pieces as well as by slitting the skin before cooking, which allowed the excess fat to render. But our biggest discovery came when we opted to salt the chicken instead of brine it; by adding salt to the rub and refrigerating the chicken pieces overnight, we allowed both the salt and the spices to penetrate the meat for even deeper flavor. Sure enough, when we oven-roasted the chicken the next day, we found the meat to be well seasoned throughout and very moist. If you plan to serve the chicken later on the same day that you cook it, refrigerate it immediately after it has cooled and let it come back to room temperature before serving. On the breast pieces, we use toothpicks to secure the skin, which otherwise shrinks considerably in the oven, leaving the meat exposed and prone to drying out. We think the extra effort is justified, but you can omit this step. For spicier chicken, use the greater amount of cayenne. This recipe halves easily.

5	pounds bone-in chicken pieces (split breasts cut in half crosswise, drumsticks, and/or thighs), trimmed
3	tablespoons packed brown sugar
2	tablespoons chili powder
2	tablespoons sweet paprika
2	tablespoons kosher salt
2	teaspoons pepper
¼–½	teaspoon cayenne pepper

1. Make 2 or 3 short slashes in skin of each piece of chicken with sharp knife, taking care not to cut into meat. Combine sugar, chili powder, paprika, salt, pepper, and cayenne in small bowl and mix thoroughly. Coat chicken pieces with spices, gently lifting skin to distribute spice rub underneath but leaving attached to chicken. Transfer chicken, skin side up, to wire rack set in rimmed baking sheet, lightly tent with foil, and refrigerate for at least 6 hours or up to 24 hours.

2. If desired, secure skin of each breast piece with 2 or 3 toothpicks placed near edges of skin.

3. Adjust oven rack to middle position and heat oven to 425 degrees. Roast chicken until smallest piece registers 140 degrees, 15 to 20 minutes. Increase oven temperature to 500 degrees and continue roasting until breasts register 160 degrees and thighs/drumsticks register 175 degrees, 5 to 13 minutes, removing pieces from oven and transferring them to clean wire rack as they finish cooking. Let cool completely before refrigerating or serving. (Chicken can be refrigerated for up to 2 days.)

Picnic Fried Chicken

Serves 4 `MAKE AHEAD`

Why This Recipe Works Fried chicken is a picnic staple but often involves making do with a soggy crust and bland meat. To achieve well-seasoned fried chicken that stayed crunchy when cold, we pulled out every trick in the book. A combination of Wondra flour and cornstarch made for a coating that kept its crunch even when the chicken was cold, and dredging the chicken twice, with a water dip in between, created a thick, craggy crust (dipping in beaten egg softened the coating too much, so we left it out and stuck with water). Double-frying the chicken permitted extra moisture to evaporate from the skin, and chilling it uncovered guarded against sogginess. Finally, since cold dulls flavors, brining and extra seasoning were in order. This recipe may not be fast, but it can be made a day ahead. Come picnic time, the chicken will still be moist and crunchy. Use a Dutch oven that holds 6 quarts or more.

- ¼ cup table salt for brining
- 3 pounds bone-in chicken pieces (split breasts cut in half crosswise, drumsticks, and/or thighs), trimmed
- 1½ cups Wondra flour
- 1½ cups cornstarch
- 1 tablespoon pepper
- 2 teaspoons white pepper
- 1½ teaspoons baking powder
- 1 teaspoon dried thyme
- 1 teaspoon dried sage leaves
- 1 teaspoon garlic powder
- 1 teaspoon table salt
- ¼ teaspoon cayenne pepper
- 3 quarts peanut or vegetable oil

1. Dissolve ¼ cup salt in 1 quart cold water in large container. Submerge chicken in brine, cover, and refrigerate for 1 hour.

2. Whisk flour and cornstarch together in large bowl. Transfer 1 cup flour mixture to shallow dish; set aside. Whisk pepper, white pepper, baking powder, thyme, sage, garlic powder, salt, and cayenne into remaining flour mixture. Add ¼ cup water to seasoned flour mixture. Rub flour and water together with your fingers until water is evenly incorporated and mixture contains craggy bits of dough. Pour 2 cups cold water into medium bowl.

3. Set wire rack in rimmed baking sheet. Working with 2 pieces of chicken at a time, remove chicken from brine and dip in unseasoned flour mixture, pressing to adhere; dunk quickly in water, letting excess drip off; and dredge in seasoned flour mixture, pressing to adhere. Place chicken on prepared wire rack and refrigerate for at least 30 minutes or up to 2 hours.

4. Add oil to large Dutch oven until it measures about 2 inches deep and heat over medium-high heat to 350 degrees. Fry half of chicken until slightly golden and just beginning to crisp, 5 to 7 minutes. Adjust burner, if necessary, to maintain oil temperature between 300 and 325 degrees. (Chicken will not be cooked through at this point.) Return parcooked chicken to wire rack. Return oil to 350 degrees and repeat with remaining raw chicken. Let each batch of chicken rest for 5 to 7 minutes.

5. Return oil to 350 degrees. Return first batch of chicken to oil and fry until breasts register 160 degrees and thighs/drumsticks register 175 degrees, 5 to 7 minutes. Adjust burner, if necessary, to maintain oil temperature between 300 and 325 degrees. Transfer chicken to clean wire rack. Return oil to 350 degrees and repeat with remaining chicken. Let chicken cool to room temperature, transfer to paper towel–lined plate, and refrigerate uncovered until ready to eat, up to 24 hours in advance. Serve cold or let chicken come to room temperature.

Picnic Fried Chicken

Green Goddess Roast Chicken

Indoor Barbecue Ribs

Green Goddess Roast Chicken
Serves 4 to 6

Why This Recipe Works Green goddess dressing, made with lots of fresh herbs, is often a creamy, tangy complement to sweet butter lettuce. But it makes a great counterpoint to chicken, too. When slathered on bone-in parts, it produces roast chicken with immense summertime flavor, perfect for an easy weeknight dinner served outside. Instead of a dressing, we blended a green goddess–inspired marinade, swapping mayonnaise for tangy buttermilk and adding fresh chives, parsley, and tarragon plus lemon juice, garlic, and anchovy fillets. We marinated the chicken in a portion of this mixture so it could drink up the herby flavor and become tangy and deeply seasoned. While the chicken roasted, we whisked some of the reserved herb mixture with mayonnaise and a splash more buttermilk to make a rich, vibrant sauce. Chop the herbs and garlic just enough to measure them, and then let the blender do the bulk of the work.

½ cup chopped fresh chives
½ cup chopped fresh parsley
¼ cup plus 1 tablespoon buttermilk, divided
2 tablespoons lemon juice
4 teaspoons chopped fresh tarragon
2 garlic cloves, chopped
2 anchovy fillets, rinsed
¼ cup mayonnaise
1½ teaspoons table salt
3 pounds bone-in chicken pieces
(2 split breasts cut in half crosswise,
2 drumsticks, and 2 thighs), trimmed

1. Process chives, parsley, ¼ cup buttermilk, lemon juice, tarragon, garlic, and anchovies in blender until smooth, about 30 seconds, scraping down sides of blender jar as needed.

2. Transfer 2 tablespoons herb mixture to bowl, add mayonnaise and remaining 1 tablespoon buttermilk, and stir to combine. Cover and set aside until ready to serve.

3. Combine salt and remaining herb mixture in 1-gallon zipper-lock bag. Add chicken to bag, press out air, seal bag, and turn to coat chicken in marinade. Refrigerate for at least 2 hours or up to 24 hours.

4. Adjust oven rack to middle position and heat oven to 475 degrees. Line rimmed baking sheet with aluminum foil. Place chicken, skin side up, on prepared sheet (do not brush off marinade that sticks to chicken). Make sure skin is not bunched up on chicken. Roast until breasts register 160 degrees and drumsticks/thighs register 175 degrees, 25 to 30 minutes.

5. Transfer chicken to platter, tent with foil, and let rest for 10 minutes. Serve chicken with sauce.

Slow Roast Beef with Horseradish–Sour Cream Sauce

Serves 6 to 8 MAKE AHEAD

Why This Recipe Works Roast beef might seem more fit for the dining room than the patio, but a platter of sliced beef dressed with a simple sauce is a fantastic dish for a dinner party al fresco. Better yet, it can be made ahead and served cold as a refreshing option for a hot summer's day. Use the leftovers for sandwiches. The test kitchen's low and slow method means you needn't buy a pricey roast. We achieved remarkably tender and juicy meat with a cut that starts out relatively tough—a boneless eye-round—by roasting the meat elevated on a wire rack at a very low 225 degrees and then turning off the oven toward the end of cooking. This allowed time for the meat's enzymes to act as natural tenderizers, breaking down the tough connective tissue. Searing the meat before roasting, as well as salting it up to a day ahead, vastly improved its flavor. If the roast has not reached the desired temperature in the time specified in step 4, reheat the oven to 225 degrees for 5 minutes, then shut it off and continue to cook the roast to the desired temperature. We don't recommend cooking this roast past medium. This recipe requires refrigerating the salted beef for at least 18 hours or up to 24 hours before cooking (a longer time is preferable). Buy refrigerated prepared horseradish, not the shelf-stable kind, which contains preservatives and additives.

Horseradish–Sour Cream Sauce

- ½ cup sour cream
- ½ cup prepared horseradish, drained
- ¾ teaspoon table salt
- ⅛ teaspoon pepper

Beef

- 1 (3½- to 4½-pound) boneless eye-round roast, trimmed
- 4 teaspoons kosher salt
- 2 teaspoons plus 1 tablespoon vegetable oil, divided
- 2 teaspoons pepper

1. For the horseradish-sour cream sauce Whisk all ingredients together in bowl. Cover and refrigerate for at least 30 minutes to allow flavors to meld. Season with salt and pepper to taste. (Sauce can be refrigerated for up to 2 days.)

2. For the beef Rub roast thoroughly with salt, wrap in plastic wrap, and refrigerate for 18 to 24 hours.

3. Adjust oven rack to middle position and heat oven to 225 degrees. Pat roast dry with paper towels, rub with 2 teaspoons oil, and sprinkle with pepper.

4. Heat remaining 1 tablespoon oil in 12-inch skillet over medium-high heat until just smoking. Brown roast well on all sides, 12 to 16 minutes; reduce heat if pan begins to scorch. Transfer roast to wire rack set in rimmed baking sheet and roast until meat registers 115 degrees (for medium-rare), 1¼ to 1¾ hours.

5. Turn oven off and leave roast in oven, without opening door, until meat registers 130 degrees (for medium-rare) or 140 degrees (for medium), 30 to 50 minutes.

6. Transfer roast to carving board and let rest for 15 to 20 minutes. (Fully cooled roast can also be refrigerated for up to 2 days.) Slice meat crosswise as thin as possible and serve with sauce.

Indoor Barbecue Ribs

Serves 4 to 6 MAKE AHEAD

Why This Recipe Works Tender ribs with a stick-to-your-fingers sauce are perfect for outdoor eating, but they're not exactly last-minute cooking; good ribs take time to achieve their uniquely complex character from the slow mingling of flavors in meat, sauce, and smoke. So rather then tending to a grill or smoker all day, we decided to bring the process indoors and create a more convenient version we could make ahead and bring to a picnic or potluck or enjoy at home. We found that we could achieve great flavor and fall-off-the-bone tenderness by first rubbing the ribs in a mixture of salt, pepper, brown sugar, smoked paprika, and a bit of cayenne and then slow-roasting them in a moderate oven for about 5 hours. During the first 2 hours in the oven we simply roasted the ribs to allow the spice rub to cook into the meat, and during the final stint in the oven, we built up layers of "bark" by painting the ribs with barbecue sauce. We tried different styles of sauce and found we got the most authentic barbecue flavor when we incorporated espresso powder, mustard, and liquid smoke into the traditional base of vinegar, ketchup, and molasses. Look for liquid smoke that contains no salt or additional flavorings. Serve with Skillet Cornbread (page 244).

Barbecue Sauce

- 1 tablespoon vegetable oil
- 1 onion, chopped fine
- ¼ teaspoon table salt
- 1 tablespoon smoked paprika
- 1½ cups chicken broth
- ¾ cup cider vinegar
- ¾ cup dark corn syrup
- ¾ cup ketchup
- ½ cup molasses
- 2 tablespoons brown mustard
- 1 tablespoon hot sauce
- 1 tablespoon instant espresso powder
- ½ teaspoon liquid smoke

Ribs

- 3 tablespoons smoked paprika
- 2 tablespoons packed brown sugar
- 1 tablespoon table salt
- 1 teaspoon pepper
- ¼ teaspoon cayenne pepper
- 2 (2½ to 3-pound) racks St. Louis-style spareribs, trimmed, membrane removed

1. For the barbecue sauce Heat oil in large saucepan over medium heat until shimmering. Add onion and salt and cook until softened, about 5 minutes. Stir in paprika and cook until fragrant, about 30 seconds. Whisk in broth, vinegar, corn syrup, ketchup, molasses, mustard, hot sauce, and espresso powder and bring to simmer. Reduce heat to medium-low and simmer, stirring occasionally, until thickened and reduced to 2 cups, 50 minutes to 1 hour. Off heat, stir in liquid smoke and season with salt and pepper to taste. Measure out ½ cup sauce and set aside for serving. (Sauce can be refrigerated up to 1 week, bring to room temperature before serving.)

2. For the ribs Combine paprika, sugar, salt, pepper, and cayenne in bowl. Pat ribs dry with paper towels. Rub evenly with spice mixture, wrap in plastic wrap, and refrigerate for at least 1 hour. (Ribs can be refrigerated up to 24 hours.)

3. Adjust oven rack to middle position and heat oven to 275 degrees. Set wire rack in aluminum foil–lined rimmed baking sheet. Place ribs, meat side up, on prepared sheet and bake for 2 hours.

4. Remove ribs from oven and brush top of each rack with ¼ cup barbecue sauce. Return ribs to oven and bake until tender and fork inserted into meat meets no resistance, 2½ to 3 hours longer, brushing with additional barbecue sauce every hour. (Ribs can be refrigerated for up to 3 days; to reheat, place ribs on wire rack set in foil-lined rimmed

baking sheet and let sit at room temperature for 30 minutes, then cover ribs with foil and reheat in 400-degree oven for 15 minutes, uncover, and continue to cook until edges of meat begin to sizzle, 5 to 10 minutes)

5. Remove ribs from oven, tent with foil, and let rest for 20 minutes. Slice meat between bones to separate ribs. Serve warm or at room temperature along with reserved sauce.

Skillet Cornbread
Serves 12

If you don't have buttermilk, you can substitute clabbered milk; whisk 2 tablespoons lemon juice into 2 cups of milk and let the mixture sit until slightly thickened, about 10 minutes. We prefer a cast-iron skillet here, but any ovensafe 10-inch skillet will work fine. Avoid coarsely ground cornmeal, as it will make the cornbread gritty.

- 2¼ cups (11¼ ounces) cornmeal
- 2 cups buttermilk
- ¼ cup vegetable oil
- 4 tablespoons unsalted butter, cut into 4 pieces
- 2 large eggs
- 1 teaspoon baking powder
- 1 teaspoon baking soda
- ¾ teaspoon table salt

1. Adjust oven racks to lower-middle and middle positions and heat oven to 450 degrees. Heat 10-inch cast-iron skillet on upper rack for 10 minutes. Spread cornmeal over rimmed baking sheet and bake on lower rack until fragrant and color begins to deepen, about 5 minutes. Transfer hot cornmeal to large bowl and whisk in buttermilk; set aside.

2. Carefully add oil to hot skillet and continue to heat until oil is just smoking, about 5 minutes. Remove skillet from oven and add butter, carefully swirling pan until butter is melted. Pour all but 1 tablespoon oil mixture into cornmeal mixture, leaving remaining oil mixture in pan. Whisk eggs, baking powder, baking soda, and salt into cornmeal mixture.

3. Pour cornmeal mixture into hot skillet and bake until top begins to crack and sides are golden brown, 12 to 16 minutes, rotating pan halfway through baking. Let cornbread cool in pan for 5 minutes, then turn out onto wire rack. Serve.

Roasted Butterflied Leg of Lamb
Serves 8 to 10 `MAKE AHEAD`

Why This Recipe Works As with the roast beef on page 243, a platter of aromatic, well-seasoned leg of lamb is delicious whether served warm or cold. And it pairs well with a variety of summery vegetable and grain dishes, such as Simple Tomato Salad (page 307), Marinated Eggplant with Capers and Mint (page 298), or Bulgur Salad with Chickpeas, Spinach, and Za'atar (page 64). To keep the process easy, we skipped the usual rolling and tying and roasted the butterflied leg pounded flat, which allowed more thorough seasoning, a great ratio of crust to meat, and faster, more even cooking. Roasting the lamb in a 250-degree oven kept the meat juicy; a final blast under the broiler was all it took to crisp and brown the exterior. We ditched the usual spice rub (which can scorch under the broiler) in favor of a slow-cooked spice-infused oil that seasoned the lamb during cooking. We prefer the subtler flavor of lamb labeled "domestic" or "American" for this recipe. We prefer this lamb cooked to medium-rare, but if you prefer it more or less done, see our guidelines on page 188.

Lemon-Yogurt Sauce
- 1 cup plain yogurt
- 1 tablespoon minced fresh mint
- 1 teaspoon grated lemon zest plus 2 tablespoons juice
- 1 garlic clove, minced

Lamb
- 1 (3½- to 4-pound) butterflied leg of lamb
- 1 tablespoon kosher salt
- ⅓ cup extra-virgin olive oil
- 3 shallots, sliced thin
- 4 garlic cloves, peeled and smashed
- 1 (1-inch) piece ginger, peeled, sliced into ½-inch-thick rounds, and smashed
- 1 tablespoon coriander seeds
- 1 tablespoon cumin seeds
- 1 tablespoon mustard seeds
- 3 bay leaves
- 2 (2-inch) strips lemon zest

1. For the lemon-yogurt sauce Whisk all ingredients in bowl until combined. Season with salt and pepper to taste. Let sit until flavors meld, about 30 minutes. (Sauce can be refrigerated for up to 2 days.)

2. For the lamb Place lamb on cutting board with fat cap facing down. Using sharp knife, trim any pockets of fat and connective tissue from underside of lamb. Flip lamb over, trim fat cap to between ⅛ and ¼ inch thick, and pound roast to

Roasted Butterflied Leg of Lamb

even 1-inch thickness. Cut slits, spaced ½ inch apart, in fat cap in crosshatch pattern, being careful to cut down to but not into meat. Rub salt over entire roast and into slits. Let sit, uncovered, at room temperature for 1 hour.

3. Meanwhile, adjust oven rack to lower-middle position and second rack 4 to 5 inches from broiler element and heat oven to 250 degrees. Stir together oil, shallots, garlic, ginger, coriander seeds, cumin seeds, mustard seeds, bay leaves, and lemon zest in rimmed baking sheet and bake on lower rack until spices are softened and fragrant and shallots and garlic turn golden, about 1 hour. Remove sheet from oven and discard bay leaves.

4. Pat lamb dry with paper towels and transfer fat side up to sheet (directly on top of spices). Roast on lower rack until lamb registers 120 degrees, 20 to 25 minutes. Remove sheet from oven and heat broiler. Broil lamb on upper rack until surface is well browned and charred in spots and lamb registers 125 degrees (for medium-rare), 3 to 8 minutes.

5. Remove sheet from oven and transfer lamb to carving board (some spices will cling to bottom of roast). Tent with aluminum foil and let rest for 20 minutes. (Fully cooled lamb can be refrigerated for up to 2 days.)

6. Slice lamb with grain into 3 equal pieces. Turn each piece and slice against grain into ¼-inch-thick slices. Serve.

Poached Side of Salmon

Boiled Lobster

Poached Side of Salmon
Serves 8 to 10 MAKE AHEAD

Why This Recipe Works A whole poached side of salmon might be the ideal centerpiece for a summer gathering. Made ahead, stored in the fridge, and served cold, it is both elegant and unfussy—at least when you use this method, which uses no special equipment and ensures perfectly cooked fish. To accomplish this, we got rid of the water and steamed the salmon in its own moisture. We wrapped the seasoned fish in heavy-duty aluminum foil and placed it directly on the oven rack, which offered more even cooking than using a baking sheet. Cooking the salmon slowly in a very low oven gave the best results—moist, rich fish. If serving a big crowd, you can oven-poach two individually wrapped sides of salmon in the same oven (on the upper-middle and lower-middle racks) without altering the cooking time. As a final flourish to this dish, consider topping the salmon with a bright, fresh salsa (see pages 234–237). White wine vinegar can be substituted for the cider vinegar.

1 (4-pound) skin-on side of salmon, pin bones removed
1 teaspoon table salt
2 tablespoons cider vinegar
6 sprigs fresh tarragon or dill, plus 2 tablespoons minced
2 lemons, sliced thin, plus lemon wedges for serving

1. Adjust oven rack to middle position and heat oven to 250 degrees. Cut 3 pieces of heavy-duty aluminum foil to be 1 foot longer than side of salmon. Working with 2 pieces of foil, fold up 1 long side of each by 3 inches. Lay sheets side by side with folded sides touching, fold edges together to create secure seam, and press seam flat. Center third sheet of foil over seam. Spray foil with vegetable oil spray.

2. Pat salmon dry with paper towels and sprinkle with salt. Lay salmon, skin side down, in center of foil. Sprinkle with vinegar, then top with tarragon sprigs and lemon slices. Fold foil up over salmon to create seam on top and gently fold foil edges together to secure; do not crimp too tightly.

3. Lay foil-wrapped salmon directly on oven rack (without baking sheet). Cook until color of salmon has turned from pink to orange and thickest part registers 135 to 140 degrees, 45 minutes to 1 hour.

4. Remove salmon from oven and open foil. Let salmon cool at room temperature for 30 minutes. Pour off any accumulated liquid, then reseal salmon in foil and refrigerate until cold, at least 1 hour or up to 2 days.

5. To serve, unwrap salmon and brush away lemon slices, tarragon sprigs, and any solidified poaching liquid. Transfer fish to serving platter, sprinkle with minced tarragon, and serve with lemon wedges.

Boiled Lobster

Serves 4 (Yields 1 pound meat) `MAKE AHEAD`

Why This Recipe Works If you have seafood crackers, melted butter, and lots of napkins, a lobster boil is an instant summer party. But cooking lobster can be a daunting process: How do you deal with that thrashing tail, and how do you know it's done? We sedated our lobsters by placing them in the freezer for 30 minutes. To determine doneness (who wants a chewy lobster?), we poked a thermometer in the underside of the meaty tail. To cook four lobsters at once, you will need a pot with a capacity of at least 3 gallons. If your pot is smaller, boil the lobsters in batches. Start timing the lobsters from the moment they go into the pot. Serve with melted butter and lemon wedges or chill the meat for New England Lobster Rolls (page 89) and salads.

4 (1¼-pound) live lobsters
⅓ cup table salt

1. Place lobsters in large bowl and freeze for 30 minutes. Meanwhile, bring 2 gallons water to boil in large pot over high heat.

2. Add lobsters and salt to pot, arranging with tongs so that all lobsters are submerged. Cover pot, leaving lid slightly ajar, and adjust heat to maintain gentle boil. Cook for 8 minutes, then, holding lobster with tongs, insert thermometer through underside of tail into thickest part; meat should register 140 degrees. If necessary, return lobster to pot for 2 minutes, until tail registers 140 degrees.

3. Serve immediately or transfer lobsters to rimmed baking sheet and set aside until cool enough to remove meat, about 10 minutes. (Lobster meat can be refrigerated in airtight container for up to 24 hours.)

COOKING LOBSTER

Add lobsters and salt to pot, arranging with tongs so that all lobsters are submerged. Cook with lid slightly ajar at gentle boil for 8 minutes.

REMOVING LOBSTER MEAT FROM THE SHELL

1. Once cooked lobster is cool enough to handle, set it on cutting board. Grasp tail with your hand and grab body with your other hand and twist to separate.

2. Lay tail on its side on counter and use both your hands to press down on tail until shell cracks.

3. Hold tail, flippers facing you and shell facing down. Pull sides back to open shell and remove meat. Rinse meat under water to remove green tomalley; pat dry with paper towels and remove dark vein.

4. Twist "arms" to remove claws and attached "knuckles". Twist to remove from claw. Break knuckles at joint using back of chef's knife or lobster-cracking tool. Use handle of teaspoon to push out meat.

5. Wiggle hinged portion of each claw to separate. If meat is stuck inside small part, remove with skewer. Break open claws, cracking 1 side and then flipping to crack other side, and remove meat.

6. Twist legs to remove. Lay flat on counter. Using rolling pin, roll toward open end, pushing out meat. Stop rolling before reaching end of legs; otherwise leg can crack and release pieces of shell.

Indoor Clambake
Serves 4 to 6

Why This Recipe Works A clambake is the ultimate summer seafood meal: clams, mussels, and lobster, nestled with sausage, corn, and potatoes, all steamed together with hot stones in a sand pit by the sea. A genuine clambake is an all-day affair and, of course, requires a beach. But we wanted to re-create the great flavors of the clambake without hours of preparation so we could enjoy this flavorful feast anywhere. A large stockpot was our cooking vessel of choice, and with careful layering, we could cook everything in the same pot and have it all finish at the same time. And we didn't need to add water, because the shellfish released enough liquid to steam everything else. Sliced kielbasa went into the pot first, so that it could sear before the steam was generated. Clams and mussels were next, wrapped in cheesecloth for easy removal. Then in went the potatoes; they were best placed near the heat source and cut into 1-inch pieces to cook more quickly. Corn, with the husks left on to protect it from seafood flavors and lobster foam, was next, followed by the lobsters. It took less than half an hour for everything to cook—and we had all the elements of a clambake (minus the sand and surf) without having spent all day preparing them. Choose a large, narrow stockpot in which you can easily layer the ingredients. The recipe can be cut in half and layered in an 8-quart Dutch oven, but it should cook for the same amount of time. We prefer small littlenecks for this recipe. If your market carries larger clams, use 4 pounds. Mussels sometimes contain a weedy beard protruding from the crack between the two shells. It's fairly small and can be difficult to tug out of place. To remove it easily, trap the beard between the side of a small paring knife and your thumb and pull to remove it. The flat surface of the knife gives you some leverage to remove the beard.

2 pounds small littleneck or cherrystone clams, scrubbed
2 pounds mussels, scrubbed and debearded
1 pound kielbasa, sliced into ⅓-inch-thick rounds
1 pound small new or red potatoes, unpeeled, cut into 1-inch pieces
6 ears corn, silk and all but last layer of husk removed
2 (1½-pound) live lobsters
8 tablespoons salted butter, melted

1. Place clams and mussels on large piece of cheesecloth and tie ends together to secure; set aside. In 12-quart stockpot, layer sliced kielbasa, sack of clams and mussels, potatoes, corn, and lobsters on top of one another. Cover with lid and place over high heat. Cook until potatoes are tender and lobsters are bright red, 17 to 20 minutes.

2. Off heat, remove lid (watch out for scalding steam). Remove lobsters and set aside until cool enough to handle. Remove corn from pot and peel off husks; arrange ears on serving platter. Using slotted spoon, remove potatoes and arrange on platter with corn. Transfer clams and mussels to large bowl and cut open cheesecloth with scissors. Using slotted spoon, remove kielbasa from pot and arrange on platter with potatoes and corn. Pour remaining steaming liquid in pot over clams and mussels. Using kitchen towel to protect your hand, twist and remove lobster tails, claws, and legs (if desired). Arrange lobster parts on platter. Serve immediately with melted butter and napkins.

South Carolina Shrimp Boil
Serves 8

Why This Recipe Works Inspired by Frogmore stew (which contains no frogs and isn't even a stew), shrimp boils make a regular appearance at backyard picnics and along South Carolina's coast in casual seaside restaurants. Though Old Bay is this stew's star seasoning, we wanted the summery notes of shrimp and corn to really shine, so we staggered their cooking times and injected bright, robust flavors along the way. We browned pieces of smoky, spicy andouille sausage and left its rendered fat in the pot to carry its flavor into the briny broth of clam juice and water. We simmered Old Bay, a bay leaf, tomatoes, potatoes, and cut-up ears of corn until the potatoes were just tender and then added the browned sausage back to the pot. To add flavor and keep them moist, we cooked seasoned, shell-on shrimp in a steamer basket set atop the vegetables. This dish is always made with shell-on shrimp, and we think peeling them is half the fun. If you prefer peeled shrimp, use only 1 teaspoon of Old Bay in step 3. You can substitute kielbasa sausage for the andouille sausage. If doing so, add ¼ teaspoon of cayenne pepper to the broth in step 2. Use small red potatoes measuring 1 to 2 inches in diameter.

1½ pounds andouille sausage, cut into 2-inch lengths
2 teaspoons vegetable oil
1½ pounds small red potatoes, unpeeled, halved
4 ears corn, husks and silk removed, cut into 2-inch rounds
4 cups water
1 (8-ounce) bottle clam juice
1 (14.5-ounce) can diced tomatoes
5 teaspoons Old Bay seasoning, divided
1 bay leaf
2 pounds extra-large shrimp (21 to 25 per pound)

1. Heat sausage and oil in Dutch oven over medium-high heat until fat is rendered and sausage is browned, about 5 minutes; using slotted spoon, transfer sausage to plate.

2. Add potatoes, corn, water, clam juice, tomatoes, 1 tablespoon Old Bay, and bay leaf to pot and bring to boil. Reduce heat to medium-low and simmer, covered, until potatoes are barely tender, about 10 minutes.

3. Return browned sausage to pot. Toss shrimp with remaining 2 teaspoons Old Bay and transfer to collapsible steamer basket. Nestle steamer basket into pot. Cook, covered, stirring shrimp occasionally, until cooked through, about 10 minutes. Strain stew and discard bay leaf. Serve.

Buttermilk Coleslaw
Serves 4 to 6 `NO COOK` `MAKE AHEAD`

Why This Recipe Works Crisp coleslaw with a light but flavorful dressing is the quintessential picnic side dish, but it's also often one of the most disappointing. Store-bought packages of coleslaw are flavorless and bland, and homemade coleslaw is prone to turning watery and wilted. We wanted our coleslaw recipe to produce crisp, evenly cut pieces of cabbage lightly coated with a flavorful buttermilk dressing that would cling to the cabbage instead of collecting in the bottom of the bowl. We found that salting and draining the cabbage removed excess water and wilted it to a pickle-crisp texture. For a dressing that was both hefty and tangy, we combined buttermilk, mayonnaise, and sour cream.

½ head red or green cabbage, cored, quartered, and shredded (6 cups)
1¼ teaspoons table salt, divided
1 carrot, peeled and shredded
½ cup buttermilk
2 tablespoons mayonnaise
2 tablespoons sour cream
1 small shallot, minced
2 tablespoons minced fresh parsley
½ teaspoon cider vinegar
½ teaspoon sugar
¼ teaspoon Dijon mustard
⅛ teaspoon pepper

1. Toss shredded cabbage and 1 teaspoon salt in colander set over large bowl and let sit until wilted, at least 1 hour or up to 4 hours. Rinse cabbage under cold running water. Press, but do not squeeze, to drain, and blot dry with paper towels.

South Carolina Shrimp Boil

Buttermilk Coleslaw

2. Combine wilted cabbage and carrot in large bowl. In separate bowl, whisk buttermilk, mayonnaise, sour cream, shallot, parsley, vinegar, sugar, mustard, pepper, and remaining ¼ teaspoon salt together. Pour dressing over cabbage and toss to combine. Refrigerate until chilled, about 30 minutes. Serve. (Coleslaw can be refrigerated for up to 3 days.)

VARIATIONS

Buttermilk Coleslaw with Scallions and Cilantro
Omit mustard. Substitute 1 tablespoon minced fresh cilantro for parsley and 1 teaspoon lime juice for cider vinegar. Add 2 thinly sliced scallions to dressing.

Lemony Buttermilk Coleslaw
Substitute 1 teaspoon lemon juice for cider vinegar. Add 1 teaspoon minced fresh thyme and 1 tablespoon minced fresh chives to dressing.

Napa Cabbage Slaw with Carrots and Sesame

Serves 4 to 6 `FAST`

Why This Recipe Works Compared to traditional green and red cabbage, napa cabbage has a more tender, delicate texture and sweeter flavor that's ideally suited for a slaw with a light, bright dressing. Its more delicate structure also means that it will leach twice as much liquid as regular cabbage. To avoid a bland, watered-down salad, we made a potent dressing with a high ratio of vinegar to oil. We also cooked down the dressing's vinegar to offset the diluting power of the cabbage's water. After we tossed the cabbage with the dressing and let it sit for about 5 minutes, the slaw reached the perfect level of bright acidity. Adding another crunchy vegetable, some colorful herbs, and a handful of seeds or nuts gave the slaw an additional layer of flavor and texture. This slaw is best served within an hour of being dressed. Use the large holes of a box grater to prepare the carrots.

⅓ cup white wine vinegar
2 teaspoons toasted sesame oil
2 teaspoons vegetable oil
1 tablespoon rice vinegar
1 tablespoon soy sauce
1 tablespoon sugar
1 teaspoon grated fresh ginger
¼ teaspoon salt

Napa Cabbage Slaw with Carrots and Sesame

1 small head napa cabbage, sliced thin (9 cups)
2 carrots, peeled and grated
4 scallions, sliced thin on bias
¼ cup sesame seeds, toasted

1. Bring white wine vinegar to simmer in small saucepan over medium heat; cook until reduced to 2 tablespoons, 4 to 6 minutes. Transfer white wine vinegar to large bowl and let cool completely, about 10 minutes. Whisk in sesame oil, vegetable oil, rice vinegar, soy sauce, sugar, ginger, and salt.

2. When ready to serve, add cabbage and carrots to dressing and toss to coat. Let stand for 5 minutes. Add scallions and sesame seeds and toss to combine. Serve.

VARIATIONS

Napa Cabbage Slaw with Apple and Walnuts
Omit sesame oil and increase vegetable oil to 4 teaspoons. Omit soy sauce and ginger. Substitute cider vinegar for rice vinegar. Decrease sugar to 2 teaspoons and increase salt to ¾ teaspoon. Substitute 2 celery ribs, sliced thin on bias, and 1 grated Fuji apple for carrots. Substitute 3 tablespoons minced fresh chives for scallions and ½ cup walnuts, toasted and chopped fine, for sesame seeds.

Napa Cabbage Slaw with Jícama and Pepitas

Omit sesame oil and increase vegetable oil to 4 teaspoons. Omit soy sauce. Substitute lime juice for rice vinegar, honey for sugar, and ½ teaspoon ground coriander for ginger. Increase salt to ¾ teaspoon. Substitute 1 seeded and minced jalapeño for ginger. Substitute 6 ounces jícama, peeled and grated, for carrots. Substitute ¼ cup coarsely chopped fresh cilantro for scallions and ½ cup roasted and salted pepitas, chopped fine, for sesame seeds.

24-Hour Picnic Salad
Serves 12 NO COOK   MAKE AHEAD

Why This Recipe Works Picnic side dishes should be simple, portable, and flavorful and this recipe checks all the boxes. It can be assembled in advance, put in the fridge for a night, and simply tossed and served the next day. Salting the layers of iceberg lettuce pulled moisture out; we used this water to thin our dressing to the perfect consistency. Soft ingredients such as mushrooms and spinach wilted into mush overnight but crunchy celery, bell pepper, and cucumber stayed crisp. Frank's RedHot Original Hot Sauce is our favorite brand of hot sauce. If using a hotter brand, such as Tabasco Sauce, reduce the amount to 1 tablespoon.

Salad
- 1 head iceberg lettuce (2 pounds), cored and chopped, divided
- 1 teaspoon table salt, divided
- ½ red onion, sliced thin
- 6 Easy-Peel Hard-Cooked Eggs (page 54), peeled and chopped
- 1½ cups frozen peas
- 4 celery ribs, sliced thin
- 1 red bell pepper, stemmed, seeded, and chopped
- 1 cucumber, halved lengthwise, seeded, and sliced thin
- 1 pound bacon, cooked and crumbled
- 6 ounces blue cheese, crumbled (1½ cups)

Dressing
- 1½ cups mayonnaise
- 3 tablespoons cider vinegar
- 2 tablespoons hot sauce
- 2 teaspoons sugar
- 1½ teaspoons pepper

1. For the salad Layer ingredients into large serving bowl as follows: half of lettuce sprinkled with ½ teaspoon salt, onion, eggs, peas, celery, bell pepper, cucumber, remaining lettuce sprinkled with remaining ½ teaspoon salt, bacon, and cheese.

2. For the dressing Whisk all ingredients together in bowl and spread evenly over top of salad. Refrigerate for at least 8 hours or up to 24 hours. Toss until salad is evenly coated with dressing and serve.

Broccoli Salad with Raisins and Walnuts
Serves 6 FAST   MAKE AHEAD

Why This Recipe Works Most recipes for this picnic classic leave the broccoli raw, but we found that cooking it briefly in boiling water improved both its flavor and its appearance. Adding the hardier stems to the boiling water before the florets leveled the playing field, so both became tender at the same time. Drying the broccoli in a salad spinner rid it of excess moisture, so the dressing—a tangy mayo-and-vinegar mixture—wouldn't get watered down. As an added benefit, when treated this way, the broccoli retained its color, flavor, and crunch for a few days, allowing us to prepare it well in advance of assembly. Toasted walnuts and golden raisins brought crunch and salty-sweet balance to this salad. If you don't own a salad spinner, lay the broccoli on a clean dish towel to dry in step 2.

- ½ cup golden raisins
- 1½ pounds broccoli, florets cut into 1-inch pieces, stalks peeled and sliced ¼ inch thick
- ½ cup mayonnaise
- 1 tablespoon balsamic vinegar
- ½ teaspoon table salt
- ¼ teaspoon pepper
- ½ cup walnuts, toasted and chopped coarse
- 1 large shallot, minced

1. Bring 3 quarts water to boil in Dutch oven. Fill large bowl halfway with ice and water. Combine ½ cup of boiling water and raisins in small bowl, cover, and let sit for 5 minutes; drain.

2. Meanwhile, add broccoli stalks to pot of boiling water and cook for 1 minute. Add florets and cook until slightly tender, about 1 minute. Drain broccoli, then transfer to ice bath and let sit until chilled, about 5 minutes. Drain again, transfer broccoli to salad spinner, and spin dry.

3. Whisk mayonnaise, vinegar, salt, and pepper together in large bowl. (Blanched broccoli, plumped raisins, and dressing can be refrigerated separately for up to 3 days.)

4. Add broccoli, raisins, walnuts, and shallot to bowl with dressing and toss to combine. (Dressed salad can be refrigerated for up to 2 hours.) Season with salt and pepper to taste, and serve.

Fresh Corn and Tomato Salad

Fresh Corn and Tomato Salad
Serves 4 to 6 MAKE AHEAD

Why This Recipe Works While corn on the cob is certainly a crowd-pleasing summertime side, we wanted to create an easy-to-serve salad that would highlight corn's sweet off-the-cob flavor. This bright salad pairing corn and tomatoes fits the bill, and as a bonus it can be made a couple of hours ahead. To avoid bland corn, limp tomatoes, and watery dressing, we salted and drained the tomatoes to remove excess moisture. Toasting the corn in a skillet brought out a delicious nutty depth while still allowing the kernels to keep some of their snappy bite, and adding the dressing and scallions while the kernels were still warm gave the corn a chance to soak up even more flavor. To give the flavors time to meld, we stirred in the remaining ingredients once the corn had cooled and allowed the salad to rest. Don't add the tomatoes to the toasted corn until it is cool, or the heat from the corn will partially cook the tomatoes.

- 2 tomatoes, cored and cut into ½-inch pieces
- 1¼ teaspoons table salt, divided
- 2½ tablespoons extra-virgin olive oil, divided
- 5 ears corn, kernels cut from cobs (5 cups)
- 2 scallions, sliced thin
- 1½ tablespoons white wine vinegar
- ½ teaspoon pepper
- ¼ cup minced fresh parsley

1. Toss tomatoes with ½ teaspoon salt in colander set over bowl and let drain for 30 minutes.

2. Meanwhile, heat 1 tablespoon oil in 12-inch nonstick skillet over medium-high heat until shimmering. Add corn and cook, stirring occasionally, until spotty brown, 5 to 7 minutes. Transfer to large bowl and stir in scallions, vinegar, pepper, remaining ¾ teaspoon salt, and remaining 1½ tablespoons oil. Let cool to room temperature, about 20 minutes.

3. Stir in drained tomatoes and parsley. Let sit until flavors meld, about 30 minutes. (Dressed salad can be refrigerated for up to 2 hours.) Season with salt and pepper to taste before serving.

VARIATIONS
Fresh Corn and Tomato Salad with Arugula and Goat Cheese
Omit parsley. Substitute lemon juice for white wine vinegar. Stir in 2 ounces chopped baby arugula and 1 cup crumbled goat cheese with tomatoes.

Farmers' Market Find   Corn

When the first ears of sweet, fresh corn start appearing in farmers' markets and local supermarkets, most of us in the test kitchen turn giddy with excitement, especially since here in the Northeast, we often have to wait until late July or August for true local corn. And then the season is practically over by Labor Day. Not so in the South and the Midwest, where corn season happily stretches across the entire summer. Regardless of where you live, look for plump ears with green, pliable husks that are closely wrapped around the ear and clean, pale golden or white silk extending from the tops (the more silk, the better, since it is an indicator of the number of kernels). Don't peel back the husk and silk (which makes ears less desirable for other shoppers). Instead, gently press on the kernels through the husk; they should feel tightly packed, plump, and firm, with no spots where it feels like there's an absence of kernels. To store corn (for up to a few days), wrap it in a wet paper bag and then in a plastic produce bag and refrigerate it.

Fresh Corn and Tomato Salad with White Beans and Basil

Substitute red wine vinegar for white wine vinegar. Toss 1 (15-ounce) can rinsed cannellini beans with vinaigrette and hot corn. Substitute 2 tablespoons chopped fresh basil for parsley.

Watermelon Salad with Basil and Feta

Serves 4 to 6 NO COOK MAKE AHEAD

Why This Recipe Works Watermelon's sweet, juicy flavor takes center stage in this savory twist on fruit salad. Salty feta, briny olives, and aromatic basil work in tandem with the watermelon for a salad full of contrasting flavors and textures. We started by macerating the fresh melon in sugar for 30 minutes; this easy step drove off excess moisture and prevented a watery salad. A simple dressing of white wine vinegar and olive oil allowed the bold flavors of the salad to shine, and soaking sliced shallot in the vinegar before tossing it in the bowl tamed its bite and infused the vinegar with plenty of flavor. Mild cucumber added fresh crunch, and red pepper flakes contributed a kick of heat. Letting the dressed watermelon and olives rest in the fridge chilled the salad and allowed the sweet and salty flavors to meld, and finishing with some basil and feta just before serving added a burst of freshness.

  6 cups 1-inch seedless watermelon pieces
1½ teaspoons sugar, divided
  1 shallot, sliced into thin rings
  3 tablespoons white wine vinegar
  ½ teaspoon table salt, divided
  ¼ teaspoon red pepper flakes
  1 English cucumber, peeled, quartered lengthwise, seeded, and cut into ½-inch pieces
  ½ teaspoon pepper
  3 tablespoons extra-virgin olive oil
  ½ cup pitted kalamata olives, chopped
  ½ cup fresh basil leaves, torn into bite-size pieces
  3 ounces feta cheese, crumbled (¾ cup)

1. Toss watermelon with 1 teaspoon sugar in colander set over large bowl and let drain for 30 minutes. Combine shallot, vinegar, ¼ teaspoon salt, pepper flakes, and remaining ½ teaspoon sugar in separate bowl and let sit while watermelon drains. Discard watermelon juice and wipe bowl clean with paper towels.

2. Pat cucumber and drained watermelon dry with paper towels and transfer to now-empty bowl. Using fork, remove shallot from vinegar mixture and add to bowl with watermelon. Add pepper and remaining ¼ teaspoon salt to vinegar mixture and slowly whisk in oil until incorporated. Add dressing and olives to bowl with watermelon and toss to combine. Refrigerate for at least 30 minutes or up to 4 hours.

3. Add basil to salad and toss to combine. Season with salt and pepper to taste. Transfer to serving platter and sprinkle with feta. Serve.

Classic Potato Salad
Serves 4 to 6 MAKE AHEAD

Why This Recipe Works All-American potato salad conjures visions of lazy picnics and summertime cookouts, and our rich, flavorful version will have you loading your plate with this classic. Potatoes absorb moisture right after they cook, which means that adding the mayonnaise too early can lead to a dry, dull salad. To avoid this pitfall, we waited to add the mayonnaise but drizzled our just-cooked potatoes with a tangy, briny mixture of pickle juice and mustard. After the potatoes cooled, we added our creamy dressing, onion, celery, and pickles. Though it's optional, we love the flavor of hard-cooked egg. Make sure not to overcook the potatoes. Keep the water at a gentle simmer and use the tip of a paring knife to judge the doneness of the potatoes. If the knife inserts easily into the potato pieces, they are done. This recipe can be easily doubled; use a Dutch oven to cook the potatoes in step 1.

  2 pounds Yukon Gold potatoes, unpeeled, cut into ¾-inch pieces
  ½ teaspoon table salt, plus salt for cooking potatoes
  ¼ cup finely chopped dill pickles, plus 3 tablespoons brine, divided
  1 tablespoon yellow mustard
  ¾ cup mayonnaise
  ½ cup finely chopped red onion
  1 celery rib, minced
  2 tablespoons distilled white vinegar, plus extra for seasoning
  ½ teaspoon celery seeds
  ¼ teaspoon pepper
  2 Easy-Peel Hard-Cooked Eggs (page 54), chopped (optional)

1. Place potatoes and 1 teaspoon salt in large saucepan and cover with cold water by 1 inch. Bring to simmer over medium-high heat and cook until potatoes are tender, 10 to 15 minutes.

2. Drain potatoes thoroughly in colander, then spread out on rimmed baking sheet. Mix 2 tablespoons pickle brine and mustard together in bowl, then drizzle over potatoes, gently tossing until evenly coated. Refrigerate potato mixture until cooled slightly, about 15 minutes.

3. Combine mayonnaise, onion, celery, vinegar, celery seeds, pickles, remaining 1 tablespoon pickle brine, salt, and pepper in large bowl. Add cooled potato mixture and toss to combine. Cover and refrigerate until well chilled, about 30 minutes. (Salad can be refrigerated for up to 2 days.) Gently fold in eggs, if using. Season with extra vinegar, salt, and pepper to taste before serving.

Lemon and Herb Red Potato Salad

Serves 8

Why This Recipe Works Mayonnaise-based potato salad needs to be served cold, but for an alternative we could serve warm or room temperature, we opted for a light dressing paired with bright herbs. We boiled chunks of red potatoes and to help them keep their shape we added vinegar to the cooking water. A mixture of briny capers and tart lemon juice complemented the earthiness of the potatoes, while tarragon, parsley, and chives gave the salad a fresh character. Adding some of the vinaigrette while the potatoes were still hot let them absorb all of its flavor. To remove some of the onion's harshness after chopping, place it in a fine-mesh strainer and run it under cold water. Drain, but do not rinse, the capers.

- 3 pounds red potatoes, unpeeled, cut into 1-inch pieces
- 2 tablespoons distilled white vinegar
- 1 teaspoon table salt, plus salt for cooking potatoes
- 2 teaspoons grated lemon zest plus 3 tablespoons juice
- ½ teaspoon pepper
- ⅓ cup extra-virgin olive oil
- ½ cup finely chopped onion, rinsed
- 3 tablespoons minced fresh tarragon
- 3 tablespoons minced fresh parsley
- 3 tablespoons minced fresh chives
- 2 tablespoons capers, minced

1. Combine potatoes, 8 cups water, vinegar, and 2 tablespoons salt in Dutch oven and bring to boil over high heat. Reduce heat to medium and cook at strong simmer until potatoes are just tender, 10 to 15 minutes.

2. Meanwhile, whisk lemon zest and juice, pepper, and salt together in large bowl. Slowly whisk in oil until emulsified; set aside.

3. Drain potatoes thoroughly, then transfer to rimmed baking sheet. Drizzle 2 tablespoons dressing over hot potatoes and gently toss until evenly coated. Let potatoes cool, about 30 minutes, stirring once halfway through cooling.

4. Whisk dressing to recombine and stir in onion, tarragon, parsley, chives, and capers. Add cooled potatoes to dressing and gently stir to combine. Season with salt and pepper to taste. Serve warm or at room temperature.

Cool and Creamy Macaroni Salad

Serves 8 to 10 MAKE AHEAD

Why This Recipe Works Pasta mixed with crunchy onion and celery and dressed with seasoned tangy mayonnaise makes for a cool and refreshing side for a summer cookout, but more often than not this classic is a mushy, unappetizing blob of overcooked pasta with too much dressing. The biggest challenge with macaroni salad is keeping the pasta from absorbing too much mayonnaise, which causes it to turn into a dry, flavorless mess. We had learned from our Classic Potato Salad (page 253) that adding the mayonnaise to a warm salad will cause the starchy potatoes to soak up all of the mayo's moisture, so for our macaroni salad we cooked the pasta until tender, and then rinsed and drained it so that there was still a little moisture remaining. Next we mixed in all of the ingredients except our mayonnaise and let the mixture sit so that the pasta could absorb not just the water, but also the flavors of the seasonings so that everything melded together. We prefer garlic powder to fresh garlic here because its flavor isn't as sharp and the powder dissolves into the smooth dressing. Cooking the pasta until it is completely tender and leaving it slightly wet after rinsing are important for the texture of the finished salad. This recipe can be easily doubled.

8 ounces (2 cups) elbow macaroni
   Table salt for cooking pasta
¼ cup finely chopped red onion
¼ cup finely chopped celery
2 tablespoons minced fresh parsley
1 tablespoon lemon juice
1½ teaspoons Dijon mustard
   Pinch garlic powder
   Pinch cayenne pepper
¾ cup mayonnaise

1. Bring 4 quarts water to boil in large pot. Add macaroni and 1 tablespoon salt and cook, stirring often, until tender. Drain macaroni, rinse with cold water, and drain again, leaving macaroni slightly wet.

2. Toss macaroni, onion, celery, parsley, lemon juice, mustard, garlic powder, and cayenne together in large bowl and let sit until flavors meld, about 2 minutes. Stir in mayonnaise and let sit until salad is no longer watery, 5 to 10 minutes. (Salad can be refrigerated for up to 2 days; adjust consistency with hot water as needed.) Season with salt and pepper to taste before serving.

VARIATIONS
Cool and Creamy Macaroni Salad with Roasted Red Peppers and Capers
Add ½ cup jarred roasted red peppers, chopped, and 3 tablespoons drained capers, chopped, to macaroni with onion.

Cool and Creamy Macaroni Salad with Sharp Cheddar and Chipotle
Add 1½ cups shredded extra-sharp cheddar cheese and 2 tablespoons minced canned chipotle chile in adobo sauce to macaroni with onion and other flavorings.

RINSING MACARONI

After draining cooked macaroni, rinse under cold water to stop cooking and rinse away excess starch, which helps prevent sticking. Let pasta drain just briefly. It should be slightly wet when you dress it.

Lemon and Herb Red Potato Salad

Cool and Creamy Macaroni Salad

Pasta Salad with Pesto

Serves 6 to 8 `MAKE AHEAD`

Why This Recipe Works Full of bold herbal flavors, pesto makes for an excellent dressing for pasta salad during the hot summer months. And it couldn't be simpler to make: Just process fresh basil, garlic, pine nuts, salty Parmesan cheese, and extra-virgin olive oil together in a food processor. But when we tossed the pesto directly with hot pasta, the sauce became separated and greasy as the pasta cooled. We found that spreading the pasta on a baking sheet for about half an hour before adding the pesto was enough to adequately cool the pasta. A handful of baby spinach helped the pesto retain a bright green color but was mild enough in flavor to let the basil shine. Adding some mayonnaise was the perfect way to give our pesto the clingy, thick texture ideal for a pasta salad. We finished off our salad by reserving some of the toasted pine nuts to add a nice nutty crunch and tossed in sweet cherry tomatoes for a bright burst of freshness. Other pasta shapes can be substituted for the farfalle.

    2 garlic cloves, unpeeled
    1 pound farfalle
    1 teaspoon table salt, plus salt for cooking pasta
    5 tablespoons extra-virgin olive oil, divided
    3 cups fresh basil leaves, lightly bruised
    1 cup baby spinach
    ¾ cup pine nuts, toasted, divided
    2 tablespoons lemon juice
    1½ ounces Parmesan cheese, grated (¾ cup),
        plus extra for serving
    6 tablespoons mayonnaise
    12 ounces cherry tomatoes, quartered

1. Bring 4 quarts water to boil in large pot. Add garlic and cook for 1 minute. Remove garlic with slotted spoon and rinse under cold water to stop cooking. Let garlic cool slightly, then peel and chop fine; set aside.

2. Meanwhile, add pasta and 1 tablespoon salt to boiling water and cook, stirring often, until tender. Reserve ¼ cup cooking water. Drain pasta, toss with 1 tablespoon oil, and spread in single layer on rimmed baking sheet. Let pasta and cooking water cool to room temperature, about 30 minutes.

3. Process basil, spinach, ¼ cup pine nuts, lemon juice, garlic, and salt in food processor until smooth, about 30 seconds, scraping down sides of bowl as needed. Add Parmesan, mayonnaise, and remaining ¼ cup oil and process until thoroughly combined; transfer to large bowl.

4. Toss cooled pasta with pesto, adding reserved cooking water, 1 tablespoon at a time, until pesto evenly coats pasta. (Cooled pasta can be tossed with half of pesto and refrigerated for up to 3 days; refrigerate remaining pesto separately, covered with 1 tablespoon olive oil. To serve, microwave pasta to remove chill, 1 to 2 minutes, then toss with reserved pesto, adding hot water 1 tablespoon at a time as needed until evenly coated. Continue with step 5.)

5. Fold in remaining ½ cup pine nuts and tomatoes. Season with salt and pepper to taste. Serve.

Tortellini Salad with Asparagus and Fresh Basil Vinaigrette

Serves 4 to 6 `MAKE AHEAD`

Why This Recipe Works For a super-easy but upscale pasta salad that would impress any picnic crowd, we paired convenient store-bought cheese tortellini with crisp asparagus and a dressing inspired by the flavors of classic pesto. First, we blanched the asparagus in the same water we later used to cook the tortellini, which instilled the pasta with the asparagus's delicate flavor. Once the tortellini were cooked, we tossed them in a bold dressing of extra-virgin olive oil, lemon juice, shallot, and garlic. To finish the salad, we tossed in some bright, juicy cherry tomatoes, fresh basil, grated Parmesan, and toasted pine nuts along with the blanched asparagus just before serving. Cooking the tortellini until it is completely tender and leaving it slightly wet after rinsing are important for the texture of the finished salad. Be sure to set up the ice water bath before cooking the asparagus, as plunging it in the cold water immediately after blanching preserves its bright green color and ensures that it doesn't overcook.

    1 pound thin asparagus, trimmed and cut into
        1-inch lengths
    1 teaspoon table salt, plus salt for cooking
        asparagus and pasta
    1 pound dried cheese tortellini
    3 tablespoons lemon juice, plus extra for seasoning
    1 shallot, minced
    2 garlic cloves, minced
    ¾ teaspoon pepper
    ½ cup extra-virgin olive oil
    12 ounces cherry tomatoes, halved
    1 ounce Parmesan cheese, grated (½ cup)
    ¾ cup chopped fresh basil, mint, or parsley
    ¼ cup pine nuts, toasted

1. Bring 4 quarts water to boil in large pot. Fill large bowl halfway with ice and water. Add asparagus and 1 tablespoon salt to boiling water and cook until crisp-tender, about 2 minutes. Using slotted spoon, transfer asparagus to ice water and let cool, about 2 minutes; drain and pat dry.

2. Return pot of water to boil. Add tortellini and cook, stirring often, until tender. Drain tortellini, rinse with cold water, and drain again, leaving tortellini slightly wet.

3. Whisk lemon juice, shallot, garlic, pepper, and salt together in large bowl. Whisking constantly, drizzle in oil. Add tortellini and toss to combine.

4. Add asparagus, tomatoes, Parmesan, basil, and pine nuts and gently toss to combine. Season with salt, pepper, and extra lemon juice to taste. Serve. (Cooled tortellini, cooked asparagus, and vinaigrette can be refrigerated separately for up to 2 days.)

Fusilli Salad with Salami, Provolone, and Sun-Dried Tomato Vinaigrette

Serves 4 to 6 `FAST` `MAKE AHEAD`

Why This Recipe Works Inspired by traditional antipasto flavors, we wanted to create a pasta salad that could take on hearty, interesting mix-ins. We started with fusilli pasta, which was substantial enough to hold up to the larger pieces of meat and cheese. Thickly cut salami and provolone added savory bite and richness, and sliced kalamata olives added a brininess to punch up the flavor. With several rich ingredients in the mix, a mayonnaise-based dressing was overkill, so we swapped it out in favor of a bright vinaigrette accented with tangy sun-dried tomatoes, red wine vinegar, garlic, and basil. When left to marinate for a day or two, the pasta took on even more flavor; to loosen the dressing and quickly take the chill off the pasta, we stirred in a little boiling water. Chopped baby spinach added just before serving lent extra color and freshness. Other pasta shapes can be substituted for the fusilli.

- 8 ounces fusilli
- ¾ teaspoon table salt, plus salt for cooking pasta
- ¾ cup oil-packed sun-dried tomatoes, rinsed, patted dry, and minced, plus 2 tablespoons packing oil
- ¼ cup red wine vinegar, plus extra for seasoning
- 2 tablespoons chopped fresh basil or parsley
- 1 garlic clove, minced
- ¾ teaspoon pepper
- ¼ cup extra-virgin olive oil

Fusilli Salad with Salami, Provolone, and Sun-Dried Tomato Vinaigrette

- 4 (¼-inch-thick) slices deli salami or pepperoni (8 ounces), cut into 1-inch-long matchsticks
- 4 (¼-inch-thick) slices deli provolone (8 ounces), cut into 1-inch-long matchsticks
- ½ cup pitted kalamata olives, sliced
- 2 ounces (2 cups) baby spinach, chopped

1. Bring 4 quarts water to boil in large pot. Add pasta and 1 tablespoon salt and cook, stirring often, until tender. Drain pasta, rinse with cold water, and drain again, leaving pasta slightly wet.

2. Whisk sun-dried tomatoes, vinegar, basil, garlic, pepper, and salt together in large bowl. Whisking constantly, drizzle in olive oil and sun-dried tomato packing oil. Add pasta, salami, cheese, and olives and toss to combine. (To make ahead, toss fusilli, salami, cheese, and olives with half of vinaigrette; refrigerate pasta mixture and remaining vinaigrette separately for up to 2 days. To serve, bring to room temperature, then stir in vinaigrette, then stir vinaigrette and ¼ cup boiling water into pasta mixture before continuing.)

3. Add spinach and gently toss to combine. Season with salt, pepper, and extra vinegar to taste. Serve.

Quinoa, Black Bean, and Mango Salad

Orzo Salad with Broccoli and Radicchio

Quinoa, Black Bean, and Mango Salad

Serves 4 to 6 `FAST` `MAKE AHEAD`

Why This Recipe Works This hearty quinoa salad doubles as a side dish and a vegetarian main. We toasted the quinoa to bring out its flavor before adding liquid. Spreading the cooked quinoa on a rimmed baking sheet allowed the residual heat to finish cooking it gently as it cooled. Mango, bell pepper, and black beans lent brightness, color, and heft. A simple but intense dressing of olive oil, lime juice, jalapeño, cumin, and cilantro added the right amount of acidity and warmth. Finally, scallions and avocado added bite and creamy richness. If you buy unwashed quinoa (or if you are unsure whether it's washed), be sure to rinse it before cooking to remove its bitter protective coating (called saponin).

1½ cups prewashed white quinoa
2¼ cups water
1½ teaspoons table salt, divided
  5 tablespoons lime juice (3 limes)
 ½ jalapeño chile, stemmed, seeded, and chopped
 ¾ teaspoon ground cumin
 ½ cup extra-virgin olive oil
 ⅓ cup fresh cilantro leaves
  1 red bell pepper, stemmed, seeded, and chopped
  1 mango, peeled, pitted, and cut into ¼-inch pieces
  1 (15-ounce) can black beans, rinsed
  2 scallions, sliced thin
  1 avocado, halved, pitted, and sliced thin

1. Toast quinoa in large saucepan over medium-high heat, stirring often, until quinoa is very fragrant and makes continuous popping sounds, 5 to 7 minutes. Stir in water and ½ teaspoon salt and bring to simmer. Cover, reduce heat to low, and simmer gently until most of water has been absorbed and quinoa is nearly tender, about 15 minutes. Spread quinoa on rimmed baking sheet and let cool completely, about 15 minutes; transfer to large bowl.

2. Process lime juice, jalapeño, cumin, and remaining 1 teaspoon salt in blender until jalapeño is finely chopped, about 15 seconds. With blender running, add oil and cilantro; continue to process until smooth and emulsified, about 20 seconds. (Cooled quinoa and dressing can be refrigerated separately for up to 3 days.)

3. Add bell pepper, mango, beans, scallions, and lime-jalapeño dressing to cooled quinoa and toss to combine. Season with salt and pepper to taste. (Dressed salad can be refrigerated for up to 2 hours.) Serve, topping individual servings with avocado.

Orzo Salad with Broccoli and Radicchio

Serves 4 to 6 `MAKE AHEAD`

Why This Recipe Works Orzo salad is a great all-purpose side for a picnic, a day at the beach, or a patio dinner. Wherever it's served, it benefits from boldly flavored additions. We included vibrant broccoli, bitter radicchio, salty sun-dried tomatoes, and crunchy pine nuts. Cooking the orzo in the water that we used to blanch the broccoli imparted a delicate vegetal flavor throughout the dish and streamlined the recipe. To ensure that the orzo was tender even when served cold, we cooked it al dente. To unite all components of the dish, we whisked up a bold dressing with balsamic vinegar and honey. Toasting the pine nuts intensified their nutty flavor. Sharp Parmesan added a salty accent, and a hefty dose of chopped basil offered a fresh finish to this hearty side. Cooking the pasta until it is completely tender and leaving it slightly wet after rinsing are important for the texture of the finished salad.

12 ounces broccoli florets, cut into 1-inch pieces
 1 teaspoon table salt, plus salt for cooking broccoli and pasta
1⅓ cups orzo
 1 head radicchio (10 ounces), cored and chopped fine
 2 ounces Parmesan cheese, grated (1 cup)
 ½ cup oil-packed sun-dried tomatoes, rinsed, patted dry, and minced, plus 3 tablespoons packing oil
 ½ cup pine nuts, toasted
 ¼ cup balsamic vinegar, plus extra for seasoning
 1 garlic clove, minced
 1 teaspoon honey
 3 tablespoons extra-virgin olive oil
 ½ cup chopped fresh basil

1. Bring 4 quarts water to boil in large pot. Fill large bowl halfway with ice and water. Add broccoli and 1 tablespoon salt to boiling water and cook until crisp-tender, about 2 minutes. Using slotted spoon, transfer broccoli to ice bath and let cool, about 2 minutes; drain and pat dry.

2. Return pot of water to boil. Add orzo and cook, stirring often, until tender. Drain orzo, rinse with cold water, and drain again, leaving orzo slightly wet. Toss orzo, broccoli, radicchio, Parmesan, tomatoes, and pine nuts together in large bowl.

3. In small bowl, whisk vinegar, garlic, honey, and salt together. Whisking constantly, drizzle in tomato oil and olive oil. Stir vinaigrette into orzo mixture. (Salad can be refrigerated for up to 1 day; refresh with warm water and additional oil as needed.) Stir in basil and season with salt and pepper to taste before serving.

Classic Three-Bean Salad

Serves 8 to 10 `MAKE AHEAD`

Why This Recipe Works Recipes for this familiar picnic standby of canned green, yellow, and kidney beans tossed in a sweet, vinegary dressing, have changed little since the salad's heyday in the 1950s. We wanted an updated, fresher-tasting three-bean salad recipe so we used a combination of canned kidney beans and fresh yellow and green beans. For the dressing, we relied on canola oil for mildness and red wine vinegar for tang. Heating the oil and vinegar with sugar, garlic, salt, and pepper intensified the vinaigrette flavor and sweetness. Refrigerating the salad overnight allows the flavors to meld. Allowing the beans to marinate in the dressing improves their flavor so prepare the salad 1 day before you plan to serve it.

 1 cup red wine vinegar
 ¾ cup sugar
 ½ cup vegetable oil
 2 garlic cloves, minced
 1 teaspoon table salt, plus salt for cooking beans
 8 ounces green beans, trimmed and cut into 1-inch lengths
 8 ounces yellow wax beans, trimmed and cut into 1-inch lengths
 1 (15-ounce) can red kidney beans, rinsed
 ½ red onion, chopped
 ¼ cup minced fresh parsley

1. Heat vinegar, sugar, oil, garlic, 1 teaspoon salt, and pepper to taste in small saucepan over medium heat, stirring occasionally, until sugar dissolves, about 5 minutes. Transfer to a large bowl and let cool to room temperature.

2. Bring 3 quarts water to boil in large saucepan over high heat. Add 1 tablespoon salt and green and yellow beans; cook until crisp-tender, about 5 minutes. Meanwhile, fill medium bowl with ice water. When beans are done, drain and immediately plunge into ice water to stop cooking process; let sit until chilled, about 2 minutes. Drain well.

3. Add green and yellow beans, kidney beans, onion, and parsley to vinegar mixture; toss well to coat. Cover and refrigerate overnight to let flavors meld. Let stand at room temperature 30 minutes before serving. (Salad can be refrigerated for up to 4 days.)

Chickpea Salad with Carrots, Arugula, and Olives

Serves 4 to 6 `FAST` `MAKE AHEAD`

Why This Recipe Works Canned chickpeas are an ideal ingredient for a salad because they absorb flavors easily and provide texture. Here a flavorful pairing of sweet carrots, peppery arugula, and briny olives transforms bland canned chickpeas into a bright and savory salad. We found that heating the chickpeas in the microwave briefly softened them just enough to allow them to quickly soak up the tangy vinaigrette. Shred the carrots on the large holes of a box grater or use a food processor fitted with the shredding disk.

 2 (15-ounce) cans chickpeas, rinsed
 ¼ cup extra-virgin olive oil
 2 tablespoons lemon juice
 ¾ teaspoon table salt
 ½ teaspoon pepper
    Pinch cayenne pepper
 3 carrots, peeled and shredded
 ½ cup pitted kalamata olives, chopped
 1 cup baby arugula, chopped

1. Microwave chickpeas in medium bowl until hot, about 1 minute 30 seconds. Stir in oil, lemon juice, salt, pepper, and cayenne and let sit for 30 minutes. Add carrots and olives and toss to combine. (Chickpea mixture can be refrigerated for up to 2 days. Bring to room temperature before continuing with step 2.)

2. Add arugula and gently toss to combine. Season with salt and pepper to taste. Serve.

VARIATION

Chickpea Salad with Roasted Red Peppers and Feta

Substitute ½ cup drained and chopped jarred roasted red peppers, ½ cup crumbled feta cheese, and ¼ cup chopped fresh parsley for carrots, olives, and arugula.

Strawberry Pretzel Salad

Serves 10 to 12 `MAKE AHEAD`

Why This Recipe Works This tri-layer Midwestern specialty doesn't much resemble salad, but the sweet-salty, creamy-crunchy combination grabbed our attention. We knew we could make this slightly offbeat potluck favorite shine with some homemade elements. We replaced the "whipped topping" with real cream, which we whipped into softened cream cheese with some sugar for a tangy, not-too-sweet middle layer. The top layer, traditionally made from boxed Jell-O, got an upgrade to plain gelatin flavored with real pureed strawberry juice and sliced frozen berries. The time it took to make these elements from scratch was well worth the extra effort. For a sturdier crust, use (thinner) pretzel sticks not (fatter) rods. Thaw the strawberries in the refrigerator the night before you begin the recipe. You'll puree 2 pounds of the strawberries and slice the remaining 1 pound.

 6½ ounces pretzel sticks
 2¼ cups (15¾ ounces) sugar, divided
 12 tablespoons unsalted butter, melted and cooled
 8 ounces cream cheese
 1 cup heavy cream
 3 pounds (10½ cups) frozen strawberries, thawed
 ¼ teaspoon table salt
 1½ tablespoons unflavored gelatin
 ½ cup cold water

1. Adjust oven rack to middle position and heat oven to 400 degrees. Spray 13 by 9-inch baking pan with vegetable oil spray. Pulse pretzels and ¼ cup sugar in food processor until coarsely ground, about 15 pulses. Add melted butter and pulse until combined, about 10 pulses. Transfer pretzel mixture to prepared pan. Using bottom of measuring cup, press crumbs into bottom of pan. Bake until crust is fragrant and beginning to brown, about 10 minutes, rotating pan halfway through baking. Set aside crust, letting it cool slightly, about 20 minutes.

2. Using stand mixer fitted with whisk, whip cream cheese and ½ cup sugar on medium speed until light and fluffy, about 2 minutes. Increase speed to medium-high and, with mixer still running, slowly add cream in steady stream. Continue to whip until soft peaks form, scraping down bowl as needed, about 1 minute. Spread whipped cream cheese mixture evenly over cooled crust. Refrigerate until set, about 30 minutes.

3. Meanwhile, process 2 pounds strawberries in now-empty food processor until pureed, about 30 seconds. Strain mixture through fine-mesh strainer set over medium saucepan, using underside of small ladle to push puree through strainer. Add remaining 1½ cups sugar and salt to strawberry puree in saucepan and cook over medium-high heat, whisking occasionally, until bubbles begin to appear around sides of pan and sugar is dissolved, about 5 minutes; remove from heat.

4. Sprinkle gelatin over water in large bowl and let sit until gelatin softens, about 5 minutes. Whisk strawberry puree into gelatin. Slice remaining strawberries and stir into strawberry-gelatin mixture. Refrigerate until gelatin thickens slightly and starts to cling to sides of bowl, about 30 minutes. Carefully pour gelatin mixture evenly over whipped cream cheese layer. Refrigerate salad until gelatin is fully set, at least 4 hours or up to 24 hours. Serve.

Best Lemon Bars
Serves 12 (Makes 12 bars)   `MAKE AHEAD`

Why This Recipe Works The sweet-tart, sunshiny taste of a good lemon bar captures the best of summer's bright flavors, and these bars make for a simple picnic dessert that travels well. To make our bars, we started at the bottom, with a pat-in-the-pan crust. Using melted—not cold—butter allowed us to simply stir the crust together instead of using a food processor. For a truly crisp texture, we used granulated sugar instead of the usual confectioners' sugar and baked the crust until it was dark golden brown to ensure that it retained its crispness even after we topped it with the lemon filling. We cooked our lemon filling on the stove to shorten the oven time and keep it from curdling or browning at the edges when it baked. The combination of lemon juice and lemon zest provided complex flavor, and a couple of teaspoons of cream of tartar (tartaric acid) gave it a bright, lingering finish. Do not substitute bottled lemon juice for fresh here.

Crust
- 1 cup (5 ounces) all-purpose flour
- ¼ cup (1¾ ounces) granulated sugar
- ½ teaspoon table salt
- 8 tablespoons unsalted butter, melted

Filling
- 1 cup (7 ounces) granulated sugar
- 2 tablespoons all-purpose flour
- 2 teaspoons cream of tartar
- ¼ teaspoon table salt
- 3 large eggs plus 3 large yolks
- 2 teaspoons grated lemon zest plus
  ⅔ cup juice (4 lemons)
- 4 tablespoons unsalted butter, cut into 8 pieces
  Confectioners' sugar (optional)

Chickpea Salad with Carrots, Arugula, and Olives

Best Lemon Bars

1. For the crust Adjust oven rack to middle position and heat oven to 350 degrees. Make foil sling for 8-inch square baking pan by folding 2 long sheets of aluminum foil so each is 8 inches wide. Lay sheets of foil in pan perpendicular to each other, with extra foil hanging over edges of pan. Push foil into corners and up sides of pan, smoothing foil flush to pan.

2. Whisk flour, sugar, and salt together in bowl. Add melted butter and stir until combined. Transfer mixture to prepared pan and press into even layer over entire bottom of pan (do not wash bowl). Bake crust until dark golden brown, 19 to 24 minutes, rotating pan halfway through baking.

3. For the filling While crust bakes, whisk sugar, flour, cream of tartar, and salt together in now-empty bowl. Whisk in eggs and yolks until no streaks of egg remain. Whisk in lemon zest and juice. Transfer mixture to saucepan and cook over medium-low heat, stirring constantly, until mixture thickens and registers 160 degrees, 5 to 8 minutes. Off heat, stir in butter. Strain filling through fine-mesh strainer set over bowl.

4. Pour filling over hot crust and tilt pan to spread evenly. Bake until filling is set and barely jiggles when pan is shaken, 8 to 12 minutes. (Filling around perimeter of pan may be slightly raised.) Let bars cool completely, at least 1½ hours. Using foil overhang, lift bars out of pan and transfer to cutting board. Cut into bars, wiping knife clean between cuts as necessary. (Lemon bars can be refrigerated for up to 2 days or frozen for up to 1 month; if frozen, thaw completely at room temperature before serving.) Before serving, dust bars with confectioners' sugar, if using.

Key Lime Bars
Serves 16 (Makes 16 bars) `MAKE AHEAD`

Why This Recipe Works The best key lime bars are packed with bold, sweet-tart lime flavor, but we wanted a version of these bars that we could make with limes from the grocery store rather than hard-to-find key limes. To get big lime flavor into our lime bars, we avoided weak, bitter-tasting bottled juice and went with the fresh stuff. It took only four supermarket limes (as opposed to 20 key limes) to yield the right amount of juice. But fresh lime juice alone didn't give us a taste of the Florida Keys; so we also added lime zest. For these bars to slice and eat neatly, we needed the filling to be firmer than that of a typical key lime pie, so we supplemented the usual sweetened condensed milk and egg yolk with cream cheese. Our crust needed to be sturdier, too, and this meant using more crumbs. We had been using graham crackers, but when we increased the amount in

the crust their flavor overpowered the filling. Animal crackers had just the right vanilla flavor, and light brown sugar added subtle caramel notes. Key limes can be substituted for the regular limes here, although they have a more delicate flavor; you'll need about 20 to make ½ cup of juice. Do not substitute bottled key lime juice. Be sure to zest the limes before juicing them.

Crust
- 5 ounces (2½ cups) animal crackers
- 3 tablespoons packed light brown sugar
- Pinch table salt
- 4 tablespoons unsalted butter, melted and cooled

Filling
- 2 ounces cream cheese, softened
- 1 tablespoon grated lime zest plus ½ cup juice (4 limes)
- Pinch table salt
- 1 (14-ounce) can sweetened condensed milk
- 1 large egg yolk
- ¾ cup (2¼ ounces) sweetened shredded coconut, toasted (optional)

1. Adjust oven rack to middle position and heat oven to 325 degrees. Make foil sling for 8-inch square baking pan by folding 2 long sheets of aluminum foil so each is 8 inches wide. Lay sheets of foil in pan perpendicular to each other, with extra foil hanging over edges of pan. Push foil into corners and up sides of pan, smoothing foil flush to pan. Grease foil.

2. For the crust Process animal crackers, sugar, and salt in food processor to fine crumbs, about 15 seconds. Add melted butter and pulse to combine, about 10 pulses. Sprinkle mixture into prepared pan and press firmly into even layer. Bake until crust is fragrant and deep golden brown, 18 to 20 minutes, rotating pan halfway through baking.

3. For the filling Stir cream cheese, lime zest, and salt in bowl until combined. Whisk in condensed milk until smooth. Whisk in egg yolk and lime juice until combined.

4. Pour filling evenly over crust. Bake until bars are set and edges begin to pull away slightly from sides of pan, 15 to 20 minutes, rotating pan halfway through baking.

5. Let bars cool completely in pan on wire rack, about 2 hours, then refrigerate until thoroughly chilled, about 2 hours. Using foil overhang, remove bars from pan. Cut into 16 pieces and top with toasted coconut, if using, before serving. (Key lime bars can be refrigerated for up to 2 days.)

Perfect Chocolate Chip Cookies
Makes 16 cookies `MAKE AHEAD`

Why This Recipe Works There's no question that the chocolate chip cookie is the most iconic American treat, and these homey cookies are perfectly portable for an easy but mouthwatering picnic dessert. While both crispy cookies and cakey ones have their place, we wanted a version reminiscent of the classic Toll House cookie, one with crisp edges and a chewy interior. But perhaps nostalgia clouded our memory, because the Toll House recipe actually produces cookies that are a bit cakey and wan. We wanted a reliably moist and chewy cookie with crisp edges and deep butterscotch notes. The key ingredient was browned butter. Melting the butter made its water content readily available to interact with the flour, thus creating more gluten and a chewier texture. Continuing to cook the butter until it browned contributed deep caramel notes, as did dissolving the sugar in the melted butter. Using two egg yolks but only one white added richness without giving the cookies a cakey texture. Studded with gooey chocolate and boasting a complex toffee flavor, these are chocolate chip cookies, perfected. Light brown sugar can be used in place of the dark, but the cookies won't be as full-flavored.

1¾ cups (8¾ ounces) all-purpose flour
½ teaspoon baking soda
14 tablespoons unsalted butter, divided
¾ cup packed (5¼ ounces) dark brown sugar
½ cup (3½ ounces) granulated sugar
2 teaspoons vanilla extract
1 teaspoon table salt
1 large egg plus 1 large yolk
1¼ cups (7½ ounces) semisweet or bittersweet chocolate chips
¾ cup pecans or walnuts, toasted and chopped (optional)

1. Adjust oven rack to middle position and heat oven to 375 degrees. Line 2 baking sheets with parchment paper. Whisk flour and baking soda together in bowl.

2. Melt 10 tablespoons butter in 10-inch skillet over medium-high heat. Continue to cook, swirling skillet constantly, until butter is dark golden brown and has nutty aroma, 1 to 3 minutes. Transfer browned butter to large bowl and stir in remaining 4 tablespoons butter until melted. Whisk in brown sugar, granulated sugar, vanilla, and salt until incorporated. Whisk in egg and yolk until smooth and no lumps remain, about 30 seconds.

Key Lime Bars

Perfect Chocolate Chip Cookies

Texas Sheet Cake

3. Let mixture sit for 3 minutes, then whisk for 30 seconds. Repeat process of resting and whisking 2 more times until mixture is thick, smooth, and shiny. Using rubber spatula, stir in flour mixture until just combined, about 1 minute. Stir in chocolate chips and pecans, if using.

4. Working with 3 tablespoons dough at a time, roll into balls and space them 2 inches apart on prepared sheets. (Dough balls can be frozen for up to 1 month; bake frozen dough balls in 300-degree oven for 30 to 35 minutes.)

5. Bake cookies, 1 sheet at a time, until golden brown and edges have begun to set but centers are still soft and puffy, 10 to 14 minutes, rotating sheet halfway through baking. Transfer baking sheet to wire rack. Let cookies cool completely before serving. Baked cookies can be stored at room temperature for up to 3 days; to refresh, place in 425-degree oven for 4 to 5 minutes.

Texas Sheet Cake
Serves 12 to 15 `MAKE AHEAD`

Why This Recipe Works A picnic or potluck standby in the Lone Star State, Texas sheet cake is a sheet pan–size, pecan-topped chocolate cake. Its appeal comes not only from the fact that it's easy to transport, uses mostly pantry ingredients, and feeds a crowd: It also offers layers of chocolaty goodness and a range of textures that come from pouring sweet chocolate icing over a cake that's still hot from the oven. Once the cake has cooled, you're left with a layer of icing on top, a fudgy middle layer where the icing and hot cake have melded, and a bottom layer of moist chocolate cake, plus the crunchy pecan topping. For the cake, we relied on a combination of butter and vegetable oil for fat, which produced a dense, brownie-like texture. We wanted the cake's fudgy chocolate flavor to match its fudgy texture, so we used both cocoa powder and melted semisweet chocolate for a cake that was ultrachocolaty yet still moist and dense. Getting the texture of the icing right was key to this cake's success—replacing milk with heavy cream gave it more body, while adding corn syrup produced a lustrous finish.

Cake
- 2 cups (10 ounces) all-purpose flour
- 2 cups (14 ounces) granulated sugar
- ½ teaspoon baking soda
- ½ teaspoon table salt
- 2 large eggs plus 2 large yolks
- ¼ cup sour cream
- 2 teaspoons vanilla extract
- 8 ounces semisweet chocolate, chopped
- ¾ cup vegetable oil

Patriotic Poke Cake

¾ cup water
½ cup (1½ ounces) Dutch-processed cocoa powder
4 tablespoons unsalted butter

Icing
8 tablespoons unsalted butter
½ cup heavy cream
½ cup (1½ ounces) Dutch-processed cocoa powder
1 tablespoon light corn syrup
3 cups (12 ounces) confectioners' sugar
1 tablespoon vanilla extract
1 cup pecans, toasted and chopped

1. For the cake Adjust oven rack to middle position and heat oven to 350 degrees. Grease 18 by 13-inch rimmed baking sheet. Whisk flour, sugar, baking soda, and salt together in large bowl. Whisk eggs and yolks, sour cream, and vanilla in second bowl until smooth.

2. Heat chocolate, oil, water, cocoa, and butter in large saucepan over medium heat, stirring occasionally, until smooth, 3 to 5 minutes. Whisk chocolate mixture into flour mixture until incorporated. Whisk egg mixture into batter, then transfer batter to prepared sheet. Bake until toothpick inserted in center comes out clean, 18 to 20 minutes, rotating sheet halfway through baking. Transfer sheet to wire rack.

3. For the icing About 5 minutes before cake is done baking, heat butter, cream, cocoa, and corn syrup in large saucepan over medium heat, stirring occasionally, until smooth. Off heat, whisk in sugar and vanilla. Spread warm icing evenly over hot cake and sprinkle with pecans. Let cake cool completely in pan on wire rack, about 1 hour, then refrigerate until icing is set, about 1 hour. Cut cake into 24 pieces before serving. (Cake can be refrigerated for up to 2 days. Bring to room temperature before serving.)

Patriotic Poke Cake
Serves 10 to 12 `MAKE AHEAD`

Why This Recipe Works For a festive and impressive Fourth of July dessert, we wanted to create a layer cake that was worthy of serving with fireworks at a summer cookout. To ensure our cake was red, white, and blue all the way through, we decided to turn our layer cake into a poke cake. We started by cooking blueberries and strawberries and then combining each with gelatin to create two colorful, brightly flavored syrups. We used a simple white cake as our base; it was tender and flavorful but also had enough structure to handle a syrup soaking. We used a skewer to poke holes into the cake layers while they were still

in their pans and then drizzled the blueberry syrup over one layer and the strawberry syrup over the other. A simple filling and frosting of whipped cream kept this cake light and refreshing for the summer holidays.

1 cup (5 ounces) blueberries
1¼ cups water, divided
¼ cup (1¾ ounces) sugar, divided
2 tablespoons berry-flavored gelatin
7½ ounces (1½ cups) strawberries, hulled
1 tablespoon strawberry-flavored gelatin
1 recipe White Cake Layers (page 266)
1 recipe Double-Batch Whipped Cream (page 406)

1. Cook blueberries, ¾ cup water, and 2 tablespoons sugar in medium saucepan over medium-low heat, covered, until blueberries are softened, about 8 minutes. Strain mixture through fine-mesh strainer into bowl; discard solids. Whisk berry-flavored gelatin into juices and let cool slightly, about 15 minutes. Repeat cooking and straining using strawberries, remaining ½ cup water, and remaining 2 tablespoons sugar. Whisk strawberry-flavored gelatin into juices and let cool slightly, about 15 minutes.

2. Using skewer, poke 25 holes in top of each cake, twisting gently to form slightly larger holes. Pour cooled blueberry syrup over 1 cake layer. Repeat with cooled strawberry syrup and remaining cake layer. Cover cake pans with plastic wrap and refrigerate until gelatin is set, at least 3 hours or up to 24 hours.

3. Run thin knife around edge of pans. Invert blueberry cake, discarding parchment, onto wire rack, then reinvert onto platter. Spread 1 cup whipped cream evenly over top. Invert strawberry cake onto rack, discarding parchment, and place, right side up, on whipped cream, pressing lightly to adhere. Spread remaining whipped cream over top and sides of cake. Serve.

MAKING POKE CAKE

1. Using skewer, poke about 25 holes over cake, being careful not to poke through to bottom. Twist skewer to enlarge holes.

2. Slowly pour cooled gelatin mixture evenly over surface of cake and it will slowly soak into cake.

White Cake Layers
Makes two 9-inch round cake layers

　1　cup whole milk, room temperature
　6　large egg whites, room temperature
　1　teaspoon vanilla extract
2¼　cups (9 ounces) cake flour
1¾　cups (12¼ ounces) sugar
　4　teaspoons baking powder
　1　teaspoon table salt
12　tablespoons unsalted butter, cut into
　　　12 pieces and softened

1. Adjust oven rack to middle position and heat oven to 350 degrees. Grease two 9-inch round cake pans, line with parchment paper, grease parchment, and flour pans. Whisk milk, egg whites, and vanilla together in bowl.

2. Using stand mixer fitted with paddle, mix flour, sugar, baking powder, and salt on low speed until combined. Add butter, 1 piece at a time, until only pea-size pieces remain, about 1 minute. Add all but ½ cup milk mixture, increase speed to medium-high, and beat until light and fluffy, about 1 minute. Reduce speed to medium-low, add remaining ½ cup milk mixture, and mix until incorporated, about 30 seconds (batter may look curdled). Give batter final stir by hand.

3. Divide batter evenly between prepared pans and smooth tops with rubber spatula. Gently tap pans on counter to settle batter. Bake until toothpick inserted in center comes out with few crumbs attached, 23 to 25 minutes, switching and rotating pans halfway through baking.

4. Let cakes cool in pans on wire rack for 10 minutes. Remove cakes from pans, discarding parchment, and let cool completely on rack, about 2 hours. (Cake layers can be stored at room temperature for up to 24 hours or frozen for up to 1 month; defrost cakes at room temperature.)

Nectarine and Raspberry Slab Galette

Serves 18 to 24　`MAKE AHEAD`

Why This Recipe Works Free-form galettes are perfect for showcasing fresh summer fruit. For a dessert that could feed a crowd we formed an extra-large galette in a baking sheet. The expansive surface left the fruit beautifully exposed, and the surface area of the sheet meant the fruit juices evaporated readily and thickened enough after cooking that we didn't need a thickener. You can toss the fruit mixture in step 4 in two bowls if it doesn't fit in one. Be sure to weigh the flour for this recipe. In the mixing stage, this dough will be moister than most pie doughs, but as it chills it will absorb much of the excess moisture. Be sure to roll the dough on a well-floured counter.

Pie Dough
24　tablespoons (3 sticks) unsalted butter, divided
2¾　cups (13¾ ounces) all-purpose flour, divided
　2　tablespoons sugar
　1　teaspoon table salt
　½　cup ice water, divided

Galette
3¼　pounds ripe but firm nectarines, halved, pitted, and sliced ½ inch thick
12½　ounces (2½ cups) raspberries
　½　cup (3½ ounces) plus 1 tablespoon sugar, divided
　¼　teaspoon table salt

1. For the pie dough Grate 5 tablespoons butter on large holes of box grater and place in freezer. Cut remaining 19 tablespoons butter into ½-inch cubes.

2. Pulse 1¾ cups flour, sugar, and salt in food processor until combined, 2 pulses. Add cubed butter and process until homogeneous paste forms, 40 to 50 seconds. Using your hands, carefully break paste into 2-inch chunks and redistribute evenly around processor blade. Add remaining 1 cup flour and pulse until mixture is broken into pieces no larger than 1 inch (most pieces will be much smaller), 4 to 5 pulses. Transfer mixture to bowl. Add grated butter and toss until butter pieces are separated and coated with flour.

3. Sprinkle ¼ cup ice water over mixture. Toss with rubber spatula until mixture is evenly moistened. Sprinkle remaining ¼ cup ice water over mixture and toss to combine. Press dough with spatula until dough sticks together. Using spatula, divide dough into 2 equal portions. Transfer each portion to sheet of plastic wrap. Working with 1 portion at a time, draw edges of plastic over dough and press firmly on sides and top to form compact, fissure-free mass. Wrap in plastic and form into

Nectarine and Raspberry Slab Galette

7. Adjust oven racks to lower-middle and lowest positions and heat oven to 375 degrees. Gently toss nectarines, raspberries, ½ cup sugar, and salt together in bowl. Spread nectarine mixture evenly over chilled dough-lined sheet. Fold overhanging dough over filling, pleating corners, trimming excess dough as needed, and pinching overlapping edges to secure. (If dough is too stiff to fold, let stand at room temperature until pliable.) Brush dough with water and sprinkle evenly with remaining 1 tablespoon sugar.

8. Place large sheet of aluminum foil directly on lower rack (to catch any bubbling juices). Place galette on upper rack and bake until crust is deep golden brown and fruit is bubbling, about 1 hour, rotating sheet halfway through baking. Let galette cool on wire rack until filling has set, about 2 hours or up to 8 hours. Serve.

ROLLING SLAB PIE DOUGH

1. Starting at short side of 1 piece of dough, loosely roll around rolling pin, then gently unroll over half of long side of sheet, leaving about 2 inches of dough overhanging 3 edges of sheet.

2. Repeat with second piece of dough, overlapping first piece of dough by ½ inch in center of sheet.

3. Ease dough into sheet by gently lifting edges of dough with your hand while pressing into sheet bottom with your other hand.

4. Brush edge where doughs overlap with water, pressing to seal.

5 by 6-inch rectangle. Refrigerate dough for at least 2 hours or up to 2 days. Let chilled dough sit on counter to soften slightly, about 10 minutes, before rolling. (Wrapped dough can be frozen for up to 1 month. If frozen, let dough thaw completely on counter before rolling.)

4. For the galette Line rimmed baking sheet with parchment paper. Roll each dough rectangle into 16 by 11-inch rectangle on floured counter; stack on prepared sheet, separated by second sheet of parchment. Cover loosely with plastic wrap and refrigerate until dough is firm but still pliable, about 10 minutes.

5. Using parchment as sling, transfer chilled dough rectangles to counter; discard parchment. Wipe sheet clean with paper towels and spray with vegetable oil spray. Starting at short side of 1 dough rectangle, loosely roll around rolling pin, then gently unroll over half of long side of prepared sheet, leaving about 2 inches of dough overhanging 3 edges. Repeat with second dough rectangle, unrolling it over empty side of sheet and overlapping first dough piece by ½ inch.

6. Ease dough into sheet by gently lifting edges of dough with your hand while pressing into sheet bottom with your other hand. Brush overlapping edge of dough rectangles with water and press to seal. Leave any dough that overhangs sheet in place. Cover loosely with plastic and refrigerate until firm, about 30 minutes.

Summertime Sips

Please note that liquid ingredients in all recipes are measured in fluid ounces.
■ FAST (30 minutes or less total time) ■ NO COOK ■ MAKE AHEAD
Photos (clockwise from top left): Frozen Hurricanes; Watermelon-Lime Agua Fresca;
Pimm's Cups; Sangria

Iced Tea

Lemonade

Sweet Iced Tea
Serves 4 to 6 `MAKE AHEAD`

Why This Recipe Works A chilled pitcher of sweet iced tea is the perfect refreshment to pair with the bold flavors and hot days of summer. Our version of iced tea shirks the traditional idea that this drink has to be prepared hot and then cooled down. We skipped the heat and created a version at room temperature that was still perfectly clear and smooth, without any bitterness. We steeped our tea bags in room-temperature water, leaving them for 45 minutes for a strong-flavored brew without bitter undertones. Without heating the tea, granulated sugar couldn't properly dissolve, leaving us with an unpleasantly grainy texture. Instead of putting the sugar straight in the tea, we sweetened with a simple syrup that kept our tea both smooth and sweet. This recipe can be easily doubled.

  6 black tea bags
 33 ounces water, room temperature, divided
  2 tablespoons sugar
  1 lemon, sliced thin, divided
     Ice

1. Tie strings of tea bags together (for easy removal) and place in large bowl along with 32 ounces water; let steep for 45 minutes.

2. Microwave sugar and remaining 1 ounce water in bowl until heated through, about 1 minute. Stir mixture constantly until sugar has dissolved completely. Discard tea bags and pour tea into serving pitcher. Add sugar mixture and half of lemon slices to tea and stir to combine. (Tea can be refrigerated for up to 1 week; lemon flavor will intensify over time.) Serve chilled over ice with remaining lemon slices.

VARIATIONS
Mint Iced Tea
Add ¼ cup fresh mint leaves, bruised with wooden spoon, to bowl along with tea bags and water. Strain before pouring into serving pitcher.

Cranberry-Orange Iced Tea
Substitute 24 ounces cranberry juice for 24 ounces of water in step 1. Substitute ½ orange, halved lengthwise and sliced thin, for lemon.

Pomegranate-Lime Iced Tea
Substitute 8 ounces pomegranate juice for 8 ounces of water in step 1. Substitute lime for lemon.

Lemonade

Serves 6 to 8 NO COOK MAKE AHEAD

Why This Recipe Works Nothing quenches thirst better than a tall ice-filled glass of tart-sweet lemonade. For punched up fruity flavor that toned down the sour taste of tart lemons, we muddled the lemon slices with granulated sugar to extract the oils in the peel. Then, we combined the lemons with some water and freshly squeezed lemon juice—no simple syrup needed—and just a bit of whisking dissolved the sugar. Straining the mixture removed the solid bits of lemon for a smooth drink with sweet, lemony flavor. For a simple and fun watermelon lemonade, we just added watermelon in while we muddled the lemon, and for a more sophisticated take on this childhood classic we created a variation with cucumber and mint that's cool and refreshing. When purchasing lemons, choose large ones that give to gentle pressure; hard lemons have thicker skin and yield less juice. Lemons are commonly waxed to prevent moisture loss, increase shelf life, and protect from bruising during shipping. Scrub them with a vegetable brush under running water to remove wax, or buy organic lemons. Don't worry about the seeds in the extracted juice; the entire juice mixture is strained at the end of the recipe.

1½ cups sugar
13 lemons (2 sliced thin, seeds and ends discarded, 11 juiced to yield 2 cups)
56 ounces cold water

Using potato masher, mash sugar and half of lemon slices in large bowl until sugar is completely wet, about 1 minute. Add water and lemon juice and whisk until sugar is completely dissolved, about 1 minute. Strain mixture through fine-mesh strainer set over serving pitcher, pressing on solids to extract as much juice as possible; discard solids. Add remaining lemon slices to lemonade and refrigerate until chilled, about 1 hour. (Lemonade can be refrigerated for up to 1 week.) Stir to recombine before serving chilled over ice.

VARIATIONS

Watermelon Lemonade

Reduce water to 48 ounces. Mash 4 cups coarsely chopped seedless watermelon with lemon slices.

Cucumber-Mint Lemonade

Mash 1 thinly sliced peeled cucumber and 1 cup fresh mint leaves with lemon slices. Add 1 thinly sliced peeled cucumber and ½ cup fresh mint leaves to strained lemonade with remaining lemon slices.

Farmers' Market Find   Watermelon

You're probably used to seeing watermelon at the supermarket, sold in halves, wedges, and precut chunks. In the summer, you'll see whole melons at supermarkets and farm stands alike. A seeded watermelon is your typical round or oblong pink-and-green melon with black seeds throughout (the seeds you'd spit out as you eat around them). There are several varieties of seedless watermelon, all of which are hybrid breeds. Miniature watermelons are cute and small with a thinner rind. At the summer farmers' market, you may also see yellow or orange watermelons, which tend to have slightly sweeter flesh than pink melons.

Watermelon-Lime Agua Fresca

Serves 8 to 10 FAST NO COOK MAKE AHEAD

Why This Recipe Works Agua fresca means "fresh water" and is the catchall term for a variety of beverages made by combining fruits, grains, seeds, or flowers with sugar and water. To make a version with one of summer's favorite fruits—watermelon—we whizzed chunks of melon with water in a blender and strained out the pulp before accenting the mixture with lime juice, agave nectar, and a pinch of salt to bring out the sweet and tart flavors. Watermelons vary in sweetness. Adjust the amounts of lime juice and sweetener to your taste.

8 cups 1-inch pieces seedless watermelon
16 ounces water
2 ounces lime juice (2 limes), plus extra for seasoning
2 tablespoons agave nectar or honey, plus extra for seasoning
¼ teaspoon table salt
   Fresh mint leaves (optional)

Working in 2 batches, process watermelon and water in blender until smooth, about 30 seconds. Strain mixture through fine-mesh strainer into 2-quart pitcher; discard solids. Stir in lime juice, agave, and salt. Season with extra lime juice and extra agave to taste. Serve chilled over ice, garnished with mint, if using. (Agua fresca can be refrigerated for up to 5 days; stir to recombine before serving.)

Hibiscus-Guava Agua Fresca

Aperol Spritz

Hibiscus-Guava Agua Fresca
Serves 8 `MAKE AHEAD`

Why This Recipe Works A popular herbal drink, hibiscus tea is an infusion made from the deep magenta–colored calyxes (outer layers) of the roselle flower, a particular species of hibiscus. It has a tart, cranberry-like flavor and is used in many different herbal tea blends as well as on its own. Our goal here was a fruity, refreshing nonalcoholic beverage that would go down easy at an outdoor party on a hot summer day. We started by brewing hibiscus tea using our favorite room-temperature brewing method for iced tea. We then sampled our hibiscus tea mixed with every variety of fruit juice we could imagine and settled on the sweet, mildly tart taste of guava nectar as the winner. To sweeten our juicy tea, we favored mint syrup, which brought an herbal lift to the flavor. A small dose of lemon juice added some citrus acidity to round out the flavors perfectly and make it even more refreshing after a long afternoon in the sun. For the best flavor, look for hibiscus tea that is 100 percent hibiscus. You can find guava nectar in the international aisle of most well-stocked supermarkets; if not, you can substitute pineapple or mango juice.

Agua Fresca
- 10 hibiscus tea bags
- 28 ounces water, room temperature
- 14 ounces guava nectar, chilled
- 2 ounces lemon juice, plus lemon slices for garnishing
- ¼ cup fresh mint leaves

Mint Syrup
- 6 tablespoons sugar
- 2½ ounces water
- ¼ cup fresh mint leaves

1. For the agua fresca Tie strings of tea bags together (for easy removal) and place in serving pitcher or large container along with water; let steep for 45 minutes.

2. For the mint syrup Meanwhile, heat sugar and water in small saucepan over medium heat, whisking often, until sugar has dissolved, about 5 minutes; do not boil. Stir in mint and let cool completely, about 30 minutes. Strain syrup through fine-mesh strainer into airtight container; discard solids.

3. Discard tea bags. Stir guava nectar, mint syrup, and lemon juice into tea. Cover and refrigerate until well chilled, at least 2 hours or up to 5 days.

4. Stir agua fresca to recombine, then serve chilled in chilled glasses filled with ice, garnishing individual portions with lemon slices and mint leaves.

Switchel

Serves 12   `MAKE AHEAD`

Why This Recipe Works From the 1700s all the way through the 1900s, switchel was traditionally served to farmers working in the fields during haying season. (In fact, another common name for switchel was haymaker's punch.) Today it is still served in some Amish communities. This drink was all about quenching thirst and fortifying the body for more work. You could consider it the original energy drink or health tonic, since both cider vinegar and maple syrup contain potassium, an electrolyte, and ginger contains curcumin, which is an anti-inflammatory. The added ginger was also a way to quell any stomach issues that might emerge as farmers drank so much water in the fields. The vinegar helped to maintain the balance of acidity already present in the body. But for our purposes, we like this refresher just as well on a lazy, hot summer afternoon. We liked a balance of 6 ounces cider vinegar to 4 ounces pure maple syrup. Two tablespoons of grated fresh ginger gave the spicy warmth we were looking for without overpowering the delicate maple flavor. Last but not least, the oats gave the drink body. Traditionally, when oats were added, they would not be strained out, and farmers would snack on their switchel-soaked oatmeal. The longer you let the switchel chill before straining, the stronger the ginger flavor will be. Do not substitute pancake syrup for the maple syrup. Feel free to adjust the tartness with water to suit your taste.

48 ounces water
6 ounces cider vinegar
4 ounces pure maple syrup
¼ cup old-fashioned rolled oats
2 tablespoons grated fresh ginger
1 teaspoon grated lemon zest, plus lemon slices for garnishing
¼ teaspoon table salt

1. Bring all ingredients to brief simmer in large saucepan over medium-high heat. Let cool to room temperature, about 1 hour. Transfer switchel to bowl, cover, and refrigerate until flavors meld, at least 6 hours or up to 1 day.

2. Strain mixture through fine-mesh strainer set over serving pitcher or large container, pressing on solids to extract as much liquid as possible; discard solids. Serve chilled in chilled glasses filled with ice, garnishing individual portions with lemon slices. (Switchel can be refrigerated for up to 1 week.)

Aperol Spritz

Serves 8   `FAST`   `NO COOK`

Why This Recipe Works Low in alcohol, and with just the right balance between bitter and sweet, the Aperol spritz is one of Italy's most popular cocktails for relaxing and cooling off. With its fiery sunset-orange hue, it's also among the most beautiful. This fizzy cocktail was created in the Veneto region of Italy in the 1950s. Sometimes other mildly bitter liqueurs are used instead of Aperol, and we tested a few: Campari made a bolder, more bitter spritz, and Cynar (an artichoke-based liqueur) made an herbaceous cocktail. But Aperol was our favorite. The secret formula for this liqueur was developed more than 100 years ago; it includes bitter and sweet oranges, herbs, and roots (including rhubarb). The spritz's popularity explosion has generated countless variations made with various ingredients, but we went back to the source for our Aperol spritz, using the three original components: Aperol, prosecco, and seltzer, gently stirred so as not to lose the fizzy splendor. (Cava or another dry sparkling wine also works well here.) When creating our version, we experimented with different proportions, but tasters agreed that adding 3 parts sparkling wine, along with 2 parts Aperol and 1 part seltzer, achieved the most balanced and complex flavor. Garnishes for the Aperol spritz can be the subject of passionate debate. An orange wedge or peel and green olives are traditional, but these days the olives are often left out, especially outside Italy. In the test kitchen, we appreciated the intriguing salty note a couple of green olives brought to our cocktail, but feel free to omit, if you prefer.

24 ounces dry sparkling wine, such as prosecco or cava, chilled
16 ounces Aperol
8 ounces seltzer, chilled
Brine-cured green olives (optional)
8 strips orange peel

Fill 8 chilled wineglasses halfway with ice. Add 3 ounces wine, 2 ounces Aperol, and 1 ounce seltzer to each glass. Using bar spoon, gently lift mixture from bottom of glasses to top to combine. Top each with additional ice and garnish with olives, if using. Pinch 1 orange peel strip over each drink and rub outer edge of glass with peel, then garnish with orange peel and serve chilled.

Mojitos

Serves 8 `FAST` `NO COOK` `MAKE AHEAD`

Why This Recipe Works Origin stories for the mojito range from it being invented during Sir Francis Drake's attempted plunder of Cuba in 1586 to it being concocted in a Havana bar that Ernest Hemingway frequented in the 1950s. But while the origins of the mojito are unclear, the deliciousness of this king of muddled drinks is not. Fresh and herbaceous from muddled mint, sweet yet tart from fresh lime juice and sugar, and with a kick of white rum and a fizzy splash of seltzer, the mojito is perennially popular and perfectly suited to hot summer nights. Yet there are some versions of a mojito that we'd rather not drink again: those with a crunchy layer of undissolved sugar at the bottom, and those where we have to strain out shreds of muddled mint with our teeth. To solve the first problem, we skipped the muddling altogether and instead processed a generous amount of mint with simple syrup instead of granulated sugar to ensure that the sweetener was fully dissolved in the cocktail. We added the rum, lime juice, and some water to the blender and pulsed the mixture until combined before straining it through a fine-mesh strainer to avoid shreds of herb clogging up our straws or our teeth. We then refrigerated the strained liquid until fully chilled. Topped with chilled seltzer and garnished with a fresh sprig of mint, our drink was both refreshing and easy to drink.

- 2½ cups fresh mint leaves, plus 8 mint sprigs for garnishing
- 8 ounces Simple Syrup (page 275)
- 16 ounces white rum
- 6 ounces lime juice (6 limes)
- 4 ounces cold water
- 32 ounces plain seltzer, chilled

1. Process mint leaves and simple syrup in blender until coarsely chopped, about 10 seconds. Add rum, lime juice, and water to blender and pulse until combined, about 2 pulses. Strain mixture through fine-mesh strainer set over serving pitcher or large container, pressing on solids to extract as much liquid as possible; discard solids. Cover and refrigerate until mixture is well chilled, at least 2 hours or up to 1 day.

2. Divide mixture into 8 chilled glasses half-filled with ice. Add 4 ounces seltzer to each glass and, using teaspoon, gently lift rum mixture from bottom of glasses to top to combine. Top with additional ice and garnish with mint sprigs. Serve chilled.

Pimm's Cups

Serves 12 `FAST` `NO COOK` `MAKE AHEAD`

Why This Recipe Works No drink is more evocative of English summertime than a Pimm's cup. In summer, go to any society event or even a regular pub and ask for one and they'll know exactly what you're talking about (they'll probably have premixed pitchers waiting). Fruit cups were a Victorian homemade concoction of fruit, liqueurs, and gin, and James Pimm is largely credited with making premixed fruit cups popular by serving them at his fashionable oyster bar in the City of London in the 1840s. By 1865, his aperitif known as Pimm's No.1—a gin-based liqueur with sweet fruit and slightly bitter herbal flavors—was sold prebottled, and now "Pimm's" is synonymous with fruit cups. A Pimm's cup is made by combining Pimm's No.1 with English-style lemonade (which is clear and sparkling, with a well-judged sweet-sour balance). It should always be lavishly garnished with fruit. The closest substitute for the lemonade we could find in the United States was lemon-lime soda or ginger ale, but neither passed muster, as both distracted from the spiced, caramelized orange flavor of the Pimm's. Making our own lemonade from Simple Syrup, fresh lemon juice, and seltzer gave us much better results—clean, balanced, and bright. We infused our Pimm's mixture in a pitcher with some fresh lemon slices, cucumber, and mint, garnishing each drink with more of the same. In order to keep the drink sparkling, we gently stirred in the seltzer just before serving. The strawberry is a traditional (and properly British) garnish.

- 20 ounces Pimm's No.1
- 8 ounces Simple Syrup (page 275)
- 5 lemons (1 sliced thin, 4 juiced to yield 6 ounces), plus lemon slices for garnishing
- 1 English cucumber, sliced thin, divided
- ½ cup fresh mint leaves, chopped, plus mint sprigs for garnishing
- 32 ounces plain seltzer, chilled
  Strawberries

1. Combine Pimm's, simple syrup, lemon slices and juice, half of cucumber, and chopped mint in serving pitcher or large container. Cover and refrigerate until flavors meld and mixture is well chilled, at least 2 hours or up to 8 hours.

2. Gently stir seltzer into Pimm's mixture. Serve chilled in chilled glasses filled with ice, garnishing individual portions with extra lemon slice, remaining cucumber slices, mint sprig, and strawberry.

Sangria

Serves 12 `NO COOK` `MAKE AHEAD`

Why This Recipe Works From its humble—and ancient—roots in Spain, sangria has grown to become a party drink mainstay around the world. Many people think of sangria as a random collection of fruit chunks in overly sweetened wine. To create a robust, winey sangria with pure flavor, we experimented with untold varieties of fruit and eventually concluded that simpler is better. With red wine, we preferred the straightforward tang of citrus in the form of oranges and lemons, discovering that the zest and pith as well as the fruit itself made an important contribution to flavor. Some orange liqueur complemented and deepened the citrus flavor of the fruit. With white wine, we preferred the crisp taste of apples and pears, highlighted with brandy instead of orange liqueur. For another twist uniquely suited for summertime, rosé seemed like a natural pairing with mixed berries; for our liqueur, we wanted something more floral and delicate, and chose elderflower. The longer sangria rests before serving, the smoother and mellower it will taste. Give it an absolute minimum of 2 hours and up to 8 hours, if possible.

> 2 (750-ml) bottles fruity red wine, such as Merlot
> 4 ounces orange liqueur
> 4 ounces Simple Syrup
> 3 oranges (2 sliced thin, 1 juiced to yield 4 ounces)
> 2 lemons, sliced thin

1. Combine all ingredients in serving pitcher or large container. Cover and refrigerate until flavors meld and mixture is well chilled, at least 2 hours or up to 8 hours.

2. Stir sangria to recombine, then serve chilled in chilled wineglasses half-filled with ice, garnishing individual portions with macerated fruit.

VARIATIONS
White Sangria

Substitute fruity white wine, such as Riesling, for red wine, brandy for orange liqueur, 8 ounces apple juice for orange juice, and 2 apples or pears, sliced thin, for orange and lemon slices.

Rosé Sangria

Rosé Sangria

Substitute rosé wine for red wine, elderflower liqueur for orange liqueur, 8 ounces pomegranate juice for orange juice, and 2 cups mixed berries for orange and lemon slices.

Simple Syrup
Makes about 8 ounces

> ¾ cup sugar
> 5 ounces warm tap water

Whisk sugar and warm water together in bowl until sugar has dissolved. Let cool completely, about 10 minutes, before transferring to airtight container. (Syrup can be refrigerated for up to 1 month.)

Margaritas

Micheladas

Margaritas
Serves 12 `NO COOK` `MAKE AHEAD`

Why This Recipe Works Margaritas are often thought of as the ultimate summer party drink, especially the frozen versions. However, in a traditional margarita the fresh citrus flavors have an even stronger chance to shine, as their brightness is not in danger of being dulled by frozen temperatures. For a superior fresh margarita worthy of being called the best, we sought a balanced blend of fresh citrus flavors and tequila. Mixes and bottled juice had no place in our cocktail. Not only did we insist on freshly squeezed juice, but we also steeped lemon and lime zest in their own juice, along with spirits and simple syrup, for a deep, tangy, refreshing flavor. The longer the zest and juice mixture is allowed to steep, the more developed the citrus flavors will be in the finished margaritas. We found that the key was using the right proportions of alcohol and citrus juice—equal parts tequila, orange liqueur, and juice. *Blanco* tequila will give the margaritas a stronger, more spirit-forward flavor. *Reposado* tequila, which is aged about 12 months, will bring a smoother, more mellow flavor. For the orange liqueur, you can use a clear-spirit-based one, such as Cointreau.

16 ounces blanco or reposado tequila
16 ounces orange liqueur
 4 teaspoons finely grated lime zest plus 8 ounces juice (8 limes), plus lime wedges for garnishing
 4 teaspoons finely grated lemon zest plus 8 ounces juice (6 lemons)
 6 ounces water
 3 ounces Simple Syrup (page 275)
 ½ cup kosher salt (optional)

1. Combine tequila, liqueur, lime zest and juice, lemon zest and juice, water, and simple syrup in bowl. Cover and refrigerate until flavors meld and mixture is well chilled, at least 2 hours or up to 1 day.

2. Strain mixture through fine-mesh strainer set over serving pitcher or large container, pressing on solids to extract as much liquid as possible; discard solids. Keep margarita chilled in refrigerator until ready to serve.

3. Spread salt, if using, into even layer in shallow bowl. Moisten about ½ inch of chilled glass or margarita glass rims by running lime wedge around outer edge; dry any excess juice with paper towel. Roll moistened rims in salt to coat. Remove any excess salt that falls into glass. Serve margaritas chilled in prepared glasses filled with ice, garnishing each with lime wedge.

House Punch

Serves 8 `MAKE AHEAD`

Why This Recipe Works This sweet-sour punch is a fresh mixture of fruity summer flavors and our more sophisticated take on the zombie cocktail. One of the original tiki drinks, the zombie was invented in Hollywood in the 1930s. Nowadays this "lethal libation" is firmly part of the classic tiki drink canon and is a mainstay at most modern tiki bars. Traditionally, it's a potent mix of different rums, citrus and other juices, and sweetener. But like many tiki drinks, the recipe has been interpreted badly over the years and has often ended up being a kitchen-sink amalgamation of whatever the barkeep has on hand. Possibly, this has led to the more imaginative tales about its madness-inducing properties. While we can't claim ours to be mind-altering, the smooth aged rum, combined with just two juices, nutty orgeat, and warmly spiced syrup, ensures that this drink does go down easy. Freshly grated nutmeg will be the more aromatic and flavorful choice, but preground nutmeg will also work. Fresh pineapple wedges make a nice additional garnish, if you like.

Spiced Syrup
- ¼ cup sugar
- 2 ounces water
- ½ cinnamon stick
- 3 allspice berries, lightly crushed
- 2 whole cloves

Punch
- 16 ounces aged rum
- 6 ounces pineapple juice
- 6 ounces lime juice (6 limes)
- 4 ounces orgeat syrup
- 1 teaspoon old-fashioned aromatic bitters
- Ground nutmeg

1. For spiced syrup Heat sugar, water, cinnamon stick, allspice berries, and cloves in small saucepan over medium heat, whisking often, until sugar has dissolved, about 5 minutes; do not boil. Let cool completely, about 30 minutes. Strain syrup through fine-mesh strainer into airtight container; discard solids.

2. For punch Combine rum, pineapple juice, lime juice, orgeat syrup, spiced syrup, and bitters in serving pitcher or large container. Cover and refrigerate until well chilled, at least 2 hours or up to 3 days.

3. Stir punch to recombine. Serve chilled in chilled glasses half-filled with ice or containing 1 large ice cube, sprinkling individual portions with nutmeg.

Micheladas

Serves 8 `FAST` `NO COOK`

Why This Recipe Works The Michelada is a spicy cold-beer cocktail meant to be drunk on a blisteringly hot day—or as a hangover cure. Originating in Mexico, the Michelada has lots of variations there, depending on what region you're in. The drink made it to America (via Texas) only relatively recently, in the 1990s. American versions often have tomato juice, but in Mexico they are just as likely to omit it. One constant is fresh lime. We found that a generous 2 ounces of lime juice added the refreshing tartness we sought. To balance that tartness, we added doses of Worcestershire sauce and hot sauce, finding that a thicker hot sauce contributed a bit of body. To ensure that everything was well blended, we combined the flavorful seasoning ingredients in the glass before pouring in the beer. Use a well-chilled Mexican lager here. Our favorite is Tecate, but Corona Extra or Modelo will also work. Depending on the size of your glass, you may have some beer left over—we'll let you decide what to do with it. We recommend Cholula and Tapatío hot sauces for their flavor and thicker consistencies. If using a thinner, more vinegary hot sauce such as Tabasco, start with half the amount called for and adjust to your taste after mixing.

- ½ cup kosher salt
- ½ teaspoon chili powder
- 16 ounces lime juice (16 limes), plus lime wedges for garnishing
- ⅓ cup hot sauce
- ¼ cup Worcestershire sauce
- 8 (12-ounce) bottles lager, chilled

1. Combine salt and chili powder on small plate and spread into even layer. Moisten about ½ inch of 8 chilled glass rims by running lime wedge around outer edge; dry any excess juice with paper towel. Roll moistened rims in salt to coat. Remove any excess salt that falls into glasses; set aside.

2. Fill prepared glasses halfway with ice. Add 2 ounces lime juice, 1½ teaspoons hot sauce, and ¾ teaspoon Worcestershire to each glass and stir to combine using tea spoon. Add 1 bottle beer to each glass and, using spoon, gently lift lime mixture from bottom of glasses to top to combine. Top with additional ice and garnish with lime wedges. Serve chilled.

Horchata Borracha

Serves 4 `NO COOK` `MAKE AHEAD`

Why This Recipe Works Every household and restaurant in Mexico boasts its own version of wildly popular *horchata*, a traditional milky drink made by steeping raw rice, and sometimes various nuts or seeds, in water with warm spices, then blending the mixture to creamy goodness. It's the perfect complement to spicy Mexican cuisine or fantastic on its own as a refreshing summer indulgence. Our *borracha* ("drunken") version started traditionally enough, but we found that adding almonds to the rice base lent more complex flavor and a creamier feel to the beverage. We combined water, almonds, sugar, and rice with vanilla extract and cinnamon. Letting the mixture soak overnight not only softened the nuts and rice (making blending easier) but also deepened the flavor infusion. We then blended the mixture until the rice and almonds broke down. The addition of heavy cream helped make the horchata even creamier. Our spirit of choice for our Horchata Borracha was clear: The lighter body and tropical toasted sugar flavors of white rum were ideal. For a nonalcoholic version of this cocktail, omit the rum and increase the water to 24 ounces.

20 ounces water
5 ounces whole, slivered, or sliced blanched almonds
½ cup sugar
¼ cup long-grain white rice
¾ teaspoon vanilla extract
½ teaspoon ground cinnamon, plus extra for garnishing
¼ teaspoon table salt
6 ounces white rum
4 ounces heavy cream
Lime slices

1. Combine water, almonds, sugar, rice, vanilla, cinnamon, and salt in bowl. Cover and let sit at room temperature for at least 12 hours or up to 24 hours.

2. Set fine-mesh strainer over 8-cup liquid measuring cup and line with triple layer of cheesecloth that overhangs edges. Process almond mixture in blender until smooth, 30 to 60 seconds, scraping down sides of blender jar as needed.

3. Transfer mixture to prepared strainer and let drain until liquid no longer runs freely, about 5 minutes. Pull edges of cheesecloth together to form pouch, then firmly squeeze pouch to extract as much liquid from pulp as possible; discard pulp. You should have 2 cups liquid. Stir in rum and cream, cover, and refrigerate until completely chilled, at least 1 hour or up to 2 days. Stir to recombine, then divide into 4 chilled glasses filled with ice. Garnish with lime slices and cinnamon and serve chilled.

Peach-Strawberry Frosé

Serves 4 `NO COOK` `MAKE AHEAD`

Why This Recipe Works Frosé, frozen rosé wine blended with other ingredients, is a hip new kid on the summer beverage block, having become popular only in the past couple of years. But oh how popular it is! People can't seem to get enough of this pretty, pink, fruit-forward wine cocktail, and with good reason. Though you may see it churning away in countertop machines at restaurants, it's simple to make at home. While some recipes call for pouring wine right from bottle to blender, we discovered that freezing some of the wine first in ice cube trays created the best slushy texture. Many recipes call for strawberries and lemon juice, but we found this to be overwhelming. Instead, combining equal parts strawberries and peaches resulted in a light, fresh fruitiness that enhanced rather than suppressed the flavor of the wine. We used frozen fruit (fruit picked at the peak of ripeness and then frozen); this, along with the wine ice cubes, eliminated the need for adding regular ice cubes (which, in testing, caused the frosé to have an unpleasantly icy consistency). The risk of brain freeze has never been more worth it! Use a fruitier rather than a drier rosé for this cocktail.

1 (750-ml) bottle rosé wine
3 ounces Simple Syrup (page 275)
4½ ounces (1 cup) frozen strawberries
4½ ounces (1 cup) frozen peaches
Fresh strawberry slices

1. Measure out and reserve 10 ounces wine. Divide remaining wine between 2 ice cube trays and freeze until firm, about 2 hours. (Frozen wine cubes can be transferred to zipper-lock bag and kept frozen for up to 2 months.)

2. Add reserved wine, simple syrup, strawberries, peaches, and frozen wine cubes to blender (in that order) and process until smooth, about 1 minute, scraping down sides of blender jar as needed. Divide into 4 chilled wineglasses. Garnish with strawberry slices and serve.

VARIATION
Peach Friesling
Substitute sweet (spätlese) Riesling for rosé, omit strawberries, and increase peaches to 2 cups.

Bourbon Cherry Slush

8 ounces bourbon
½ cup frozen orange juice concentrate
1 teaspoon old-fashioned aromatic bitters
1 pound (4 cups) frozen sweet cherries
20 ounces (5 cups) ice cubes
   Orange wedges
   Cocktail cherries

Add bourbon, orange juice concentrate, bitters, cherries, and ice to blender (in that order) and process until smooth, about 1 minute, scraping down sides of blender jar as needed. Divide into 4 chilled glasses. Garnish with orange wedges and cocktail cherries and serve.

Florentine Freeze
Serves 4 FAST NO COOK

Why This Recipe Works In any Italian piazza in the predinner hour, at any time of year, you will find friends catching up over *aperitivi*. Often that early evening drink is a Negroni. But for scorching summer days, we wanted to create a frozen riff on this classic cocktail, which is traditionally equal parts Campari, gin, and sweet vermouth. To lighten up the strong flavors a bit, we opted to use fruit juice in place of the vermouth. We favored orange juice since its sweet flavor tempered both the herbal spiciness of Campari and the botanical notes of the gin. But simply dumping a lot of ice into the blender along with the juice and other ingredients resulted in a soupy, decidedly unslushy concoction. A trick we learned during our testing of frozen drinks was to swap out fresh juice for frozen concentrate. We tried that here, and the orange juice concentrate added its sweet flavor to the Campari and gin while also helping create the proper smoothly icy texture without excess dilution of flavor. Proving that not all frozen drinks need to be sweet-tart, our Florentine Freeze achieved a complex herbal-bittersweet flavor that was *molto delizioso*.

4 ounces Campari
4 ounces gin
1 (12-ounce) container frozen orange juice concentrate
20 ounces (5 cups) ice cubes
   Orange slices

Add Campari, gin, orange juice concentrate, and ice to blender (in that order) and process until smooth, about 1 minute, scraping down sides of blender jar as needed. Divide into 4 chilled glasses. Garnish with orange slices and serve.

Bourbon Cherry Slush
Serves 4 FAST NO COOK

Why This Recipe Works Cherry slush from the ice cream truck ranks among the fondest of summertime childhood memories for many. We wanted a thoroughly grown-up version of this icy treat to help recall thoughts of those simpler times. Starting with a full pound of frozen sweet cherries guaranteed strong, delicious cherry flavor while ensuring that this cocktail would be summery but not seasonally dependent. Because the red-fruit flavor of cherries goes so well with the oaky, caramel-vanilla notes of bourbon (think about the old-fashioned or the Manhattan), this whiskey was a clear choice for our adult slush. To add a touch of tartness to balance the rich flavors of the cherries and bourbon, we turned to frozen orange juice concentrate. The OJ boosted that fruity, fun flavor we've come to expect from traditional (that is, nonalcoholic) slush. For a more complex flavor profile, we added several drops of old-fashioned aromatic bitters. With every frosty sip, this Bourbon-Cherry Slush conjured up that familiar ice cream truck jingle and reminded us that, even as grown-ups, it's good to relax and enjoy lazy summers in the present.

Frozen Hurricanes

Serves 4 FAST NO COOK

Why This Recipe Works This tropical, brightly hued beverage is a tiki drink beloved for its sweet, fruity flavors and festive vibe. However, the frozen versions you typically find these days are pumped from giant machines, mix-based, garishly red from dye, and laden with artificial ingredients and harsh, cheap booze. For our Frozen Hurricanes, we wanted to bring this drink back to its quality roots. We tried many iterations with various fruit juices and eventually narrowed our version down to three: passion fruit, orange, and lime. To get the frozen consistency just right, ice alone wasn't enough, so we adjusted our cocktail with frozen passion fruit puree and a freezer staple, orange juice concentrate. This drink typically has a combination of rums, but after testing several mixtures, we discovered that we preferred just one type in our Frozen Hurricanes: aged rum, which provided deep, rich flavor while still allowing the fruit juices to shine. A bit of sweetness from grenadine balanced the sour notes of the passion fruit, keeping this frozen rum punch delightfully balanced.

- ½ cup frozen passion fruit puree
- ½ cup frozen orange juice concentrate
- 8 ounces aged rum
- 1½ ounces lime juice (2 limes), plus lime wedges for garnishing
- 1½ ounces grenadine
- 16 ounces (4 cups) ice cubes
  Cocktail cherries

Add passion fruit puree, orange juice concentrate, rum, lime juice, grenadine, and ice to blender (in that order) and process until smooth, about 1 minute, scraping down sides of blender jar as needed. Divide into 4 chilled glasses. Garnish with lime wedges and cocktail cherries and serve.

Piña Coladas

Serves 4 FAST NO COOK

Why This Recipe Works The piña colada is a magical combination of pineapple, coconut, and rum and can be enjoyed either shaken over ice or frozen. We wanted to create a frozen version bursting with real tropical fruit flavor. With that in mind, we first compared fresh pineapple, frozen pineapple, canned pineapple, and pineapple juice. We found the natural flavor of fresh pineapple more appealing than the processed flavor of canned or juice. Since we were making a frozen drink, frozen pineapple offered the best of both worlds,

providing the flavor of fresh while reducing the amount of additional ice needed for texture. Next we experimented with cream of coconut, coconut milk, and coconut cream. Cream of coconut made our drink taste like sunblock and coconut milk was too thin and watery. We chose coconut cream for its mouth-feel and rich coconut flavor. Choosing the rum from the array of colors and grades was no easy task (though it was a fun one). White rum provided the right flavor, holding its own with the pineapple and coconut without overpowering them. For a dramatic presentation that adds complexity, we suggest floating some aged rum on top. Do not substitute cream of coconut for the coconut cream, as the former is heavily sweetened.

- 1 (15-ounce) can coconut cream
- 6 ounces white rum
- 2 ounces Simple Syrup (page 275)
- 12 ounces (3 cups) frozen pineapple chunks
- 8 ounces (2 cups) ice cubes
  Fresh pineapple slices

Add coconut cream, rum, simple syrup, pineapple, and ice to blender (in that order) and process until smooth, about 1 minute, scraping down sides of blender jar as needed. Divide into 4 chilled glasses. Garnish with pineapple and serve.

VARIATION
Nonalcoholic Piña Coladas
Substitute pineapple juice for rum.

Vanilla Milkshakes

Serves 2 (Makes about 4 cups) FAST NO COOK

Why This Recipe Works For an old-fashioned soda fountain–style milkshake, we moved from the traditional blender to the food processor. The larger bowl of the food processor exposed more of the ice cream mixture to air and to the walls of the workbowl; this resulted in extra air being incorporated into the milkshakes, which made them lighter, frothier, and easier to sip through a straw. The slightly higher heat generated by the food processor's blade caused more of the ice cream's crystals to melt slightly, creating a smoother milkshake that remained cold but fluid. To ramp up the vanilla flavor in our milkshake, we added a pinch of salt, which also offset the sweetness. Our simple ingredient list and food processor method made it easy to mix up different flavors. Serving these milkshakes in chilled glasses helps them stay colder longer. This recipe can be easily doubled; simply process the milkshakes in two batches.

4 cups vanilla ice cream
4 ounces milk
  Pinch table salt

Let ice cream soften on counter for 15 minutes. Combine all ingredients in food processor and process until smooth, about 1 minute, scraping down sides of bowl as needed. Divide between 2 chilled glasses and serve.

VARIATIONS

Coffee Milkshakes
Add 2 teaspoons instant espresso powder to food processor with other ingredients.

Strawberry Milkshakes
Process 1 pound (3½ cups) thawed frozen strawberries in food processor until smooth, about 1 minute, scraping down sides of bowl as needed. Reduce ice cream to 2 cups and milk to ¼ cup, and add to processor with pureed strawberries.

Chocolate-Banana Milkshakes
Process 1 ripe banana, peeled and halved crosswise, in food processor until smooth, about 1 minute, scraping down sides of bowl as needed. Reduce ice cream to 3 cups and milk to ¼ cup. Add ice cream, milk, ¼ cup malted milk powder, and 1 tablespoon unsweetened cocoa powder to food processor with pureed banana.

INGREDIENT SPOTLIGHT

VANILLA ICE CREAM
You think vanilla is plain? Take a good look at the freezer section of your supermarket—the sheer number of vanilla ice cream choices could make your head spin. With nearly 40 brands on the market nationwide and a slew of different styles, who knows which to pick? In our opinion, what matters most boils down to one thing: vanilla taste. Our favorite vanilla ice cream, **Turkey Hill Original Vanilla Premium Ice Cream**, is silky and full of rich vanilla flavor. It is spoonable and airy but still velvety.

Piña Colada

Chocolate-Banana Milkshakes

CHAPTER 9

Seasonal Sides

■ FAST (30 minutes or less total time)　■ NO COOK　■ MAKE AHEAD
Photos (clockwise from top left): Peach Caprese Salad; Sugar Snap Peas with Pine Nuts, Fennel, and Lemon Zest; Watermelon-Tomato Salad; Sautéed Summer Squash Ribbons; Broiled Eggplant with Basil

While often thought of as a spring vegetable, asparagus is now available year-round and can be found in the early summer months at farmers' markets. There are many asparagus varieties, offshoot varieties, and hybrids, but the basic types you'll most frequently see at the farm stand or grocery store are identifiable by color. You might assume that thinner asparagus spears are younger and more tender than thicker ones. However, the thickness of an asparagus spear has nothing to do with its age— a thin spear will not mature into a thick spear. Instead, the diameter is determined by the age of the entire plant (younger crowns produce more slender stalks) and its variety. We only eat young asparagus—the new shoots of the plant crown. As mature asparagus begins to bud out, the stems become woody and nearly inedible. When shopping for asparagus, look for medium-thick spears, which work best in most recipes, since larger spears must be peeled and pencil-thin spears overcook easily. Much of the flavor and prized texture of asparagus resides in the tips, which are comprised of leaf-like cladodes, or stems. Thick or thin, asparagus is sweet, nutty, and grassy, with a pleasing texture. To maintain asparagus's bright color and crisp texture, trim the bottom ½ inch of the stalks and stand the spears upright in a glass or jar filled with 1 inch of water. Cover with plastic wrap and place the glass in the refrigerator. Asparagus stored this way should remain relatively fresh for about four days; you may need to add a little more water every few days. Retrim the very bottom of the stalks before using.

Green Asparagus The most commonly sold variety, traditional green asparagus is the type from which most other varieties descend.

Purple Asparagus Purple asparagus, a cultivar of green asparagus, gets its violet color from anthocyanins, a beneficial type of antioxidant. Purple asparagus turn green when cooked.

White Asparagus The same variety as green, white asparagus is artificially cultivated under soil, where the spears are shielded from sunlight and prevented from photosynthesizing, which would turn them green from chlorophyll. White asparagus is more tender and has a sweeter, buttery flavor; it is considerably more expensive than green asparagus.

Pan-Steamed Asparagus with Garlic

Serves 6 FAST

Why This Recipe Works To preserve the fresh grassy flavor and color of early-summer asparagus and ensure a crisp-tender texture without leaving it washed out and bland, we combined two cooking methods. We started by briefly sautéing the asparagus in butter in a skillet to add flavor and to keep the color. Adding a little water to the pan and steaming the pieces cooked them through more evenly. Allowing the water to evaporate left the asparagus perfectly crisp-tender and glossed with garlicky butter. This recipe works best with asparagus spears that are about ½ inch thick. If using thinner spears, reduce the uncovered cooking time to 1½ to 2 minutes. Peeling the bottom halves of the spears ensures that the cooked asparagus is tender. This recipe can easily be halved; use a 10-inch skillet if you halve the recipe.

- 2 pounds thin asparagus, trimmed
- 1 tablespoon unsalted butter
- 2 tablespoons water
- 1 garlic clove, minced
- ½ teaspoon table salt

1. Peel bottom halves of spears until white flesh is exposed. Cut spears on bias into 2-inch lengths. Melt butter in 12-inch nonstick skillet over medium-high heat. Add water, garlic, and salt and stir to combine. Add asparagus, shaking skillet to evenly distribute. Cover and cook, without stirring, for 2 minutes.

2. Uncover and continue to cook, stirring occasionally, until skillet is almost dry and asparagus is crisp-tender, 2½ to 3 minutes longer. Serve.

VARIATIONS

Pan-Steamed Asparagus with Anchovies and Red Pepper Flakes

Substitute extra-virgin olive oil for butter and heat until shimmering. Add 2 rinsed and minced anchovy fillets and ¼ teaspoon red pepper flakes to skillet with garlic. Decrease salt to ¼ teaspoon.

Pan-Steamed Asparagus with Lemon and Parmesan

Combine 1 teaspoon grated lemon zest plus 1 tablespoon juice and ¼ teaspoon pepper in small bowl. Stir lemon zest mixture into asparagus and sprinkle with ¼ cup shredded Parmesan before serving.

Pan-Steamed Asparagus with Mint and Almonds

Combine ¼ cup chopped fresh mint, 2 teaspoons sherry vinegar, and ¼ teaspoon smoked paprika in small bowl. Stir mint mixture into asparagus and sprinkle with ¼ cup sliced almonds, toasted, cooled, and lightly crushed, just before serving.

Pan-Steamed Asparagus with Shallots and Herbs

Substitute ¼ cup minced shallots for garlic. Stir ¼ cup chopped fresh chives and 2 teaspoons chopped fresh dill into asparagus before serving.

Asparagus Salad with Radishes, Pecorino Romano, and Croutons

Serves 4 to 6   FAST

Why This Recipe Works Raw asparagus is just as delicious as cooked; it's mildly sweet and nutty, with a delicate crunch and none of the sulfurous flavors that cooked asparagus sometimes has. And when paired with the right dressing or sauce, it can make a supereasy side-dish salad. Many recipes for raw asparagus salads call for cut-up lengths of raw asparagus, but even when we peeled the spears, they were too fibrous. As long as we chose the right spears (bright green, firm, and crisp, with tightly closed tips) and sliced them very thin on the bias, we could avoid woodiness but still keep things crunchy. To complement the fresh asparagus, we wanted a no-cook summery dressing; inspired by the herb garden, we chose mint and basil for a bright, herbaceous flavor. A high ratio of herbs to oil created a pesto-style dressing potent enough to enhance but not mask the flavor of the asparagus. A food processor made it easy to chop the herbs together with Pecorino Romano cheese, garlic, lemon, and seasonings before stirring in extra-virgin olive oil. A few radishes, more Pecorino, and buttery croutons rounded out the salad. Look for asparagus spears between ½ and ¾ inch in diameter. Parmesan can be substituted for the Pecorino Romano. Grate the cheese for the dressing with a rasp-style grater or use the small holes of a box grater; shave the cheese for the salad with a vegetable peeler.

Croutons

- 2 tablespoons unsalted butter
- 1 tablespoon extra-virgin olive oil
- 2 slices hearty white sandwich bread, crusts discarded, cut into ½-inch pieces (1⅓ cups)
- ⅛ teaspoon table salt

Asparagus Salad with Radishes, Pecorino Romano, and Croutons

Pesto Dressing

- 2 cups fresh mint leaves
- ¼ cup fresh basil leaves
- ¼ cup grated Pecorino Romano cheese
- 1 teaspoon grated lemon zest plus 2 teaspoons juice
- 1 garlic clove, minced
- ¾ teaspoon table salt
- ½ cup extra-virgin olive oil

Salad

- 2 pounds thick asparagus, trimmed
- 5 radishes, trimmed and sliced thin
- 2 ounces Pecorino Romano cheese, shaved (¾ cup)

1. For the croutons Heat butter and oil in 12-inch nonstick skillet over medium heat until butter is melted. Add bread pieces and salt and cook, stirring frequently, until golden brown, 7 to 10 minutes. Season with salt and pepper to taste, and set aside.

2. For the pesto dressing Process mint, basil, Pecorino, lemon zest and juice, garlic, and salt in food processor until smooth, about 20 seconds, scraping down sides of bowl as needed. With processor running, slowly add oil until incorporated; transfer to large bowl and season with salt and pepper to taste.

3. For the salad Cut asparagus tips from spears into ¾-inch-long pieces. Slice asparagus spears ⅛ inch thick on bias. Add asparagus tips and spears, radishes, and Pecorino to dressing and toss to combine. Season with salt and pepper to taste. Transfer salad to serving platter and top with croutons. Serve.

VARIATIONS

Asparagus Salad with Grapes, Goat Cheese, and Almonds

Omit croutons. Substitute 6 ounces thinly sliced grapes for radishes and 1 cup crumbled goat cheese for Pecorino in the salad. Add ¾ cup almonds, toasted and chopped, to salad in step 3.

Asparagus Salad with Oranges, Feta, and Hazelnuts

Omit croutons and radishes. Substitute 1 cup crumbled feta cheese for Pecorino in the salad. Cut away peel and pith from 2 oranges. Holding fruit over bowl, use paring knife to slice between membranes to release segments. Add to salad in step 3. Add ¾ cup hazelnuts, toasted, skinned, and chopped, to salad in step 3.

Green Bean Salad with Cherry Tomatoes and Feta

Green Bean Salad with Cherry Tomatoes and Feta

Serves 4 to 6 FAST MAKE AHEAD

Why This Recipe Works With their vibrant color and pleasant texture, in-season green beans are a summer delight. To make the beans in this summer-perfect salad tender, bright green, and deeply flavored, we blanched them in highly concentrated salt water (¼ cup of salt to 2 quarts of water). This quickly softened the pectin in the beans' skins, so they became tender before losing their vibrant color; it also seasoned them inside and out. We paired them with another flavorful summer vegetable—cherry tomatoes—and added mint and parsley for fresh-from-the-garden brightness. Lemon juice added a citrusy lift, and feta cheese lent a salty note. If you don't own a salad spinner, lay the green beans on a clean dish towel to dry in step 2.

1½ pounds green beans, trimmed and cut into 1- to 2-inch lengths
¼ teaspoon table salt, plus salt for cooking green beans
12 ounces cherry tomatoes, halved
¼ cup extra-virgin olive oil
2 tablespoons chopped fresh mint
2 tablespoons chopped fresh parsley
1 tablespoon lemon juice
¼ teaspoon pepper
2 ounces feta cheese, crumbled (½ cup)

1. Bring 2 quarts water to boil in large saucepan over high heat. Add green beans and ¼ cup salt, return to boil, and cook until green beans are bright green and tender, 5 to 8 minutes.

2. While green beans cook, fill large bowl halfway with ice and water. Drain green beans in colander and immediately transfer to ice bath. When green beans are no longer warm to touch, drain in colander and dry thoroughly in salad spinner. (Green beans can be refrigerated in a zipper-lock bag for up to 2 days.)

3. Place green beans, tomatoes, oil, mint, parsley, lemon juice, pepper, and ¼ teaspoon salt in bowl and toss to combine. Transfer to serving platter, sprinkle with feta, and serve.

Green Bean Salad with Cilantro Sauce

Serves 6 to 8 FAST MAKE AHEAD

Why This Recipe Works Fresh green beans make an interesting base for a simple vegetable salad. We came up with a new take on pesto by swapping the traditional basil for bright, grassy cilantro. A single scallion brightened the color of the sauce, and walnuts and garlic cloves, toasted in a skillet, added nutty depth. The fruity flavor of extra-virgin olive oil complemented the other flavors in the dressing nicely. Finally, a touch of lemon juice rounded out the flavors and helped to loosen the sauce to just the right consistency. We blanched the beans in salted water and shocked them to set their vibrant green color and ensure that they were evenly cooked. Don't worry about drying the beans before tossing them with the sauce; any water that clings to the beans will help to thin out the sauce.

- ¼ cup walnuts
- 2 garlic cloves, unpeeled
- 2½ cups fresh cilantro leaves and stems, tough stem ends trimmed (about 2 bunches)
- ½ cup extra-virgin olive oil
- 4 teaspoons lemon juice
- 1 scallion, sliced thin
- ½ teaspoon table salt, plus salt for cooking green beans
- ⅛ teaspoon pepper
- 2 pounds green beans, trimmed

1. Cook walnuts and garlic in 8-inch skillet over medium heat, stirring often, until toasted and fragrant, 5 to 7 minutes; transfer to bowl. Let garlic cool slightly, then peel and roughly chop.

2. Process walnuts, garlic, cilantro, oil, lemon juice, scallion, salt, and pepper in food processor until smooth, about 1 minute, scraping down sides of bowl as needed; transfer to large bowl.

3. Bring 2 quarts water to boil in large pot over high heat. Meanwhile, fill large bowl halfway with ice and water. Add ¼ cup salt and green beans to boiling water and cook until crisp-tender, 3 to 5 minutes. Drain green beans, transfer to ice bath, and let sit until chilled, about 2 minutes. Transfer green beans to bowl with cilantro sauce and gently toss until coated. Season with salt and pepper to taste. Serve. (Salad can be refrigerated for up to 4 hours.)

Spicy Salad with Mustard and Balsamic Vinaigrette

Serves 8 to 10 FAST NO COOK

Why This Recipe Works With wide-ranging varieties of greens—from popular arugula to lesser known types like mustard greens and mizuna—showing up at the summer farmers' markets, we wanted to create a salad to showcase farm-fresh greens that we don't see year-round in addition to our favorite standbys. Many of these summer greens are spicy, peppery, and bitter; we incorporated a number of them in our salad and dressed them with a pungent, mustardy vinaigrette. We envisioned this salad as standing up to rich main dishes like grilled steaks or pasta with summer vegetables, so we used both balsamic vinegar and Dijon mustard as the acidic components. Minced shallot provided another strong flavor and added a bit of texture to our vinaigrette. We mixed the greens and vinaigrette together a little at a time to ensure that all the greens were well covered. Boldly flavored, this spicy salad with mustard and balsamic vinaigrette will wake up any dulled palate.

- 6 tablespoons extra-virgin olive oil
- 4 teaspoons balsamic vinegar
- 1 tablespoon Dijon mustard
- 1 teaspoon minced shallot
- ¼ teaspoon table salt
- ⅛ teaspoon pepper
- 16 ounces (16 cups) spicy greens, such as arugula, watercress, mizuna, and baby mustard greens

Whisk oil, vinegar, mustard, shallot, salt, and pepper in bowl until combined. Place greens in large bowl, drizzle vinaigrette over greens a little at a time, and toss to coat evenly, adding more vinaigrette if greens seem dry. Serve.

Stir-Fried Bok Choy with Soy Sauce and Ginger

Serves 4 to 6 FAST

Why This Recipe Works Bok choy, also known as Chinese cabbage, is one of those vegetables that you'll often see at the farmers' market in summer months but that you might not always know what to do with. Our answer? Stir-frying, which nicely preserves the crisp-tender texture of bok choy stalks.

Broccoli Rabe with Garlic and Red Pepper Flakes

We sliced the bok choy heads and started the stalks first in the skillet, then added the greens later. This way, both stalks and greens ended up perfectly cooked. A combination of soy sauce and sugar dressed the vegetable with subtly sweet umami flavors, and some grated fresh ginger gave the dish an assertive lift. Be sure to add the ginger, and then the soy sauce mixture, just as the edges of the stalks turn translucent; otherwise, the stalks won't retain their bite.

2 tablespoons soy sauce
1 teaspoon sugar
2 tablespoons vegetable oil
1½ pounds bok choy, stalks halved lengthwise then cut crosswise into ½-inch pieces, greens sliced into ½-inch-thick pieces
1 tablespoon grated fresh ginger

1. Whisk soy sauce and sugar in small bowl until sugar has dissolved.

2. Heat oil in 12-inch nonstick skillet over high heat until just smoking. Add bok choy stalks and cook, stirring constantly, until edges begin to turn translucent, about 5 minutes. Stir in ginger and cook until fragrant, about 30 seconds. Add bok choy greens and soy sauce mixture and cook, stirring frequently, until greens are wilted and tender, about 1 minute. Serve.

VARIATION
Stir-Fried Bok Choy with Oyster Sauce and Garlic
Substitute 2 tablespoons oyster sauce (or substitute hoisin sauce, if desired) and 1 tablespoon rice vinegar for soy sauce. Add 2 minced garlic cloves with ginger.

Broccoli Rabe with Garlic and Red Pepper Flakes

Serves 4 FAST

Why This Recipe Works We love this cousin of broccoli because it's easy to prepare in minutes and makes for a satisfying side dish that is compatible with an array of flavors. We were after a quick and dependable method of cooking this aggressive vegetable that would tamp down the bitterness in favor of rounder, more balanced flavor. Blanching the broccoli rabe in a large amount of salted water tamed its bitterness without eliminating its depth of flavor. Then we sautéed the blanched rabe with garlic and red pepper flakes, summertime standbys that complemented the vegetable's strong flavor beautifully.

Sautéed Cabbage with Parsley and Lemon

14 ounces broccoli rabe, trimmed and
cut into 1-inch pieces
Table salt for cooking broccoli rabe
2 tablespoons extra-virgin olive oil
3 garlic cloves, minced
¼ teaspoon red pepper flakes

1. Bring 3 quarts water to boil in large saucepan. Fill large bowl halfway with ice and water. Add broccoli rabe and 2 teaspoons salt to boiling water and cook until wilted and tender, about 2½ minutes. Drain broccoli rabe, then transfer to ice bath and let sit until chilled. Drain again and thoroughly pat dry.

2. Cook oil, garlic, and pepper flakes in 10-inch skillet over medium heat, stirring often, until garlic begins to sizzle, about 2 minutes. Increase heat to medium-high, add broccoli rabe, and cook, stirring to coat with oil, until heated through, about 1 minute. Season with salt and pepper to taste, and serve.

Sautéed Cabbage with Parsley and Lemon

Serves 4 to 6 `FAST`

Why This Recipe Works Cabbage might not be the first vegetable to spring to mind when you think of summer, but you can find various types of seasonal cabbage at farmers' markets. This simple preparation of humble green cabbage brought out the vegetable's natural sweetness and preserved its crisp-tender texture. We pan-steamed and sautéed the cabbage over relatively high heat to cook it quickly, which also added extra flavor from browning. Soaking the cabbage reduced bitterness while providing extra moisture to help the cabbage steam. Onion reinforced the cabbage's sweetness and lemon and parsley lent brightness.

1 small head green cabbage (1¼ pounds), cored and sliced thin
2 tablespoons extra-virgin olive oil, divided
1 onion, halved and sliced thin
¾ teaspoon table salt, divided
¼ teaspoon pepper
¼ cup chopped fresh parsley
1½ teaspoons lemon juice

1. Place cabbage in large bowl and cover with cold water. Let sit for 3 minutes; drain well.

2. Heat 1 tablespoon oil in 12-inch nonstick skillet over medium-high heat until shimmering. Add onion and ¼ teaspoon salt and cook until softened and lightly browned, 5 to 7 minutes; transfer to bowl.

3. Heat remaining 1 tablespoon oil in now-empty skillet over medium-high heat until shimmering. Add cabbage and sprinkle with remaining ½ teaspoon salt and pepper. Cover and cook, without stirring, until cabbage is wilted and lightly browned on bottom, about 3 minutes. Stir and continue to cook, uncovered, until cabbage is crisp-tender and lightly browned in places, about 4 minutes, stirring once halfway through cooking. Off heat, stir in onion, parsley, and lemon juice. Season with salt and pepper to taste, and serve.

VARIATION
Sautéed Cabbage with Fennel and Garlic

Omit pepper. Substitute 1 small head savoy cabbage for green cabbage and 1 fennel bulb, fronds minced, stalks discarded, bulb halved, cored, and sliced thin, for onion. Cook fennel until softened, 8 to 10 minutes, then add 2 minced garlic cloves and ¼ teaspoon red pepper flakes and cook until fragrant, about 30 seconds. Substitute fennel fronds for parsley and increase lemon juice to 2 teaspoons. Drizzle cabbage with extra 1 tablespoon oil and sprinkle with 2 tablespoons grated Parmesan cheese before serving.

SLICING CABBAGE

1. Cut cabbage into quarters, then trim and discard core. Separate cabbage into small stacks of leaves that flatten when pressed.

2. Use chef's knife to cut each stack of cabbage leaves into thin shreds.

Slow-Cooked Whole Carrots
Serves 6

Why This Recipe Works When fresh-from-the-ground carrots grace your local farmers' market, it seems a shame to coat them in anything that will drown their innate sweetness. We wanted a recipe that would utilize carrots' natural sweet flavor while slightly softening them to perfection, and also wanted to keep them whole for an elegantly rustic appearance. Instead of just boiling them, we gently "steeped" the carrots in warm water before cooking to firm up the vegetable's cell walls, making them more resistant to breaking down when cooked at a higher temperature. This activated an enzyme within the carrots that strengthened their pectin. Before their warm soak, we topped the carrots with a fitted piece of parchment paper, called a cartouche, which ensured they cooked evenly from end to end and didn't become mushy. Just a bit of oil in the cooking water provided a slight sheen—no extra sugar necessary. Serve with a simple, flavor-packed relish for a perfect finishing touch. Use carrots that measure ¾ inch to 1¼ inches across at the thickest end. You will need a 12-inch skillet with a tight-fitting lid for this recipe.

>   3 cups water
>   1 tablespoon extra-virgin olive oil
>   ½ teaspoon table salt
>   1½ pounds carrots, trimmed and peeled

1. Cut parchment paper into 11-inch circle, then cut 1-inch hole in center, folding paper as needed.

2. Bring water, oil, and salt to simmer in 12-inch skillet over high heat. Off heat, add carrots, top with parchment, cover skillet, and let sit for 20 minutes.

3. Uncover, leaving parchment in place, and bring to simmer over high heat. Reduce heat to medium-low and cook until most of water has evaporated and carrots are very tender, about 45 minutes.

4. Discard parchment, increase heat to medium-high, and cook carrots, shaking skillet often, until lightly glazed and no water remains, 2 to 4 minutes. Serve.

FOLDING PARCHMENT FOR SLOW-COOKED CARROTS

1. Cut parchment into 11-inch circle, then cut 1-inch hole in center, folding paper as needed to cut out hole.

2. Lay parchment circle on top of carrots, underneath lid, to help retain and evenly distribute moisture during cooking.

Pine Nut Relish
Makes about ¾ cup

>   ⅓ cup pine nuts, toasted
>   1 shallot, minced
>   1 tablespoon sherry vinegar
>   1 tablespoon minced fresh parsley
>   1 teaspoon honey
>   ½ teaspoon minced fresh rosemary
>   ¼ teaspoon smoked paprika
>   ¼ teaspoon table salt
>   Pinch cayenne pepper

Combine all ingredients in small bowl.

Red Pepper and Almond Relish
Makes about ¾ cup

>   ½ cup finely chopped jarred roasted red peppers
>   ¼ cup slivered almonds, toasted and chopped coarse
>   2 tablespoons extra-virgin olive oil
>   2 tablespoons minced fresh parsley
>   1 tablespoon white wine vinegar
>   1 teaspoon minced fresh oregano
>   ¼ teaspoon table salt

Combine all ingredients in small bowl.

Moroccan-Style Carrot Salad

Serves 4 to 6 `FAST` `NO COOK`

Why This Recipe Works Our Moroccan-style salad combines grated carrots with olive oil, citrus, and warm spices like cumin and cinnamon. We tried grating the carrots both with a coarse grater and with a food processor and found that the coarse grater worked better. To complement the earthy carrots, we added juicy orange segments, reserving some of the orange juice to add to the salad dressing. We balanced the sweet orange juice with a squeeze of lemon juice and small amounts of cumin, cayenne, and cinnamon. The musty aroma and slight nuttiness of the cumin nicely complemented the sweetness of the carrots. A touch of honey provided a pleasing floral note. To add color and freshness, we stirred in some minced cilantro before serving. Use the large holes of a box grater to shred the carrots.

    2   oranges
    1   tablespoon lemon juice
    1   teaspoon honey
    ¾   teaspoon ground cumin
    ½   teaspoon table salt
    ⅛   teaspoon cayenne pepper
    ⅛   teaspoon ground cinnamon
    1   pound carrots, peeled and shredded
    3   tablespoons minced fresh cilantro
    3   tablespoons extra-virgin olive oil

1. Cut away peel and pith from oranges. Holding fruit over bowl, use paring knife to slice between membranes to release segments. Cut segments in half crosswise and let drain in fine-mesh strainer set over large bowl, reserving juice.

2. Whisk lemon juice, honey, cumin, salt, cayenne, and cinnamon into reserved orange juice. Add drained oranges and carrots and gently toss to coat. Let sit until liquid starts to pool in bottom of bowl, 3 to 5 minutes.

3. Drain salad in fine-mesh strainer and return to now-empty bowl. Stir in cilantro and oil and season with salt and pepper to taste. Serve.

Slow-Cooked Whole Carrots

Farmers' Market Find   Carrots

Commercially cultivated carrots as we know them—with their bright orange color and crispy-juicy texture—represent just a few of the types of carrots that exist. Bunches containing carrots of various colors can now be found in both farmers' markets and supermarkets. Whether yellow or purple, they can be substituted for orange carrots in any recipe. Purple carrots can lose their color when cooked, so some people prefer to use them in raw preparations only. Perky-looking greens still attached to carrots is a sign of freshness. At home, twist off the greens and store them separately from the carrots for sautéing or using in pestos or salads. The "baby carrots" that you see in supermarkets are actually full-grown carrots that are mechanically cut into smaller pieces and sculpted into small rounded batons. Actual baby carrots that have not fully matured are available at summer farmers' markets. Carrots keep for a least a week in an open plastic produce bag in the refrigerator.

Chopped Carrot Salad with Mint, Pistachios, and Pomegranate Seeds

Skillet Roasted Cauliflower with Garlic and Lemon

Chopped Carrot Salad with Mint, Pistachios, and Pomegranate Seeds

Serves 4 to 6 `FAST` `NO COOK`

Why This Recipe Works This salad showcases raw carrots, using them as an innovative canvas for contrasting flavors and textures. Instead of chopping or grating the carrots by hand, we found that finely chopping them in the food processor produced a delicately crunchy, light-textured base for our salad. We saved even more time on prep by not peeling the carrots; scrubbing them was sufficient, and the skins contributed a subtle but pleasant bitterness to the dish. We added bulk and contrasting flavor with lots of fresh mint (chopped by hand to avoid overprocessing the leaves in the food processor), pomegranate seeds for bright color and bursts of sweet-tart flavor, and toasted pistachios for some nutty crunch. A bright dressing bound it all together. We prefer the convenience and the hint of bitterness that leaving the carrots unpeeled lends to this salad; just be sure to scrub the carrots well before using them.

¾ cup shelled pistachios, toasted
¼ cup extra-virgin olive oil
3 tablespoons lemon juice
1 tablespoon honey
1 teaspoon table salt
½ teaspoon pepper
½ teaspoon smoked paprika
⅛ teaspoon cayenne pepper
1 pound carrots, trimmed and cut into 1-inch pieces
1 cup pomegranate seeds, divided
½ cup minced fresh mint

1. Pulse pistachios in food processor until coarsely chopped, 10 to 12 pulses; transfer to small bowl. Whisk oil, lemon juice, honey, salt, pepper, paprika, and cayenne in large bowl until combined.

2. Process carrots in now-empty processor until finely chopped, 10 to 20 seconds, scraping down sides of bowl as needed. Transfer carrots to bowl with dressing; add ½ cup pomegranate seeds, mint, and half of pistachios and toss to combine. Season with salt to taste. Transfer to serving platter, sprinkle with remaining ½ cup pomegranate seeds and pistachios, and serve.

Chopped Carrot Salad with Radishes and Sesame Seeds

Omit pistachios. Substitute 3 tablespoons vegetable oil and 2 teaspoons toasted sesame oil for olive oil. Substitute rice vinegar for lemon juice and 1½ teaspoons Korean red pepper flakes for paprika, cayenne, and pepper. Increase honey to 2 tablespoons and salt to 1¼ teaspoons. Before processing carrots, pulse 8 ounces radishes, trimmed and halved, in food processor until coarsely but evenly chopped, 10 to 12 pulses; add to dressing. Substitute ¼ cup toasted sesame seeds for pomegranate seeds and cilantro for mint.

Skillet-Roasted Cauliflower with Garlic and Lemon

Serves 4 to 6

Why This Recipe Works Cauliflower florets are irresistible when roasted to perfect crispness. But in the summer months, we always appreciate an opportunity to make dinner without turning on the oven and heating up the kitchen. For a version of roasted cauliflower that would bypass the oven, we opted instead for pan roasting. This seemed like the perfect way to achieve the texture we were after and give the florets a nutty, caramelized flavor while keeping cool. We began by cutting cauliflower into planks and then into flat-sided florets to maximize their exposed surface area for plenty of flavorful browning. Starting in a cold, covered pan allowed the slices to gradually steam in their own moisture before we removed the lid and let them brown. To give our side dish some standout flavor, we finished cooking the florets with minced garlic, lemon zest, and fresh parsley, and to add some crunch, we sprinkled on toasted fresh bread crumbs. For the first 5 minutes of cooking, the cauliflower steams in its own released moisture, so it is important not to lift the lid from the skillet during this time.

- 1 head cauliflower (2 pounds)
- 1 slice hearty white sandwich bread, torn into 1-inch pieces
- 5 tablespoons extra-virgin olive oil, divided
     Pinch plus 1 teaspoon table salt, divided
     Pinch plus ½ teaspoon pepper, divided
- 1 garlic clove, minced
- 1 teaspoon grated lemon zest, plus lemon wedges for serving
- ¼ cup chopped fresh parsley

1. Trim outer leaves of cauliflower and cut stem flush with bottom of head. Turn head so stem is facing down and cut head into ¾-inch-thick slices. Cut around core to remove florets; discard core. Cut large florets into 1½-inch pieces. Transfer florets to bowl, including any small pieces that may have been created during trimming, and set aside.

2. Pulse bread in food processor to coarse crumbs, about 10 pulses. Heat bread crumbs, 1 tablespoon oil, pinch salt, and pinch pepper in 12-inch nonstick skillet over medium heat, stirring frequently, until bread crumbs are golden brown, 3 to 5 minutes. Transfer crumbs to bowl and wipe skillet clean with paper towels.

3. Combine 2 tablespoons oil and cauliflower florets in now-empty skillet and sprinkle with remaining 1 teaspoon salt and remaining ½ teaspoon pepper. Cover skillet and cook over medium-high heat until florets start to brown and edges just start to become translucent (do not lift lid), about 5 minutes. Remove lid and continue to cook, stirring every 2 minutes, until florets turn golden brown in many spots, about 12 minutes.

4. Push cauliflower to sides of skillet. Add remaining 2 tablespoons oil, garlic, and lemon zest to center and cook, stirring with rubber spatula, until fragrant, about 30 seconds. Stir garlic mixture into cauliflower and continue to cook, stirring occasionally, until cauliflower is tender but still firm, about 3 minutes. Off heat, stir in parsley and season with salt and pepper to taste. Transfer cauliflower to serving platter and sprinkle with bread crumbs. Serve with lemon wedges.

VARIATIONS
Skillet-Roasted Cauliflower with Capers and Pine Nuts

Omit bread and reduce oil to ¼ cup. Reduce salt in step 3 to ¾ teaspoon. Substitute 2 tablespoons rinsed, minced capers for garlic. Substitute 2 tablespoons minced fresh chives for parsley and stir in ¼ cup toasted pine nuts with chives in step 4.

Skillet-Roasted Cauliflower with Cumin and Pistachios

Omit bread and reduce oil to ¼ cup. Heat 1 teaspoon cumin seeds and 1 teaspoon coriander seeds in 12-inch nonstick skillet over medium heat, stirring frequently, until lightly toasted and fragrant, 2 to 3 minutes. Transfer to spice grinder or mortar and pestle and coarsely grind. Wipe out skillet. Substitute ground cumin-coriander mixture, ½ teaspoon paprika, and pinch cayenne pepper for garlic; lime zest for lemon zest; and 3 tablespoons chopped fresh mint for parsley. Sprinkle with ¼ cup shelled pistachios, toasted and chopped, before serving with lime wedges.

North African Cauliflower Salad with Chermoula

North African Cauliflower Salad with Chermoula

Serves 4 to 6

Why This Recipe Works Chermoula is a traditional Moroccan marinade made with hefty amounts of cilantro, lemon, and garlic that packs a big punch of summer flavors. While this dressing is traditionally used as a marinade for meat and fish, here we decided to make it the flavor base for a zippy cauliflower salad in an effort to zest up a vegetable that can be bland and boring. We focused first on the cooking method of the starring vegetable. Roasting was the best choice to add deep flavor to the cauliflower and balance the bright chermoula. To keep the cauliflower from overbrowning on the exterior before the interior was cooked, we started it covered and let it steam until barely tender. Then we removed the foil, added sliced onions, and returned the pan to the oven to let both the onions and the cauliflower caramelize. Adding the onions to the same pan once the cauliflower was uncovered eased their preparation and ensured that they would finish cooking at the same time. To highlight the natural sweetness of the cooked vegetables, we added shredded carrot and raisins, two traditional North African ingredients. We now had a warm and flavorful salad sure to spice up any meal. Use the large holes of a box grater to shred the carrot.

Foolproof Boiled Corn

Chermoula
Makes about 1½ cups

¾ cup fresh cilantro leaves
¼ cup extra-virgin olive oil
2 tablespoons lemon juice
4 garlic cloves, minced
½ teaspoon ground cumin
½ teaspoon paprika
¼ teaspoon table salt
⅛ teaspoon cayenne pepper

Process all ingredients in food processor until smooth, about 1 minute, scraping down sides of bowl as needed. Transfer to large bowl. (Chermoula can be refrigerated for up to 2 days. Bring to room temperature before using.)

1 head cauliflower (2 pounds), cored and
   cut into 2-inch florets
2 tablespoons extra-virgin olive oil
½ teaspoon table salt
¼ teaspoon pepper
½ red onion, sliced ¼ inch thick
1 cup shredded carrot
½ cup raisins
2 tablespoons chopped fresh cilantro
2 tablespoons sliced almonds, toasted
1 recipe Chermoula (page 295)

1. Adjust oven rack to lowest position and heat oven to 475 degrees. Toss cauliflower with oil and sprinkle with salt and pepper. Arrange cauliflower in single layer in parchment paper–lined rimmed baking sheet. Cover tightly with aluminum foil and roast until softened, 5 to 7 minutes. Remove foil and spread onion evenly on sheet. Roast until vegetables are tender, cauliflower is deep golden brown, and onion slices are charred at edges, 10 to 15 minutes, stirring halfway through roasting. Let cool slightly, about 5 minutes.

2. Gently toss cauliflower-onion mixture, carrot, raisins, and cilantro with chermoula until coated. Transfer to serving platter and sprinkle with almonds. Serve warm or at room temperature.

Foolproof Boiled Corn
Serves 4 to 6

Why This Recipe Works Fresh corn is one of those vegetables that's really only worth eating at its peak season in the summer. It might not seem like you need a recipe to boil corn, but with such a short window of off-the-cob opportunity, we don't like to take any chances. We needed a dependable method for cooking corn that wouldn't turn these gems mushy or leave them too raw and starchy. To produce perfectly crisp, juicy corn every time, we figured out that the ideal doneness range is 150 to 170 degrees—when the starches have gelatinized but a minimum amount of the pectin (the glue that holds the cell walls together) has dissolved. We also realized that we shouldn't boil the corn. Instead, we brought a measured amount of water to a boil, shut off the heat, dropped in six ears, and let them stand for at least 10 minutes. The temperature of the water decreased quickly enough that there was never any chance of the corn overcooking, while the temperature of the corn increased to the ideal zone. Even better, we found that the method is flexible: It can accommodate between six and eight ears of different sizes, and the corn can sit in the water for as long as 30 minutes without overcooking. The result: perfectly sweet, snappy kernels every time. Serve with one of our flavored salts, if desired.

6 ears corn, husks and silk removed
  Unsalted butter, softened

1. Bring 4 quarts water to boil in large Dutch oven. Turn off heat, add corn to water, cover, and let sit for at least 10 minutes or up to 30 minutes.

2. Serve corn immediately, passing butter, salt, and pepper separately.

Chili-Lime Salt
Makes 3 tablespoons

2 tablespoons kosher salt
4 teaspoons chili powder
¾ teaspoon grated lime zest

Combine all ingredients in small bowl. (Salt can be refrigerated for up to 1 week.)

Cumin-Sesame Salt
Makes 3 tablespoons

1 tablespoon cumin seeds
1 tablespoon sesame seeds
1 tablespoon kosher salt

Toast cumin seeds and sesame seeds in 8-inch skillet over medium heat, stirring occasionally, until fragrant and sesame seeds are golden brown, 3 to 4 minutes. Transfer mixture to cutting board and let cool for 2 minutes. Mince mixture fine until well combined. Transfer mixture to small bowl and stir in salt. (Salt can be stored at room temperature for up to 1 month.)

Pepper-Cinnamon Salt
Makes 2 tablespoons

1 tablespoon kosher salt
1 tablespoon coarsely ground pepper
¼ teaspoon ground cinnamon

Combine all ingredients in small bowl. (Salt can be stored at room temperature for up to 1 month.)

Southwestern Tomato and Corn Salad

Serves 4   FAST   NO COOK

Why This Recipe Works The combination of ripe summer tomatoes and fresh corn can't be beat and luckily they both reach their peak season at about the same time. The key to a superior salad starring this iconic duo is choosing the best tomatoes and corn you can find, easy to do at the farmers' market or a farm stand. We tried adding the corn to the salad three ways: blanched, sautéed, and raw. We preferred the version with the raw kernels to the two others because the kernels added little bursts of sweetness that countered the acidic tomatoes. For a robust southwestern profile, we finished the salad with spicy minced jalapeño, a sprinkling of rich *queso fresco*, and some vibrant fresh cilantro leaves. For the best results, use the ripest in-season tomatoes you can find. If queso fresco is unavailable, you can substitute farmer's cheese or a mild feta.

1½   pounds ripe mixed tomatoes, cored
  1   ear corn, kernels cut from cob
 ¼   cup extra-virgin olive oil
  1   tablespoon minced shallot
  1   tablespoon minced jalapeño
  2   teaspoons lime juice
 ½   teaspoon table salt
 ¼   teaspoon pepper
  2   ounces queso fresco, crumbled (½ cup)
  2   tablespoons fresh cilantro leaves

1. Cut tomatoes into ½-inch-thick wedges, then cut wedges in half crosswise. Arrange tomatoes on large, shallow platter, alternating colors. Season with salt and pepper to taste. Sprinkle corn over top.

2. Whisk oil, shallot, jalapeño, lime juice, salt, and pepper together in medium bowl. Spoon dressing evenly over tomatoes. Sprinkle with queso fresco and cilantro. Serve.

CUTTING KERNELS FROM THE COB

After removing husk and silk from each ear of corn, stand ear upright in large bowl and use paring knife to carefully slice kernels off of cob.

Sesame-Lemon Cucumber Salad

Serves 4   NO COOK

Why This Recipe Works Cucumbers make a cool, crisp, and ultra-refreshing salad to pair with main dishes like grilled chicken, fish, or tacos. But often cucumbers can turn soggy from their own moisture. We often salt cucumber slices to draw out excess moisture, but for a salad with the best crunch, we found that weighting the salted cucumbers with a gallon zipper-lock bag filled with water forced more moisture from the slices than salting alone. Using a bag of water, instead of something rigid, to weight the cucumbers allowed the weight to mold and adjust to the shrinking slices as they drained. After many tests, we determined that 1 to 3 hours of weighted draining worked best: Even after 12 hours, the cucumbers gave up no more water than they had after 3 hours. For a bit of zip, we liked pairing the cucumbers with a rice vinegar and lemon juice dressing. Sesame seeds added some nutty flavor that complemented the bright dressing. This salad is best served within 1 hour of being dressed.

  3   cucumbers, peeled, halved lengthwise, seeded, and sliced ¼ inch thick
  1   tablespoon table salt, for salting cucumbers
 ¼   cup rice vinegar
  2   tablespoons toasted sesame oil
  1   tablespoon lemon juice
  1   tablespoon sesame seeds, toasted
  2   teaspoons sugar
 ⅛   teaspoon red pepper flakes, plus extra for seasoning

1. Toss cucumbers with salt in colander set over large bowl. Weight cucumbers with 1 gallon-size zipper-lock bag filled with water; let drain for 1 to 3 hours. Rinse and pat dry.

2. Whisk vinegar, oil, lemon juice, sesame seeds, sugar, and pepper flakes together in large bowl. Add cucumbers and toss to coat. Season with salt and pepper to taste. Serve.

VARIATION

Yogurt-Mint Cucumber Salad

Add 1 small red onion, thinly sliced, in with cucumbers. Omit rice vinegar, sesame oil, lemon juice, sesame seeds, sugar, and pepper flakes. Whisk 1 cup plain low-fat yogurt, ¼ cup minced fresh mint, 2 tablespoons extra-virgin olive oil, 1 minced garlic clove, and ½ teaspoon ground cumin together in large bowl. Add cucumber-onion mixture and toss to coat. Season with salt and pepper to taste. Serve at room temperature or chilled.

Country-Style Greek Salad

Serves 6 to 8   `NO COOK`

Why This Recipe Works Our Greek salad features a mix of fresh vegetables and herbs—minus the iceberg lettuce. This "country-style" version is popular throughout Greece. Even with the absence of the iceberg's crunch, we maintained the classic salad's trademark flavors and textures by combining ripe tomatoes and slices of red onion and cucumbers with fresh mint and parsley, roasted red peppers, and a generous sprinkling of feta and olives. For a bright-tasting dressing, we used a mixture of lemon juice and red wine vinegar and added fresh oregano, olive oil, and a clove of garlic. Marinating the cucumbers and onion in the vinaigrette both toned down the onion's harshness and flavored the cucumbers.

- 6 tablespoons extra-virgin olive oil
- 1½ tablespoons red wine vinegar
- 2 teaspoons minced fresh oregano
- 1 teaspoon lemon juice
- 1 garlic clove, minced
- ½ teaspoon table salt
- ⅛ teaspoon pepper
- 2 cucumbers, peeled, halved lengthwise, seeded, and sliced thin
- ½ red onion, sliced thin
- 6 large ripe tomatoes, cored, seeded, and cut into ½-inch-thick wedges
- 1 cup jarred roasted red peppers, rinsed, patted dry, and cut into ½-inch strips
- ½ cup pitted kalamata olives, quartered
- ¼ cup chopped fresh parsley
- ¼ cup chopped fresh mint
- 5 ounces feta cheese, crumbled (1¼ cups)

1. Whisk oil, vinegar, oregano, lemon juice, garlic, salt, and pepper together in large bowl. Add cucumbers and onion, toss to coat, and let sit for 20 minutes.

2. Add tomatoes, red peppers, olives, parsley, and mint to bowl with cucumber-onion mixture and toss to combine. Season with salt and pepper to taste. Transfer salad to wide, shallow serving bowl or platter and sprinkle with feta. Serve immediately.

Southwestern Tomato and Corn Salad

Country-Style Greek Salad

Marinated Eggplant with Capers and Mint

Serves 4 to 6 `MAKE AHEAD`

Why This Recipe Works Marinated eggplant is a classic meze dish popular for sharing and right at home as a side to any number of summery main dishes. It has a surprisingly creamy texture and a deep yet tangy flavor. We wanted an easy recipe that would keep the eggplant in the spotlight, with a complementary, brightly flavored marinade. To make use of the eggplant cropping up at farm stands, we chose Italian eggplant here, which is smaller than the standard supermarket size and more readily available in the summer months. Broiling the marinated eggplant helped us achieve flavorful browning while it cooked through perfectly. To encourage even more browning, we first salted the eggplant, which drew out excess moisture. As for the marinade, a Greek-inspired combination of extra-virgin olive oil (using only a few tablespoons kept the eggplant from turning greasy), red wine vinegar, capers, lemon zest, oregano, garlic, and mint worked perfectly. We prefer using kosher salt because residual grains can be easily wiped away from the eggplant; if using table salt, be sure to reduce the amount in the recipe by half.

1½ pounds Italian eggplant, sliced into 1-inch-thick rounds
½ teaspoon kosher salt, for salting eggplant
¼ cup extra-virgin olive oil, divided
4 teaspoons red wine vinegar
1 tablespoon capers, rinsed and minced
1 garlic clove, minced
½ teaspoon grated lemon zest
½ teaspoon minced fresh oregano
¼ teaspoon pepper
3 tablespoons minced fresh mint

1. Spread eggplant on paper towel–lined baking sheet, sprinkle both sides with salt, and let sit for 30 minutes.

2. Adjust oven rack 4 inches from broiler element and heat broiler. Thoroughly pat eggplant dry with paper towels, arrange on aluminum foil–lined rimmed baking sheet in single layer, and lightly brush both sides with 1 tablespoon oil. Broil eggplant until mahogany brown and lightly charred, 6 to 8 minutes per side.

3. Whisk remaining 3 tablespoons oil, vinegar, capers, garlic, lemon zest, oregano, and pepper together in large bowl. Add eggplant and mint and gently toss to combine. Let eggplant cool to room temperature, about 1 hour. Season with pepper to taste, and serve. (Marinated eggplant can be refrigerated for up to 3 days. Bring to room temperature before serving.)

Marinated Eggplant with Capers and Mint

Broiled Eggplant with Basil

Serves 4 to 6

Why This Recipe Works While you can jazz up broiled eggplant if you want, all you really need is a sprinkling of fresh summery herbs to make it shine. But if you try to simply slice and broil eggplant, it will steam in its own juices rather than brown. For eggplant with great color and texture, we started by salting it to draw out its moisture. After 30 minutes, we patted the slices dry, moved them to a baking sheet (lined with aluminum foil for easy cleanup), and brushed them with oil. A few minutes per side under the blazing-hot broiler turned the slices a beautiful mahogany color. The only accent needed was a sprinkling of fresh basil. It is important to slice the eggplant thin so that the slices will cook through by the time the exterior is browned. We prefer using kosher salt because residual grains can be easily wiped away from the eggplant; if using table salt, be sure to reduce the amount in the recipe by half.

1½ pounds eggplant, sliced into ¼-inch-thick rounds
1½ teaspoons kosher salt, for salting eggplant
3 tablespoons extra-virgin olive oil
2 tablespoons chopped fresh basil

1. Spread eggplant on paper towel–lined baking sheet, sprinkle both sides with salt, and let sit for 30 minutes.

2. Adjust oven rack 4 inches from broiler element and heat broiler. Thoroughly pat eggplant dry with paper towels, arrange on aluminum foil–lined rimmed baking sheet in single layer, and brush both sides with oil. Broil eggplant until mahogany brown and lightly charred, about 4 minutes per side. Transfer eggplant to serving platter, season with pepper to taste, and sprinkle with basil. Serve.

Fennel Salad
Serves 4 to 6 `NO COOK`

Why This Recipe Works This bright and lively salad is a great way to get to know fresh fennel with its mild licorice flavor and celery-like crunch. Since fennel is a classic Mediterranean ingredient, we looked there for inspiration. We wanted an assertive salad with a balance of sweet, salty, slightly sour, and bitter flavors. Right off we learned that there is a right way and a wrong way to cut fennel. As with meat, cutting fennel against the grain—or in this case, fibers—shortens the fibers, which makes the slices less stringy. For sweetness we threw raisins into our salad bowl and for the salty component, capers; thinly sliced red onion added pungency while whole leaves of Italian flat-leaf parsley added an herbal note. For the vinaigrette, extra-virgin olive oil was a given, and we added fresh lemon juice and balanced its brightness with a little honey. Dijon mustard helped emulsify the vinaigrette and added bite. We let the vegetables macerate in the vinaigrette for 30 minutes, which softened the onion's harshness and seasoned the fennel slices. When ready to serve, we stirred in the parsley and some almonds for extra crunch.

- ¼ cup extra-virgin olive oil
- 3 tablespoons lemon juice
- 2 teaspoons Dijon mustard
- 2 teaspoons honey
- 1 teaspoon table salt
- 1 teaspoon pepper
- 2 fennel bulbs, stalks discarded, bulbs halved, cored, and sliced thin crosswise
- ½ red onion, halved through root end and sliced thin crosswise
- ½ cup golden raisins, chopped
- 3 tablespoons capers, rinsed and minced
- ½ cup fresh parsley leaves
- ½ cup sliced almonds, toasted

1. Whisk oil, lemon juice, mustard, honey, salt, and pepper together in large bowl. Add fennel, onion, raisins, and capers and toss to combine. Cover and refrigerate for 30 minutes to allow flavors to blend.

2. Stir in parsley and almonds. Season with salt and pepper to taste, and serve.

Garlicky Braised Kale
Serves 8

Why This Recipe Works Kale sounds like a great side dish in theory, but in practice it can be tricky to tame its toughness. We came up with a one-pot approach to turn kale tender without taking hours or leaving it awash in excess liquid. To make the most of a farmers' market haul or generous harvest, we started with a whopping 4 pounds of kale. We added the greens one handful at a time to a seasoned broth and let them wilt before adding more. When the kale had nearly reached the tender-firm texture we wanted, we removed the lid and raised the heat to cook off the liquid. Onion and a substantial amount of garlic gave our greens some aromatic character. This will look like a mountain of raw kale before it's cooked, but it wilts down and will eventually all fit into the pot.

- 6 tablespoons extra-virgin olive oil, divided
- 1 large onion, chopped fine
- 10 garlic cloves, minced
- ¼ teaspoon red pepper flakes
- 2 cups chicken or vegetable broth
- 1 cup water
- ½ teaspoon table salt
- 4 pounds kale, stemmed and cut into 3-inch pieces, divided
- 1 tablespoon lemon juice, plus extra for seasoning

1. Heat 3 tablespoons oil in Dutch oven over medium heat until shimmering. Add onion and cook until softened and lightly browned, 5 to 7 minutes. Stir in garlic and pepper flakes and cook until fragrant, about 1 minute. Stir in broth, water, and salt and bring to simmer.

2. Add one-third of kale, cover, and cook, stirring occasionally, until wilted, 2 to 4 minutes. Repeat with remaining kale in 2 batches. Continue to cook, covered, until kale is tender, 13 to 15 minutes.

3. Remove lid and increase heat to medium-high. Cook, stirring occasionally, until most liquid has evaporated and greens begin to sizzle, 10 to 12 minutes. Off heat, stir in remaining 3 tablespoons oil and lemon juice. Season with salt, pepper, and extra lemon juice to taste. Serve.

Fried Okra

Serves 4 to 6 `MAKE AHEAD`

Why This Recipe Works Hailed as a Southern staple, fried okra is an indulgent treat that, for many, is simply the only way to eat okra. For the ultimate crunchy bite, we cut the pods into pieces so that the interior mucilage would evaporate when it hit the hot oil. For a light and crispy fried exterior that wouldn't crumble and fall off the okra when we bit into it, we made a "glue" of buttermilk and egg in which to dip the pieces before dredging. The ratio of cornmeal to cornstarch to all-purpose flour was key in creating a crunchy outer fried shell that adhered well. The cornmeal was crucial for the classic Southern fried flavor profile, the cornstarch added a light crispy effect, and the flour added the glutinous structure needed to ensure that the coating stayed put. We added a final flavorful stir-in of garlic powder and cayenne to the blend before dredging and frying the pods. While we prefer the flavor and texture of fresh okra in this recipe, you can substitute frozen cut okra, thawed and thoroughly patted dry, for fresh. We recommend frying in three batches if using frozen okra.

- ⅔ cup buttermilk
- 1 large egg
- ¾ cup cornmeal
- ½ cup cornstarch
- ¼ cup all-purpose flour
- 1½ teaspoons table salt
- 1 teaspoon garlic powder
- ½ teaspoon cayenne pepper
- ¼ teaspoon pepper
- 1 pound okra, stemmed and cut into 1-inch pieces
- 3 quarts peanut or vegetable oil
  Lemon wedges
  Hot sauce

1. Adjust oven rack to middle position and heat oven to 200 degrees. Line rimmed baking sheet with parchment paper. Set wire rack in second rimmed baking sheet and line with triple layer of paper towels.

2. Whisk buttermilk and egg together in shallow dish. Whisk cornmeal, cornstarch, flour, salt, garlic powder, cayenne, and pepper together in second shallow dish. Working in batches, dip okra in buttermilk mixture, letting excess drip back into dish. Dredge in cornmeal mixture, pressing firmly to adhere; transfer to parchment-lined sheet. Refrigerate, uncovered, for at least 30 minutes or up to 4 hours.

3. Add oil to large Dutch oven until it measures about 2 inches deep and heat over medium-high heat to 375 degrees. Carefully add half of okra to oil and fry, stirring as needed to prevent sticking, until okra is golden and crisp, 2 to 4 minutes.

Adjust burner if necessary to maintain oil temperature between 350 and 375 degrees. Using wire skimmer or slotted spoon, transfer okra to prepared rack. Season with salt and transfer to oven to keep warm.

4. Return oil to 375 degrees and repeat with remaining okra. Serve immediately with lemon wedges and hot sauce.

Greek Stewed Okra with Tomatoes

Serves 6 to 8

Why This Recipe Works For a fresh way to turn okra into an irresistible side dish perfect for serving with fish or meat dishes, we paired this satisfying vegetable with a deeply flavored tomatoey sauce similar to those popular in Greece. The bright-tasting but warmly spiced tomato sauce enveloped the whole okra pods and allowed the vegetal green freshness of the okra to shine through. Greek-style tomato sauce is often seasoned with cinnamon, allspice, and other warm baking spices. For our version, we also included onion, garlic, and lemon juice, for a sweet-savory balance. We found that salting the okra pods before stewing them minimized their slippery qualities. While we prefer the flavor and texture of fresh okra in this recipe, you can substitute frozen whole okra, thawed, for fresh.

- 2 pounds okra, stemmed
- ¾ teaspoon table salt, plus salt for salting okra
- 2 (28-ounce) cans whole peeled tomatoes, drained
- ½ cup extra-virgin olive oil
- 1 onion, chopped fine
- 5 garlic cloves, sliced thin
- ½ teaspoon ground allspice
- ¼ teaspoon ground cinnamon
- ¼ teaspoon pepper
- 2 tablespoons lemon juice
- ¼ cup minced fresh parsley

1. Toss okra with 2 teaspoons salt in colander and let sit for 1 hour, tossing again halfway through. Rinse well and set aside.

2. Process tomatoes in food processor until smooth, about 1 minute. Heat oil in Dutch oven over medium heat until shimmering. Add onion and cook until softened and lightly browned, 5 to 7 minutes. Stir in garlic, ¾ teaspoon salt, allspice, cinnamon, and pepper and cook until fragrant, about 30 seconds. Stir in tomatoes and lemon juice and bring to simmer. Cook, stirring occasionally, until thickened slightly, about 10 minutes.

3. Stir in okra and return to simmer. Reduce heat to medium-low, cover, and cook, stirring occasionally, until okra is just tender, 20 to 25 minutes. Season with salt and pepper to taste. Sprinkle with parsley and serve.

Sautéed Radishes
Serves 4 to 6 `FAST`

Why This Recipe Works Vibrant radishes of various colors overflow summertime farm stands. But other than slicing them up for a salad, slaw, or taco-topper, what can you do with them? Enter the mellow, sweet flavor of cooked radishes—greens and all. Heat concentrates the natural sugars in radishes while toning down many of the compounds responsible for their pungent, peppery flavor. Here we started by cooking quartered radishes in butter over moderate heat. The butter provided substantial browning and lent subtle, nutty notes to the radishes. And since radishes contain relatively little water, within 10 minutes they were golden brown all over and perfectly tender, with a slight bite. Radish greens are often overlooked, but we wanted to take advantage of this multi-dimensional vegetable, so we decided to incorporate them into our side dish. To provide some textural variety and color, we cooked the greens at the end so that they retained a slight crispness that complemented the heartier radish pieces. If you can't find radishes with their greens or they don't yield enough greens to amount to 8 cups, you can substitute baby arugula or watercress.

  3 tablespoons unsalted butter, cut into
      3 pieces, divided
1½ pounds radishes with their greens, radishes
      trimmed and quartered, 8 cups greens reserved
 ¼ teaspoon plus ⅛ teaspoon table salt, divided
 ¼ teaspoon pepper, divided
  1 garlic clove, minced
      Lemon wedges

1. Melt 2 tablespoons butter in 12-inch skillet over medium-high heat. Add radishes, ¼ teaspoon salt, and ⅛ teaspoon pepper and cook, stirring occasionally, until radishes are lightly browned and crisp-tender, 10 to 12 minutes. Stir in garlic and cook until fragrant, about 30 seconds; transfer to bowl.

Sautéed Radishes with Vadouvan Curry and Almonds

2. Melt remaining 1 tablespoon butter in now-empty skillet over medium heat. Add radish greens, remaining ⅛ teaspoon salt, and remaining ⅛ teaspoon pepper and cook, stirring frequently, until wilted, about 1 minute. Off heat, stir in radishes and season with salt and pepper to taste. Serve with lemon wedges.

VARIATIONS
Sautéed Radishes with Chili and Lime
Stir 1 teaspoon paprika and ½ teaspoon chili powder into radishes with garlic. Substitute lime wedges for lemon.

Sautéed Radishes with Vadouvan Curry and Almonds
Omit lemon wedges. Substitute 1½ teaspoons vadouvan curry for garlic. Sprinkle with 2 tablespoons chopped toasted almonds before serving.

Look for fresh peas at farmers' markets in the late springtime and early summer. Once you get them home, use them as soon as possible. If you find pea greens in any form in the spring or summer, they should look fresh and vibrant, with no signs of wilting, browning, or yellowing. They are very perishable, so wrap them in paper towels and store them in the refrigerator for a day or two.

English Peas Plump and sweet, fresh English peas—the green garden peas we're all familiar with—are a quintessential vegetable of late spring and early summer. Freshly picked peas are as sweet as candy, so snap them up when you can. Supermarkets seldom carry whole English peapods, both because they're a bit of work to shell and because the pods are too tough to eat. But there are two edible peapods you will readily find: snow peas and sugar snap peas.

Snow Peas Snow peas are recognizable for their flat, almost translucent pods in which no peas (or tiny peas) have developed. They cook in a flash, so they're ideal for sautéing for simple side dishes or adding to stir-fries.

Sugar Snap Peas These are a hybrid of English peas and snow peas, and they combine the best of both worlds—crunchy, juicy pods with plump, sweet peas inside. Stir-fry them or use them in salads.

Pea Shoots Pea shoots are the first growth of the plant and are extremely delicate; they are sometimes shelved and labeled as "pea sprouts" in markets. They are sweet and mild and are great used raw as a topping for salads and sandwiches.

Pea Tendrils Pea tendrils are the next stage of growth. Tender leaves have developed, and long, thin coils (the tendrils) spring out in every direction, all the better to capture sunlight for growth. Pea tendrils are more intense in flavor than pea shoots and are great in stir-fries.

Pea Greens Pea greens are the third stage of growth. The rounded, bright green leaves are grassy and faintly bitter, tasting of fresh peas but without the sweetness. They are excellent salad greens, and they also can be used instead of basil or other herbs to make a pesto.

Sugar Snap Peas with Pine Nuts, Fennel, and Lemon Zest

Serves 4 FAST

Why This Recipe Works Sugar snap peas are a cross between English peas and snow peas and are a farmers' market mainstay. They have sweet, crisp edible pods with small juicy peas inside. To ensure that the pods and their peas cooked through at the same rate, we used a hybrid method to steam the sugar snap peas briefly before quickly sautéing them; the trapped steam transferred heat more efficiently than air, so the peas cooked through faster. Cutting the sugar snap peas in half further reduced the cooking time, so the pods retained more of their snap, and as a bonus, the pockets captured the seasonings rather than letting them slide to the bottom of the platter. Sprinkling the snap peas with a dukkah-like mix of finely chopped pine nuts, fennel seeds, and seasonings dressed up this simple preparation with distinct (but not overwhelming) flavor and crunch. Do not substitute ground fennel for the fennel seeds in this recipe.

3 tablespoons pine nuts
1 teaspoon fennel seeds
½ teaspoon grated lemon zest
½ teaspoon kosher salt
⅛ teaspoon red pepper flakes
2 teaspoons vegetable oil
12 ounces sugar snap peas, strings removed, halved crosswise on bias
2 tablespoons water
1 garlic clove, minced
3 tablespoons chopped fresh basil

1. Toast pine nuts in 12-inch skillet over medium heat, stirring frequently, until just starting to brown, about 3 minutes. Add fennel seeds and continue to toast, stirring constantly, until pine nuts are lightly browned and fennel is fragrant, about 1 minute. Transfer pine nut mixture to cutting board. Sprinkle lemon zest, salt, and pepper flakes over pine nut mixture. Chop mixture until finely minced and well combined. Transfer to bowl and set aside.

2. Heat oil in now-empty skillet over medium heat until shimmering. Add snap peas and water, immediately cover, and cook for 2 minutes. Uncover, add garlic, and continue to cook, stirring frequently, until moisture has evaporated and snap peas are crisp-tender, about 2 minutes. Remove skillet from heat; stir in three-quarters of pine nut mixture and basil. Transfer snap peas to serving platter, sprinkle with remaining pine nut mixture, and serve.

Sugar Snap Peas with Almonds, Coriander, and Orange Zest

Slivered almonds can be used in place of sliced almonds. Do not use ground coriander in this recipe.

Substitute sliced almonds for pine nuts, coriander seeds for fennel seeds, ¼ teaspoon orange zest for lemon zest, and cilantro for basil. Omit red pepper flakes.

Sugar Snap Peas with Sesame, Ginger, and Lemon Zest

Black or white sesame seeds can be used in this recipe.

Substitute 2 tablespoons sesame seeds for pine nuts, ½ teaspoon grated fresh ginger for garlic, and 1 thinly sliced scallion for basil. Omit fennel seeds and red pepper flakes.

Spinach and Strawberry Salad with Poppy Seed Dressing

Serves 4 to 6

Why This Recipe Works We love to brighten up a summer salad with fresh, vibrant berries. Spinach and strawberries are a popular salad pairing, but they need to be combined in the right way to let both components shine. In our salad, we cut back on the spinach and swapped in crisp chopped romaine for color and crunch. We also bumped up the amount of strawberries to a full pound so there would be berries in every bite. For a dressing that was neither too thick nor over-the-top sweet but had plenty of flavor, we toasted the poppy seeds to enhance their nuttiness and used them in a simple vinaigrette of red wine vinegar, a minimal amount of sugar, and mild vegetable oil. Red onion and toasted almonds rounded out the salad's ingredients. Poppy seeds are dark so it's hard to see when they're fully toasted. Instead, use your nose: They should smell nutty.

½ cup red wine vinegar
⅓ cup sugar
¾ teaspoon table salt
½ red onion, sliced thin
1 tablespoon poppy seeds
½ cup sliced almonds, divided
¼ cup vegetable oil
1 teaspoon dry mustard
½ teaspoon pepper

Spinach and Strawberry Salad with Poppy Seed Dressing

1 pound strawberries, hulled and quartered (2½ cups)
1 romaine lettuce heart (6 ounces), torn into bite-size pieces
5 ounces (5 cups) baby spinach

1. Whisk vinegar, sugar, and salt together in bowl. Transfer ¼ cup vinegar mixture to small bowl and microwave until hot, about 1 minute. Add onion, stir to combine, and let sit for at least 30 minutes. (Pickled onion can be refrigerated, covered, for up to 2 days.)

2. Meanwhile, toast poppy seeds in 8-inch nonstick skillet over medium heat until fragrant and slightly darkened, 1 to 2 minutes; transfer to bowl and set aside. Add almonds to now-empty skillet, return to medium heat, and toast until fragrant and golden, 3 to 5 minutes.

3. Whisk oil, mustard, poppy seeds, and pepper into remaining vinegar mixture. Combine strawberries, lettuce, spinach, and ¼ cup almonds in large bowl. Using fork, remove onions from vinegar mixture and add to salad. Add poppy seed dressing to salad and toss to combine. Season with salt and pepper to taste. Transfer salad to serving platter and top with remaining ¼ cup almonds. Serve.

Sautéed Spinach with Yogurt and Dukkah

Roasted Baby Pattypan Squash with Lemon and Basil

Sautéed Spinach with Yogurt and Dukkah

Serves 4 FAST

Why This Recipe Works A combination found throughout the eastern Mediterranean region, earthy, tender spinach and creamy, tangy yogurt are a perfect match. We found that we greatly preferred the hearty flavor and texture of curly-leaf spinach—a favorite farmers' market green—to baby spinach here, as the more tender baby spinach wilted down into mush. We cooked the spinach in extra-virgin olive oil and, once it was cooked, used tongs to squeeze the excess moisture out of the leaves. Lightly toasted minced garlic, cooked after the spinach in the same pan, added a sweet nuttiness. We emphasized the yogurt's tanginess with lemon zest and juice and drizzled it over our garlicky spinach. To elevate the flavor and give it some textural contrast, we sprinkled on some dukkah, an Egyptian blend of ground seeds, nuts, and spices that enhances all kinds of dishes. Two pounds of flat-leaf spinach (about three bunches) can be substituted for the curly-leaf spinach. We prefer to use our homemade Dukkah (page 305), but you can substitute store-bought dukkah if you wish.

½ cup plain yogurt
1½ teaspoons lemon zest plus 1 teaspoon juice
3 tablespoons extra-virgin olive oil, divided
20 ounces curly-leaf spinach, stemmed
2 garlic cloves, minced
¼ cup Dukkah (page 305)

1. Combine yogurt and lemon zest and juice in bowl; set aside for serving. Heat 1 tablespoon oil in Dutch oven over high heat until shimmering. Add spinach, 1 handful at a time, stirring and tossing each handful to wilt slightly before adding more. Cook spinach, stirring constantly, until uniformly wilted, about 1 minute. Transfer spinach to colander and squeeze between tongs to release excess liquid.

2. Wipe pot dry with paper towels. Add remaining 2 tablespoons oil and garlic to now-empty pot and cook over medium heat until fragrant, about 30 seconds. Add spinach and toss to coat, gently separating leaves to evenly coat with garlic oil. Off heat, season with salt and pepper to taste. Transfer spinach to serving platter, drizzle with yogurt sauce, and sprinkle with dukkah. Serve.

3 tablespoons unsalted butter, melted
1 teaspoon honey
¼ teaspoon table salt
⅛ teaspoon pepper
1½ pounds baby pattypan squash, halved horizontally

Adjust oven rack to lowest position, place rimmed baking sheet on rack, and heat oven to 500 degrees. Whisk melted butter, honey, salt, and pepper in large bowl until honey has fully dissolved. Add squash and toss to coat. Working quickly, arrange squash cut side down on hot sheet. Roast until cut side is browned and squash is tender, 15 to 18 minutes. Season with salt and pepper to taste. Serve.

VARIATIONS
Roasted Baby Pattypan Squash with Lemon and Basil
Whisk ½ teaspoon lemon zest and 1 tablespoon lemon juice into butter mixture. Sprinkle squash with 2 tablespoons chopped fresh basil before serving.

Roasted Baby Pattypan Squash with Chile and Lime
Omit pepper. Whisk 1 minced Thai chile pepper, ½ teaspoon lime zest, and 1 tablespoon lime juice into butter mixture. Sprinkle squash with 2 tablespoons chopped fresh mint before serving.

Roasted Baby Pattypan Squash
Serves 4 to 6 FAST

Why This Recipe Works You might not know what to make of these beautiful round and squat squashes when you come across them, but when you're thinking about cooking yellow squash or zucchini, take advantage of these summer baby squash. Green and yellow like their cousins, pattypans come in a variety of sizes; here we chose baby ones for their tender skin and vibrant flavor (some say the squash loses flavor as it matures) and, quite frankly, because they are so cute. We wanted to create a recipe where the squash would retain its beautiful shape and color while getting good browning. Roasting was the fastest and easiest way to cook a decent amount of squash in one batch, and we used a couple of tricks to help things along. First, we cut the squashes in half horizontally, creating flower-shaped slabs. Then we cranked the oven to 500 degrees and preheated a sheet pan for maximum searing. Tossing the squash in butter and honey both complemented the squash's own sweet and creamy profile and promoted browning. We didn't even have to flip the squash—the pieces were beautifully browned on the cut side, retained their bright color on top, and were fully cooked through. Use baby pattypan squashes between 1½ and 2 inches in diameter.

Sautéed Swiss Chard with Currants and Pine Nuts
Serves 4 FAST

Why This Recipe Works Swiss chard is a sturdy green with a bitter, beet-like flavor that mellows when cooked. The key to sautéing this hearty vegetable is to get the stems to finish cooking at the same time as the leaves. Swiss chard stems fall somewhere in the middle between spinach's quick-cooking stems and kale's tough ribs. To encourage the stems to cook efficiently and evenly, we sliced them thin on the bias. We gave the stems a head start, sautéing them with garlic and warm cumin over relatively high heat to create a crisp-tender texture and complex, lightly caramelized flavor. We introduced the tender leaves later and in two stages, allowing the first batch to begin wilting before adding the rest. This hearty green is often served simply seasoned or with garlic. To introduce some new flavors and textures to this simple vegetable, we chose to incorporate sweet currants and crunchy pine nuts, which we stirred in off the heat with some sherry vinegar. The result was a bright, nuanced side of greens with a range of appealing textures in every bite. You can use any variety of Swiss chard for this recipe.

- 2 tablespoons extra-virgin olive oil
- 1 garlic clove, minced
- ¼ teaspoon ground cumin
- 1½ pounds Swiss chard, stems sliced ¼ inch thick on bias, leaves sliced into ½-inch-wide strips, divided
- ⅛ teaspoon table salt
- 2 teaspoons sherry vinegar
- 3 tablespoons dried currants
- 3 tablespoons pine nuts, toasted

1. Heat oil in 12-inch nonstick skillet over medium-high heat until just shimmering. Add garlic and cumin and cook, stirring constantly, until lightly browned, 30 to 60 seconds. Add chard stems and salt and cook, stirring occasionally, until spotty brown and crisp-tender, about 6 minutes.

2. Add two-thirds of chard leaves and cook, tossing with tongs, until just starting to wilt, 30 to 60 seconds. Add remaining chard leaves and continue to cook, stirring frequently, until leaves are tender, about 3 minutes. Off heat, stir in vinegar, currants, and pine nuts. Season with salt and pepper to taste. Serve.

Socca with Swiss Chard, Pistachios, and Apricots

Serves 6 to 8 (Makes 5 flatbreads)

Why This Recipe Works Whether visiting a summer farmers' market or the supermarket we're always impressed by the giant leaves of Swiss chard and regularly bring home a colorful bunch, but once home we can struggle to find interesting ways to prepare it. Looking for an innovative approach, we went outside the box and thought of socca—a satisfying, savory French flatbread made with chickpea flour. A mound of sautéed Swiss chard piled on this savory flatbread would be a delicious way to add some excitement to the table. Socca's loose, pancake-like batter comes together in less than a minute: Simply whisk together chickpea flour, water, olive oil, turmeric, salt, and pepper. Traditionally the batter is poured into a cast-iron skillet and baked in a wood-burning oven. But in a home oven, this technique produced socca that was dry and limp, and also heated up the kitchen more than we'd like on a hot day. We also loved the idea of

smaller flatbreads for individual servings, so we ditched the oven for the higher direct heat of the stovetop and made small, crispy, golden-brown socca. As an added bonus, these smaller flatbreads had a higher ratio of crunchy crust to tender interior. For a Swiss chard topping, we combined the sautéed greens with dried apricots and toasted pistachios for sweet-savory flavor and a bit of texture. Stirring in warm spices—cumin and allspice—balanced the bright notes of the chickpea flatbreads.

Batter
- 1½ cups (6¾ ounces) chickpea flour
- ½ teaspoon table salt
- ½ teaspoon pepper
- ½ teaspoon turmeric
- 1½ cups water
- 6 tablespoons plus 1 teaspoon extra-virgin olive oil, divided

Topping
- 1 tablespoon extra-virgin olive oil
- 1 onion, chopped fine
- 2 garlic cloves, minced
- ¾ teaspoon ground cumin
- ¼ teaspoon table salt
- ⅛ teaspoon allspice
- 12 ounces Swiss chard, stemmed and chopped
- 3 tablespoons finely chopped dried apricots
- 2 tablespoons finely chopped toasted pistachios
- 1 teaspoon white wine vinegar

1. For the batter Adjust oven rack to middle position and heat oven to 200 degrees. Set wire rack in rimmed baking sheet and place in oven. Whisk chickpea flour, salt, pepper, and turmeric together in bowl. Slowly whisk in water and 3 tablespoons oil until combined and smooth.

2. Heat 2 teaspoons oil in 8-inch nonstick skillet over medium-high heat until shimmering. Add ½ cup batter to skillet, tilting pan to coat bottom evenly. Reduce heat to medium and cook until crisp at edges and golden brown on bottom, 3 to 5 minutes. Flip socca and continue to cook until second side is browned, about 2 minutes. Transfer to wire rack in warm oven and repeat, working with 2 teaspoons oil and ½ cup batter at a time.

3. For the topping Heat oil in 12-inch nonstick skillet over medium heat until shimmering. Add onion and cook until softened, about 5 minutes. Stir in garlic, cumin, salt, and allspice and cook until fragrant, about 30 seconds. Stir in Swiss chard and apricots and cook until chard is wilted, 4 to 6 minutes. Off heat, stir in pistachios and vinegar and season with salt and pepper to taste. Top each cooked socca with ⅓ cup chard mixture, slice, and serve.

Simple Tomato Salad

1 teaspoon lemon juice
½ teaspoon table salt
¼ teaspoon pepper
2 tablespoons toasted pine nuts
1 tablespoon torn fresh basil leaves

Arrange tomatoes on large, shallow platter. Whisk oil, shallot, lemon juice, salt, and pepper together in bowl. Spoon dressing over tomatoes. Sprinkle with pine nuts and basil. Serve immediately.

Tomato Salad with Feta and Cumin-Yogurt Dressing

Serves 6

Why This Recipe Works For another fresh salad that uses plump and juicy summer tomatoes, we created one with complementary flavors and a creamy dressing. Tomatoes exude lots of liquid when cut, which can quickly turn a salad into soup. To get rid of some of the tomato juice without losing all its valuable flavor, we salted the tomato wedges before making the salad. Letting them sit for 15 minutes provided enough time for the juice to drain. Salting also seasoned both the tomatoes and their juice, some of which we reserved to add to our creamy Greek yogurt dressing, along with lemon juice to boost its tang. To infuse the dressing with more flavor we added fresh oregano, cumin, and garlic. A quick zap in the microwave was all it took to effectively bloom the spice and cook the garlic, mellowing their flavors. We tossed the tomatoes with the dressing, finishing with just the right amount of briny feta to add richness and another layer of flavor. Both regular and lowfat Greek yogurt will work well here; do not use nonfat yogurt. For the best results, use the ripest in-season tomatoes you can find.

2½ pounds ripe tomatoes, cored and
    cut into ½-inch-thick wedges
½ teaspoon table salt
1 tablespoon extra-virgin olive oil
1 garlic clove, minced
1 teaspoon ground cumin
¼ cup plain Greek yogurt
1 tablespoon lemon juice
1 scallion, sliced thin
1 tablespoon minced fresh oregano
3 ounces feta cheese, crumbled (¾ cup)

Simple Tomato Salad

Serves 4 `FAST` `NO COOK`

Why This Recipe Works A simple tomato salad is one of the elemental joys of summer, when tomatoes are juicy and flavorful. We started ours with the ripest tomatoes we could get our hands on. Because tomatoes are already fairly acidic, we found that a dressing made with the typical 3:1 ratio of oil to acid was too sharp here. Adjusting the amount of lemon juice to minimize the acidity perfectly balanced the salad. A minced shallot added a bit of sweetness while toasted pine nuts added a buttery nuttiness and some textural diversity. Basil and tomato is an iconic summer combination, so we topped the tomatoes with torn basil leaves to complete the salad with a fresh herbal note. For the best results, use the ripest in-season tomatoes you can find. Serve this salad with crusty bread to sop up the dressing.

1½ pounds mixed ripe tomatoes,
    cored and sliced ¼ inch thick
3 tablespoons extra-virgin olive oil
1 tablespoon minced shallot

1. Toss tomatoes with salt and let drain in colander set over bowl for 15 to 20 minutes.

2. Microwave oil, garlic, and cumin in bowl until fragrant, about 30 seconds; let cool slightly. Transfer 1 tablespoon tomato liquid to large bowl; discard remaining liquid. Whisk in yogurt, lemon juice, scallion, oregano, and oil mixture until combined. Add tomatoes and feta and gently toss to coat. Season with salt and pepper to taste. Serve at room temperature.

Best Summer Tomato Gratin
Serves 6 to 8

Why This Recipe Works Some think it's sacrilege to cook a perfect summer tomato, but we disagree. Cooking intensifies the tomato's natural flavor, and it's an excellent way to use great tomatoes at the time of year when there are plenty of them around. That's why tomato gratin is so appealing. It combines fresh tomatoes with bread to soak up all the juices released as the tomatoes cook, and it's topped off with Parmesan for both flavor and contrasting texture. Starting on the stovetop initiated the breakdown of the tomatoes, drove off some moisture that would have sogged out the bread, and shortened the overall cooking time. We then finished the dish in the even heat of the oven. Toasting cubes of a crusty baguette ensured that the bread didn't get soggy once combined with the tomatoes. We set aside the toasted bread and added the chopped tomatoes as well as garlic, a small amount of sugar, and salt and pepper. Just before moving the skillet to the oven, we folded in most of the toasted bread and scattered the remainder over the top along with some Parmesan. Fresh basil provided color and bright flavor. For the best results, use the ripest in-season tomatoes you can find. Supermarket vine-ripened tomatoes will work, but the gratin won't be as flavorful as one made with locally grown tomatoes. Do not use plum tomatoes, which contain less juice than regular round tomatoes and will result in a dry gratin. For the bread, we prefer a crusty baguette with a firm, chewy crumb.

- 6 tablespoons extra-virgin olive oil, divided
- 6 ounces crusty baguette, cut into ¾-inch cubes (4 cups)
- 3 garlic cloves, sliced thin
- 3 pounds ripe tomatoes, cored and cut into ¾-inch pieces
- 2 teaspoons sugar
- 1 teaspoon table salt
- 1 teaspoon pepper
- 1½ ounces Parmesan cheese, grated (¾ cup)
- 2 tablespoons chopped fresh basil

Best Summer Tomato Gratin

1. Adjust oven rack to middle position and heat oven to 350 degrees. Heat ¼ cup oil in 12-inch ovensafe skillet over medium-low heat until shimmering. Add bread and stir to coat. Cook, stirring constantly, until bread is browned and toasted, about 5 minutes. Transfer bread to bowl.

2. Return now-empty skillet to low heat and add remaining 2 tablespoons oil and garlic. Cook, stirring constantly, until garlic is golden at edges, 30 to 60 seconds. Add tomatoes, sugar, salt, and pepper and stir to combine. Increase heat to medium-high and cook, stirring occasionally, until tomatoes have started to break down and have released enough juice to be mostly submerged, 8 to 10 minutes.

3. Remove skillet from heat and gently stir in 3 cups bread until completely moistened and evenly distributed. Using spatula, press down on bread until completely submerged. Arrange remaining 1 cup bread evenly over surface, pressing to partially submerge. Sprinkle evenly with Parmesan.

4. Bake until top of gratin is deeply browned, tomatoes are bubbling, and juice has reduced, 40 to 45 minutes; after 30 minutes, run spatula around edge of skillet to loosen crust and release any juice underneath. (Gratin will appear loose and jiggle around outer edges but will thicken as it cools.)

5. Remove skillet from oven and let sit for 15 minutes. Sprinkle with basil and serve hot, warm, or at room temperature.

Roasted Tomatoes

Serves 4 `MAKE AHEAD`

Why This Recipe Works When tomatoes are in season, oven roasting is a great way to intensify their flavor while also increasing their shelf life—they can be refrigerated or frozen and kept on hand to serve as a chilled or rewarmed side dish, mixed into a green or grain salad, blended into a homemade hummus, or placed atop crusty toasted bread with a smear of ricotta cheese. Many recipes call for a low oven temperature and hours of cooking, only to yield leathery tomatoes. To cut down on the cooking time without sacrificing quality of flavor, we cut the tomatoes into thick slices to create lots of exposed surface area from which water could escape. Oil transfers heat with great efficiency, so we poured some extra-virgin olive oil over the slices to help drive more moisture away and to concentrate the tomatoes' flavor. We started roasting the tomatoes in a 425-degree oven and then reduced the temperature to 300 degrees to gently finish cooking. For the best results, use the ripest in-season tomatoes you can find.

- 3 pounds large ripe tomatoes, cored, bottom ⅛ inch trimmed, and sliced ¾ inch thick
- 2 garlic cloves, peeled and smashed
- ¼ teaspoon dried oregano
- ¼ teaspoon kosher salt
- ¾ cup extra-virgin olive oil

1. Adjust oven rack to middle position and heat oven to 425 degrees. Line rimmed baking sheet with aluminum foil. Arrange tomatoes in even layer on prepared sheet, with larger slices around edge and smaller slices in center. Place garlic cloves on tomatoes. Sprinkle with oregano and salt and season with pepper to taste. Drizzle oil evenly over tomatoes.

2. Bake for 30 minutes, rotating sheet halfway through baking. Remove sheet from oven. Reduce oven temperature to 300 degrees and prop open door with wooden spoon to cool oven. Using thin spatula, flip tomatoes.

3. Return tomatoes to oven, close oven door, and continue to cook until spotty brown, skins are blistered, and tomatoes have collapsed to ¼ to ½ inch thick, 1 to 2 hours. Remove from oven and let cool completely, about 30 minutes. Discard garlic and transfer tomatoes and oil to airtight container. Serve warm, at room temperature, or cold. (Tomatoes can be refrigerated for up to 5 days or frozen for up to 2 months.)

Sautéed Summer Squash Ribbons

Serves 4 to 6 `FAST`

Why This Recipe Works To create a fresh, simple summer squash recipe with as much visual appeal as pleasant flavor, we started with very thinly sliced squash, using a peeler to make even "ribbons" and discarding the waterlogged seeds. The ultrathin ribbons browned and cooked so quickly that they didn't have time to break down and release their liquid, eliminating the need to salt them before cooking. The cooked squash needed little embellishment; a quick, tangy vinaigrette of extra-virgin olive oil, garlic, and lemon and a sprinkle of fresh parsley rounded out the flavors. We like a mix of yellow summer squash and zucchini, but you can use just one or the other. To avoid overcooking the squash, start checking for doneness at the lower end of the cooking time.

- 1 small garlic clove, minced
- 1 teaspoon grated lemon zest plus 1 tablespoon juice
- 4 (6- to 8-ounce) yellow summer squash and/or zucchini, trimmed
- 2 tablespoons plus 1 teaspoon extra-virgin olive oil, divided
- ¼ teaspoon table salt
- ⅛ teaspoon pepper
- 1½ tablespoons chopped fresh parsley

1. Combine garlic and lemon juice in large bowl and set aside for at least 10 minutes. Using vegetable peeler, shave off 3 ribbons from 1 side of summer squash, then turn summer squash 90 degrees and shave off 3 more ribbons. Continue to turn and shave ribbons until you reach seeds; discard core. Repeat with remaining summer squash.

2. Whisk 2 tablespoons oil, salt, pepper, and lemon zest into garlic–lemon juice mixture.

MAKING SUMMER SQUASH RIBBONS

Use vegetable peeler to shave squash lengthwise into 3 thin ribbons on 1 side, rotating squash 90 degrees and repeating on next side. Continue to rotate and peel squash into thin ribbons until you reach core. Discard core.

3. Heat remaining 1 teaspoon oil in 12-inch nonstick skillet over medium-high heat until just smoking. Add summer squash and cook, tossing occasionally with tongs, until summer squash has softened and is translucent, 3 to 4 minutes. Transfer summer squash to bowl with dressing, add parsley, and gently toss to coat. Season with salt and pepper to taste. Serve.

VARIATION
Sautéed Summer Squash Ribbons with Mint and Pistachios
Omit lemon zest and substitute 1½ teaspoons cider vinegar for lemon juice. Substitute ⅓ cup chopped fresh mint for parsley and sprinkle summer squash with 2 tablespoons chopped toasted pistachios before serving.

Stewed Zucchini
Serves 6 to 8

Why This Recipe Works Looking for a new way to take advantage of the abundance of zucchini in the summer, we landed on a stewed preparation, which makes this crisp vegetable pleasantly soft and almost creamy in texture while still retaining its natural flavor. Stewing zucchini is popular in Greece, so we looked to the traditional Greek combination of zucchini and tomatoes. We started by browning seeded zucchini on the stovetop (in batches to ensure thorough, even browning) and set it aside while we built a savory tomato sauce. Canned whole peeled tomatoes, processed until smooth, gave the dish the right balance of tomato flavor and silky texture. A smattering of olives complemented the sauce and enhanced the Greek flavor profile. Once our sauce had simmered and thickened, we stirred in the browned zucchini and transferred the pot to the oven to allow it to gently finish cooking and develop deep, concentrated flavor. A garnish of shredded fresh mint, stirred in at the end, added brightness. If possible, use smaller, in-season zucchini, which have thinner skins and fewer seeds.

- 1 (28-ounce) can whole peeled tomatoes
- 3 tablespoons extra-virgin olive oil, divided
- 5 zucchini (8 ounces each), trimmed, quartered lengthwise, seeded, and cut into 2-inch lengths
- 1 onion, chopped fine
- ¾ teaspoon table salt
- 3 garlic cloves, minced
- 1 teaspoon minced fresh oregano or ¼ teaspoon dried
- ¼ teaspoon red pepper flakes
- 2 tablespoons chopped pitted kalamata olives
- 2 tablespoons shredded fresh mint

1. Adjust oven rack to lower-middle position and heat oven to 325 degrees. Process tomatoes and their juice in food processor until completely smooth, about 1 minute; set aside.

2. Heat 2 teaspoons oil in Dutch oven over medium-high heat until just smoking. Brown one-third of zucchini, about 3 minutes per side; transfer to bowl. Repeat with 4 teaspoons oil and remaining zucchini in 2 batches; transfer to bowl.

3. Add remaining 1 tablespoon oil, onion, and salt to now-empty pot and cook, stirring occasionally, over medium-low heat until onion is very soft and golden brown, 9 to 11 minutes. Stir in garlic, oregano, and pepper flakes and cook until fragrant, about 30 seconds. Stir in olives and tomatoes, bring to simmer, and cook, stirring occasionally, until sauce has thickened, about 30 minutes.

4. Stir in zucchini and any accumulated juices, cover, and transfer pot to oven. Bake until zucchini is very tender, 30 to 40 minutes. Stir in mint and adjust sauce consistency with hot water as needed. Season with salt and pepper to taste. Serve.

Zucchini and Feta Fritters
Serves 4 to 6

Why This Recipe Works During the summer there never seems to be enough ways to cook zucchini. These fritters fall between pancakes and latkes and make a great side dish, or vegetarian main, when you want something crispy. We shredded and salted the zucchini, let it drain, and squeezed it in a dish towel to eliminate moisture, which can make the fritters soggy. To allow the zucchini's flavor to shine, we bound the zucchini with eggs and a little flour. Fresh dill and feta cheese were ideal add-ins for an herbal note and salty richness. Use a coarse grater or the shredding disk of a food processor to shred the zucchini. Make sure to squeeze the zucchini until it is completely dry, or the fritters will fall apart in the skillet. Do not let the zucchini sit for too long after it has been squeezed dry or it will turn brown. Fritters can be served warm or at room temperature. Serve with Tzatziki (page 20), if desired.

- 1 pound zucchini, shredded
- 1 teaspoon table salt
- 4 ounces feta cheese, crumbled (1 cup)
- 2 scallions, minced
- 2 large eggs, lightly beaten
- 2 tablespoons minced fresh dill
- 1 garlic clove, minced
- ¼ teaspoon pepper
- ¼ cup all-purpose flour
- 6 tablespoons extra-virgin olive oil, divided
  Lemon wedges

1. Adjust oven rack to middle position and heat oven to 200 degrees. Toss zucchini with salt and let drain in fine-mesh strainer for 10 minutes.

2. Wrap zucchini in clean dish towel, squeeze out excess liquid, and transfer to large bowl. Stir in feta, scallions, eggs, dill, garlic, and pepper. Sprinkle flour over mixture and stir to incorporate.

3. Heat 3 tablespoons oil in 12-inch nonstick skillet over medium heat until shimmering. Drop 2-tablespoon-size portions of batter into skillet and use back of spoon to press batter into 2-inch-wide fritter (you should fit about 6 fritters in skillet at a time). Fry until golden brown, about 3 minutes per side.

4. Transfer fritters to paper towel–lined baking sheet and keep warm in oven. Wipe skillet clean with paper towels and repeat with remaining 3 tablespoons oil and remaining batter. Serve with lemon wedges.

Peach Caprese Salad

Serves 6 `FAST` `NO COOK`

Why This Recipe Works Caprese salad is traditionally made with slices of tomatoes and mozzarella and fresh basil with a simple dressing of extra-virgin olive oil and balsamic vinegar. To give this salad a new twist, we swapped in a different juicy summer fruit: ripe fresh peaches. If you're lucky, you'll be able to find both the peaches and fresh mozzarella at the farmers' market. A lemony dressing highlighted the best flavors in both the peaches and the creamy cheese. Tossing the peach slices with the dressing before assembling the salad ensured that the peaches were deeply seasoned. For the best results, use the ripest in-season peaches you can find. We like using 4-ounce balls of fresh mozzarella in this recipe.

- 3 tablespoons extra-virgin olive oil
- 1½ tablespoons lemon juice
- ¼ teaspoon table salt
- ⅛ teaspoon pepper
- 1 pound ripe peaches, quartered and pitted, each quarter cut into 4 slices
- 12 ounces fresh mozzarella cheese, halved and sliced ¼ inch thick
- 6 large fresh basil leaves, torn into small pieces

1. Whisk oil, lemon juice, salt, and pepper together in large bowl. Add peaches and gently toss to coat.

2. Shingle peaches and mozzarella on serving platter. Drizzle any remaining dressing from bowl over top. Sprinkle with basil. Season with salt and pepper to taste. Serve.

Stewed Zucchini

Zucchini and Feta Fritters

Peach and Tomato Salad

Purslane and Watermelon Salad

Peach and Tomato Salad
Serves 4 to 6 `NO COOK`

Why This Recipe Works At the height of summer, we like to take advantage of both in-season fruits and vegetables, but it's especially gratifying to enjoy them in combination. We combined ripe, plump peaches and tomatoes for a savory-sweet salad. Salting the tomatoes helped concentrate the flavors by removing excess liquid that would have watered down the salad. Their acidity balanced the natural sweetness of the peaches, as did cider vinegar, lemon juice, and lemon zest in the dressing. Thinly sliced shallot kept the salad on the savory side, and torn mint leaves added a fresh herbal note. For the best results, use the ripest in-season peaches and tomatoes you can find.

- 1 pound ripe tomatoes, cored, cut into ½-inch-thick wedges, and wedges halved crosswise
- 1 teaspoon table salt, divided
- 3 tablespoons extra-virgin olive oil, plus extra for drizzling
- 2 tablespoons cider vinegar
- ½ teaspoon grated lemon zest plus 1 tablespoon juice
- ½ teaspoon pepper
- 1 pound ripe peaches, halved, pitted, cut into ½-inch-thick wedges, and wedges halved crosswise
- 1 shallot, sliced into thin rings
- ⅓ cup fresh mint leaves, torn

1. Combine tomatoes and ½ teaspoon salt in bowl and toss to coat; transfer to colander and let drain in sink for 30 minutes.

2. Whisk oil, vinegar, lemon zest and juice, remaining ½ teaspoon salt, and pepper together in large bowl. Add peaches, shallot, and drained tomatoes to dressing and toss gently to coat. Season with salt and pepper to taste. Transfer to serving platter and sprinkle with mint. Drizzle with extra oil. Serve.

VARIATION
Peach and Tomato Salad with Pancetta and Basil
Increase oil to ¼ cup. Cook 4 ounces pancetta, cut into ½-inch pieces, in 1 tablespoon oil in 10-inch skillet over medium heat until crisp, 7 to 9 minutes. Transfer pancetta to paper towel–lined plate to drain. Substitute 2 scallions, sliced thin on bias, for shallot and basil for mint. Sprinkle pancetta over salad with basil.

Purslane and Watermelon Salad
Serves 4 to 6 `NO COOK`

Why This Recipe Works You've probably seen purslane growing all around—in open fields, in sidewalk cracks, maybe even in your backyard—without realizing that this common foraged green is not only edible but also delicious. Its crisp, juicy stems and leaves and slightly tart, tangy flavor make it a special ingredient perfect for highlighting in a fresh salad. Since purslane is available only in the summer, we created a salad that celebrates a pairing of two fresh, summery ingredients. To start, we cubed watermelon into 1-inch chunks, tossed the cubes with sugar, and let them drain of any excess liquid. This ensured that we wouldn't have a soupy mess on our hands. To gently balance the melon's sweetness and the purslane's tangy bite, we added thinly sliced shallot for delicate onion flavor. Tearing the purslane into pieces ensured that every bite would have purslane flavor. Fresh basil lent brightness, torn bits of fresh mozzarella added creamy substance, and a simple vinaigrette of olive oil, cider vinegar, and lemon brought everything together. This salad benefits from a liberal sprinkling of salt and pepper, so don't be shy when seasoning the mozzarella.

- 4 cups 1-inch seedless watermelon pieces
- 2 teaspoons sugar
- 2 tablespoons extra-virgin olive oil, plus extra for drizzling
- 1 tablespoon cider vinegar
- ½ teaspoon grated lemon zest plus 1 tablespoon juice
- ½ teaspoon table salt
- ¼ teaspoon pepper
- 6 ounces purslane, trimmed and torn into 1½-inch pieces (6 cups)
- ¼ cup fresh basil leaves, torn
- 1 shallot, sliced thin
- 6 ounces fresh mozzarella cheese, torn into 1-inch pieces

1. Toss watermelon with sugar in colander set over bowl; set aside for 30 minutes.

2. Whisk oil, vinegar, lemon zest and juice, salt, and pepper together in large bowl. Add purslane, basil, shallot, and drained watermelon and toss gently to combine. Transfer to serving platter and scatter mozzarella over top. Drizzle with extra oil and season with salt and pepper to taste. Serve.

Watermelon-Tomato Salad
Serves 4 `NO COOK`

Why This Recipe Works This salad shouts summer, but to ensure that the vibrant flavors of the watermelon and tomatoes didn't get drowned out, we had to devise a way to tame the juiciness of both fruits before combining them in a lightly dressed salad. To do this, we tossed cubes of watermelon with some sugar and let them drain. We tossed cherry tomatoes—ideally, farm-fresh ones—with a little salt and set them aside while the watermelon drained. Since both of our salad components were bright red, we chose yellow cherry tomatoes for nice color contrast. Shallot gently balanced the melon's sweetness and basil lent brightness. Finally, we added bits of fresh mozzarella for substance and a simple vinaigrette to bring everything together. This salad benefits from a liberal sprinkling of salt and pepper, so don't be shy when seasoning the mozzarella.

- 4 cups 1-inch seedless watermelon pieces
- 2 teaspoons sugar
- 12 ounces yellow cherry tomatoes, halved
- ¾ teaspoon table salt, divided
- ½ teaspoon pepper, divided
- 2 tablespoons extra-virgin olive oil, plus extra for drizzling
- 1 tablespoon cider vinegar
- ½ teaspoon grated lemon zest plus 1 tablespoon juice
- 1 shallot, sliced thin
- ¼ cup fresh basil leaves, torn
- 6 ounces fresh mozzarella cheese, torn into 1-inch pieces

1. Toss watermelon with sugar in colander set over bowl; set aside for 30 minutes.

2. Toss tomatoes, ¼ teaspoon salt, and ¼ teaspoon pepper together in small bowl; set aside.

3. Whisk oil, vinegar, lemon zest and juice, remaining ½ teaspoon salt, and remaining ¼ teaspoon pepper together in large bowl. Add shallot, basil, drained watermelon, and tomatoes and toss gently to combine. Transfer to platter and evenly scatter mozzarella over top. Drizzle with extra oil and season with salt and pepper to taste. Serve.

Preserve the Season

▦ MAKE AHEAD
Photos (clockwise from top left): Whole Peeled Tomatoes; Quick Pickle Chips;
Classic Blueberry Jam; Classic Plum Preserves; Tangy Corn Relish

No-Commitment Strawberry Jam

Makes two 1-cup jars `MAKE AHEAD`

Why This Recipe Works No-commitment jams are perfect for trying out jam making as they are pretty simple to prepare. They generally make a small batch, which means you don't need to invest in bushels of fruit, and there's no need to process jars in boiling water for long-term storage; you can keep the two jars of jam the recipe makes in the fridge and finish them off in a few weeks. Also, a small batch of fruit will cook down quickly to the proper consistency, resulting in a vibrant and fresh-tasting jam. And because the cooking time is so short, there's no danger that the naturally occurring pectin in the fruit won't do its job (a risk when cooking larger batches). In addition to the pectin in the fruit itself, hefty doses of lemon juice and sugar helped this strawberry jam set up perfectly. Crushing the strawberries with a potato masher before cooking jump-started the release of pectin and further decreased the cooking time, ensuring maximum fresh fruit flavor. The jam will continue to thicken as it cools, so it's best to err on the side of undercooking. Overcooked jam that is dark, thick, and smells of caramelized sugar cannot be saved. Be sure to use bottled lemon juice, not fresh-squeezed juice, in this recipe, or the jam might not set up properly. This jam cannot be processed for long-term storage.

1½ pounds strawberries, hulled and
     cut into ½-inch pieces (5 cups)
1 cup sugar
3 tablespoons bottled lemon juice

1. Place 2 small plates in freezer to chill. In large saucepan, mash strawberries with potato masher until fruit is mostly broken down. Stir in sugar and lemon juice and bring to boil, stirring often, over medium-high heat.

2. Once sugar is completely dissolved, boil mixture, stirring and adjusting heat as needed, until thickened and registers 217 to 220 degrees, 15 to 20 minutes. (Temperature will be lower at higher elevations; see page 328 for more information.) Remove pot from heat.

3. To test consistency, place 1 teaspoon jam on chilled plate and freeze for 2 minutes. Drag your finger through jam on plate; jam has correct consistency when your finger leaves distinct trail. If runny, return pot to heat and simmer for 1 to 3 minutes before retesting. Skim any foam from surface of jam using spoon.

4. Meanwhile, place two 1-cup jars in bowl and place under hot running water until heated through, 1 to 2 minutes; shake dry.

No-Commitment Jams

5. Using funnel and ladle, portion hot jam into hot jars. Let cool to room temperature, cover, and refrigerate until jam is set, 12 to 24 hours. (Jam can be refrigerated for up to 2 months.)

VARIATIONS

No-Commitment Berry Jam
Substitute 1 pound (3 cups) blueberries, raspberries, or blackberries for strawberries and leave berries whole. Reduce boiling time in step 2 as follows: 8 to 12 minutes for blueberries, and 10 to 15 minutes for raspberries or blackberries.

No-Commitment Stone Fruit Jam
We like to leave the skins on our stone fruits because they add color and flavor to the jam. Substitute 1 pound thinly sliced yellow peaches (do not use white peaches), nectarines, apricots, or plums (3 cups) for berries. In step 2, boil mixture for 10 to 15 minutes.

Classic Strawberry Jam
Makes four 1-cup jars `MAKE AHEAD`

Why This Recipe Works When summer gifts us with an abundance of fresh strawberries, there's no better way to extend enjoyment of them than making jam. Naturally low in pectin, strawberries are often cooked too long, causing the fruit to lose its bright flavor. We shortened the cooking time by cutting the strawberries into smaller pieces and then mashing them to release their juices and jump-start the cooking process. Shredded apple added natural pectin and fresh flavor to the mix. Lemon juice added acidity to balance the sugar's sweetness and helped the natural pectin to gel. Small, fragrant berries produce the best jam. For safety reasons, be sure to use bottled lemon juice, not fresh-squeezed juice, in this recipe (see page 324). To double this recipe make two single batches in separate pots. Do not try not to make a double batch in a single large pot; it will not work.

- 3 pounds strawberries, hulled and cut into ½-inch pieces (10 cups)
- 3 cups sugar
- 1¼ cups peeled and shredded Granny Smith apple (1 large apple)
- 2 tablespoons bottled lemon juice

1. Place 2 small plates in freezer to chill. Set canning rack in canning pot, place four 1-cup jars in rack, and add water to cover by 1 inch. Bring to simmer over medium heat, then turn off heat and cover to keep hot.

2. In Dutch oven, crush strawberries with potato masher until fruit is mostly broken down. Stir in sugar, apple, and lemon juice and bring to boil, stirring often, over medium-high heat. Once sugar is completely dissolved, boil mixture, stirring and adjusting heat as needed, until thickened and registers 217 to 220 degrees, 20 to 25 minutes. (Temperature will be lower at higher elevations; see page 328 for more information.) Remove pot from heat.

3. To test consistency, place 1 teaspoon jam on chilled plate and freeze for 2 minutes. Drag your finger through jam on plate; jam has correct consistency when your finger leaves distinct trail. If runny, return pot to heat and simmer for 1 to 3 minutes before retesting. Skim any foam from surface of jam using spoon.

4. Place dish towel flat on counter. Using jar lifter, remove jars from pot, draining water back into pot. Place jars upside down on towel and let dry for 1 minute. Using funnel and ladle, portion hot jam into hot jars, leaving ¼ inch headspace. Slide wooden skewer along inside edge of jar and drag upward to remove air bubbles.

5A. For short-term storage Let jam cool to room temperature, cover, and refrigerate until jam is set, 12 to 24 hours. (Jam can be refrigerated for up to 2 months.)

5B. For long-term storage While jars are hot, wipe rims clean, add lids, and screw on rings until fingertip-tight; do not overtighten. Return pot of water with canning rack to boil. Lower jars into water, cover, bring water back to boil, then start timer. Cooking time will depend on your altitude: Boil 10 minutes for up to 1,000 feet, 15 minutes for 1,001 to 3,000 feet, 20 minutes for 3,001 to 6,000 feet, or 25 minutes for 6,001 to 8,000 feet. Turn off heat and let jars sit in pot for 5 minutes. Remove jars from pot and let cool for 24 hours. Remove rings, check seal, and clean rims. (Sealed jars can be stored for up to 1 year.)

Classic Blueberry Jam
Makes four 1-cup jars `MAKE AHEAD`

Why This Recipe Works When fresh blueberries are plentiful, preserve a bit of summer year-round with blueberry jam. The trick to our jam was making sure not to overcook the fruit. Blueberries have thick skins and numerous tiny seeds within, so when overcooked they can easily take on a leathery texture and mealy taste. To combat this, we simmered the blueberries for just 5 minutes to let them release their natural juices before adding pectin (mixed with a little sugar), followed by the rest of the sugar, to create the perfect gel set. We were left with silky jam and a few intact blueberries that burst in your mouth with bright taste. Freshly picked ripe-yet-firm blueberries are best. For safety reasons, be sure to use bottled lemon juice, not fresh-squeezed juice, in this recipe (see page 324). To double this recipe make two single batches in separate pots. Do not try not to make a double batch in a single large pot; it will not work.

- 2¾ cups sugar, divided
- 2 tablespoons Sure-Jell for Less or No Sugar Needed Recipes (see page 324)
- 25 ounces (5 cups) blueberries
- 2 tablespoons bottled lemon juice
- 1 teaspoon grated lemon zest

1. Set canning rack in canning pot, place four 1-cup jars in rack, and add water to cover by 1 inch. Bring to simmer over medium heat, then turn off heat and cover to keep hot.

2. Combine ¼ cup sugar and Sure-Jell in bowl. Bring blueberries, lemon juice, and lemon zest to simmer in Dutch oven over medium-high heat. Reduce heat to medium-low and simmer, stirring occasionally, until blueberries have softened and released their juice, about 5 minutes.

Classic Raspberry Jam

3. Bring mixture to boil over high heat. Whisk in Sure-Jell mixture and bring to boil. Whisk in remaining 2½ cups sugar and bring to vigorous boil. Once boiling, cook for 1 minute, whisking constantly. Remove pot from heat and skim any foam from surface of jam using spoon.

4. Place dish towel flat on counter. Using jar lifter, remove jars from pot, draining water back into pot. Place jars upside down on towel and let dry for 1 minute. Using funnel and ladle, portion hot jam into hot jars, leaving ¼ inch headspace. Slide wooden skewer along inside edge of jar and drag upward to remove air bubbles.

5A. For short-term storage Let jam cool to room temperature, cover, and refrigerate until jam is set, 12 to 24 hours. (Jam can be refrigerated for up to 2 months.)

5B. For long-term storage While jars are hot, wipe rims clean, add lids, and screw on rings until fingertip-tight; do not overtighten. Return pot of water with canning rack to boil. Lower jars into water, cover, bring water back to boil, then start timer. Cooking time will depend on your altitude: Boil 10 minutes for up to 1,000 feet, 15 minutes for 1,001 to 3,000 feet, 20 minutes for 3,001 to 6,000 feet, or 25 minutes for 6,001 to 8,000 feet. Turn off heat and let jars sit in pot for 5 minutes. Remove jars from pot; let cool for 24 hours. Remove rings, check seal, and clean rims. (Sealed jars can be stored for up to 1 year.)

Classic Peach Jam

Classic Raspberry Jam
Makes four 1-cup jars `MAKE AHEAD`

Why This Recipe Works For a raspberry jam bursting with fresh fruit flavor, we started by finding the perfect balance of fruit to sugar. For intense fruit flavor, we added a grated Granny Smith apple. Traditionally, apple adds body to fruit jams, but in this recipe we also found it created great bright flavor. Lemon juice boosted the brightness while also adding acidity to help the pectin set. We boiled our jam for just 10 to 15 minutes to achieve the perfect consistency. Slightly unripe or "just ripe" fruit will form a jam more easily than very ripe fruit, as it contains more pectin and is more acidic. For safety reasons, be sure to use bottled lemon juice, not fresh-squeezed juice, in this recipe (see page 324). To double this recipe make two single batches in separate pots. Do not try to make a double batch in a single large pot; it will not work.

- 2 pounds (6½ cups) raspberries
- 3 cups sugar
- 1 cup peeled and shredded Granny Smith apple (1 apple)
- 1 tablespoon bottled lemon juice

1. Place 2 small plates in freezer to chill. Set canning rack in canning pot, place four 1-cup jars in rack, and add water to cover by 1 inch. Bring to simmer over medium heat, then turn off heat and cover to keep hot.

2. In Dutch oven, bring raspberries, sugar, apple, and lemon juice to boil, stirring often, over medium-high heat. Once sugar is completely dissolved, boil mixture, stirring and adjusting heat as needed, until thickened and registers 217 to 220 degrees, 10 to 15 minutes. (Temperature will be lower at higher elevations; see page 328 for more information.) Remove pot from heat.

3. To test consistency, place 1 teaspoon jam on chilled plate and freeze for 2 minutes. Drag your finger through jam on plate; jam has correct consistency when your finger leaves distinct trail. If runny, return pot to heat and simmer for 1 to 3 minutes before retesting. Skim any foam from surface of jam using spoon.

4. Place dish towel flat on counter. Using jar lifter, remove jars from pot, draining water back into pot. Place jars upside down on towel and let dry for 1 minute. Using funnel and ladle, portion hot jam into hot jars, leaving ¼ inch headspace. Slide wooden skewer along inside edge of jar and drag upward to remove air bubbles.

5A. For short-term storage Let jam cool to room temperature, cover, and refrigerate until jam is set, 12 to 24 hours. (Jam can be refrigerated for up to 2 months.)

5B. For long-term storage While jars are hot, wipe rims clean, add lids, and screw on rings until fingertip-tight; do not overtighten. Return pot of water with canning rack to boil. Lower jars into water, cover, bring water back to boil, then start timer. Cooking time will depend on your altitude: Boil 10 minutes for up to 1,000 feet, 15 minutes for 1,001 to 3,000 feet, 20 minutes for 3,001 to 6,000 feet, or 25 minutes for 6,001 to 8,000 feet. Turn off heat and let jars sit in pot for 5 minutes. Remove jars from pot and let cool for 24 hours. Remove rings, check seal, and clean rims. (Sealed jars can be stored for up to 1 year.)

THE FROZEN PLATE TEST

If the jam runs back into the area just cleared by your finger, it needs to be cooked longer.

If your finger leaves a distinct trail through the jam, it will set properly when cooled.

Classic Peach Jam
Makes four 1-cup jars MAKE AHEAD

Why This Recipe Works In our classic peach jam, sugar brings out the sweetness of summer-ripe peaches and lemon juice adds brightness and acidity. A shredded apple provided enough natural pectin for just the right set. Leaving the skins on the peaches created a pretty rose-tinted jam and intensified the peach flavor, and a shortened cooking time retained that flavor. Do not use white peaches here; they are not acidic enough for safe canning using this recipe. For safety reasons, be sure to use bottled lemon juice, not fresh-squeezed juice, in this recipe (see page 324). To double this recipe make two single batches in separate pots. Do not try not to make a double batch in a single large pot; it will not work.

> 2 pounds ripe but firm yellow peaches, halved, pitted, and cut into ½-inch pieces (6 cups)
> 2½ cups sugar
> 1 cup peeled and shredded Granny Smith apple (1 apple)
> 3 tablespoons bottled lemon juice

1. Place 2 small plates in freezer to chill. Set canning rack in canning pot, place four 1-cup jars in rack, and add water to cover by 1 inch. Bring to simmer over medium heat, then turn off heat and cover to keep hot.

2. Stir peaches, sugar, apple, and lemon juice together in Dutch oven until well combined. Cover and let sit for 20 minutes. Bring mixture to boil, stirring often, over medium-high heat. Once sugar is completely dissolved, reduce heat to medium-low, cover, and simmer, stirring occasionally, until peaches have softened, about 15 minutes.

3. Off heat, crush fruit with potato masher until mostly smooth. Return mixture to boil over medium-high heat and cook, stirring and adjusting heat as needed, until mixture registers 217 to 220 degrees, 5 to 7 minutes. (Temperature will be lower at higher elevations; see page 328 for more information.) Remove pot from heat.

4. To test consistency, place 1 teaspoon jam on chilled plate and freeze for 2 minutes. Drag your finger through jam on plate; jam has correct consistency when your finger leaves distinct trail. If runny, return pot to heat and simmer for 1 to 3 minutes before retesting. Skim any foam from surface of jam using spoon.

5. Place dish towel flat on counter. Using jar lifter, remove jars from pot, draining water back into pot. Place jars upside down on towel and let dry for 1 minute. Using funnel and ladle, portion hot jam into hot jars, leaving ¼ inch headspace. Slide wooden skewer along inside edge of jar and drag upward to remove air bubbles.

6A. For short-term storage Let jam cool to room temperature, cover, and refrigerate until jam is set, 12 to 24 hours. (Jam can be refrigerated for up to 2 months.)

6B. For long-term storage While jars are hot, wipe rims clean, add lids, and screw on rings until fingertip-tight; do not overtighten. Return pot of water with canning rack to boil. Lower jars into water, cover, bring water back to boil, then start timer. Cooking time will depend on your altitude: Boil 10 minutes for up to 1,000 feet, 15 minutes for 1,001 to 3,000 feet, 20 minutes for 3,001 to 6,000 feet, or 25 minutes for 6,001 to 8,000 feet. Turn off heat and let jars sit in pot for 5 minutes. Remove jars from pot and let cool for 24 hours. Remove rings, check seal, and clean rims. (Sealed jars can be stored for up to 1 year.)

Classic Apricot Preserves
Makes four 1-cup jars MAKE AHEAD

Why This Recipe Works Our apricot preserves are bright, texturally pleasing, and full of fruit flavor. For a strong start, we created a puree by cooking down half the chopped apricots, along with sugar, water for moisture, and lemon juice. We kept the fresh fruit flavor by adding half the apricots later in the cooking process. Coarsely mashing the cooked mixture left some discernible apricot pieces and a satisfying texture. Choose ripe but firm apricots. For safety reasons, be sure to use bottled lemon juice, not fresh-squeezed juice, in this recipe (see page 324). To double this recipe make two single batches in separate pots. Do not try to make a double batch in a single large pot; it will not work.

- 3 pounds ripe but firm apricots, pitted and cut into ½-inch pieces (about 8½ cups), divided
- 2 cups sugar
- 3 tablespoons bottled lemon juice

1. Place 2 small plates in freezer to chill. Set canning rack in canning pot, place four 1-cup jars in rack, and add water to cover by 1 inch. Bring to simmer over medium heat, then turn off heat and cover to keep hot.

2. In Dutch oven, bring half of apricots, sugar, ½ cup water, and lemon juice to boil, stirring often, over medium-high heat. Once sugar is completely dissolved, reduce heat to medium-low and simmer, stirring often, until mixture is thick with some pieces of fruit intact, about 25 minutes.

3. Stir in remaining apricots and simmer until they are just softened, 5 to 7 minutes. Off heat, crush fruit coarse with potato masher, leaving some larger pieces intact. Return mixture to

Classic Apricot Preserves

boil over medium-high heat and cook, stirring and adjusting heat as needed, until mixture registers 217 to 220 degrees, about 5 minutes. (Temperature will be lower at higher elevations; see page 328 for more information.) Remove pot from heat.

4. To test consistency, place 1 teaspoon preserves on chilled plate and freeze for 2 minutes. Drag your finger through preserves on plate; preserves have correct consistency when your finger leaves distinct trail. If runny, return pot to heat and simmer for 1 to 3 minutes before retesting. Skim any foam from surface of preserves using spoon.

5. Place dish towel flat on counter. Using jar lifter, remove jars from pot, draining water back into pot. Place jars upside down on towel and let dry for 1 minute. Using funnel and ladle, portion hot preserves into hot jars, leaving ¼ inch headspace. Slide wooden skewer along inside edge of jar and drag upward to remove air bubbles.

6A. For short-term storage Let preserves cool to room temperature, cover, and refrigerate until jam is set, 12 to 24 hours. (Preserves can be refrigerated for up to 2 months.)

6B. For long-term storage While jars are hot, wipe rims clean, add lids, and screw on rings until fingertip-tight; do not overtighten. Return pot of water with canning rack to boil.

Lower jars into water, cover, bring water back to boil, then start timer. Cooking time will depend on your altitude: Boil 10 minutes for up to 1,000 feet, 15 minutes for 1,001 to 3,000 feet, 20 minutes for 3,001 to 6,000 feet, or 25 minutes for 6,001 to 8,000 feet. Turn off heat and let jars sit in pot for 5 minutes. Remove jars from pot and let cool for 24 hours. Remove rings, check seal, and clean rims. (Sealed jars can be stored for up to 1 year.)

Classic Plum Preserves
Makes four 1-cup jars MAKE AHEAD

Why This Recipe Works To yield plum preserves with the most intense fresh plum flavor, we cooked all the ingredients together for just a short time. Leaving the skins on the plums contributed a lot of natural pectin as well as a lot of plum flavor. Using 2 cups of sugar muted the plums' tartness and high-lighted their natural sweetness. We opted for lime juice, which provided vibrant flavor. For safety reasons, be sure to use bottled lime juice, not fresh-squeezed juice, in this recipe (see page 324). To double this recipe make two single batches in separate pots. Do not try to make a double batch in a single large pot; it will not work.

2½   pounds ripe but firm plums, pitted and
      cut into ½-inch pieces (8 cups)
2   cups sugar
2   tablespoons bottled lime juice

1. Place 2 small plates in freezer to chill. Set canning rack in canning pot, place four 1-cup jars in rack, and add water to cover by 1 inch. Bring to simmer over medium heat, then turn off heat and cover to keep hot.

2. In Dutch oven, bring plums, sugar, and lime juice to boil, stirring often, over medium-high heat. Once sugar has completely dissolved, remove pot from heat and crush fruit coarse with potato masher, leaving some larger pieces intact.

3. Return mixture to boil over medium-high heat and cook, stirring and adjusting heat as needed, until mixture registers 217 to 220 degrees, 5 to 7 minutes. (Temperature will be lower at higher elevations; see page 328 for more information.) Remove pot from heat.

4. To test consistency, place 1 teaspoon preserves on chilled plate and freeze for 2 minutes. Drag your finger through preserves on plate; preserves have correct consistency when your finger leaves distinct trail. If runny, return pot to heat and simmer for 1 to 3 minutes before retesting. Skim any foam from surface of preserves using spoon.

5. Place dish towel flat on counter. Using jar lifter, remove jars from pot, draining water back into pot. Place jars upside down on towel and let dry for 1 minute. Using funnel and ladle, portion hot preserves into hot jars, leaving ¼ inch headspace. Slide wooden skewer along inside edge of jar and drag upward to remove air bubbles.

6A. For short-term storage Let preserves cool to room temperature, cover, and refrigerate until preserves are set, 12 to 24 hours. (Preserves can be refrigerated for up to 2 months.)

6B. For long-term storage While jars are hot, wipe rims clean, add lids, and screw on rings until fingertip-tight; do not overtighten. Return pot of water with canning rack to boil. Lower jars into water, cover, bring water back to boil, then start timer. Cooking time will depend on your altitude: Boil 10 minutes for up to 1,000 feet, 15 minutes for 1,001 to 3,000 feet, 20 minutes for 3,001 to 6,000 feet, or 25 minutes for 6,001 to 8,000 feet. Turn off heat and let jars sit in pot for 5 minutes. Remove jars from pot and let cool for 24 hours. Remove rings, check seal, and clean rims. (Sealed jars can be stored for up to 1 year.)

Cherry Preserves
Makes four 1-cup jars MAKE AHEAD

Why This Recipe Works One of the highlights of the summer fruit season is the arrival of juicy sweet cherries, which can be transformed into succulent preserves packed with deep cherry flavor. We tried cutting the cherries to various sizes and found that simply halving them gave us the best chunky texture. To soften the cherries and help them release their flavorful juices, we simmered them in a covered pot before whisking in just enough pectin and sugar to create a thickened, velvety back-drop for the fruit. We blended the liquid ingredients with a whisk while also gently mashing the fruit with it. We used Bing cherries to develop this recipe, but any variety of sweet cherries can be used; do not use sour cherries. For safety reasons, be sure to use bottled lemon juice, not fresh-squeezed juice, in this recipe (see page 324). To double this recipe make two single batches in separate pots. Do not try to make a double batch in a single large pot; it will not work.

3   cups sugar, divided
3   tablespoons Sure-Jell for Less or No Sugar
      Needed Recipes (see page 324)
2   pounds sweet cherries, pitted and halved (4 cups)
2   tablespoons bottled lemon juice

1. Set canning rack in canning pot, place four 1-cup jars in rack, and add water to cover by 1 inch. Bring to simmer over medium heat, then turn off heat and cover to keep hot.

2. Combine ¼ cup sugar and Sure-Jell in bowl. In Dutch oven, bring cherries and lemon juice to boil, stirring often, over medium-high heat. Reduce heat to medium, cover, and simmer, stirring occasionally, until cherries soften and release some of their juices, about 3 minutes.

3. Bring mixture to boil over high heat. Whisk in Sure-Jell mixture and return to boil. Whisk in remaining 2¾ cups sugar and bring to vigorous boil. Once boiling, cook for 1 minute, whisking constantly. Remove pot from heat and skim any foam from surface of preserves using spoon.

4. Place dish towel flat on counter. Using jar lifter, remove jars from pot, draining water back into pot. Place jars upside down on towel and let dry for 1 minute. Using funnel and ladle, portion hot preserves into hot jars, leaving ¼ inch headspace. Slide wooden skewer along inside edge of jar and drag upward to remove air bubbles.

5A. For short-term storage Let preserves cool to room temperature, cover, and refrigerate until preserves are set, 12 to 24 hours. (Preserves can be refrigerated for up to 2 months.)

5B. For long-term storage While jars are hot, wipe rims clean, add lids, and screw on rings until fingertip-tight; do not overtighten. Return pot of water with canning rack to boil. Lower jars into water, cover, bring water back to boil, then start timer. Cooking time will depend on your altitude: Boil 10 minutes for up to 1,000 feet, 15 minutes for 1,001 to 3,000 feet, 20 minutes for 3,001 to 6,000 feet, or 25 minutes for 6,001 to 8,000 feet. Turn off heat and let jars sit in pot for 5 minutes. Remove jars from pot and let cool for 24 hours. Remove rings, check seals, and clean rims. (Sealed jars can be stored for up to 1 year.)

Concord Grape Jelly
Makes four 1-cup jars MAKE AHEAD

Why This Recipe Works When Concord grapes show up in late summer through early fall, we like to make jelly. We simmered fresh grapes to steam them quickly and then crushed them gently as they released their juices. We strained out the solids and refrigerated the juice for a day before straining it again to ensure a crystal-clear jelly. We added just enough sugar to enhance the natural sweetness of the grapes, and just enough pectin to produce a clear, smooth set. Look for grapes that are firm, plump, and securely attached to their stems. To double this recipe double all of the ingredients except the grapes; increase the amount of grapes to 7 pounds. Use a 12-quart pot when making the juice in step 1 and jelly in step 4.

Measure out 7 cups juice before making the jelly. Increase the amount of sugar mixed with the pectin to ½ cup; add the remaining 4½ cups sugar as directed in step 4.

 4 pounds Concord grapes, stemmed
1½ cups water
2½ cups sugar, divided
 5 tablespoons Sure-Jell for Less or No Sugar Needed Recipes (see page 324)

1. Bring grapes and water to boil in Dutch oven over high heat. Reduce heat to medium, cover, and simmer, crushing grapes occasionally with potato masher, until grapes are soft and separated from their skins, 5 to 10 minutes.

2. Working in batches, strain mixture through fine-mesh strainer into large bowl, pressing firmly on solids to extract as much liquid as possible; discard solids. Clean strainer, line with triple layer of cheesecloth, and strain juice again into large measuring cup. Let juice cool, then cover and refrigerate for 24 to 48 hours. Before making jelly, strain juice again through cheesecloth-lined strainer and measure out 3½ cups; reserve any extra juice for another use.

3. Set canning rack in canning pot, place four 1-cup jars in rack, and add water to cover by 1 inch. Bring to simmer over medium heat, then turn off heat and cover to keep hot.

4. Combine ¼ cup sugar and Sure-Jell in bowl. Bring juice to boil in clean Dutch oven over high heat. Whisk in Sure-Jell mixture and bring to boil. Whisk in remaining 2¼ cups sugar and bring to vigorous boil. Once boiling, cook for 1 minute, whisking constantly. Remove pot from heat and skim any foam from surface of jelly using large spoon.

5. Place dish towel flat on counter. Using jar lifter, remove jars from pot, draining water back into pot. Place jars upside down on towel and let dry for 1 minute. Using funnel and ladle, portion hot jelly into hot jars, leaving ¼ inch headspace. Slide wooden skewer along inside edge of jar and drag upward to remove air bubbles.

6A. For short-term storage Let jelly cool to room temperature, cover, and refrigerate until jelly is set, 12 to 24 hours. (Jelly can be refrigerated for up to 3 months.)

6B. For long-term storage While jars are hot, wipe rims clean, add lids, and screw on rings until fingertip-tight; do not overtighten. Return pot of water with canning rack to boil. Lower jars into water, cover, bring water back to boil, then start timer. Cooking time will depend on your altitude: Boil 10 minutes for up to 1,000 feet, 15 minutes for 1,001 to 3,000 feet, 20 minutes for 3,001 to 6,000 feet, or 25 minutes for 6,001 to 8,000 feet. Turn off heat and let jars sit in pot for 5 minutes. Remove jars from pot and let cool for 24 hours. Remove rings, check seals, and clean rims. (Sealed jars can be stored for up to 1 year.)

Red Pepper Jelly

Makes four 1-cup jars `MAKE AHEAD`

Why This Recipe Works Homemade red pepper jelly is a terrific way to make use of garden-fresh bell peppers. We wanted our recipe to highlight two ingredients: red bell peppers and chiles. We favored habaneros for their lingering, full-bodied flavor and spiciness. We started out by chopping, then pulsing the peppers in a food processor. To soften the peppers, we added them to a Dutch oven with a small amount of water and allowed them to steam. The heat from the habaneros helped balance the sweetness of the red bell peppers and sugar. Distilled white vinegar gave us a clean, acidic tang and a combination of pectin and sugar produced the perfect consistency. Do not substitute other types of vinegar for the distilled white vinegar. To make this jelly spicier, reserve and add the chile seeds. Do not substitute other brands of low-sugar pectin for the Sure-Jell. To double this recipe make two single batches in separate pots. Do not try to make a double batch in a single large pot; it will not work.

3½ cups sugar, divided
¼ cup Sure-Jell for Less or No Sugar Needed Recipes (page 324)
1 pound red bell peppers, stemmed, seeded, and cut into 1-inch pieces
3 habanero chiles, halved, stemmed, and seeded
¼ cup water
2 cups distilled white vinegar

1. Set canning rack in canning pot, place four 1-cup jars in rack, and add water to cover by 1 inch. Bring to simmer over medium-high heat, then turn off heat and cover to keep hot.

2. Whisk ¼ cup sugar and Sure-Jell together in bowl; set aside. Pulse bell peppers and habaneros in food processor until finely chopped, 12 to 15 pulses, scraping down bowl as necessary. Transfer peppers to Dutch oven and stir in water. Cover and cook over medium heat until peppers have softened, 10 to 15 minutes. Uncover and simmer until water has evaporated, about 1 minute.

3. Add vinegar and Sure-Jell mixture and bring to boil, whisking constantly. Add remaining 3¼ cups sugar and bring to vigorous boil, whisking constantly. Once boiling, cook for 1 minute, whisking constantly. Remove pot from heat and skim foam from surface using large spoon.

Red Pepper Jelly

4. Place dish towel flat on counter. Using jar lifter, remove jars from pot, draining water back into pot. Place jars upside down on towel and let dry for 1 minute. Using funnel and ladle, portion hot jelly into hot jars, leaving ¼ inch headspace.

5A. For short-term storage Let jelly cool to room temperature, cover, and refrigerate until set, 12 to 24 hours. Stir to redistribute peppers before serving. (Jelly can be refrigerated for up to 4 months.)

5B. For long-term storage While jars are hot, wipe rims clean, add lids, and screw on rings until fingertip-tight; do not overtighten. Return pot of water with canning rack to boil. Lower jars into water, cover, bring water back to boil, then start timer. Cooking time will depend on your altitude: Boil 10 minutes for up to 1,000 feet, 15 minutes for 1,001 to 3,000 feet, 20 minutes for 3,001 to 6,000 feet, or 25 minutes for 6,001 to 8,000 feet. Turn off heat and let jars sit in pot for 5 minutes. Remove jars from pot and let cool for 24 hours. Remove rings, check seal, and clean rims. (Sealed jars can be stored in cool, dark place for up to 1 year.)

Key Ingredients in Preserving

Other than fresh fruits and vegetables, there are just a few key ingredients you need for home preserving and pickling success. Here's what they are, what they do, and why you need them.

PECTIN

There are two basic types of pectin: regular pectin and low-sugar pectin. Regular pectin requires high amounts of sugar and acidity in order to set. In the test kitchen we prefer low-sugar pectin (which is only available in powdered form) as it contains all of the ingredients necessary to form a gel; this allows us to choose a level of sugar based on the preserve and not the pectin. Our favorite pectin is **Sure-Jell for Less or No Sugar Needed Recipes**; it comes in a bright pink box and is widely available. It's often found in the baking aisle near the gelatin and cornstarch.

SUGAR

Sugar is a natural preservative. It contributes to flavor and adds sweetness to jams and jellies as well as helps to bring out the fruits' flavor. When simmered, it also affects the texture of mixtures and makes them thicker. In addition, sugar interacts with natural pectin and encourages it to set. When jams are cooked, sugar bonds with the pectin and provides structure and spreadability. When preserving fruit, a syrup of sugar and water helps the fruit retain its flavor, color, and shape. We like to use granulated sugar in our recipes and tend to use less sugar because we prefer our jams and jellies less sweet.

BOTTLED LEMON JUICE AND LIME JUICE

Achieving the proper acidity (pH) level is key for preservation. Without the right pH, boiling water canning is not considered safe. Likewise, without enough acid, unprocessed foods will have a short lifespan, even in the fridge. Acidity also plays a key role in the gelling abilities of pectin; without a consistent pH it can be difficult to predict how a jam or jelly will set. Fresh lemon juice varies too much from lemon to lemon to consistently predict how much it will increase the acidity of a given preserve; bottled lemon juice has a tightly controlled pH that is always consistent.

VINEGAR

When making pickles, vinegar provides not only flavor but also acidity, which helps preserve the pickles and ensure they're safe to eat. Getting pickles to the proper pH is particularly important when boiling water canning, which is only safe for high-acid foods. The two most common vinegars for pickling are cider vinegar and distilled white vinegar; both are available at a 5 percent acetic acid level, meaning they have a consistent pH. Always use the variety of vinegar called for in the recipe.

SALT

The additives commonly found in table salt can produce off-flavors and hazy brines and, in fermented pickles, can inhibit the growth of good microbes. Canning salt, often called pickling or preserving salt, is specifically designed for pickle making and doesn't have any iodine or anti-caking agents. This salt also has a very fine grain, which dissolves quickly in water. However, you can swap kosher salt for pickling salt without any adverse effects. If substituting Morton's Kosher Salt for canning salt, increase the measurement by 50 percent (for example, from 1 teaspoon to 1½ teaspoons); if using Diamond Crystal Kosher Salt, increase by 100 percent (from 1 teaspoon to 2 teaspoons).

WATER

Pickles are made using water, vinegar, and salt, so the quality of the water matters. Fluoride and other elements may interfere with the pickling process, and water may contain enough chlorine to delay fermentation. If the water is highly chlorinated, that smell can carry through to the food. Soft tap water or filtered tap water are preferable for pickling. The minerals in hard water can interfere with the formation of acid and might also discolor the pickles. If you have any concerns about your water, use bottled.

The ATK DIY Canning Kit

The amount of canning equipment now available has grown, including premade canning kits. We found most canning-specific items to be a waste of money, so we put together our own set of essential items. You don't need to buy anything too fancy or expensive; you really only need to invest in a good canning pot and a handful of other key pieces to help you can successfully in your own kitchen. You can typically find everything you need at a good kitchen supply store or online.

A large (18- to 21-quart) canning pot is handy for heating the jars and key for processing the filled jars. We like a pot that has silicone-coated handles for easy gripping and a clear lid so we can monitor what is going on inside. Our winning canning pot is the **Victorio Stainless Steel Multi-Use Canner**.

A canning rack with tall handles that fits inside the pot keeps the jars off the bottom of the pot and makes pulling the hot jars out of boiling water easier. Canning pots are often sold with a rack; our winning pot comes with one.

Glass canning jars (aka Mason jars) are sold with flat metal lids and threaded metal screw rings that hold the lids in place during processing.

A canning-specific jar lifter works better than tongs when putting hot filled jars in and out of boiling water because it allows you to grasp the jars firmly. Our favorite jar lifter is the **Ball Secure-Grip Jar Lifter**.

A wide-mouth stainless-steel funnel makes pouring liquids, like jams and brines, and channeling pieces of fruit into jars easier and tidier. Don't bother with plastic funnels.

A ladle makes transferring cooked foods and pouring hot cooking liquid or brine into jars much simpler and neater. Our best buy is the **OXO Good Grips Stainless Steel Ladle**.

Wooden skewers help to release the air bubbles around the inside of each jar once the jars are filled. (We also use them to poke fruits and vegetables to test for doneness.)

A timer is important for monitoring cooking and processing times. While you can certainly use your watch or a clock, a timer takes away the guesswork and lessens the risk of mistakes. We rely on the **OXO Good Grips Triple Timer**.

Canning Step by Step

Canning is a great way to preserve foods at their peak of summer freshness, from jams and jellies to tomatoes and fruits to all kinds of pickles. The boiling water canning process can seem daunting—since you are dealing with a huge pot of boiling water and multiple glass jars of food—but each step along the way is in fact quite simple.

1 HEAT THE JARS

Many recipes call for sterilizing the jars and lids before filling them; however, the U.S. Department of Agriculture (USDA) says that this is only necessary when processing jars for less than 10 minutes. We don't sterilize jars in this book because all of our recipes are processed for at least 10 minutes. Yet, the jars do need to be heated before being filled with hot jam or the room-temperature glass may shatter. Jars can either be warmed in the canning pot that will be used for processing or placed under hot running tap water. As for the lids, they do not need to be heated before using, and in fact many manufacturers warn against it.

2 FILL THE JARS

As soon as the jam has finished cooking, it needs to be portioned into the hot jars. Given that both the jam and the jars are hot, we found it very helpful to use a wide-mouth canning funnel, or you can make a real mess and possibly burn yourself. A canning funnel works better than a traditional kitchen funnel for this task because a large opening makes filling the jars go quickly (which helps to keep the jam hot), and the funnel nestles securely into the jar so it's less likely to top over when full. Because the timing is so important here, we like to have the jars warmed and waiting for the jam.

3 MEASURE THE HEADSPACE

It is very important to leave some space between the top of the food and the rim of the jar, known as headspace. If canning larger pieces of fruit or vegetables in liquid, make sure the solids are fully covered by the liquid and then measure the distance between the liquid and the rim of the jar. Each recipe will spell out exactly how much headspace is required (usually between ¼ inch and 1 inch). The headspace allows for the food to expand as it heats up during processing. If you have either too much or too little headspace, it can prevent the lid from sealing properly to the jar.

4 RELEASE THE AIR BUBBLES

After filling the jars and measuring the headspace, use a wooden skewer to remove any air bubbles trapped in the jar. For thick jams and jellies, draw the skewer upward to release the bubbles. For larger pieces of fruit or vegetables in liquid, press the skewer against the food to press the air bubbles out. If left unchecked, the air bubbles will collect at the top of the jar during processing and alter the headspace, which can prevent the jar from sealing properly. Once the air bubbles have been removed, be sure to add extra jam or liquid as needed so that the headspace measurement is correct.

5 ADD THE LIDS AND RINGS

Before adding the lids and rings, it is important to wipe the rim of the jar clean of any drips. Once clean, place the lids on top and screw on the rings until just fingertip-tight. Do not overtighten the rings, or you will prevent any air from escaping the jars during processing, which is a key part of the canning process. Note that the lids can only be used once; they cannot be reused. The rings, however, can be used several times as long as they are in good shape.

6 PROCESS THE JARS

Using a jar lifter, lower the hot, filled jars into the rack inside the pot of boiling water. Make sure the jars are covered by at least 1 inch of water; if necessary add more water. Bring the water back to a boil and then process (boil) the jars for the amount of time as prescribed in each recipe. Be sure to start the timer only after the water has returned to a boil. Processing times will vary based on the size of the jars, your altitude, and the type of food inside the jars. Smaller jars and lower elevations have shorter processing times than larger jars and higher elevations. The USDA has determined safe processing times for all different types of food, and we follow their guidelines in all of our recipes.

7 LET THE JARS SEAL THEMSELVES

After the processing time is up, turn off the heat and let the jars sit in the hot water for 5 minutes. This allows the boiling-hot food inside the jars to settle down and starts the lid-sealing process. After 5 minutes, remove the jars from the pot and allow them to cool at room temperature for 24 hours. As the food cools, it contracts, which makes a small vacuum form inside the jar. The pull of this vacuum pops the flexible metal lid inward, an indication that the jar has been hermetically sealed and oxygen can no longer pass through. To test the seal, press on the lid with your finger; a sealed lid will feel firm, while an unsealed lid will flex under the pressure and make a small popping sound.

8 STORE THE JARS

The combination of the sterilized jam and the hermetically sealed lid is the reason the jar can be stored for at least one year in a dark, cool place. We recommend storing the jars without their rings. This way, you can quickly tell if the seal has been broken before using, indicating that the jam is not safe to eat. If the seal pops at any time during storage, you must discard the jam; it could contain harmful bacteria or toxins that could make you sick.

Making Jam

TEMP THE JAM

When making jam without commercial pectin, we like to monitor the jam's temperature as it cooks. This isn't a great way to determine if the jam's done, but it is a good indication of how close it is to the set point. The set point for jam is roughly 8 degrees above the boiling point of water, but we suggest removing the pot from the heat 2 to 3 degrees early and performing the frozen plate test (see below). The boiling point of water changes with elevation; listed below are the jam set temperatures for varying altitudes. The temperature within the pot can range up to 10 degrees; to get an accurate reading, whisk the jam thoroughly and move the thermometer back and forth as you take the temperature.

JAM SET TEMPERATURES BY ELEVATION

Elevation	Temperature
Sea level	217–220 degrees
1,000 feet	215–218 degrees
2,000 feet	213–216 degrees
3,000 feet	211–214 degrees
4,000 feet	209–212 degrees
5,000 feet	208–211 degrees
6,000 feet	206–209 degrees

PERFORM THE FROZEN PLATE TEST

To determine the doneness of a jam made without commercial pectin we use the "frozen plate" test. Spoon hot jam onto a frozen plate, place it in the freezer for 2 minutes, and then drag your finger through the jam. The jam has the correct consistency if your finger leaves a distinct trail (see page 319).

USE THE RIGHT PECTIN

For all of the jelly recipes, and a few of the jam recipes, we use store-bought pectin to thicken the mixture to the right consistency. After testing a few different brands and types of pectin, we found it best to use **Sure-Jell for Less or No Sugar Needed Recipes** (see page 324); it was the most consistent and worked well in all of our recipes. Do not substitute other brands or types of pectin for the pink box of Sure-Jell (not even the yellow box of Sure-Jell) or the recipes may not work. After whisking in the pectin, it's important to return the mixture to a boil and let it dissolve. Only then can you whisk in the remaining sugar and boil the jam for 1 to 2 minutes to activate the pectin and dissolve the sugar.

LEAVE HEADSPACE

The space between the surface of the jam and the lid is known as headspace, and each recipe spells out exactly how much headspace is needed. (Headspace is only important for jams that are going to be processed.) The headspace allows for the hot bubbling jam to expand in the jar during processing. As the jam expands, it forces the air in the headspace out through the edges of the lid, which has not yet sealed to the jar. The lid is held in place by the rings, but the rings are not very tight so that this air is allowed to escape. If you don't leave enough headspace, the jam will leak out of the jar; leave too much headspace and the lid may not seal properly.

MIND THE PROCESSING TIME

Processing jars of jam is only necessary if you want to be able to store them for a long time at room temperature; the processing neutralizes any bacteria or toxins inside the jar and hermetically seals the lid to the jar. The processing times listed for each recipe in the book will vary depending on the size of the jars, your altitude, and the type of food inside the jar. Small jars require less processing than larger jars, and lower altitudes require less processing than higher altitudes. The U.S. Department of Agriculture (USDA) has determined safe processing times for all different types of food, and we follow their guidelines in all of our recipes. After lowering the jars into the water, be sure to wait until the water has returned to a boil before starting the timer for processing.

CHECK THE SEAL

After the processing time is up, the heat is turned off and the jars are left to sit in the hot water for 5 minutes. This allows the boiling hot food inside the jars to settle down and starts the lid sealing process. The jars are then removed from the pot and allowed to cool at room temperature for 24 hours, during which time the food shrinks, causing a small vacuum inside the jar. The pull of this vacuum pops the flexible metal lid inward, signaling that the jar has been hermetically sealed and oxygen can no longer pass through. The combination of the sterilized jam and the hermetically sealed lid is the reason the jar can be stored at room temperature for at least one year before opening. You can tell if the lid is sealed or not by pressing down in the center; a sealed lid won't move, while an unsealed lid will be flexible and make a small popping noise. If the seal pops at any time during storage, you must discard the jam.

Making Pickles

**Dill Pickle Chips
and Spears**

KEEP 'EM CRISP

A crisp texture is key in recipes such as Bread-and-Butter Pickles (page 330), Dill Pickle Chips (page 331), Sweet Zucchini Pickle Chips (page 334), and Giardiniera (page 337). To help the vegetables retain their fresh, crisp texture, we found it beneficial to add Ball Pickle Crisp, which is simply a granulated form of calcium chloride, to our vinegar-based pickles. It reinforces the naturally occurring pectin in vegetables and helps to keep pickles crunchy after being processed and stored for months in brine.

LOW-TEMPERATURE PROCESSING

For delicate vegetables, such as cucumbers and zucchini, we found it best to process the jars in hot water rather than boiling water. This process is called "low-temperature pasteurization treatment" by the USDA and is used to help keep pickles crisp. Although it requires a thermometer and a watchful eye to maintain the water in the canning pot between 180 and 185 degrees during the processing time, we loved the snappy texture this technique produces in our pickles.

COVER IT UP

When making fermented pickles, it is important to keep the cucumbers completely submerged in the brine so that they ferment evenly and don't get moldy. To prevent the cucumbers from floating above the surface of the brine, we press a parchment round flush to the surface of the brine in the jar, then place a zipper-lock bag filled with brine as a weight on top. The bag is filled with brine so that just in case it leaks, the brine in the jar won't get watered down. Finally, we cover the jar with a triple layer of cheesecloth so that fermentation gases can be released while keeping out any dust or debris.

KEEP COOL

The flavor of a fermented pickle depends heavily on the temperature of the fermenting room. We found that temperatures between 50 and 70 degrees Fahrenheit were in the ideal range for fermentation; any warmer and the pickles will have a fishy off-flavor, and the texture of the cucumbers will begin to turn mushy. Keeping your pickles in a basement or cool, dark place is one of the easiest ways to maintain these temperatures, while a wine cooler outfitted with a digital thermostat is the most accurate (and high-end) method. If fermenting in the basement, be sure to invest in a good room thermometer that keeps track of temperature fluctuations and place it next to the jar of fermenting pickles.

WHAT ABOUT BOTULISM?

Food-borne botulism is a rare but serious illness, and most cases are due to improperly home-canned foods. Luckily, avoiding botulism is very easy if you follow our recipes exactly. The processing times given in our recipes are derived from the *USDA Complete Guide to Home Canning*; these times are long enough to neutralize any dangerous toxins inside the jars.

We measured the pH of every recipe in the book and have been careful to stay well below the minimum level (pH of 4.6) for food safety and botulism in canned goods. The pH for your batches at home will be the same as long as you use bottled lemon or lime juice and don't substitute other types of vinegar.

Be sure to work cleanly. Thoroughly wash the food, jars, rings and lids, counter, sink, and your hands before starting a home-canning project to reduce the possibility of contamination.

Lastly, when in doubt, throw it out. Always discard food from jars that have lost their seal during storage, as it is a sign that bacteria, mold, or other toxins might be growing inside the jar. Also, if a jar is still sealed but the food inside looks or smells off when you open it, you should discard it.

Quick Pickle Chips
Makes one 1-pint jar `MAKE AHEAD`

Why This Recipe Works A snap to make, these quick-pickled cucumber slices are ready to jump in on short notice to brighten up a picnic, barbecue, or weeknight meal. They are a great fuss-free pickle for a novice, and a super go-to recipe for anyone looking to satisfy a craving without the effort involved in larger-scale pickling projects. Just a few easy steps will transform a handful of cucumbers into perfect pickle chips—crunchy, tangy, a bit sweet, and loaded with fresh, aromatic flavor. Like a classic bread and butter pickle, these chips get a hint of warm spice from black peppercorns, mustard seeds, and turmeric. Fresh dill sprigs add a mild anise flavor, befitting a classic hamburger pickle. To streamline our preparation time, we chose seasoned rice vinegar—which contains vinegar, sugar, and salt—and eliminated the work of separately measuring three ingredients. We sliced our cucumbers into ¼-inch chips using a chef's knife, though a mandoline or cutter for making crinkle cuts can also be used for added flair. We heated our glass jar in hot water to ensure that it wouldn't crack when we filled it with hot brine. After 3 hours, these pickles were thoroughly suffused with a lively combination of sweet, sour, and aromatic tones. Be sure to choose the freshest, firmest pickling cucumbers available, for guaranteed crunch. These pickles cannot be processed for long-term storage.

- ¾ cup seasoned rice vinegar
- ¼ cup water
- 1 garlic clove, peeled and halved
- ¼ teaspoon ground turmeric
- ⅛ teaspoon black peppercorns
- ⅛ teaspoon yellow mustard seeds
- 8 ounces pickling cucumbers, ends trimmed, sliced ¼ inch thick
- 2 sprigs fresh dill

1. Bring vinegar, water, garlic, turmeric, peppercorns, and mustard seeds to boil in medium saucepan over medium-high heat.

2. Place one 1-pint jar under hot running water until heated through, about 1 minute; shake dry. Pack cucumbers and dill into hot jar. Using funnel and ladle, pour hot brine over cucumbers to cover. Let jar cool to room temperature, about 30 minutes.

3. Cover jar with lid and refrigerate for at least 2½ hours before serving. (Pickles can be refrigerated for up to 6 weeks; pickles will soften significantly after 6 weeks.)

Bread-and-Butter Pickles
Makes four 1-pint jars `MAKE AHEAD`

Why This Recipe Works Bread-and-butter pickles have a crisp texture and the perfect balance of sweet and sour—a great addition to burgers or a picnic spread of sandwiches. Most recipes combine cucumbers and onions in a spiced, syrupy brine; we cut back on the sugar and added red bell pepper for its fresh flavor and color. Cucumbers can lose their crunch when processed; we found that combining several crisping techniques gave us the best results. We tossed our sliced vegetables in salt to draw out excess water and added a small amount of Ball Pickle Crisp, which helps keep the natural pectin from breaking down, resulting in firmer pickles. Finally, rather than processing in a boiling-water bath, we used a technique known as low-temperature pasteurization, which involved maintaining our pickles in a hot-water bath at 180 to 185 degrees Fahrenheit for 30 minutes; in this temperature range microorganisms are destroyed and pectin remains largely intact. To double the recipe double all of the ingredients and use a larger pot when making the brine; the processing time will remain the same.

- 2 pounds pickling cucumbers, ends trimmed, sliced ¼ inch thick
- 1 onion, quartered and sliced thin
- 1 red bell pepper, stemmed, seeded, and cut into 1½-inch matchsticks
- 2 tablespoons canning and pickling salt (see page 324)
- 3 cups apple cider vinegar
- 2 cups sugar
- 1 cup water
- 1 tablespoon yellow mustard seeds
- ¾ teaspoon ground turmeric
- ½ teaspoon celery seeds
- ¼ teaspoon ground cloves
- ½ teaspoon Ball Pickle Crisp (see page 329)

1. Toss cucumbers, onion, and bell pepper with salt in large bowl and refrigerate for 3 hours. Drain vegetables in colander (do not rinse), then pat dry with paper towels.

2. Meanwhile, set canning rack in canning pot, place four 1-pint jars in rack, and add water to cover by 1 inch. Bring to simmer over medium-high heat, then turn off heat and cover to keep hot.

3. Bring vinegar, sugar, water, mustard seeds, turmeric, celery seeds, and cloves to boil in large saucepan over medium-high heat; cover and remove from heat.

4. Place dish towel flat on counter. Using jar lifter, remove jars from pot, draining water back into pot. Place jars upside down on towel and let dry for 1 minute. Add ⅛ teaspoon Pickle Crisp to each hot jar, then pack tightly with vegetables.

5. Return brine to brief boil. Using funnel and ladle, pour hot brine over cucumbers to cover, distributing spices evenly and leaving ½ inch headspace. Slide wooden skewer along inside of jar, pressing slightly on vegetables to remove air bubbles, and add extra brine as needed.

6A. For short-term storage Let jars cool to room temperature, cover with lids, and refrigerate for 1 day before serving. (Pickles can be refrigerated for up to 3 months; flavor will continue to mature over time.)

6B. For long-term storage While jars are warm, wipe rims clean, add lids, and screw on rings until fingertip-tight; do not overtighten. Before processing jars, heat water in canning pot to temperature between 120 and 140 degrees. Lower jars into water, bring water to 180 to 185 degrees, then cook for 30 minutes, adjusting heat as needed to maintain water between 180 and 185 degrees. Remove jars from pot and let cool for 24 hours. Remove rings, check seal, and clean rims. (Sealed jars can be stored for up to 1 year.)

Dill Pickle Chips
Makes four 1-pint jars `MAKE AHEAD`

Why This Recipe Works The savory cousins of bread-and-butter pickles, these iconic pickle chips are tart and full of dill flavor. To give our chips their characteristic punch, we found dill seeds and fresh dill to be the best combination. Mustard seeds and garlic added heat, while a bit of sugar balanced the acidity of the apple cider vinegar. To preserve the crunch, we salted our cucumbers for several hours to draw out water and then packed the raw slices into jars, along with a bit of Ball Pickle Crisp, before covering them with hot brine. We processed the cucumber slices using the low-temperature pasteurization method, maintaining them in a hot-water bath at 180 to 185 degrees Fahrenheit for 30 minutes to produce crisp pickles. To double the recipe double all of the ingredients and use a larger pot when making the brine; the processing time will remain the same.

2½ pounds pickling cucumbers, ends trimmed, sliced ¼ inch thick
2 tablespoons canning and pickling salt (see page 324)
2 cups chopped dill plus 4 large sprigs, divided
3 cups cider vinegar
3 cups water
¼ cup sugar
1 tablespoon yellow mustard seeds
2 teaspoons dill seeds
½ teaspoon Ball Pickle Crisp (see page 329)
4 garlic cloves, peeled and quartered

Bread-and-Butter Pickles

1. Toss cucumbers with salt in bowl and refrigerate for 3 hours. Drain cucumbers in colander (do not rinse), then pat dry with paper towels.

2. Bundle chopped dill in cheesecloth and secure with kitchen twine. Bring dill sachet, vinegar, water, sugar, mustard seeds, and dill seeds to boil in large saucepan over medium-high heat. Cover, remove from heat, and let steep for 15 minutes; discard sachet.

3. Meanwhile, set canning rack in canning pot, place four 1-pint jars in rack, and add water to cover by 1 inch. Bring to simmer over medium-high heat, then turn off heat and cover to keep hot.

4. Place dish towel flat on counter. Using jar lifter, remove jars from pot, draining water back into pot. Place jars upside down on towel and let dry for 1 minute. Add ⅛ teaspoon Pickle Crisp to each hot jar, then pack tightly with dill sprigs, garlic, and drained cucumbers.

5. Return brine to brief boil. Using funnel and ladle, pour hot brine over cucumbers to cover, distributing spices evenly and leaving ½ inch headspace. Slide wooden skewer along inside of jar, pressing slightly on vegetables to remove air bubbles, and add extra brine as needed.

6A. For short-term storage Let jars cool to room temperature, cover with lids, and refrigerate for 1 day before serving. (Pickles can be refrigerated for up to 3 months; flavor will continue to mature over time.)

6B. For long-term storage While jars are warm, wipe rims clean, add lids, and screw on rings until fingertip-tight; do not overtighten. Before processing jars, heat water in canning pot to temperature between 120 and 140 degrees. Lower jars into water, bring water to 180 to 185 degrees, then cook for 30 minutes, adjusting heat as needed to maintain water between 180 and 185 degrees. Remove jars from pot and let cool for 24 hours. Remove rings, check seal, and clean rims. (Sealed jars can be stored for up to 1 year.)

VARIATION
Dill Pickle Spears
After trimming both ends from cucumbers, quarter cucumbers lengthwise and cut into 4-inch-long spears. Pack cucumber spears vertically into jars; salting and processing times will remain the same.

Dilly Beans
Makes four 1-pint jars   MAKE AHEAD

Why This Recipe Works Dilly beans are crunchy, sweet-sour pickled green beans flavored with plenty of fresh dill, plus garlic and black peppercorns. We tried various techniques for preparing our beans before packing them into jars, and we found that raw packing gave us leathery beans, while hot packing resulted in overly soft beans. To tenderize our beans and preserve their crunch, we found that a quick blanch in boiling water (followed by an ice bath) did the trick. Just 1 minute of boiling gave us the texture we were looking for in our pickles. We experimented with different ways of infusing our beans with dill and found that a large bunch of chopped fresh dill steeped in the brine for 15 minutes produced the most well-rounded and satisfying flavor. For added bite, we divided garlic cloves among our jars before adding the beans. To double the recipe double all of the ingredients and use a larger pot when making the brine; the processing time will remain the same.

- **3** tablespoons canning and pickling salt (see page 324), plus salt for blanching green beans
- **2** pounds green beans, trimmed and cut into 4-inch lengths
- **2** cups chopped fresh dill
- **3** cups distilled white vinegar
- **6** tablespoons sugar
- **1** tablespoon black peppercorns
- **6** garlic cloves, peeled and quartered

1. Fill large bowl with ice water. Bring 6 quarts water and 1 tablespoon salt to boil in Dutch oven over high heat. Add beans and cook until crisp-tender but still crunchy at core, about 1 minute. Transfer beans to ice water and let cool for 2 minutes; drain well, discard ice, and pat dry with paper towels.

2. Bundle dill in cheesecloth and secure with kitchen twine. Bring dill sachet, vinegar, 3 cups water, sugar, peppercorns, and 3 tablespoons salt to boil in large saucepan over medium-high heat. Cover, remove from heat, and let steep for 15 minutes; discard sachet.

3. Meanwhile, set canning rack in canning pot, place four 1-pint jars in rack, and add water to cover by 1 inch. Bring to simmer over medium-high heat, then turn heat off and cover to keep hot.

4. Place dish towel flat on counter. Using jar lifter, remove jars from pot, draining water back into pot. Place jars upside down on towel and let dry for 1 minute. Distribute garlic evenly among jars, then pack tightly with beans.

Dilly Beans

5. Return brine to brief boil. Using funnel and ladle, pour hot brine over beans to cover, distributing peppercorns evenly and leaving ½ inch headspace. Slide wooden skewer along inside of jar, pressing slightly on beans to remove air bubbles, and add extra brine as needed.

6A. For short-term storage Let jars cool to room temperature, cover with lids, and refrigerate for at least 1 week before serving. (Beans can be refrigerated for up to 3 months; flavor will continue to mature over time.)

6B. For long-term storage While jars are warm, wipe rims clean, add lids, and screw on rings until fingertip-tight; do not overtighten. Return pot of water with canning rack to boil. Lower jars into water, cover, bring water back to boil, then start timer. Cooking time will depend on your altitude: Boil 10 minutes for up to 1,000 feet, 15 minutes for 1,001 to 3,000 feet, 20 minutes for 3,001 to 6,000 feet, or 25 minutes for above 6,000 feet. Turn off heat and let jars sit in pot for 5 minutes. Remove jars from pot and let cool for 24 hours. Remove rings, check seal, and clean rims. (Sealed jars can be stored for up to 1 year.)

Green beans are legumes, which are plants that produce a pod with edible seeds inside. Green beans are grown and eaten for their pods rather than for what's inside them. Different varieties—yellow wax, purple, Romano, haricots verts—may vary in texture, color, and size, but all have a sweet, grassy flavor and crisp texture. "Green beans," "snap beans," and "string beans" are general terms that cover many different varieties of beans. Their traditional garden season runs from midsummer through fall. When shopping, select thinner beans if possible, since those will be more crisp and sweet. Store green beans wrapped in paper towels in an open plastic produce bag in the crisper drawer for no more than a few days.

Blue Lake The most commonly available bean variety is Blue Lake. As they age, regular green beans can become tough and start to develop a stronger, slightly bitter flavor edge. Several purple varieties are also available; they're very pretty when raw but turn plain green when cooked.

Haricots Verts Haricots verts, also called French beans, are a thinner, shorter variety. They have a more delicate texture than regular green beans and a fresh, lightly sweet flavor. They cook much more quickly than regular green beans and are even tender enough to eat raw.

Wax Beans Wax beans, like green beans, encompass many varieties. They are pale yellow snap beans with a flavor that's similar to green beans but slightly milder and sweeter. Wax beans have none of the chlorophyll pigment that makes green beans green. You might also sometimes see yellow wax beans with vivid purple streaks. Wax beans can be substituted for green beans in any dish.

Romano Beans Romano beans, also called Italian flat beans or Italian pole beans, are flatter and broader than regular green beans and have a crisp texture and sweet flavor. Like regular green beans, they also come in yellow wax and purple varieties. They can be used similarly to regular green beans.

Chinese Long Beans Chinese long beans can grow up to nearly 3 feet in length. They have a flavor that's a little more mellow than regular green beans and a softer, chewier texture, which is best highlighted by stir-frying or deep frying.

**Sweet Zucchini
Pickle Chips**

**Pink Pickled
Turnips**

Sweet Zucchini Pickle Chips
Makes four 1-pint jars `MAKE AHEAD`

Why This Recipe Works Zucchini are great for pickling, and unlike pickling cucumbers, are available year-round. Plus, when gardeners have more zucchini than they know what to do with, making pickles is a great way to use them. We wanted a zucchini pickle with a familiar sweet-and-sour profile, but with added elegance. We chose shallots instead of onions for their more delicate flavor and made a tangy yet sweet brine with classic pickling spices. Like cucumbers, zucchini required special treatment to ensure crispness. We salted the slices to draw out water, which helped them stay firm. We packed them into jars along with Ball Pickle Crisp, which helps retain pectin. We opted for low-temperature pasteurization, which made our pickles shelf-stable while ensuring their crispness. To double the recipe double all of the ingredients and use a larger pot when making the brine; the processing time will remain the same.

2¾ pounds small zucchini (6 ounces each), trimmed and
     sliced ¼ inch thick
  4 shallots, sliced thin
  2 tablespoons canning and pickling salt (see page 324)
  3 cups apple cider vinegar
  2 cups sugar
  1 cup water
  1 tablespoon yellow mustard seeds
  ¾ teaspoon turmeric
  ½ teaspoon celery seeds
  ½ teaspoon Ball Pickle Crisp (see page 329)

1. Toss zucchini and shallots with salt in bowl and refrigerate for 3 hours. Drain vegetables in colander (do not rinse), then pat dry with paper towels.

2. Meanwhile, set canning rack in canning pot, place four 1-pint jars in rack, and add water to cover by 1 inch. Bring to simmer over medium-high heat, then turn off heat and cover to keep hot.

3. Bring vinegar, sugar, water, mustard seeds, turmeric, and celery seeds to boil in large saucepan over medium-high heat; cover and remove from heat.

4. Place dish towel flat on counter. Using jar lifter, remove jars from pot, draining water back into pot. Place jars upside down on towel and let dry for 1 minute. Add ⅛ teaspoon Pickle Crisp to each hot jar, then pack tightly with drained vegetables.

5. Return brine to brief boil. Using funnel and ladle, pour hot brine over vegetables to cover, distributing spices evenly and leaving ½ inch headspace. Slide wooden skewer along inside of jar, pressing slightly on vegetables to remove air bubbles, then add extra brine as needed.

6A. For short-term storage Let jars cool to room temperature, cover with lids, and refrigerate for at least 1 day before serving. (Pickles can be refrigerated for up to 1 month; flavor will continue to mature over time.)

6B. For long-term storage While jars are warm, wipe rims clean, add lids, and screw on rings until fingertip-tight; do not overtighten. Before processing jars, heat water in canning pot to temperature between 120 and 140 degrees. Lower jars into water, bring water to 180 to 185 degrees, then cook for 30 minutes, adjusting heat as needed to maintain water between 180 and 185 degrees. Remove jars from pot and let cool for 24 hours. Remove rings, check seal, and clean rims. (Sealed jars can be stored for up to 1 year.)

VARIATION
Sweet and Spicy Zucchini Pickle Chips
Add 3 red jalapeño chiles, stemmed and sliced into rings, to zucchini mixture before salting in step 1. Divide 8 garlic cloves, peeled and quartered, between jars before packing with vegetables.

Pink Pickled Turnips
Makes two 1-pint jars `MAKE AHEAD`

Why This Recipe Works Refreshing pickled turnips are traditionally served as an accompaniment to falafel (page 96) and rolled up in shawarmas. A staple across the Middle East, they are also at home on a picnic spread. These pickled turnips are whimsically fuchsia in color (from intermingling with beets) and provide just the right crunch to complement any dip or spread. Because these pickles are typically served with robust, flavorful foods, we chose to keep them mild with just a bit of garlic, allspice, and black peppercorns. Once we were happy with the flavor profile, we turned to the question of how to best impart a bright pink color to our otherwise boring white turnips. Betacyanin, the pigment responsible for beetroot's deep red color, brightens into a vibrant pink when in contact with acid. Our vinegar brine was the perfect medium to impart the beet's color to our turnips. We mixed pieces of beet with the turnips in the jars and poured the hot brine over them. The acidic brine coaxed a beautiful hot-pink color from the beets, while the lack of cooking minimized any dulling. The beets left behind in the jar will eventually become pickled as well and make for a tasty treat. The turnips need to be refrigerated for two days to allow the brine to fully penetrate and pickle the vegetable. These pickled turnips cannot be processed for long-term storage.

1¼ cups white wine vinegar
1¼ cups water
2½ tablespoons sugar
1½ tablespoons canning and pickling salt (see page 324)
3 garlic cloves, smashed and peeled
¾ teaspoon whole allspice berries
¾ teaspoon black peppercorns
1 pound turnips, peeled and cut into 2 by ½-inch sticks
1 small beet, trimmed, peeled, and cut into 1-inch pieces

1. Bring vinegar, water, sugar, salt, garlic, allspice, and peppercorns to boil in medium saucepan over medium-high heat. Cover, remove from heat, and let steep for 10 minutes. Strain brine through fine-mesh strainer, then return to saucepan.

2. Place two 1-pint jars in bowl and place under hot running water until heated through, 1 to 2 minutes; shake dry. Pack turnips vertically into hot jars with beet pieces evenly distributed throughout.

3. Return brine to brief boil. Using funnel and ladle, pour hot brine over vegetables to cover. Let jars cool to room temperature, cover with lids, and refrigerate for at least 2 days before serving. (Pickled turnips can be refrigerated for up to 1 month; turnips will soften over time.)

Cajun Pickled Okra
Makes two 1-pint jars `MAKE AHEAD`

Why This Recipe Works Southerners fry, smother, and bake okra, but outside of the South most know it for its role as a thickener in gumbo, thanks to the viscous liquid inside the pods. When you pickle okra, the salt pulls out moisture, giving the pods a nice crunch. As the okra sits in the pickle brine, it becomes less sticky inside and more crisp. The liquid that has been drawn out of the okra creates a glue on the outside of the pod for the spices and aromatics to cling to. For a pickle packed with punchy Cajun flavor, we needed to make a spicy, aromatic brine; we started with red pepper flakes and oregano. While we loved the roundness that the oregano brought, the red pepper flakes didn't provide the heat or depth we associate with Cajun cuisine. We swapped in a hefty ½ teaspoon of cayenne pepper for the red pepper flakes and added smoked paprika to the mix. The cayenne provided a fiery heat and brightness, while the paprika offered a little sweetness and a smoky dimension. Lastly, spooning raw minced garlic straight into the jars alongside the okra (rather than steeping it in the brine) gave us the sharp, peppery backbone needed to make these pickles the ultimate Cajun treat. We found that this pickle needs one week for the brine to fully penetrate the okra and for the flavors to develop, but it will continue to get more crisp as it sits in the refrigerator. Use these to serve alongside fried chicken (page 241), chopped and stirred into macaroni salad (page 254), or to garnish a Bloody Mary.

1½ cups white wine vinegar
  1 cup water
  2 tablespoons sugar
  2 tablespoons canning and pickling salt (see page 324)
  1 teaspoon smoked paprika
  1 teaspoon dried oregano
  ½ teaspoon cayenne pepper
  6 garlic cloves, minced
 14 ounces small fresh okra (3 inches or smaller), trimmed

1. Bring vinegar, water, sugar, salt, paprika, oregano, and cayenne to boil in medium saucepan over medium-high heat; cover and remove from heat.

2. Place two 1-pint jars in bowl and place under hot running water until heated through, 1 to 2 minutes; shake dry.

3. Portion garlic into hot jars. Tightly pack okra vertically into jars, alternating them upside down and right side up for best fit.

4. Return brine to brief boil. Using funnel and ladle, pour hot brine over vegetables to cover, leaving ½ inch headspace. Slide wooden skewer along inside of jar, pressing slightly on vegetables, to remove air bubbles, then add extra brine as needed.

5A. For short term storage Let jars cool to room temperature, cover with lids, and refrigerate for 1 week before serving. (Pickled okra can be refrigerated for at least 6 months; okra will become more crisp, and flavor will mature over time.)

5B. For long-term storage While jars are warm, wipe rims clean, add lids, and screw on rings until fingertip-tight; do not overtighten. Set canning rack in canning pot, fill three-quarters full of water, and bring to boil. Lower hot, filled jars into water and make sure they are covered by at least 1 inch of water (if necessary add more water), cover pot, and bring water back to boil, then start timer. Cooking time will depend on your altitude: Boil 10 minutes for up to 1,000 feet, 15 minutes for 1,001 to 3,000 feet, 20 minutes for 3,001 to 6,000 feet, or 25 minutes for above 6,000 feet. Turn off heat and let jars sit in pot for 5 minutes. Remove jars from pot and let cool for 24 hours. Remove rings, check seal, and clean rims. (Sealed jars can be stored for up to 1 year.)

Pickled Watermelon Rind
Makes four 1-pint jars `MAKE AHEAD`

Why This Recipe Works Pickled watermelon rind is a classic Southern treat. We knew we wanted to avoid the cloyingly sweet, syrupy brines we found in most recipes, so we also looked at several savory versions—some herbal, some citrusy, some spiced—but ultimately we chose a more traditional, sweet profile, only with more tang, less sugar, and a bit of cinnamon and cloves. Many recipes call for salting the cut rind overnight before pickling; we wanted to streamline this process but still produce a pickled rind that was firm yet tender. We had great results as long as we paid close attention to certain visual and textural clues along the way. We soaked our rind in a salt-water solution for 3 hours to tenderize and season it. Next we simmered it in fresh water to purge the salt and soften the watermelon. We transferred the rind to our flavorful pickling brine and simmered it until it just began to turn translucent. To double the recipe double all of the ingredients and use a larger pot (or two pots) when making the brine and cooking the rind; the processing time will remain the same.

  ½ cup canning and pickling salt (see page 324)
  1 (12- to 15-pound) watermelon, peeled and quartered, rind removed from flesh, scraped clean, and cut into 1-inch pieces (12 cups)
  3 cinnamon sticks, broken in half
  1 teaspoon whole cloves
  3 cups distilled white vinegar
  3 cups sugar
  1 cup water

1. Dissolve salt in 2 quarts water in bowl. Add rind and refrigerate for 3 hours; drain and rinse. Bring 2 quarts water to boil in Dutch oven over high heat, add rind, and cook until just tender, about 3 minutes; drain.

2. Meanwhile, set canning rack in canning pot, place four 1-pint jars in rack, and add water to cover by 1 inch. Bring to simmer over medium-high heat, then turn off heat and cover to keep hot.

3. Bundle cinnamon and cloves in cheesecloth and secure with kitchen twine. Bring spice sachet, vinegar, sugar, and 1 cup water to boil in now-empty Dutch oven over medium-high heat. Cover, remove from heat, and let steep for 15 minutes; discard sachet. Return brine to simmer, add cooked rind, and simmer until it begins to turn translucent, 2 to 4 minutes.

4. Place dish towel flat on counter. Using jar lifter, remove jars from pot, draining water back into pot. Place jars upside down on towel and let dry for 1 minute. Using slotted spoon, pack rind into hot jars. Using funnel and ladle, pour hot brine over rind to cover, leaving ½ inch headspace. Slide wooden skewer along inside of jar, pressing slightly on rind to remove air bubbles, and add extra brine as needed.

5A. For short-term storage Let jars cool to room temperature, cover with lids, and refrigerate for 1 day before serving. (Pickled watermelon rind can be refrigerated for up to 3 months; texture will continue to soften over time.)

5B. For long-term storage While jars are warm, wipe rims clean, add lids, and screw on rings until fingertip-tight; do not overtighten. Return pot of water with canning rack to boil. Lower jars into water, cover, bring water back to boil, then start timer. Cooking time will depend on your altitude: Boil 10 minutes for up to 1,000 feet, 15 minutes for 1,001 to 3,000 feet, 20 minutes for 3,001 to 6,000 feet, or 25 minutes for above 6,000 feet. Turn off heat and let jars sit in pot for 5 minutes. Remove jars from pot and let cool for 24 hours. Remove rings, check seal, and clean rims. (Sealed jars can be stored for up to 1 year.)

Giardiniera
Makes four 1-pint jars `MAKE AHEAD`

Why This Recipe Works *Giardiniera* is an Italian mix of spicy pickled vegetables featuring carrots, cauliflower, red bell peppers, and celery. We hoped to fix what plagues most supermarket brands: harsh brines and flat flavors. We started with the traditional vegetables in a white vinegar brine, but found our pickles lacking. The addition of serrano peppers delivered heat, while sliced garlic and coriander seeds provided depth. We opted for white wine vinegar over distilled white vinegar to give the brine a well-rounded flavor. Adding water, sugar, and salt balanced out the harsh vinegar. We loved the flavor of fresh dill, but it turned slimy in the brine. Bundling the herbs in cheesecloth before steeping fixed this and allowed them to be easily discarded. We simply packed the raw vegetables into jars and topped them with hot brine. This method was successful at keeping the vegetables crisp over short-term storage, but the carrots and celery softened after a month. Adding a bit of Ball Pickle Crisp solved our crispness problem. To double the recipe double all of the ingredients and use a larger pot when making the brine; the processing time will remain the same.

Pickled Watermelon Rind

Giardiniera

½ head cauliflower (1 pound), cored and cut into
  1-inch florets
3 carrots, peeled and sliced ¼ inch thick on bias
3 celery ribs, cut crosswise into ½-inch pieces
1 red bell pepper, stemmed, seeded,
  and cut into ½-inch-wide strips
2 serrano chiles, stemmed and sliced thin
6 garlic cloves, sliced thin
1½ cups chopped fresh dill
1 teaspoon whole coriander seeds
2¾ cups white wine vinegar
2¼ cups water
¼ cup sugar
2 tablespoons canning and pickling salt (see page 324)
½ teaspoon Ball Pickle Crisp (see page 329)

1. Set canning rack in canning pot, place four 1-pint jars in rack, and add water to cover by 1 inch. Bring to simmer over medium-high heat, then turn off heat and cover to keep hot.

2. Combine cauliflower, carrots, celery, bell pepper, serranos, and garlic in bowl. Bundle dill and coriander in cheesecloth and secure with kitchen twine. Bring dill-coriander sachet, vinegar, water, sugar, and salt to boil in large saucepan over medium-high heat. Cover, remove from heat, and let steep for 10 minutes; discard sachet.

3. Place dish towel flat on counter. Using jar lifter, remove jars from pot, draining water back into pot. Place jars upside down on towel and let dry for 1 minute. Add ⅛ teaspoon Pickle Crisp to each hot jar, then pack tightly with vegetables.

4. Return brine to brief boil. Using funnel and ladle, pour hot brine over vegetables to cover, leaving ½ inch headspace. Slide wooden skewer along inside of jar, pressing slightly on vegetables, to remove air bubbles, then add extra brine as needed.

5A. For short-term storage Let jars cool to room temperature, cover with lids, and refrigerate for at least 2 days before serving. (Giardiniera can be refrigerated for at least 5 months; flavor will continue to get spicier over time.)

5B. For long-term storage While jars are warm, wipe rims clean, add lids, and screw on rings until fingertip-tight; do not overtighten. Return pot of water with canning rack to boil. Lower jars into water, cover, bring water back to boil, then start timer. Cooking time will depend on your altitude: Boil 10 minutes for up to 1,000 feet, 15 minutes for 1,001 to 3,000 feet, 20 minutes for 3,001 to 6,000 feet, or 25 minutes for above 6,000 feet. Turn off heat and let jars sit in pot for 5 minutes. Remove jars from pot and let cool for 24 hours. Remove rings, check seal, and clean rims. (Sealed jars can be stored for up to 1 year.)

Sour Dill Pickles
Makes 12 pickles MAKE AHEAD

Why This Recipe Works Fermented pickles have a unique and complex flavor. Often salted or submerged in a salty brine, they are left to sit for anywhere from a few days to a few weeks. When it comes to "full sour" dill pickles, it's all about the tang—and the crunch. To get crisp pickles, we tried every technique we could find. We added a grape leaf and a black-tea bag; these contain tannic acid that deactivates the enzymes responsible for softening. We used pricey sea salts containing minerals which inhibit softening. We also added Ball Pickle Crisp to our brine. While delivering slightly more crisp pickles, these techniques either added off-flavors or were too expensive. Lastly, we salted the cucumbers for 3 hours before pickling. These pickles were significantly crunchier, without tasting off. For flavor we added fresh dill, dill seeds, garlic, and black peppercorns. The ideal environment to create the classic sour dill flavor is between 50 and 70 degrees (do not ferment above 70 degrees). The fermentation temperature will affect the timing and flavor of the pickle; warmer temperatures will ferment more quickly and produce sharper, more pungent flavors. For a balanced flavor, we prefer a fermentation temperature of 65 degrees. Be sure to let the brine cool to room temperature before pouring it over the cucumbers. These pickles cannot be processed for long-term storage. These pickles need to ferment for at least 7 days or up to 14 days.

12 small pickling cucumbers (3 to 4 ounces each),
  ends trimmed
3 tablespoons canning and pickling salt
  (see page 324), divided
7 cups water
20 sprigs fresh dill
5 garlic cloves, smashed and peeled
1 tablespoon dill seeds
1½ teaspoons black peppercorns

1. Toss cucumbers with 1 tablespoon salt in bowl and refrigerate for 3 hours. Drain cucumbers in colander; do not rinse.

2. Meanwhile, bring water and remaining 2 tablespoons salt to boil in medium saucepan over high heat. Remove from heat and let cool to room temperature.

3. Cut out parchment paper round to match diameter of ½-gallon wide-mouth jar. Tightly pack cucumbers, dill sprigs, garlic, dill seeds, and peppercorns into jar, leaving 2½ inches headspace. Pour cooled brine over cucumbers to cover. Press parchment round flush against surface of brine.

Sour Dill Pickles

4. Fill 1-quart zipper-lock bag with ½ cup brine, squeeze out air, and seal well; discard excess brine. Place bag of brine on top of parchment and gently press down to submerge cucumbers. Cover jar with triple layer of cheesecloth and secure with rubber band.

5. Place jar in 50- to 70-degree location away from direct sunlight and let ferment for 7 days; check jar daily, skimming residue from surface and pressing to keep pickles submerged. After 7 days, taste pickles daily until they have reached desired flavor (this may take up to 7 days; pickles will look darker with an earthy and tangy flavor).

6. When pickles have reached desired flavor, remove cheesecloth, bag of brine, and parchment, and skim off any residue. Serve. (Pickles and brine can be transferred to clean jar, covered, and refrigerated for up to 1 month; once refrigerated, flavor of pickles will continue to mature.)

VARIATION
Garlic Sour Dill Pickles
Increase garlic to 20 smashed cloves.

Pickled Jalapeños
Makes 10 jalapeños `MAKE AHEAD`

Why This Recipe Works Pickled jalapeños, commonly served with many Mexican dishes, are typically pickled in a vinegar brine and flavored with bay leaf and onion. While we appreciate the classic, we developed a recipe that was a bit more adventurous. We chose to ferment the jalapeños in order to add deep flavors to an inherently grassy, bright chile. Shallot and garlic provided depth and pungency, the addition of cumin brought earthiness, and strips of lime zest brightened the mix. The pickles took on complex floral notes and an intense heat. Removing the seeds of the chiles before pickling made for pleasantly spicy pickles; for atomic heat, don't remove the seeds. The ideal environment for fermenting is between 50 and 70 degrees (do not ferment above 70 degrees). The fermentation temperature will affect the timing and flavor of the jalapeños; warmer temperatures will ferment more quickly and produce sharper, more pungent flavors. For a balanced flavor, we prefer a fermentation temperature of 65 degrees. These fermented jalapeños cannot be processed for long-term storage. These pickles need to ferment for at least 10 days or up to 14 days. Use these on tacos or nachos, spice up a Bloody Mary, or chop and add to tuna or chicken salad.

 3 cups water
 7 teaspoons canning and pickling salt (see page 324)
1½ tablespoons sugar
 1 tablespoon cumin seeds
10 small jalapeño chiles (2 to 3 inches long), halved lengthwise and seeded
 1 shallot, peeled and halved through root end
 6 (2-inch) strips lime zest
 4 garlic cloves, smashed and peeled

1. Bring water, salt, sugar, and cumin to boil in small saucepan over high heat. Remove from heat and let cool to room temperature. Cut out parchment paper round to match diameter of 1-quart wide-mouth jar.

2. Tightly pack jalapeños, shallot, zest, and garlic into jar, leaving 1½-inch headspace. Pour cooled brine over jalapeños to cover and leave 1 inch headspace; vegetables should be so tightly packed that chiles don't float. Press parchment round flush to surface of brine and press gently to submerge. Cover jar with triple layer of cheesecloth and secure with rubber band.

3. Place jar in 50- to 70-degree location away from direct sunlight and let ferment for 10 days; check jar daily, skimming residue from surface. After 10 days, taste jalapeños daily until they have reached desired flavor (this may take up to 4 days; jalapeños should be softened with tangy, floral flavor).

4. When jalapeños have reached desired flavor, remove cheesecloth and parchment, and skim off any residue. Serve. (Pickled jalapeños and brine can be transferred to clean jar, covered, and refrigerated for up to 5 months; once refrigerated, flavor of jalapeños will continue to mature and they will darken in color.)

SEEDING JALAPEÑOS

Cut the jalapeño in half lengthwise. Then, starting at the end opposite the stem, use a melon baller to scoop out the seeds and ribs from each half.

Crushed Tomatoes
Makes four 1-quart jars   `MAKE AHEAD`

Why This Recipe Works Our recipe for crushed tomatoes highlights the vibrancy of ripe tomatoes. To yield 4 quarts, we started with 14 pounds of tomatoes. We couldn't simply throw this pile of tomatoes into the pot all at once; instead we added the tomatoes in batches, crushing them down as they cooked. After crushing all the tomatoes, we boiled them for 30 minutes just to concentrate the flavors without cooking off the fresh tomato texture and brightness. The addition of lemon juice to each jar helped to acidify the crushed tomatoes so we could can them safely. For safety reasons, be sure to use bottled lemon juice, not fresh-squeezed juice, in this recipe (see page 324). For more information on peeling tomatoes, see page 377. To double the recipe double all of the ingredients. The batches of tomatoes must be cooked and processed in 2 separate batches. All of the tomatoes can be peeled, cored, and quartered at the same time; refrigerate the second batch until ready.

- 14 pounds tomatoes, cored, peeled, and cut into 2-inch pieces, divided
- ¾ cup bottled lemon juice
- 2 teaspoons table salt

1. Cook one-quarter of tomatoes in large Dutch oven over medium-high heat, stirring often, until they release their juices, about 5 minutes. Crush tomatoes with potato masher and cook until no large pieces remain, about 5 minutes. Working in batches, add handful of tomatoes to pot and crush with potato masher; bring to boil before adding next handful.

2. Once all tomatoes have been crushed into pot, continue to boil mixture, reducing heat as needed, until slightly thickened and measures slightly more than 4 quarts, 20 to 30 minutes.

3. Meanwhile, set canning rack in canning pot, place four 1-quart jars in rack, and add water to just cover jars. Bring to simmer over medium-high heat, then turn off heat and cover to keep hot.

4. Place dish towel flat on counter. Using jar lifter, remove jars from pot, draining water back into pot. Place jars upside down on towel and let dry for 1 minute. Add 3 tablespoons lemon juice and ½ teaspoon salt to each hot jar. Using funnel and ladle, portion hot tomatoes into jars, leaving ½ inch head-space. Slide wooden skewer along inside of jar, pressing slightly on tomatoes to remove air bubbles, and add more tomatoes as needed.

5. While jars are hot, wipe rims clean, add lids, and screw on rings until fingertip-tight; do not overtighten. Return pot of water with canning rack to boil. Lower jars into water, cover, bring water back to boil, then start timer. Cooking time will depend on your altitude: Boil 45 minutes for up to 1,000 feet, 50 minutes for 1,001 to 3,000 feet, 55 minutes for 3,001 to 6,000 feet, or 1 hour for 6,001 to 8,000 feet. Turn off heat and let jars sit in pot for 5 minutes. Remove jars from pot and let cool for 24 hours. Remove rings, check seal, and clean rings. (Sealed jars can be stored for up to 1 year.)

Whole Peeled Tomatoes
Makes four 1-quart jars   `MAKE AHEAD`

Why This Recipe Works To get the freshest flavor from our whole peeled tomatoes, we created a homemade tomato juice to use as a flavorful cooking and packing liquid. Instead of packing the tomatoes raw into jars, we changed our canning method to a "hot pack," meaning we cooked the tomatoes in juice before gently packing them into jars. This short precooking let the tomatoes release juices and air in the pot rather than in the jars. The addition of Pickle Crisp helped keep the tomatoes firm. You will have a few cups of juice left over that will not fit into the jars. For safety reasons, be sure to use bottled lemon juice, not fresh-squeezed juice, in this recipe (see page 324). For more information on peeling tomatoes, see page 377. To double the recipe double all of the ingredients. The batches of tomatoes must be cooked and processed in 2 separate batches. All of the tomatoes can be peeled and cored at the same time, and the double batch of juice can be made in step 2; refrigerate the second batch of tomatoes and juice until ready.

13 pounds plum tomatoes, cored and peeled
¾ cup bottled lemon juice
1 tablespoon table salt
1 teaspoon Ball Pickle Crisp (see page 329)

1. Set canning rack in canning pot, place four 1-quart jars in rack, and add water to just cover jars. Bring to simmer over medium-high heat, then turn off heat and cover to keep hot.

2. Working in 2 batches, process half of tomatoes in blender until smooth, about 30 seconds. Strain mixture through fine-mesh strainer into Dutch oven, pressing on solids to extract juice; discard solids.

3. Bring juice to boil over medium-high heat. Stir in remaining tomatoes, bring to simmer, and cook until tomatoes have softened slightly, about 5 minutes; skim foam from surface using large spoon.

4. Meanwhile, place dish towel flat on counter. Using jar lifter, remove jars from pot, draining water back into pot. Place jars upside down on towel and let dry for 1 minute. Add 3 tablespoons lemon juice, ¾ teaspoon salt, and ¼ teaspoon Pickle Crisp to each hot jar. Using slotted spoon, gently pack tomatoes into hot jars. Using funnel and ladle, pour hot juice over tomatoes to cover, leaving 1½ inches headspace. Slide wooden skewer along inside of jar, pressing slightly on tomatoes to remove air bubbles, and add extra juice as needed.

5. While jars are hot, wipe rims clean, add lids, and screw on rings until fingertip-tight; do not overtighten. Lower jars into water, cover, bring water back to boil, then start timer. Cooking time will depend on your altitude: Boil 1 hour 25 minutes for up to 1,000 feet, 1½ hours for 1,001 to 3,000 feet, 1 hour 35 minutes for 3,001 to 6,000 feet, or 1 hour 40 minutes for 6,001 to 8,000 feet. Turn off heat and let jars sit in pot for 10 minutes. Remove jars from pot and let cool for 24 hours. Remove rings, check seal, and clean rims. (Sealed jars can be stored for up to 1 year.)

Summer Tomato Sauce
Makes four 1-pint jars `MAKE AHEAD`

Why This Recipe Works This tomato sauce makes great use of an end-of-summer tomato bounty. We loved the idea of canning a large batch of this fresh sauce so we could open up a jar on a dreary February night. While many rustic tomato sauce recipes include the skins, we found them bitter and their texture distracting from the final product. We infused the sauce with garlic and basil and cooked it down for a more vibrant, intensified flavor. In order to ensure the safety of canning this tomato product, we added 2 tablespoons red wine vinegar to each pint jar; this amount of vinegar ensured the sauce's pH was

Crushed Tomatoes

Summer Tomato Sauce

in the sweet spot. Just a teaspoon of sugar was enough to coax out the natural sweetness of the tomatoes and balance the acidity of the vinegar. While all types of tomatoes work with this recipe, we preferred this sauce made with plum tomatoes. One jar is enough sauce to coat ½ pound of pasta. For more richness, add a bit of extra-virgin olive oil to the sauce before serving. For more information on peeling tomatoes, see page 377. To double the recipe double all of the ingredients. Substitute a large stockpot for the Dutch oven and increase the sauce cooking time in step 2 to about 2 hours.

- 10 pounds tomatoes, cored, peeled, and cut into 1½-inch pieces
- 4 garlic cloves, minced
- ⅓ cup tomato paste
- ⅓ cup chopped fresh basil
- 1 tablespoon table salt
- 1 teaspoon sugar
- ½ cup red wine vinegar

1. Set canning rack in canning pot, place four 1-pint jars in rack, and add water to cover by 1 inch. Bring to simmer over medium-high heat, then turn off heat and cover to keep hot.

2. Working in 4 batches, process tomatoes in blender until almost smooth, 10 to 15 seconds; transfer to Dutch oven. Stir in garlic, tomato paste, basil, salt, and sugar, and bring to boil over medium-high heat. Boil, stirring often and reducing heat as needed, until sauce has thickened and measures slightly more than 2 quarts, 1¼ to 1½ hours.

3. Place dish towel flat on counter. Using jar lifter, remove jars from pot, draining water back into pot. Place jars upside down on towel and let dry for 1 minute. Add 2 tablespoons vinegar to each hot jar. Using funnel and ladle, portion hot sauce into hot jars, leaving ½ inch headspace. Slide wooden skewer along inside of jar to remove air bubbles and add more sauce as needed.

4A. For short-term storage Let jars cool to room temperature. Cover with lids, refrigerate, and serve. (Sauce can be refrigerated for up to 1 month.)

4B. For long-term storage While jars are hot, wipe rims clean, add lids, and screw on rings until fingertip-tight; do not overtighten. Return pot of water with canning rack to boil. Lower jars into water, cover, bring water back to boil, then start timer. Cooking time will depend on your altitude: Boil 35 minutes for up to 1,000 feet, 40 minutes for 1,001 to 3,000 feet, 45 minutes for 3,001 to 6,000 feet, or 50 minutes for 6,001 to 8,000 feet. Turn off heat and let jars sit in pot for 5 minutes. Remove jars from pot and let cool for 24 hours. Remove rings, check seal, and clean rims. (Sealed jars can be stored for up to 1 year.)

Spicy Tomato Jam
Makes two 1-cup jars MAKE AHEAD

Why This Recipe Works Spicy tomato jam is a flavorful and unique way to transform your next tray of tomatoes. A great project for anyone new to jam making, this sticky spread is a cinch to make: Just combine everything in a large pot and cook the mixture down to a sweet and spicy ruby-red jam. Leaving the peels on the tomatoes gave our chunky jam a pleasant chew. To achieve the right amount of heat to stand up to the sweet tomato flavors, we found that a single seeded habanero did the trick. This pepper packed the heat we were looking for, and brought a complementary fruity flavor. For an even spicier tomato jam, include the habanero seeds. Serve tomato jam with sharp cheddar cheese or add it to an omelet. It can also zip up a meatloaf or spice up a pizza or flatbread. This jam cannot be processed for long-term storage.

- 2½ pounds tomatoes, cored and chopped coarse
- 1 cup red wine vinegar
- ¾ cup sugar
- 7 garlic cloves, minced
- 1 habanero chile, stemmed, seeded, and minced
- ½ teaspoon ground cumin
- ½ teaspoon table salt

1. Combine all ingredients in large saucepan and bring to boil over medium-high heat. Reduce heat to medium-low and simmer vigorously, stirring often and adjusting heat as needed, until mixture has thickened, darkened in color, and measures slightly more than 2 cups, 1 to 1¼ hours.

2. Let jam cool slightly. Using funnel and spoon, portion jam into two 1-cup jars, then let cool to room temperature. Cover, refrigerate, and serve. (Jam can be refrigerated for at least 4 months; flavor will become milder over time.)

Green Tomato Chutney
Makes two 1-cup jars MAKE AHEAD

Why This Recipe Works Accented with the citrusy warmth of crushed coriander seeds, vibrant green tomato chutney is a perfect, and easy, way to use unripe end-of-season tomatoes. Green tomatoes are naturally a little bit sweet and a tad tart, so our recipe plays off these flavors. Much of the green tomato flavor is bound up in the juice, seeds, and peel, so we certainly didn't want to toss any of that out; instead, we just chopped our tomatoes, combined everything, and simmered. We added a hint of lemon juice, cranked up the heat with red pepper flakes, and used equal parts granulated sugar and white vinegar to round out the flavor. The chutney is ready when the tomatoes have broken down, the vinegar has evaporated, and there are thick, sticky preserves left in the pot. For safety reasons, be sure to use bottled lemon juice, not fresh-squeezed juice, in this recipe (see page 324). This chutney is great to serve alongside grilled chicken or pork, to use as a relish for hot dogs, or to add to a cheese sandwich.

2¼ pounds green tomatoes, cored and cut into
     1-inch pieces
 ¾ cup sugar
 ¾ cup distilled white vinegar
  1 teaspoon coarsely cracked coriander seeds
  1 teaspoon table salt
 ¼ teaspoon red pepper flakes
  2 teaspoons bottled lemon juice

1. Bring tomatoes, sugar, vinegar, coriander, salt, and pepper flakes to boil in large pot over medium-high heat. Reduce heat to medium-low and simmer vigorously, stirring occasionally, until mixture thickens to jam-like consistency and rubber spatula leaves trail when dragged across bottom of pot, about 1 hour.

2. Off heat, stir in lemon juice. Let chutney cool slightly. Using funnel and spoon, portion chutney into two 1-cup jars.

3A. For short-term storage Let jars cool to room temperature. Cover with lids, refrigerate, and serve. (Chutney can be refrigerated for up to 5 months; flavor will mellow over time.)

3B. For long-term storage While jars are warm, wipe rims clean, add lids, and screw on rings until fingertip-tight; do not overtighten. Set canning rack in canning pot, fill three-quarters full of water, and bring to boil. Lower hot, filled jars into water and make sure they are covered by at least 1 inch of water (if necessary add more water), cover pot, and bring water back to boil, then start timer. Cooking time will depend on your altitude: Boil 10 minutes for up to 1,000 feet, 15 minutes for 1,001 to 3,000 feet, 20 minutes for 3,001 to 6,000 feet, or 25 minutes for 6,001 to 8,000 feet. Turn off heat and let jars sit in pot for 5 minutes. Remove jars from pot and let cool for 24 hours. Remove rings, check seal, and clean rims. (Sealed jars can be stored for up to 1 year.)

Spicy Tomato Jam

Green Tomato Chutney

Roasted Tomato–Lime Salsa
Makes four 1-cup jars `MAKE AHEAD`

Why This Recipe Works To achieve the spicy, smoky-sweet flavor of traditional *salsa asada*, or "roasted salsa," we broiled halved tomatoes and red jalapeños, sliced onion, and whole garlic cloves. Cilantro added brightness, while ground cumin provided earthy undertones. Cooking our salsa on the stovetop intensified its flavors and developed a saucier base. To safely process this salsa, we acidified it with lime juice, which also gave it a fresh tang. For safety reasons, be sure to use bottled lime juice, not fresh squeezed juice, in this recipe (see page 324). This salsa is fairly spicy; to make it milder, remove and discard the chile seeds. To double the recipe double all of the ingredients. Broil the vegetables in 4 batches in step 2 and increase the salsa cooking time in step 4 until it measures slightly more than 8 cups, 20 to 25 minutes.

2½ pounds tomatoes, cored and halved
1 onion, sliced into ½-inch-thick rounds
5 red jalapeño or Fresno chiles,
   stemmed and halved lengthwise
6 garlic cloves, peeled
⅓ cup bottled lime juice
2½ teaspoons table salt
2 teaspoons sugar
2 teaspoons chopped fresh cilantro
1 teaspoon ground cumin

1. Set canning rack in canning pot, place four 1-cup jars in rack, and add water to cover by 1 inch. Bring to simmer over medium-high heat, then turn off heat and cover to keep hot.

2. Adjust oven rack 4 inches from broiler element and heat broiler. Line rimmed baking sheet with aluminum foil. Place tomatoes, cut side down, and onion on prepared sheet. Broil until tomatoes are well charred, about 15 minutes; transfer to bowl. Place chiles, cut side down, and garlic on now-empty sheet and broil until chiles are well charred, about 8 minutes.

3. Transfer chiles, garlic, half of tomatoes, and half of onions to food processor and process until thick puree, about 10 seconds; transfer to Dutch oven. Transfer remaining broiled tomatoes and onions to now-empty food processor and pulse into ½-inch pieces, 2 or 3 pulses; add to pot.

4. Stir in lime juice, salt, sugar, cilantro, and cumin. Boil over medium-high heat, stirring often, until salsa has thickened slightly and measures slightly more than 4 cups, about 10 minutes.

Roasted Tomato–Lime Salsa

5. Place dish towel flat on counter. Using jar lifter, remove jars from pot, draining water back into pot. Place jars upside down on towel and let dry for 1 minute. Using funnel and ladle, portion hot salsa into hot jars, leaving ½ inch headspace. Slide wooden skewer along inside of jar to remove air bubbles, adding more salsa as needed.

6A. For short-term storage Let jars cool to room temperature. Cover with lids, refrigerate, and serve. (Salsa can be refrigerated for up to 1 month.)

6B. For long-term storage While jars are hot, wipe rims clean, add lids, and screw on rings until fingertip-tight; do not overtighten. Return pot of water with canning rack to boil. Lower jars into water, cover, bring water back to boil, then start timer. Cooking time will depend on your altitude: Boil 15 minutes for up to 1,000 feet, 20 minutes for 1,001 to 3,000 feet, 25 minutes for 3,001 to 6,000 feet, or 30 minutes for 6,001 to 8,000 feet. Turn off heat and let jars sit in pot for 5 minutes. Remove jars from pot and let cool for 24 hours. Remove rings, check seal, and clean rims. (Sealed jars can be stored for up to 1 year.)

Pickle Relish
Makes four 1-cup jars MAKE AHEAD

Why This Recipe Works No cookout is complete without pickle relish. A great relish should have bright flavor, a little crunch, and a balanced combination of tanginess and sweetness. Chopping the vegetables into 1-inch pieces before pulsing them in a food processor gave us the texture we were looking for. To avoid a watered-down and mushy relish, we salted the vegetables before a 3-hour rest in the refrigerator. We then rid them of more moisture by squeezing them in a clean dish towel. For flavor, we liked white vinegar along with sugar, yellow mustard seeds, and celery seeds. We added turmeric to impart a warm, bright flavor. To deepen the flavors before canning, we found that a simmer on the stovetop was necessary. To double the recipe double all of the ingredients. Pulse the cucumbers in 3 batches, pulse the peppers in 1 batch, and pulse the onions in 2 batches. Increase the simmering time in step 3 to about 30 minutes.

- 2 pounds pickling cucumbers, ends trimmed, cut into 1-inch pieces
- 1 green bell pepper, stemmed, seeded, and cut into 1-inch pieces
- 1 onion, chopped
- 1 tablespoon canning and pickling salt (page 324)
- 2 cups distilled white vinegar
- 1 cup sugar
- 4 teaspoons yellow mustard seeds
- 2 teaspoons celery seeds
- ¾ teaspoon ground turmeric

1. Working in 2 batches, pulse cucumbers in food processor until coarsely chopped into ¼-inch pieces, 8 to 10 pulses; transfer to large bowl. Pulse bell pepper until coarsely chopped into ¼-inch pieces, about 6 pulses; transfer to bowl with cucumbers. Pulse onion until coarsely chopped into ¼-inch pieces, about 10 pulses; transfer to bowl with vegetables. Stir in salt, cover, and refrigerate for 3 hours.

2. Set canning rack in canning pot, place four 1-cup jars in rack, and add water to cover by 1 inch. Bring to simmer over medium-high heat, then turn off heat and cover to keep hot.

3. Drain vegetables in colander, transfer to dish towel, and squeeze to remove excess liquid. Bring vinegar, sugar, mustard seeds, celery seeds, and turmeric to boil in Dutch oven over medium-high heat. Add vegetables, reduce heat to medium, and simmer until vegetables are translucent and mixture has thickened slightly, 10 to 15 minutes.

4. Place dish towel flat on counter. Using jar lifter, remove jars from pot, draining water back into pot. Place jars upside down on towel and let dry for 1 minute. Using funnel and ladle, portion relish into hot jars, leaving ½ inch headspace. Slide wooden skewer along inside of jar, pressing slightly on relish, to remove air bubbles.

5A. For short-term storage Let jars cool to room temperature. Cover with lids, refrigerate, and serve. (Relish can be refrigerated for up to 4 months; flavor will deepen over time.)

5B. For long-term storage While jars are hot, wipe rims clean, add lids, and screw on rings until fingertip-tight; do not overtighten. Return pot of water with canning rack to boil. Lower jars into water, cover, bring to boil, then start timer. Cooking time will depend on your altitude: Boil 10 minutes for up to 1,000 feet, 15 minutes for 1,001 to 3,000 feet, 20 minutes for 3,001 to 6,000 feet, and 25 minutes for 6,001 to 8,000 feet. Turn off heat and let jars sit in pot for 5 minutes. Remove jars from pot and let cool for 24 hours. Remove rings, check seal, and clean rims. (Sealed jars can be stored for up to 1 year.)

Tangy Corn Relish
Makes four 1-cup jars MAKE AHEAD

Why This Recipe Works This bright and tangy corn relish adds a summery flair to hot dogs, burgers, and sandwiches. To maintain the freshness of the corn, we used raw corn and let the warm pickling brine do its work. We simmered our aromatics in vinegar until softened, and stirred in the corn off the heat. This kept the corn fresh and crisp, especially after the processing time. To punch up the flavor, we used poblano peppers and added red jalapeño chiles for a hint of heat and bright color. Cumin seeds and ground coriander added the right spice without overpowering the mild corn flavor, and sugar brought out the natural sweetness of the corn and helped to balance the tangy vinegar. To double the recipe double all of the ingredients; the simmering time will not change.

- 1¼ cups cider vinegar
- ¼ cup water
- ¼ cup sugar
- 2½ teaspoons canning or pickling salt (page 324)
- ¾ teaspoon cumin seeds
- ¼ teaspoon ground coriander
- 2 poblano chiles, stemmed, seeded, and cut into ¼-inch pieces
- 2 red jalapeño or Fresno chiles, stemmed, seeded, and chopped fine
- 1 small onion, chopped fine
- 4 ears corn, kernels cut from cobs (3 cups)

1. Set canning rack in large pot, place four 1-cup jars in rack, and add water to cover by 1 inch. Bring to simmer over medium-high heat, then turn off heat and cover to keep hot.

2. Bring vinegar, water, sugar, salt, cumin seeds, and coriander to boil in Dutch oven over high heat. Add poblanos, jalapeños, and onion, reduce heat to medium, and simmer until softened, about 5 minutes. Off heat, stir in corn.

3. Place dish towel flat on counter. Using jar lifter, remove jars from pot, draining water back into pot. Place jars upside down on towel and let dry for 1 minute. Using funnel and ladle, portion relish into hot jars, leaving ½ inch headspace. Slide wooden skewer along inside of jar, pressing slightly on relish, to remove air bubbles.

4A. For short-term storage Let relish cool to room temperature. Cover, refrigerate, and serve. (Relish can be refrigerated for up to 1 month; flavor will deepen over time.)

4B. For long-term storage While jars are hot, wipe rims clean, add lids, and screw on rings until fingertip-tight; do not overtighten. Return pot of water with canning rack to boil. Lower jars into water, cover, bring water back to boil, then start timer. Cooking time will depend on your altitude: Boil 15 minutes for up to 1,000 feet, 20 minutes for 1,001 to 3,000 feet, 25 minutes for 3,001 to 6,000 feet, and 30 minutes for 6,001 to 8,000 feet. Turn off heat and let jars sit in pot for 5 minutes. Remove jars from pot and let cool for 24 hours. Remove rings, check seal, and clean rims. (Sealed jars can be stored for up to 1 year.)

Chow-Chow
Makes four 1-cup jars MAKE AHEAD

Why This Recipe Works Chow-chow is a sweet green tomato relish packed with mustard seeds and celery seeds. There are countless regional variations, some with cauliflower, others with cabbage or peppers. While Pennsylvania chow-chow is sweeter, we liked the Southern take with a kick to balance the syrupy juices in this relish. We chose a combination of jalapeño and cayenne for heat. Bell peppers provided a mild fruitiness, and cabbage lent crispness. We found that using a food processor gave us the perfect size pieces. Salting the vegetables for 3 hours pulled out any excess moisture. Our other pickle relish recipes often squeeze the salted vegetables out with a towel to remove any excess moisture. We found this to be too rough with the cabbage; it drew too much liquid from the tomatoes, leaving nothing behind to make a juicy brine. We waited to add the vegetables to the brine until it was off the heat; this kept the cabbage crisp and the peppers and tomatoes firm. To double the recipe double all of the ingredients. Pulse the vegetables in 6 batches. Increase the brine simmering time in step 3 to about 8 minutes.

3 green tomatoes, cored and chopped coarse
1 cup coarsely chopped green cabbage
1 cup coarsely chopped green bell pepper
½ cup coarsely chopped red bell pepper
½ cup coarsely chopped onion
1 jalapeño chile, stemmed, seeded, and chopped
1½ tablespoons canning and pickling salt (see page 324)
½ cup distilled white vinegar
½ cup sugar
1¼ teaspoons yellow mustard seeds
½ teaspoon celery seeds
¼ teaspoon turmeric
¼ teaspoon cayenne pepper

1. Combine tomatoes, cabbage, bell peppers, onion, and jalapeño in bowl. Working in 3 batches, pulse vegetables in food processor until pieces measure ¼ to ½ inch, 4 to 6 pulses; transfer to separate bowl. Stir in salt, cover, and refrigerate for 3 hours.

2. Set canning rack in canning pot, place four 1-cup jars in rack, and add water to cover by 1 inch. Bring to simmer over medium-high heat, then turn off heat and cover to keep hot.

3. Transfer vegetables to colander and let drain for 20 minutes. Bring vinegar, sugar, mustard seeds, celery seeds, turmeric, and cayenne to boil in large saucepan over high heat. Reduce to simmer and cook until slightly thickened, about 5 minutes. Off heat, stir in drained vegetables.

4. Place dish towel flat on counter. Using jar lifter, remove jars from pot, draining water back into pot. Place jars upside down on towel and let dry for 1 minute. Using funnel and ladle, portion relish into hot jars, leaving ½ inch headspace. Slide wooden skewer along inside of jar, pressing slightly on relish, to remove air bubbles.

5A. For short-term storage Let jars cool to room temperature. Cover with lids, refrigerate, and serve. (Relish can be refrigerated for at least 6 months.)

5B. For long-term storage While jars are hot, wipe rims clean, add lids, and screw on rings until fingertip-tight; do not overtighten. Return pot of water with canning rack to boil. Lower jars into water, cover, bring water back to boil, then start timer. Cooking time will depend on your altitude: Boil 10 minutes for up to 1,000 feet, 15 minutes for 1,001 to 3,000 feet, 20 minutes for 3,001 to 6,000 feet, and 25 minutes for 6,001 to 8,000 feet. Turn off heat and let jars sit in pot for 5 minutes. Remove jars from pot and let cool for 24 hours. Remove rings, check seal, and clean rims. (Sealed jars can be stored for up to 1 year.)

Peach Mostarda

Makes two 1-pint wide-mouth jars `MAKE AHEAD`

Why This Recipe Works *Mostarda* is an Italian condiment featuring candied fruit in a mustardy syrup. It can be served with grilled meats, added to a sandwich, or spooned over couscous or rice. Our version preserves cooked peaches in a syrup created from the peaches' juices. With the kick from dry and whole-grain mustard, the warmth from spices, and the sweet-tart hit from cider vinegar, sugar, and orange juice, our mostarda packs a flavorful punch. For more information on peeling peaches, see page 377. Do not use white peaches in this recipe; they are not acidic enough for safe long-term storage. Both freshly squeezed and store-bought orange juice will work in this recipe. This fruit cannot be processed for long-term storage.

- 2 pounds ripe but firm yellow peaches, peeled, halved, and pitted
- 2 cups sugar
- ⅔ cup orange juice
- ¾ teaspoon table salt
- 5 whole cloves
- 3 star anise pods
- 3 bay leaves
- ¼ cup dry mustard
- ¼ cup whole-grain mustard
- 3 tablespoons cider vinegar
- ¼ teaspoon cayenne pepper

1. Combine peaches, sugar, orange juice, salt, cloves, star anise, and bay leaves in large bowl. Cover and refrigerate for 24 hours.

2. Using slotted spoon, gently transfer peaches to separate bowl. Transfer juice to large saucepan and cook over medium heat until sugar is completely dissolved, about 3 minutes. Add peaches to syrup and bring to boil. Reduce heat to low and simmer until peaches are just tender and tip of knife inserted into peach meets with very little resistance, 10 to 15 minutes. Remove pot from heat.

3. Meanwhile, place two 1-pint wide-mouth jars in bowl and place under hot running water until heated through, 1 to 2 minutes; shake dry.

4. Using slotted spoon, gently pack peaches into hot jars. Return syrup to boil over medium heat and cook until syrup measures 1⅔ cups, 5 to 10 minutes; remove from heat. Combine dry mustard, whole-grain mustard, vinegar, and cayenne in bowl, then whisk into syrup.

5. Using funnel and ladle, pour hot syrup over peaches to cover, distributing spices evenly among jars. Let cool to room temperature, cover, and refrigerate for 1 week before serving. (Mostarda can be refrigerated for up to 3 months.)

Chow-Chow

Peach Mostarda

Summer Fruit Desserts

■ FAST (30 minutes or less total time)   ■ NO COOK   ■ MAKE AHEAD
Photos (clockwise from left): Individual Fresh Berry Gratins; Summer Berry Pie;
Honey-Glazed Peaches with Hazelnuts; Easy Apricot and Blueberry Tart

Melon, Plums, and Cherries with Mint and Vanilla

Strawberries with Balsamic Vinegar

Melon, Plums, and Cherries with Mint and Vanilla

Serves 4 to 6 `FAST` `NO COOK`

Why This Recipe Works A fresh fruit salad is the perfect light dessert to finish off a summer meal or to enjoy as a sweet treat on a hot afternoon. We were after a salad with balanced fruit flavor and sweetness. A combination of cantaloupe, plums, and cherries not only offered a range of complementary flavors but also looked beautiful. A small amount of sugar encouraged the fruit to release its juices, creating a more cohesive salad. We balanced the sweetness with fresh lime juice, but tasters wanted more complexity. Mashing the sugar with fresh mint before stirring it into the fruit worked perfectly and ensured even distribution of flavor throughout the salad. Since our fruit salad had come together so easily, we decided to apply the same techniques to a combination of peaches and berries, using fresh basil in place of the mint and a small amount of pepper to bring the flavors to life. Blueberries can be substituted for the cherries.

- 4 teaspoons sugar
- 1 tablespoon minced fresh mint
- 3 cups ½-inch cantaloupe pieces
- 2 plums, halved, pitted, and cut into ½-inch pieces
- 8 ounces fresh sweet cherries, pitted and halved
- ¼ teaspoon vanilla extract
- 1 tablespoon lime juice, plus extra for seasoning

Combine sugar and mint in large bowl. Using rubber spatula, press mixture into side of bowl until sugar becomes damp, about 30 seconds. Add cantaloupe, plums, cherries, and vanilla and gently toss to combine. Let sit at room temperature, stirring occasionally, until fruit releases its juices, 15 to 30 minutes. Stir in lime juice and season with extra lime juice to taste. Serve.

VARIATION
Peaches, Blackberries, and Strawberries with Basil and Pepper
Nectarines can be substituted for the peaches.

- 2 tablespoons chopped fresh basil
- 4 teaspoons sugar
- ½ teaspoon pepper
- 3 peaches, halved, pitted, and cut into ½-inch pieces
- 10 ounces (2 cups) blackberries
- 10 ounces strawberries, hulled and quartered (2 cups)
- 1 tablespoon lime juice, plus extra for seasoning

Combine basil, sugar, and pepper in large bowl. Using rubber spatula, press mixture into side of bowl until sugar becomes damp, about 30 seconds. Add peaches, blackberries, and strawberries and gently toss to combine. Let sit at room temperature, stirring occasionally, until fruit releases its juices, 15 to 30 minutes. Stir in lime juice and season with extra lime juice to taste. Serve.

Strawberries with Balsamic Vinegar

Serves 4 to 6 FAST

Why This Recipe Works To pay homage to the traditional Italian combination of strawberries and balsamic, we created a dessert in which the vinegar enhanced the flavor of bright summer berries. High-end aged balsamic vinegars can cost a pretty penny, so we opted instead to use an inexpensive vinegar and employ a few tricks to coax more flavor from it. First, we simmered the vinegar with sugar to approximate the syrupy texture of an aged vinegar. Next we found that a squirt of fresh lemon juice brought just the right amount of brightness. We tossed the berries with light brown sugar—rather than the traditional granulated sugar—and a pinch of pepper for the most complex flavor. Once we mixed the sliced berries and sugar together, it took about 15 minutes for the sugar to dissolve and the berries to release their juice; if the berries sat any longer, they continued to soften and became mushy. If you don't have light brown sugar on hand, sprinkle the berries with an equal amount of granulated white sugar. Serve the berries and syrup as is or with a scoop of vanilla ice cream or a dollop of lightly sweetened mascarpone cheese.

⅓ cup balsamic vinegar
2 teaspoons granulated sugar
½ teaspoon lemon juice
2 pounds strawberries, hulled and sliced lengthwise ¼ inch thick (6½ cups)
¼ cup (1¾ ounces) packed light brown sugar
Pinch pepper

1. Bring vinegar, granulated sugar, and lemon juice to simmer in small saucepan over medium heat and cook, stirring occasionally, until thickened and measures about 3 tablespoons, about 3 minutes. Transfer syrup to small bowl and let cool completely.

2. Gently toss strawberries with brown sugar and pepper in large bowl. Let sit at room temperature, stirring occasionally, until strawberries begin to release their juices, 10 to 15 minutes. Pour syrup over strawberries and gently toss to combine. Serve.

Nectarines and Berries in Prosecco

Serves 6 to 8 FAST NO COOK

Why This Recipe Works For a celebratory yet light fruit dessert, we wanted to combine fresh fruit with sparkling wine. After some enjoyable experimentation, we settled on nectarines and berries as our fruit and prosecco for the wine. But simply pouring prosecco over lightly sugared fruit resulted in disappointingly disparate flavors. Instead, we tossed the fruit with sugar and allowed the mixture to macerate. The nectarines and berries softened and released some of their juices, which, when combined with the chilled wine, contributed to a more cohesive flavor profile. Orange liqueur added depth as well as some nice citrus notes. Our harmonious blend of fruit and fizz made a refreshing ending to a summer meal. Peaches or plums can be substituted for the nectarines. While we prefer to use prosecco here, any young, fruity sparkling wine will work.

10 ounces (2 cups) blackberries or raspberries
10 ounces strawberries, hulled and quartered (2 cups)
1 pound nectarines, pitted and cut into ¼-inch wedges
¼ cup (1¾ ounces) sugar, plus extra as needed
1 tablespoon orange liqueur, such as Grand Marnier or triple sec
1 tablespoon chopped fresh mint
¼ teaspoon grated lemon zest
1 cup chilled prosecco

Gently toss blackberries, strawberries, nectarines, sugar, orange liqueur, mint, and lemon zest together in large bowl. Let sit at room temperature, stirring occasionally, until fruit begins to release its juices, 10 to 15 minutes. Just before serving, pour prosecco over fruit and season with extra sugar to taste. Serve.

HULLING STRAWBERRIES

If you don't own a strawberry huller (see page 11), you can improvise with a plastic drinking straw.

To remove the hull from the strawberry, simply push the straw through the bottom of the berry and up through the leafy stem end. The straw will remove the core as well as the leafy top.

Strawberry-Rhubarb Compote with Ice Cream

Serves 6 `FAST` `MAKE AHEAD`

Why This Recipe Works A compote transforms summer fruit into the simplest of desserts: a lightly sweet topping for ice cream (it's also good on Greek yogurt or ricotta cheese). Gentle cooking releases the fruit's juices without breaking it down into jam. We translated the classic duo of strawberries and rhubarb to a sweet-tart compote and followed with colorful stone fruit and berry combos. Adding the delicate fruit off the heat prevented an overly soft compote, as did transferring the compote to a bowl to cool. Do not overcook the rhubarb or it will become stringy. To make your own ice cream or frozen yogurt, see the recipes on pages 403–409.

- ½ vanilla bean
- 6 tablespoons honey
- ¼ cup water
- Pinch table salt
- 8 ounces rhubarb, peeled and cut into 1-inch lengths
- 20 ounces strawberries, hulled and quartered (4 cups)
- 1 tablespoon unsalted butter
- 3 cups vanilla ice cream or frozen yogurt
- 1 tablespoon minced fresh mint

1. Cut vanilla bean in half lengthwise. Using tip of paring knife, scrape out seeds and reserve bean. Bring vanilla seeds and bean, honey, water, and salt to simmer in 12-inch nonstick skillet over medium heat. Stir in rhubarb and cook until it begins to soften and sauce thickens slightly, 4 to 6 minutes.

2. Off heat, gently stir in strawberries and butter until butter has melted. Discard vanilla bean, transfer compote to bowl, and let cool to room temperature, 10 to 15 minutes. (Compote can be refrigerated for up to 1 day; return to room temperature or before serving.)

3. Scoop ice cream into individual bowls and top with about ½ cup of compote. Sprinkle with mint and serve immediately.

VARIATIONS

Plum-Blackberry Compote with Ice Cream

Try to buy plums of similar ripeness so that they cook evenly. To prevent the compote from overcooking, be sure to transfer it to a bowl to cool.

- ½ vanilla bean
- 6 tablespoons water
- ¼ cup honey

Plum-Blackberry Compote with Ice Cream

- Pinch table salt
- 1½ pounds plums, pitted, sliced ⅓ inch thick, then halved crosswise
- 10 ounces (2 cups) blackberries
- 1 tablespoon unsalted butter
- 3 cups vanilla ice cream or frozen yogurt
- 1 tablespoon minced fresh mint

1. Cut vanilla bean in half lengthwise. Using tip of paring knife, scrape out seeds and reserve bean. Bring vanilla seeds and bean, water, honey, and salt to simmer in 12-inch nonstick skillet over medium heat. Stir in plums and cook until they begin to soften and sauce thickens slightly, 5 to 7 minutes.

2. Stir in blackberries and continue to cook until they begin to soften, about 1 minute. Off heat, stir in butter until melted. Discard vanilla bean, transfer compote to bowl, and let cool to room temperature, 10 to 15 minutes. (Compote can be refrigerated for up to 1 day; return to room temperature before serving.)

3. Scoop ice cream into individual bowls and top with about ½ cup of compote. Sprinkle with mint and serve immediately.

Blueberry-Nectarine Compote with Ice Cream

Try to buy nectarines of similar ripeness so that they cook evenly. To prevent the compote from overcooking, be sure to transfer it to a bowl to cool.

½ vanilla bean
3 tablespoons honey
2 tablespoons water
Pinch table salt
1½ pounds nectarines, pitted, sliced ⅓ inch thick, then halved crosswise
10 ounces (2 cups) blueberries
1 tablespoon lemon juice
1 tablespoon unsalted butter
3 cups vanilla ice cream or frozen yogurt
1 tablespoon minced fresh mint

1. Cut vanilla bean in half lengthwise. Using tip of paring knife, scrape out seeds and reserve bean. Bring vanilla seeds and bean, honey, water, and salt to simmer in 12-inch nonstick skillet over medium heat. Stir in nectarines and cook until they begin to soften and sauce thickens slightly, 3 to 5 minutes. Stir in blueberries and continue to cook until they begin to release their juice, 2 to 4 minutes.

2. Off heat, stir in lemon juice and butter until butter has melted. Discard vanilla bean pod, transfer compote to bowl, and let cool to room temperature, 10 to 15 minutes. (Compote can be refrigerated for up to 1 day; return to room temperature before serving.)

3. Scoop ice cream into individual bowls and top with about ½ cup of compote. Sprinkle with mint and serve immediately.

Honey-Glazed Peaches with Hazelnuts

Serves 6 `FAST`

Why This Recipe Works This simple broiled dessert puts fragrant summer peaches in the spotlight, with just enough added sweetness to amplify the fruit's complex flavors. For tender peaches and a flavorful glaze, we tried tossing the halved and pitted peaches with sugar and baking them until the sugar caramelized. However, the peaches turned to mush by the time we achieved any browning. We found our solution in the direct, intense heat of the broiler. We tossed the peaches with a little sugar, salt, and lemon juice for balance; this seasoned the fruit and extracted some juice that began the glazing process.

After broiling them briefly, we brushed them with a mixture of honey and fruity extra-virgin olive oil and then returned them to the broiler until they were beautifully glazed. Reducing the accumulated juice until it was syrupy intensified the peach flavor and made for an attractive, shiny glaze. Toasted hazelnuts added a contrasting crunch to the dessert. Select peaches that yield slightly when pressed. For more information on peeling peaches, see page 377. These peaches are best served warm with ice cream or Greek yogurt.

2 tablespoons lemon juice
1 tablespoon sugar
¼ teaspoon table salt
6 ripe but firm peaches, peeled, halved, and pitted
⅓ cup water
¼ cup honey
1 tablespoon extra-virgin olive oil
¼ cup hazelnuts, toasted, skinned, and chopped coarse

1. Adjust oven rack 6 inches from broiler element and heat broiler. Combine lemon juice, sugar, and salt in large bowl. Add peaches and toss to combine, making sure to coat all sides with sugar mixture.

2. Arrange peaches cut side up in 12-inch broiler-safe skillet and spoon any remaining sugar mixture into peach cavities. Pour water around peaches in skillet. Broil until peaches are just beginning to brown, 11 to 15 minutes.

3. Combine honey and oil in bowl and microwave until warm, about 20 seconds, then stir to combine. Remove skillet from oven. Being careful of hot skillet handle, brush half of honey mixture on peaches. Return peaches to oven and continue to broil until spotty brown, 5 to 7 minutes.

4. Carefully remove skillet from oven, brush peaches with remaining honey mixture, and transfer to serving platter, leaving juice behind. Bring accumulated juice in skillet to simmer over medium heat and cook, whisking frequently to combine, until syrupy, about 1 minute. Pour syrup over peaches and sprinkle with hazelnuts. Serve.

HALVING AND PITTING PEACHES

Cut peach in half, pole to pole, using crease in peach skin as guide. Grasp both halves of fruit and twist apart. Halves will come apart cleanly so pit can be easily removed.

Roasted Plums with Dried Cherries and Almonds

Warm Figs with Goat Cheese and Honey

Roasted Plums with Dried Cherries and Almonds

Serves 4 to 6

Why This Recipe Works Roasting plums turns them into an unexpectedly easy dessert that's the perfect use of one of summer's most irresistible stone fruits. Our two-stage cooking process yielded tender, beautifully caramelized fruit. The plums required almost no prep work; to help them retain their shape, we kept the skins on and simply halved and pitted them. We browned the halves cut side down in a skillet on the stovetop to build a bit of color and banish some of the plums' moisture; we then moved the skillet to the oven where the surrounding heat gently roasted the fruit and created deeper browning. After 5 minutes, we flipped the halves and allowed them to finish softening. The juices in the pan were perfect for a sauce, so we reduced them with white wine. A handful of dried cherries added the right amount of fruity sweetness and tender chew; a touch of cinnamon and a bit of lemon juice added a kick that complemented the plums. Toasted almonds supplied a contrasting crunchy garnish. This recipe works equally well with red or black plums. You will need a 12-inch ovensafe skillet for this recipe. The fruit can be served as is or with ice cream or Greek yogurt.

2½ tablespoons unsalted butter, divided
 4 ripe but firm red or black plums, halved and pitted
1¼ cups dry white wine
½ cup dried cherries
⅓ cup (2⅓ ounces) sugar
¼ teaspoon ground cinnamon
⅛ teaspoon table salt
 1 teaspoon lemon juice
⅓ cup sliced almonds, toasted

1. Adjust oven rack to middle position and heat oven to 450 degrees. Melt 1½ tablespoons butter in 12-inch ovensafe skillet over medium-high heat. Place plum halves, cut side down, in skillet. Cook, without moving, until plums are just beginning to brown, about 3 minutes.

2. Transfer skillet to oven and roast for 5 minutes. Flip plums and continue to roast until fork easily pierces fruit, about 5 minutes.

3. Remove skillet from oven (skillet handle will be hot); transfer plums to serving platter. Being careful of hot skillet handle, return skillet to medium-high heat and add wine, cherries, sugar, cinnamon, salt, and remaining 1 tablespoon butter. Bring to vigorous simmer, whisking to scrape up any browned bits. Cook until sauce is reduced and has consistency of maple syrup, 7 to 10 minutes. Off heat, stir in lemon juice. Pour sauce over plums, sprinkle with almonds, and serve.

Peaches and Cherries Poached in Spiced Red Wine

Serves 6   FAST

Why This Recipe Works Poaching fruit allows its beautiful shape and texture to remain intact while improving its tenderness and enhancing rather than masking its flavor. Sweet cherries and floral peaches made a perfectly elegant pair when poached in a red wine syrup. We found that a 2:1 ratio of wine to sugar was necessary to achieve a glossy syrup that would nicely coat the fruit. We boiled the syrup first to dissolve the sugar and then allowed the fruit to cook gently by pouring the hot syrup over it. Slicing the peaches thin ensured that they would cook at the same rate as the cherries. To infuse the fruit with flavor as it cooled in the wine syrup, we added half a cinnamon stick (a whole one was overpowering) and a couple of whole cloves to the mix. Select peaches that yield slightly when pressed. For more information on peeling peaches, see page 377. Serve this compote as is, with a bit of the poaching syrup, or with ice cream, Greek yogurt, or crème fraîche.

  1 pound ripe but firm peaches, peeled, halved, pitted, and sliced ¼ inch thick
  1 pound fresh sweet cherries, pitted and halved
  ½ cinnamon stick
  2 whole cloves
  2 cups dry red wine
  1 cup (7 ounces) sugar

Combine peaches, cherries, cinnamon stick, and cloves in large bowl. Bring red wine and sugar to boil in small saucepan over high heat and cook, stirring occasionally, until sugar has dissolved, about 5 minutes. Pour syrup over fruit, cover, and let cool to room temperature. Discard cinnamon stick and cloves. Serve.

Warm Figs with Goat Cheese and Honey

Serves 4 to 6   FAST

Why This Recipe Works Fresh figs have sweet, juicy flesh and a delicate flavor that need little adornment, so to create a light fruit dessert that was just sweet enough to end a summer dinner, we baked the figs for a few minutes to warm them through. We started by choosing the ripest, plumpest figs we could find. Halving them and topping them with a bit of tangy goat cheese offset their sweetness nicely. A brief stint in a hot oven was enough to warm the figs and cheese through, and topping each one with a walnut half, toasted to bring out its flavor, offered pleasant crunchy contrast. Finally, a drizzle of honey (tasters preferred milder-flavored options like clover) brought all the elements together with a hit of floral sweetness.

 1½ ounces goat cheese
  8 fresh figs, halved lengthwise
 16 walnut halves, toasted
  3 tablespoons honey

  1. Adjust oven rack to middle position and heat oven to 500 degrees. Spoon heaping ½ teaspoon goat cheese onto each fig half and arrange in parchment paper–lined rimmed baking sheet. Bake figs until heated through, about 4 minutes; transfer to serving platter.

  2. Place 1 walnut half on top of each fig half and drizzle with honey. Serve.

Individual Fresh Berry Gratins
Serves 4

Why This Recipe Works *Zabaglione* is an ethereal Italian custard flavored with wine and often accompanied by fresh berries. To turn this simple combination into a dessert worthy of serving to guests at a summer dinner party, we baked it as a gratin. We macerated the berries with a little bit of sugar to encourage them to release their flavorful juices. For the custard, we whisked together egg yolks, sugar, and wine over a pot of barely simmering water. Keeping the heat low and using a glass bowl rather than a metal one guarded against overcooking. Tasters preferred the flavor of light, crisp white wine to the more traditional Marsala, but the decreased sugar made our custard runny. To make up for the loss of structure without making the custard achingly sweet, we folded in some whipped cream. Dividing the berries and custard among individual gratin dishes made for a pretty presentation and easier serving. Running the gratins briefly under the broiler produced warm, succulent berries and a golden-brown crust on the zabaglione. You will need four shallow 6-ounce broiler-safe gratin dishes, but a broiler-safe pie plate or gratin dish can be used instead. When making the zabaglione, make sure to cook the egg mixture in a glass bowl over water that is barely simmering; glass conducts heat more evenly and gently than metal. Although we prefer to make this recipe with a mixture of blackberries, blueberries, raspberries, and strawberries, you can use 3 cups of just one type of berry. Do not use frozen berries for this recipe. To prevent scorching, pay close attention to the gratins when broiling. Use a medium-bodied dry white wine such as Sauvignon Blanc or Chardonnay in this recipe.

Berry Mixture

- 11 ounces (2¼ cups) blackberries, blueberries, and/or raspberries
- 4 ounces strawberries, hulled and halved lengthwise if small or quartered if large (¾ cup)
- 2 teaspoons granulated sugar
  Pinch table salt

Zabaglione

- 3 large egg yolks
- 3 tablespoons granulated sugar, divided
- 3 tablespoons dry white wine
- 2 teaspoons packed light brown sugar
- 3 tablespoons heavy cream, chilled

1. For the berry mixture Line rimmed baking sheet with aluminum foil. Toss berries, strawberries, sugar, and salt together in bowl. Divide berry mixture evenly among 4 shallow 6-ounce gratin dishes and place on prepared sheet; set aside.

2. For the zabaglione Whisk egg yolks, 2 tablespoons plus 1 teaspoon granulated sugar, and wine in medium bowl until sugar has dissolved, about 1 minute. Set bowl over saucepan of barely simmering water and cook, whisking constantly, until mixture is frothy. Continue to cook, whisking constantly, until mixture is slightly thickened, creamy, and glossy, 5 to 10 minutes (mixture will form loose mounds when dripped from whisk). Remove bowl from saucepan and whisk constantly for 30 seconds to cool slightly. Transfer bowl to refrigerator and chill until egg mixture is completely cool, about 10 minutes.

3. Meanwhile, adjust oven rack 6 inches from broiler element and heat broiler. Combine brown sugar and remaining 2 teaspoons granulated sugar in bowl.

4. Whisk heavy cream in large bowl until it holds soft peaks, 30 to 90 seconds. Using rubber spatula, gently fold whipped cream into cooled egg mixture. Spoon zabaglione over berries and sprinkle sugar mixture evenly on top. Let sit at room temperature for 10 minutes, until sugar dissolves.

5. Broil gratins until sugar is bubbly and caramelized, 1 to 4 minutes. Serve immediately.

Strawberry Shortcakes
Serves 6 to 8 `MAKE AHEAD`

Why This Recipe Works Strawberry shortcake is a must-have summer dessert. We wanted a juicy strawberry filling that would stay put in between our biscuits. The solution? We chose the ripest berries we could find (for the best flavor), and then mashed some of them into a chunky sauce and sliced the rest. Left to sit for a bit with a little sugar, the berry mixture macerated, exuding even more flavorful juice, making for a thick, chunky filling that soaked into, and didn't slip off, our tender biscuits. Preparing the fruit first gave it a chance to become truly juicy—just what you want on the fresh-made biscuits. This recipe will yield six biscuits and scraps can be gathered and patted out to yield another biscuit or two; these, though, will not be as tender as the first.

- 2½ pounds strawberries, hulled (8 cups), divided
- ½ cup (3½ ounces) plus 3 tablespoons sugar, divided
- 2 cups (10 ounces) all-purpose flour
- 1 tablespoon baking powder
- ½ teaspoon table salt
- 8 tablespoons unsalted butter, cut into ½-inch pieces and chilled
- ⅔ cup half-and-half
- 1 large egg plus 1 large egg white, lightly beaten
- 1 recipe Whipped Cream (page 406)

1. Crush 3 cups strawberries with potato masher. Slice remaining berries and stir into crushed berries with 6 tablespoons sugar. Let sit at room temperature, stirring occasionally, until fruit begins to release its juices, about 30 minutes or up to 2 hours.

2. Meanwhile, adjust oven rack to lower-middle position and heat oven to 425 degrees. Pulse flour, 3 tablespoons sugar, baking powder, and salt in food processor until combined.

Scatter butter pieces over top and pulse until mixture resembles coarse cornmeal, about 15 pulses. Transfer to large bowl.

3. In separate bowl, whisk half-and-half and egg together. Add half-and-half mixture to flour mixture and stir with rubber spatula until large clumps form. Turn mixture onto lightly floured counter and knead lightly until dough comes together.

4. Using your fingertips, pat dough into 9 by 6-inch rectangle about 1 inch thick. Cut out 6 biscuits using floured 2¾-inch biscuit cutter. Pat remaining dough into 1-inch thick piece and cut out 2 more biscuits. Place biscuits on parchment-lined baking sheet, spaced 1 inch apart.

5. Brush top of biscuits with egg white and sprinkle with remaining 2 tablespoons sugar. Bake biscuits until golden brown, 12 to 14 minutes. Let biscuits cool on baking sheet for about 10 minutes. (Biscuits can be stored at room temperature for up to 3 days or frozen for up to 1 month; to serve, refresh in 350-degree oven for 3 to 5 minutes, or 7 to 10 minutes for frozen biscuits.)

6. Split each biscuit in half and place bottoms on individual serving plates. Spoon portion of fruit over each bottom, then top with dollop of whipped cream. Cap with biscuit tops and serve immediately.

Strawberry Shortcakes

Summer Berry Trifle
Serves 12 to 16   MAKE AHEAD

Why This Recipe Works When done right, trifle—a towering dish of cake layered with pastry cream, whipped cream, and fruit—is a stellar summer showstopper featuring light, cool, creamy, and fruity elements. For a standout berry trifle, we streamlined the components so that the entire dessert could be made from scratch in just a few hours. We added a little extra flour to a chiffon cake batter (chiffon cake is sturdier than butter cake when soaked); the added structure meant we could bake the cake in a rimmed baking sheet, which allowed it to bake and cool very quickly. Pastry cream often becomes runny during assembly, but adding some extra cornstarch to the cream helped it stay put and remain a distinct layer. We liked the balance of sweet, tart, and earthy flavors that a mixture of strawberries, raspberries, and blackberries provided. Rather than leaving all our berries whole, we mashed one-third of them so their juices could help the components meld. A bit of cream sherry, mixed into the whipped cream and drizzled over the cake, further unified the layers. Assemble the trifle at least 6 hours before serving. Make sure to use a glass bowl with at least a 3½-quart capacity; straight sides are preferable.

Summer Berry Trifle

Pastry Cream

3½ cups whole milk, divided
1 cup (7 ounces) sugar
6 tablespoons cornstarch
Pinch table salt
5 large egg yolks (reserve whites for cake)
4 tablespoons unsalted butter, cut into
½-inch pieces and chilled
4 teaspoons vanilla extract

Cake

1⅓ cups (5⅓ ounces) cake flour
¾ cup (5¼ ounces) sugar
1½ teaspoons baking powder
¼ teaspoon table salt
⅓ cup vegetable oil
¼ cup water
1 large egg, plus 5 large whites
(reserved from pastry cream)
2 teaspoons vanilla extract
¼ teaspoon cream of tartar

Fruit Filling

1½ pounds strawberries, hulled and cut into
½-inch pieces (4 cups), divided, plus
3 halved berries reserved for garnish
12 ounces (2⅓ cups) blackberries, large
berries halved crosswise, divided, plus
3 whole berries reserved for garnish
12 ounces (2⅓ cups) raspberries, divided,
plus 3 reserved for garnish
¼ cup (1¾ ounces) sugar
½ teaspoon cornstarch
Pinch table salt
½ cup cream sherry, divided
1 recipe Whipped Cream (page 406)

1. For the pastry cream Heat 3 cups milk in medium saucepan over medium heat until just simmering. Meanwhile, whisk sugar, cornstarch, and salt together in bowl. Whisk egg yolks and remaining ½ cup milk into sugar mixture until smooth. Remove milk from heat and, whisking constantly, slowly add 1 cup milk to sugar mixture to temper. Whisking constantly, add tempered sugar mixture to milk in saucepan.

2. Return saucepan to medium heat and cook, whisking constantly, until mixture is very thick and bubbles burst on surface, 4 to 7 minutes. Off heat, whisk in butter and vanilla until incorporated. Strain pastry cream through fine-mesh strainer set over bowl. Press lightly greased parchment paper directly on surface and refrigerate until set, at least 2 hours or up to 24 hours.

3. For the cake Adjust oven rack to middle position and heat oven to 350 degrees. Lightly grease 18 by 13-inch rimmed baking sheet, line with parchment, and lightly grease parchment. Whisk flour, sugar, baking powder, and salt together in large bowl. Whisk oil, water, egg, and vanilla into flour mixture until smooth batter forms.

4. Using stand mixer fitted with whisk attachment, whip egg whites and cream of tartar on medium-low speed until foamy, about 1 minute. Increase speed to medium-high and whip until soft peaks form, 2 to 3 minutes.

5. Whisk one-third of whites into batter. Using rubber spatula, gently fold remaining whites into batter until no white streaks remain. Transfer batter to prepared sheet and spread into even layer. Bake until top is golden brown and cake springs back when pressed lightly in center, 13 to 16 minutes, rotating sheet halfway through baking.

6. Let cake cool in pan on wire rack for 5 minutes. Invert cake onto rack, discarding parchment, then carefully reinvert cake onto second rack. Let cool completely, at least 30 minutes.

7. For the fruit filling Place 1½ cups strawberries, 1 cup blackberries, 1 cup raspberries, sugar, cornstarch, and salt in medium saucepan. Place remaining berries in large bowl; set aside. Using potato masher, thoroughly mash berries in saucepan. Cook over medium heat until sugar is dissolved and mixture is thick and bubbling, 4 to 7 minutes. Transfer mixture to bowl with remaining berries and stir to combine; set aside.

8. Using serrated knife, trim ¼ inch off each side of cake; discard trimmings. Cut cake into 24 equal pieces (each piece about 2½ inches square).

9. Briefly whisk pastry cream until smooth. Spoon ¾ cup pastry cream into 3½-quart trifle dish or glass bowl; spread over bottom. Shingle 12 cake pieces, fallen domino–style, on top of pastry cream, placing 10 pieces against dish wall and 2 remaining pieces in center. Drizzle ¼ cup sherry evenly over cake. Spoon half of berry mixture evenly over cake, making sure to use half of liquid. Using back of spoon, spread half of remaining pastry cream over berries, then spread half of whipped cream over pastry cream (whipped cream layer will be thin). Repeat layering with remaining 12 cake pieces, sherry, berries, pastry cream, and whipped cream. Cover bowl with plastic wrap and refrigerate for at least 6 hours or up to 36 hours. Just before serving, arrange remaining berries in center of trifle.

Blackberry–Key Lime Trifle

Serves 12 `NO COOK` `MAKE AHEAD`

Why This Recipe Works Our laid-back, late-summer black-berry trifle is inspired by the refreshing flavors of key lime pie. We created a convenient make-ahead version we could prepare without turning on the oven by swapping the traditional cake and pastry cream for graham crackers and a no-cook pudding. To make the pudding, we combined fresh lime juice, sugar, cream cheese, condensed milk, and a secret ingredient: instant vanilla pudding. After the pudding had thickened and chilled in the fridge, we layered it with graham crackers and fresh blackberries. Decorated with lime slices, this trifle makes for an impressive end to any meal. Assemble the trifle at least 6 hours before serving. Make sure to use a glass bowl with at least a 3½-quart capacity; straight sides are preferable.

¼ cup (1¾ ounces) granulated sugar
1 tablespoon grated lime zest plus 1 cup juice (8 limes), plus 5 limes sliced ⅛ inch thick, divided
8 ounces cream cheese, softened
1 (14-ounce) can sweetened condensed milk
⅓ cup instant vanilla pudding mix
1 teaspoon vanilla extract
12 whole graham crackers, broken in half
1 recipe Double Batch Whipped Cream (page 406)
30 ounces (6 cups) blackberries, divided

1. Process sugar and lime zest in food processor until sugar turns bright green, about 30 seconds. Set aside 2 teaspoons lime sugar. Add cream cheese to remaining lime sugar and process until combined, about 30 seconds. Add condensed milk and pudding mix and process until smooth, about 30 seconds, scraping down sides of bowl as needed. With processor running, add lime juice and vanilla and process until thoroughly combined, about 30 seconds. Transfer custard to bowl, cover with plastic wrap, and refrigerate until thickened, about 1 hour.

2. Shingle 12 cracker halves along bottom of 3½-quart trifle dish or glass bowl. Arrange half of lime slices upright around bottom of dish, wedged between cracker halves and wall of dish. Spread 1½ cups custard in even layer over cracker halves, followed by 2 cups whipped cream. Sprinkle 5 cups blackberries in even layer over whipped cream. Shingle 11 cracker halves over blackberries along edge of trifle and place remaining 1 cracker half in center. Arrange remaining lime slices upright around dish. Spread remaining custard over cracker halves, followed by remaining 2 cups whipped cream. Cover bowl with plastic and refrigerate for at least 6 hours or up to 24 hours. Just before serving, arrange remaining 1 cup blackberries in center of trifle and sprinkle top of trifle with reserved lime sugar.

Blueberry Cobbler

Blueberry Cobbler

Serves 8

Why This Recipe Works We wanted a cobbler that put the blueberry flavor front and center, with a light, tender biscuit topping that could hold its own against the fruit filling. We started by preparing a filling using 6 cups of fresh berries and just enough sugar to sweeten them. Cornstarch worked well to thicken the fruit's juices. Parbaking the biscuit topping ensured that the biscuits wouldn't become soggy once placed on top of the fruit, and precooking the fruit filling meant all we had to do was set the parbaked biscuits on the hot filling and bake them together for 15 minutes until bubbly. Taste the fruit before adding sugar; use less if it is very sweet, more if it is tart. Do not let the biscuit batter sit for longer than 5 minutes or so before baking.

Biscuit Topping

- 1½ cups (7½ ounces) all-purpose flour
- ¼ cup (1¾ ounces) plus 2 teaspoons sugar, divided
- 1½ teaspoons baking powder
- ¼ teaspoon baking soda
- ¼ teaspoon table salt
- ¾ cup buttermilk, chilled
- 6 tablespoons unsalted butter, melted and hot
- ⅛ teaspoon ground cinnamon

Fruit Filling

- ⅓–⅔ cup (2⅓–4⅔ ounces) sugar
- 4 teaspoons cornstarch
- 30 ounces (6 cups) blueberries
- 1 tablespoon lemon juice
- ½ teaspoon ground cinnamon

1. For the biscuit topping Adjust oven rack to middle position and heat oven to 400 degrees. Line rimmed baking sheet with parchment paper. Whisk flour, ¼ cup sugar, baking powder, baking soda, and salt together in large bowl.

2. In separate bowl, stir buttermilk and melted butter together until butter forms small clumps. Using rubber spatula, stir buttermilk mixture into flour mixture until just incorporated and dough pulls away from sides of bowl.

3. Using greased ¼-cup measure, scoop out and drop 8 mounds of dough onto prepared baking sheet, spaced about 1½ inches apart. Combine remaining 2 teaspoons sugar with cinnamon, then sprinkle over biscuits. Bake biscuits until puffed and lightly browned on bottom, about 10 minutes, rotating sheet halfway through baking. Remove parbaked biscuits from oven; set aside.

4. For the fruit filling Whisk sugar and cornstarch together in large bowl. Add blueberries, lemon juice, and cinnamon and toss gently to combine. Transfer fruit mixture to 9-inch pie plate, cover with aluminum foil, and place on foil-lined rimmed baking sheet. Bake until filling is hot and berries have released their juice, 20 to 25 minutes.

5. Remove fruit from oven, uncover, and stir gently. Arrange parbaked biscuits over top, squeezing them slightly as needed to fit into dish. Bake cobbler until biscuits are golden brown and fruit is bubbling, about 15 minutes. Transfer to wire rack and let cool for 15 minutes before serving.

VARIATIONS
Peach or Nectarine Cobbler

In the filling, substitute 3 pounds peaches or nectarines, peeled, halved, pitted, and cut into ½-inch-thick wedges, for blueberries, and 1 teaspoon vanilla extract for cinnamon. Reduce cornstarch to 1 tablespoon and lemon juice to 1 teaspoon.

Fresh Sour Cherry Cobbler

In the filling, substitute 3 pounds pitted fresh sour cherries for blueberries. Omit lemon juice and cinnamon. Increase cornstarch to 1½ tablespoons and sugar to ¾ cup. Add 2 tablespoons red wine and ¼ teaspoon almond extract to bowl with cherries before baking.

No-Bake Cherry Crisp
Serves 6

Why This Recipe Works Most fruit crisps are baked in the oven, but we wanted a summer cherry dessert as good as the baked version that didn't require us to turn on the oven at all. After testing various methods, we found that the best was actually the easiest: After browning a topping of almonds, sugar, flour, and butter in a skillet on the stovetop, we use the same pan to cook the filling. We cooked pitted cherries with sugar, lemon juice, and almond and vanilla extracts. Some cornstarch thickened the filling to a syrupy consistency, and dried cherries soaked up excess moisture while adding texture and more cherry flavor.

Topping

- ¾ cup sliced almonds, divided
- ⅔ cup (3⅓ ounces) all-purpose flour
- ¼ cup packed (1¾ ounces) light brown sugar
- ¼ cup (1¾ ounces) granulated sugar
- ½ teaspoon vanilla extract
- ¼ teaspoon ground cinnamon
- ¼ teaspoon table salt
- 6 tablespoons unsalted butter, melted

Filling

- ⅓ cup (2⅓ ounces) granulated sugar, divided
- 1 tablespoon cornstarch
- 2 pounds cherries, pitted and halved
- 1 tablespoon lemon juice
- 1 teaspoon vanilla extract
- ½ teaspoon table salt
- ¼ teaspoon almond extract
- ⅔ cup dried cherries

1. For the topping Finely chop ¼ cup almonds. Combine chopped almonds, flour, brown sugar, granulated sugar, vanilla, cinnamon, and salt in bowl. Stir in melted butter until mixture resembles wet sand and no dry flour remains.

2. Toast remaining ½ cup almonds in 10-inch nonstick skillet over medium-low heat until just beginning to brown, about 4 minutes. Add flour mixture and cook, stirring constantly, until lightly browned, 6 to 8 minutes; transfer to plate to cool. Wipe skillet clean with paper towels.

3. For the filling Combine 2 tablespoons sugar and cornstarch in small bowl; set aside. Combine cherries, lemon juice, vanilla, salt, almond extract, and remaining sugar in now-empty skillet. Cover and cook over medium heat until cherries release their juice, about 7 minutes, stirring halfway through cooking. Uncover, stir in dried cherries, and simmer until cherries are very tender, about 3 minutes.

4. Stir in cornstarch mixture and simmer, stirring constantly, until thickened, 1 to 3 minutes. Off heat, distribute topping evenly over filling. Return skillet to medium-low heat and cook until filling is bubbling around edges, about 3 minutes. Let cool off heat for at least 30 minutes before serving.

Peach Melba Crisp
Serves 6

Why This Recipe Works For an easy dessert with bold fruit flavor, we wanted to translate the classic flavors of peach Melba (peaches and raspberries) into a warm summer crisp. But we found that the peaches' variable juiciness could produce a perfect crisp one day and a soupy one the next. Meanwhile, the raspberries disintegrated with baking. Macerating and draining the peaches, and then adding back 2 tablespoons of juice with ground tapioca, ensured a full-flavored, properly thickened filling. Sprinkling the delicate raspberries on top of the peaches instead of folding them in created a pretty layered effect and prevented them from being crushed. A simple topping of oats, flour, and nuts made a crisp and buttery crown for the sweet fruit filling. Do not use quick or instant oats in this recipe. Measure the tapioca before grinding in a spice grinder or mini food processor. For more information on peeling peaches, see page 377. Serve with vanilla ice cream.

Filling
- 2½ pounds fresh peaches, peeled, halved, pitted, and cut into ½-inch wedges
- ¼ cup (1¾ ounces) granulated sugar
- ⅛ teaspoon table salt
- 2 tablespoons instant tapioca, ground
- 1 tablespoon lemon juice
- 1 teaspoon vanilla extract
- 10 ounces (2 cups) raspberries

No-Bake Cherry Crisp

Peach Melba Crisp

Strawberry Sonker

Easy Peach and Blackberry Tart

Topping

- ½ cup (2½ ounces) all-purpose flour
- ¼ cup packed (1¾ ounces) brown sugar
- ¼ cup (1¾ ounces) granulated sugar
- ¼ teaspoon ground cinnamon
- ¼ teaspoon ground ginger
- ¼ teaspoon table salt
- 6 tablespoons unsalted butter, cut into ½-inch pieces and chilled
- ½ cup (1½ ounces) old-fashioned rolled oats
- ½ cup pecans, chopped

1. For the filling Gently toss peaches with sugar and salt in bowl and let sit, stirring occasionally, for 30 minutes. Drain peaches in colander set in bowl; reserve peach juice. Return drained peaches to original bowl and toss with 2 tablespoons reserved peach juice, tapioca, lemon juice, and vanilla. Transfer to 8-inch square baking dish and press gently into even layer. Top peaches with raspberries. Adjust oven rack to upper-middle position and heat oven to 400 degrees.

2. For the topping While peaches are macerating, combine flour, brown sugar, granulated sugar, cinnamon, ginger, and salt in food processor and process until combined, about 15 seconds. Add butter and pulse until mixture resembles wet sand, about 8 pulses. Add oats and pecans and pulse until mixture forms marble-size clumps and no dry flour remains, about 15 pulses. Chill mixture for at least 15 minutes.

3. Distribute topping evenly over fruit. Bake until topping is well browned and fruit is bubbling around edges, about 30 minutes, rotating dish halfway through baking. Let cool on wire rack for at least 30 minutes. Serve.

Strawberry Sonker
Serves 6

Why This Recipe Works Not quite a pie and not quite a cobbler, sonker is a juicy, fruit-filled deep-dish dessert rarely found outside Surry County, North Carolina. While toppings vary, a subset of sonker recipes dub themselves "lazy" sonkers, in which the fruit is cooked into a sweet stew and topped with a pancake batter that bakes into a distinct, lightly crisp layer of cake. For our version, we tossed strawberries with sugar, salt, water, and cornstarch and then baked them until they bubbled and thickened. We then poured the batter over the filling and returned it to the oven. The thick stewed strawberries gave the batter a sturdy, level surface on which to bake, and the hot filling baked the batter from underneath. Eight tablespoons of melted butter made the batter light and floatable so that it baked into a tender-yet-crisp raft of cake. If you're using frozen strawberries in this recipe, there's no need to let them thaw. In steps 2 and 3, be sure to stir the strawberry filling as directed, scraping the bottom of the dish to incorporate the cornstarch so that it evenly and thoroughly thickens the mixture. In step 3, add the butter to the batter while it is still hot so it remains pourable, and be sure to mix the batter only right before pouring it over the filling. Serve with vanilla ice cream.

2 pounds fresh strawberries, hulled (6½ cups)
1 cup (7 ounces) sugar, divided
½ teaspoon table salt, divided
¼ cup water
3 tablespoons cornstarch
1 cup (5 ounces) all-purpose flour
1 teaspoon baking powder
½ cup whole milk
8 tablespoons unsalted butter, melted and hot
¼ teaspoon vanilla extract

1. Adjust oven rack to middle position and heat oven to 350 degrees. Line rimmed baking sheet with parchment paper. Combine strawberries, ¼ cup sugar, and ¼ teaspoon salt in bowl. Whisk water and cornstarch together in second bowl; add to strawberry mixture and toss until strawberries are evenly coated.

2. Transfer strawberry mixture to 8-inch square baking dish and place dish on prepared sheet. Bake until filling is bubbling around sides of dish, 35 to 40 minutes, stirring and scraping bottom of dish with rubber spatula halfway through baking.

3. Remove sheet from oven and stir filling, being sure to scrape bottom and corners of dish with rubber spatula. Whisk flour, baking powder, remaining ¾ cup sugar, and remaining ¼ teaspoon salt together in bowl. Whisk in milk, melted butter, and vanilla until smooth. Pour batter evenly over filling.

4. Bake until surface is golden brown and toothpick inserted in center comes out with no crumbs attached, 35 to 40 minutes, rotating dish halfway through baking. Let sonker cool on wire rack for 15 minutes. Serve.

VARIATIONS
Blueberry Sonker
Substitute 2 pounds (6½ cups) fresh blueberries for strawberries.

Peach Sonker
Substitute 2½ pounds peaches, peeled, halved, pitted, and cut into ½-inch-thick wedges, for strawberries.

Easy Peach and Blackberry Tart
Serves 6 MAKE AHEAD

Why This Recipe Works This appealingly rustic free-form tart (also known as a galette) requires no special pan; it is simply rolled out and folded around a generous fruit filling. To ensure it had proper structure, we needed a pliable but flaky crust. We used the food processor to cut cold butter into flour and then stirred in ice water by hand to avoid overworking the dough (which would have rendered it tough). To limit the amount of liquid drawn out of the fruit by the sugar we added to sweeten the filling, we tossed the filling ingredients together just before assembling and baking the tart. We loved the color and flavor contrast of deep, dark blackberries and vibrant orange peaches. Taste the fruit before adding sugar; use less if it is very sweet, more if it is tart. Do not toss the sugar with the fruit until you are ready to form the tart.

1½ cups (7½ ounces) all-purpose flour
½ teaspoon table salt
10 tablespoons unsalted butter, cut into ½-inch pieces and chilled
7–8 tablespoons ice water, divided
1 pound peaches, halved, pitted, and cut into ½-inch-thick wedges
5 ounces (1 cup) blackberries
6 tablespoons (2⅔ ounces) sugar, divided

1. Process flour and salt in food processor until combined, about 3 seconds. Scatter butter over top and pulse until mixture resembles coarse crumbs, about 10 pulses. Transfer to bowl. Sprinkle 6 tablespoons ice water over mixture. Using rubber spatula, stir and press dough until it sticks together, adding up to 1 tablespoon more ice water if it will not come together.

2. Turn dough onto lightly floured counter, form into 4-inch disk, wrap tightly in plastic wrap, and refrigerate for 1 hour. (Wrapped dough can be refrigerated for up to 2 days or frozen for up to 1 month.)

3. Adjust oven rack to lower-middle position and heat oven to 375 degrees. Line rimmed baking sheet with parchment paper. Let chilled dough sit on counter to soften slightly, about 10 minutes, before rolling. Roll dough into 12-inch circle on lightly floured counter, then transfer to prepared sheet.

4. Gently toss peaches, blackberries, and 5 tablespoons sugar together in bowl. Mound fruit in center of dough, leaving 2-inch border around edge. Carefully grasp 1 edge of dough and fold up 2 inches over fruit. Repeat around circumference of tart, overlapping dough every 2 inches; gently pinch pleated dough to secure, but do not press dough into fruit.

5. Brush dough with remaining 1 tablespoon water and sprinkle remaining 1 tablespoon sugar evenly over dough and fruit. Bake until crust is deep golden brown and fruit is bubbling, 45 to 50 minutes. Transfer sheet to wire rack and let tart cool for 10 minutes. Using metal spatula, loosen tart from parchment and slide onto wire rack; let cool until warm, about 30 minutes. Cut into wedges and serve.

VARIATIONS
Easy Plum and Raspberry Tart
Substitute plums for peaches and raspberries for blackberries.

Easy Apricot and Blueberry Tart
Substitute apricots for peaches and blueberries for blackberries.

Strawberry Galette with Candied Basil and Balsamic

Serves 6 to 8 MAKE AHEAD

Why This Recipe Works Whereas pie fillings run the gamut from custards and creams to fruit, chocolate, and nuts, galettes typically feature fruit alone. There's a good reason for this: The exposed fruit does more than just meld into a cohesive filling—it roasts! This deepens the flavor of the fruit and evaporates moisture quickly, so there's usually no need for an added thickener. But we discovered that strawberries are an exception. We followed the standard method of our fruit galettes and what came from the oven was a watery mess severely lacking in strawberry flavor; we needed a thickener of some kind. Tossing cornstarch with the berries did the trick, and incorporating some strawberry jam intensified the berry flavor while adding viscosity. This tart was beautifully fresh, but its flavor was further elevated by a drizzle of balsamic glaze made by reducing vinegar with some sugar: The balsamic's acidity heightened the flavor of the strawberries while its woodsy fruitiness deepened it. Some ground black pepper provided sharp contrast. And to gild the lily, we finished with some candied basil leaves that took less than 2 minutes to make in the microwave. We love these garnishes, but you could substitute 1 tablespoon chopped fresh basil for all of them if you prefer.

Galette
- 1½ cups (7½ ounces) all-purpose flour
- ½ teaspoon table salt
- 10 tablespoons unsalted butter, cut into ½-inch cubes and chilled
- 3–6 tablespoons ice water
- ⅓ cup strawberry jam
- ¼ cup (1¾ ounces) plus 1 tablespoon sugar, divided
- ¼ teaspoon table salt
- 1½ tablespoons cornstarch
- 1½ pounds strawberries, hulled and halved (5 cups)

Garnishes
- ½ cup balsamic vinegar
- 1½ teaspoons sugar, divided
  Vegetable oil spray
- ¼ cup fresh basil leaves
- 1 teaspoon coarsely ground pepper

1. For the galette Process flour and salt in food processor until combined, about 5 seconds. Scatter butter over top and pulse until mixture resembles coarse sand and butter pieces are about size of small peas, about 10 pulses. Continue to pulse, adding ice water 1 tablespoon at a time, until dough begins to form small curds that hold together when pinched with your fingers, about 10 pulses.

2. Transfer mixture to lightly floured counter and gather into rectangular-shaped pile. Starting at farthest end, use heel of your hand to smear small amount of dough against counter. Continue to smear dough until all crumbs have been worked. Gather smeared crumbs together in another rectangular-shaped pile and repeat process.

3. Form dough into 6-inch disk, wrap tightly in plastic wrap, and refrigerate for at least 1 hour or up to 2 days. Let chilled dough sit on counter to soften slightly, about 10 minutes, before rolling. (Wrapped dough can be frozen for up to 1 month. If frozen, let dough thaw completely on counter before rolling.)

4. Roll dough into 12-inch circle between 2 large sheets of floured parchment paper. (If dough sticks to parchment, gently loosen dough with bench scraper and dust parchment with additional flour.) Slide dough, still between parchment, onto rimmed baking sheet and refrigerate until firm, 15 to 30 minutes.

5. Adjust oven rack to lower-middle position and heat oven to 375 degrees. Microwave jam, ¼ cup sugar, and salt in large bowl until warm, about 30 seconds. Whisk in cornstarch. Add strawberries and gently toss to coat. Mound fruit in center of chilled dough, leaving 2-inch border around edge. Fold outermost 2 inches of dough over fruit, pleating it every 2 to 3 inches as needed. Gently pinch pleated dough to secure, but do not press dough into fruit.

6. Brush top and sides of dough lightly with water and sprinkle with remaining 1 tablespoon sugar. Bake until crust is deep golden brown and fruit is bubbling, 1 hour to 1 hour 10 minutes. Let tart cool on baking sheet for 10 minutes. Using parchment, carefully slide tart onto wire rack and let cool until just warm, about 30 minutes.

7. For the garnishes While tart cools, bring vinegar and 1 teaspoon sugar to simmer in 8-inch skillet over medium heat. Cook until vinegar is reduced to 2 tablespoons, 5 to 7 minutes; set aside to cool slightly, about 5 minutes. Line large plate with parchment and lightly spray with oil spray. Arrange basil in single layer on plate, then lightly spray with oil spray and sprinkle evenly with remaining ½ teaspoon sugar. Microwave until bright green and crisp, about 90 seconds; transfer to paper towel–lined plate to cool completely, about 5 minutes. Serve tart, topping with basil and pepper and drizzling with balsamic reduction.

Fresh Fruit Tart
Serves 8 `MAKE AHEAD`

Why This Recipe Works A fresh fruit tart is often a showpiece highlighting vibrant summer fruits, but baking one can be a time-consuming affair. We traded traditional rolled pastry and pastry cream filling for easier, faster alternatives to produce an appealing (and easier) fresh summer fruit tart. Stirring melted butter into the dry ingredients yielded a malleable dough that could be pressed into the pan; for extra flavor, we browned the butter first and added back the water that had cooked off so that there was enough moisture for the flour to form enough gluten to give the crust structure. A mix of mascarpone, melted white baking chips, and lime juice and zest gave us a quick-to-make filling that was lush and creamy but also full-bodied and firm enough to slice cleanly. Arranging thin-sliced peaches in lines radiating from the center of the tart to its outer edge created cutting guides between which we artfully arranged a mix of berries. These guides ensured that we could slice the tart into neat portions without marring the arrangement of the fruit. A glaze of apricot preserves and lime juice brightened the fruit and gave the tart a polished, professional look. This recipe calls for extra berries to account for any bruising. For more information on peeling peaches, see page 377. Ripe, unpeeled nectarines can be substituted for the peaches, if desired. Use white baking chips here and not white chocolate bars, which contain cocoa butter and will result in a loose filling. Use a light hand when dabbing on the glaze; too much force will dislodge the fruit. If the glaze begins to solidify while dabbing, microwave it for 5 to 10 seconds.

Strawberry Galette with Candied Basil and Balsamic

Fresh Fruit Tart

Crust

1⅓ cups (6⅔ ounces) all-purpose flour
¼ cup (1¾ ounces) sugar
⅛ teaspoon table salt
10 tablespoons unsalted butter
2 tablespoons water

Tart

⅓ cup (2 ounces) white baking chips
¼ cup heavy cream
1 teaspoon grated lime zest, plus 7 teaspoons juice (2 limes), divided
Pinch table salt
6 ounces (¾ cup) mascarpone cheese, room temperature, divided
2 ripe peaches, peeled
20 ounces (4 cups) raspberries, blackberries, and blueberries
⅓ cup apricot preserves

1. For the crust Adjust oven rack to middle position and heat oven to 350 degrees. Whisk flour, sugar, and salt together in bowl. Melt butter in small saucepan over medium-high heat. Cook, stirring and scraping bottom of saucepan with heatproof spatula, until milk solids are dark golden brown and butter has nutty aroma, 1 to 3 minutes. Remove saucepan from heat and add water. When bubbling subsides, transfer butter to bowl with flour mixture and stir until well combined. Transfer dough to 9-inch tart pan with removable bottom and let dough sit until just warm, about 10 minutes.

2. Use your hands to evenly press and smooth dough over bottom and up side of pan (using two-thirds of dough for bottom crust and remaining third for side). Place pan on wire rack set in rimmed baking sheet and bake until crust is golden brown, 25 to 30 minutes, rotating pan halfway through baking. Let crust cool completely, about 1 hour. (Cooled crust can be wrapped loosely in plastic wrap and stored at room temperature for up to 24 hours.)

3. For the tart Microwave baking chips, cream, lime zest, and salt in medium bowl, stirring every 10 seconds, until baking chips are melted, 30 to 60 seconds. Whisk in one-third of mascarpone, then whisk in 2 tablespoons lime juice and remaining mascarpone until smooth. Transfer filling to tart shell and spread into even layer.

4. Place peach, stem side down, on cutting board. Placing knife just to side of pit, cut down to remove 1 side of peach. Turn peach 180 degrees and cut off opposite side. Cut off remaining 2 sides. Place pieces cut side down and slice ¼ inch thick. Repeat with second peach. Select best 24 slices.

5. Evenly space 8 berries around outer edge of tart. Using berries as guide, arrange 8 sets of 3 peach slices in filling, slightly overlapping slices with rounded sides up, starting at center and ending on right side of each berry. Arrange remaining berries in attractive pattern between peach slices, covering as much of filling as possible and keeping fruit in even layer.

6. Microwave preserves and remaining 1 teaspoon lime juice in small bowl until fluid, 20 to 30 seconds. Strain mixture through fine-mesh strainer. Using pastry brush, gently dab mixture over fruit, avoiding crust. Refrigerate tart for 30 minutes.

7. Remove outer metal ring of tart pan. Slide thin metal spatula between tart and pan bottom to loosen tart, then carefully slide tart onto serving platter. Let tart sit at room temperature for 15 minutes. Using peaches as guide, cut tart into wedges and serve. (Tart can be refrigerated for up to 24 hours. If refrigerated for more than 1 hour, let tart sit at room temperature for 1 hour before serving.)

MAKE AN EDIBLE SLICING GUIDE

Strategically arranging the fruit isn't all about looks. It can make it easier to cut clean slices, too.

1. Evenly arrange 8 berries around outer edge of tart.

2. Arrange 8 sets of 3 overlapping peach slices from center to edge of tart on right side of each berry.

3. Arrange remaining berries in attractive pattern between peach slices in even layer to cover filling.

Peach Tarte Tatin
Serves 8

Why This Recipe Works To put a summery spin on classic tarte tatin, we substituted peaches for the traditional apples. But peaches produced a cloying tart that was awash in juice; this soft fruit would require a different approach. To make peaches work, we started by cooking them in the skillet for slightly less time. We also decided to use pie crust instead of tart crust, as its flaky texture was a better match for the delicate peaches. Once it was baked, we poured off the excess juice before inverting our tart. Then we reduced the juices with a bit of bourbon and brushed the mixture over the peaches. Firm peaches are important here, as they hold their shape when cooked. When pouring off the liquid in step 4, the peaches may shift; shake the skillet to redistribute them. For more information on peeling peaches, see page 377.

1 recipe Foolproof All-Butter Single-Crust Pie Dough (page 372)
3 tablespoons unsalted butter, softened
½ cup (3½ ounces) plus 2 tablespoons sugar, divided
¼ teaspoon table salt
2 pounds ripe but firm peaches, peeled, quartered, and pitted
1 tablespoon bourbon (optional)

Peach Tarte Tatin

1. Invert rimmed baking sheet and place sheet of parchment paper or waxed paper on top. Roll dough into 10-inch circle on well-floured counter. Loosely roll dough around rolling pin and gently unroll it onto prepared sheet. Working around circumference, fold outer ½ inch of dough under itself and pinch to create 9-inch round with raised rim. Cut three 2-inch slits in center of dough and refrigerate until needed.

2. Adjust oven rack to middle position and heat oven to 400 degrees. Smear butter over bottom of 10-inch ovensafe skillet. Sprinkle ½ cup sugar over butter and shake skillet to distribute sugar in even layer. Sprinkle salt over sugar. Arrange peaches in circular pattern around edge of skillet, nestling fruit snugly. Tuck remaining peaches into center, squeezing in as much fruit as possible (it is not necessary to maintain circular pattern in center).

3. Place skillet over high heat and cook, without stirring fruit, until juice is released and turns from pink to deep amber, 8 to 12 minutes. (If necessary, adjust skillet's placement on burner to even out hot spots and encourage even browning.) Off heat, carefully slide prepared dough over fruit, making sure dough is centered and does not touch edge of skillet.

Brush dough lightly with water and sprinkle with remaining 2 tablespoons sugar. Transfer skillet to oven and bake until crust is very well browned, 30 to 35 minutes. Transfer skillet to wire rack set in rimmed baking sheet and let cool for 20 minutes.

4. Place inverted plate on top of crust. With your hand firmly securing plate, carefully tip skillet over bowl to drain juice (skillet handle may still be hot). When all juice has been transferred to bowl, return skillet to wire rack, remove plate, and shake skillet firmly to redistribute peaches. Carefully invert tart onto plate, then slide tart onto wire rack. (If peaches have shifted during unmolding, gently nudge them back into place with spoon.)

5. Pour juice into now-empty skillet (handle may be hot). Stir in bourbon, if using, and cook over high heat, stirring constantly, until mixture is dark and thick and starting to smoke, 2 to 3 minutes. Return mixture to bowl and let cool until mixture is consistency of honey, 2 to 3 minutes. Brush mixture over peaches. Let tart cool for at least 20 minutes. Transfer to serving platter and serve.

At the end of summer, farmers' markets are often abundant with ripe, juicy stone fruits—a group of fruits with juicy flesh surrounding a pit (or stone) in the center. Store apricots, nectarines, peaches, and plums on the counter. Store cherries in the fridge.

Apricots Apricots have a unbeatable sweet-tart flavor that makes this stone fruit versatile to eat as a snack or use for baking. When shopping for apricots at the market, look for fruit with a dark orange, or even red, skin color and a firm texture.

Cherries Fresh cherries are one of our favorite signs of summer since this stone fruit is typically available only mid-May through August. There are hundreds of varieties of cherries, both sweet and tart, and the most common is the sweet Bing. When buying Bing cherries, look for deeply colored fruit that is reddish-black and shiny rather than matte. Other popular sweet cherries include the heart-shaped Lambert and gold-toned Rainier. Although sour cherries are less widely available than their sweet cousins, Montmorency and Morello are the varieties you're likely to find in markets.

Nectarines Though nectarines are similar to peaches, the main difference between these two stone fruits is their skin. While peaches have a fuzzy coating, nectarines have a smooth, fuzz-free skin. Much like peaches, nectarines can either be white or yellow (and sometimes even red) and can be clingstone or freestone. Compared to peaches, nectarines are usually smaller and firmer, and they can usually be found at the market in late summer.

Peaches Peach varieties are distinguished by the color of their flesh (white or yellow) and whether that flesh clings to the pit (clingstone) or not (freestone). Yellow peaches, with red-orange skin and golden flesh, and white peaches, with rosy-yellow skin and butter-colored flesh, are the most common options in markets. When selecting peaches, look for heavy but slightly soft fruit and be sure to give them a whiff; ripe peaches are aromatic.

Plums Juicy, sweet plums at the farmer's market can come in a range of colors from deep purple and ruby red to yellow. When shopping for plums, look for fruit that feels soft when gently squeezed.

Roasted Plum and Mascarpone Tart

Serves 6 to 8

Why This Recipe Works For this elegant but simple tart made with store-bought puff pastry, we first roasted plums—which gave them great complexity and a richly caramelized exterior—before adding them to a prebaked shell for an easy-to-assemble multilayer tart. We jump-started the process by searing the plums in butter before transferring the skillet to a hot oven for 10 minutes. We deglazed the pan with white wine, adding sugar, thyme, and currants to create a lacquering sauce. For a rich, plush filling that tied the components together, we incorporated creamy, lightly sweetened mascarpone cheese flavored with a little lemon zest. To thaw frozen puff pastry, let it sit either in the refrigerator for 24 hours or on the counter for 30 minutes to 1 hour. Be gentle when stirring the mascarpone in step 1; stirring aggressively can cause the cheese to become too loose or even break.

12 ounces (1½ cups) mascarpone cheese, room temperature
2 tablespoons confectioners' sugar
1 teaspoon grated lemon zest plus ½ teaspoon juice
1 (9½ by 9-inch) sheet puff pastry, thawed
1 large egg, lightly beaten with 1 tablespoon water
3 tablespoons unsalted butter, divided
6 ripe but firm plums, halved and pitted
¾ cup dry white wine
¼ cup dried currants
¼ cup (1¾ ounces) granulated sugar
1 teaspoon fresh thyme leaves, divided
⅛ teaspoon table salt

1. Adjust oven rack to middle position and heat oven to 425 degrees. Gently stir mascarpone, confectioners' sugar, and lemon zest in bowl until combined, then cover with plastic wrap and refrigerate until ready to serve.

2. Roll pastry into 14 by 10-inch rectangle on floured counter and transfer to parchment paper–lined rimmed baking sheet. Poke dough all over with fork, then brush surface with egg wash. Bake until puffed and golden brown, 12 to 15 minutes, rotating sheet halfway through baking.

3. Using tip of paring knife, cut ½-inch-wide border around top edge of pastry (being careful not to cut through to bottom), then press center down with your fingertips. Transfer tart shell to wire rack and let cool completely, about 30 minutes.

Roasted Plum and Mascarpone Tart

Summer Berry Pie
Serves 8 `MAKE AHEAD`

Why This Recipe Works This pie captures the flavors of summer with a simple pat-in-the-pan crust that is incredibly easy to make. There's no bouncy gelatin or dairy-heavy pudding here to overshadow the sweet-tart flavor of perfectly ripe berries. Rather, the filling is simply fresh whole berries piled on a puree of more berries that we cooked down with some sugar and just enough cornstarch to hold the filling together. A flavorful graham cracker crust provided the perfect complement to the bright mix of berries. The result was a pie that sliced neatly and had great berry texture and flavor. Tossing the whole berries with a bit of jelly gave them a beautiful sheen and contributed the perfect amount of sweetness. If you are short on one type of berry but have extras of another, you can always make up the difference with the extras. If blackberries are not available, use 3 cups each of raspberries and blueberries. When pureeing the berries, be sure to process them for a full minute; otherwise, they may not yield enough puree.

- 10 ounces (2 cups) raspberries
- 10 ounces (2 cups) blackberries
- 10 ounces (2 cups) blueberries
- ½ cup (3½ ounces) sugar
- 3 tablespoons cornstarch
- ⅛ teaspoon table salt
- 1 tablespoon lemon juice
- 1 recipe Graham Cracker Crust (page 373), baked and cooled
- 2 tablespoons red currant or apple jelly

1. Gently toss berries together in large bowl. Process 2½ cups berries in food processor until very smooth, about 1 minute (do not underprocess). Strain puree through fine-mesh strainer into small saucepan, pressing on solids to extract as much liquid as possible (you should have about 1½ cups); discard solids.

2. Whisk sugar, cornstarch, and salt together in bowl, then whisk into strained puree. Bring puree mixture to boil, stirring constantly, and cook until thickened to the consistency of pudding, about 7 minutes. Off heat, stir in lemon juice and let cool slightly.

3. Pour warm berry puree into cooled crust. Melt jelly in clean, dry small saucepan over low heat, then pour over remaining 3½ cups berries and toss to coat. Spread berries evenly over puree and lightly press them into puree. Cover pie loosely with plastic wrap and refrigerate until filling is chilled and set, at least 3 hours or up to 24 hours. Serve chilled or at room temperature.

4. Melt 2 tablespoons butter in 12-inch ovensafe skillet over medium-high heat. Place plum halves cut side down in skillet and cook, without moving, until plums are beginning to brown, about 3 minutes. Transfer skillet to oven and roast for 5 minutes. Flip plums cut side up and continue to roast until fork easily pierces fruit, about 5 minutes.

5. Remove skillet from oven and transfer plums to plate. Being careful of hot skillet handle, whisk in wine, currants, granulated sugar, ½ teaspoon thyme, and salt. Bring to vigorous simmer over medium-high heat, whisking to scrape up any browned bits, and cook until sauce has consistency of maple syrup and measures about ½ cup, 3 to 5 minutes. Off heat, stir in lemon juice. Let cool slightly, about 10 minutes.

6. Spread mascarpone mixture evenly over cooled tart shell, avoiding raised border, then arrange plums over top. Drizzle with sauce and sprinkle with remaining ½ teaspoon thyme. Serve.

Blueberry Pie
Serves 8

Why This Recipe Works If the filling for blueberry pie doesn't gel, a sliced wedge can collapse into a soupy puddle topped by a sodden crust. But use too much thickener and cutting through the filling is like slicing through gummi bears. We wanted a pie with a firm, glistening filling and still-plump blueberries. To thicken the pie, we favored tapioca because it didn't mute the blueberry flavor; but as with other thickeners, too much made the filling stiff. Cooking and reducing half of the berries helped us cut down on the tapioca required, but not enough. A second inspiration came from a peeled, grated Granny Smith apple. Apples are high in pectin, which acts as a thickener when cooked. Combined with a modest 2 tablespoons of instant tapioca, the apple helped the filling take on a soft, even consistency. We still needed a bit of moisture evaporation as more liquid was released during baking; cutouts atop the pie were a simple and attractive alternative to a lattice crust. This recipe was developed using fresh blueberries, but unthawed frozen blueberries will work. In step 2, cook half the frozen berries over medium-high heat, without mashing, until reduced to 1¼ cups, 12 to 15 minutes. Use the large holes of a box grater to shred the apple. Measure the tapioca before grinding in a spice grinder or mini food processor.

    1 recipe Foolproof All-Butter Double-Crust Pie
       Dough (page 372)
   30 ounces (6 cups) blueberries, divided
    1 Granny Smith apple, peeled and shredded
   ¾   cup (5¼ ounces) sugar
    2 tablespoons instant tapioca, ground
    2 teaspoons grated lemon zest plus 2 teaspoons juice
       Pinch table salt
    2 tablespoons unsalted butter, cut into ¼-inch pieces
    1 large egg, lightly beaten with 1 tablespoon water

1. Roll 1 disk of dough into 12-inch circle on floured counter. Loosely roll dough around rolling pin and gently unroll it onto 9-inch pie plate, letting excess dough hang over edge. Ease dough into plate by gently lifting edge of dough with your hand while pressing into plate bottom with your other hand. Leave any dough that overhangs plate in place. Wrap dough-lined plate loosely in plastic wrap and refrigerate until firm, about 30 minutes. Roll other disk of dough into 12-inch circle on floured counter. Using 1¼-inch round biscuit cutter, cut round from center of dough. Cut 6 more rounds from dough, 1½ inches from edge of center hole and equally spaced around center hole. Transfer dough to parchment paper–lined baking sheet; cover with plastic and refrigerate for 30 minutes.

2. Place 3 cups blueberries in medium saucepan and set over medium heat. Using potato masher, mash blueberries several times to release juice. Continue to cook, stirring often and mashing occasionally, until about half of blueberries have broken down and mixture is thickened and reduced to 1½ cups, about 8 minutes; let cool slightly.

3. Adjust oven rack to lowest position and heat oven to 400 degrees. Place apple in clean dish towel and wring dry. Transfer apple to large bowl and stir in sugar, tapioca, lemon zest and juice, salt, cooked blueberries, and remaining 3 cups uncooked blueberries until combined.

4. Spread mixture into dough-lined plate and scatter butter over top. Loosely roll remaining dough round around rolling pin and gently unroll it onto filling. Trim overhang to ½ inch beyond lip of plate. Pinch edges of top and bottom dough firmly together. Tuck overhang under itself; folded edge should be flush with edge of plate.

5. Crimp dough evenly around edge of plate. Brush surface with egg wash. Place pie on aluminum foil–lined rimmed baking sheet and bake until crust is light golden brown, about 25 minutes. Reduce oven temperature to 375 degrees, rotate sheet, and continue to bake until juices are bubbling and crust is deep golden brown, 35 to 50 minutes. Let pie cool on wire rack until filling has set, about 4 hours. Serve.

Sweet Cherry Pie
Serves 8

Why This Recipe Works Cherry pies are often made with sour cherries, and for good reason: Their soft, juicy flesh and bright, punchy flavor aren't dulled by oven heat or sugar. But even in the summer sour cherries rarely make an appearance. Sweet cherries are easier to find, but their mellow flavor and meaty flesh—traits that make them ideal for snacking—aren't well suited to baking. To develop a sweet cherry pie with the intense, jammy flavor of the best sour cherry pie, we incorporated plums; their tartness helped balance the cherries' sweetness. Cutting the cherries in half encouraged them to soften and give up some of their juices. We pureed some of the cherries with the plums to create a cohesive filling, straining out the skins so the plum flesh wouldn't be noticeable. Rather than the lattice crust often seen on cherry pies, we used a traditional top crust to prevent too much moisture from evaporating, ensuring a juicy filling. You can substitute 2 pounds of frozen sweet cherries for the fresh cherries. If you are using frozen fruit, measure it frozen, but let it thaw before filling the pie; otherwise you run the risk of partially cooked fruit and undissolved tapioca. Measure the tapioca before grinding in a spice grinder or mini food processor.

Blueberry Pie

1 recipe Foolproof All-Butter Double-Crust Pie Dough (page 372)

2 red plums, halved and pitted

2½ pounds fresh sweet cherries, pitted and halved, divided

½ cup (3½ ounces) sugar

2 tablespoons instant tapioca, ground

1 tablespoon lemon juice

2 teaspoons bourbon (optional)

⅛ teaspoon table salt

⅛ teaspoon ground cinnamon (optional)

2 tablespoons unsalted butter, cut into ¼-inch pieces

1 large egg, lightly beaten with 1 teaspoon water

1. Roll 1 disk of dough into 12-inch circle on floured counter. Loosely roll dough around rolling pin and gently unroll it onto 9-inch pie plate, letting excess dough hang over edge. Ease dough into plate by gently lifting edge of dough with your hand while pressing into plate bottom with your other hand. Leave any dough that overhangs plate in place. Wrap dough-lined plate loosely in plastic wrap and refrigerate until firm, about 30 minutes. Roll other disk of dough into 12-inch circle on floured counter, then transfer to parchment paper–lined rimmed baking sheet; cover with plastic and refrigerate until firm, about 30 minutes.

2. Adjust oven rack to lowest position and heat oven to 400 degrees. Process plums and 1 cup cherries in food processor until smooth, about 1 minute, scraping down sides of bowl as needed. Strain puree through fine-mesh strainer into large bowl, pressing on solids to extract as much liquid as possible; discard solids. Stir remaining cherries; sugar; tapioca; lemon juice; bourbon, if using; salt; and cinnamon, if using, into strained puree. Let stand for 15 minutes.

3. Spread cherry mixture with its juices into dough-lined plate and scatter butter over top. Loosely roll remaining dough round around rolling pin and gently unroll it onto filling. Trim overhang to ½ inch beyond lip of plate. Pinch edges of top and bottom dough firmly together. Tuck overhang under itself; folded edge should be flush with edge of plate. Crimp dough evenly around edge of plate. Cut eight 1-inch slits in top of dough. Brush surface with egg wash.

4. Place pie on aluminum foil–lined rimmed baking sheet and bake until crust is light golden brown, about 30 minutes. Reduce oven temperature to 350 degrees, rotate sheet, and continue to bake until juices are bubbling and crust is deep golden brown, 35 to 50 minutes. Let pie cool on wire rack until filling has set, about 4 hours. Serve.

Sweet Cherry Pie

Foolproof Pie Crusts

MAKE AHEAD

The abundance of fresh fruit in the summer months makes it an ideal time for baking pie. But as every experienced pie baker knows, a good dough can make or break a pie crust. We wanted foolproof go-to recipes that would work with just about any pie filling imaginable.

Foolproof All-Butter Single-Crust Pie Dough

Makes one 9-inch single crust

Be sure to weigh the flour. This dough will be moister than most pie doughs, but it will absorb a lot of excess moisture as it chills. Roll out the dough on a well-floured counter.

 10 tablespoons unsalted butter, chilled, divided
1¼ cups (6¼ ounces) all-purpose flour, divided
  1 tablespoon sugar
 ½ teaspoon table salt
 ¼ cup (2 ounces) ice water, divided

1. Grate 2 tablespoons butter on large holes of box grater and place in freezer. Cut remaining 8 tablespoons butter into ½-inch cubes.

2. Pulse ¾ cup flour, sugar, and salt in food processor until combined, 2 pulses. Add cubed butter and process until homogeneous paste forms, about 30 seconds. Using your hands, carefully break paste into 2-inch pieces and redistribute evenly around processor blade. Add remaining ½ cup flour and pulse until mixture is broken into pieces no larger than 1 inch (most pieces will be much smaller), 4 to 5 pulses. Transfer mixture to bowl. Add grated butter and toss until butter pieces are separated and coated with flour.

3. Sprinkle 2 tablespoons ice water over mixture. Toss with rubber spatula until mixture is evenly moistened. Sprinkle remaining 2 tablespoons ice water over mixture and toss to combine. Press dough with spatula until dough sticks together. Transfer dough to sheet of plastic wrap. Draw edges of plastic over dough and press firmly on sides and top to form compact, fissure-free mass. Wrap in plastic and form into 5-inch disk. Refrigerate dough for at least 2 hours or up to 2 days. Let chilled dough sit on counter to soften slightly, about 10 minutes, before rolling. (Wrapped dough can be frozen for up to 1 month. If frozen, let dough thaw completely on counter before rolling.)

Foolproof All-Butter Double-Crust Pie Dough

Makes one 9-inch double crust

Be sure to weigh the flour. This dough will be moister than most pie doughs, but it will absorb a lot of excess moisture as it chills. Roll out the dough on a well-floured counter.

 20 tablespoons (2½ sticks) unsalted butter, chilled, divided
2½ cups (12½ ounces) all-purpose flour, divided
  2 tablespoons sugar
  1 teaspoon table salt
 ½ cup (4 ounces) ice water, divided

1. Grate 4 tablespoons butter on large holes of box grater and place in freezer. Cut remaining 16 tablespoons butter into ½-inch cubes.

2. Pulse 1½ cups flour, sugar, and salt in food processor until combined, 2 pulses. Add cubed butter and process until homogeneous paste forms, 40 to 50 seconds. Using your hands, carefully break paste into 2-inch chunks and redistribute evenly around processor blade. Add remaining 1 cup flour and pulse until mixture is broken into pieces no larger than 1 inch (most pieces will be much smaller), 4 to 5 pulses. Transfer mixture to bowl. Add grated butter and toss until butter pieces are separated and coated with flour.

3. Sprinkle ¼ cup ice water over mixture. Toss with rubber spatula until mixture is evenly moistened. Sprinkle remaining ¼ cup ice water over mixture and toss to combine. Press dough with spatula until dough sticks together. Using spatula, divide dough into 2 equal portions. Transfer each portion to sheet of plastic wrap. Working with 1 portion at a time, draw edges of plastic over dough and press firmly on sides and top to form compact, fissure-free mass. Wrap in plastic and form into 5-inch disk. Refrigerate dough for at least 2 hours or up to 2 days. Let chilled dough sit on counter to soften slightly, about 10 minutes, before rolling. (Wrapped dough can be frozen for up to 1 month. If frozen, let dough thaw completely on counter before rolling.)

Graham Cracker Crust

Makes one 9-inch crust

We don't recommend using store-bought graham cracker crumbs here, as they can often be stale.

- 8 whole graham crackers, broken into 1-inch pieces
- 3 tablespoons sugar
- 5 tablespoons unsalted butter, melted and cooled

1. Adjust oven rack to middle position and heat oven to 325 degrees. Process graham cracker pieces and sugar in food processor to fine, even crumbs, about 30 seconds. Sprinkle melted butter over crumbs and pulse to incorporate, about 5 pulses.

2. Sprinkle mixture into 9-inch pie plate. Using bottom of dry measuring cup, press crumbs into even layer on bottom and sides of pie plate. Bake until crust is fragrant and beginning to brown, 12 to 18 minutes; transfer to wire rack. Following particular pie recipe, use crust while it is still warm or let it cool completely. (Crust can be stored at room temperature for up to 24 hours.)

Chocolate Cookie Crust

Makes one 9-inch crust

We prefer to use Oreo cookies; other brands of chocolate sandwich cookies may be substituted, but avoid "double-filled" cookies as the proportion of cookie to filling won't be correct.

- 16 Oreo cookies, broken into rough pieces
- 4 tablespoons unsalted butter, melted

1. Adjust oven rack to middle position and heat oven to 325 degrees. Process cookie pieces in food processor until finely ground, about 30 seconds. Add butter and pulse until crumbs are evenly moistened, about 10 pulses.

2. Sprinkle mixture into 9-inch pie plate. Using bottom of measuring cup, firmly pack crust into even layer on bottom and sides of pie plate. Bake crust until fragrant and set, 13 to 18 minutes, rotating pie plate halfway through baking. Let crust cool completely on wire rack, about 30 minutes. (Crust can be stored at room temperature for up to 24 hours.)

Peach Pie

Peach Pie
Serves 8

Why This Recipe Works Eaten out of hand, a juicy peach is one of summer's greatest pleasures. But to incorporate peaches into a pie that wasn't soupy, we needed to corral the moisture exuded by this juicy fruit. For most pies one of the following techniques does the trick: macerating or cooking the fruit, adding a thickener, or supplementing the fruit's natural pectin. We discovered that with peaches we had to use all three. First, we macerated the peaches to draw out their juices. Then we used both cornstarch and pectin (the latter of which we cooked with some of the peach liquid) to bind our filling; this gave us a clear, silky filling without the gumminess or gelatinous texture that larger amounts of either one alone produced. For more information on peeling peaches, see page 377. We recommend both Sure-Jell for Less or No Sugar Needed Recipes and Ball RealFruit Low or No-Sugar Needed Pectin.

- 1 recipe Foolproof All-Butter Double-Crust Pie Dough (page 372)
- 3 pounds ripe but firm peaches, peeled, halved, pitted, and cut into 1-inch pieces
- ½ cup (3½ ounces) plus 3 tablespoons sugar, divided
- 1 teaspoon grated lemon zest plus 1 tablespoon juice
- ⅛ teaspoon table salt
- 2 tablespoons low- or no-sugar-needed fruit pectin
- ¼ teaspoon ground cinnamon
  Pinch ground nutmeg
- 1 tablespoon cornstarch
- 1 large egg, lightly beaten with 1 tablespoon water

1. Roll 1 disk of dough into 12-inch circle on floured counter. Loosely roll dough around rolling pin and gently unroll it onto 9-inch pie plate, letting excess dough hang over edge. Ease dough into plate by gently lifting edge of dough with your hand while pressing into plate bottom with your other hand. Leave any dough that overhangs plate in place. Wrap dough-lined plate loosely in plastic wrap and refrigerate until firm, about 30 minutes.

2. Roll other piece of dough into 13 by 10½-inch rectangle on floured counter, then transfer to parchment paper–lined rimmed baking sheet; cover loosely with plastic and refrigerate until firm, about 30 minutes.

3. Using pizza wheel, fluted pastry wheel, or paring knife, trim ¼ inch dough from long sides of rectangle, then cut lengthwise into eight 1¼-inch-wide strips. Cover loosely with plastic and refrigerate until firm, about 30 minutes. Adjust oven rack to middle position and heat oven to 400 degrees.

Rustic Plum Cake

4. Toss peaches, ½ cup sugar, lemon zest and juice, and salt in bowl and let sit for at least 30 minutes or up to 1 hour. Combine pectin, cinnamon, nutmeg, and 2 tablespoons sugar in small bowl; set aside. Measure out 1 cup peach pieces and mash with fork to coarse paste. Drain remaining peach pieces in colander set in bowl, reserving ½ cup peach juice. Return peach pieces to now-empty bowl and toss with cornstarch.

5. Whisk reserved peach juice and pectin mixture together in 12-inch skillet. Cook over medium heat, stirring occasionally, until thickened slightly and pectin is dissolved (liquid should become less cloudy), 3 to 5 minutes. Transfer peach-pectin mixture and peach paste to bowl with peach pieces and stir to combine. Spread peach mixture into dough-lined plate.

6. Remove dough strips from refrigerator; if too stiff to be workable, let sit at room temperature until softened slightly but still very cold. Lay 2 longest strips across center of pie perpendicular to each other. Using 4 shortest strips, lay 2 strips across pie parallel to 1 center strip and 2 strips parallel to other center strip, near edges of pie; you should have 6 strips in place. Using remaining 4 strips, lay each one across pie parallel and equidistant from center and edge strips. (If dough becomes too soft to work with, refrigerate pie and dough strips until firm.)

7. Trim overhang to ½ inch beyond lip of pie plate. Press edges of bottom crust and lattice strips together and fold under. Folded edge should be flush with edge of pie plate. Crimp dough evenly around edge of pie using your fingers. (If dough is very soft, refrigerate for 10 minutes before baking.) Using spray bottle, evenly mist lattice with water and sprinkle with remaining 1 tablespoon sugar.

8. Place pie on aluminum foil–lined rimmed baking sheet and bake until crust is light golden, 20 to 25 minutes. Reduce oven temperature to 350 degrees, rotate sheet, and continue to bake until juices are bubbling and crust is deep golden brown, 30 to 50 minutes. Let pie cool on wire rack until filling has set, about 4 hours. Serve.

MAKING A LATTICE TOP

1. Roll dough into 13 by 10-inch rectangle, transfer to parchment paper–lined baking sheet, and cut into eight 1¼-inch-wide strips with fluted pastry wheel, pizza wheel, or paring knife. Refrigerate for 30 minutes.

2. Lay 2 longest strips perpendicular to each other across center of pie to form cross. Place 4 shorter strips along edges of pie, parallel to center strips.

3. Lay 4 remaining strips between each edge strip and center strip. Trim off excess lattice ends, press edges of bottom crust and lattice strips together, and fold under.

Rustic Plum Cake
Serves 8 to 10

Why This Recipe Works Plum cake can be anything from an Alsatian tart to a German yeasted bread, but our preference is for an almond cake base. Replacing some of the all-purpose flour with homemade almond flour created a rich, moist cake that was sturdy enough to hold the plums aloft. Poaching the plums in a few tablespoons of brandy and red currant jelly along with their own juices heightened their floral flavor and ensured they didn't dehydrate during baking. Arranging the plum slices, slightly overlapped, in two rings on top of the batter made for an elegant presentation. This recipe works best with Italian prune plums. If substituting regular red or black plums, use an equal weight of plums, cut them into eighths, and stir them a few times while cooking in step 1. Don't use canned Italian plums. Don't add the leftover plum cooking liquid to the cake before baking; reserve it and serve with the finished cake. The cake can be served warm or at room temperature; if serving warm, remove the sides of the pan after letting the cake cool for 30 minutes and serve as directed. We like to serve this cake with Whipped Cream (page 406).

3 tablespoons brandy

2 tablespoons red currant jelly or seedless raspberry jam

1 pound Italian prune plums, halved and pitted

¾ cup (5¼ ounces) granulated sugar

⅓ cup slivered almonds

¾ cup (3¾ ounces) all-purpose flour

½ teaspoon baking powder

¼ teaspoon table salt

6 tablespoons unsalted butter, cut into 6 pieces and softened

1 large egg plus 1 large yolk, room temperature

1 teaspoon vanilla extract

¼ teaspoon almond extract (optional)

Confectioners' sugar (optional)

1. Cook brandy and jelly in 10-inch nonstick skillet over medium heat until thick and syrupy, 2 to 3 minutes. Remove skillet from heat and add plums, cut side down. Return skillet to medium heat and cook, shaking pan to prevent plums from sticking, until plums release their juices and liquid reduces to thick syrup, about 5 minutes. Let plums cool in skillet for 20 minutes.

2. Adjust oven rack to middle position and heat oven to 350 degrees. Grease and flour 9-inch springform pan. Process granulated sugar and almonds in food processor until nuts are finely ground, about 1 minute. Add flour, baking powder, and salt and pulse to combine, about 5 pulses. Add butter and pulse until mixture resembles coarse sand, about 10 pulses. Add egg and yolk, vanilla, and almond extract, if using, and process until smooth, about 5 seconds, scraping down sides of bowl as needed (batter will be very thick and heavy).

3. Transfer batter to prepared pan and smooth top with rubber spatula. Stir plums to coat with syrup. Arrange plum halves, skin side down, evenly over surface of batter (reserve leftover syrup). Bake until golden and toothpick inserted in center comes out with few crumbs attached, 40 to 50 minutes, rotating pan halfway through baking. Run thin knife around edge of pan to loosen cake. Let cake cool completely in pan on wire rack, about 2 hours. Remove sides of pan and dust cake with confectioners' sugar, if using. Slide thin metal spatula between cake bottom and pan bottom to loosen, then slide cake onto platter. Serve with reserved plum syrup.

Peach Cornmeal Upside-Down Cake

Peach Cornmeal Upside-Down Cake

Serves 8

Why This Recipe Works Skillet upside-down cakes are simple affairs: Sauté the fruit, top the fruit with batter, and pop the skillet in the oven. If all goes well, the cake releases from the skillet to reveal beautifully caramelized fruit perched atop a rustic, not-too-sweet cake. But too often the result is overly sweet or, worse, a soggy mess. To avoid the latter, we added toasted cornmeal to the cake batter for both flavor and texture and nestled the peaches in a sauce of sugar and butter before baking to ensure a top layer of caramelized peaches with the perfect amount of sweetness. If using frozen peaches, be sure to thaw and drain them before using; otherwise, they will produce a mushy cake. For more information on peeling peaches, see page 377. We like to serve this cake with Whipped Cream (page 406).

½ cup (2½ ounces) cornmeal

2 tablespoons unsalted butter plus
  6 tablespoons melted and cooled

⅓ cup (2⅓ ounces) sugar plus
  ¾ cup (5¼ ounces), divided
  Pinch plus ½ teaspoon table salt, divided

1 pound peaches, peeled, halved, pitted,
  and cut into ¾-inch wedges

1 cup (5 ounces) all-purpose flour

1 teaspoon baking powder

⅛ teaspoon baking soda

½ cup whole milk

2 teaspoons grated orange zest plus ¼ cup juice

1 large egg plus 1 large yolk

1. Adjust oven rack to middle position and heat oven to 350 degrees. Toast cornmeal in ovensafe 10-inch nonstick skillet over medium heat until fragrant, 2 to 3 minutes, stirring frequently. Transfer to large bowl and let cool slightly.

2. Wipe skillet clean with paper towels. Melt 2 tablespoons butter in now-empty skillet over medium heat. Add ⅓ cup sugar and pinch salt and cook, whisking constantly, until sugar is melted, smooth, and deep golden brown, 3 to 5 minutes. (Mixture may look broken but will come together.) Off heat, carefully arrange peaches cut side down in tight pinwheel around edge of skillet. Arrange remaining peaches in center of skillet.

3. Whisk flour, baking powder, baking soda, and remaining ½ teaspoon salt into cornmeal. In separate bowl, whisk milk, orange zest and juice, egg and yolk, melted butter, and remaining ¾ cup sugar until smooth. Stir milk mixture into flour mixture until just combined.

4. Pour batter over peaches and spread into even layer. Bake until cake is golden brown and toothpick inserted in center comes out clean, 28 to 33 minutes, rotating skillet halfway through baking.

5. Let cake cool in skillet on wire rack for 15 minutes. Run knife around edge of skillet to loosen cake. Place large, flat serving platter over skillet. Using potholders and holding platter tightly, invert skillet and platter together; lift off skillet (if any peaches stick to skillet, remove and position on top of cake). Let cake cool completely, about 1 hour. Serve.

PEELING PEACHES (AND TOMATOES)

1. With paring knife, score small X at base of each peach.

2. Lower peaches into boiling water and simmer until skins loosen, 30 to 60 seconds.

3. Transfer peaches immediately to ice water and let cool for about 1 minute.

4. Use paring knife to remove strips of loosened peel, starting at X on base of each peach.

INGREDIENT SPOTLIGHT

CORNMEAL

To find our favorite cornmeal, we baked five nationally available products in cornbread and conducted a blind tasting. Even though some people shudder at the word "moist," tasters commonly used it to describe the cornbread made with our winner, **Anson Mills Antebellum Fine Yellow Cornmeal**. It was soft and tender, with a smooth, cakey texture that "holds together nicely" and was "not too crumbly." Tasters also noted a "nice butter flavor."

CHAPTER 12

Icebox and Frozen Sweets

■ NO COOK   ■ MAKE AHEAD
Photos (clockwise from top left): Lemon Posset with Berries; Raspberry Sorbet;
Icebox Margarita Cheesecake; Cookies and Cream Ice Cream Pie

Coconut Paletas

Strawberry Cream Paletas
Serves 6 (Makes 6 paletas) `NO COOK` `MAKE AHEAD`

Why This Recipe Works A cousin of Popsicles, paletas are Mexican-style frozen treats that usually rely on fresh fruit juice as their base with chunks of fresh fruit stirred in. Inspired by an early summer fruit harvest, we built our recipe using fresh strawberries as the focal point. We used the berries in two ways: First, we pureed half of them to a smooth consistency with a small amount of honey for sweetness. We pulsed the rest of the berries to a coarse chop to ensure bites of fresh fruit throughout our pops. For richness, we added heavy cream for just the right velvety texture. This recipe was developed using 3-ounce ice pop molds.

- 1 pound strawberries, hulled (3 cups), divided
- ½ cup heavy cream
- ¼ cup honey
- 1 teaspoon lemon juice
- ⅛ teaspoon table salt

1. Process 1½ cups strawberries, cream, honey, lemon juice, and salt in food processor until smooth, about 30 seconds, scraping down sides of bowl as needed. Add remaining 1½ cups strawberries and pulse until coarsely chopped, about 5 pulses. Transfer mixture to large liquid measuring cup.

2. Divide strawberry mixture evenly among six 3-ounce ice pop molds. Insert Popsicle stick in center of each mold, cover, and freeze until firm, at least 6 hours or up to 5 days. To serve, hold mold under warm running water for 30 seconds to thaw.

Striped Fruit Ice Pops

Coconut Paletas
Serves 6 (Makes 6 paletas) `NO COOK` `MAKE AHEAD`

Why This Recipe Works We wanted a rich, creamy, and decadent frozen treat, perfect for a light poolside snack. Using richly flavored coconut milk as our base, we added a small amount of honey for sweetness, vanilla extract for deeply nuanced undertones, and salt for balance. Adding unsweetened flaked coconut amped up the coconut flavor and gave our paletas some textural contrast. Do not substitute low-fat coconut milk or the paletas will taste watery and have an icy texture. This recipe was developed using 3-ounce ice pop molds.

- 2 cups canned coconut milk
- 3 tablespoons honey
- 1 tablespoon vanilla extract
- ¼ teaspoon table salt
- 3 tablespoons unsweetened flaked coconut

1. Whisk coconut milk, honey, vanilla, and salt together in large liquid measuring cup to dissolve honey and salt. Stir in flaked coconut.

2. Divide coconut mixture evenly among six 3-ounce ice pop molds. Insert Popsicle stick in center of each mold, cover, and freeze until firm, at least 6 hours or up to 5 days. To serve, hold mold under warm running water for 30 seconds to thaw.

VARIATIONS
Horchata Paletas
Add ½ teaspoon ground cinnamon and ⅛ teaspoon ground cloves to coconut mixture in step 1. Substitute 3 tablespoons toasted sliced almonds for flaked coconut.

Coconut, Lime, and Cardamom Paletas
Add 2 teaspoons grated lime zest, 1 tablespoon lime juice, and ½ teaspoon cardamom to coconut mixture in step 1.

Striped Fruit Ice Pops
Serves 6 (Makes 6 ice pops) `NO COOK` `MAKE AHEAD`

Why This Recipe Works Multicolored Popsicles bring to mind carefree summer vacations. But with all that nostalgia comes sugar, corn syrup, and artificial coloring—we wanted an ultraflavorful, naturally colored and sweetened version that you would feel good about giving your kids as a snack. We used berries as our main ingredient, and honey for a subtle sweetener. We made a vibrant red raspberry puree for one layer; a blueberry puree made for a beautifully contrasting purple layer. For the middle layer, we aimed for a clean-looking white to make the red and purple stand out. We tested several bases, and settled on using a little bit of cream along with lemon juice for the perfect balance of flavor and texture. A small amount of water in each layer ensured that the ice pops froze solid. For clean, well-defined stripes, be sure to let each layer freeze completely before adding the next layer, and be careful not to spill the mixture onto the sides of the molds when pouring. This recipe was developed using 3-ounce ice pop molds.

Raspberry Layer
- 4 ounces (¾ cup) raspberries
- ¼ cup water
- 1 tablespoon honey
- Pinch table salt

Lemon Layer
- ¼ cup water
- 3 tablespoons heavy cream
- 4 teaspoons honey
- 1 tablespoon lemon juice
- Pinch table salt

Blueberry Layer
- 4 ounces (¾ cup) blueberries
- ¼ cup water
- 1 tablespoon honey
- Pinch table salt

1. For the raspberry layer Process all ingredients in food processor until smooth, about 1 minute. Using 1 tablespoon measuring spoon, carefully pour 2 tablespoons of raspberry mixture evenly into each of six 3-ounce ice pop molds, being careful to keep walls of molds free from drips. Cover molds and freeze until firm, about 4 hours.

2. For the lemon layer Whisk all ingredients together in bowl. Using 1 tablespoon measuring spoon, carefully pour 2 tablespoons lemon mixture into each ice pop mold. Cover molds tightly with double layer of aluminum foil. Push Popsicle stick through foil into center of each mold until tip hits frozen raspberry mixture. Freeze until firm, about 4 hours.

3. For the blueberry layer Process all ingredients in food processor until smooth, about 1 minute. Using 1 tablespoon measuring spoon, carefully pour 2 tablespoons blueberry mixture into each ice pop mold. Cover molds and freeze until solid, at least 6 hours or up to 5 days. To serve, hold mold under warm running water for 30 seconds to thaw.

Best Butterscotch Pudding
Serves 8 `MAKE AHEAD`

Why This Recipe Works This homey classic can't be beat—with a homemade caramel combined with custard, it's miles away from the painfully sweet puddings in hermetically sealed pouches from your youth. We were determined to take the scare out of making caramel—the usual approach of boiling it from start to finish is tricky in a blink-and-you've-burned-it way. Our more forgiving method: Boil the caramel to jump-start it, then reduce the heat and gently simmer it until it reaches the desired temperature. Next, to turn butterscotch into pudding, most recipes have you temper the yolks and cornstarch, add everything to the remaining dairy in the pot, and stir constantly as the mixture slowly thickens. We swapped this fussy method in favor of pouring the boiling caramel sauce directly over the thickening agents (egg yolks and cornstarch thinned with a little milk).

When taking the temperature of the caramel in step 1, tilt the saucepan and move the thermometer back and forth to equalize hot and cool spots.

- 12 tablespoons unsalted butter, cut into ½-inch pieces
- ½ cup (3½ ounces) granulated sugar
- ½ cup packed (3½ ounces) dark brown sugar
- ¼ cup water
- 2 tablespoons light corn syrup
- 1 teaspoon lemon juice
- ¾ teaspoon table salt
- 1 cup heavy cream, divided
- 2¼ cups whole milk, divided
- 4 large egg yolks
- ¼ cup cornstarch
- 2 teaspoons vanilla extract
- 1 teaspoon dark rum

1. Bring butter, granulated sugar, brown sugar, water, corn syrup, lemon juice, and salt to boil in large saucepan over medium heat, stirring occasionally to dissolve sugar and melt butter. Once mixture is at full rolling boil, cook, stirring occasionally, for 5 minutes (caramel should register about 240 degrees). Immediately reduce heat to medium-low and gently simmer (caramel should maintain steady stream of lazy bubbles—if not, adjust heat accordingly), stirring frequently, until mixture is color of dark peanut butter, 12 to 16 minutes (caramel should register about 300 degrees and have slight burnt smell).

2. Remove saucepan from heat; carefully pour ¼ cup cream into caramel mixture and swirl to incorporate (mixture will bubble and steam); let bubbling subside. Whisk vigorously and scrape corners of saucepan until mixture is completely smooth, at least 30 seconds. Return saucepan to medium heat and gradually whisk in remaining ¾ cup cream until smooth. Whisk in 2 cups milk until mixture is smooth, scraping corners and edges of saucepan to remove any remaining bits of caramel.

3. Microwave remaining ¼ cup milk until simmering, 30 to 45 seconds. Whisk egg yolks and cornstarch in large bowl until smooth. Gradually whisk in hot milk until smooth; set aside.

4. Return saucepan to medium-high heat and bring mixture to full rolling boil, whisking frequently. Once mixture is boiling rapidly and beginning to climb toward top of saucepan, working quickly, immediately pour into bowl with yolk mixture in 1 motion (do not add gradually). Whisk thoroughly for 10 to 15 seconds (mixture will thicken after few seconds). Whisk in vanilla and rum.

5. Spray piece of parchment paper with vegetable oil spray and press directly against surface of pudding. Cover and refrigerate until fully set, at least 3 hours or up to 3 days. Whisk pudding until smooth before serving.

Dark Chocolate–Avocado Pudding
Serves 6 `MAKE AHEAD`

Why This Recipe Works Sometimes a summertime treat calls for something lighter and a bit more healthful than a typical dessert, and making a luscious chocolate pudding by substituting good-for-you avocados for the cream and eggs has become something of a craze of late. But more often than not, these puddings are a far cry from the silky-smooth, ultrachocolaty pudding we want, yielding a grainy texture and lackluster chocolate flavor that doesn't conceal the vegetal notes. We knew we could do better without making the recipe too complicated. Rather than simply blending everything together, we started by creating a simple hot cocoa syrup in a saucepan (with a touch of espresso powder, vanilla, and salt to enhance the chocolate flavor). Meanwhile, we processed the flesh of two large avocados for a full 2 minutes until they were absolutely smooth. Next, with the food processor running, we carefully streamed in the cocoa syrup until the mixture was velvety and glossy. We finished by blending in a moderate amount of melted dark chocolate to give our pudding a wonderfully full chocolate flavor and additional richness.

- 1 cup water
- ¾ cup (5¼ ounces) sugar
- ¼ cup (¾ ounce) unsweetened cocoa powder
- 1 tablespoon vanilla extract
- 1 teaspoon instant espresso powder (optional)
- ¼ teaspoon table salt
- 2 large ripe avocados (8 ounces each), halved and pitted
- 3½ ounces bittersweet chocolate, chopped

1. Combine water, sugar, cocoa, vanilla, espresso powder (if using), and salt in small saucepan. Bring to simmer over medium heat and cook, stirring occasionally, until sugar and cocoa dissolve, about 2 minutes. Remove saucepan from heat and cover to keep warm.

2. Scoop flesh of avocados into food processor bowl and process until smooth, about 2 minutes, scraping down sides of bowl as needed. With processor running, slowly add warm cocoa mixture in steady stream until completely incorporated and mixture is smooth and glossy, about 2 minutes.

3. Microwave chocolate in bowl at 50 percent power, stirring occasionally, until melted, 2 to 4 minutes. Add to avocado mixture and process until well incorporated, about 1 minute. Transfer pudding to clean bowl, cover, and refrigerate until chilled and set, at least 2 hours or up to 24 hours. Serve.

Chocolate Pots de Crème

Serves 8 `MAKE AHEAD`

Why This Recipe Works Classic pots de crème are the perfect way to end a summertime soiree—they're cold, creamy, and pack an intense hit of chocolate. But traditionally, making these petite chocolate custards calls for cooking them in a fussy water bath in an oven, and who wants to turn on the oven on a sweltering day? So we took an unconventional approach: cooking the custard on the stovetop and then pouring it into ramekins. We skipped right over semisweet chocolate, which was too mild for our dark chocolate dreams. Bittersweet chocolate, and lots of it—50 percent more than most recipes—gave our custards the rich flavor we sought. We prefer pots de crème made with 60 percent cacao bittersweet chocolate, but 70 percent bittersweet chocolate can also be used—you will need to reduce the amount of chocolate to 8 ounces.

10	ounces bittersweet chocolate, chopped fine
1	tablespoon vanilla extract
1	tablespoon water
½	teaspoon instant espresso powder
5	large egg yolks
5	tablespoons (2¼ ounces) sugar
¼	teaspoon table salt
1½	cups heavy cream
¾	cup half-and-half
1	recipe Half-Batch Whipped Cream (page 406)
	Cocoa powder and/or chocolate shavings (optional)

1. Place chocolate in medium heatproof bowl and set fine-mesh strainer over top. Combine vanilla, water, and espresso powder in second bowl.

2. Whisk egg yolks, sugar, and salt in medium saucepan until combined. Whisk in cream and half-and-half. Cook over medium-low heat, not letting mixture simmer, stirring constantly and scraping bottom of pot with wooden spoon, until thickened and silky and registers 175 to 180 degrees, 8 to 12 minutes.

3. Immediately pour custard through fine-mesh strainer over chocolate, then let sit until chocolate is melted, about 5 minutes. Add espresso mixture and whisk until smooth. Divide chocolate custard evenly among eight 5-ounce ramekins and gently tap each ramekin against counter to remove air bubbles.

4. Let pots de crème cool completely, then cover with plastic wrap and refrigerate until chilled, at least 4 hours or up to 3 days. (Before serving, let pots de crème stand at room temperature for 10 minutes.)

5. Divide whipped cream evenly among pots de crème and garnish with cocoa and/or chocolate shavings, if using. Serve.

Dark Chocolate-Avocado Pudding

Chocolate Pots de Crème

Strawberry Mousse

Panna Cotta

Strawberry Mousse
Serves 4 to 6 `MAKE AHEAD`

Why This Recipe Works There are few things better than a juicy, sweet strawberry fresh from the market. We wanted to highlight these jewels of early summer, so we set out to achieve a mousse with a creamy yet firm texture with amped-up strawberry flavor. We used a mix of cream cheese and cream as our base, and we processed the berries into small pieces and macerated them with sugar and a little salt to draw out their juice. We then reduced the released liquid to a syrup before adding it to the mousse, which standardized the amount of moisture in the dessert and also concentrated the berry flavor. Fully pureeing the juiced berries contributed bright, fresh berry flavor. In step 1, be careful not to overprocess the berries For more-complex berry flavor, replace the 3 tablespoons of raw strawberry juice in step 2 with strawberry or raspberry liqueur. In addition to the diced berries you can serve the mousse with Whipped Cream (page 406).

2 pounds strawberries, hulled (6½ cups), divided
½ cup (3½ ounces) sugar, divided
  Pinch table salt
1¾ teaspoons unflavored gelatin
4 ounces cream cheese, cut into 8 pieces and softened
½ cup heavy cream, chilled

1. Dice enough strawberries into ¼-inch pieces to measure 1 cup; refrigerate until ready to serve. Pulse remaining strawberries in food processor in 2 batches until most pieces are ¼ to ½ inch thick (some larger pieces are fine), 6 to 10 pulses. Transfer strawberries to bowl and toss with ¼ cup sugar and salt. (Do not clean processor.) Cover bowl and let sit, stirring occasionally, for 45 minutes.

2. Drain processed strawberries in fine-mesh strainer set over bowl (you should have about ⅔ cup juice). Measure out 3 tablespoons juice into small bowl, sprinkle gelatin over juice, and let sit until gelatin softens, about 5 minutes. Transfer remaining juice to small saucepan and cook over medium-high heat until reduced to 3 tablespoons, about 10 minutes. Off heat, whisk in softened gelatin mixture until gelatin dissolves. Whisk in cream cheese until smooth, then transfer to large bowl.

3. While juice is reducing, return strawberries to now-empty processor and process until smooth, 15 to 20 seconds. Strain puree through fine-mesh strainer into medium bowl, pressing on solids to remove seeds (you should have about 1⅔ cups puree). Discard any solids in strainer. Add strawberry puree to juice-gelatin mixture and whisk until incorporated.

4. Using stand mixer fitted with whisk, whip cream on medium-low speed until foamy, about 1 minute. Increase speed to high and whip until soft peaks form, 1 to 3 minutes. Gradually add remaining ¼ cup sugar and whip until stiff peaks form, 1 to 2 minutes. Whisk whipped cream into strawberry mixture until no white streaks remain. Portion into individual dessert dishes and chill for at least 4 hours or up to 48 hours. (If chilled longer than 6 hours, let mousse sit at room temperature for 10 minutes before serving.) Serve, garnishing with reserved diced strawberries.

Panna Cotta
Serves 8 MAKE AHEAD

Why This Recipe Works Impress your backyard barbecue guests with this cool, creamy, and elegant dessert. But for all its elegance, panna cotta is not complicated to prepare. We created a simple recipe that would guarantee a pudding with the rich flavor of cream and vanilla and a delicate texture. The amount of gelatin proved critical; we used a light hand, adding just enough to make the dessert firm enough to unmold. Because gelatin sets more quickly at cold temperatures, we minimized the amount of heat by softening the gelatin in cold milk, then heating it very briefly until it was melted. To avoid premature hardening, we gradually added cold vanilla-infused cream to the gelatin mixture and stirred everything over an ice bath to incorporate the gelatin. A vanilla bean gives the panna cotta the deepest flavor, but 2 teaspoons of vanilla extract can be used instead. Serve the panna cotta with lightly sweetened berries.

2¾ teaspoons unflavored gelatin
1 cup cold whole milk
3 cups cold heavy cream
1 vanilla bean
6 tablespoons (2⅔ ounces) sugar
  Pinch table salt

1. Sprinkle gelatin over milk in medium saucepan and let sit until gelatin softens, about 5 minutes. Meanwhile, place cream in large measuring cup. Cut vanilla bean in half lengthwise. Using tip of paring knife, scrape out vanilla seeds. Add vanilla bean and seeds to cream. Set eight 4-ounce serving dishes on rimmed baking sheet. Fill large bowl halfway with ice and water.

2. Heat milk and gelatin mixture over high heat, stirring constantly, until gelatin is dissolved and mixture registers 135 degrees, about 1½ minutes. Off heat, stir in sugar and salt until dissolved, about 1 minute.

3. Stirring constantly, slowly strain cream through fine-mesh strainer into milk mixture. Transfer mixture to clean bowl and set over bowl of ice water. Stir mixture often until slightly thickened and mixture registers 50 degrees, about 10 minutes. Strain mixture through fine-mesh strainer into second large liquid measuring cup, then distribute evenly among serving dishes.

4. Cover baking sheet with plastic wrap and refrigerate until custards are just set (mixture should wobble when shaken gently), at least 4 hours or up to 24 hours. (If unmolding, run paring knife around perimeter of each serving dish. Hold serving plate over top of each serving dish and invert; set plate on counter and gently shake serving dish to release panna cotta.) Serve.

VARIATION
Lemon Panna Cotta
Add four 2-inch strips lemon zest, cut into thin strips, to cream with vanilla bean. Add ¼ cup lemon juice (2 lemons) to strained cream mixture before dividing among serving dishes.

Lemon Posset with Berries
Serves 6 MAKE AHEAD

Why This Recipe Works This chilled British dessert with the plush texture of a mousse comes together almost by magic with little more than cream, sugar, and lemons. We found that using just the right proportion of sugar to lemon juice was the key to a smooth, luxurious consistency and a bright enough flavor to balance the richness of the cream. Lemon zest was essential to making the lemon flavor even more prominent. We paired the dessert with fresh, seasonal berries for textural contrast and to keep it from feeling overly rich. Reducing the cream mixture to exactly 2 cups creates the best consistency. Transfer the liquid to a 2-cup heatproof liquid measuring cup once or twice during boiling to monitor the amount. Do not leave the cream unattended, as it can boil over easily.

2 cups heavy cream
⅔ cup (4⅔ ounces) sugar
1 tablespoon grated lemon zest plus
  6 tablespoons juice (2 lemons)
7½ ounces (1½ cups) blueberries or raspberries

1. Combine cream, sugar, and lemon zest in medium saucepan and bring to boil over medium heat. Continue to boil, stirring frequently to dissolve sugar, until mixture is reduced to 2 cups, 8 to 12 minutes. (If at any point mixture begins to boil over, remove from heat.)

2. Remove saucepan from heat and stir in lemon juice. Let sit until mixture is cooled slightly and skin forms on top, about 20 minutes. Strain through fine-mesh strainer into bowl; discard zest. Divide mixture evenly among 6 individual ramekins or dessert dishes.

3. Refrigerate, uncovered, until set, at least 3 hours. Once chilled, possets can be wrapped in plastic wrap and refrigerated for up to 2 days. Unwrap and let sit at room temperature for 10 minutes before serving. Garnish with blueberries and serve.

Icebox Cheesecake
Serves 10 to 12 `MAKE AHEAD`

Why This Recipe Works Creamy, tangy, cheesecake is the perfect way to showcase summer fruits. But there's no denying cheesecake is typically a bit of a project. It's also incredibly rich and decadent. We wanted the essence of a cheesecake with less fuss, and the tang of a cream cheese–based cake without the weight—something lighter and creamier to finish a meal. Enter icebox cheesecake: The filling is lightened with whipped cream and the absence of eggs makes for a less rich cake (and apart from the crust, it requires no baking). We achieved the best flavor and texture when we stuck to the tried-and-true combination of heavy cream and cream cheese thickened with gelatin. Allowing the gelatin to hydrate in a portion of the cream and then bringing it to a boil in the microwave fully activated its thickening power. Lemon juice, lemon zest, and a little vanilla added just enough spark to perk up the tangy cream cheese. Serve with strawberries or your favorite fruit topping.

Crust
- 8 whole graham crackers, broken into rough pieces
- 1 tablespoon sugar
- 5 tablespoons unsalted butter, melted

Filling
- 2½ teaspoons unflavored gelatin
- 1½ cups heavy cream, divided
- ⅔ cup (4⅔ ounces) sugar
- 1 pound cream cheese, cut into 1-inch pieces and softened
- 1 teaspoon grated lemon zest plus 2 tablespoons juice
- 1 teaspoon vanilla extract
  Pinch table salt

Icebox Cheesecake

1. For the crust Adjust oven rack to middle position and heat oven to 325 degrees. Pulse crackers and sugar in food processor until finely ground, about 15 pulses. Add melted butter and pulse until combined, about 8 pulses. Transfer crumb mixture to greased 9-inch springform pan. Using bottom of dry measuring cup, press crumb mixture firmly into bottom of pan. Bake until fragrant and beginning to brown, about 13 minutes. Let crust cool completely, about 30 minutes.

2. For the filling Sprinkle gelatin over ¼ cup cream in 2-cup liquid measuring cup and let sit until gelatin softens, about 5 minutes. Microwave until mixture is bubbling around edges and gelatin dissolves, about 30 seconds; whisk to combine and set aside.

3. Using stand mixer fitted with whisk attachment, whip remaining 1¼ cups cream and sugar on medium-low speed until foamy, about 1 minute. Increase speed to high and whip until soft peaks form, 1 to 3 minutes. Fit stand mixer with paddle, reduce speed to medium-low, add cream cheese, and beat until combined, about 1 minute, scraping down bowl once (mixture may not be completely smooth). Add lemon juice, vanilla, and salt and continue to beat until combined, about 1 minute, scraping down bowl as needed.

Increase speed to medium-high and beat until smooth, about 3 minutes. Add dissolved gelatin mixture and lemon zest and continue to beat until smooth and airy, about 2 minutes.

4. Pour filling into crust and spread into even layer with spatula. Wrap cheesecake tightly in plastic wrap and refrigerate until set, at least 6 hours or up to 24 hours.

5. To unmold cheesecake, wrap hot, damp dish towel around pan and let sit for 1 minute. Remove sides of pan and slide thin metal spatula between crust and pan bottom to loosen, then slide cheesecake onto serving platter. Serve.

VARIATIONS

Peppermint Chip Icebox Cheesecake

For crust, substitute 16 Oreo Chocolate Mint Creme cookies for graham crackers, omit sugar, and reduce melted butter to 2 tablespoons. For filling, reduce sugar to ½ cup and omit lemon juice, lemon zest, and vanilla; add 2 tablespoons crème de menthe with salt; and stir 1 cup mini semisweet chocolate chips into filling before pouring into crust.

Peanut Butter Icebox Cheesecake

For crust, substitute 16 Nutter Butter cookies, broken into rough pieces, for graham crackers. Process cookie pieces in food processor until evenly ground, about 45 seconds (you should have about 1¼ cups crumbs) before combining with butter in step 1. Reduce butter to 2 tablespoons and omit sugar. For filling, omit lemon zest and juice and reduce sugar to ½ cup. In step 3, after adding dissolved gelatin mixture, add 1 cup creamy unsalted peanut butter and beat until smooth, about 1 minute. Press ½ cup finely chopped salted peanuts onto sides of cake after unmolding and before serving.

NOTES FROM THE TEST KITCHEN

SLICING CREAMY CAKES

Cheesecakes, icebox cakes, and ice cream cakes have supercreamy fillings that will stick to the knife, making it difficult to cut neat pieces. We like to dip our knife in a container of hot water or run it under a hot tap and quickly dry it before cutting so it glides through the cake. Wipe the knife clean before making another cut. Repeat heating the knife as needed.

Icebox Margarita Cheesecake
Serves 10 to 12 MAKE AHEAD

Why This Recipe Works In this dessert, cool, creamy icebox cheesecake meets the salty, pucker-inspiring flavors of the best poolside companion: a margarita. We started by dissolving gelatin in a mixture of margarita mix, tequila, and triple sec to create a kind of margarita Jell-O (perhaps the best kind of Jell-O). We mixed some of this into the cheesecake filling for flavor and structure, and we strained the remainder to create a glassy "shot" on top of the cake. For a crust that was more in line with our theme, we replaced the traditional graham cracker crust with a pretzel one to hint at the salted rim of a margarita glass. To finish, we garnished the sides of the cake with a mixture of coconut and lime zest and topped it off with slices of lime. This tart and creamy cheesecake is so good and refreshing we'd strongly consider skipping cocktail hour and enjoying a slice of cake instead.

1	cup (3 ounces) sweetened shredded coconut
1	teaspoon grated lime zest plus 1 lime, sliced thin
4½	ounces pretzel sticks (3 cups)
6	tablespoons unsalted butter, melted
4	teaspoons unflavored gelatin
¾	cup water, divided
1	(10-ounce) can frozen margarita mix, thawed
¼	cup tequila
¼	cup triple sec
1½	cups heavy cream, chilled
1	(14-ounce) can sweetened condensed milk
4	ounces cream cheese, softened

1. Adjust oven rack to middle position and heat oven to 350 degrees. Grease 9-inch springform pan and line wall of springform pan with 3-inch-wide strip of parchment paper. Process coconut and lime zest in food processor until coarsely ground, 25 to 30 seconds; reserve ½ cup and set aside. Add pretzels to remaining coconut mixture and process until finely ground, about 1 minute. Add melted butter and pulse to combine, about 5 pulses. Transfer crumb mixture to springform pan. Using bottom of dry measuring cup, press crumb mixture firmly into bottom of pan. Bake until edges are golden, 10 to 12 minutes. Let crust cool completely, about 30 minutes.

2. Sprinkle gelatin over ¼ cup water in small saucepan and let sit until gelatin softens, about 5 minutes. Add margarita mix, tequila, and triple sec and cook over low heat, stirring frequently, until gelatin dissolves, about 5 minutes. Let cool for 15 minutes; set aside.

Chocolate Eclair Cake

3. Using stand mixer fitted with whisk attachment, whip cream on medium-low speed until foamy, about 1 minute. Increase speed to high and whip until soft peaks form, 1 to 3 minutes. Transfer whipped cream to bowl; set aside. Using clean, dry mixer bowl and whisk attachment, whip condensed milk and cream cheese until combined, about 1½ minutes. Add 1 cup margarita mixture and whip until incorporated, about 25 seconds. Use whisk to mix in one-third of whipped cream, then use rubber spatula to gently fold in remaining whipped cream. Pour filling into crust. Refrigerate until just set, about 1 hour.

4. Stir remaining ½ cup water into remaining margarita mixture. Strain mixture through fine-mesh strainer into 2-cup liquid measuring cup. Pour over filling and refrigerate until set, at least 4 hours or up to 24 hours. Remove sides of pan and parchment. Press reserved coconut mixture onto sides of cake and top with lime slices. Slide thin metal spatula between crust and pan bottom to loosen, then slide cheesecake onto serving platter. Serve.

Chocolate Eclair Cake
Serves 15 MAKE AHEAD

Why This Recipe Works This crowd-pleasing no-bake dessert incorporates all of the creamy decadence and rich chocolate flavor of the popular pastry, but with a fraction of the work. It's typically made by layering a mixture of instant vanilla pudding and Cool Whip between graham crackers, topping it with chocolate frosting, and letting the refrigerator take care of the rest. With a couple of easy techniques (a quick stovetop pudding, whipped cream, and a microwave-and-stir glaze) and very little active time, we produced a from-scratch version that easily trumped its inspiration. Six ounces of finely chopped semisweet chocolate can be used in place of the chips.

1¼ cups (8¾ ounces) sugar
   6 tablespoons (1½ ounces) cornstarch
   1 teaspoon table salt
   5 cups whole milk
   4 tablespoons unsalted butter, cut into 4 pieces
   5 teaspoons vanilla extract
1¼ teaspoons unflavored gelatin
   2 tablespoons water
2¾ cups heavy cream, chilled, divided
 23 graham crackers
   1 cup (6 ounces) semisweet chocolate chips
   5 tablespoons light corn syrup

Basic Ice Cream Cake

1. Combine sugar, cornstarch, and salt in large saucepan. Whisk milk into sugar mixture until smooth and bring to boil over medium-high heat, scraping bottom of pan with rubber spatula. Immediately reduce heat to medium-low and cook, continuing to scrape bottom, until thickened and large bubbles appear on surface, 4 to 6 minutes. Off heat, whisk in butter and vanilla. Transfer pudding to large bowl and place parchment directly on surface of pudding. Refrigerate until cool, about 2 hours.

2. Sprinkle gelatin over water in bowl and let sit until gelatin softens, about 5 minutes. Microwave until mixture is bubbling around edges and gelatin dissolves, about 30 seconds. Using stand mixer fitted with whisk attachment, whip 2 cups cream on medium-low speed until foamy, about 1 minute. Increase speed to high and whip until soft peaks form, 1 to 3 minutes. Add gelatin mixture and whip until stiff peaks form, about 1 minute.

3. Whisk one-third of whipped cream into chilled pudding until smooth. Fold remaining whipped cream into chilled pudding until only a few white streaks remain. Cover bottom of 13 by 9-inch baking dish with layer of graham crackers, breaking crackers as necessary to line bottom of pan. Top with half of pudding–whipped cream mixture (about 5½ cups) and another layer of graham crackers. Repeat with remaining pudding–whipped cream mixture and remaining graham crackers.

4. Combine chocolate chips, corn syrup, and remaining ¾ cup cream in bowl and microwave on 50 percent power, stirring occasionally, until smooth, 1 to 2 minutes. Let glaze cool completely, about 10 minutes. Spread glaze evenly over graham crackers and refrigerate cake for at least 6 hours or up to 2 days before serving.

Basic Ice Cream Cake
Serves 8 to 10   MAKE AHEAD

Why This Recipe Works The appeal of ice cream cake is obvious: These two beloved desserts are a match made in heaven, and a cold, creamy slice of ice cream cake is far more satisfying than a scoop of ice cream haphazardly dolloped onto a slice of cake. We wanted to develop a basic ice cream cake that would be a hit at any party. We started with three crowd-pleasing flavors—chocolate, vanilla, and strawberry—to create a striped Neapolitan cake. Oreo crumbs served as a sturdy bottom crust and also provided a welcome bit of chocolaty crunch between each layer of ice cream. When it came to assembling the cake, we found that the key was patience. We didn't start until the crust was completely cool, and allowing the ice cream to soften

to a spreadable consistency ensured it wouldn't mar the crust. For clean lines and to avoid a melty mess, it was essential to freeze each layer before adding the next. We dressed up our cake by pressing party-ready rainbow sprinkles into the sides, but you could also use chopped nuts or crushed candies or cookies. You can also pipe a greeting on top once the cake is fully frozen. Use the entire Oreo—filling and all—for the crust.

25 Oreo cookies, broken into rough pieces
 3 tablespoons unsalted butter, melted
 1 pint strawberry ice cream
 1 pint vanilla ice cream
 1 pint chocolate ice cream
½ cup rainbow sprinkles

1. Adjust oven rack to middle position and heat oven to 325 degrees. Process Oreos in food processor until finely ground, about 30 seconds. Add melted butter and process until mixture resembles wet sand, about 10 seconds.

2. Using your hands, press ⅔ cup crumb mixture evenly into bottom of greased 9-inch springform pan. Using bottom of measuring cup, firmly pack crust into pan. Bake until crust is fragrant and set, 5 to 10 minutes. Let crust cool completely on wire rack, about 30 minutes.

3. Scoop strawberry ice cream into large bowl and, using large rubber spatula or wooden spoon, break up scoops of ice cream. Stir and fold ice cream to achieve smooth consistency. Spread softened ice cream evenly over crust. Sprinkle ⅔ cup Oreo crumbs over ice cream and pack down lightly. Wrap pan tightly with plastic wrap and freeze until ice cream is just firm, about 30 minutes. Repeat with vanilla ice cream and remaining ⅔ cup Oreo crumbs; wrap tightly and freeze for another 30 minutes. Soften chocolate ice cream, spread evenly in pan, and smooth top. Wrap cake tightly in plastic and freeze until firm, at least 8 hours or up to 1 week.

4. To unmold cake, dip slicing knife in very hot water and wipe dry. Run knife around edge of pan. Remove sides of pan and slide thin metal spatula between crust and pan bottom to loosen, then slide cake onto serving platter. Press sprinkles onto sides of cake. Serve immediately.

VARIATION
Mexican Chocolate Ice Cream Torte
Substitute coffee ice cream for strawberry ice cream. Mix 1 teaspoon cinnamon in with vanilla ice cream. Substitute 1½ cups sliced toasted almonds for rainbow sprinkles, sprinkling some over top as well.

Banana Split Cake

S'mores Ice Cream Cake

Tiramisu Ice Cream Cake

Serves 8 to 10 `NO COOK` `MAKE AHEAD`

Why This Recipe Works We love the classic Italian dessert tiramisu and wanted to reinterpret it for summer as an ice cream cake, filling a ring of coffee-soaked ladyfingers with coffee chip ice cream and crowning it with whipped cream enriched by mascarpone cheese and flavored with rum. To assemble the cake, we needed to take care to soften the ice cream until it was easily spreadable so it wouldn't rip the delicate soaked ladyfinger cookies. While some Italian bakeries make fresh ladyfingers, their soft, cakelike texture became even softer when soaked, which prevented them from standing up straight in the pan. Store-bought dried ladyfingers were sturdier and worked much better. Depending on the brand, 14 ounces of ladyfingers is 42 to 60 cookies.

2½	cups brewed coffee, room temperature
1½	tablespoons instant espresso powder
6	tablespoons dark rum, divided
14	ounces dried ladyfingers
4	pints coffee ice cream
¼	cup (1½ ounces) mini chocolate chips
8	ounces (1 cup) mascarpone cheese
¾	cup heavy cream, chilled
¼	cup (1¾ ounces) sugar
	Unsweetened cocoa powder

1. Set wire rack in rimmed baking sheet. Combine coffee, espresso powder, and 5 tablespoons rum in large bowl. Working with 1 cookie at a time, quickly dunk ladyfingers in coffee mixture and transfer to wire rack; let sit for 5 minutes.

2. Spray 16-cup tube pan with vegetable oil spray and line bottom with parchment paper. Lightly spray parchment with oil spray. Line outer wall of prepared pan with soaked ladyfingers, flat sides facing in, packing gently to ensure that there are no spaces between cookies; freeze until firm, about 1 hour. When cookies are firm, scoop ice cream into large bowl and, using large rubber spatula or wooden spoon, break up scoops of ice cream. Stir and fold ice cream to achieve smooth consistency; fold in chocolate chips. Transfer softened ice cream to cookie-lined pan and smooth top. Wrap pan tightly with plastic wrap and freeze until ice cream is firm, at least 4 hours or up to 1 week.

3. Using stand mixer fitted with whisk attachment, whip mascarpone, cream, sugar, and remaining 1 tablespoon rum on medium-high speed until stiff peaks form, about 2 minutes. Gently invert pan to turn cake onto serving platter, discarding parchment. Using rubber spatula, top cake with 1 cup mascarpone mixture, then dust lightly with cocoa. Serve immediately with remaining mascarpone mixture.

Banana Split Cake

Serves 8 to 10 `NO COOK` `MAKE AHEAD`

Why This Recipe Works Served with a topping of old-school nostalgia, the banana split is the ultimate ice cream sundae. Our festive ice cream cake is like a massive banana split; it duplicates its flavor and offers an ultracharming appearance. To give the sundae the structure of a cake, we lined the edge of a springform pan with cut store-bought ice cream sandwiches. That took care of the chocolate and vanilla; we then filled the center of the cake with bright strawberry ice cream. We froze the cake at this stage and patiently waited to get to the fun part: the topping. Hot fudge was a must, and was the perfect frosting substitute for this cake. A generous fluff of whipped cream dolloped in the center, a sprinkling of chopped walnuts, and, of course, banana slices, were iconic adornments. A cherry on top was the finishing touch for our sundae cake. We prefer to use our homemade Hot Fudge Sauce (page 407), but you can use store-bought if desired.

```
 8  ice cream sandwiches
 3  pints strawberry ice cream
 1  cup heavy cream
 1  cup Hot Fudge Sauce (page 407), warmed
⅓  cup walnuts, chopped
 1  ripe banana, peeled, halved lengthwise,
     and sliced thin
 1  maraschino cherry (optional)
```

1. Chill 9-inch springform pan in freezer. Cut each ice cream sandwich in half lengthwise, then cut in half crosswise to yield 4 pieces. Transfer sandwich pieces to plate and freeze until very firm, about 2 hours. Line outer edge of chilled springform pan with sandwich pieces, standing them upright with thin sides against pan. Scoop ice cream into large bowl and, using large rubber spatula or wooden spoon, break up scoops of ice cream. Stir and fold ice cream to achieve smooth consistency. Fill center with softened ice cream and smooth surface. Wrap pan tightly with plastic wrap and freeze until firm, at least 4 hours or up to 1 week.

2. Using stand mixer fitted with whisk attachment, whip cream on medium-low speed until foamy, about 1 minute. Increase speed to high and whip until soft peaks form, 1 to 3 minutes. To unmold cake, remove sides of pan and slide thin metal spatula between cake bottom and pan bottom to loosen, then slide cake onto serving platter. Spoon warmed fudge sauce onto center of cake and spread almost to edge. Dollop with whipped cream and top with walnuts and banana. Top with cherry, if using. Serve immediately.

S'mores Ice Cream Cake

Serves 8 to 10 `MAKE AHEAD`

Why This Recipe Works The combination of chocolate, graham crackers, and marshmallows is irresistible. We wanted to take each element of s'mores and reimagine this beloved campfire snack as a magnificent ice cream cake. Combining warm, gooey s'mores with ice cream may sound like a mess, but we found a way to add the heat without causing a meltdown. The base of our cake was simple: just a graham cracker crust covered with fudge. The fudge layer provided plenty of chocolate flavor, gave the cake a sundae-like quality, and kept the crust from becoming soggy under the remaining layers. Between the fudge-covered crust and a generous filling of chocolate ice cream, we spread a layer of sweet marshmallow crème—but it wouldn't be s'mores without toasted marshmallows too. We halved large marshmallows so they'd lie flat and covered the top of our cake with them. After freezing the cake until it was very firm, it took just a quick run under a hot broiler to toast the marshmallows without melting the cake. A ring of graham crackers around the outside provided the finishing touch to this playful dessert. When working with the marshmallow crème, grease both the inside of your measuring cup and a spatula with vegetable oil spray to prevent sticking.

```
 4  ounces bittersweet chocolate, chopped fine
½  cup heavy cream
¼  cup light corn syrup
16  graham crackers (8 broken into pieces,
     8 quartered along dotted seams)
 4  tablespoons unsalted butter, melted
 1  tablespoon sugar
 1  cup marshmallow crème
 3  pints chocolate ice cream
26  large marshmallows, halved crosswise
```

1. Combine chocolate, cream, and corn syrup in bowl and microwave at 50 percent power until melted and smooth, about 1 minute, stirring halfway through microwaving. Let cool completely, about 30 minutes.

2. Adjust oven rack to middle position and heat oven to 325 degrees. Spray 9-inch springform pan with vegetable oil spray and line wall of springform pan with 2½-inch-wide strip of parchment paper. Pulse broken crackers in food processor until finely ground, about 15 pulses. Combine cracker crumbs, melted butter, and sugar in bowl until mixture resembles wet sand. Using your hands, press crumb mixture evenly into pan bottom. Using bottom of measuring cup, firmly pack crust into pan. Bake until fragrant and beginning to brown, about 12 minutes. Let crust cool completely in pan on wire rack, about 30 minutes.

3. Pour chocolate mixture over crust and smooth into even layer; freeze until firm, about 30 minutes. Spread marshmallow crème over chocolate mixture in even layer; freeze until firm, about 15 minutes. Scoop ice cream into large bowl and, using large rubber spatula or wooden spoon, break up scoops of ice cream. Stir and fold ice cream to achieve smooth consistency. Spread softened ice cream evenly over marshmallow crème layer. Cover with plastic wrap and freeze until ice cream is very firm, at least 4 hours or up to 24 hours.

4. Adjust oven rack 6 inches from broiler element and heat broiler. Dip slicing knife in very hot water and wipe dry. Run knife around edge of pan. Place cake on rimmed baking sheet, discarding plastic, and arrange marshmallow halves, cut sides down, in snug layer over top. Broil until marshmallows are lightly browned, 30 to 60 seconds, rotating sheet halfway through broiling. (Refreeze cake if necessary.) Working quickly, remove sides of pan, discarding parchment, and slide thin metal spatula between cake bottom and pan bottom to loosen, then slide cake onto serving platter. Arrange cracker pieces vertically along sides of cake. Serve immediately.

MAKING THE MARSHMALLOW TOPPING

1. Place cake, still in pan, on baking sheet. Remove plastic wrap and arrange marshmallow halves, cut side down, snugly over top of cake.

2. Broil until marshmallows are lightly browned, 30 to 60 seconds, rotating sheet halfway through broiling for even browning.

Frozen Lemonade Cake
Serves 12 MAKE AHEAD

Why This Recipe Works There's nothing more refreshing than an ice-cold glass of lemonade on a hot summer day . . . or is there? Mixing lemonade concentrate into vanilla ice cream made an even more satisfying lemon-kissed treat. For a rich and zippy contrasting layer, we stirred lemon curd into whipped topping (we found Cool Whip brand worked best in this recipe) and sandwiched it between two layers of the lemonade ice cream.

We used animal crackers to make a slightly sweet, crisp crust that contrasted nicely with the creamy ice cream layers. For a decorative flourish, we used a paintbrush that we'd dipped in yellow food coloring to brush the top of the cake with a modern and abstract pop of color.

5 ounces animal crackers
3 tablespoons sugar
Pinch table salt
4 tablespoons unsalted butter, melted
2 pints vanilla ice cream
16 ounces Cool Whip Whipped Topping, thawed, divided
1 (12-ounce) container frozen lemonade concentrate, thawed
2 (10.5-ounce) jars lemon curd
1 teaspoon yellow gel food coloring, divided

1. Adjust oven rack to middle position and heat oven to 325 degrees. Process crackers, sugar, and salt in food processor until finely ground, about 30 seconds. Add melted butter and pulse until combined, about 8 pulses. Transfer crumb mixture to greased 9-inch springform pan. Using bottom of dry measuring cup, press crumb mixture firmly into bottom of pan. Bake crust until fragrant and beginning to brown, 12 to 14 minutes. Let cool completely, about 30 minutes.

2. Scoop vanilla ice cream into large bowl and, using rubber spatula or wooden spoon, break up scoops of ice cream. Stir and fold ice cream to achieve smooth consistency. Stir ice cream, 2½ cups whipped topping, and lemonade concentrate in bowl until combined. Pour half of ice cream mixture into cooled crust and smooth top with offset spatula. Transfer pan and bowl with remaining ice cream mixture to freezer and freeze until firm, about 1 hour. Stir lemon curd, ½ teaspoon food coloring, and remaining 2½ cups whipped topping in separate bowl until combined. Spread lemon curd mixture in even layer over frozen ice cream layer. Return pan to freezer until firm, about 1 hour. Scoop remaining half of ice cream mixture into large bowl and, using rubber spatula or wooden spoon, break up scoops of ice cream. Stir and fold ice cream to achieve smooth consistency, then spread over frozen lemon curd layer, smoothing top with offset spatula. Freeze cake until fully firm, at least 6 hours or up to 24 hours.

3. Remove sides of pan and slide thin metal spatula between crust and pan bottom to loosen, then slide cake to cake plate or pedestal. Smooth sides of cake with offset spatula. Dip 1-inch paintbrush in remaining ½ teaspoon food coloring and lightly drag across top of cake, painting straight yellow stripes 2 to 3 inches long, refreshing brush with food coloring as needed. Slice and serve.

Chocolate Chip Ice Cream Sandwiches

Serves 12 (Makes 12 Sandwiches) `MAKE AHEAD`

Why This Recipe Works Most homemade ice cream sandwiches need to be eaten at the perfect time. Miss that window, and you've got oozy soft ice cream or rock-hard cookies. Not ours, though. Straight out of the freezer, these ice cream sandwiches feature full-flavored cookies, tender enough to bite through but sturdy enough to hold a heaping helping of ice cream. Our secret? We added more water to the dough. The sugar in the dough lowered the freezing temperature of the water, keeping it fluid. Plus, freezing the assembled sandwiches for 8 hours allowed a small amount of water to migrate from the ice cream to the cookies, softening the cookies even further. These sandwiches should be made at least 8 hours before serving. We prefer the deeper flavor of dark brown sugar here, but light brown sugar will also work. If using a premium ice cream such as Ben & Jerry's or Häagen-Dazs, which is likely to be harder than a less-premium brand when frozen, let the ice cream soften slightly in the refrigerator before scooping. If you have one, a #16 scoop works well for portioning the ice cream.

- 10 tablespoons unsalted butter
- ¾ cup packed (5¼ ounces) dark brown sugar
- ¾ teaspoon table salt
- 1 cup plus 2 tablespoons (5⅔ ounces) all-purpose flour
- ¼ teaspoon baking soda
- 1 large egg
- 2 tablespoons water
- 2 teaspoons vanilla extract
- ½ cup (3 ounces) mini semisweet chocolate chips, plus 1 cup for optional garnish
- 3 pints vanilla ice cream

1. Adjust oven rack to middle position and heat oven to 325 degrees. Melt butter in 10-inch skillet over medium-high heat. Cook, stirring and scraping skillet constantly with rubber spatula, until milk solids are dark golden brown and butter has nutty aroma, 1 to 3 minutes. Immediately transfer to heatproof large bowl. Whisk in sugar and salt until fully incorporated and let mixture cool for 10 minutes. Meanwhile, line 2 rimmed baking sheets with parchment paper. Stir flour and baking soda together in second bowl; set aside.

2. Add egg, water, and vanilla to browned butter mixture and whisk until smooth, about 30 seconds. Using rubber spatula, stir in flour mixture until combined. Stir in ½ cup chocolate chips. (Dough will be very soft.)

Frozen Lemonade Cake

Chocolate Chip Ice Cream Sandwiches

Fresh Strawberry Pie

3. Using #60 scoop or 1 tablespoon measure, evenly space 12 mounds of dough on each prepared sheet. Bake cookies, 1 sheet at a time, until puffed and golden brown, 9 to 12 minutes, rotating sheet halfway through baking. Let cookies cool on sheet for 5 minutes, then transfer to wire rack and let cool completely, about 45 minutes. Place 1 sheet, still lined with parchment, in freezer.

4. Place 4 cookies upside down on counter. Quickly deposit 2-inch-tall, 2-inch-wide scoop of ice cream in center of each cookie. Place 1 cookie from wire rack right side up on top of each scoop. Gently press and twist each sandwich between your hands until ice cream spreads to edges of cookies (this doesn't have to be perfect; ice cream can be neatened after chilling). Transfer sandwiches to sheet in freezer. Repeat with remaining cookies and remaining ice cream. Place 1 cup chocolate chips, if using, in shallow bowl or pie plate.

5. Remove first 4 sandwiches from freezer. Working with 1 sandwich at a time, hold sandwiches over bowl of chocolate chips and gently press chocolate chips into sides of sandwiches with your other hand, neatening ice cream if necessary. Return garnished sandwiches to freezer and repeat with remaining 8 sandwiches in 2 batches. Freeze sandwiches for at least 8 hours before serving. (Sandwiches can be individually wrapped tightly in plastic wrap, transferred to zipper-lock bag, and frozen for up to 2 months.)

Lemon Icebox Pie

Fresh Strawberry Pie
Serves 8 MAKE AHEAD

Why This Recipe Works This pie of high-piled, gleaming strawberries is the perfect pie to showcase your farmers' market haul. What's the secret to preventing the berry mountain from tumbling? The thickener has to be just right— or rather, thickeners, as we soon discovered. Together, pectin and cornstarch—combined with a puree of some of the strawberries—produced a supple, lightly clingy glaze that held the berries together. To account for imperfect fruit, we call for several more ounces than will be used in the pie. If possible, seek out local, in-season berries. For fruit pectin, we recommend both Sure-Jell for Less or No Sugar Needed Recipes and Ball RealFruit Low or No-Sugar Needed Pectin. The pie is at its best after 2 hours of chilling; longer and the glaze becomes softer and wetter, though the pie will taste good. You can use the Foolproof All-Butter Single-Crust Pie Dough (page 372) or a store-bought pie dough in this recipe.

1 recipe Foolproof All-Butter Single-Crust Pie Dough (page 372)
3 pounds strawberries, hulled (9½ cups)
¾ cup (5¼ ounces) sugar
2 tablespoons cornstarch
1½ teaspoons low- or no-sugar-needed fruit pectin
   Pinch table salt
1 tablespoon lemon juice

1. Roll dough into 12-inch circle on well-floured counter. Loosely roll dough around rolling pin and gently unroll it onto 9-inch pie plate, letting excess dough hang over edge. Ease dough into plate by gently lifting edge of dough with your hand while pressing into plate bottom with your other hand.

2. Trim overhang to ½ inch beyond lip of plate. Tuck overhang under itself; folded edge should be flush with edge of plate. Crimp dough evenly around edge of plate. Wrap dough-lined plate loosely in plastic wrap and refrigerate until firm, about 30 minutes. Adjust oven rack to middle position and heat oven to 350 degrees.

3. Line chilled pie shell with double layer of aluminum foil, covering edges to prevent burning, and fill with pie weights. Bake on foil-lined rimmed baking sheet until edges are set and just beginning to turn golden, 25 to 30 minutes, rotating sheet halfway through baking. Remove foil and weights, rotate sheet, and continue to bake crust until golden brown and crisp, 10 to 15 minutes longer. Transfer sheet to wire rack and let cool completely, about 45 minutes.

4. Select 6 ounces misshapen, underripe, or otherwise unattractive strawberries, halving those that are large; you should have about 1½ cups. Process strawberries in food processor to smooth puree, 20 to 30 seconds, scraping down bowl as needed (you should have about ¾ cup puree). Whisk sugar, cornstarch, pectin, and salt together in medium saucepan. Stir in berry puree, making sure to scrape corners of saucepan. Bring to boil over medium-high heat, stirring constantly. Boil, scraping bottom and sides of pan to prevent scorching, for 2 minutes (mixture will appear frothy when it first reaches boil, then will darken and thicken with further cooking). Transfer glaze to large bowl and stir in lemon juice; let cool completely.

5. Meanwhile, pick over remaining strawberries and measure out 2 pounds of most attractive ones; halve only extra-large strawberries. Add strawberries to bowl with glaze and fold gently with rubber spatula until berries are evenly coated. Scoop strawberries into cooled crust, piling into mound. Turn any cut sides face down. If necessary, rearrange strawberries so that holes are filled and mound looks attractive. Refrigerate until chilled and set, at least 2 hours or up to 5 hours. Serve.

Lemon Icebox Pie
Serves 8 MAKE AHEAD

Why This Recipe Works Much like Key lime pie, lemon icebox pie boasts a buttery graham cracker crust that holds a tart, citrusy filling made with sweetened condensed milk and egg yolks. Older versions are no-bake pies that are served chilled: cool, oh-so-creamy, sweet yet tart, and easy to make. Many Americans, however, are nervous about eating raw eggs, so modern recipes call for a brief bake time. Food safety worries aside, we found that the baking innovation was a good one: Baked pies set up and sliced much better than unbaked pies. After a few tests, we settled on baking for 15 minutes at a relatively gentle 325 degrees. Now we just needed to figure out the right amount of lemon. Recipes called for as little as 2 tablespoons of lemon juice (these pies were bland) and as much as 2 cups (these pies were inedibly sour). The perfect pucker appeared at 1 cup. We were going to sweeten the whipped cream with sugar but we realized we could get the same effect from using some of the sweetened condensed milk from the filling. Stealing 3 tablespoons threw off the pie's balance, so we decreased the lemon juice slightly to reestablish harmony. You can use the Graham Cracker Crust (page 373) or a store-bought graham cracker crust in this recipe.

2 (14-ounce) cans sweetened condensed milk, divided
3 large egg yolks
¾ cup plus 2 tablespoons lemon juice (5 lemons)
1 recipe Graham Cracker Crust (page 373), baked and cooled
1 cup heavy cream
½ teaspoon vanilla extract

1. Adjust oven rack to middle position and heat oven to 325 degrees. Set aside 3 tablespoons condensed milk. Whisk egg yolks and remaining condensed milk in bowl until smooth. Slowly whisk in lemon juice.

2. Pour filling into cooled crust. Bake until edges are beginning to set but center still jiggles when shaken, about 15 minutes. Let pie cool on wire rack for 1 hour. Refrigerate until chilled and set, at least 3 hours or up to 24 hours.

3. Using stand mixer fitted with whisk attachment, whip cream, vanilla, and reserved condensed milk on medium-low speed until foamy, about 1 minute. Increase speed to high and whip until stiff peaks form, 1 to 3 minutes. Spread whipped cream attractively over pie before serving.

The official start of summer is a hotly debated topic. Purists say it begins with the summer solstice, while others say Memorial Day. We think nothing signals the start of the summer season quite like the square turquoise paper containers piled high with berries at the farmers' market. Transformed into jams and jellies, baked into pies, and (of course) simply eaten out of hand, summer berries just can't be beat.

Blackberries Blackberries are a bramble fruit well loved for their deep purple-black color and their elegantly sweet-yet-tart, almost woodsy, flavor. What's more, they're packed with nutrients. Look for them at their peak season right around Memorial Day.

Strawberries These heart-shaped cuties are among the most popular summer berries. Their time to shine is early in the season—and you need to grab them fast. They start appearing at farm stands in early June and then start dwindling once July rolls around. When buying, choose vibrant, shiny berries that are firm and plump.

Raspberries Sweet and tangy (but less tart than blackberries), raspberries have hollow cores and are among the most delicate of all the berries—they're best eaten quickly as they're prone to spoiling and don't keep well. Red raspberries are the most common, but you may also find golden or yellow varieties.

Blueberries Jewel-like blueberries have a longer season than the other berries on this list—they are perfectly delicious starting in June, but get even sweeter as the season goes on. The darker the berry, the sweeter the fruit. Wild blueberries (common in Maine) are smaller, with concentrated flavor, while other varieties are larger and juicier.

FREEZING INSTRUCTIONS
Spread unwashed berries in an even layer on a baking sheet or plate and freeze. After they are frozen solid, transfer the berries to a zipper-lock plastic bag and freeze them for up to two months. This method ensures that your berries won't freeze in clumps, so you can defrost just as many as you need. A quick rinse helps jump-start the defrosting process.

Raspberry Chiffon Pie
Serves 8 MAKE AHEAD

Why This Recipe Works Raspberry chiffon pie celebrates the sweetly tart berries, featuring them in two distinct layers— a fruit-forward jam-like layer and a light and frothy whipped raspberry concoction on top. Whipped cream spread on the very top kept the pie light and lovely. For fruit pectin, we recommend both Sure-Jell for Less or No Sugar Needed Recipes and Ball RealFruit Low or No-Sugar Needed Pectin. For an accurate measurement of boiling water, bring a full kettle of water to a boil and then measure out the desired amount. You can use the Foolproof All-Butter Single-Crust Pie Dough (page 372) or a store-bought pie dough in this recipe.

1 recipe Foolproof All-Butter Single-Crust Pie Dough (page 372)

Fruit
17 ounces fresh raspberries, divided
3 tablespoons low- or no-sugar-needed fruit pectin
1½ cups (10½ ounces) sugar
Pinch table salt

Chiffon
3 tablespoons raspberry-flavored gelatin
3 tablespoons boiling water
3 ounces cream cheese, softened
1 cup heavy cream, chilled

1 recipe Whipped Cream (page 406)

1. Roll dough into 12-inch circle on floured counter. Loosely roll dough around rolling pin and gently unroll it onto 9-inch pie plate, letting excess dough hang over edge. Ease dough into plate by gently lifting edge of dough with your hand while pressing into plate bottom with your other hand.

2. Trim overhang to ½ inch beyond lip of plate. Tuck overhang under itself; folded edge should be flush with edge of plate. Crimp dough evenly around edge of plate. Wrap dough-lined plate loosely in plastic wrap and refrigerate until firm, about 30 minutes. Adjust oven rack to middle position and heat oven to 350 degrees.

3. Line chilled pie shell with double layer of aluminum foil, covering edges to prevent burning, and fill with pie weights. Bake on foil-lined rimmed baking sheet until edges are set and just beginning to turn golden, 25 to 30 minutes, rotating sheet halfway through baking. Remove foil and weights, rotate sheet, and continue to bake crust until golden brown and crisp, 10 to 15 minutes longer. Transfer sheet to wire rack and let cool completely, about 30 minutes.

Raspberry Chiffon Pie

Icebox Chocolate Cream Pie
Serves 8 `MAKE AHEAD`

Why This Recipe Works Chocolate cream pies usually look superb, but they're often gluey and overly sweet and require standing over the stove to make the filling. We wanted a sweet, creamy filling that fell somewhere between a pudding and a mousse, and we wanted much of the work to be hands-off. Blooming the gelatin in milk and cream and then heating it briefly in the microwave created just the texture we were after. We played with varying amounts of milk and cream. Too much made the pie bland; too little and it tasted watery. We settled on a 3:1 ratio for the best creaminess. A combination of bittersweet chocolate and cocoa powder gave us the best chocolate flavor and texture. The food processor helped us make a perfectly silky-smooth mixture, and then the refrigerator took care of the rest, setting it up into the chocolate filling of our dreams. You can use the Chocolate Cookie Crust (page 373) or a store-bought chocolate cookie crust in this recipe.

1½ cups heavy cream
½ cup whole milk
½ teaspoon vanilla extract
1¾ teaspoons unflavored gelatin
2 ounces bittersweet chocolate, coarsely chopped
3 tablespoons sugar
2 tablespoons unsweetened cocoa powder
⅛ teaspoon table salt
1 recipe Chocolate Cookie Crust (page 373), baked and cooled
1 recipe Whipped Cream (page 406)

1. Combine cream, milk, and vanilla in 2-cup liquid measuring cup. Sprinkle gelatin over top and let sit until gelatin softens, about 5 minutes. Microwave cream mixture, stirring occasionally, until hot but not boiling and gelatin is completely dissolved, about 2 minutes.

2. Add chocolate, sugar, cocoa, and salt to food processor. With processor running, slowly add hot cream mixture and process until chocolate is melted and filling is smooth, about 1 minute, scraping down sides of bowl as needed. Pour filling into cooled crust and smooth top. Spray piece of parchment paper with vegetable oil spray and press directly against surface of pie. Cover and refrigerate until filling is chilled and set, at least 3 hours or up to 24 hours.

3. Spread whipped cream attractively over top of pie before serving.

4. For the fruit Cook 12 ounces raspberries in medium saucepan over medium-high heat, stirring occasionally, until berries begin to give up their juices, about 3 minutes. Stir in pectin and bring to boil, stirring constantly. Stir in sugar and salt and return to boil. Cook, stirring constantly, until slightly thickened, about 2 minutes. Strain mixture through fine-mesh strainer into bowl, pressing on solids to extract as much puree as possible. Scrape puree off underside of strainer into bowl.

5. Transfer ⅓ cup raspberry puree to small bowl and let cool completely. Gently fold remaining 5 ounces raspberries into remaining puree and spread evenly over bottom of cooled crust; set aside.

6. For the chiffon Sprinkle gelatin over boiling water in bowl of stand mixer and let sit until gelatin softens, about 5 minutes. Fit stand mixer with paddle, add cream cheese and reserved ⅓ cup raspberry puree, and beat on high speed, scraping down bowl once or twice, until smooth, about 2 minutes. Add cream and beat on medium-low speed until incorporated, about 30 seconds. Scrape down bowl. Increase speed to high and beat until cream holds stiff peaks, 1 to 2 minutes. Spread evenly over fruit in pie shell. Cover pie with plastic. Refrigerate until set, at least 3 hours or up to 2 days. Spread whipped cream attractively over pie before serving.

Caramel Turtle Icebox Pie

Caramel Turtle Icebox Pie

Serves 8 `MAKE AHEAD`

Why This Recipe Works We wanted all of the contrasting flavors and textures of turtle candies—smooth, deep chocolate; sweet, chewy caramel; and rich, crunchy nuts—but in pie form. For the base we opted for a chocolate cookie crust, which was only mildly sweet so the pie could handle a rich filling and a thick pecan-caramel sauce. We poured a layer of the sauce right onto the baked crust so it was integrated into the pie. On top of the sauce we spread our filling: a combination of marshmallow crème, cream cheese, heavy cream, peanut butter, and butter. The cream cheese tempered the sweetness of the marshmallow, while the heavy cream ensured that our filling was fluffy and light. Do not use products labeled marshmallow sauce or marshmallow topping. When working with the marshmallow crème, grease both the inside of your measuring cup and a spatula with vegetable oil spray to prevent sticking. The sauce will need to be warm so that it is pourable. When taking the temperature of the caramel in step 1, tilt the saucepan and move the thermometer back and forth to equalize hot and cool spots. You can use the Chocolate Cookie Crust (page 373) or a store-bought chocolate cookie crust in this recipe.

Caramel-Chocolate-Pecan Sauce

- 1 cup (7 ounces) sugar
- ⅓ cup water
- 3 tablespoons light corn syrup
- ¾ cup heavy cream
- 2 ounces bittersweet chocolate, chopped
- 1 tablespoon unsalted butter, chilled
- ½ cup pecans, toasted and chopped
- 1 teaspoon vanilla extract
- ⅛ teaspoon table salt

Pie

- 1 recipe Chocolate Cookie Crust (page 373), baked and cooled
- 8 ounces cream cheese, softened
- 1 cup marshmallow crème
- ½ cup heavy cream
- ½ cup creamy peanut butter
- 2 tablespoons unsalted butter, softened

1. For the caramel-chocolate-pecan sauce Bring sugar, water, and corn syrup to boil in large saucepan over medium-high heat. Cook, without stirring, until mixture is straw-colored, 6 to 8 minutes. Reduce heat to low and continue to cook, swirling saucepan occasionally, until caramel is amber-colored, 2 to 5 minutes. (Caramel should register between 360 and 370 degrees.)

Peanut Butter Pie

2. Off heat, carefully stir in cream; mixture will bubble and steam. Stir in chocolate and butter and let sit for 3 minutes. Whisk sauce until smooth and chocolate is fully melted. Stir in pecans, vanilla, and salt. Let cool slightly. (Sauce can be refrigerated for up to 2 weeks; gently warm in microwave, stirring every 10 seconds, until pourable, before using.)

3. For the pie Pour 1 cup sauce into bottom of crust and refrigerate, uncovered, until set, about 30 minutes.

4. Using stand mixer fitted with paddle, beat cream cheese, marshmallow crème, heavy cream, peanut butter, and butter on medium-high speed until light and fluffy, about 5 minutes, scraping down sides of bowl as needed. Transfer filling to cooled crust, smoothing top with spatula. Cover pie and refrigerate until filling is chilled and set, at least 2 hours or up to 24 hours. Drizzle remaining sauce attractively over top of pie and serve.

Peanut Butter Pie
Serves 8 `NO COOK` `MAKE AHEAD`

Why This Recipe Works Peanut butter is a natural filling for pie, but keeping its flavor strong while creating a light, almost airy texture took some finessing. We started by whipping peanut butter with cream cheese (for tang and to aid sliceability), confectioners' sugar, and a touch of cream, which loosened the mixture just enough for a fluffy consistency; folding in whipped cream lightened the filling even further. We sprinkled honey-roasted peanuts directly onto the crust for textural contrast before layering in the filling, and after topping the pie with more whipped cream, we took it over the top with a second dose of crunchy nuts. All-natural peanut butters will work in this recipe. You can use the Graham Cracker Crust (page 373) or a store-bought graham cracker crust in this recipe.

- ½ cup honey roasted peanuts, chopped, divided
- 1 recipe Graham Cracker Crust (page 373), baked and cooled
- ¾ cup (3 ounces) plus 2 tablespoons confectioners' sugar, divided
- ¾ cup creamy peanut butter
- 6 ounces cream cheese, softened
- 1¾ cups heavy cream, divided
- 1 teaspoon vanilla extract

1. Spread ⅓ cup peanuts evenly over bottom of crust. Using stand mixer fitted with whisk attachment, mix ¾ cup sugar, peanut butter, cream cheese, and 3 tablespoons cream on low speed until combined, about 1 minute. Increase speed to medium-high and whip until fluffy, about 1 minute. Transfer to large bowl; set aside.

2. In now-empty mixer bowl, whip ¾ cup cream on medium-low speed until foamy, about 1 minute. Increase speed to high and whip until stiff peaks form, 1 to 3 minutes. Gently fold whipped cream into peanut butter mixture in 2 additions until no white streaks remain. Spoon filling into crust and spread into even layer with spatula.

3. In now-empty mixer bowl, whip vanilla, remaining cream, and remaining 2 tablespoons sugar on medium-low speed until foamy, about 1 minute. Increase speed to high and whip until stiff peaks form, 1 to 3 minutes. Spread whipped cream attractively over pie. Refrigerate until set, about 2 hours. Sprinkle with remaining peanuts. Serve.

NOTES FROM THE TEST KITCHEN

ICEBOX DESSERTS
Made from layering cookies with a creamy filling and letting it rest in the refrigerator until the cookies absorbed the moisture from the filling, transforming them into a cake-like layer, recipes for icebox cakes started showing up in the 1930s with the advent of the modern-day refrigerator. The most famous recipe involved Nabisco chocolate wafers, and recipes were printed on the back of the wafer boxes. Nowadays, icebox desserts are more than just cakes. Requiring little baking (sometimes none at all if you use store-bought crust), these cool, refreshing desserts come together quickly, with very little work up front.

Cookies and Cream Ice Cream Pie
Serves 8 `MAKE AHEAD`

Why This Recipe Works When done right, cookies and cream ice cream pie conjures up childhood ice cream parlor memories. But all too often this dessert tastes stale and freezer-burned. For a fresher take, we used crushed sugar cones to make the crust, turning an ice cream cone into a plated affair. The flavor was a better match for the ice cream than the more conventional graham cracker crust, and it didn't overshadow the texture of the cookies in the pie the way a chocolate cookie crust would. Instead of using prepared cookies-and-cream ice cream, we made our own by adding our favorite crushed chocolate sandwich cookies to ice cream that we softened in a bowl with a spatula. (Leaving the container out to soften resulted in an unevenly melted mess.) We like to serve the pie with Hot Fudge Sauce (page 407) for a sundae-like effect.

12 sugar cones
5 tablespoons unsalted butter, melted
2 tablespoons sugar
2 pints vanilla ice cream
16 Oreo cookies, coarsely chopped (about 2 cups)
1 recipe Whipped Cream (page 406)

1. Adjust oven rack to middle position and heat oven to 350 degrees. Process sugar cones in food processor to fine crumbs, about 30 seconds. (You should have 1 ⅓ cups.) Transfer crumbs to bowl and stir in melted butter and sugar until crumbs are moistened. Using bottom of dry measuring cup, press crumbs evenly into bottom and up sides of plate. Bake crust until crisp, 6 to 8 minutes. Let crust cool completely on wire rack, about 30 minutes. (Crust can be wrapped in plastic wrap and frozen for up to 1 month.)

2. Scoop ice cream into large bowl and, using rubber spatula or wooden spoon, break up scoops of ice cream. Stir and fold ice cream to achieve smooth consistency. Add Oreos to bowl and mash mixture with back of spoon until well combined. Spread ice cream mixture into crust in even layer. Place plastic directly on surface of ice cream and freeze until completely frozen, at least 4 hours or up to 1 week.

3. Spread whipped cream attractively over top of pie before serving.

Coconut-Raspberry Gelato Pie

Coconut-Raspberry Gelato Pie
Serves 8   MAKE AHEAD

Why This Recipe Works Our Cookies and Cream Ice Cream Pie (page 399) is a fun cross between an ice cream cone and an ice cream sundae in sliceable form. But ice cream pie isn't just for kids; we wanted to make an easy yet sophisticated version using store-bought ingredients, for a layered ice cream pie with complex flavors. Our graham cracker crust was an easy starting point. And for a refreshing twist, we decided to use sweet-tart sorbet paired with coconut gelato for contrasting richness. We spread an even layer of sorbet into the crust followed by the gelato; mashing some fresh raspberries into the gelato before layering it into our pie allowed the two flavors to meld. Toasted and chopped macadamia nuts sprinkled on top gave a nod to the tropics and contributed crunch. You can use coconut ice cream in place of gelato, but it may be a little icy. Serve the pie with Hot Fudge Sauce (page 407), if desired. You can use the Graham Cracker Crust (page 373) or a store-bought graham cracker crust in this recipe.

1 cup raspberry sorbet
1 recipe Graham Cracker Crust (page 373), baked and cooled
1 pint coconut gelato
7½ ounces (1½ cups) raspberries, divided
½ cup macadamia nuts, toasted and chopped

1. Scoop raspberry sorbet into large bowl and, using rubber spatula or wooden spoon, break up scoops of sorbet. Stir and fold sorbet to achieve smooth consistency. Spread raspberry sorbet into crust in even layer. Transfer to freezer while making coconut layer.

2. Scoop coconut gelato into clean bowl and work with rubber spatula to soften. Stir in 1 cup raspberries, mashing mixture with spatula until well combined. Remove pie from freezer and spread gelato mixture over sorbet in even layer. Place plastic wrap directly on surface of gelato and freeze until filling is completely frozen, at least 4 hours or up to 1 week.

3. Let pie sit at room temperature for 30 minutes. Halve remaining ½ cup raspberries, then sprinkle raspberries and macadamia nuts over top of pie. Serve.

Lemon Ice

Serves 8 (Makes 1 quart) `NO COOK` `MAKE AHEAD`

Why This Recipe Works This refreshing dessert is sure to quench your thirst on a hot day. But with so few ingredients, lemon ice is regularly plagued by the harsh and unbalanced flavors that often afflict lemon desserts. The way we see it (or taste it), lemon ice should melt on the tongue with abandon, strike a perfect sweet-tart balance, and hit lots of high notes before quickly disappearing without so much as a trace of bitterness. A cup of sugar gave our lemon ice the ideal amount of sweetness; less sugar left it with a pronounced bitterness, and more sugar made it taste like frozen lemonade. Colorless, odorless, and relatively tasteless vodka was added for its anti-freezing properties—it ensured that the finished ice was soft and creamy, with a slightly slushy texture. Of course, the single most important determinant of the texture of lemon ice is the freezing method. Freezing the lemon mixture in ice cube trays and then processing the cubes in a food processor and transferring the mixture to a chilled bowl produced a fluffy, coarse-grained texture. The addition of vodka yields the best texture, but it can be omitted.

2¼ cups water
1 cup lemon juice (6 lemons)
1 cup (7 ounces) sugar
2 tablespoons vodka (optional)
⅛ teaspoon table salt

1. Whisk all ingredients together in bowl until sugar has dissolved. Pour mixture into 2 ice cube trays and freeze until solid, at least 3 hours or up to 5 days.

2. Place medium bowl in freezer. Pulse half of ice cubes in food processor until creamy and no large lumps remain, about 18 pulses. Transfer mixture to chilled bowl and return to freezer. Repeat pulsing remaining cubes; transfer to bowl. Serve immediately.

VARIATIONS
Orange Ice
Reduce lemon juice to 2 tablespoons and add ¾ cup orange juice (2 oranges). Reduce sugar to ¾ cup.

Lemon-Lime Ice
Substitute ½ cup lime juice (4 limes) for ½ cup lemon juice.

Minted Lemon Ice
Bring 1 cup water, sugar, and salt to simmer in small saucepan over medium-high heat, stirring occasionally. Off heat, stir in ½ cup fresh mint leaves, roughly torn; let steep for 5 minutes, then strain mixture through fine-mesh strainer into medium bowl. Stir in remaining 1¼ cups water, lemon juice, and vodka, if using; let cool to room temperature, about 15 minutes. Freeze as directed.

Lemon-Lavender Ice
Bring 1 cup water, sugar, and salt to simmer in small saucepan over medium-high heat, stirring occasionally. Off heat, stir in 2½ teaspoons dried lavender; let steep for 5 minutes, then strain mixture through fine-mesh strainer into medium bowl. Stir in remaining 1¼ cups water, lemon juice, and vodka, if using; let cool to room temperature, about 15 minutes. Freeze as directed.

Raspberry Sorbet

Serves 8 (Makes 1 quart) `MAKE AHEAD`

Why This Recipe Works To make a light, refreshing raspberry sorbet that was beautifully creamy and smooth, we had to avoid both the jagged, unpleasant ice crystals that often develop in homemade sorbets and the tendency toward crumbly, dull results. Finding the right balance of water and sugar was key; corn syrup helped to create a smooth texture without over-sweetening. Freezing a small amount of the base separately and then adding it back to the rest helped superchill the mix, making it freeze faster and more smoothly. We also added some pectin to bump up the raspberries' natural pectin, which helped keep the whole thing from turning into a puddle too quickly at room temperature. If using a canister-style ice cream machine, be sure to freeze the empty canister for at least 24 hours and preferably 48 hours before churning. For self-refrigerating machines, prechill the canister by running the machine for 5 to 10 minutes before pouring in the sorbet mixture. For fruit pectin we recommend both Sure-Jell for Less or No Sugar Needed Recipes and Ball RealFruit Low or No-Sugar Needed Pectin. You can use a food processor instead of a blender if you prefer.

1 cup water
1 teaspoon low- or no-sugar-needed fruit pectin
⅛ teaspoon table salt
1¼ pounds (4 cups) fresh raspberries
½ cup plus 2 tablespoons (4⅓ ounces) sugar
¼ cup light corn syrup

1. Heat water, pectin, and salt in medium saucepan over medium-high heat, stirring occasionally, until pectin has fully dissolved, about 5 minutes. Remove saucepan from heat and let mixture cool slightly, about 10 minutes.

2. Process raspberries, sugar, corn syrup, and cooled water mixture in blender until smooth, about 30 seconds. Strain mixture through fine-mesh strainer, pressing on solids to extract as much liquid as possible. Transfer 1 cup mixture to small bowl and place remaining mixture in large bowl. Cover both bowls with plastic wrap. Place large bowl in refrigerator and small bowl in freezer and chill for at least 4 hours or up to 24 hours. (Small bowl of base will freeze solid.)

3. Remove mixtures from refrigerator and freezer. Scrape frozen base from small bowl into large bowl of base. Stir occasionally until frozen base has fully dissolved. Transfer mixture to ice cream machine and churn until mixture has consistency of thick milkshake and color lightens, 15 to 25 minutes.

4. Transfer sorbet to airtight container and freeze until firm, at least 2 hours or up to 5 days. Let sorbet sit at room temperature for 5 minutes before serving.

SUPERCHILLING RASPBERRY SORBET

1. Transfer 1 cup berry puree to small bowl. Cover bowls; freeze small bowl and refrigerate large bowl for at least 4 hours or up to 1 day.

2. Scrape frozen base into large bowl. Stir until completely combined. Transfer to ice cream maker and churn until color lightens.

Chocolate Semifreddo
Serves 12 `MAKE AHEAD`

Why This Recipe Works *Semifreddo*, a classic frozen mousse–like sliced Italian dessert, is a silky, elegant treat that will wow your guests. It's rich and decadently creamy, and requires no special equipment to make—airy whipped cream gives semifreddo its signature light texture, with no churning in an ice cream maker required. Then it's frozen in a loaf pan until solid, unmolded, and cut into neat slices. But instead of being hard and densely packed, semifreddo is soft enough that

it easily caves to the pressure of a spoon. Better yet, unlike ice cream, it can sit out of the freezer for an extended period of time without melting, which makes it ideal for serving to company. Do not whip the heavy cream until the chocolate mixture has cooled. If the semifreddo is difficult to release from the pan, run a thin offset spatula around the edges of the pan or carefully run the sides of the pan under hot water for 5 to 10 seconds. If frozen more than 6 hours, the semifreddo should be tempered before serving for the best texture. To temper, place slices on individual plates or a large tray, and refrigerate for 30 minutes.

> 8 ounces bittersweet chocolate, chopped fine
> 1 tablespoon vanilla extract
> ½ teaspoon instant espresso powder
> 3 large eggs
> 5 tablespoons (2¼ ounces) sugar
> ¼ teaspoon table salt
> 2 cups heavy cream, chilled, divided
> ¼ cup water

1. Lightly spray loaf pan with vegetable oil spray and line with plastic wrap, leaving 3-inch overhang on all sides. Place chocolate in large heatproof bowl and set fine-mesh strainer over top. Combine vanilla and espresso powder in small bowl.

2. Whisk eggs, sugar, and salt in medium saucepan until combined. Whisk in ½ cup cream. Cook over medium-low heat, not letting mixture simmer, stirring constantly and scraping bottom of pot with wooden spoon, until thickened and silky and registers 160 to 165 degrees, about 5 minutes.

3. Immediately pour mixture through strainer set over chocolate. Let mixture sit to melt chocolate, about 5 minutes. Whisk until chocolate is melted and smooth, then whisk in vanilla-espresso mixture. Let chocolate mixture cool completely, about 15 minutes.

4. Using stand mixer fitted with whisk attachment, beat remaining 1½ cups cream on medium-low speed until foamy, about 1 minute. Increase speed to high and whip until soft peaks form, 1 to 3 minutes.

5. Whisk one-third of whipped cream into chocolate mixture. Using rubber spatula, gently fold remaining whipped cream into chocolate mixture until incorporated and no streaks of whipped cream remain. Transfer mixture to prepared pan and spread evenly with rubber spatula. Fold overhanging plastic over surface. Freeze until firm, at least 6 hours or up to 2 weeks.

6. When ready to serve, remove plastic from surface and invert pan onto serving platter. Remove plastic and smooth surface with spatula as necessary. Dip slicing knife in very hot water and wipe dry. Slice semifreddo ¾ inch thick, transferring slices to individual plates and dipping and wiping knife after each slice. Serve immediately.

Vanilla No-Churn Ice Cream
Serves 8 (Makes about 1 quart)

`NO COOK` `MAKE AHEAD`

Why This Recipe Works With little more than a blender and some basic pantry ingredients, you can have velvety, creamy, scoopable ice cream. Whipping heavy cream in a blender incorporated air in a way that mimicked the effect of churning in an ice cream maker. We added sweetened condensed milk and corn syrup (to keep the ice cream soft) and a hefty 1 tablespoon of vanilla extract and a bit of salt (to enhance the flavor), which produced an intense vanilla ice cream in about a minute of work. Then, we just popped the blended mixture in the freezer and waited. The cream mixture freezes more quickly in a loaf pan than in a taller, narrower container. If you don't have a loaf pan, use an 8-inch square baking pan.

2	cups heavy cream, chilled
1	cup sweetened condensed milk
¼	cup whole milk
¼	cup light corn syrup
2	tablespoons sugar
1	tablespoon vanilla extract
¼	teaspoon table salt

1. Process cream in blender until soft peaks form, 20 to 30 seconds. Scrape down sides of blender jar and continue to process until stiff peaks form, about 10 seconds. Using rubber spatula, stir in condensed milk, whole milk, corn syrup, sugar, vanilla, and salt. Process until thoroughly combined, about 20 seconds, scraping down sides of blender jar as needed.

2. Pour cream mixture into 8½ by 4½-inch loaf pan. Press plastic wrap flush against surface of cream mixture. Freeze until firm, at least 6 hours or up to 5 days. Serve.

VARIATIONS
Dark Chocolate No-Churn Ice Cream
Decrease vanilla to 1 teaspoon. Add 6 ounces melted bittersweet chocolate and ½ teaspoon instant espresso powder with condensed milk.

Mint Cookie No-Churn Ice Cream

Birthday Cake No-Churn Ice Cream
Decrease vanilla to 2 teaspoons. Add ½ cup store-bought vanilla frosting and ⅛ teaspoon yellow food coloring with condensed milk. After transferring cream mixture to loaf pan, gently stir in 2 tablespoons rainbow sprinkles before freezing.

Strawberry Buttermilk No-Churn Ice Cream
Substitute ½ cup buttermilk for whole milk and 1 teaspoon lemon juice for vanilla. After transferring cream mixture to loaf pan, dollop ⅓ cup strawberry jam over top. Swirl jam into cream mixture using tines of fork before freezing.

Mint Cookie No-Churn Ice Cream
Substitute ¾ teaspoon peppermint extract for vanilla. Add ⅛ teaspoon green food coloring with condensed milk. After transferring cream mixture to loaf pan, gently stir in ½ cup coarsely crushed Oreo cookies before freezing.

Foolproof Vanilla Ice Cream

Pistachio Gelato

Foolproof Vanilla Ice Cream
Serves 8 (Makes about 1 quart) MAKE AHEAD

Why This Recipe Works While we love the ease of our No-Churn Ice Cream, there's nothing quite like a traditional custard-based homemade ice cream—thick, rich, and luxuriously creamy, it's a bit of a project with an elegant payoff. Our main discovery in the test kitchen was that the quicker the ice cream freezes, the smoother and creamier the results. So, we took a two-pronged approach. First, we supplemented the sugar with corn syrup, which ensured a faster freezing time, and second, we used the same superchilling method as our Raspberry Sorbet (page 401), freezing a small amount of the base separately and then adding it back into the rest before churning. The result was an ice cream that remained hard at home-freezer temperatures, and was devoid of large ice crystals. If using a canister-style ice cream machine, be sure to freeze the empty canister for at least 24 hours or preferably 48 hours before churning. For self-refrigerating ice cream machines, prechill the canister by running the machine for 5 to 10 minutes before pouring in the custard.

1 vanilla bean
1¾ cups heavy cream
1¼ cups whole milk
½ cup plus 2 tablespoons (3½ ounces) sugar, divided
⅓ cup light corn syrup
¼ teaspoon table salt
6 large egg yolks

1. Place 8- or 9-inch square baking pan in freezer. Cut vanilla bean in half lengthwise. Using tip of paring knife, scrape out seeds. Combine vanilla bean and seeds, cream, milk, 6 tablespoons sugar, corn syrup, and salt in medium saucepan. Heat over medium-high heat, stirring occasionally, until mixture is steaming steadily and registers 175 degrees, 5 to 10 minutes. Remove saucepan from heat.

2. While cream mixture heats, whisk egg yolks and remaining ¼ cup sugar in bowl until smooth, about 30 seconds. Slowly whisk 1 cup heated cream mixture into egg yolk mixture. Return mixture to saucepan and cook over medium-low heat, stirring constantly, until mixture thickens and registers 180 degrees, 7 to 14 minutes. Immediately pour custard into large bowl and let cool until no longer steaming, 10 to 20 minutes. Transfer 1 cup custard to small bowl. Cover both bowls with plastic wrap. Place large bowl in refrigerator and small bowl in freezer and let cool completely, at least 4 hours or up to 24 hours. (Small bowl of custard will freeze solid.)

3. Remove custards from refrigerator and freezer. Scrape frozen custard from small bowl into large bowl of custard. Stir occasionally until frozen custard has fully dissolved.

Strain custard through fine-mesh strainer and transfer to ice cream machine. Churn until mixture resembles thick soft-serve ice cream and registers about 21 degrees, 15 to 25 minutes. Transfer ice cream to frozen baking pan and press plastic on surface. Return to freezer until firm around edges, about 1 hour.

4. Transfer ice cream to airtight container, pressing firmly to remove any air pockets, and freeze until firm, at least 2 hours or up to 5 days. Serve.

VARIATIONS
Foolproof Triple Ginger Ice Cream
Freeze the crystallized ginger for at least 15 minutes before adding it to the churning ice cream.

Substitute one 3-inch piece fresh ginger, peeled and sliced into thin rounds, and 2 teaspoons ground ginger for vanilla bean. Add ½ cup chopped crystallized ginger to ice cream during last minute of churning.

Foolproof Coffee Crunch Ice Cream
Look for chocolate-covered cacao nibs (roasted pieces of the cacao bean) in chocolate shops or well-stocked supermarkets. Freeze the cacao nibs for at least 15 minutes before adding them to the churning ice cream.

Substitute ½ cup coarsely ground coffee for vanilla bean. Add ¾ cup chocolate-covered cacao nibs to ice cream during last minute of churning.

Pistachio Gelato
Serves 8 (Makes about 1 quart) `MAKE AHEAD`

Why This Recipe Works Gelato is the Italian version of ice cream, and is its luxurious, more grown-up cousin. We wanted to make a nutty, elegant treat that was quintessentially Italian, so we turned to buttery pistachios. Many recipes call for pistachio paste, a challenging-to-find specialty Sicilian product made from sweetened ground pistachios and oil. While pistachio paste is generally delicious and intensely flavored, we found that the percentages of sugar and fat varied from brand to brand, which would affect the texture of the gelato. Instead, we turned to raw pistachios. Grinding the nuts and steeping them in the warmed milk and cream released their volatile oils and deeply flavored the base, and straining the solids through cheesecloth ensured a velvety smooth texture. The gelato stayed within the ideal temperature range for up to 6 hours of freezing time, but after that we needed to temper the frozen gelato in the refrigerator until it warmed to the ideal serving temperature of 10 to 15 degrees for a creamy, intensely pistachio-flavored treat, perfect for bringing sunny Sicilian afternoons home. If using a canister-style ice cream maker, be sure to freeze the empty canister for at least 24 hours and preferably for 48 hours before churning. For self-refrigerating ice cream makers, prechill the canister by running the machine for 5 to 10 minutes before pouring in the custard.

2½ cups (11¼ ounces) shelled pistachios
3¾ cups whole milk, divided
¾ cup (5¼ ounces) sugar
⅓ cup heavy cream
⅓ cup light corn syrup
¼ teaspoon table salt
5 teaspoons cornstarch
5 large egg yolks

1. Process pistachios in food processor until finely ground, about 20 seconds. Combine 3½ cups milk, sugar, cream, corn syrup, and salt in large saucepan. Cook, stirring frequently, over medium-high heat until tiny bubbles form around edge of saucepan, 5 to 7 minutes. Off heat, stir in pistachios, cover, and let steep for 1 hour.

2. Line fine-mesh strainer with triple layer of cheesecloth that overhangs edges and set over large bowl. Transfer pistachio mixture to prepared strainer and press to extract as much liquid as possible. Gather sides of cheesecloth around pistachio pulp and gently squeeze remaining liquid into bowl; discard spent pulp.

3. Whisk cornstarch and remaining ¼ cup milk together in small bowl; set aside. Return pistachio-milk mixture to clean saucepan. Whisk in egg yolks until combined. Bring custard to gentle simmer over medium heat and cook, stirring occasionally and scraping bottom of saucepan with rubber spatula, until custard registers 190 degrees, 4 to 6 minutes.

4. Whisk cornstarch mixture to recombine, then whisk into custard. Cook, stirring constantly, until custard thickens, about 30 seconds. Immediately pour custard into bowl and let cool until no longer steaming, about 20 minutes.

5. Cover with plastic wrap and refrigerate for at least 6 hours or up to 24 hours.

6. Whisk custard to recombine, then transfer to ice cream maker and churn until mixture resembles thick soft-serve ice cream and registers 21 degrees, 15 to 30 minutes. Transfer gelato to airtight container, pressing firmly to remove any air pockets, and freeze until firm, at least 6 hours or up to 5 days. Serve. (If frozen for longer than 6 hours, let gelato sit in refrigerator for 1 to 2 hours until it registers 10 to 15 degrees before serving.)

Ice Cream Sundae Bar

While we'll never say no to a classic cone, there's nothing quite as decadent as an ice cream sundae. And it's an easy-to-assemble dessert that you can whip together for your guests—just set out bowls of ice cream, your favorite toppings, and spoons, and let your friends and family create their own special treats.

Whipped Cream
Makes about 2 cups

Light and airy whipped cream is the quintessential finish to an ice cream sundae. Whipping the ingredients on medium-low speed to start ensured that the sugar, vanilla, and salt were evenly dispersed in the cream before we increased the mixer speed to achieve soft peaks (our preference for a decadent dollop).

- 1 cup heavy cream, chilled
- 1 tablespoon sugar
- 1 teaspoon vanilla extract
- Pinch table salt

Using stand mixer fitted with whisk attachment, whip cream, sugar, vanilla, and salt on medium-low speed until foamy, about 1 minute. Increase speed to high and whip until soft peaks form, 1 to 3 minutes. (Whipped cream can be refrigerated in fine-mesh strainer set over small bowl and covered with plastic wrap for up to 8 hours.)

VARIATIONS
Half-Batch Whipped Cream
Makes about 1 cup

Halve all ingredients. (Whipped cream can be refrigerated in fine-mesh strainer set over small bowl and covered with plastic wrap for up to 8 hours.)

Double-Batch Whipped Cream
Makes about 4 cups

Double all ingredients. (Whipped cream can be refrigerated in fine-mesh strainer set over small bowl and covered with plastic wrap for up to 8 hours.)

Hot Fudge Sauce

Makes about 2 cups

Intense and complex, a luxurious chocolate sauce can transform a simple scoop of ice cream into a decadent dessert. Our classic hot fudge sauce relies on cocoa powder and unsweetened chocolate for complexity and richness. We used milk rather than cream to help preserve the intense chocolate flavor; butter imparted an attractive sheen.

1¼ cups (8¾ ounces) sugar
⅔ cup whole milk
¼ teaspoon table salt
⅓ cup (1 ounce) unsweetened cocoa powder, sifted
3 ounces unsweetened chocolate, chopped fine
4 tablespoons unsalted butter, cut into 8 pieces and chilled
1 teaspoon vanilla extract

1. Heat sugar, milk, and salt in medium saucepan over medium-low heat, whisking gently, until sugar has dissolved and liquid starts to bubble around edges of saucepan, about 6 minutes. Reduce heat to low, add cocoa, and whisk until smooth.

2. Off heat, stir in chocolate and let sit for 3 minutes. Whisk sauce until smooth and chocolate is fully melted. Whisk in butter and vanilla until fully incorporated and sauce thickens slightly. (Sauce can be refrigerated for up to 1 month; gently warm in microwave, stirring every 10 seconds, until pourable, before using.)

Easy Caramel Sauce

Makes about 1½ cups

When taking the temperature of the caramel in step 1, tilt the saucepan and move the thermometer back and forth to equalize hot and cool spots.

1¾ cups (12¼ ounces) sugar
½ cup water
¼ cup light corn syrup
1 cup heavy cream
1 teaspoon vanilla extract
¼ teaspoon salt

1. Bring sugar, water, and corn syrup to boil in large saucepan over medium-high heat. Cook, without stirring, until mixture is straw-colored, 6 to 8 minutes. Reduce heat to low and continue to cook, swirling saucepan occasionally, until caramel is amber-colored, 2 to 5 minutes. (Caramel will register between 360 and 370 degrees.)

2. Off heat, carefully stir in cream, vanilla, and salt; mixture will bubble and steam. Continue to stir until sauce is smooth. Let cool slightly. (Sauce can be refrigerated for up to 2 weeks; gently warm in microwave, stirring every 10 seconds, until pourable, before using.)

Peanut Butter Sauce

Makes 2 cups

1 cup (7 ounces) sugar
¾ cup evaporated milk
8 tablespoons unsalted butter
½ cup creamy peanut butter
1 teaspoon vanilla extract
⅛ teaspoon table salt

Bring sugar, milk, butter, peanut butter, vanilla, and salt to simmer in medium saucepan over medium heat. Reduce heat to low and cook, stirring often, until sauce is smooth and thick, about 3 minutes. Serve warm. (Sauce can be refrigerated for up to 1 week; gently warm in microwave, stirring every 10 seconds, until pourable, before using.)

Magic Chocolate Shell

Makes about ¾ cup

This sauce is meant to be served over ice cream; the cold ice cream causes the sauce to solidify into a thin shell almost like (dare we say it!) magic.

¼ teaspoon vanilla extract
⅛ teaspoon instant espresso powder
Pinch table salt
4 ounces semisweet chocolate, chopped fine
⅓ cup coconut oil
1 teaspoon unsweetened cocoa powder

Stir vanilla, espresso powder, and salt in small bowl until espresso dissolves. Microwave chocolate and coconut oil in medium bowl at 50 percent power, stirring occasionally, until melted, 2 to 4 minutes. Whisk in vanilla mixture and cocoa until combined. Let cool to room temperature, about 30 minutes, before using. (Sauce can be stored at room temperature in airtight container for up to 2 months; gently warm in microwave, stirring every 10 seconds, until pourable but not hot, before using.)

Vegan Coconut Ice Cream
Serves 8 (Makes 1 quart) `MAKE AHEAD`

Why This Recipe Works Developing a recipe for ice cream without milk, cream, or eggs seemed like a tall order, but we were determined to make a thick, creamy vegan frozen treat with the dense texture of the premium ice creams we love. Using canned coconut milk as the base gave us clean coconut flavor and silky texture. In addition to sugar, we added corn syrup, which interfered with ice crystal formation. Including cornstarch also prevented ice crystal formation and acted as a stabilizer. But tasters noticed a persistent grainy, starchy texture, from unemulsified bits of fat. The solution? We blended the hot mixture after cooking, so the fat became fully emulsified. We prefer to make this recipe in a canister-style ice cream maker; the ice cream was grainy when made in self-refrigerating models. Be sure to freeze the empty canister for at least 24 hours and preferably for 48 hours before churning. Make sure your blender is only two-thirds full or less, open the lid vent, and hold in place with a dish towel in step 2. Do not use light canned coconut milk in this recipe.

2 (14-ounce) cans coconut milk, divided
2 tablespoons cornstarch
½ cup (3½ ounces) sugar
¼ cup light corn syrup
1 teaspoon vanilla extract
¼ teaspoon table salt

1. Shake unopened cans of coconut milk to form homogeneous mixture. Whisk ¼ cup coconut milk and cornstarch together in small bowl and set aside. Combine remaining coconut milk, sugar, corn syrup, vanilla, and salt in large saucepan. Cook over medium-high heat, whisking often to dissolve sugar, until small bubbles form around edge of saucepan and mixture registers 190 degrees, 5 to 7 minutes. Reduce heat to medium. Whisk cornstarch mixture to recombine, then whisk into coconut milk mixture in pan. Cook, constantly scraping bottom of pan with rubber spatula, until thickened slightly, about 30 seconds.

2. Carefully transfer mixture to blender, let cool slightly, about 1 minute, then process on high speed for 1 minute. Pour ice cream base into large bowl and let cool until no longer steaming, about 20 minutes. Cover with plastic wrap and refrigerate for at least 6 hours or up to 24 hours.

3. Whisk chilled ice cream base until recombined and smooth, then transfer to ice cream machine and churn until mixture has consistency of soft-serve ice cream and registers 21 degrees. Transfer to airtight container, cover, and freeze until firm, at least 6 hours or up to 2 weeks. Serve.

VARIATIONS
Vegan Coconut Horchata Ice Cream
Add ¾ teaspoon ground cinnamon and ⅛ teaspoon ground cloves to coconut milk mixture in saucepan before cooking in step 1. Serve topped with toasted sliced almonds.

Vegan Coconut Lime Ice Cream
Substitute 1 tablespoon lime juice for vanilla extract. Add 2 teaspoons grated lime zest to coconut milk mixture with lime juice in step 1.

Frozen Yogurt
Serves 8 (Makes about 1 quart) `MAKE AHEAD`

Why This Recipe Works Fro yo experienced a resurgence in popularity in the early aughts, but we think it's more than just a flash in the . . . freezer. For a frozen yogurt that would be dense and creamy—not icy and rock-hard like most versions—the key was controlling the water in the base to minimize the number of large ice crystals that formed during freezing. Since Greek yogurt is strained of excess liquid during processing, it seemed like a logical starting point, but it produced a chalky frozen yogurt. We got much creamier results when we used plain whole-milk yogurt that we strained ourselves. We also found that using Lyle's Golden Syrup in addition to the granulated sugar played an important role in reducing ice crystals, as did dissolving and heating just 1 teaspoon of gelatin in a portion of the strained whey. Together, these techniques delivered a frozen yogurt that was scoopable straight from the freezer. This recipe requires draining the yogurt for 8 to 12 hours. We prefer the flavor and texture that Lyle's Golden Syrup lends this frozen yogurt, but if you can't find it, you can substitute light corn syrup. You can substitute low-fat yogurt for whole-milk yogurt, but the results will be less creamy and flavorful.

1 quart plain whole-milk yogurt
1 teaspoon unflavored gelatin
¾ cup (5¼ ounces) sugar
3 tablespoons Lyle's Golden Syrup
⅛ teaspoon table salt

1. Line colander or fine-mesh strainer with triple layer of cheesecloth and place over large bowl or measuring cup. Place yogurt in colander, cover with plastic wrap (plastic should not touch yogurt), and refrigerate until 1¼ cups whey has drained from yogurt, at least 8 hours or up to 12 hours. (If more than 1¼ cups whey drains from yogurt, simply stir extra back into yogurt.)

2. Discard ¾ cup drained whey. Sprinkle gelatin over remaining ½ cup whey in bowl and let sit until gelatin softens, about 5 minutes. Microwave until mixture is bubbling around edges and gelatin dissolves, about 30 seconds. Let cool for 5 minutes. In large bowl, whisk sugar, syrup, salt, drained yogurt, and cooled whey-gelatin mixture until sugar is completely dissolved. Cover and refrigerate (or place bowl over ice bath) until yogurt mixture registers 40 degrees or less.

3. Churn yogurt mixture in ice cream maker until mixture resembles thick soft-serve frozen yogurt and registers about 21 degrees, 25 to 35 minutes. Transfer frozen yogurt to airtight container and freeze until firm, at least 2 hours or up to 5 days. Serve.

VARIATIONS
Ginger Frozen Yogurt
Stir 1 tablespoon grated fresh ginger and 1 teaspoon ground ginger into whey-gelatin mixture as soon as it is removed from microwave. After mixture has cooled for 5 minutes, strain through fine-mesh strainer, pressing on solids to extract all liquid. Proceed with recipe as directed.

Orange Frozen Yogurt
Substitute ½ cup orange juice for ½ cup whey in step 2. Stir ½ teaspoon grated orange zest into orange juice–gelatin mixture as soon as it is removed from microwave.

Strawberry Frozen Yogurt
Substitute ¾ cup strawberry puree for ½ cup whey in step 2.

Vegan Coconut Ice Cream

Strawberry Frozen Yogurt

Nutritional Information for Our Recipes

We calculate the nutritional values of our recipes per serving; if there is a range in the serving size, we used the highest number of servings to calculate the nutritional values. We entered all the ingredients, using weights for important ingredients such as most vegetables. We also used our preferred brands in these analyses. We did not include additional salt or pepper for food that's "seasoned to taste."

	Calories	Total Fat (G)	Sat Fat (G)	Chol (MG)	Sodium (MG)	Total Carb (G)	Dietary Fiber (G)	Total Sugars (G)	Protein (G)
SMALL BITES									
Hummus	140	10	1.5	0	160	9	2	0	4
Butterbean and Pea Dip with Mint	97	2	1	1	210	15	4	1	6
Beet Muhammara	150	12	1.5	0	330	9	2	6	2
Baba Ghanoush	80	6	1	0	220	8	3	4	2
Caponata	90	4.5	0.5	0	150	12	3	17	2
Tzatziki	20	1.5	1	0	40	1	0	2	1
Tabbouleh	190	14	2	0	210	14	3	2	3
Whipped Feta Dip	109	10	5	26	263	2	0	1	4
Pita Chips	181	14	2	0	102	13	2	0	2
Marinated Olives	170	18	2	0	510	3	1	0	0
Quick Pickled Carrots	10	0	0	0	20	3	1	1	0
Fig-Balsamic Jam	80	0	0	0	15	19	1	1	0
Cheese Straws	200	13	6	5	400	20	1	1	7
Prosciutto-Wrapped Figs with Gorgonzola	130	4.5	2	25	680	18	2	15	8
Caprese Skewers	120	11	4	15	70	1	0	1	4
Blistered Shishito Peppers	136	6	1	0	8	24	10	0	4
Bruschetta with Arugula Pesto and Goat Cheese Topping	240	14	2.5	5	420	24	1	4	6
Serrano and Manchego Crostini with Orange Honey	210	7	4	20	640	25	0	9	12
Baguette with Radishes, Butter, and Herbs	120	11	6	25	90	6	1	1	1
Chicken Satay with Spicy Peanut Dipping Sauce	190	10	1.5	45	450	9	1	7	16
Peruvian Fish Ceviche with Radishes and Orange	324	20	3	28	568	19	5	7	21
Grilled Clams, Mussels, or Oysters with Mignonette Sauce	70	1	0	25	460	4	0	1	10
Smoked Salmon Rolls	80	3.5	1	15	400	1	0	0	10
Broiled Coriander-Lemon Shrimp	180	16	2.5	90	730	1	0	0	9
Mexican Shrimp Cocktail (Cóctel de Camarón)	166	6	1	119	832	15	3	8	15
Vietnamese Summer Rolls	604	21	4	98	771	76	5	8	28
Vietnamese Dipping Sauce (Nuoc Cham)	54	0	0	0	1770	13	0	11	1

	Calories	Total Fat (G)	Sat Fat (G)	Chol (MG)	Sodium (MG)	Total Carb (G)	Dietary Fiber (G)	Total Sugars (G)	Protein (G)
SMALL BITES (cont.)									
Chilled Cucumber and Yogurt Soup	150	9	7	15	620	9	2	7	8
Gazpacho	75	4	1	0	494	9	2	6	2
Herbed Croutons	69	3	1	5	99	9	1	1	2
DINNER-SIZE SALADS									
Chicken Salad with Pickled Fennel, Watercress, and Macadamia Nuts	280	16	2.5	85	290	5	2	2	28
Chicken and Arugula Salad with Figs and Warm Spices	440	24	3	85	460	26	6	14	31
Shredded Cooked Chicken	100	2	0	60	110	0	0	0	19
Classic Vinaigrette	100	11	1.5	0	90	0	0	0	0
Lemon Vinaigrette	100	11	1.5	0	90	0	0	0	0
Balsamic-Mustard Vinaigrette	110	11	1.5	0	140	1	0	1	0
Tahini-Lemon Vinaigrette	90	9	1.5	0	150	1	0	0	1
Green Goddess Dressing	223	24	4	17	197	1	0	0	1
Parmesan-Peppercorn Dressing	35	3	0.5	5	70	0	0	0	1
Chicken Salad with Whole-Grain Mustard Vinaigrette	364	24	5	73	572	13	3	10	26
Moroccan Chicken Salad with Apricots and Almonds	580	36	5	85	490	32	6	20	32
Kale Caesar Salad with Chicken	510	32	6	75	930	25	2	2	29
Beet and Carrot Noodle Salad with Chicken	420	21	3.5	60	860	35	8	20	28
Asian Chicken and Cellophane Noodle Salad	512	22	4	53	1255	54	4	6	24
Wedge Salad with Steak Tips	540	35	15	155	990	7	1	5	46
Arugula Salad with Steak Tips and Gorgonzola	570	46	16	115	1130	8	2	4	35
Steak Taco Salad	650	36	13	99	1343	45	15	8	43
Grilled Steak and Vegetable Salad	538	40	13	126	981	11	3	7	32
Grilled Thai Beef Salad	120	3	1	23	505	14	4	5	10
Bistro Salad with Fried Egg	413	39	11	225	509	5	2	2	15
Bitter Greens and Fig Salad with Warm Shallot Dressing	646	26	5	22	897	43	8	27	15
Smoked Salmon Niçoise Salad	342	17	7	219	953	28	5	5	22
Easy-Peel Hard-Cooked Eggs	71	5	2	186	71	0	0	0	6
Mediterranean Couscous Salad with Smoked Trout	360	16	2.5	30	950	37	3	1	17
Seared Tuna Salad with Olive Dressing	310	15	2	40	540	12	3	3	29
Fennel and Bibb Salad with Scallops and Hazelnuts	430	31	4	40	1180	15	4	4	24
Shrimp and White Bean Salad with Garlic Toasts	510	19	3	145	1490	55	8	6	29
Mediterranean Chopped Salad	367	21	6	25	912	34	10	10	14
Vegetarian Cobb Salad	591	36	7	377	919	44	12	9	26
Marinated Tofu and Vegetable Salad	360	22	3	0	510	22	2	13	21

	Calories	Total Fat (G)	Sat Fat (G)	Chol (MG)	Sodium (MG)	Total Carb (G)	Dietary Fiber (G)	Total Sugars (G)	Protein (G)
DINNER-SIZE SALADS (cont.)									
Fattoush	315	25	3	0	632	23	4	5	4
Tomato and Burrata Salad with Pangrattato and Basil	300	24	7	25	400	15	2	6	10
Salad with Pickled Tomatillos, Sun-Dried Tomatoes, and Goat Cheese	100	7	2	5	260	7	2	3	4
Farro Salad with Sugar Snap Peas and White Beans	310	9	1	0	460	50	8	6	11
Quinoa Taco Salad	420	22	3.5	5	740	45	13	5	14
Bulgur Salad with Chickpeas, Spinach, and Za'atar	200	8	1	0	410	28	5	2	5
Pearl Couscous Salad with Radishes and Watercress	440	20	4.5	10	370	52	2	2	14
Wheat Berry and Endive Salad with Blueberries and Goat Cheese	450	28	5	10	250	43	9	4	11
Egyptian Barley Salad	263	10	3	9	206	39	8	10	7
Brown Rice Salad with Jalapeños, Tomatoes, and Avocado	280	13	1.5	0	200	44	6	4	5
Chilled Soba Noodle Salad with Cucumber, Snow Peas, and Radishes	350	10	1	0	380	56	1	10	9
BURGERS, SANDWICHES, AND TACOS									
Classic Beef Burgers	493	28	10	116	496	21	1	3	36
Well-Done Burgers	480	37	13	120	450	4	0	1	30
Grilled Bacon Burgers with Caramelized Onions and Blue Cheese	837	58	23	175	1032	25	1	5	49
Classic Turkey Burgers	443	23	8	133	527	22	1	3	38
Buffalo Chicken Burgers	596	33	14	187	565	30	2	9	38
Grilled Harissa Lamb Burgers	719	53	19	128	378	25	2	4	33
Crispy Salmon Burgers with Tomato Chutney	405	13	2	78	722	38	3	10	35
Grilled Tuna Burgers with Wasabi and Pickled Ginger	371	26	4	57	578	4	2	1	30
South Carolina Shrimp Burgers	751	53	7	234	1599	37	2	5	29
Tartar Sauce	140	15	2.5	5	190	0	0	0	0
Southwestern Black Bean Burgers	637	21	4	62	457	87	16	5	27
Classic Burger Sauce	114	11	2	6	162	4	0	3	0
Pub-Style Burger Sauce	161	17	2	8	366	2	0	2	0
Chipotle Sauce	120	12	2.5	10	110	1	0	1	0
Sautéed Mushroom Topping	104	9	5	23	147	4	1	2	1
Crispy Bacon	180	17	6	30	280	1	0	0	5
Vegan Pinto Bean and Beet Burgers	451	15	1	0	380	65	10	7	15
Grilled Portobello Burgers with Goat Cheese and Arugula	282	16	3	7	349	26	2	5	8
Chicken Avocado Salad Sandwiches	412	42	10	145	1216	39	7	8	45
Curried Chicken Salad with Cashews	459	26	4	140	208	13	1	7	44
Chicken Caesar Salad Wraps	530	34	6	115	570	17	0	3	37

	Calories	Total Fat (G)	Sat Fat (G)	Chol (MG)	Sodium (MG)	Total Carb (G)	Dietary Fiber (G)	Total Sugars (G)	Protein (G)
BURGERS, SANDWICHES, AND TACOS (cont.)									
Grilled Steak Sandwiches	869	68	16	96	914	34	2	2	30
Tuna Niçoise Salad Sandwiches	340	17	3	130	690	17	1	1	26
Crispy Fish Sandwiches	730	35	7	115	1320	74	1	8	27
Shrimp Po' Boys	1000	51	8	305	1750	102	2	12	34
New England Lobster Rolls	244	10	4	108	561	21	1	3	17
Tomato Sandwiches	467	34	5	11	499	33	4	6	7
Avocado Toast	330	23	3	0	390	28	8	2	5
Israeli Eggplant and Egg Sandwiches	640	36	7	280	2120	58	13	7	27
Tahini-Yogurt Sauce	80	6	1.5	0	230	3	0	0	3
Roasted Eggplant and Mozzarella Panini	486	30	9	38	723	40	7	10	17
French Summer Sandwiches with Zucchini and Olive Tapenade	350	27	7	15	680	19	1	3	9
Philly-Style Broccoli Rabe, Portobello, and Cheese Sandwich	440	27	11	50	1380	23	4	9	22
Tofu Banh Mi	580	29	3.5	5	1000	66	1	11	18
Chickepea Salad Sandwiches	340	17	2	0	790	37	3	5	11
Crispy Falafel Pitas	360	19	3	55	1180	37	4	5	11
Easy Chipotle Chicken Tacos	500	16	6	145	160	46	0	8	43
Mexican Crema	90	10	2	10	75	1	0	1	0
Avocado Crema	20	2	0	0	0	1	1	0	0
Quick Pickled Shallot and Radishes	30	0	0	0	150	8	1	4	1
Quick Pickled Red Onions	88	0	0	0	148	20	1	18	0
Pickled Onion and Cabbage	30	0	0	0	200	7	1	4	1
Grilled Chicken Tacos with Salsa Verde	507	13	2	199	1035	31	6	5	65
Grilled Skirt Steak and Poblano Tacos	560	23	7	100	900	55	1	11	37
Baja Fish Tacos	640	27	4	80	1070	64	1	10	34
Grilled Fish Tacos	606	25	4	100	1228	64	11	20	37
Salmon Tacos with Avocado Crema	650	33	6	95	750	50	5	7	41
Soft Corn Tacos with Sweet Potatoes, Poblano, and Corn	740	42	8	30	880	87	6	17	13
MAINS INSPIRED BY THE FARMERS' MARKET									
Asparagus and Goat Cheese Tart	420	31	13	15	500	32	3	2	11
Stir-Fried Shrimp and Broccoli	214	9	1	143	1147	14	3	3	19
Everyday White Rice	210	0	0	0	0	48	0	0	5
Roasted Salmon and Broccoli Rabe with Pistachio Gremolata	630	44	9	125	610	6	4	1	52
Whole Romanesco with Berbere and Tahini-Yogurt Sauce	300	25	12	50	230	16	5	6	7
Cauliflower Steaks with Salsa Verde	320	29	4.5	0	500	14	6	5	5
Roast Chicken with Cauliflower and Tomatoes	650	44	10	205	860	22	7	9	43
Steak Tips with Spicy Cauliflower	698	50	16	177	1129	13	5	5	50

	Calories	Total Fat (G)	Sat Fat (G)	Chol (MG)	Sodium (MG)	Total Carb (G)	Dietary Fiber (G)	Total Sugars (G)	Protein (G)
MAINS INSPIRED BY THE FARMERS' MARKET (cont.)									
Chorizo, Corn, and Tomato Tostadas with Lime Crema	850	49	20	90	1760	73	8	12	30
Creamy Corn Bucatini with Ricotta and Basil	400	8	3	15	350	69	4	7	17
Spice-Rubbed Pork Chops with Corn, Summer Squash, and Poblano Sauté	330	15	3	75	400	18	3	7	34
Orecchiette with Baby Dandelion Greens in Lemony Cream Sauce	550	28	14	65	640	61	4	3	17
Classic Stir-Fried Eggplant	200	11	1	0	500	20	5	9	4
Braised Eggplant with Paprika, Coriander, and Yogurt	190	12	1	3	637	20	9	12	4
Eggplant Involtini	320	21	5	20	860	23	8	11	11
Stuffed Eggplant with Bulgur	310	15	4	15	680	39	12	14	11
Whole-Wheat Pasta with Italian Sausage and Fennel	480	22	3	10	720	53	10	4	18
Braised Halibut with Fennel and Tarragon	460	20	12	143	1084	23	7	11	41
Teriyaki Stir-Fried Garlic Scapes with Chicken	340	18	2.5	85	690	14	2	4	29
Stir-Fried Sichuan Green Beans	206	15	3	20	465	12	4	5	8
Pearl Couscous with Clams, Leeks, and Tomatoes	670	8	3	60	1220	106	4	12	34
Thai-Style Chicken Salad Lettuce Wraps	225	4	1	97	610	16	2	12	32
Korean Sizzling Beef Lettuce Wraps	550	39	12	120	1100	12	2	9	35
Nettle Soup	230	16	9	35	490	14	2	2	7
Madras Okra Curry	260	22	8	0	320	14	4	4	5
Eggs Pipérade	240	16	3.5	280	770	11	3	6	11
Pepper and Onion Frittata with Arugula Salad	411	31	9	569	673	9	2	5	23
Pasta with Pesto, Potatoes, and Green Beans	587	26	6	13	584	75	6	5	15
Roasted Chicken with Radishes, Spinach, and Bacon	640	42	12	240	960	6	3	2	56
Pan-Roasted Cod with Amarillo Sauce	300	9	1	75	800	18	2	4	34
Tomatillo and Pinto Bean Nachos	710	46	15	60	1260	56	11	7	24
Fresh Tomato Soup with Basil	160	8	1	0	310	21	6	13	5
Pan-Seared Shrimp with Tomatoes and Avocado	260	16	2	160	1030	12	5	4	20
Fresh Tomato Galette	442	31	17	101	532	31	3	4	12
Penne with Garden Vegetable Sauce	420	11	1.5	0	830	70	3	9	13
One-Pan Pork Tenderloin and Panzanella Salad	551	26	5	109	893	38	3	9	42
Red Curry Noodles with Shrimp, Summer Squash, and Bell Peppers	680	25	12	145	1440	92	4	9	23
Skillet Summer Vegetable Lasagna	440	15	6	25	1040	59	1	9	18
Summer Vegetable Gratin	188	13	3	5	617	15	4	8	6
Pan-Seared Skirt Steak with Zucchini and Scallion Sauce	605	49	12	109	848	7	3	3	36

	Calories	Total Fat (G)	Sat Fat (G)	Chol (MG)	Sodium (MG)	Total Carb (G)	Dietary Fiber (G)	Total Sugars (G)	Protein (G)
MAINS INSPIRED BY THE FARMERS' MARKET (cont.)									
Cod Baked in Foil with Zucchini and Tomatoes	302	9	1	99	1027	9	3	5	43
Vegetable and Orzo Tian	360	11	4	15	870	50	3	8	19
Zucchini Noodles with Roasted Tomatoes and Cream Sauce	610	43	21	90	1320	45	5	14	16
Soupe au Pistou	298	16	3	3	1049	30	7	4	10
KEEP COOL WITH COUNTERTOP COOKING									
Slow-Cooker Thai Chicken with Asparagus and Mushrooms	540	23	13	200	1690	14	2	5	67
Slow-Cooker Lemony Chicken and Rice with Spinach and Feta	926	50	14	247	1234	67	2	3	49
Slow-Cooker Jerk Chicken	778	55	14	227	609	11	1	6	57
Slow-Cooker Sweet and Tangy Pulled Chicken	465	18	4	87	702	41	3	17	34
Sweet and Tangy Coleslaw	123	7	0	0	137	15	1	14	0
Slow-Cooker Tomatillo Chicken Chili	300	8	1.5	110	480	16	3	5	37
Slow-Cooker Shredded Beef Tacos with Cabbage-Carrot Slaw	530	27	10	100	530	39	3	8	34
Slow-Cooker Korean Lettuce Wraps	979	85	36	173	757	17	2	8	35
Slow-Cooker Street Fair Sausages with Peppers and Onions	530	20	6	50	1380	52	3	11	36
Slow-Cooker Pork Carnitas	313	21	6	87	527	6	2	1	25
Slow-Cooker Classic Barbecued Spareribs	860	62	20	210	750	30	2	25	42
Slow-Cooker Salmon with Mediterranean White Rice Salad	912	48	11	122	1144	68	2	7	48
Slow-Cooker Sicilian Fish Stew	246	12	2	56	600	11	3	6	22
Slow-Cooker Poached Swordfish with Warm Tomato and Olive Relish	465	29	5	131	870	9	3	4	41
Slow-Cooker Shrimp with Spiced Quinoa and Corn Salad	388	14	4	157	916	40	6	4	26
Slow-Cooker Garden Minestrone	200	3	0.5	0	970	32	7	2	12
Slow-Cooker Black Bean Chili	290	5	0.5	0	430	48	3	12	15
Slow-Cooker Southern Braised Collard Greens with Pork	220	12	3	50	840	12	6	2	20
Slow-Cooker Summer Barley Salad	212	8	1	2	430	32	7	4	5
Slow-Cooker Lentil Salad with Radishes, Cilantro, and Pepitas	391	20	4	10	379	39	7	5	17
Slow-Cooker Refried Beans	340	4.5	1.5	5	830	53	19	5	19
Pressure-Cooker Spanish-Style Chicken and Couscous	780	22	6	225	1280	59	6	3	79
Pressure-Cooker Teriyaki Chicken Thighs with Carrots and Snow Peas	440	11	2	160	2140	45	3	33	40
Pressure-Cooker Chicken in a Pot with Lemon-Herb Sauce	400	16	6	165	890	8	1	2	48
Pressure-Cooker Braised Pork with Broccoli Rabe and Sage	340	16	5	115	490	7	3	1	37

	Calories	Total Fat (G)	Sat Fat (G)	Chol (MG)	Sodium (MG)	Total Carb (G)	Dietary Fiber (G)	Total Sugars (G)	Protein (G)
KEEP COOL WITH COUNTERTOP COOKING (cont.)									
Pressure-Cooker North Carolina–Style Pulled Pork	364	18	6	101	1356	15	2	10	36
Pressure-Cooker Lamb Meatballs with Couscous, Pickled Onions, and Tahini	650	36	13	85	820	53	4	10	29
Tahini Sauce	35	3	0	0	0	2	0	0	1
Pressure-Cooker Braised Striped Bass with Zucchini and Tomatoes	320	11	2	70	1090	19	2	10	36
Pressure-Cooker Poached Salmon with Cucumber and Tomato Salad	490	35	7	95	580	6	2	3	36
Pressure-Cooker Shrimp with Tomatoes and Warm Spices	210	9	1.5	105	970	16	4	7	14
Pressure-Cooker Mussels with White Wine and Garlic	280	12	6	85	750	10	0	0	27
Garlic Toasts	216	9	1		295	28	2	3	6
Pressure-Cooker Beet and Watercress Salad with Orange and Dill	270	15	6	10	500	27	8	18	10
Pressure-Cooker Green Beans with Tomatoes and Basil	280	10	1.5	0	880	42	8	11	7
Pressure-Cooker Rustic Garlic Toasts with Stewed Tomatoes, Shaved Fennel, and Burrata	540	31	10	40	1190	53	4	10	20
Pressure-Cooker Ratatouille	290	19	3	0	920	24	7	13	6
Couscous	250	4	2.5	0	490	45	3	0	8
Pressure-Cooker Boston Baked Beans	620	29	9	25	1440	72	12	28	19
DINNER OFF THE GRILL									
Grilled Chicken Kebabs with Garlic and Herb Marinade	551	41	7	160	749	10	3	5	35
Chicken Souvlaki	460	19	3.5	85	620	39	2	4	32
Grilled Lemon-Parsley Chicken Breasts	556	32	5	199	739	3	0	2	62
Grilled Bone-In Chicken	290	6	1.5	175	500	0	0	0	54
Teriyaki Chicken with Grilled Bok Choy and Pineapple	354	9	1	124	1465	26	3	18	42
Classic Barbecued Chicken	390	7	1	110	1130	44	0	39	35
Paprika-and-Lime-Rubbed Chicken with Grilled Vegetable Succotash	850	54	12	230	1150	35	8	10	60
Indian-Spiced Chicken with Radicchio and Grilled Naan	760	44	12	235	1100	29	1	4	59
Grilled Butterflied Lemon Chicken	430	25	4.5	150	930	1	0	1	47
Grill-Roasted Beer Can Chicken	600	37	10	173	794	16	6	2	46
Grilled Boneless Steaks	380	19	8	155	400	0	0	0	48
Grilled Porterhouse or T-Bone Steaks	278	12	5	103	416	0	0	0	40
Grilled Beef Kebabs with Lemon-Rosemary Marinade	490	34	10	118	786	13	2	8	32
Grilled Flank Steak with Vegetables and Salsa Verde	510	33	9	115	610	13	6	6	40
Grilled Mojo-Marinated Skirt Steak	344	24	8	98	602	2	0	0	31

	Calories	Total Fat (G)	Sat Fat (G)	Chol (MG)	Sodium (MG)	Total Carb (G)	Dietary Fiber (G)	Total Sugars (G)	Protein (G)
DINNER OFF THE GRILL (cont.)									
Grill-Smoked Herb-Rubbed Flat-Iron Steaks	198	11	4	76	360	2	1	0	23
Smoked Roast Beef	300	8	2.5	135	760	2	0	1	51
Barbecued Burnt Ends	480	29	11	135	820	14	0	11	39
Texas Barbecue Brisket	390	12	4.5	195	1120	1	0	0	65
Grilled Pork Cutlets and Zucchini with Feta and Mint Compound Butter	401	24	11	159	797	5	1	3	42
Grilled Pork Chops with Plums	417	33	3	86	492	14	2	11	18
Grilled Pork Tenderloin and Summer Squash with Chimichurri	490	26	4.5	145	710	11	2	8	50
Grill-Roasted Bone-In Pork Rib Roast	280	17	3.5	85	640	0	0	0	30
Barbecued Pulled Pork	72	3	1	9	71	9	3	4	4
Barbecued Baby Back Ribs	320	17	6	110	920	5	2	2	36
Kansas City Sticky Ribs	1100	65	20	210	2370	86	2	80	43
Sweet and Tangy Grilled Country-Style Pork Ribs	430	15	4	130	1340	32	1	27	37
Grilled Sausages with Bell Peppers and Onions	633	20	6	45	1486	75	5	10	37
Vietnamese Grilled Pork Patties with Rice Noodles and Salad (Bun Cha)	406	17	6	54	1641	46	3	11	18
Grilled Lamb Shoulder Chops with Zucchini and Corn Salad	590	44	11	105	990	16	3	7	33
Grilled Lamb Kofte	496	39	13	88	460	8	2	3	24
Swordfish Kebabs with Zucchini Ribbon Salad	617	42	9	161	1065	10	3	5	50
Grilled Salmon Steaks with Lemon-Caper Sauce	740	53	14	180	870	3	1	1	58
Grill-Smoked Salmon	410	25	6	105	670	4	0	4	39
Grilled Blackened Red Snapper	344	15	6	104	555	4	2	0	46
Grilled Whole Red Snapper	440	15	2.5	125	1090	0	0	0	70
Grilled Scallops	190	8	0.5	40	810	9	0	1	21
Grilled Jalapeño and Lime Shrimp Skewers	222	12	2	214	965	4	0	1	24
New England Clambake	780	49	19	265	2570	44	4	9	46
Grilled Paella	680	26	6	165	1900	63	3	3	46
Grilled Vegetable Kebabs with Grilled Lemon Dressing	200	15	2	0	340	13	4	8	5
Grilled Vegetable and Halloumi Salad	280	20	8	30	710	17	3	12	10
Grilled Artichokes with Lemon Butter	162	16	8	31	157	5	2	1	1
Grilled Asparagus	100	8	5	25	290	5	2	2	3
Grilled Broccoli with Lemon and Parmesan	230	16	3	5	619	17	7	4	9
Grilled Brined Carrots with Cilantro-Yogurt Sauce	156	6	2	5	1138	22	6	11	6
Husk-Grilled Corn	190	14	7	30	190	18	2	5	4
Mexican-Style Grilled Corn	220	16	3	10	270	19	2	5	6
Grilled Eggplant with Chermoula	329	32	4	0	86	12	5	6	2

	Calories	Total Fat (G)	Sat Fat (G)	Chol (MG)	Sodium (MG)	Total Carb (G)	Dietary Fiber (G)	Total Sugars (G)	Protein (G)
DINNER OFF THE GRILL (cont.)									
Grilled Caesar Salad	458	34	6	12	592	32	4	4	9
Grill-Roasted Peppers	190	15	2	0	300	12	4	7	2
Grilled Potatoes with Garlic and Rosemary	300	14	2	0	620	38	4	3	5
Grilled Radicchio	160	14	2	0	420	6	1	1	2
Brined Grilled Zucchini with Mint Salsa Verde	180	15	2	0	570	10	3	5	4
Grilled Pizza	699	39	12	43	639	63	3	5	23
PICNIC-TABLE FAVORITES									
Fresh Tomato Salsa	15	0	0	0	0	3	1	2	1
One-Minute Tomato and Black Bean Salsa	30	0	0	0	290	7	2	2	2
Guacamole	120	11	1.5	0	160	7	5	1	2
Roasted Tomatillo Salsa	40	2.5	0	0	90	5	1	3	1
Fresh Corn Salsa with Tomato	30	1.5	0	0	110	4	1	2	1
Creamy Herbed Spinach Dip	130	13	2.5	10	310	3	1	1	2
Seven-Layer Dip	370	31	14	65	580	15	6	4	14
Pimento Cheese Spread	300	28	13	65	430	1	0	0	12
Turkey Picnic Sandwich with Sun-Dried Tomato Spread	777	43	11	68	1164	67	6	4	32
Spice-Rubbed Picnic Chicken	635	43	12	213	677	6	1	4	53
Picnic Fried Chicken	1698	119	19	255	1186	84	3	0	69
Green Goddess Roast Chicken	568	42	11	175	612	2	0	1	43
Slow Roast Beef with Horseradish–Sour Cream Sauce	300	11	3.5	125	960	3	1	2	45
Indoor Barbecue Ribs	1040	65	20	210	2120	71	2	65	42
Skillet Cornbread	213	10	3	43	227	25	1	2	5
Roasted Butterflied Leg of Lamb	520	25	8	205	380	3	1	2	66
Poached Side of Salmon	260	12	2	100	250	0	0	0	36
Boiled Lobster	130	1.5	0	215	860	0	0	0	28
Indoor Clambake	768	40	17	245	2129	38	3	6	64
South Carolina Shrimp Boil	485	28	9	192	1639	29	4	6	31
Buttermilk Coleslaw	119	7	2	7	433	12	4	7	3
Napa Cabbage Slaw with Carrots and Sesame	80	4.5	0.5	0	210	7	2	4	2
24-Hour Picnic Salad	482	44	12	123	732	8	2	4	13
Broccoli Salad with Raisins and Walnuts	250	19	2.5	5	340	18	3	12	4
Fresh Corn and Tomato Salad	165	8	1	0	410	25	3	9	4
Watermelon Salad with Basil and Feta	157	9	3	13	401	17	2	13	4
Classic Potato Salad	327	23	3	11	516	28	4	2	3
Lemon and Herb Red Potato Salad	207	9	1		83	29	3	3	4
Cool and Creamy Macaroni Salad	413	27	4	14	224	35	2	2	6

	Calories	Total Fat (G)	Sat Fat (G)	Chol (MG)	Sodium (MG)	Total Carb (G)	Dietary Fiber (G)	Total Sugars (G)	Protein (G)
PICNIC-TABLE FAVORITES (cont.)									
Pasta Salad with Pesto	371	21	3	6	280	37	2	3	9
Tortellini Salad with Asparagus and Fresh Basil Vinaigrette	570	35	7	50	1240	51	3	6	16
Fusilli Salad with Salami, Provolone, and Sun-Dried Tomato Vinaigrette	400	24	7	35	970	32	1	1	15
Quinoa, Black Bean, and Mango Salad	450	27	3.5	0	740	45	8	3	9
Orzo Salad with Broccoli and Radicchio	440	27	4	5	710	41	3	7	14
Classic Three-Bean Salad	140	7	1	0	320	17	4	7	4
Chickpea Salad with Carrots, Arugula, and Olives	180	11	1.5	0	570	17	4	3	4
Strawberry Pretzel Salad	482	26	16	78	322	62	3	44	4
Best Lemon Bars	260	13	8	125	170	32	0	21	4
Key Lime Bars	193	9	6	29	130	26	0	20	3
Perfect Chocolate Chip Cookies	312	19	9	50	154	36	2	24	3
Texas Sheet Cake	388	22	8	39	88	49	2	38	3
Patriotic Poke Cake	614	23	8	18	490	94	2	60	10
White Cake Layers	310	12	7	30	380	47	0	30	4
Nectarine and Raspberry Slab Galette	210	11	7	30	120	26	2	11	2
SUMMERTIME SIPS									
Sweet Iced Tea	18	0	0	0	7	5	0	4	0
Lemonade	159	0	0	0	9	42	0	39	0
Watermelon-Lime Agua Fresca	51	0	0	0	32	13	1	11	1
Hibiscus-Guava Agua Fresca	70	0	0	0	5	18	1	16	0
Switchel	66	0	0	0	84	15	0	12	0
Aperol Spritz	280	0	0	0	5	26	0	24	0
Mojitos	220	0	0	0	0	22	1	19	0
Pimm's Cups	160	0	0	0	0	14	0	13	0
Sangria	170	0	0	0	5	16	1	11	0
Simple Syrup	70	0	0	0	0	19	0	19	0
Margaritas	250	0	0	0	0	21	0	20	0
House Punch	200	0	0	0	0	18	0	15	0
Micheladas	120	0	0	0	640	11	0	2	1
Horchata Borracha	540	28	8	30	160	43	5	28	9
Peach-Strawberry Frosé	220	0	0	0	10	22	1	17	1
Bourbon Cherry Slush	220	0	0	0	5	21	2	17	1
Florentine Freeze	200	0	0	0	10	32	1	28	2
Frozen Hurricanes	250	0	0	0	15	23	3	18	1
Piña Coladas	550	17	16	0	40	75	1	64	2
Vanilla Milkshakes	584	31	19	122	383	65	2	59	11

	Calories	Total Fat (G)	Sat Fat (G)	Chol (MG)	Sodium (MG)	Total Carb (G)	Dietary Fiber (G)	Total Sugars (G)	Protein (G)
SEASONAL SIDES									
Pan-Steamed Asparagus with Garlic	48	2	1	5	197	6	3	3	3
Asparagus Salad with Radishes, Pecorino Romano, and Croutons	330	29	7	20	560	13	4	4	8
Green Bean Salad with Cherry Tomatoes and Feta	152	11	3	8	194	11	4	6	4
Green Bean Salad with Cilantro Sauce	190	16	2	0	230	9	3	0	3
Spicy Salad with Mustard and Balsamic Vinaigrette	112	10	1	0	215	4	1	2	1
Stir-Fried Bok Choy with Soy Sauce and Ginger	60	5	0	0	370	3	1	2	2
Broccoli Rabe with Garlic and Red Pepper Flakes	90	8	1	0	180	4	3	0	3
Sautéed Cabbage with Parsley and Lemon	80	4.5	0.5	0	320	8	3	3	1
Slow-Cooked Whole Carrots	67	2	1	5	283	12	3	6	1
Moroccan-Style Carrot Salad	120	7	1	0	240	13	3	9	1
Chopped Carrot Salad with Mint, Pistachios, and Pomegranate Seeds	236	17	2	0	331	21	5	12	4
Skillet-Roasted Cauliflower with Garlic and Lemon	160	12	2	0	480	10	3	3	3
North African Cauliflower Salad with Chermoula	190	11	1.5	0	160	22	5	15	4
Chermoula	130	14	2	0	125	2	0	0	0
Foolproof Boiled Corn	98	3	1	3	241	19	2	6	3
Chili-Lime Salt	5	0	0	0	1170	1	1	0	0
Southwestern Tomato and Corn Salad	219	18	4	10	539	13	3	7	5
Sesame-Lemon Cucumber Salad	100	8	1	0	290	6	1	4	1
Country-Style Greek Salad	190	15	4	15	430	10	2	6	4
Marinated Eggplant with Capers and Mint	120	10	1.5	0	130	7	3	4	1
Broiled Eggplant with Basil	90	7	1	0	280	7	3	4	1
Fennel Salad	202	13	2	0	321	21	5	13	3
Garlicky Braised Kale	190	12	1.5	0	340	18	6	5	8
Fried Okra	480	39	3	35	630	30	3	2	5
Greek Stewed Okra with Tomatoes	200	14	2	0	1110	16	5	6	3
Sautéed Radishes	80	6	3.5	15	200	6	3	3	2
Sugar Snap Peas with Pine Nuts, Fennel, and Lemon Zest	102	7	0	0	240	8	3	4	3
Pine Nut Relish	50	4.5	0	0	100	3	0	2	1
Spinach and Strawberry Salad with Poppy Seed Dressing	225	14	1	0	469	23	5	16	4
Sautéed Spinach with Yogurt and Dukkah	180	14	2.5	5	240	10	4	2	6
Dukkah	40	3	0	0	230	2	1	0	1
Roasted Baby Pattypan Squash	70	6	3.5	15	95	5	1	4	1
Sautéed Swiss Chard with Currants and Pine Nuts	100	7	1	0	440	7	3	7	3

	Calories	Total Fat (G)	Sat Fat (G)	Chol (MG)	Sodium (MG)	Total Carb (G)	Dietary Fiber (G)	Total Sugars (G)	Protein (G)
SEASONAL SIDES (cont.)									
Socca with Swiss Chard, Pistachios, and Apricots	70	3.5	0.5	0	220	7	2	5	2
Simple Tomato Salad	151	13	2	0	300	8	2	5	2
Tomato Salad with Feta and Cumin-Yogurt Dressing	110	7	3.5	15	340	9	3	6	5
Best Summer Tomato Gratin	206	12	2	4	488	19	3	7	6
Roasted Tomatoes	300	28	4	0	160	10	3	9	2
Sautéed Summer Squash Ribbons	70	6	1	0	110	5	1	4	2
Stewed Zucchini	100	6	1	0	420	10	2	6	3
Zucchini and Feta Fritters	230	20	5	80	400	7	1	3	6
Peach Caprese Salad	271	21	10	50	403	9	1	7	13
Peach and Tomato Salad	115	7	1	0	415	13	3	9	2
Purslane and Watermelon Salad	170	12	4.5	20	220	11	1	8	6
Watermelon-Tomato Salad	279	18	8	38	725	21	2	16	11
PRESERVE THE SEASON									
No-Commitment Strawberry Jam	30	0	0	0	0	8	0	7	0
Classic Strawberry Jam	45	0	0	0	0	11	1	11	0
Classic Blueberry Jam	40	0	0	0	0	10	0	10	0
Classic Raspberry Jam	90	0	0	0	0	23	0	21	0
Classic Peach Jam	40	0	0	0	0	10	0	9	0
Classic Apricot Preserves	35	0	0	0	0	9	0	8	0
Classic Plum Preserves	35	0	0	0	0	9	0	8	0
Cherry Preserves	45	0	0	0	5	12	0	11	0
Concord Grape Jelly	50	0	0	0	10	13	0	12	0
Red Pepper Jelly	45	0	0	0	10	11	0	11	0
Quick Pickle Chips	5	0	0	0	0	1	0	0	0
Bread-and-Butter Pickles	60	0	0	0	55	14	0	13	0
Dill Pickle Chips	20	0	0	0	450	3	0	2	0
Dilly Beans	35	0	0	0	670	7	1	3	2
Sweet Zucchini Pickle Chips	60	0	0	0	450	15	0	14	1
Pink Pickled Turnips	20	0	0	0	580	5	1	3	0
Cajun Pickled Okra	15	0	0	0	870	4	1	2	1
Giardiniera	30	0	0	0	910	7	1	5	1
Sour Dill Pickles	10	0	0	0	200	2	1	1	1
Pickled Jalapeños	30	0	0	0	170	7	0	7	0
Crushed Tomatoes	20	0	0	0	80	4	1	3	1
Whole Peeled Tomatoes	15	0	0	0	115	4	1	2	1
Summer Tomato Sauce	30	0	0	0	250	6	2	4	1
Spicy Tomato Jam	25	0	0	0	40	6	0	6	0
Green Tomato Chutney	139	0	0	0	408	33	2	31	2

	Calories	Total Fat (G)	Sat Fat (G)	Chol (MG)	Sodium (MG)	Total Carb (G)	Dietary Fiber (G)	Total Sugars (G)	Protein (G)
PRESERVE THE SEASON (cont.)									
Roasted Tomato–Lime Salsa	20	0	0	0	370	5	1	3	1
Pickle Relish	60	0	0	0	470	15	1	14	1
Tangy Corn Relish	122	1	0	0	342	26	2	15	3
Chow-Chow	35	0	0	0	670	9	1	8	1
Peach Mostarda	35	0	0	0	50	8	0	7	0
SUMMER FRUIT DESSERTS									
Melon, Plums, and Cherries with Mint and Vanilla	70	0	0	0	15	18	2	16	1
Strawberries with Balsamic Vinegar	100	0	0	0	5	25	3	20	1
Nectarines and Berries in Prosecco	110	0	0	0	0	20	3	15	1
Strawberry-Rhubarb Compote with Ice Cream	360	18	11	95	105	43	3	36	5
Honey-Glazed Peaches with Hazelnuts	170	6	0.5	0	100	31	3	27	2
Roasted Plums with Dried Cherries and Almonds	220	7	3	15	55	29	1	23	2
Peaches and Cherries Poached in Spiced Red Wine	270	0	0	0	0	55	3	50	2
Warm Figs with Goat Cheese and Honey	150	7	1.5	5	35	22	2	19	3
Individual Fresh Berry Gratins	190	8	4	150	40	26	4	21	3
Strawberry Shortcakes	500	25	15	95	440	57	3	31	13
Summer Berry Trifle	423	19	8	117	185	56	4	38	7
Blackberry–Key Lime Trifle	330	17	10	55	200	40	4	32	6
Blueberry Cobbler	300	9	5	25	220	53	3	27	4
No-Bake Cherry Crisp	493	18	8	31	302	82	5	62	5
Peach Melba Crisp	462	19	8	31	150	64	8	41	5
Strawberry Sonker	418	17	10	43	603	66	4	42	4
Easy Peach and Blackberry Tart	387	20	12	51	198	49	3	20	5
Strawberry Galette with Candied Basil and Balsamic	410	19	12	50	270	56	2	25	4
Fresh Fruit Tart	410	25	15	72	162	44	6	19	5
Peach Tarte Tatin	350	18	11	50	220	44	2	26	3
Roasted Plum and Mascarpone Tart	420	31	17	65	160	32	2	17	6
Summer Berry Pie	220	8	4.5	20	60	39	5	28	1
Blueberry Pie	590	31	19	85	310	75	3	35	5
Sweet Cherry Pie	590	31	19	85	330	75	3	35	6
Peach Pie	520	24	15	85	370	69	3	33	7
Foolproof All-Butter Single-Crust Pie Crust	410	28	18	75	290	35	0	3	5
Foolproof All-Butter Double-Crust Pie Crust	210	14	9	40	150	18	0	2	2
Graham Cracker Crust	100	7	4.5	20	20	7	0	6	0
Chocolate Cookie Crust	160	10	5	15	95	17	0	9	1
Rustic Plum Cake	401	12	6	69	110	70	5	45	5
Peach Cornmeal Upside-Down Cake	192	4	2	32	271	35	2	14	4

	Calories	Total Fat (G)	Sat Fat (G)	Chol (MG)	Sodium (MG)	Total Carb (G)	Dietary Fiber (G)	Total Sugars (G)	Protein (G)
ICEBOX AND FROZEN SWEETS									
Strawberry Cream Paletas	140	8	4.5	25	55	18	2	15	1
Coconut Paletas	180	13	12	0	125	11	0	10	1
Striped Fruit Ice Pops	80	3	1.5	10	75	15	2	12	1
Best Butterscotch Pudding	443	33	20	186	272	34	0	30	4
Dark Chocolate–Avocado Pudding	210	15	5	0	82	19	7	10	3
Chocolate Pots de Crème	490	41	25	190	110	30	2	11	6
Strawberry Mousse	248	14	8	48	128	29	3	25	3
Panna Cotta	368	34	21	125	85	13	0	14	3
Lemon Posset with Berries	381	29	18	109	31	30	1	28	2
Icebox Cheesecake	347	30	17	95	207	17	0	15	4
Icebox Margarita Cheesecake	693	33	20	93	967	84	3	31	12
Chocolate Eclair Cake	499	28	16	76	335	58	2	41	6
Basic Ice Cream Cake	340	18	8	40	150	43	0	30	3
Tiramisu Ice Cream Cake	714	36	21	208	254	82	2	53	13
Banana Split Cake	523	28	16	91	226	64	3	30	7
S'mores Ice Cream Cake	469	22	13	55	145	68	2	52	5
Frozen Lemonade Cake	416	27	16	109	126	41	1	31	5
Chocolate Chip Ice Cream Sandwiches	354	20	12	70	237	42	1	31	4
Fresh Strawberry Pie	340	14	9	40	170	51	3	29	3
Lemon Icebox Pie	390	24	15	140	95	38	0	34	6
Raspberry Chiffon Pie	640	39	25	120	240	67	4	46	6
Icebox Chocolate Cream Pie	660	49	28	235	220	48	1	36	11
Caramel Turtle Icebox Pie	610	42	21	85	270	56	2	42	7
Peanut Butter Pie	600	49	24	105	250	30	2	23	11
Cookies and Cream Ice Cream Pie	580	40	24	115	220	50	0	33	6
Coconut-Raspberry Gelato Pie	290	18	8	35	45	29	2	23	3
Lemon Ice	110	0	0	0	40	27	0	26	0
Raspberry Sorbet	130	0	0	0	50	33	5	27	1
Chocolate Semifreddo	269	22	13	101	84	19	1	17	3
Whipped Cream	110	11	7	35	25	2	0	2	1
Hot Fudge Sauce	130	6	3.5	10	40	19	1	16	1
Easy Caramel Sauce	200	7	4.5	25	60	35	0	35	1
Peanut Butter Sauce	160	10	4.5	15	70	15	0	14	3
Magic Chocolate Shell	200	18	15	0	25	12	0	11	1
Vanilla No-Churn Ice Cream	253	17	11	64	103	23	0	23	3
Foolproof Vanilla Ice Cream	330	24	14	200	120	27	0	27	5
Pistachio Gelato	480	28	8	140	140	48	4	39	14
Vegan Coconut Ice Cream	280	21	19	0	95	25	0	21	2
Frozen Yogurt	172	4	3	16	99	31	0	24	4

Conversions and Equivalents

Some say cooking is a science and an art. We would say that geography has a hand in it, too. Flours and sugars manufactured in the United Kingdom and elsewhere will feel and taste different from those manufactured in the United States. So we cannot promise that the loaf of bread you bake in Canada or England will taste the same as a loaf baked in the States, but we can offer guidelines for converting weights and measures. We also recommend that you rely on your instincts when making our recipes. Refer to the visual cues provided. If the dough hasn't "come together in a ball" as described, you may need to add more flour—even if the recipe doesn't tell you to. You be the judge.

The recipes in this book were developed using standard U.S. measures following U.S. government guidelines. The charts below offer equivalents for U.S. and metric measures. All conversions are approximate and have been rounded up or down to the nearest whole number.

Example

1 teaspoon	=	4.9292 milliliters, rounded up to 5 milliliters
1 ounce	=	28.3495 grams, rounded down to 28 grams

VOLUME CONVERSIONS

U.S.	Metric
1 teaspoon	5 milliliters
2 teaspoons	10 milliliters
1 tablespoon	15 milliliters
2 tablespoons	30 milliliters
¼ cup	59 milliliters
⅓ cup	79 milliliters
½ cup	118 milliliters
¾ cup	177 milliliters
1 cup	237 milliliters
1¼ cups	296 milliliters
1½ cups	355 milliliters
2 cups (1 pint)	473 milliliters
2½ cups	591 milliliters
3 cups	710 milliliters
4 cups (1 quart)	0.946 liter
1.06 quarts	1 liter
4 quarts (1 gallon)	3.8 liters

WEIGHT CONVERSIONS

Ounces	Grams
½	14
¾	21
1	28
1½	43
2	57
2½	71
3	85
3½	99
4	113
4½	128
5	142
6	170
7	198
8	227
9	255
10	283
12	340
16 (1 pound)	454

CONVERSIONS FOR COMMON BAKING INGREDIENTS

Baking is an exacting science. Because measuring by weight is far more accurate than measuring by volume, and thus more likely to produce reliable results, in our recipes we provide ounce measures in addition to cup measures for many ingredients. Refer to the chart below to convert these measures into grams.

Ingredient	Ounces	Grams
Flour		
1 cup all-purpose flour*	5	142
1 cup cake flour	4	113
1 cup whole-wheat flour	5½	156
Sugar		
1 cup granulated (white) sugar	7	198
1 cup packed brown sugar (light or dark)	7	198
1 cup confectioners' sugar	4	113
Cocoa Powder		
1 cup cocoa powder	3	85
Butter†		
4 tablespoons (½ stick or ¼ cup)	2	57
8 tablespoons (1 stick or ½ cup)	4	113
16 tablespoons (2 sticks or 1 cup)	8	227

* U.S. all-purpose flour, the most frequently used flour in this book, does not contain leaveners, as some European flours do. These leavened flours are called self-rising or self-raising. If you are using self-rising flour, take this into consideration before adding leaveners to a recipe.

† In the United States, butter is sold both salted and unsalted. We generally recommend unsalted butter. If you are using salted butter, take this into consideration before adding salt to a recipe.

OVEN TEMPERATURES

Fahrenheit	Celsius	Gas Mark
225	105	¼
250	120	½
275	135	1
300	150	2
325	165	3
350	180	4
375	190	5
400	200	6
425	220	7
450	230	8
475	245	9

CONVERTING TEMPERATURES FROM AN INSTANT-READ THERMOMETER

We include doneness temperatures in many of the recipes in this book. We recommend an instant-read thermometer for the job. Refer to the table above to convert Fahrenheit degrees to Celsius. Or, for temperatures not represented in the chart, use this simple formula:

Subtract 32 degrees from the Fahrenheit reading, then divide the result by 1.8 to find the Celsius reading.

Example

"Roast chicken until thighs register 175 degrees."

To convert:

160°F − 32 = 128°

128° ÷ 1.8 = 71.11°C, rounded down to 71°C

TEXAS BARBECUE BRISKET

Index

Note: Page references in *italics* indicate photographs.

N

Naan and Radicchio, Grilled, Indian-Spiced Chicken with, *184,* 184–85

Nachos, Tomatillo and Pinto Bean, 131

Nectarine(s)
  about, 368
  and Berries in Prosecco, 351
  -Blueberry Compote with Ice Cream, 353
  No-Commitment Stone Fruit Jam, 316, *316*
  or Peach Cobbler, 360
  and Raspberry Slab Galette, 266–67, *267*

Nettle(s)
  handling safely, 125
  Soup, 124–25, *125*

New England Clambake, 216–17, *217*

New England Lobster Rolls, *89,* 89–90

No Bake Cherry Crisp, 360–61, *361*

No-Commitment Berry Jam, 316, *316*

No-Commitment Stone Fruit Jam, 316, *316*

No-Commitment Strawberry Jam, 316, *316*

Nonalcoholic Piña Coladas, 280

Nonstick skillet, 11

Noodle(s)
  Cellophane, and Chicken Salad, Asian, 47
  Chilled Soba, Salad with Cucumber, Snow Peas, and Radishes, *68,* 69
  Red Curry, with Shrimp, Summer Squash, and Bell Peppers, *135,* 135–36
  Rice, and Salad, Vietnamese Grilled Pork Patties with (Bun Cha), *206,* 206–7
  Vietnamese Summer Rolls, *34,* 35–36

North African Cauliflower Salad with Chermoula, *294,* 294–95

North African Marinade, Grilled Beef Kebabs with, *189,* 190

North Carolina–Style Pulled Pork, Pressure-Cooker, 164, *165*

Nuoc Cham (Vietnamese Dipping Sauce), 36

Nuts
  for cheese boards, 24
  see also specific nuts

O

Oil, premium extra-virgin olive, about, 44

Okra
  about, 126
  buying and storing, 126
  Cajun Pickled, 335–36
  Curry, Madras, 126, *126*
  Fried, 300
  Greek Stewed, with Tomatoes, 300–301

Olive oil, premium extra-virgin, about, 44

Olive(s)
  Carrots, and Arugula, Chickpea Salad with, 260, *261*
  Country-Style Greek Salad, 297, *297*
  Dressing, Seared Tuna Salad with, 56, *56*
  Farro Salad with Sugar Snap Peas and White Beans, *38,* 63
  Fusilli Salad with Salami, Provolone, and Sun-Dried Tomato Vinaigrette, 257, *257*
  Marinated, *24,* 25
  Mediterranean Chopped Salad, 58–59
  Pepper and Onion Frittata with Arugula Salad, 127–28
  Pressure-Cooker Poached Salmon with Cucumber and Tomato Salad, 167, *167*
  Pressure-Cooker Shrimp with Tomatoes and Warm Spices, *168,* 168–69
  Smoked Salmon Niçoise Salad, 54, *55*
  Spread, Ham Picnic Sandwich with, 240
  Tapenade and Roasted Tomatoes, French Summer Sandwich with, 94
  Tapenade and Zucchini, French Summer Sandwich with, *93,* 93–94
  Tomatoes, and Ricotta Salata, Pearl Couscous Salad with, 66
  and Tomato Relish, Warm, Slow-Cooker Poached Swordfish with, 154
  Watermelon Salad with Basil and Feta, *232,* 253

One-Minute Tomato and Black Bean Salsa, 234

Onion(s)
  and Bell Peppers, Grilled Sausages with, *205,* 205–6
  and Cabbage, Pickled, 100
  Caramelized, and Blue Cheese, Grilled Bacon Burgers with, *70,* 74–75
  Grilled Skirt Steak and Poblano Tacos, 98–99, *99*
  and Pepper Frittata with Arugula Salad, 127–28
  and Peppers, Slow-Cooker Street Fair Sausages with, 150
  Pickled, Couscous, and Tahini, Pressure-Cooker Lamb Meatballs with, 164–65, *165*
  Quick Pickled Red, 100
  varieties of, 74

Orange liqueur
  Margaritas, 276, *276*
  Sangria, *268,* 275

Orange(s)
  -Cranberry Iced Tea, 270
  and Dill, Pressure-Cooker Beet and Watercress Salad with, *170,* 170–71
  Feta, and Hazelnuts, Asparagus Salad with, 286
  Florentine Freeze, 279
  Frozen Hurricanes, *268,* 280
  Frozen Yogurt, 409
  -Ginger Sauce, Grilled Salmon Steaks with, 211
  Grilled Mojo-Marinated Skirt Steak, *191,* 191–92
  Ice, 401
  Moroccan-Style Carrot Salad, 291
  and Radishes, Peruvian Fish Ceviche with, *30,* 31
  Salsa with Cuban Flavors, Grill-Roasted Bone-In Pork Rib Roast with, 200
  Sangria, *268,* 275
  -Tarragon Chicken Breasts, Grilled, 179

Orecchiette with Baby Dandelion Greens in Lemony Cream Sauce, *114,* 114–15

Orzo Salad with Broccoli and Radicchio, *258,* 259

Oysters, Grilled, with Mignonette Sauce, 32

Oyster Sauce and Garlic, Stir-Fried Bok Choy with, 288

P

Paella, Grilled, *174,* 217–18
Paletas
Coconut, *380,* 380–81
Coconut, Lime, and Cardamom, 381
Horchata, 381
Strawberry Cream, 380
Pancetta and Basil, Peach and Tomato Salad with, 312
Panini, Roasted Eggplant and Mozzarella, 92, *93*
Panna Cotta, *384, 385*
Panna Cotta, Lemon, 385
Pan-Roasted Cod with Amarillo Sauce, 130, *130*
Pan-Seared Shrimp with Tomatoes and Avocado, 132
Pan-Seared Skirt Steak with Zucchini and Scallion Sauce, *104,* 138–39
Pan-Steamed Asparagus
with Anchovies and Red Pepper Flakes, 284
with Garlic, 284
with Lemon and Parmesan, 284
with Mint and Almonds, 285
with Shallots and Herbs, 285
Paprika
Coriander, and Yogurt, Braised Eggplant with, 116, *117*
Grilled Bone-In Chicken with Cajun Spice Rub, 180
Parmesan
Best Summer Tomato Gratin, 308, *308*
Cheese Straws, *24,* 25
Chicken Caesar Salad Wraps, 85–86
Grilled Caesar Salad, *174,* 225–26
Grilled Pizza, *230,* 230–31
Kale Caesar Salad with Chicken, *45,* 45–46
and Lemon, Grilled Broccoli with, 221–22
and Lemon, Pan-Steamed Asparagus with, 284
Orecchiette with Baby Dandelion Greens in Lemony Cream Sauce, *114,* 114–15
Pasta Salad with Pesto, 256
-Peppercorn Dressing, 43
-Rosemary Pita Chips, 22, *22*

Parmesan *(cont.)*
Summer Vegetable Gratin, *137,* 137–38
Vegetable and Orzo Tian, *104,* 140
Parsley
Baguette with Radishes, Butter, and Herbs, *14,* 29
Brined Grilled Zucchini with Mint Salsa Verde, *229,* 229–30
Cauliflower Steaks with Salsa Verde, *104,* 109–10
and Dill, Whipped Feta Dip with, 21, *21*
Grilled Flank Steak with Vegetables and Salsa Verde, 190, *191*
Grilled Pork Tenderloin and Summer Squash with Chimichurri, *198,* 198–99
and Lemon, Sautéed Cabbage with, *288,* 289
Pearl Couscous Salad with Radishes and Watercress, *65,* 65–66
Spiced Tabbouleh, 21
Tabbouleh, 20–21
Passion fruit
Frozen Hurricanes, *268,* 280
Pasta
Cool and Creamy Macaroni Salad, 254–55, *255*
Cool and Creamy Macaroni Salad with Roasted Red Peppers and Capers, 255
Cool and Creamy Macaroni Salad with Sharp Cheddar and Chipotle, 255
Creamy Corn Bucatini with Ricotta and Basil, 112–13, *113*
Fusilli Salad with Salami, Provolone, and Sun-Dried Tomato Vinaigrette, 257, *257*
Orecchiette with Baby Dandelion Greens in Lemony Cream Sauce, *114,* 114–15
Orzo Salad with Broccoli and Radicchio, *258,* 259
Penne with Garden Vegetable Sauce, 133–34
with Pesto, Potatoes, and Green Beans, 128, *129*
Salad with Pesto, 256
Slow-Cooker Garden Minestrone, 155
Soupe au Pistou, 141
Tortellini Salad with Asparagus and Fresh Basil Vinaigrette, 256–57, *257*

Pasta *(cont.)*
Vegetable and Orzo Tian, *104,* 140
Whole-Wheat, with Italian Sausage and Fennel, 119
see also Couscous
Patriotic Poke Cake, *264, 265*
Peach(es)
Blackberries, and Strawberries with Basil and Pepper, 350–51
and Blackberry Tart, Easy, *362,* 363–64
buying, 368
Caprese Salad, *282,* 311
and Cherries Poached in Spiced Red Wine, 355
Cornmeal Upside-Down Cake, *376,* 377
Fresh Fruit Tart, *365,* 365–66
Friesling, 278
halving and pitting, 353
Honey-Glazed, with Hazelnuts, *348,* 353
Jam, Classic, *318,* 319–20
Melba Crisp, *361,* 361–62
Mostarda, *347, 347*
No-Commitment Stone Fruit Jam, *316, 316*
or Nectarine Cobbler, 360
peeling, 375
Pie, *374,* 374–75
and Radishes, Fresh Corn Salsa with, 237
Sonker, 363
-Strawberry Frosé, 278
Tarte Tatin, 367, *367*
and Tomato Salad, 312, *312*
and Tomato Salad with Pancetta and Basil, 312
Peanut Butter
Beet and Carrot Noodle Salad with Chicken, *46,* 46–47
Caramel Turtle Icebox Pie, *398,* 398–99
Icebox Cheesecake, 387
Peanut-Hoisin Sauce, *34,* 35
Pie, *398,* 399
Sauce, *406,* 407
Spicy Peanut Dipping Sauce, *30,* 30–31
Pearl Couscous
with Clams, Leeks, and Tomatoes, 122–23, *123*
Salad with Radishes and Watercress, *65,* 65–66
Salad with Tomatoes, Olives, and Ricotta Salata, 66